D1535258

MANPOWER IN ECONOMIC GROWTH

The American Record since 1800

ECONOMICS HANDBOOK SERIES

SEYMOUR E. HARRIS, EDITOR

THE BOARD OF ADVISORS

NEIL W. CHAMBERLAIN
Yale University—Labor

JOHN M. CULBERTSON
University of Wisconsin—Monetary Theory

SEYMOUR E. HARRIS
*Harvard University—International Economics,
International Trade Theory;* all other areas not specified

FRANCO MODIGLIANI
Massachusetts Institute of Technology—Economic Theory

RICHARD A. MUSGRAVE
Princeton University—Public Policy

MARC NERLOVE
Stanford University—Econometrics and Mathematical Economics

MANPOWER IN ECONOMIC GROWTH:

the american record since 1800

STANLEY LEBERGOTT
WESLEYAN UNIVERSITY

McGraw-Hill Book Company
New York   San Francisco   Toronto   London

MANPOWER IN ECONOMIC GROWTH:

The American Record since 1800

Copyright © 1964 by McGraw-Hill Inc. All Rights Reserved. Printed in the United States of America. This book, or parts thereof, may not be reproduced in any form without permission of the publishers. *Library of Congress Catalog Card Number* 62-14865

36975

For R

Quand vous serez bien vieille, au soir a la chandelle . . .

"*If such a* scientia media *might be allowed to man, which is beneath certainty, and above conjecture, such should I call our persuasion. . . .*"

Fuller, The Worthies of England

"*Like those architects, pupils of Viollet-le-Duc, who, fancying that they can detect, beneath a Renaissance rood-loft and an eighteenth century altar, traces of a Norman choir, restore the whole church to the state in which it probably was in the twelfth century.*"

Proust, Swann's Way

PREFACE

The growth of nations draws vitality from the many and diverse fields of human endeavor. One may therefore hope for some insights into the growth process by studying almost any of these. The present work is addressed to two primary questions. How has manpower in the United States been utilized and rewarded since 1800? And what have proved to be some of the more significant consequences that this pattern of use and reward has imposed on the course of our growth? To build a better base for attempting such inquiry, we have developed a substantial set of new series on wages, employment, labor force, unemployment, and prices for the decades from 1800 to 1960. In studying these aspects of the labor force, we necessarily treat of human beings who were not merely employees—or slaves or entrepreneurs—but also parents, churchgoers, voters, and members of a striking new society. Hence, to give a fuller insight into what created the shifting pattern of labor-force and wage change, we have sought to make some contact with the historical aspects of growth, as well as with economic and statistical ones.

An economist concerned with national growth will typically review the changing distribution of resources. Of interest for any such study of United States growth should be our review of how one major resource—labor—was allocated among the several industries of the nation between 1800 and 1960. Among the relevant questions considered are the following: What determinants dominated the secular advance of productivity in this nation? How did the competition of mind and of market complement each other in stimulating growth? Did varying levels of uncertainty in the labor market create external economies, thereby affecting wage rates? What does the long-term supply of labor look like under vigorously competitive conditions? How closely do shifts of labor among the regions link to the pattern of wage differentials among those regions?

For those whose primary interest is in the driving forces of American history, there may be advantage in considering the tides of employment shifts and migration change. The connection, for example, between our adherence to the "career open to talents" and the world's wide wonder for more than a century—American material productivity—is no fortuitous one. Some discussion of it appears in the present study. For those who find that the most clairvoyant insights into, say, our maritime history are given by Melville or Morison, there may nonetheless be some benefits to be gleaned from our measures of the number employed at sea, and their pay scale. Those who find that Rhodes or Randall illuminate the great issues of the 1850s may find complementary insights from data on the changing ratio of free to slave labor, from comparison of wage rates paid in Kansas, California, and Texas with those paid in Massachusetts and Virginia. And those who are devoted to a study of how the nation was gradually unified, the frontier eroded, may find some value in our review of the links between interstate wage variation and interstate migration flows.

In parts II and III a basis of vantage is provided for those who would construct their own inference and conclusions. The variety of new statistical series on employment, unemployment, wages, and cost of living presented there suggest new measures of the trend in our real output. They point to somewhat different conclusions as to the extent and timing of our growth advances than do existing measures of real product. The new wage measures report a pattern of stability and advance that differs from earlier estimates, which typically applied only to factory workers or to other partial totals of the labor force. And the new employment measures, when combined with new GNP estimates of Kuznets, imply different changes in labor requirements per unit of output than those asserted by prior studies.

The present work probably has too much history for most statisticians, too many statistics for most historians, and too much economics to suit either group. Yet its major shortcoming is probably that it benefits too little from what these separate yet complementary disciplines can offer. Hopefully the exceptionally able group beginning to rewrite economic history for our generation will remedy this lack. And it is to be anticipated that a partial effort of one person will be superseded by substantial endeavors that take full advantage of both modern machine computation procedures and the multitudinous materials in archives and libraries that are ready for the gleaning.

Fortunately "the greater number" are always present to help those engaged in research. Dependence on the work of such indefatigable pioneers as Wesley Mitchell and Francis Walker, such distant luminaries as Alba Edwards, Daniel Carson, and Joseph Weeks will be obvious. The author trusts that footnote references emphasize the persistent use made of work by such distinguished contemporary scholars as Kuznets, Durand, Fabricant, Barger, Douglas, Rees, Palmer, and others. Penetrating comments by Moses Abramowitz and Melvin Reder were of significant value in removing some of the shortcomings of an earlier draft. Reliance on the indispensable advice and unpublished materials provided by David L. Kaplan and many other staff members of the Bureau of the Census has been great, as have benefits from expert guidance given by the Bureau of Labor Statistics, where work on the present labor-force series began some years ago. Unpublished data, plus guidance in interpreting published figures, have been given most generously by Dorothy Thomas; by Lillian Epstein, Elizabeth Jenks, and Robert Lipsey of the National Bureau of Economic Research; by the able staff of the Office of Business Economics; and by the Agricultural Marketing Service, the Forest Service, the Fish and Wildlife Service, the Office of Education, Western Union, Prudential Life, and the Anaconda Copper Company. Permission to reprint materials from earlier work published by the Princeton University Press and the National Bureau of Economic Research is acknowledged as well.

Every research worker knows, with Burton, how much "are we all bound that are scholars, to those munificent Ptolemies, bountiful Macecenases, heroical patrons . . . that have provided for us so many well furnished libraries." But without equally fine librarians these would be mere accumulations of inflammable materials. The present work has benefited repeatedly from assistance by the incomparable staff of the library of the Bureau of the Budget, under Ruth Fine (in particular, Helen Brook and Dorothy Catling), their kindness being exceeded only by their competence. It is no less a pleasure to acknowledge courtesies extended by Robert Lovett of the Harvard Business School, the staffs of the Essex Institute, Harvard's Houghton Library, the National Archives, the Bureau of Railway Economics, and the libraries of Congress, Princeton, Stanford, Yale, and the University of Colorado.

Any work prepared during spare hours and during more than a decade will possess its share of inconsistency and flat error. Such proportion as may nonetheless appear will reflect the author's nine fortunate months as a recipient of a Rockefeller Public Service Award, an experience hereby gratefully acknowledged.

Stanley Lebergott

CONTENTS

PART **I**

SOURCES AND

CONSEQUENCES OF GROWTH

This good land, which stretches around us to such a vast extent, whose copious product we are enjoying so richly. . . . Lift up your eyes and behold its magnitude! It is large like the munificence of heaven. Stretching from sea to sea, and from southern climes to the pole, it composes no inconsiderable portion of the whole globe. Such a noble present never before was given to any people.
The Reverend Stanley Griswold, 1802†

† *The Good Land We Live In, a Sermon* (Suffield: Edward Gray, 1802), p. 5.

1

THE MATRIX

A NEW SOCIETY

Passing through the Kentucky wilderness in 1832, a traveler came upon the camp of "a petit bon homme and his wife," who had just arrived from France. Life in the rugged land that Boone had only recently left was surely strange, unsettling. Yet it was certain that even the newest nation required a cafe and restaurant. And so "there they were on the banks of the Mississippi, standing guard over their little pile of trunks full of napkins, liqueur glasses, coffee cups, curacao, anisette and parfait amour, with looks of infinite sang froid and gaiety; and long ere this they have doubtless found their nest." [1] This quick note of arrant confidence leads to the great theme of American history, that of the open society. It is impossible to understand our changing patterns of manpower use and reward without seeing how they sprang from the broader patterns of national belief and action—which they in turn deflected. We consider three elements in this broader system: hope, ignorance, and space.

Hope. And the greatest of these is hope. Hope springs from many an obscure source, and the motives of those men who became America's entrepreneurs and laborers have been described with many a differing insight. Dipping his eighteenth-century pen in acid, the Reverend James Mac-Sporran wrote that "Great numbers have chose this province [Rhode Island] for their habitation not to avoid any violence to their persons or principles (as is more commonly than truly alledged, in New England

[1] Charles Joseph Latrobe, *The Rambler in North America, 1832–1833* (New York: 1835).

especially) but to improve their fortunes in those parts." [2] A century later an observer of the new West wondered: "Will laborers be wanting" to develop these territories? and concluded that "where food is abundant and cheap, there cannot long be a deficiency of laborers. What brought our ancestors (with the exception of the few who fled from persecution) from the other side of the Atlantic, but the greater abundance of the means of subsistence on this side? What other cause has so strongly operated in bringing to our valley [of the Mississippi] the 10 or 11 million who now inhabit it? The cause continuing, will the effect cease?" [3] Of course, differences in wages offer a perfectly straightforward explanation of labor mobility. But hope of improvement is not to be equated with rational calculation. Some who arrived came with skills almost classically unsuited to American needs. Our earliest official report on immigrant entrances (for 1821) reports a falconer, a dancing master, a hairdresser, even a rope dancer.[4] In the following year two rope dancers arrived, plus an elephant keeper.[5] And so they came from every country on earth. Unequal in wealth, station, or the talents required in a new nation, they were equal in the intensity of their expectations. And it was this intensity that caught the attention of almost every European who came to observe this new land and its people. They found a settled belief that "there is not an avenue to wealth or distinction which is closed—not a post unattainable." In America "there existed no prerogative rights. . . . There was a completely open field; neither the immunities of an ancient hereditary nobility, nor the privileges of a reigning church, nor the difference of colour as in South America, presented obstacles to a new organization; for at that time [1776] the whites constituted alone the citizens of the state. . . ." [6] Looking to the "fertile country . . . in and around the Illinois Valley" where lay the bounty lands due the soldiers of the Revolution, one dreamer wrote in 1819: "We deem it not romantic nor visionary to predict that the man who shall live twenty years to come may anticipate with confidence the voyages of steam boats from the Gulf of Mexico . . . to the falls of Niagara. . . . What a prospect of commercial advancement! What mo-

---

[2] *America Dissected—Published as a caution to unsteady people who may be tempted to leave their native country* (Dublin: 1753). Reprinted in Wilkins Updike, *A History of the Episcopal Church in Narragansett* (1907), vol. II, p. 16.

[3] J. W. Scott, "The Internal Trade of the United States," *Hunt's Magazine* (April, 1843), p. 326.

[4] Peter Force, *The National Calendar for MDCCCXXI* (Davis & Force, 1821), p. 237.

[5] Peter Force, *The National Calendar and Annals of the United States for MDCCCXXIII* (1823), pp. 265–267.

[6] C. F. von Schmidt-Phiseldek, *Europe and America, or the Relative State of the Civilized World at a Future Period* (Copenhagen: Bernhard Schlesinger, 1820), pp. 25–26.

tives to the industrious and skilful cultivation of the soil does the contemplation of this stupendous enterprise open to the views of the people of the west!" [7]

From hope came energy. As late as 1850 a French visitor marveled at the obvious: The Puritans "have remained the dominant element in the American society. . . . They have carried everywhere their spirit of initiative and their indomitable energy." [8] Cobbett, in lauding "the great quantity of work performed by the American laborer," declared his wages high but his day's work unscanted: "The sun, who seldom hides his face, tells him when to begin in the morning and when to leave off at night." [9] All things, of course, have deteriorated since that happy day, including the weather. But the contrast between high-money wages and low efficiency wages still appears to be sharper in the United States than in many parts of the world.

Ignorance.   Next only to hope as a constructive factor in our economic development has been that of ignorance—and the recognition of ignorance. "What a blessing to mankind it is," Justice Holmes once wrote, "that men begin life ignorant. . . . Everyone knows that it often happens that, from historical causes, analogous cases are governed by dissimilar rules, and that forms which have lost their significance by lapse of time remain as technicalities." [10] The elder Holmes, for once, put the matter better than his son: "To think of trying to waterproof the American mind against the questions that Heaven rains down upon it shows a misapprehension of our new condition. . . . What the Declaration means is the right to question everything." [11]

In Europe the answers were all known. Entrepreneurs and workmen alike had discovered the best methods of production; the centuries had taught them. American attempts to reproduce English and continental patterns of production did not work. The resource pattern was so different, costs of land so much lower, costs of labor so much greater, that new solutions offered fantastic promise. Mere technological invention was not the key: The ingenuity of Oliver Evans was great, but that of James Watt was fully as great. The most dismal years of the reign of Justinian, Suleiman, or the Ming emperors saw vital technical advances discerned. Every

---

[7] Edmund Dana, *A Description of the Bounty Lands in the State of Illinois* (Cincinnati: Looker, Reynolds and Co., 1819), p. 13.

[8] B. Dureau, *Les Etats Unis en 1850* (Paris: 1891), p. 499. Dureau's preface, dated Cincinnati, Mar. 1, 1851, shows his work completed in 1850 after his stay in the United States.

[9] William Cobbett, *A Year's Residence in the United States of America* (New York: Clayton and Kingsland, 1819), vol. II, pp. 225, 229.

[10] Mark DeWolfe Howe, *Justice Oliver Wendell Holmes, The Shaping Years* (1957), p. 278.

[11] *Ibid.*, p. 18.

added inquiry into the past finds still more technical innovation, precursors, "mute inglorious Miltons" in the most unlikely nations and periods.[12] Inventions occur everywhere; innovations do not. Nor are innovations adopted with impartial and equal frequency. For it is not the man but the nation that is the significant innovator—in Schumpeter's sense—adopting new technologies, new ways of doing business, new systems of action.

The most brilliant innovation in economic growth may well be the willingness to consider innovation itself as a permanent regimen. What was strikingly new about America was such willingness. Here was no established production system in which the classical entrepreneur made one marginal change in a factor input after another, improving an established process. Here was the very choice of the process itself, in every industry and region. Perry Miller's description of the ceaseless adaptability of our Puritan forebears is no less precise a description of the eighteenth- and nineteenth-century labor force. "Men who started as millers, being paid in grain, were compelled to find buyers and so grew to be traders, perceiving therein the guiding hand of providence; men who started as artisans settled down in workshops, took apprentices and shortly were made capitalists." [13]

Travelers accustomed to the guild traditions of Europe were amazed at the reckless adaptiveness of the American labor force. From an English migrant in 1818: Besides the "great quantity of work performed by the American laborer his skill and the versatility of his talent is a great thing. Every man can use an axe, a saw and a hammer. Scarcely one who cannot do any job of rough carpentering, and mind a plough or a wagon." [14] From a Frenchman in 1836: The American workman may be inferior in particular skills to the British workman but he has a "more general aptitude." [15] From a British *vade mecum* for immigrants to the United States: "Most mechanics of the 'Old Country' are wedded as it were to the old order of things, but in each particular profession the workmen should be prepared at least to meet with new and peculiar, if not improved, modes and ideas. . . . Most of the variations he may meet with in the manner of his work have had their origin in something either of necessity or use." [16] From a Swiss visitor in 1848: Everything in America is in a

---

[12] The extensive review merely for the nations of Europe in Singer and Holmyard, *History of Technology* is more than suggestive on the point. The discussions by Gilfillan, Usher, and others of the gap between invention and application are well known.

[13] Perry Miller, "Declension in a Bible Commonwealth," *Proceedings of the American Antiquarian Society* (1941), vol. 51, p. 78.

[14] Cobbett, *loc. cit.*

[15] Michel Chevalier, *Lettres sur L'Amerique du Nord* (Paris: 1836), vol. II, 515.

[16] *The British Mechanics and Labourers Hand Book and True Guide to the*

"transitory state." Here, a wine merchant who had been a railway director, a watch merchant who now sold shoes; there a farmer selling butter but formerly the proprietor of a factory for making calicoes; and a postman who became a flour merchant! No one seemed to remain in his proper occupation: "The Yankees believe themselves suited to anything, there is no status to which they do not feel themselves predestined, not a situation which they do not feel they understand to its depths. . . . Everything here speaks in dollars, everything is measured in dollars, everything is done for dollars." [17]

He who has tasted only the staid pleasures of the quadrille can hardly anticipate the delights of the waltz; they are too far from his ken. And in a country where for twenty centuries seasonal workers have been hired for the harvest, a farmer's vision of his productive alternatives is bleakly narrowed to such questions as precisely when to hire such workers. Such traditional wisdom may divest him of the ability to consider one dizzying possibility: dispensing altogether with a summer harvest force, and its high wage rates. But given a new country, where a multitude of alternative work opportunities present themselves, a mechanical reaper to cut 12 acres of wheat a day (compared to 2 acres by hand) is not only conceived of, but put into production.[18] In a new country, with so varied a mixture of migrants that the technological or guild tradition of no single European nation could be adopted, vastly different production methods and factor combinations could be and were attempted. The result was revolutionary change—revolutionary not in the hackneyed tradition of invoking elderly theories where they do not apply, but in the sense of adopting new solutions suited to new conditions. We may summarize in the words of a Danish observer in 1820: "History is unable to produce a more evident proof . . . that in order to develop the energies of a nation quickly and from all sides, the removing of every obstacle and the full enjoyment of independence and property, are alone requisite." [19]

Space.   Third of the major sections of that matrix within which our labor force developed was the land. In 1800, nearly 900,000 square miles; after the Louisiana Purchase, nearly double that area. Land of boundless

---

United States (London: Charles Knight, 1840), pp. 14, 16. The writer continues: "He should also, without delay, learn to 'get up the steam.' Mechanics work harder and labour in most occupations is greater . . . than in any other part of the world."

[17] Leo Lesquereux, *Lettres Ecrites d'Amerique Destinees aux Emigrants* (Neuchatel: H. Wolfrath, 1849, 1850), p. 48.

[18] An estimate of ¾ of an acre by sickle near the end of the eighteenth century, of 2 acres by the cradle, and of 12 to 15 acres by the first Hussey reapers, can be derived from data in Leo Rogin, *An Introduction to Farm Machinery,* University of California Publications in Economics (1931), vol. 9, pp. 125, 133.

[19] Schmidt-Phiseldek, *op. cit.,* p. 27.

fertility, it was available to those with strength to settle it. How few the Indians, how many the acres, the pioneers observed. In 1789 (according to Secretary of War Knox) there were only 76,000 Indians in the East.[20] By 1817 a mere 100,000 Pani, Chackshahs, Soukies, Foxes roamed the plains beyond the Appalachians—fewer than the number in some major Indian tribes of our own day.[21]

Against this enormous background of possibility a mere handful of Americans were at work, leaving almost infinite room for the hopeful migrant. In 1812 the hunting and trading parties up the Missouri and Mississippi totaled perhaps 300 persons—to tap one of the greatest supplies of furs in the world.[22] By 1831 the number did not reach above 500.[23] In 1819 the total number working the lead mines of Missouri, long destined to be the greatest in the nation, totaled slightly over 1,100.[24] In 1800 the entire codfishing industry of the nation, after a century of colonial development, occupied—part year—fewer than 4,000 people.[25] Above all, the number of farmers was decisive—perhaps 900,000 in 1810, or about one farmer for 2 square miles. What an incredible ratio to those who lived in European countries where densities a hundred times as great prevailed.

And the land, in addition to being sparsely settled, was rich. So rich, William Dunbar wrote rhapsodically (about his explorations for President Jefferson), that "a couple of acres of Indian corn" suffices to stock the pioneers' "magazine with bread for the year; the forest supplies venison, bear, turkey. . . . In a year or two he arrives at a state of independence; he purchases horses, cows and other domestic animals, perhaps a slave also who shares with him the labours and productions of his fields and the adjoining forests. How happy the contrast, when we compare the fortune of the new settler in the United States with the misery of the half starving, oppressed and degraded peasant of Europe!" [26]

[20] U.S. Bureau of the Census, *A Century of Population Growth* (1909), p. 40.

[21] H. M. Brackenridge, *Views of Louisiana* (Baltimore: Shaeffer and Maund, 1817), p. 146. Brackenridge itemizes the Indian tribes and estimates the number in each. His figures total about 105,000. As of 1813, two missionaries estimated 70,000 west of the Alleghenies. *Transactions and Collections of the American Antiquarian Society* (1820), vol. I, p. 270.

[22] Brackenridge, *op. cit.,* p. 215.

[23] Warren Ferris, *Life in the Rocky Mountains 1830–35* (reprint 1940), p. 228. Ferris estimates 300, as does the Wetmore Report, while the 1831 Pilcher Report figures 500 to 600, including those from Santa Fe as well as Missouri. *Message of the President of the United States on the Fur Trade,* 22d Cong., 1st Sess., Sen. Doc. 90 (February, 1832), pp. 37, 31. The American Fur Company apparently had about 1,000 employees in the field and in its office in the late 1830s. *Steele's Western Guide Book and Emigrants Directory* (Buffalo: Oliver G. Steele, 1836).

[24] Henry R. Schoolcraft, *A View of the Lead Mines of Missouri* (New York: Charles Wiley, 1819), p. 127.

[25] *American State Papers, Commerce and Navigation,* vol. I, p. 511.

[26] *Documents Relating to the Purchase and Exploration of Louisiana* (Boston:

With space and opportunity came growth—ebullient, swift, irresistible. Did not Charles Carroll, who had signed the Declaration of Independence, live to see Baltimore (a "village of only seven houses within his memory") become a city of 70,000? [27] And did not Griffith Yeatman, who had built one of the first huts on the banks of the Ohio, see Cincinnati grow from a handful of people to more than 200,000 before he died? [28]

The growth was dominated by successive waves of migration. For three centuries, from 1602 to 1922, men migrated freely to the United States— those who sought Dunbar's Greek democracy, the Mike Fink types in search of mere open land for hunting, and the solid citizens who desired a landed heritage to pass on to their descendants. All were welcomed in a flood of immigration without parallel in modern history. For the rest of the world's nations, whether or not close to the point of diminishing returns from land, have usually limited the type and quantity of migrants during their periods of substantial economic growth. Of America alone in the modern world can it be said: This nation was built by immigrants and by the children of immigrants.

While American history has been marked by conflicting attitudes toward particular components of the labor supply, there was for long a widespread agreement on the desirability of retaining and increasing the supply. On the one hand a Northern promanufacturing group could wish that "if it please heaven to redeem the thousands and tens of thousands, that groan in the land of bondage [i.e., Europe], and open them a passage through the waves, as to the Israelites of old, this shall be their land of promise. . . . They may shape their course to any part of a territory as expansive as the ocean they have traversed, find a thousand ways to bestow their industry to their advantage, with land, free and unoccupied, on which to settle." [29] With equal vigor and identical reference, one who addressed the Virginia State Agricultural Society in 1852 urged letting slavery "fulfill its mission until the same Power that opened the water of the Red Sea . . . [should] make dry the waters of the great deep for the passage of the African to his native shores." [30] The promanufacturing group wished to increase its labor supply. The proslavery group wished to retain its labor supply—the best that could be done when the slave trade was forbidden.

1904), p. 13. This book contains a reprinting of Dunbar's 1804 Journal, *The Exploration of the Red, the Black and the Washita River.*

[27] Captain Basil Hall, *Travels in America in the Years 1827 and 1828* (Edinburgh: Cadell and Co., 1829), vol. II, p. 394.

[28] Lesquereux, *op. cit.,* p. 20.

[29] *Address of the American Society for the Encouragement of Domestic Manufactures to the People of the United States* (New York: Van Winkle, Wiley and Co., 1817), p. 12.

[30] Willoughby Newton (in February, 1852), quoted in Avery O. Craven, *Soil Exhaustion as a Factor in the Agricultural History of Virginia and Maryland, 1606–1860* (1926), p. 153.

The fact that the point of reference for both was the exodus through the Red Sea is a happy demonstration that some North-South differences involved no basic theological but only economic aspects.

Whether American economic growth could have been what it was failing these three elements—hope, ignorance, space—there is no way of knowing. But they appeared throughout our growth and, as Thoreau remarked about finding trout in the milk can, there is some circumstantial evidence that can be awfully convincing. The mere prospect of available lands would not per se have brought the dynamic growth of the American economy. (Indeed, some could rationalize a contrary argument.)[31]

The broad acres of rich soil, the exuberant rivers, and the dimly concealed mineral wealth of America attracted migrants and helped create a new economy because with the land went a new social order open to all talents. After all, what did the European immigrant need to do? Little enough. As the Prince Royal of the Two Sicilies mused near Tallahassee in 1833: "Let him harden himself against privations by a passing effort. If he destine himself to trade let him establish a market where none are in existence. . . . If he be a physician, let him establish his reputation where he will have nobody, not even the dead, to contradict him; if he would be an agriculturalist let him grub about in new soils alone, without a neighbor, depending upon himself; he will be very liberally recompensed." [32] Possibly the Prince was too sanguine; royalty was not always properly informed about this new nation.[33] But the endless extravagant stories—some false, but many true—when told to those who found no places for them at nature's table in the Old World reported the differential advantage that spurred immigration and the development of a new nation.

[31] A nineteenth-century writer from another continent, Anton Chekhov, concluded: "In Western Europe people perish because they find life cramped and stifling; in Russia people perish because they find life too spacious. There is so much space that a little man has not got the strength to find his way about." Quoted in David Magarshack, *Chekhov* (1952), p. 142.

[32] Achille Murat, *The United States of North America* (London: 1833), p. 19.

[33] In the days when the delicate and retiring Nathaniel Hawthorne was an American consul in the United Kingdom, Queen Victoria found "Bowie knives in profusion" at the Great Exhibition, "made entirely for Americans, who never move without one." Quoted in C. R. Fay, *Palace of Industry, 1851* (1951), p. 52.

ECONOMIC DEVELOPMENT AND LABOR MOBILITY

Thou web of will, whose end is never wrought.
Sir Philip Sidney, *Desire.*

Gold is excellent. Gold is Treasure, and he who possesses it does whatever he wishes in this life, and succeeds in helping souls into Paradise.
Christopher Columbus†

To develop a new process a mild but discernible differential of economic advantage is enough. To develop an industry a greater differential may be needed. But to develop an unknown and dangerous continent, beset with savages, dangerous rivers, cholera, malaria, and "agues" of every description, a more substantial lure is surely required. America offered that opportunity, posing prospects so lurid that Dick Whittington seemed a pinched and rational calculator.

The schooner *Rajah* clears for India in 1795. After an 18-month voyage it returns with the first cargo of pepper direct to America—"yielding a profit of seven hundred percent." Two more voyages, the secret is out, and other vessels enter the Sumatra trade. But the *Rajah*'s entrepreneurs are $1,750,000 ahead of their competitors.[1] Fordham meets a river trader in 1818 and gets an itemization sufficient for an accountant, given the mutual interest in how a man could make himself $1,490 clear profit on $3,240 charged for freighting a Kentucky ark downriver from Louisville to New Orleans.[2] Captain Perkins of the Missouri Fur Company comes downriver in 1822 after a few months trading with a packet of furs valued at $14,000 and another to follow worth $10,000—virtually all clear profit—and expeditions begin fitting out for this golconda.[3] Most improbable of all, gold is discovered in California and the stories come filtering back. A man resting on a boulder after a day's work gives it to a passerby who thinks he sees flakes in it; later he learns that the final purchaser sold it for $3,000.[4] The stories multiply, persist, and men begin sailing, riding, walking to California.

Such stories appear throughout our history. The frequency is high, their geographic and industrial focus, richly varied. Men had moved before for

† Quoted by Carl Becker, *Progress and Power* (1949), p. 79.
[1] James D. Phillips, *Salem and the Indies* (1946), p. 95.
[2] Elias Fordham, *Personal Narrative . . . 1817–1818* (Reprint 1906), p. 121.
[3] *Missouri Intelligencer* (Oct. 29, 1822), quoted in Harrison E. Dale (ed.), *The Ashley-Smith Exploration and the Discovery of a Central Route to the Pacific, 1822–29* (1941), p. 62n.
[4] Anna P. Hannum (ed.), *A Quaker Forty-Niner* (1930), p. 29.

minor differentials of income. Colonists had settled in Oregon and California before 1849, attracted by high wheat yields. Ships had cleared for the Far East before 1795. And men had laboriously extracted gold from North Carolina mines for decades. What gave the distinctive temper to American labor mobility was that it was associated with the hope of such major differentials in return. The most durable, continuous, long-lasting, and important differentials in terms of settlement were undoubtedly those relating to the vast differences in crop yield—Iowa versus Massachusetts wheat, Texas versus South Carolina cotton. Indeed, so deeply did these experiences burn into the consciousness of Americans that much earlier thinking is epitomized in a very recent comment by a leading observer: "Who wants to spend his life making a reasonable profit? The great achievements have been made by people who wanted to do better than that." [5]

Mobility of labor and capital is essential in adjusting resources to new market demands and to changing resource availabilities. Complete mobility is a concept of considerable use as an archetype, indicating the direction in which maximum productive efficiency may be attained. Resistance to human mobility, which implies labor immobility, is of long standing. "As a bird that wandereth from her nest, so is a man that wandereth from his place," says Proverbs (27:8). Mobility has always been infrequent, briefly apparent. Moreover, during the mercantilist decades of the sixteenth to eighteenth centuries, European man may have approached as closely to complete immobility as ever he did to complete mobility.

What a brilliant contrast was offered by the growth of America during the nineteenth century. The restless of the earth seem to have foregathered within its limits, while the social order further transformed those who arrived.

Migration, wrote a shrewd resident of Illinois in 1835, "has become almost a habit. . . . Hundreds of men can be found, not fifty years of age, who have settled for the fourth, fifth, or sixth time on a new spot. To sell out, and remove only a few hundred miles, makes up a portion of the variety of backwoods life and manners." [6] With a touch of querulousness, John Randolph observed in 1813 that "in a few years more, those of us who are alive will move off to Kaintuck or the Mississippi, where corn can be had for sixpence a bushel and pork for a penny a pound. I do not

---

[5] W. Randolph Burgess, Undersecretary of the Treasury, "U.S. Economic Policy," remarks at the Agricultural Outlook Conference (Oct. 25, 1954), p. 3. An old illustration may be apposite: "The Discovery of McNulty gulch, a few miles off, drew 500 loose footed men in a single day" to the new quartz veins. Ovando J. Hollister, *The Mines of Colorado* (1867), p. 115.

[6] J. M. Peck, *A New Guide for Emigrants to the West, Continuing Sketches of Michigan, Ohio, Indiana, Illinois* (Boston: Gould, Kendall and Lincoln, 1837), p. 121. Peck's original preface was written in January, 1836, and only minor changes were made for the 1837 edition.

wonder at the rage for emigration. What do the bulk of the people get here that they cannot have there for one fifth the labor in the western country?" [7]

Here lay the groundwork for America's unprecedented levels of productivity. It is no mere happenstance that countries known typically for their high productivity have been small nations—Switzerland, the Netherlands, Sweden, the United Kingdom. Allocating labor effectively requires relatively more migration in large countries, more breaking with past ties of home and family. The examples of Germany and Russia in more recent decades indicate that it can be done. But of the larger nations only the United States has done so for more than a century, and without drastic social consequences. The very ground of this accomplishment has been the immense labor force of immigrants newly provided in each decade, plus the high mobility of those born in the nation.

As resource discoveries were made (iron in Michigan, silver in Nevada, gold in California), as new technologies developed in Europe (the Bessemer process, the railroad) or in America (the steamboat), they could be exploited in America with far greater promptness than in nations with lesser mobility. All other things being equal, capital is always willing to move to greater rewards. Labor is not. But since 1800 America came close to that optimum mobility because of the willingness of the nation to receive migrants, because of the willingness of its natives to move freely and frequently. Indeed, many critics have become bemused with our high mobility to the point where they consider "the West" as the key to American history. So far as the economic aspects are concerned, however, the West is merely a symbol of that mobility. There have been many "Wests." At an early date men from Connecticut were pioneering as far north as Vermont. Later, Vermonters explored New York State; New Yorkers sought out the prospects in Michigan; Michiganders left for Kansas; and men from Kansas joined the trek to Oregon. As early as 1809 it was observed that "New England may with propriety be called a nursery of men, whence are annually transported, into other parts of the United States, thousands of its natives." [8] And Daniel Webster described "with thrilling effect" how "New England farms, houses, villages and churches, spread over and adorn the immense extent from Ohio to Lake Erie. . . . Two thousand miles, West from the rock where their fathers landed, may now be found the sons of the Pilgrims." [9]

But in what part of the land, and in what decade do we not find Ameri-

[7] Quoted in Ulrich Phillips, *American Negro Slavery* (1918), p. 183. See also the informative discussion by Randle Truett, *Trade and Travel around the Southern Appalachians before 1830* (1935), chap. 3.

[8] Jedediah Morse and Elijah Parish, *A Compendious History of New England* (Newburyport: Thomas and Whipple, 1809), p. 328. A lively review of many decades appears in Stewart Holbrook, *The Yankee Exodus.*

[9] Abiel Holmes, *The Annals of America* (Cambridge: Hilliard and Brown), vol. II, p. 493.

cans and foreign visitors staggered by the apparently resistless stream of migration? In 1796 a terse American finds that "men frequently change their habitations in quest of a better place." [10] In 1822 the Bishop of Louisiana describes "these nomadic families that one has seen for several years now, descending the Ohio and Mississippi by the hundreds, and undertaking voyages of a thousand to twelve hundred leagues, furnished only with arks 60 feet in length." [11] In 1825–1826 Timothy Flint likens "the immigration from the Western and Southern states" to the area around St. Louis to "a flood, the power and strength of which could only be adequately conceived by persons on the spot. We have numbered a hundred persons passing through the village of St. Charles in one day." On the Brazos near Colonel Austin's new settlement "We saw them marching in shoals for that country [where] Land is obtained for one 'bit' or 12½ cents an acre." [12] In 1829 the indefatigable Niles reports not less than 8,000 persons passing through Charleston, Virginia, between September 1 and November 6, heading out to Indiana, Illinois, Michigan: "They jog on careless of the varying climate . . . seeking forests to fell and a new country to settle." He goes on to state that 3,000 reached Buffalo in one week, as 6,000 passed through Indianapolis for the Wabash country.[13]

Meanwhile, down on the Eastern farms, the same story is heard: "For fifty years, the emigrations from this country [Berkshire, Mass.] have been almost perpetual. The people moved at first chiefly to Vermont, and then to the State of New York." [14] In 1834 the "flood of emigration, constantly pouring onward to the far west is immense": 60,000 left Buffalo by water in 1833; in 1834 not less than 80,000 "there embarked"; while by land a "gentleman counted two hundred and fifty wagons in one day" passing a point on the South Shore. In 1835 the Camden, South Carolina, *Journal* finds that in a single week "no less than 800 persons have passed through the place for the West," while a decade or so later Professor Hedrick of the University of North Carolina saw pass his home on the Yadkin River "as many as 2,000 slaves in a single day going South mostly in the hands of speculators." [15] The process was ubiquitous, unceasing throughout our history.

[10] Daniel Smith, *A Short Description of the State of Tennessee* (1796), p. 18.

[11] L. Guil, *Notice sur l'etat Actuel de la Mission de la Louisiane* (Lyon: Chez Rusand, 1822), p. 39.

[12] Timothy Flint, *Recollections of the Last Ten Years* (1826; reprint 1932), pp. 194, 360.

[13] *Niles Magazine*, vol. 37, p. 195, quoted in Arthur C. Baggess, *The Settlement of Illinois, 1778–1830* (1908), p. 190.

[14] *A History of the County of Berkshire, Massachusetts, by Gentlemen in the County, Clergymen and Laymen* (Pittsfield: Samuel W. Bush, 1829), p. 178.

[15] Quoted in the invaluable study by Rosser H. Taylor, *Slaveholding in North Carolina: An Economic View* (1926), p. 53. Chapter IV, Migration to the Southwest, is full of relevant, vivid detail.

Men knew they wished to move, lock, stock, and chattel, the only question then being "Where?" "Dr Sir," began one letter, "I expect to start in all next month a number of Slaves either to Mississippi or Louisiana, to make an establishment for my son James M. Wright, who sets out on Wednesday week to select a spot for permanent residence. . . . What can you tell me about the advantages of each?" [16] In addition to permanent settlement, however, labor mobility was increased by temporary moves. Slaves, for example, were hired out of state when rising demand made wages elsewhere higher.[17]

When Texas was an independent republic a correspondent of Lord Palmerston's found that "many of the slaves now labouring in Texas are only hired out by their owners in the United States to the Texan planters, who can afford a much higher rate of wages to laborers than is paid in the Union." [18] Nathan Appleton observed in 1832: "It is well known [that] mechanics [i.e., carpenters, machinists, masons] go from the North to the South to get employment during the winter." [19] Even temporary transatlantic migrations took place, with thousands of English mechanics coming to the States for the boom season.[20]

Some moved for reasons clear only to the historian, the social psychologist, or the novelist. Typifying all such is the classic story attributed to Daniel Boone: The country was getting too crowded. "I had not been two years at the Licks before a dd. Yankee came and settled down within an hundred miles of me." [21] But we must take such tales with a grain of salt, for Brackenridge describes meeting "the venerable Colonel Boon . . . in the eighty-fifth year of his age [who] resides on the Salt River . . . surrounded by about forty families, who respect him as a father and who live under a kind of patriarchal government, ruled by his advice and example." [22]

[16] J. W. Wright to John Scott, Oct. 12, 1832, quoted in Henry T. Shanks (ed.), *The Papers of Willie Person Mangum* (1950), vol. I, p. 577. Another letter, to Congressman Mangum in 1834, was equally direct: "Dear Sir, I have it in contemplation to settle some of my negroes on the Red River in Louisiana, and am therefore desirous of obtaining all the information I can previous to my doing so." *Ibid.,* vol. II, p. 84.

[17] *Ibid.,* vol. II, p. 79. Shanks notes Mangum hiring his North Carolina slaves to Georgia for higher rates. Other examples of hiring for railroad construction, steamboat operation, tobacco factories can be cited from plantation records.

[18] Hook to Palmerston, April, 1841. Quoted in E. D. Adams, "Correspondence from the British Archives concerning Texas, 1837–1846," *Quarterly of the Texas State Historical Association* (January, 1912), vol. 15, p. 238.

[19] *Congressional Globe* (May 30, 1832), p. 3205.

[20] Charlotte Erickson, *American Industry and the European Immigrant, 1860–1885* (1957), p. 216, n. 29.

[21] Henry Nash Smith, *Virgin Land* (1950), p. 54. Rowland T. Berthoff, *British Immigrants in Industrial America* (1953), pp. 80–82.

[22] H. M. Brackenridge, *Views of Louisiana* (Baltimore: Shaeffer and Maund, 1817), p. 214.

To an English forty-niner a Texas physician declared that "Americans are very much disposed to change and leave their locations every eighteen months. If a settler hears his neighbors axe or the lowing of his oxen, he thinks that there is not room for both, and that one of them must leave." [23] Others moved because of want in the Eastern areas. "Fly," cried Greeley in agitated tones to the unemployed in 1837, "Scatter through the country. . . . Go to the Great West . . . anything rather than remain here." [24] How many flew, we do not know. But without entering into the contentious and interminable discussions of the Turner thesis in recent years,[25] we may assert that such migration as did take place did so with a lag— laborers waiting until it was feasible to migrate, until opportunities beckoned.

Our first systematic data on migration report that about 16 percent of all free Americans born in the Eastern and Middle states had left for other regions; 10 percent of those born in the Southwest, a mere 2 percent of those in Northwestern states and territories, and more than 25 percent of those from Southern states had left their native state for another.[26]

We lack comparable data for slave migration, but a report by the House of Representatives of South Carolina found that from 1847 to 1857 (a decade when migration was not at its peak) some 235,000 slaves were sent by ship, or marched in overland coffles from the five export to the nine import states.[27] These data are consistent with estimates of Edward Atkinson for 1840–1850, and 1850–1860, and we shall combine them (with due allowance for a high 1830–1840 rate) to infer that perhaps 600,000 slaves were moved in the 1830–1850 period.[28] Since the nonwhite population of the breeding states in 1850 was just over 1.5 million, we might

[23] Edward Smith, *Account of a Journey through North-eastern Texas Undertaken in 1849 for the Purposes of Emigration* (London: 1849), p. 141.

[24] In the *New Yorker* for June 3, 1837, quoted in Roy Marvin Robbins, "Horace Greeley and Land Reform," *Agricultural History* (January, 1933).

[25] Recent works on the safety-valve thesis, touching on migration, include the excellent study by Helen S. Zahler, *Eastern Working Men and National Land Policy, 1829–1862* (1941), chap. 2; Smith, *op. cit.,* which richly reviews the aura; and Arnold Zellner and George Murphy, "Sequential Growth . . . ," *Journal of Economic History* (September, 1959).

[26] J. D. B. DeBow, *Statistical View of the United States . . . A Compendium of the Seventh Census* (1854), p. 115.

[27] *Report of the Special Committee of the House of Representatives of South Carolina on . . . Slavery and the Slave Trade* (Charleston: Walker, Evans and Company, 1857), p. 28.

[28] Edward Atkinson, in *American Exchange and Review* (October, 1866), p. 88, estimates 298,000 for the 1840–1850 period and 191,000 for 1850–1860. These estimates are believed more reliable than those which might be derived from the anecdotal literature of the time. The report of an old woman who had 21 children, all of whom were sold, she herself being sold in her sixties, is an example of such unrepresentative if accurate reports. S. A. Ferrall, *A Ramble of 6,000 Miles through the United States of America* (London, 1832), p. 194.

well conclude that the proportion of 1850 slaves that had been born in these five Southern states but moved to others was at least equal to the 27 percent migration rate for Southern whites.[29] The magnitude of this movement can better be appreciated when it is realized it took place despite the impediments put in its way in the acts of individual states forbidding inmigration for fear of slave revolts. (In 1831 Governor Roman of Louisiana, for example, forbade the importation of slaves for sale, allowing in only those brought by owners for their own use.)[30]

Judging by the data on state of birth, the impulse to move has not declined over the years; the proportion of the native born living in other states has actually risen in recent decades over the 1850 level.[31] On the other hand, of course, the decline in the foreign born from 11 percent of our population in 1850 and 15 percent in 1860 to 7 percent by 1950 has reduced the overall mobility somewhat.[32]

Small wonder that Americans could assert flatly that "the right to emigrate is not only a natural, but a chartered right; we will maintain at every hazard, the privilege of seeking subsistence and happiness, wherever we please to think they may be found," confident that "our citizens are secured in the privilege of removing from one state to another." [33] In his last major speech to the United States Senate before withdrawing to the Confederacy, Robert Toombs began by declaring, "I will now read my own demands." Of these the first was "that the people of the United States shall have an equal right to emigrate and settle in the present or any future acquired territory with whatever property they possess, including slaves." [34] These attitudes were summed and their essence revealed with classic simplicity near the end of the century by a treaty provision in which this nation stipulated "the inalienable rights of man to change his residence and religion." [35]

[29] The 600,000 figure, of course, must be reduced to allow for mortality before we can estimate survivors among the population enumerated in 1850.

[30] Wendell Holmes Stephenson, *Isaac Franklin, Slave Trader and Planter of the Old South* (Baton Rouge: Louisiana State University Press, 1938), pp. 74, 76.

[31] U.S. Bureau of the Census, *Historical Statistics of the United States* (1946), p. 30.

[32] U.S. Bureau of the Census, *1957 Statistical Abstract*, pp. 32, 38.

[33] James Hall, *Notes on the Western States* (Philadelphia: Harrison Hall, 1838), p. 195.

[34] "I have, then, [he concluded] established the proposition—it is admitted—that you seek to outlaw $4,000,000,000 of property of our people in the Territories of the United States. Is not that a cause of war?" *Congressional Globe,* 36th Cong., 2d Sess., pp. 270–271. See also Ulrich Phillips, *The Life of Robert Toombs* (1913), p. 217ff. Similarly, Senator Green of Kentucky stated that no state "can go into a Territory but the citizens may. Does he [Senator Trumbull] accord to each of those citizens the same right to take property, to hold and enjoy it there under the provisions of law?" *Congressional Globe,* Jan. 10, 1861, p. 313.

[35] Edith Abbott, "Recent Immigration," *Educational Review* (March, 1905), p. 246.

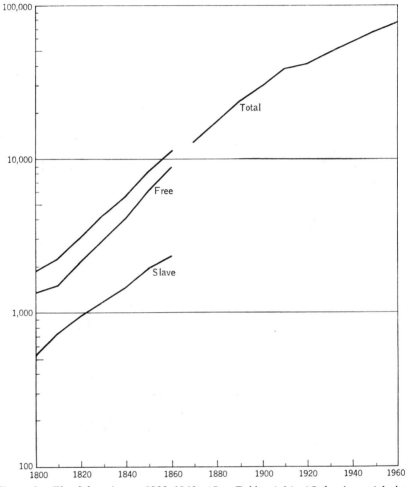

Figure 1. The labor force, 1800–1960. (See Table A-1.) (Only decennial data plotted.)

2

THE MATERIALS

THE PROVISION OF LABOR SERVICES

The provision of an assured quantity of labor service is a difficult matter in a market as imperfect as that of the United States in its first half century. Labor, scarce and mobile, was provided in three main forms.

I. Slave Labor

The most predictable continuity of labor supply is offered under slavery —and there were about 80 slaves to every 100 free wage earners in the United States labor force of 1800.[1] This supply, however, was limited and almost completely invariant to changes in economic conditions. The supply of slave labor throughout the period 1808 to 1865 was in large measure determined by the natural tides of birth and death among the slave population already present in 1808. The Louisiana Purchase increased the supply of slaves by perhaps 40,000; the war with Mexico added not much over 60,000.[2] The efforts of the American Colonization Society from 1820 to 1856, on the other hand, reduced the native stock of slaves by 3,676.[3] Manumissions disproportionately affected older slaves and hence had

---

[1] We estimate 525,000 gainfully occupied slaves, about 650,000 free employees in 1800, and 615,000 farmers.

[2] The estimate for the Louisiana Purchase, by Representative King of New York, adopted by Smith of South Carolina, appears in *Annals of Congress,* February, 1820, col. 377. See also 1860 Census, *Population of the United States in 1860,* p. xviii. The number of slaves in Texas in 1850 was enumerated at 58,161 (1870 *Census of Population,* vol. I, p. 66). Any reduction of this figure to apply to an earlier date would be more than offset by the inclusion of those slaves in the territory that had been shipped to other slaveholding states by 1850.

[3] 1860 Census, *op. cit.,* p. lx.

19

limited effect on the labor supply. Moreover, laws were passed to forbid emancipations, and the numbers to be deducted from the supply totals on this account could not have been great.[4]

The substantial flow of slaves from Africa to Cuba ran well above that country's requirements and in the long course of the illegal slave trade provided some portion of the United States slave increase after 1808. But how large a contribution they made is unknown. In 1819, Representative Middletown of South Carolina estimated the annual importation at from 13,000 to 15,000; Wright of Virginia, at 15,000; while Justice Story asserted the trade "was still carried on with all the implacable rapacity of former times."[5] A similar volume of importation is estimated for Texas in 1837, when Texas was still independent.[6] But we also know how persistent was the opposition by many Southern leaders to such importation, tending as it did to drive down both cotton prices and the value of slaves.[7] The best estimate of slaves smuggled in from 1808 to 1860 (whether by slave traders or by individual entrepreneurs such as the Hon. C. A. Lamar of the *Wanderer*) would be "a minimum of 270,000."[8] It is most likely, in sum, that the variations in supply were dominated by natural increases and factors related to that increase.[9]

[4] See Robert Toombs, in *Congressional Globe,* Jan. 7, 1861, p. 270: "Washington during all his lifetime held hundreds of slaves. He kept them as long as he lived, and left them to his wife with the provision that after her death, they should be free, a very common custom with the gentlemen in our country who have no immediate descendants and from attachment to their slaves, are reluctant to let them pass into the hands of collateral relatives. So strong was the sentiment, that my State was compelled to pass a law to prohibit emancipation, or by this time a large part of the slaves might have become free under the operation of that sentiment."

[5] Quoted in William L. Mathieson, *Great Britain and the Slave Trade, 1839–1865* (1929), pp. 138–139.

In 1804 Senator Jackson informed the "gentlemen from the north and east [that] "within less than a year 10,000 slaves have against law been imported into South Carolina and Georgia." E. E. Brown (ed.), *William Plumer's Memorandum . . . 1803–1807* (1923), p. 120.

[6] Thomas F. Buxton, *The African Slave Trade* (1839), p. 24. Buxton was "informed upon high authority" but adds that he himself did not have proof on the point.

[7] Governor Foote of Mississippi opposed reopening the slave trade, saying that it would bring "a reduction in the price of cotton, a tremendous reduction in the value of slaves, and consequently their almost exclusive acquirement by the capitalist." Quoted by William W. Davis, "Ante-bellum Southern Commercial Conventions" in *Transactions of the Alabama Historical Society for 1904* (1906), vol. VI, p. 89.

[8] Ernest P. Hutchinson, "Notes on Immigration Statistics of the United States," *Journal of the American Statistical Association* (December, 1958), p. 994.

[9] In *The Pro-slavery Argument* (Charleston, 1852), p. 369, Dew quotes Clay in 1830 to the effect that prior to the annexation of Louisiana her slaves were worth no more than $100; but after the end of the slave trade "greater attention was

It was foreseen relatively early that the limitation of slave immigration, plus the normal conditions of domestic supply, would reduce the role of slave labor. In 1827 one of the great Southern statesmen, shortly before his historic sequence of debates with Daniel Webster, spoke out against proposals to resettle some slaves in Africa. His opposition was on the ground

> that the Almighty, in the wide order of his providence, has worked out the course of events . . . [so] that when the relative proportion of the colored population to the white is greatly diminished slaves cease to be valuable, and emancipation follows as a matter of course. . . . Wherever free labor is put in full and successful operation, slave labor ceases to be profitable. . . . Time and patience are only wanting to effect the great object . . . [of relieving] the country from the danger resulting from the large proportion which the African population in this country bears to the rest.[10]

While 2 million slaves were gainfully occupied in 1860, their ratio to the total had dwindled, as implied in Hayne's prevision. On the other hand, the great rise in slave prices, in hiring rates, and in world consumption of cotton all pointed to a large increase in the demand for slaves to meet the pressing need for labor in cotton farming. Only one out of every 60 Southern acres that was adapted to cotton cultivation was so cultivated, the rest being left untilled because, in the words of an English contemporary,

> Although you had climate and sun, you had no labour. The institution of slavery forbade free-labour men in the North to come to the South; and every emigrant that landed in New York from Europe knew that the Slave States were no states for him, and therefore he went North or West. The laws of the United States, the sentiments of Europe and the world, being against any reopening of the slave-trade, the planters of the South were shut up, and the annual increase in the supply of cotton could increase only in the same proportion as the annual increase in the number of their negroes.[11]

That rate being 2½ percent per year, the limit on the supply of labor was given. The steady profitability of slavery offered increased opportunity

---

consequently bestowed on their children, and now nowhere is the African female more prolific than she is in Louisiana."

[10] R. Y. Hayne, in *Register of Debates,* U.S. Senate, col. 332, Feb. 1, 1827.

[11] John Bright, "Mr. Roebuck's Motion for Recognition of the Southern Confederacy" (June 30, 1863), and "America" (June 16, 1863), in J. E. Thorold Rogers (ed.), *Speeches on Questions of Public Policy by the Right Honourable John Bright, M.P.* (London: 1878), pp. 130, 138–139.

for the use of slaves,[12] but (minor piracy apart) the supply of slave labor expanded at only this limited rate.

II. Indentured Labor

Second in degree of stability as a source of labor was the group of indentured workers, whose contracts of employment ranged up to 3 years in most instances. The long colonial tradition of indenturing, though encompassing only a limited group of employees, is well known.[13] At one extreme the young workers might be indentured for long periods; Asa Sheldon, of Wilmington, Massachusetts, was bound out in 1797 for an immediate $20 in cash plus $100 a dozen years later when he became twenty-one.[14] As late as 1830 David Smith was bound out at $100 for his services from age thirteen to sixteen.[15] The indenture proved a most flexible legal instrument for adjusting labor supply and demand. Thus, although the Northwest ordinance forbid slavery in the Louisiana territory, "slaves were considered so convenient, that the territorial legislature authorized their introduction. For this purpose indentures were employed. The negro was directed to sign an article, binding himself to serve his master for some specified term of years, refusal could avail nothing, and compliance was termed voluntary servitude." [16]

Similarly, the constitution of Illinois which was presented to the Congress in 1818 provided that those who had "been bound to service by contract or indenture" under prior law would be held to specific performance; that "such negroes and mulattoes . . . shall serve out the time appointed by such laws, Provided, however, that the children hereafter born of such persons, negroes, or mulattoes, shall become free, the males at the age of 21 years, the females at the age of 18 years." [17]

[12] The well-known Georgia historian, Ulrich Phillips, in his classic study, *American Negro Slavery* (1918), has argued forcefully that the high prices of slaves must have meant their unprofitability. The issue of profitability has been considered more rigorously by Alfred Conrad and John Meyer, "The Economics of Slavery in the Ante-bellum South," *Journal of Political Economy* (April, 1958), and by Robert Evans, "The Economics of Negro Slavery, 1830–1860," in National Bureau of Economic Research, *Aspects of Labor Economics* (1962).

[13] It is very well described by Richard B. Morris, *Labor in Colonial America,* and the earlier study by C. A. Herrick, *White Servitude in Pennsylvania* (1926).

[14] *Life of Asa G. Sheldon: Wilmington Farmer* (Woburn: E. T. Moody, 1862; reprint 1959).

[15] U.S. Congress, Serial Set 210.

[16] David Thomas, *Travels through the Western Country in the Summer of 1816* (Auburn, N.Y.: David Rumsey, 1819), p. 167.

[17] *Annals of Congress,* November, 1818, col. 306. In 1806 the Legislative Council and House of Representatives of the Territory of Indiana resolved that the provision of the Northwest Ordinance which forbade the introduction of slaves should be suspended for 10 years to enable the new territory to acquire a stock of slaves, and to free the older states of a surplus. The resolution appears in *Congressional Globe,* Jan. 14, 1847, appendix p. 117.

Much more common was the practice of emigrants working out their passage money over a period of months—being bound to those who paid the ship's captain their passage money, or, in later years, to a labor contractor or steamship company.

But the beckoning frontier and the open social order made enforcing such contracts difficult in the extreme. Where the laborer carried the mark of his servitude inalienably about him—whether Negro, Chinese, or Mexican—indenturing was possible if difficult. But where he was indistinguishable from the surrounding free population, it was hardly feasible to single him out unless he lacked means of transport or had so crude a language facility that he could not lose himself amid that population. In 1830 the C and O Canal Company paid for importing laborers from Ireland, Holland, and Germany, the costs to be worked out. When the emigrants arrived

. . . there was a reenactment of the scenes which had so irritated Captain John Smith at Jamestown just two hundred years before. The newcomers were often idle and quarrelsome . . . insubordination and general disorder became common. The contracts which the laborers had been compelled to sign could not be enforced, while in some instances the laborers ran away and were brought back only at great expense, if indeed they could be captured and returned at all.[18]

Within a few brief years Texas provided a classic example of the limitations of indenturing. Three men, who had acquired a 45-million-acre land grant from the Mexican state of Coahuila and Texas (near what were to become Kansas and Colorado), attempted to hold their franchise by putting settlers on it. Starting with 100 families under indenture (who were to work half time for the company, and thereby repay the cost of their transportation and keep), they soon found that even the inducement of land allotments was not enough to keep the settlers under indenture. The settlers drifted away, and the enterprise collapsed.[19]

One of the last schemes for directed immigration to America foundered on the same rock: "a very large proportion" of emigrants brought over by the American Emigrant Company in 1864–1866 "failed to fulfill their contracts," drifting away for higher wages.[20] An extensive investigation by the Congress of indenturing, contract labor, and the padrone system in the 1880s served (beyond its immediate purpose of revealing the unsavory practices involved) to emphasize how tiny a contribution to the national labor supply was made by labor so recruited.[21]

[18] George W. Ward, *The Early Development of the Chesapeake & Ohio Canal Project* (1899), p. 92.

[19] Carl C. Rister, *Comanche Bondage* (1955), pp. 22, 57, 179.

[20] Charlotte Erickson, *American Industry and the European Emigrant 1860–1885* (1957), p. 46.

[21] *Contract Labor*, 50th Cong., 1st Sess., Misc. Doc. 572 (1888).

III. The Free Market: Migration

The bold and central characteristic of the supply of labor in North
America from 1800 to 1931 was migration—migration from overseas,
migration down from Newfoundland, migration up from Spanish Mexico.
True, in the more leisurely days of the Indian everyone migrated. But
migration from hunting ground to hunting ground (when capital investment was trivial and the roundabout process of production all but un-
dreamed of) offered little precedent for what was to come.

Particularly after the formation of the United States of America, migration became the modal means for adjusting an imperfect market and a
limited supply of labor to the intense possibilities of economic gain. How
to find farm laborers for the new territory Jefferson acquired? "As to obtaining labourers . . . if many families settle together . . . let them import English labourers, or make advantageous proposals to such as are
continually arriving at the eastern ports." [22] So writes Birkbeck in 1819.

At New Orleans in 1845 contractors would board a newly arrived ship
and face the crowd of migrants: " 'Look hyar—hev ye got any bricklayers
or stonemasons in this crowd,' says one. 'Gentlemen, I'm in search of
carpenters, if you've got any here, let him speak out,' said another." [23]
Specialized skills were in acute demand. Skilled workmen, so the story
went, might be hidden in barrels and smuggled past English customs inspectors to provide competitive skills to the new nation.[24]

When in 1825 a handful of entrepreneurs were attempting to break the
immensely profitable English monopoly of power weaving, printing, and
export of calicoes, one offered the leading English printer $10,000 to come
to America and take charge of his print works.[25] A mere decade before, an
entrepreneur turned down a skilled mechanic who asked $2 a day to de-
sign the machinery for one of the new mills, giving him instead only 9
shillings ($1.50) and exclusive of the customary board.[26] Although the
critical contribution of the skilled machine maker at this initial appearance
of the power loom has been warmly emphasized by Wright, the gross
difference in pay reflects the fact that in the America of those decades the
supply of able mechanics was hardly as exiguous as that of calico printers.[27]

[22] Morris Birkbeck, *Letters from Illinois* (Boston: Wells and Lilly, 1818), p. 15.

[23] John Regan, *The Emigrants Guide* (Edinburgh: Oliver and Boyd, ca. 1846),
p. 30.

[24] Theodore Marburg, "Management Problems and Procedures of a Manufacturing
Enterprise, 1802–1852," unpublished Clark University thesis, p. 266.

[25] William R. Bagnall, *Sketches of Manufacturing and Textile Establishments* (1908,
typescript, in Manuscript Room, Baker Library, Harvard), p. 2172.

[26] Kenneth W. Porter, *The Jacksons and the Lees* (1937), vol. I, pp. 750–751.
Porter reprints a manuscript letter from Patrick Tracy Jackson, Mar. 7, 1814, to
Lemuel Chase, the mechanic.

[27] Carroll Wright, in 1880 Census, *Manufactures,* p. 540, discussed the importance
of Paul Moody's work as a skilled mechanic for Lowell.

(And, of course, the rate for a single master printer did not affect the rest of the wage structure as did the mechanics' rate.)

A cotton planter in 1866, seeking to reestablish a Sea Island plantation, found the local labor to be "easy and unreliable"; reported briskly that "I have sent to the Ionian Islands to get fifteen Greeks at an expense of $2,000 and I hope they are on their way now."[28]

The ground theme running through these, and a multitude of other examples, was the same. With the nation so much smaller[29] and the supply of labor (skilled and unskilled) so much more limited, any attempts to organize steady production—certainly large-scale production—tended to require massive increases in wage rates unless migration could be stimulated. For each of the major industries the same elements emerged.

Heavy construction was perhaps the most obvious example. In a nation with six persons per square mile, with travel so crude that a man riding to the new city of Pittsburgh in 1813 could lose his horse in a mudhole on the way, it became an enormously difficult endeavor to collect a large supply of labor.[30] Henry Latrobe, when providing an estimate of the cost of a navy yard for the capitol of the nation, urged the Congress to make haste:

Should the works be undertaken immediately while the very numerous skilful and experienced workmen, who have been collected and in great part educated in the execution of large and difficult works at the Pennsylvania Bank and works for supplying the city of Philadelphia with water are within reach, I have not the smallest doubt that the assistance of those collected in the city of Washington and in a tolerable favorable season

could complete the naval arsenal by the end of 1804.[31]

The era of massive public works began with the canal-building fever of the late 1820s. And canals provide the common example of sponsored migration, of attempts to recruit large bodies of labor in Europe so that the cost of the work might be kept down. Thus C. F. Mercer, President of the Chesapeake and Ohio Canal Company (near successor to the company's first president, George Washington), could write to his European agent in 1829: "I wish to reduce the price of labour on the Canal to ten dollars

---

[28] Edward S. Philbrick, in *Report of the United States Revenue Commission on Cotton*, Spec. Rep. 3, appendix (U.S. Treasury Dept., 1866).

[29] It is necessary to scale down, quite drastically, our present intuitive understanding of orders of magnitude in the economy. See the numbers for 1800 in Table A-1, and in chap. 1 above.

[30] Population density from U.S. Census, *Historical Statistics*, vol. II, p. 8. For the loss of a horse, see the travel notes in Claude Bowers (ed.), *The Diary of Elbridge Gerry, Jr.* (1927), p. 96.

[31] *Message from the President of the United States Transmitting Plans and Estimates of a Dry Dock* (Washington city: William Duane and Son, 1802), p. 13.

per month of 26 working days. It is now 12 and 13 dollars a month." [32] When canals began in Pennsylvania and Maryland at the same time, the competing demands made costs double the initial cost estimates. In midsummer, 1839, the number of laborers at work along the Pennsylvania "canal lines" was supposed to be not far from 10,000, while a recent writer estimates that a total of 15,000 were employed in the three major canal-building states (Pennsylvania, New York, Ohio) at the peak of the canal construction.[33] Mercer sought to import labor, but could count only on the end of the Pennsylvania canals for an adequate supply of labor at rates within his purview.[34] A few years later, however, France's greatest ministerial economist noted that the high prices charged by slaveholders had induced the James River and Kanawha Canal builders to seek 400 masons in Scotland and 1,000 laborers in Germany.[35]

Heavy bunched demands for labor also appeared when the first giant textile mills were being established in Lowell. Compared to the earliest mills in Rhode Island, where locally recruited labor might be collected without inordinate impact on wage costs, how to recruit for mills 10 or 20 times the size? The answer was the black "slaver's wagon" of New England tradition, the establishing of boardinghouses, close supervision, and checkoffs for tithes—all making it possible to recruit thousands of young women for the Lowell mills within the space of a few years and at wages only slightly above those they could earn in alternative pursuits.

Next only to agriculture as a major United States employer for many years was the merchant marine. The tradition of a merchant marine manned by foreigners is ancient of days. A historian of Rome notes that "both fo'c'sle and quarterdeck must, more often than not, have been manned by Frisians, Greeks, Levantines, Arabs and others who, like Kipling's Parnesius has 'never seen Rome except in a picture.' " [36]

When that nautical novelist, Captain Frederick Marryat, visited the United States in 1838 he observed how dominant was the role of foreigners —residents and nationals of other countries—in our merchant marine. Exclusive of masters, mates, and other specialists who were Americans, he concluded that seven out of every ten men aboard United States ships coasting to and from foreign ports were British, with some admixture of

[32] Mercer to Richards, July 8, 1829, *C & O Letterbook*, p. 84, U.S. National Archives.

[33] Harvey H. Segal, "Canal Cycles, 1834–1861," unpublished Columbia University thesis (1956), pp. 46, 300.

[34] U.S. Congress, Serial Set 210.

[35] Michel Chevalier, *Histoire et Description des Voies de Communication aux Etats Unis* (Paris: Librairie de Charles Gosselin, 1840), vol. II, p. 107. In fact, the ending of public works in the North and East released such supplies of labor that a mere 32 masons and 346 laborers were imported.

[36] Mortimer Wheeler, *Rome beyond the Imperial Frontiers* (1954), p. 16.

Swedes and Danes. One-third of the whalers immortalized in Moby Dick were probably British. And, in his opinion, fully half of the fishermen who sailed American ships to the dangerous waters of the Grand Banks and farther North were likewise British.[37] It was but a few years later that the Chairman of the Committee on Naval Affairs went so far as to assert flatly that 100,000 of the 109,000 men in the Navy and merchant marine were, in fact, foreigners.[38] Indeed, in the mid-1840s many believed that two-thirds of our sailors were not native.[39]

An interesting light is cast on the subject of British impressment of American sailors by the statement of an officer of the *USS Franklin* in 1820, who told a friend that the ship had 400 English sailors on board, a number nearly as large as its complement.[40]

An equal tradition relates to the Army. Foreigners, of course, constituted not only King George's Hessians but also the honored leaders of our Revolutionary Army. When reviewing the Mexican War in 1849, the Adjutant General was informative and concise on the same point.

In the states where the greatest number of men have been recruited, [we find] our large commercial cities, where most numbers of the class of men who enter the ranks of the army report for employment, and where, also, vast numbers of emigrants are constantly arriving. Many of them, disappointed in obtaining hired employment, enter the army, and owing to these causes, one-half if not three-quarters of those who enlist in the States of New York, Pennsylvania, Maryland and Ohio are not native citizens.[41]

A distinguished historian has concluded that from one-quarter to one-third of the regular army in 1840 were aliens.[42] Now if so large a portion of the regular army were aliens and we allow for an even greater proportion among the volunteers (given Adjutant Jones's statement), it might be concluded that the Mexican War was largely a set of battles between foreigners. In any event the role of immigrants as a component in the Army as well as the merchant marine at this early date seems excessively clear.

[37] Frederick Marryat, *A Diary in America* (New York: Appleton, 1839), vol. I, p. 183.
[38] Chairman Reed, quoted in *Remarks on the Scarcity of American Seaman and the Remedy,* by the gentleman connected with the *New York Press* (New York: printed at the Herald Office, 1845), p. 17.
[39] *Hunt's Magazine* (August, 1845), p. 142.
[40] William Dalton, *Travels in the United States of America* (Appleby, 1821), p. 7.
[41] Letter from the Secretary of War, *Regular Troops Engaged in the Mexican War,* 30th Cong., 2d Sess., Serial Set 540, Exec. Doc. 38, p. 5.
[42] Edward Channing, *A History of the United States* (*1921*), vol. V, p. 598. Channing uncharacteristically gives no source; since his family burned his papers after his death, we can only speculate on his source.

Later, immigrant recruiting was also evident. When recruiting officers at Ellis Island induced immigrants to join the Union forces, their success, in some degree, is evident from the variety of Southern complaints that this was an unfair practice.[43]

Somewhat surprisingly, the greatest direct beneficiary of the flow of immigrant labor was never agriculture, though farming was our primary industry for a century and more. It was instead the construction of canals, roads, and railroads in the early decades and mining, service, and factory trades in the later ones. Immigrants entered at urban ports—New York, Boston, New Orleans. When they did not remain there they moved to other areas where the foreign born lived. Just as groups of Vermonters moved to an area in the Midwest settled by their friends and relatives in the 1820s, as men moved from South Carolina to Mississippi in the 1830s, so the foreign born moved to where their kinsmen had settled. The result was a supply of labor to a specific group of industries. We can note the trend shown in the following table, from 1870 (the first census providing such detail) to 1930 (the most recent census at which the foreign born still constituted a numerically significant group).[44]

Percent of Foreign Born in Specified Occupations

	1870	1900	1930
Miners..................	60	44	25
Domestic servants........	20	26	36
Unskilled labor..........	40	28	19
Agriculture..............	10	13	11

Only a small share of farm jobs were filled by the foreign born. And even these were not immigrant settlers who moved before they had a stake or had become acclimated to a degree. "We have not for years had any agent in Europe," reported Colonel Charles Lamborn, land commissioner of the Northern Pacific, in 1894. Why not? Because "the raw im-

[43] This recruiting is discussed briefly in Erickson, *op. cit.*

[44] 1870 Census, vol. I, pp. 704ff. We use the data for domestic servants, laborers not specified, and miners. We estimate elsewhere that 555,000 of the 1,032,084 "laborers not specified" were in agriculture. Applying this same ratio to those classified as foreign born and adding to those reported in agriculture gives a total of 6.5 million, with 0.8 million foreign born.

1900 Census, *Occupations,* pp. clxxxvii–clxxxix. For this year we similarly add 1,456,000 of the "laborers not specified" to the total for agriculture, of whom 28.8 percent, or 419,000, were estimated as foreign born.

1930 Census, vol. V, *Occupations,* pp. 76ff. We add to foreign-born white the "other races" category, deducting Mexicans. The ratios were computed for agriculture, extraction of minerals, servants, and laborers not otherwise specified.

migrant very rarely goes out to settle on lands in our country or, if he does, his destination is already fixed before he leaves home. . . . The German or Scandinavian who has been in America for a few years, and acquired a little money, is the foreigner who settles on land in the northwest and stays there." [45]

Over the years the share of domestic service jobs, and unskilled jobs in cities and mines filled by migrants was disproportionately great.[46] So excessive a flow to nonfarm occupations bespoke mixed forces. Surely the skills demanded for farm labor were not so much deeper than those that many immigrants brought with them as to be an explanation.[47] While many were attracted by the opportunity to be "giants in the earth," many more were repelled by the loneliness and the uncertainty of income. In the end foreign labor provided the key skilled personnel for establishing our early industries; it provided millions of persons to the farms that sprang up in the new lands beyond the Mississippi; but it provided most of all a supply of those who would hew wood and fetch water for the industries of city and town.

THE LABOR SUPPLY

Political and Social Limitations of Labor Supply

The structure and dimensions of the labor supply are fixed by economic forces, forces that operate within political and social limits. The bounds set by political decision have been most strikingly demonstrated within the lifetime of many persons now living. Century after century immigration flowed persistently into the American labor market, until a political decision in 1921 halted migration as a significant source of labor. A more recent example appears in the Social Security Act of 1936. That act cut athwart a long tradition of men attempting to work on into their seventies—which meant, given the mortality table, that they intended to work until they died. Federal pensions have proved a significant element in cutting the supply of labor by men over sixty-five. A third example of

[45] Quoted in Kenneth O. Bjork, *West of the Great Divide* (Norwegian-American Historical Association, 1958), p. 383, n. 2.
[46] A succinct summary appears in A. Ross Eckler and Jack Zlotnick, "Immigration and the Labor Force," *The Annals of the American Academy of Political and Social Science* (March, 1949). A fuller review appears in the excellent, pointed, study by E. P. Hutchison, *Immigrants and Their Children* (1956), tables 21, 25a, etc.
[47] For the occupations of immigrants in earlier decades, see Herbert Heaton, "Industrial Immigrants in the United States, 1783–1812," *Proceedings of the American Philosophical Society* (October, 1951). The registration data there presented must be used with caution. It is striking that no alien sailors were reported, although other evidence suggests a sizable number in the American marine.

political limitation has been the accumulated set of school-leaving regulations—laws that have persistently reduced early entrance into the labor market.

Social forces have been no less significant in bounding the dimensions of the labor force. The custom of adult males working, though taken for granted in today's world, is by no means universal. In some respects it is un-American. Long before the first white settlers landed, the regular work of the country was, in accordance with Indian custom, done by women; the men, if travelers' tales are to be believed, concentrated on the varied responsibilities of hunting, resting, gaming, and the chase.[1]

A second social force has been the resistless endeavor of each generation of Americans to dower their children with more book learning than they had received. Their success, decade after decade, has effectively cut the percentage of young workers in the labor force.

A third social force has been the faltering belief in the desirability of farming and independent entrepreneurship as a way of life. This decline may, of course, be only the reverse of a coin whose obverse is an economic force. Yet, it is by no means clear that men have sought entrepreneurship for its money return alone. Usually one must also invoke the giant shade of "equalizing advantages," which prove to be the psychic advantages of being one's own boss, of sitting under one's own fig tree and having no one to say him nay. Disenchantment with the scope and depth of such advantages has grown with each passing decade, has surely been a factor in the decline of the entrepreneur. What follows from this? That because the entrepreneur, unlike the wage earner, becomes employed as soon as he chooses to, he creates both the supply of and demand for his own labor. Hence such a decline in entrepreneurial numbers brings a decline in labor supply. The man who becomes an employee typically puts in fewer hours of work a year than does the entrepreneur; hence aggregate man-hour input tends to decline with the decline in the entrepreneurial group.[2]

The Labor Force: Definition

The labor force in the United States is most usefully defined tautologically: It consists of those persons in the labor market at any given time.[3] The scope of the group is defined by economic, political, and social forces. It is not defined by demographic criteria, such as x percent of persons

---

[1] Bernard DeVoto, *Across the Wild Missouri; Narrative of the Adventures of Zenas Leonard* (1839; reprint 1934).

[2] It should be unnecessary to add that this assertion carries no necessary implications for the trend in output, welfare, etc.

[3] Dealing with the labor force we do not consider the additional dimensions of labor supply—including hours worked, labor effort, skill, etc.

in a given age interval. On a medieval fief, on a plantation run with slaves, in a nation of labor camps quite other definitions apply. For there the labor force can be defined as definite (nearly invariant) proportions of persons in each age-sex category. A child is born, at a certain age enters the labor force, and continues to contribute his labor until he dies or becomes totally disabled. But such a pattern has only a distant and doubtful relevance to the United States labor market. Entry into our labor force is a matter of need, choice, expediency. And the limits on the supply of labor are fixed by the ingenuity and financial resources of entrepreneurs seeking labor for the mills, mines, and TV studios of the economy. The size of the labor force is bounded by cost limitations. These are similar to those which determine at what point on the wide spectrum of potential supply for any input we find the quantity offered under specific conditions of time, tide, and the market.

This arbitrary definition of the labor force in a free nation is, of course, on all fours with a definition of the national product. The latter, similarly, does not derive from any measurement of wealth or illth; nor is it limited to the production of goods or useful products. It measures merely the value of certain market transactions—without resorting to a higher or more abstruse criterion. We have no more elegant procedure for defining those who are in the labor force.

The baby has contributed more to the gaiety of nations than have all the nightclub comics in history. We include the comic in the labor force but not the baby, as we include the former's wages in the national income but set no value on the endearing talents provided by the baby. Similarly much of the world's work is done by housewives. But they are excluded from the labor-force count, as their services are excluded from the gross product estimate. Any definition of the labor force that would include them would yield a rigid labor-force measure, largely invariant to the most massive economic changes, and hence of little analytic value. But when we study the labor-force pattern we must keep the fact of such exclusions in mind. This is particularly true if we refer to the early decades of the nineteenth century, when a substantial share of the nation's clothing and food was prepared, its farm chores and housework completed, by the women and children omitted from our customary estimates of the labor force. (Conversely, of course, the mere receipt of pay does not indicate that persons in a variety of occupations were making what a majority of Americans might consider to be a productive contribution.)

No more does the labor force measure what manpower resources are available to a nation. Through the exchanges of foreign trade a nation may call upon manpower in every part of the world. Depending on its relative resource position, it will draw more or less upon those workers indirectly through trade, directly through regular migration. By affecting the terms of trade in its favor, a nation might supplement its manpower resources far more helpfully than by seeking additional hands at home. However, nationalism, flourishing with such ebullience since the late eighteenth century, has made any such possibility less and less relevant, for we usually consider our manpower resources as limited by the nation's boundaries.

Through the provision of added incentives, a nation may secure additional hours of work from those already in the labor force, may draw in women, children, and older men not currently in the labor force.[4]

Determinants of the Labor Supply

Within the broad boundaries marked off by political and social forces, will the supply of labor vary in response to changing economic incentives? Three main answers are possible. One, that the supply is almost invariant —an answer developed extensively in recent years. The second, that it is negatively related to wage rates. The third, that it is positively linked to wage-rate levels.[5] We consider each of these in principle, and then turn to a review of the major trends in labor supply over the past century and a half. By reviewing the categories subject to potential variation—additions through migration, reductions from shorter hours worked and fewer children working, increases in worker rates for women—we hope to cast light on the extent to which the supply does vary, and in what direction its major components have shifted.

The Invariant Supply Function.   Perhaps the most extensive, detailed, and forceful recent analysis of the labor force concludes that the proportion of the population in the labor force varies little over time, that such variation as does occur is a response to the hot pressures of armed-forces recruitment rather than to changing economic conditions.[6]

"The overall proportion of the working-age population in the labor force has been rather impressively stable from one high-employment census year to another: the stability has held for the United States as a whole

[4] An excellent discussion of definitions appears in Louis Ducoff and Margaret Hagood, *Labor Force Definition and Measurement* (1947), Social Science Research Council Bulletin 56, chaps. 2, 4. See too the helpful analysis by Richard Wilcock, "The Secondary Labor Force and the Measurement of Unemployment," in Universities–National Bureau of Economic Research, *The Measurement and Behavior of Unemployment* (1957), and Bureau of Labor Statistics, *The Extent and Nature of Frictional Unemployment* (1959), Study Paper 6 for the Joint Economic Committee, Study on Employment, Growth, and Price Levels.

[5] By wages we mean real wages, not assuming money illusion. However, our discussion focuses on historical changes, and the wage data for this period (as developed below) show a high correlation between money and real-wage changes.

[6] Clarence D. Long, *The Labor Force under Changing Income and Employment* (1958), *passim,* especially pp. 19, 243.

since 1890 and possibly since 1820." Since 1946 "the whole range of peacetime fluctuation in labor participation between quarterly dates . . . has been less than 2½ percent of the working age population." [7]

The present estimates (Table A-3) do indicate that the percentage of population aged fourteen and over in the labor force has varied by only a few points in any year from 1900 through 1960. A related analysis finds that an economy can reach a state of full employment—a state constituting a technical limitation and barrier to further growth. The rate of growth of the labor supply is defined as a remorseless constant, and no equilibrating adjustments occur through it.[8] (Such analyses call to mind ones that find a balance-of-payments equilibrium unattainable for a nation without a decrease in consumption—production gains being impossible because the "full employment limit has been reached," a limit treated as some technically fixed boundary.)

All these studies have, of course, very considerable fascination. A novelty among economic theories, surely, is one premising that a major input for the production of marketed goods is itself invariant to economic forces. Seen as coldly insensitive to anything less than the pressures of armed-forces recruitment, the labor force in peacetime is described as simply a function of the changes in the population in being. As each age-sex group reaches a fixed appropriate age, a given percentage of that group enters the labor force. After a fixed term, it leaves the labor force. This "bloodless ballet of mechanical forces" is inconsistent with classical theories, as Power notes.[9] Whether it can be used to create more fruitful theories, to bring better insights into the labor-market process, is a further consideration. (Such conceptual insulation of the labor-force change from other economic change may, for example, be advantageous in the study

[7] Clarence D. Long, testimony before the Joint Economic Committee, *Hearings on Employment Growth and Price Levels,* Apr. 25–28, 1959, part 3, p. 542.

[8] Thomas Power, "The Economic Framework of a Theory of Growth," *Economic Journal* (March, 1958). In sec. IV of his study, Power defines *g* both as "the annual percentage increment to the free labour supply" and also as "the rate of population growth," finding that "the relevant ceiling [on the rate of growth] is the limit of the available labour force." In sec. V he states "In the classical theory of economic growth the saving function and the rate of growth of population were assumed to adjust to each other. . . . It is more realistic, however, to assume that population growth is a given datum. . . ." Implicitly his definitions of *g* indicate that he assumes a constant percent of the population in the labor force, as well as a constant rate of growth in the labor force.

[9] A more precise analysis appears in K. W. Rothschild, *Theory of Wages* (1954), p. 46. Rothschild notes that the summation of individual and family supply schedules which decline can yield a labor supply which increases in response to rising wages provided that "workers' minimum wage demands are fairly widely spaced"—an assumption that he finds unlikely. However, American experience reflects just such spacing—not for family, but for individual schedules.

of countries afflicted with the Byzantine rigidities so dear to Spenglerian analysis.)

A useful introduction to these issues appears in *The Importance of Being Earnest.* The butler introduces the problem:

> LANE: I have often observed that in married households the champagne is rarely of a first rate brand.
>
> ALGERNON: Good Heavens! Is marriage so demoralizing as that?
>
> LANE: I believe it is a very pleasant state, sir. I have had very little experience of it myself up to the present. I have only been married once.

The difference between one marriage in a lifetime and two is numerically very small—but it is great enough. The United States Cavalry was sent to the State of Utah because of the difference between a ratio of 1.0 wives per husband and a slightly greater number. Whether a significant difference separates two percentages, or numbers, will turn on quite other considerations than absolute size.

Now any surprise at the rough stability of the percent of the adult population in the labor force from decade to decade, or changes over shorter periods, must be initially tempered by one observation. It is a basic aspect of our way of life for men (excepting only the disabled) to enter the labor force sometime between fifteen and twenty years of age and remain until they reach an advanced age. We find worker rates of 95 percent for men between twenty and sixty as far back as 1850, when our first census data become available (Table A-14).[10] And the rates are similar for other years. Differences even for a particular age group from one census to the next more probably reflect changes in census procedure, or short-term differences in morbidity, etc., than any change in worker rates. Because men have constituted 75 percent or more of our labor force over the decades, it follows that the total labor force will likewise have great stability, appearing to vary only slightly in ratio to population. If we wish to determine what forces shape the total for the economically active population, we must look to the categories within which the main lines of our social organization permit variation.

Now if the labor force were sensitive to economic change and incentive, where would such responsiveness appear, and how great would it be? For the decades prior to 1914 it should appear most immediately in the

---

[10] The 1850 data relate only to white males. A possible qualification applies to the somewhat low rates for white males in the Southern states in 1850. These lower rates may reflect enumerative error, or they may testify to a real difference under conditions characteristic of a plantation way of life. In his *Notes on Virginia,* Jefferson found that of the proprietors of slaves "a very small proportion indeed are ever seen to labor."

immigration data, and in hours worked.[11] After 1921 it would appear in both hours worked and in labor-force participation rates. Before we consider the historic changes in each, we must turn first to another, longer-established approach to labor-supply analysis.

The Negative Supply Function. In considering the supply function for final products or other productive inputs than labor, it is common to assume that these functions are positive, and that (within reasonable limits) the higher the price paid, the greater the volume provided by suppliers. But it is equally common when considering the supply of labor to emphasize a function that is reentrant at some point, becoming unequivocally negative.[12] While all other inputs and outputs are described with pedestrian forward-sloping curves, varied only occasionally with a kink here and there, discussion of the supply of labor normally induces an *elan* that results in the presentation of a negatively sloped curve. Now clearly this change involves more than mere desire for elegant variation in curve analysis. Such emphasis must be prompted by an assumption that in the real world labor supply does tend to diminish after the wage unit reaches some level.

It is of interest to consider how unequally analysis treats these productive factors. When the supply of other input items is analyzed it is total supply—all suppliers, all firms producing, all interacting markets. But when the analysis relates to the supply of labor, it suddenly becomes the theory of the supply of labor from one man. It relates not to all persons, in or potentially in, the labor force but to one person who, more depressed by the prospect of working 24 hours a day than he is elated by the incessant upward course of wage rates, decides to supply less labor as the wage rate rises.[13] Now we could hypothesize an individual firm, producing final products, that found costs mounting so at three-shift operation that, as the price of its product rose, it did not produce up to the 24-hour limit, but at some point decreased the amount it offered. (In fact, of course, it is most typical of our economy for additional establishments to provide ad-

[11] It should also appear, to some extent, in the worker rates for the native labor force. However, data prior to recent years are so intermittent as to make them unsuitable for the study of intermediate term adjustments.

[12] A characteristic discussion appears in John B. Williams, "The Theory of Wages," *Econometrica* (April, 1946). In Hicks, *Theory of Wages,* the limitation is explicitly to the "individual supply of labour" in recognition of the difficulty of saying much that is useful about aggregate supply.

[13] Occasionally it describes a native community coming under foreign domination in the nineteenth century, from which the extrapolation to a negatively sloped curve is an easy one. Even such examples may lose their cogency when the alternative uses of time for other economic purposes are considered. See, for example, Walter Elkan, "Incentives in East Africa," in H.R.H. the Duke of Edinburgh's Study Conference on the Human Problems of Industrial Communities, vol. II, *Background Papers* (1957).

ditional supply rather than for the same units to operate three shifts—suggesting that there are such developing costs.)

It is more useful, however, to treat the labor-supply function on all fours with the supply of other productive factors. If we consider not the theory of the supply of labor from one man but more generally the supply of labor (from whatever source) to the labor markets, we find little basis for such a general conclusion. In the short run, the typical labor-market response in the United States has been that of a positive-sloping supply curve.[14] The total labor supply in the nineteenth century was dominated by variations in migration; when wages rose, migration rose. For the twentieth century, our information on short-period changes in labor supply begins only with 1940, and it is common knowledge how the rising wages of 1941 to 1945 were associated with an extraordinary increase in the number of working women and the total labor supply. In 1944 the civilian labor force was as great as that in 1941, although more than 11 million men were under arms. Aside from a limited contribution by population growth, the major source was an intense increase in worker rates for women and youngsters. However significant the role of other contributing forces, it is impossible to read this graphic example as an indication of a negatively sloped labor-supply function. The substantial decrease in the number of women in the labor force in 1946 (when wage rates declined), as well as the steady increase in their number during the 1950s (when wage rates rose), alike point to a positive relationship.

For one significant group in the labor force, however, a negative pattern seems to appear at several points in our history, namely, Negro females. This substantial component of our labor force was for many years concentrated in farm labor and domestic service. The analysis of competitive or even imperfect markets is hardly applicable to that concentration under slavery. On the other hand the transition to postslavery conditions is another matter. At the end of the Civil War, a firm of cotton brokers wrote to leading planters in every state and in almost every county in the South. The replies they received expressed unequivocal and uniform dissatisfaction on one point: Once emancipation took place, female slaves did not wish to work as they had under slavery. From western Alabama: "The women and children have ceased to work." From Aiken, South Carolina: "Women seldom now work in the fields; they all ambition 'keeping house.'" From Baldwin County, Georgia: "The women have quite retired, and so too have the children." From Oglethorpe County, Georgia:

---

[14] Long-run relationships do not certainly, but probably, reflect positions on different curves. An analysis of quarter-to-quarter changes in labor-force rates from 1949 to 1960 shows a very clear response to increases in wage rates. The subject is discussed at greater length in a paper by the author for the 1963 Annual Meeting of the American Statistical Association, Business and Economics Section.

"One third of the hands [before the war] were women who now do not work at all." [15]

A second instance appeared in World War II, when again higher wage rates and higher family income offered nonwhite women a real alternative to continuation in the labor force. While worker rates for white women rose in all parts of the nation and in three major Southern cities—Norfolk, Charleston, and Mobile—the available data show that the rate for nonwhite women in these three cities plummeted from 1940 to 1944.[16] Moreover, the decline in domestic service after 1940 (Table A-4) in the face of a rising demand for servants is explicable in part by a decline in nonwhite worker rates.[17] We hypothesize that the range of alternatives open to nonwhite females in the three cities, as in other areas, was limited largely to domestic service work and work of similar low skill and low status. Hence higher family incomes offered an opportunity for them to leave such low-status occupations.

That domestic service was felt to be dishonorable work in a nation that had been a world leader in treating work per se as honorable, was noted early by visitors to America. "Service," wrote one in 1843, "is not esteemed honorable among the Americans and it is ill paid." [18] As early as 1820, a Philadelphia manufacturer found that while he had no difficulty in finding women for arduous factory work, such was the aversion to housework that he had to pay twice the going factory rate for servants.[19] And one Southern visitor to the North in the late 1850s found that "Domestic service is certainly held to be so degrading at the North that no natives will do it." [20]

To the normal disutility of work was added, for this group, a heavy contribution of social opprobrium. Offer nonwhites, however, a wider range of work and higher wage rates and you evoke a higher labor input, as appears to have been the case since World War II. It is worth adding, however, that even this possible example of a negative supply function for a substantial group is weak proof. For during the massive transition both from slavery to freedom and from a peacetime market to that of World

---

[15] F. W. Loring and C. F. Atkinson, *Cotton Culture and the South* (1869), pp. 14, 15, 20, 106, 109.

[16] U.S. Bureau of the Census, *Characteristics of the Population, Labor Force, Families and Housing* (Congested Production Area surveys, 1943–1944), Series CA-3, no. 4, table 5; no. 7, table 5; and no. 1, table 5.

[17] In large measure only a shift to alternative work was involved.

[18] George Combe, *Notes on the United States of America during a Phrenological Visit in 1838–39–40* (Philadelphia: 1841), vol. I, p. 93.

[19] William Tudor, *Letters on the Eastern States* (Boston: Wells and Lilly, 1821), p. 262.

[20] Thomas Kettell, *Southern Wealth and Northern Profits* (New York: George W. and John A. Wood, 1860), p. 102.

War II, marked changes in family incomes were concurrently taking place. Slaves who traditionally had only a few dollars' income from trading the products of their Sunday labors (omitting the limited number who were hired out in factories and other urban pursuits where they might receive a small cash incentive), suddenly found themselves receiving $10 cash wages a month. Despite a rising cost of living and failures to adhere to contracts, a marked rise in nonwhite male incomes after slavery seems surely indicated. During World War II, the addition of soldiers' allotments to family incomes created a similar effect. It is quite conceivable, therefore, that even for nonwhite females the two apparent instances of a negative labor-supply function may not be such.

COMPONENTS OF LABOR SUPPLY: MIGRATION

We turn now to those areas of our national life where variations in the labor force in response to varying economic conditions might most reasonably be found, and, if found, determined to be significant or not. We consider first the role of immigration.

Migration: The Forces

In the nineteenth century the United States labor force was still fluid. As our national boundaries were in motion, so were those of the labor force. Apart from the sudden accessions of territory bought, or wrested, from Spanish, Indian, French, or English hands, there were more important accessions in the immigrant streams. The specific causes that brought a given migrant to the United States during the nineteenth century were as multifarious as the charms that link one youth and one maid in marriage.

Here in the United States, as Festus Foster declared in 1812, "was every allurement to emigration, and the means of subsistence so easy as to produce a rapid increase of population." [1] Many came in bright hope, drawn by the "facility of land acquisition. . . . Every 5 pounds that a man saves may at once be invested in land. He need run no risk of bank failures; and his landed investment is constantly improving in value. . . . Every necessary of life is sluttishly plentiful. . . . It is not possible here to find a man hungry." [2]

It is invariably the practice of the American, observed the Shamrock Society in 1817, "and well suited to his love of independence, to purchase a piece of land as soon as he can, and cultivate his own farm, rather than live on wages. It is equally within the power of an emigrant to do the

[1] Festus Foster, *An Oration* (Brookfield: E. Merriam Co., July, 1812), p. 1.
[2] James Caird, *Prairie Farming* (New York: 1859), p. 94.

same, after a few years of labour and economy. From that moment he secures all the means to happiness." [3]

"In 1820 when lands were worth $50 per acre in Massachusetts and one dollar in Ohio, the New England farmer improved his condition by emigrating to Ohio, and when in 1840 the best lands of Ohio were worth $50 per acre and those of Illinois one dollar and a quarter he could again move with profit to Illinois; and again in 1850 from lands worth $50 in Illinois to the cheap lands of Minnesota and Kansas." [4]

Many came, too, because of the immense opportunity that an open society offered to their children. They could enter any trade without long and expensive apprenticeships; or they might become independent as farmers after only a few short years.[5]

Many another came in cold despair, having discovered that "in the land of his birth, as a Malthusian would say, 'The tables are all occupied'— that there is neither knife, fork nor wooden spoon to spare for him." No sooner would he discover this than he would find that "the love of home is smothered in his heart," and take off for the new land.[6]

In other instances the driving force of directed migration complemented such incentives. In 1828 migration agents were sent to Dublin, Cork, Belfast, and Holland to collect laborers for the Chesapeake and Ohio Canal. Their promise of "meat three times a day, a plenty of bread and vegetables, with a reasonable allowance of liquor, and eight, ten or twelve dollars a month for wages would," the President of the Company shrewdly supposed, "prove a powerful attraction to those who, narrowed down in the circle of their employment have, at this moment, a year of scarcity presented to them." [7]

In 1832 the Directors of the Delaware and Hudson Canal, disturbed

[3] Shamrock Society of New York, *Emigration to America; Hints to Emigrants from Europe* (London: William Hone, 1817), p. 11.

[4] *Minnesota, Its Place among the States, Being the First Annual Report of the Commissioner of Statistics* (Hartford, Minnesota: 1860), pp. 30–31. "Whenever great facilities exist for becoming a land-owner, men will not willingly submit to the drudgery of menial or mechanical occupations, or at least so long only as will afford them the means of taking up what they will consider a preferable mode of life." Lieut. Francis Hall, *Travels in Canada and the U.S. in 1816 and 1817* (Boston: Wells and Lilly, 1818), p. 2.

[5] Ezra Seaman, *Essays on The Progress of Nations* (New York: 1868).

[6] John Regan, *The Emigrants Guide* (Edinburgh: Oliver and Boyd, 1846), p. 10. If its residents "could migrate en masse" from Ireland, wrote another traveler in 1824, "they could become superior beings; I would strongly advise every one of them . . . to work or beg his passage over . . . so that at all events he may quit his native island . . . that den of human wretchedness." (Newnham Blane) *An Excursion through the United States and Canada during the years 1822–23 by an English Gentleman* (London: Baldwin, Cradock and Joy, 1824), pp. 169–170.

[7] Mercer to Maury, Nov. 28, 1828, *C & O Letterbook*, pp. 38–39. U.S. National Archives.

by demands for high wages, found that "against this evil the only effectual remedy was the introduction of additional miners from abroad. This was done as promptly as possible and to such extent that it is believed a recurrence of the evil will not be experienced." [8]

Migration: Some Determinants

These and a thousand other examples, motives, and forces eventually become summarized in the aggregate figures on migration. What appear to have been the dominant forces that shaped the changing volume of migration? One of the earliest answers was given by Friederich Kapp in 1870, after years of observing the flow of immigrants into the United States: "In short, bad times in Europe regularly increase, and bad times in America invariably diminish, immigration." [9]

This linkage was expounded to the Industrial Commission by John R. Commons in 1901, and has been developed extensively in recent analyses by Jerome, Thomas, and others.[10] Their work has elaborated Jerome's conclusion that "this movement is on the whole dominated by conditions in the United States. The 'pull' is stronger than the 'push.' " [11] There would, of course, have been no migration at all without the "push" of foreign economic and political pressures. But the difference between opportunities in the New and Old World was almost always great enough to make migration tempting. It was only when opportunities in the United States changed significantly that immigration was most likely to be speeded or slowed. It may be suggestive on this point that we find only a limited relationship between changes in nonfarm earnings and migration. The difference between wage levels in the two worlds was always substantial; short-term changes in wages (particularly small ones) made little difference in this ratio of advantage. Aside from climactic changes such as outright national crop failure (Ireland) or systematized and energetic government prosecution (Russia, Germany), changes in European crop yields

---

[8] *Annual Report of the Board of Managers of the Delaware and Hudson Canal Company for the Year 1832* (New York: 1833), p. 35.

[9] Friederich Kapp, *Immigration and the Commissioners of Emigration of the State of New York* (1870), p. 15.

[10] U.S. Industrial Commission, *Reports,* vol. XV, p. 305. Harry Jerome, *Migration and Business Cycles* (1926), chaps. 4, 7. Brinley Thomas, *Migrations and Economic Growth* (1954). Other sources include President's Commission on Immigration and Naturalization, *Whom We Shall Welcome* (1953), pp. 27–28; Simon Kuznets and Ernest Rubin, *Immigration and the Foreign Born* (1954), pp. 34–37; A. Ross Eckler and Jack Zlotnick, "Immigration and the Labor Force," *Annals of the American Academy of Political and Social Science* (March, 1949).

[11] Jerome, *op. cit.,* p. 208.

or social pressures made similarly small differences in the massive ratio of advantage that normally prevailed. (As a prerequisite for migration from farm to city within the United States, a major gap in economic advantage is a first requirement. But variations in the size of that gap are unimportant for determining when migration takes place. Instead variation of employment opportunities in the urban areas becomes the decisive complementary factor.)

If we recognize that endless amounts of free or nearly free land were available throughout the nineteenth century, offering brighter opportunities at nearly any time than the European migrant could have had at home, we may question why short-term variations even in American opportunities affected migration at all substantially. The answer would appear to lie in the fact that migrants first took jobs as employees—as workers in Eastern cities, hired hands on farms. Having accumulated a minimum competence, only then could they move on both geographically and economically. Immigrants left Europe in rough proportion to economic circumstance in the United States, then accumulated in Eastern cities and did not seek the way west until conditions in the United States warranted that further move.[12]

Data for our first full-blown depression as a nation, that of 1819, indicate a marked slackening of migration to the West.[13] The retardation of the immigrant flow to the United States in the recession of 1837–1839 and in the mid-1840s is likewise apparent. Our first measures of both immigration flows to the United States and internal migration flows within the United States in response to cyclical changes, however, appear to be for the recession of 1857–1858. April, 1858, arrivals at Ellis Island were 85 percent below April, 1857, levels; May was about half as great as a year before. June was only 40 percent of the prior June; and the year as a whole proved to be 41 percent as great.[14] As an indicator of the tides of internal migration, we may note the number of lots platted in Minnesota in these years. On a rising tide during the bumper years of the early

[12] A corollary would be the periodic accumulation of migrants in the reception states. The present state of our knowledge does not permit close examination of this point. Thus data on net migration of foreign-born males into New York as given in Everett Lee et al., *Population Redistribution and Economic Growth, 1870–1950* (1957), vol. I, p. 183, are larger for some decades than total migration to the United States as shown in the official immigration figures. There is perhaps greater reason to doubt the immigration data than the net migration figures, but both have their limitations.

[13] Rodney C. Loehr, "Moving Back from the Atlantic Seaboard," *Agricultural History* (April, 1943), p. 91.

[14] Computed from data in *Annual Reports of the Commissioners of Emigration of the State of New York, 1847–1860* (New York, 1861), p. 343.

Table 2-1. Migration and Production: 1854 to 1894

Year	Emigrant passengers (PRR)	Immigrants to the U.S. (000) (calendar year)	Pig-iron shipments (000 short tons)	Manufacturing production index (Frickey)
1854	23,948*	428	736	
1855	20,187*	201	784	
1856	21,524*	200	883	
1857	21,619*	251	798	
1858	16,862*	123	705	
1859	10,761*	121	841	
1860	11,831*	154	920	
1860	12,781	154	920	16
1861	11,867	92	732	16
1862	12,621	92	788	15
1863	17,432	177	948	17
1864	23,217	193	1,136	18
1865	27,791	248	932	17
1866	30,395	319	1,350	21
1867	28,625	316	1,462	22
1868	23,844	285	1,603	23
1869	28,756	386	1,917	25
1870	37,657	358	1,865	25
1871	36,451	346	1,912	26
1872	58,861	433	2,855	31
1873	56,513	427	2,868	30
1874	46,416	263	2,689	29
1875	30,187	192	2,267	28
1876	29,985	158	2,093	28
1877	36,964	133	2,315	30
1878	49,676	152	2,577	32
1879	56,973	253	3,071	36
1880	83,957	588	4,295	42
1881	97,970	713	4,642	46
1882	69,762	733	5,178	49
1883	46,283	566	5,147	50
1884	33,127	458	4,590	47
1885	135,253	348	4,530	47
1886	34,877	399	6,365	57
1887	49,255	514	7,187	60
1888	42,191	517	7,269	62
1889	30,281	436	8,516	66
1890	35,147	498	10,307	71
1891	38,442	584	9,273	73
1892	33,191	516	10,256	79
1893	40,324	435	7,979	70
1894	20,902	217	7,456	68

* Baltimore through passengers not included.

Table 2-2. Unemployment and Immigration: 1890 to 1914

Year	Unemployment (percent of labor force)	Immigrant arrivals* (000)
1890	4.0	579
1891	5.4	644
1892	3.0	544
1893	11.7	347
1894	18.4	301
1895	13.7	363
1896	14.4	244
1897	14.5	250
1898	12.4	335
1899	6.5	519
1900	5.0	563
1901	4.0	731
1902	3.7	921
1903	3.9	841
1904	5.4	1060
1905	4.3	1166
1906	1.7	1438
1907	2.8	925
1908	8.0	944
1909	5.1	1198
1910	5.9	1030
1911	6.7	1017
1912	4.6	1427
1913	4.3	1403
1914	7.9	434

* Year ending June 30 of subsequent year.

1850s, the number fell drastically with the break in economic conditions:[15]

1856   39,683
1857   90,584
1858   18,076
1859   4,932

We can attempt a more systematic look at the relationship by investigating the series in Tables 2-1 and 2-2. For immigration to the United States, we adjust the official series to a calendar-year basis.[16] For an indicator of internal migration, we use the number of emigrant passengers

[15] *Minnesota, Its Place among the States, Being the First Annual Report of the Commissioner of Statistics,* p. 1.
[16] We divided Jerome's calendar-year totals for male immigrants (*op. cit.,* p. 245) by interpolated ratios for the (fiscal-year) proportion of males to total immigration from *Historical Statistics,* vol. II, p. 62.

on the Pennsylvania Railroad, one of the great forwarders of emigrants from the Atlantic Coast farther west.[17] As one indicator of cycle change we take pig iron shipments; for another we use Frickey's output series, which begins with 1860.[18] The depressing effects of the downturns in 1873, 1882, 1885, and 1893, as signaled in the production series, appear no less clearly in the migration data for the same or the subsequent years. The forceful trends that buoy up each series make collinearity likely. Figure 2 therefore focuses on year-to-year changes in each series. It reveals a close parallelism of short-term changes. Despite the linkage, of course, other forces were at work. During the Civil War the roving *Alabama* and menacing opposition of blockade and blockade runner slowed the current of immigration. The better protected flow of internal migrants declined hardly at all from 1860 to 1861, then rose persistently till the war's end.

The course of internal migration in general ran more smoothly than did that of immigration, and showed a closer consiliency with business cycle change. It is unlikely that competing errors in the data accounted for this contrast. True, the failure of the immigration data to reflect precisely illegal entrances is known, classification errors (for example, 1854–1855) flourished, etc. Yet even if the Pennsylvania Railroad data were perfectly reported, the road's share in total migrant traffic should surely have varied. Hence the fairly tight relationship that nevertheless manifests itself in these data must truly reflect a reality, namely, a closer link between internal migration and internal economic conditions than between United States national economic conditions and its immigration.[19]

The latter was responsive as well to conditions abroad as diverse as the price of wheat under Peel, the musical tastes of Ludwig II, and the national plan of Stolypin.[20] Internal migration, moreover, would presumably

---

[17] Data from *Annual Reports of the Pennsylvania Railroad,* year and page as follows: 1855, p. 78; 1857, p. 68; 1858, p. 97; 1860, p. 85; 1861, p. 104; 1862, pp. 17 and 85; 1864, p. 22; 1866, p. 32; 1868, p. 25; 1870, p. 24; 1871, p. 32; 1872, p. 34; 1873, p. 44; 1874, p. 52; 1875, p. 112; 1876, p. 111; 1878, p. 159; 1879, p. 101; 1880, p. 100; 1882, p. 96; 1883, p. 88; 1885, p. 88; 1887, p. 91; 1889, p. 104; 1891, p. 134; 1893, p. 130; 1895, p. 68.

[18] *Historical Statistics,* vol. II, pp. 366, 409. The marked deviation in Figure 2 for 1893 may reflect some error in this output series. The more recent estimate of William H. Shaw in his *Value of Commodity Output since 1869* (1947), p. 76, shows no marked 1892–1893 decline, but a mild rise in finished goods output.

[19] Cairncross points to a similar conclusion from British data on decennial trends: "The mobility of the population was much less variable than emigration, although it varied in the same direction." A. K. Cairncross, *Home and Foreign Investment, 1870–1913* (1953), p. 217.

[20] As one graphic illustration: The number of emigrants to the Midwest via the Syracuse and Utica railroad averaged 25,000 in 1847 and 27,000 in 1848. But in 1849, the year after the revolutions in Europe, their number rose to 45,000. Syracuse and Utica, *Annual Report, 1849,* p. 14 (estimates rounded).

link even more closely to a direct measure of labor-market conditions, or a more comprehensive measure of economic activity. (For example, Frickey's output series rises significantly from 1881 to 1882, whereas the National Bureau of Economic Research dates the cycle peak at March, 1882. The immigrant total falls heavily from 1881 to 1882.)

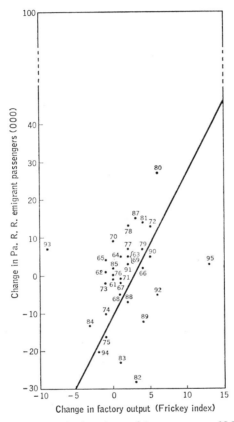

Figure 2.   Westward migration and factory output, 1861–1894.

In Figure 3 we move on to the 1890–1913 period. The railroad data are no longer available. We compare immigration changes with those in our unemployment series, which begins with 1890 (Tables A-15, A-3). Rising unemployment from one year to the next is clearly linked to declines in immigration over the year ending 6 months later.[21]

[21] The spectacular exception for July, 1907–1908, may reflect an error in the immigration figures. Beginning in 1907, the law directed the reporting officers to begin excluding temporary immigrants from the arrival data. The heavy rise in the ratio of nonimmigrants to arriving aliens (Jerome, *op. cit.,* p. 138) suggests some impact. So too does the failure of immigration from many countries to decline in 1907–

With the outbreak of World War I, the value of such year-to-year analysis ends abruptly. The 1913–1914 decline is surely to be associated not merely with United States depression but with war in Europe; and from then until the Immigration Act of 1924 drastically limited immigration, war, reconstruction, and recession make this decade useless for such short-term analysis.

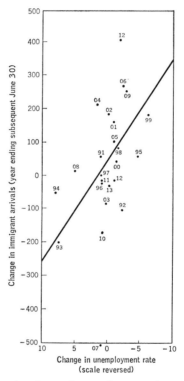

Figure 3.   Immigration and unemployment changes, 1890–1913.

We conclude that from 1789 to 1914 immigrants came to the United States seeking many goals, from a fuller measure of religious freedom to a greater economic advantage than they could foresee in their homeland. At any time in these many years such incentives were overwhelmingly important to hundreds of thousands of people. As a result the absolute volume of migration to the United States in any decade was substantial, and on an upward trend. But the fluctuations around that trend—how

---

1908, whereas the decline for Italians was spectacular. Since it was known that many Italians did not arrive intending to settle permanently, it is possible that the new act led officials to begin classifying many of them in this year as nonimmigrants.

much this year compared to last—were clearly shaped by varying economic conditions in the United States. As closely as can be seen, it was not variations in wages or working conditions that were so determinative, since these were far above alternatives in Europe and Asia even during the depths of United States depression. Rather was it variation in job opportunities in the United States that brought about short-term changes. Although cheap land, and even free land, was available for much of the period, the immediate prospect before the immigrant was work as an employee—and frequently as an employee on arrival at the coast before proceeding inland. Hence the condition of the job market bounded his immediate horizon. A measure of internal migration flows for the years from 1854 to 1894 indicates a similar, even closer, link between migration within the nation and changing job opportunities.

Hours of Work

By force of custom and need, most men of adult years are commonly in the labor force, but there is no inflexible conformity in the hours they work. Has the supply of man-hours varied in response to changing wage levels? Our experience since 1940, when reliable short-term data begin, does show such variation—marked increases during the war years as wage rates shot up, mild and inconsequential declines in the years since the war. But something can usefully be concluded by a look at the indirect indications given by the long-term historical trend.

From 1800 on through certainly to 1900, the hours worked in our major industry—agriculture—were unchanged: sunrise to sunset. In the first factory industries, the possibilities of early "lighting up" made an even longer day feasible. In 1840 an acute observer, reporting on the great strikes of 1835–1836, stated that the 10-hour day had not been established by the strikes, that 11 and 12 hours were taken as "hardly sufficient" in the Eastern factories, while "for all out of door employment in the middle and western states the duration was almost from the rise to the set of the sun." Elsewhere he noted that the factory hours had been 14 and 15 before the strike, that mechanics' work averaged 12 hours of actual work—giving a 13-hour workday.[22] And there were occasions and industries where even longer hours prevailed. The voyageurs, on a hard run into fur country, might work "about 20 hours a day for 2 to 3 weeks, resting only every 2 hours for 5 or 10 minutes to refill their pipes." [23] The continuous-process industries of the nineteenth century did not rely on two- or three-shift operation, as modern petroleum or chemical process

[22] *The British Mechanics and Labourers Hand Book and True Guide to the United States* (London: Charles Knight, 1840), pp. 18, 190. On p. 203, he notes that hours for bricklayers since the strike ran from 7 A.M. to 6 P.M. minus the dinner hour.
[23] Gordon C. Davidson, *The NorthWest Company* (1918), p. 218.

plants do; brewery hours (well into the 1880s) ran from 4 in the morning till 6 in the evening.[24]

As of 1830, a workday of 13 hours is suggested by reports from a handful of firms in the dominant textile industries, an average of 11 to 12 hours in the others.[25] For 1844 we have a detailed report for the typical Lowell mills, averaging 12 hours and 15 minutes, work beginning at 5 in the morning from May 1 to August 31; and, from September 1 to April 30, "as soon as they can see." [26] By 1860 the textile mills had decreased hours to 11, and metal industries, to 10.[27] By 1900 textiles and all manufacturing had both reached a level of just under 10 hours a day.[28] In 1960 the typical adult male worked about 7.3 hours a day.[29]

Hours worked by men have therefore been about cut in half since 1800. This decline is large, and significant, by any criterion. (We do not consider short-term changes in hours here—although sharp rises, such as in 1941–1942 and 1950, do tend to be associated with rising wage rates— largely because these changes may reflect changes in demand rather than in supply.) But the persistent pattern of declines over the years, speeding up in periods of continued wage rises, does seem to be linked to rises in wage rates—to the taking of part of the rising real incomes in the form of leisure. Changing attitudes toward what employers considered to be an efficient workday played their part. So too did a transvaluation of values among the employee group, plus a dozen other forces. But whatever its causes, the long-term decline in hours much more reasonably testifies in favor of a labor-force response to changing economic conditions than to any insulation from them.

COMPONENTS OF LABOR SUPPLY: CHILDREN

Where is the man with soul so dead that he can interest himself only in the economic aspects of children's role in the family? But these are the

[24] Fred Pabst, quoted in Thomas C. Cochran, *The Pabst Brewing Company* (1948), p. 272. An hour and a half was allowed out for meals.

[25] 1880 Census, *Report on Wages,* p. xxxiii.

[26] Statements by the agents for Merrimac manufacturing and boot manufacturing companies, in Massachusetts (General Court) House Doc. 50 (March, 1845) Report.

[27] David A. Wells, *Report of the Special Commissioner of the Revenue for 1868,* appendix D. See too the Weeks data (1880 Census, *Statistics of Wages*) suggesting an average for factory work of 10½ hours, and the confirmatory textile data in Robert G. Layer, *Earnings of Cotton Mill Operatives, 1825–1914* (1955), p. 43.

[28] Albert Rees, *Real Wages in Manufacturing, 1890–1914* (1961), tables 10, 13.

[29] Robert L. Stein and Herman Travis, *Labor Force and Employment in 1960,* U.S. Bureau of Labor Statistics, Special Labor Force Report no. 14, table D-7. We use data for males aged 25–64.

aspects on which the economist—who is, by profession, neither bachelor nor married man—can most usefully comment. For weary generations it has been noted that an increase in the number of children will eventually increase the labor supply, and thereby work to drive down wages. Poor law administrators, since Malthus and before, have warned the working class against the abysmal folly of reaching for higher living standards without also limiting philoprogenitiveness. Yet while an abstract "working class" will suffer, any given family may benefit. The family must take the labor market as it finds it; and in past centuries more children has usually meant more income per family. "Considerations of the economic and social advantages to be derived from children were once powerful motives in encouraging large families. Of patriarchal society it was said 'Happy is he who has his quiver full of them'; in agricultural communities, especially new ones, the farmer literally produces his own farm hands." [1] The economic contribution that children could make in their parents' old age was an additional factor of lively importance.[2]

Those who inhabit a labor-scarce country, such as the United States in the nineteenth century, will find—to say the least—that a natural desire for children does not run contrary to what a cold calculation of their mere economic value would indicate. In the United States today, with fewer farmers than Chicagoans, it is difficult to look back to a period when population in the Midwest was "so thinly scattered" that "there were but twelve human habitations in two hundred square miles, and these occupied principally by hunters." [3] In such echoing vacancy, "no assistance worthy of notice can be obtained from others outside the family." [4] Under such circumstances a high birth rate is not wholly unlikely. Thus, a late nineteenth-century publication of the Department of Agriculture, noting an 1846 record of "a family of 26 strong healthy boys," adds that "Today a family of five children is a rarity. This, of course, affects the amount of help." [5]

A five-year-old youngster could receive 6¼ cents a day in 1793 for throwing stones into a cart, at a time when common labor averaged perhaps 65 cents a day; and a ten-year-old, in 1798, could work as a farm

---

[1] James A. Field, *Essays on Population and Other Papers* (1931), pp. 278–279. See also Isaiah Bowman, *The Pioneer Fringe* (1931), p. 251, on children in other pioneering societies.

[2] Speaking of another way of life, but not a wholly different one, is the finding of a recent survey of Japanese opinion, in which the proportion of adult males expecting to depend on their children in their old age was 25 percent in the major cities and more than double—57 percent—in rural areas. Quoted in Horace Belshaw, *Population Growth and Levels of Consumption* (1956), p. 33.

[3] John Lorain, *Hints to Emigrants* (1819), p. 78.

[4] *Ibid.*

[5] *Wages of Farm Labor in the United States,* U.S. Department of Agriculture, misc. ser., Report 4 (1892).

laborer for a year in exchange for a cow worth $22, farm labor then being paid an average of something like $8 a month.[6]

Free Labor

As United States factories began to proliferate, the economic value of children became still greater. Cotton factories created new demands for child labor. "It is well known," a writer in 1815 noted hopefully, "that in this country . . . children, from their birth until they are of an age to go into apprenticeship [say, fourteen or sixteen] render little service to their parents; this is more especially the case in towns. But it is this description of persons who are required in cotton and woolen workers." [7] In 1811 Thomas Hazard at sixteen years of age was receiving 7 cents a day for work; but from 1835 till 1840 (when he was writing) a boy could make $1 a week and board—compared to $2 and $2.50 for female labor.[8]

After visiting our earliest cotton mill in 1800, Josiah Quincy noted that "all processes of turning cotton from its rough into every variety of marketable thread state . . . are here performed by machinery operating by water wheels, assisted only by children from four to ten years old, and one superintendent." [9] As late as 1820 the typical United States textile worker was still a child: 43 percent of all textile workers in Massachusetts, 47 percent in Connecticut, and 55 percent in Rhode Island were children.[10] (An advertisement for a Rhode Island cotton mill as late as 1828 read bluntly: "Wanted. Four families with not less than four children each to work in the mill." [11])

As the factory system grew it reached out "for the labor of young persons," withdrawing "many children from the public schools" of Philadelphia (and other urban centers?), where free public education for laboring men's children was being pioneered.[12] In Rhode Island, where the mills began, 42 percent of those who staffed the cotton mills in 1832 were in fact boys under twelve; the total proportion of children was still greater.

[6] Life of Asa G. Sheldon: Wilmington Farmer (Woburn: E. T. Moody, 1862; reprint 1959), pp. 13, 27.
[7] Niles Magazine (Oct. 7, 1815), p. 96.
[8] Thomas R. Hazard, Facts for the Laboring Man by a Laboring Man (Newport: James Atkinson, printer, 1840), pp. 16, 23.
[9] "Account of Journey of Josiah Quincy in 1800," Massachusetts Historical Society, Proceedings, 1887–1889, p. 124.
[10] 1820 Census summary in U.S. Bureau of Labor, Report on Condition of Women and Child Wage Earners in the United States (1910), vol. VI, p. 52.
[11] Providence Patriot and Columbia Phoenix (Mar. 29, 1828), quoted in Editha Hancock, "Labor Problems in Rhode Island," unpublished Brown University thesis, 1946.
[12] Roberts Vaux, President of the Philadelphia Public Schools, Report for 1822, quoted in Nicholas Wainwright, History of the Philadelphia National Bank (1953), p. 60.

The average for New England and the country as a whole was about 20 percent.[13] These children provided a substantial supplement to family income, receiving 18 cents a day in Massachusetts and 25 cents a day in Rhode Island (which may be compared to female rates of 44 and 37 cents, respectively).[14]

Children were likewise used in industries other than farming and manufacturing, but to a more limited extent. "Boys" were, of course, commonly listed on the ships' articles in any year from 1800 to 1860, some of them as young as ten, but many ranged through the teens. (Sometimes, indeed, the word was a mere synonym for "light hand.") At an arbitrary salary ranging from $4 to $10 a month, they received from one-fifth to one-third the wages paid an able-bodied seaman.[15]

It was boys who drove the Erie Canal boats; in 1845, a thirteen-year-old could earn $10 a month doing so during the months the canal was open, or about what many farm laborers of the time earned.[16]

Slave Labor

Children were no less valuable under slavery. As a great Southern architect and engineer noted, "It may indeed be justly considered one of the excellencies of the cultivation of cotton, that in its collection no manual labour is lost. Neither age nor childhood, if in health, is prevented from giving its aid in this innocent and useful pursuit. Children from eight years old can be employed to advantage." [17] The eight- and nine-year-olds, however, were not considered as part of the group from which a substantial volume of work could be expected, and Forstall in 1845 defined "children under 10 or 12 years of age" as not being among the "effectives" on a sugar estate.[18] Ruffin found that the total cost of raising a Negro slave from birth "to ten years of age . . . cannot be less than $14 a year—and that age is as early as the labor of a child can begin to pay for its

[13] These figures are weighted averages of reports appearing in U.S. Congress, Serial Set 222, 223, *Documents Relative to the Statistics of Manufactures in the U.S.* (Washington: Duff Green, 1833), vols. I and II. The definition of "boys" as being those under twelve is indicated by the Report of the New York Convention of Friends of the Manufacturing Interest appearing in *Niles Register,* vol. XLII, addendum (1832) March–August, p. 7.

[14] Rates computed from data in U.S. Congress, Serial Set 222, 223.

[15] Taking some examples from manuscripts in the Essex Institute, we have: Kimball Manuscripts, Ships H-M: Brig. *Mary,* 1801, $4; *Reward,* 1804, $8. Pingree Manuscripts, Ship *William and Henry,* 1838, $5; Bark *Eliza,* 1839, $4.

[16] Deacon M. Eaton, *Five Years on the Erie Canal* (Utica: Bennet, Backus and Hawley, 1845), pp. 32, 37.

[17] Robert Mills, *Statistics of South Carolina* (Charleston: Hurlburt and Lloyd, 1826), p. 153.

[18] Edmund J. Forstall, *Agricultural Productions of Louisiana* (New Orleans: Tropic Print, 1845), p. 6.

support."[19] In his memoirs of "A Plantation Boyhood," D. E. Huger Smith carefully noted that the quarter hands and larger children were commonly "added to the gin men as herd minders," while the general use of the young children in the trash gang, cleaning up between furrows, is widely reported.[20] Such labor was clearly part of the labor supply since the work would otherwise have required adult labor.

The "excellency" to which Mills referred was not lost sight of on most plantations. Even after heavy discounting for future mortality, the sales value of children suggests the nontrivial value of their labor.

Babies under a year were valued at a nominal sum of $100 in 1850 in Virginia; "uniform valuations of $220 for boys and $180 for girls" as "they arrived at sizes fit to begin work [nine to ten years old]" were used by an eminent Virginia scholar and farmer, Edmund Ruffin.[21] "A likely [Piute Indian] girl in her teens brings often $300 or $400," wrote a widely known explorer and businessman in the 1840s.[22] Even as late as 1865, $400 and more was paid in New Mexico for "a likely girl of not more than eight years old, healthy and intelligent."[23] Considering how uncertain the continuation of slavery then was, most of this price must have reflected advantages expected to be realized in the very near term.

Percentage of Children in the Labor Force

How may we convert such diffuse information into a reasonable count of the dimensions of the child labor force? For the period prior to 1860, we must be content with the general conclusion that children formed a significant component of the labor force in farming and in manufacturing, and worked as well in gristmills, grocery stores, mines, ships, and most of the other commercial enterprises of the day.

Our first summary data of any consequence are for 1870, and they suggest that something like 13 percent of children aged 10–15 were then gainful workers.[24]

[19] *Farmers Register* (1835), vol. II, p. 253.

[20] Quoted in Herbert R. Sass, *A Carolina Rice Plantation in the '50s* (1936), p. 71.

[21] Edmund Ruffin, "Profits in Agriculture," in *The American Farmer and Spirit of the Agricultural Journals of the Day* (Baltimore: Sands and Mills, 1849), vol. 5, new series, pp. 99, 102.

[22] Thomas Farnham, *Travels in the Great Western Prairies* (New York: Greeley and McElrath, 1843), p. 58. Farnham, partner in a leading St. Louis firm's fur-trading ventures and distinguished explorer, added that these creatures "are hunted in the spring of the year, when weak and helpless, by a certain class of men, and when taken are fattened, carried to Santa Fe and sold as slaves during their minority. . . . The males are valued less."

[23] According to Kirby Benedict, Chief Justice of the New Mexico Supreme Court, quoted in LeRoy R. Hafen and Ann W. Hafen, *The Old Spanish Trail* (1954), p. 280.

[24] Alba Edwards, *Comparative Occupations Statistics, 1870–1940* (1943), p. 97. This

Without attaching any importance to the apparent upward course from 1870 to 1880, we may note the following trends:[25]

Ratio of Children Aged 10–15 to Total Gainfully Occupied

Year	All occupations	Agriculture	Manufacturing	Mining
1870	13.2	9.3	5.6	7.1
1880	16.8	11.6	6.7	
1890	18.1	11.5	2.8	
1900	18.2	11.4	3.2	2.1
1910	15.0	9.8	2.4	0.8
1920	11.3	8.0	1.3	*
1930	4.7	3.3	*	*

* Less than 1 percent.

A marked decline during the 1880s in the ratio of child labor in manufacturing (and probably in mining) was the harbinger of a mild decline for agriculture during the 1900–1910 decade. But a really perceptible fall for both total and components began with the prosperity of World War I and the years of the 1920s: The overall rate plummeted by two-thirds from 1910 to 1930.

Given the solid contribution that child labor long made to the family and plantation exchequer, it seems most unlikely that the child labor market dwindled because the economy became unable to utilize such labor efficiently. We must look instead to concurrent changes in family incomes, values, and social attitudes.

Was one such factor the ever-increasing level of education sought for children, as evidenced by the spread of free public schools? The rise from 1850 to 1950 was as follows:[26]

volume of the 1940 Population Census summarizes the data for 1870 through 1930. The 1870 ratio may be too low because of the underenumeration of that year. However, the adjustment of 1870 Population Census figures by Everett Lee would not obviously change the population count greatly and its implications for worker rates are uncertain.

[25] All occupations, agriculture: Edwards, *loc. cit.* Manufacturing: 1900 *Census of Manufactures,* vol. VII, p. cxxvi; 1920 *Census of Manufactures,* vol. VIII, p. 20. Mining: 1870 Census, *Industry and Wealth,* pp. 392–393; 1902 Census, *Mines and Quarries, 1902,* pp. 91, 706; 1910 Census, vol XI, *Mines and Quarries, 1909,* p. 29; 1920 Census, *Mines and Quarries,* vol. XI, p. 45. We assume the 1930 mining rate to be no greater than the 1920 rate.

[26] The 1850 data are from *The Seventh Census of the United States: 1850* (1854), pp. xlii–xliv, lx. Based on school reports, they were considered more reliable than the Population Census count. The 1950 data are from the 1950 Census, *Characteristics of the Population,* vol. II, part 1, tables 38 and 111, and relate only to those aged 5–14.

Children in Public Schools

Year	Children aged 5–14	Enrollment in public schools	Ratio, percent
1850	6,132,000	3,354,000	55
1950	24,329,000	20,242,000	83

Some parents had repeated the calculation made by John Stuart Mill, if not by Horace Mann, of the advantage to the individual of foregoing an immediate income to assure an eventually higher one.[27] Many had been moved by other factors. In either event the rise in educational horizons seems to have gone on for decades. Yet no discernible decline in the child labor force appears before 1900: Worker rates for children declined not at all from 1870 to 1900.[28] Even as late as 1901, one urban family in five had working children.[29]

No more decisive factor in reducing the nineteenth-century child labor force was the steady decline in birth rates, which fell from roughly 55 to 20 per thousand population between 1820 and 1940.[30] We can compare the contribution of this fertility change to the decline in child workers with the effects of the drop in the proportion of children working, using data from Table 2-3.[31]

| Mothers' year of birth | Indices of | | |
	Number of children (ever born per 1,000 native white females)	Child worker rate in year first child becomes 10 years of age	Number of child workers
1835–1844	100.0	100.0	100
1865–1869	78.3	108.3	85
1895–1899	52.9	28.0	15

[27] Entering school in 1807, Sophia Simpson was unable to pronounce the letter *H*. "Do try," said her teacher, "for it will be a thousand pounds in your pocket." Sophia S. Simpson, *Two Hundred Years Ago* (Boston: Otis Clapp, 1859), p. 47.

[28] *Supra*, p. 53. For convenience the shorter phrase "worker rates" will be used instead of "labor-force participation rates."

[29] *Eighteenth Annual Report of the Commissioner of Labor, 1903* (1904), p. 363. Because this survey included a disproportionately great number of families with heads employed in manufacturing, heads that were union members, etc., it is likely that the proportion for all urban families was somewhat greater.

[30] Conrad Taeuber and Irene Taeuber, *The Changing Population of the United States* (1958), p. 249.

[31] Fertility data from Table 2-3. Worker rate data from Edwards, *op. cit.*, p. 92. This assumes, for arithmetic convenience, that the first child is born when the mother is aged twenty. Other assumptions would make little difference. More important, the 1870 worker rate seems unreasonably low, the adjustment made by Edwards for the

The number of child workers is estimated simply as the product of the worker rate and the number of children ever born.[32] It measures the average number of children, of those born to each group of mothers, that worked between the ages of ten and fifteen. Its decline from the first to the second period is produced solely by the fertility decline, since worker rates actually rose. The subsequent drop in child workers from the period around 1900 (mothers born between 1865 and 1869) to the depression years reflects primarily the fall in worker rates, for had there been no change in the number of children ever born, the number of child workers would have fallen by 74 percent—as compared to its actual 85 percent decline.[33]

From the earliest years of settlement, American children made their significant contribution to the work and output of the nation. There is little warrant for believing that the decline in child labor since 1800 reflected a failing market for such labor, or that the decline in fertility cut supply greatly. Moreover, the proportion of children at work appears not to have declined until the vague dawn of the twentieth century. A mild contribution probably was made by the declining employment of children in factories and mines. But the major factor at work was a decline in the size of the farm-labor force, and of the share that children composed in that group. A complementary factor (suggested by the fact that the major declines came after the 1910 Census) was the decline of the immigrant group, with its tradition of family labor. Neither the fruits of philosophy

---

1870 undercount being perhaps insufficient. The 1880 rate is therefore used for 1870, being more meaningful for a longer view even if the 1870 figure properly reflects the immediate postwar disturbances.

[32] Because the worker rate relates to all children, the absolute levels are meaningless and therefore not shown.

[33] 1940 Census, *Differential Fertility, 1940 and 1910: Women by Number of Children Ever Born,* table III. This report gives differing figures from the 1940 and from the 1910 Censuses on the number of children born to the same groups of women. The causes of these differences are discussed lucidly in Taeuber and Taeuber, *Op. cit.,* p. 255.

The method of adjusting the census data used here was as follows: In the 1910 Census, 3,128 women born in 1865–1874 reported an average of 3.769 children; in the 1940 Census, 1,771 women born in the same period reported an average of 3.544 children. The two averages would be quite consistent if we could assume that 2,357 women (3,128 minus 1,771) had died by the latter date and had had an average of 4.030 children. Neither assumption seems grossly unreasonable. The 6.35 percent excess between the 1910 and 1940 reports was therefore taken to reflect the steady toll of selective female mortality, and was assumed to have developed at a steady rate. The contemporary 1910 report was therefore taken as standard, the rate of excess interpolated for the group born in 1865–1874 through the 1895–1899 group.

Some mortality bias would have appeared even in the 1910 reports. Failing a better measure, the same 6.35 percent excess was applied to the 1835–1844 group (which stands in the same relation to the 1910 Census as the 1865–1874 one does to the 1940) with interpolation to give the excess for the other years. This implicitly assumes a stable trend in selective mortality.

nor those of education brought a decline in child labor. It was instead the decline of the family farm.

Table 2-3. Number of Children Ever Born
(Per 1,000 women, by color)

Mothers' year of birth	Adjusted		Native white		Negro	
	Native white	Negro	1910 Census	1940 Census	1910 Census	1940 Census
1835–1844	5,172	7,433	4,863		7,000	
1845–1854	5,034	7,216	4,805		6,897	
1855–1859	4,729	6,783	4,583		6,580	
1860–1864	4,408	6,257	4,339		6,162	
1865	4,050	5,484	4,050	3,544	5,484	4,678
1870–1874	3,538	4,515	3,538		4,515	
1875–1884	3,375	4,169		3,221		3,985
1885–1889	3,118	3,802		3,022		3,688
1890–1894	2,966	3,391		2,920		3,340
1895–1899	2,738	3,091		2,738		3,091

THE FEMALE LABOR SUPPLY

I myself have never had my sense of fitness jarred, nor a spark of animosity aroused in me by a woman practicing any of the fine arts, except the art of writing. That she should write a few little poems, or pensees, or some impressions of a trip in a dahabieh as far as (say) Biskra, or even a short story or two, seems to me not wholly amiss. . . .

Max Beerbohm (1957) †

Why, sir, it is our fault that our girls are decked out in the absurd costumes of a French milliner; we do not furnish them with employment, and we must not be surprised that their better natures thus run to waste.

Theodore C. Peters (1857) ‡

In most nonmatriarchal societies it is frequently assumed that women should not work—meaning work outside the home. The corollary is fre-

† *Mainly on the Air* (1958), p. 248.
‡ *Remarks in Dedication of the New York State Agricultural Rooms*, Albany, Feb. 12, 1857 (Albany: van Benthuysen, 1857). Peters was speaking in favor of the development of dairy farms, with the opportunity they offered for utilizing female labor. He concluded, "If we do not teach them to hoop cheese ought we to wonder that they turn to hoop themselves?"

quently drawn that women do not in fact work. One of the problems in reviewing census materials on the gainfully occupied during the nineteenth and even the early twentieth century is the extent to which they do measure the full extent of women's contribution to the labor force. There is no question here of whether to include the vital tasks of raising a family and keeping house. Such work is excluded from our national income estimates. It is also excluded from our twentieth-century labor-force series. There is considerable warrant for considering such work as no less real—and far more vital—than work outside the home.[1] However, there would be little analytic value to measures that always showed about 100 percent of women in the labor force, varying not at all through the business cycle or through time.

The problem of measuring female labor supply concerns, instead, whether the early censuses included work of women apart from housework. An inspection of the census schedules for 1820 and 1840—preliminary to making the present estimate for 1830—showed very few entries for women with occupations outside the manufacturing centers and big cities.[2] Since this pattern appears in 1820, 1840, 1860, 1870, 1880, and 1890 (each having a census conducted by a temporary organization completely independent of the prior censuses), we take this consistent repetition as a considerable demonstration that hundreds of thousands of enumerators and respondents at these periods agreed in not finding that many white women had occupations or were in the gainfully occupied group. Even allowing for male cultural bias, we find this result less improbable than some writers do.[3]

First of all, it must be remembered that even by present definitions unpaid labor of 15 hours a week (or less) on the family enterprise does not qualify a person for inclusion in the labor-force count. Hence even 2 hours a day tending chickens and pigs, keeping a vegetable garden going, or milking cows, would not qualify farm housewives for inclusion in the labor-force count. Secondly, the average white married woman had four children.[4] Taking care of four children is relatively time-consuming—an un-

[1] See the excellent review in National Manpower Council, *Woman Power* (1957), pp. 46ff.
[2] By reference to a nonrandom sample of unpublished schedules now in the U.S. National Archives.
[3] A case for understatement is forcefully put in A. J. Jaffe, "Trends in the Participation of Women in the Working Force," *Monthly Labor Review* (May, 1956) and Robert W. Smuts, "The Female Labor Force: A Case Study in the Interpretation of Historical Statistics," *Journal of the American Statistical Association* (March, 1960).
[4] The average white family had 5.5 persons. Excluding single individuals from the family category would make at least an average of 6 per family with husband and wife.

derstatement by any standard. Thirdly, the typical married woman in nineteenth-century America made all the children's clothes (the factory output of children's clothing being trivial prior to 1900) as well as her own; baked the family bread; prepared its soups and preserves (and even the family soap through most of the century); washed clothes for six persons without benefit of anything more than a washboard; dusted, cleaned, and performed a variety of other domestic chores. (In 1830 she even wove most of the cloth for the family's garments as well, since factory production had just gotten under way.) Under the circumstances, we find it not unreasonable to accept the judgment of generation after generation of respondents who told the census enumerators they had no occupation outside the home. We, therefore, accept the census data for the years 1870ff. when they are available. For prior years, actually only 1830 in Table A-11, we do not rely on Population Census reports but use employer reports on the composition of the work force and other sources, as noted below.

Trends for White Females (Table A-11)

In Table A-11 we show the broad course of change in female participation rates from 1830 to the present. For white women the rates almost doubled from 1830 to 1890, then tripled over the next 60 years. Because of the uncertainty of the data, however, it is more useful to contrast the rise of about 5 percentage points over the first period with the 20-point gain over the second.[5] The incredible gain in female worker rates from 1940 to 1960 (reported by the reliable, consistent measures of the Census Bureau's *Current Population Survey*) is seen as the end of a gradually rising curve. The growth over the 60 years from 1830 to 1890 was less than that in the 17 years from 1940 to 1957. The data by marital status show that the spectacular part of this gain was in the rate for married women. That rate changed hardly at all from 1830 to 1890 (it could not have been less than zero in 1830) but rose tenfold in the next 60 years. (The data for the central 35–44 age group are sufficiently similar to those for the total to suggest that the rise was no mere product of changes in the age composition of the population.) That the rise was real, striking, may be admitted. But what produced this transformation? We address ourselves to this question after first considering how similar, or how different, was the trend for nonwhite females.

[5] These contrasting gains derive from accepting census and Current Population Survey materials for 1890 and 1951. The 1830 figure, as outlined in the methodology discussion, rests on the count of factory workers reported in the factory census of the New York Convention and independent estimates of domestic servants and teachers. Hence the contrasting gains over the two periods do not arise from acceptance of 1830 Population Census figures, which are, in fact, nonexistent.

Trends for Nonwhite Females

The major problem in measuring the trends for nonwhite females is the definition of labor supply under slavery. We estimate that 90 percent of nonwhite female slaves aged ten and over were in the labor supply in 1830, as in other decennial years from 1800 to 1860. We do so on the basis of two alternative modes of estimate.

The first census to record the occupations of slaves was 1820.[6] Since the census reported occupations not for all slaves, but only for those gainfully occupied in agriculture, commerce, and manufactures, it omitted the large number of house servants and those in other pursuits. We can, nonetheless, derive an indicative estimate from that census as follows. We derive an estimate for 1820 of the ratio of female gainfully occupied slaves to total female slaves aged ten and over, using data for 12 counties in the major slave states.[7] In each of these counties, a very substantial number of slaves was recorded in proportion to the number of adult white males. Now the number of house servants (which must have been a function of the number of white families—represented by the number of adult white males) would have constituted a small proportion of all slaves in these counties. We are, therefore, safe in assuming that the house slaves omitted by the census in these counties would have formed a small proportion both of all slaves and of the total occupied.

By then deducting the estimated number of (1) white and free Negro gainfully occupied from (2) the total occupied in each county, we derive an estimate for the number of occupied slaves.[8] In Jones County, Georgia, for example, the estimate for occupied slaves thus derived is 4,218, but the number of slaves aged 14 and over was only 3,600. It is clear, therefore, that all slaves 14 and over and probably those aged 10–13 as well were included as having an occupation.[9] Net balances for the other selected

---

[6] We do not rely on the 1840 Census (which also purported to measure the occupations of slaves), because of the significant inadequacies that that census possessed. For example, examination of unpublished schedules shows areas reporting no occupational entries, while even the published volumes show whole counties with no occupation entries.

[7] Jones, Jasper, Georgia; Monroe, Alabama; Feliciana, Point Coupee, St. Charles, Louisiana; Davidson, Tennessee; St. James-Colleton, St. Thomas, Georgetown, Beaufort, South Carolina; Wilkinson, Mississippi.

[8] The proportion of white males aged 10 and over gainfully occupied in each county was estimated to be the same as in the 1850 Census, the proportion changing little over subsequent years for this group. This number was then deducted from the total reported by the 1820 Census as having an occupation. Examination of a sample of the 1820 Census schedules in the U.S. National Archives indicated no white women with occupations reported for these areas, and a trivial handful of free Negro. Hence, deducting a white male occupied count from the total would give a close figure for slave occupied.

[9] Specific examples may make the point clearer. Micajah Pickett, Sr. (of Franklin

counties all indicate this result. The inclusion of children from the age of 8 or 10 is amply confirmed by the contemporary literature (some of it cited above in the preceding section on child labor). We, therefore, conclude that the broad testimony of the 1820 Census is in favor of all slaves aged 10 and over as having occupations.

Did this particular group of counties have an unusually high proportion of slaves that were gainfully occupied? Possibly so. Yet there is little reason to hold that eleemosynary traditions were any stronger in the remaining counties where slaves were held. To allow for the number in the labor force at any time, we must deduct for illness and temporary disability. We do so by reference to the worker rates in the same areas for male whites in 1850, thus arriving at a 95 percent worker rate for Negro female slaves in the prime age group. A compatible rate for all aged 10 and over would be 90 percent.[10]

A second, confirmatory, method for estimating the number of nonwhite females in the labor force from 1800 to 1860 is given by the slave purchase data. From the very beginning of the century a clear monetary value was set upon female slaves. In 1807, for example, a female slave bought for a hogshead of rum in Africa sold for $278 in the United States, or within 10 percent of the male price, while girls sold for $244.[11] Throughout the century the value of females rose, both absolutely and relative to prices for males.[12] As in any competitive market, we must assume that the buying and selling of female slaves would not have occurred unless the purchasers, in general, expected a financial return from the transaction. This return could be realized in a variety of income-producing activities, but any of them would involve the participation of the females thus bought in what was then the labor force.[13]

County, Mississippi) reported 27 persons in agriculture in 1820—a figure larger than that obtained by counting all whites in his family aged 10 and over plus all slaves 14 and over. James Jackson, of Green County, Georgia, reported, in 1840, 144 in agriculture, but had only two whites in his family and 131 slaves aged 10 and over. Elizabeth McLendon, of Harris County, Georgia, reported 14 in agriculture in 1840 but had only one white person in the family, ten slaves aged 10 and over, and four under 10 years of age.

[10] The Census Bureau's Current Population Survey currently includes in the labor force all persons who work 1 hour or more for nonfamily enterprise during the survey week. We assume, from contemporary material noted below, that elderly Negro slaves made sufficient contributions of labor during the week to reach such a standard, or exceed it.

[11] "Account of Sales of 106 Africans Brought into Charleston, South Carolina on *Bird Three Sisters*," 1807, W.H.M., in Rhode Island Historical Society, *Collections* (January, 1919).

[12] For the rising ratio, see Robert Evans Jr., "The Economics of American Negro Slavery, 1830–1860" (1960), table 28, a paper prepared for the Universities–National Bureau of Economic Research, *Conference on Labor Economics*.

[13] We are not restricted to present industrial coverage of the labor force, but

Two apparent qualifications appear. One relates to the older females, the "idlers and drones" who (in contemporary accounts) toiled not, yet consumed. Are we right in assuming a high labor-force rate for the group? The evidence suggests that we are. Older workers were viewed as unproductive, but the standard of comparison was the average net return realized from a female in the prime ages. Measuring by hours worked, we must conclude that the older slaves did enough work to qualify their inclusion in the labor force. On Governor Roman's plantation in Louisiana, for example, a contemporary report notes that "the trash gang, consisting of children in the neighborhood of 10 years of age, picked peas, gathered corn, raked up hay or fodder or performed other light tasks under the direction of 2 or 3 old women." [14] On Valcour Aime's plantation in addition to the field hands, house servants and nurses, there were 11 old men and women "who attended the stables." [15] A second question on the estimate for female participation rates relates to periods of pregnancy. It seems unlikely that women were out of the labor force for any substantial period prior to delivery. A manual for the management of slaves recommended that 6 to 8 weeks before delivery, "they should be put among the grass gang, to bring a few bundles of grass, or vines for the stock. To the last hour they should be kept in motion." [16]

After delivery, female field hands returned to work in the field, but with more limited tasks. Reminiscing about "A Plantation Boyhood," one writer described how "the nursing mothers were relieved of much of their work, and at stated hours would be seen coming out of the field in a crowd for their maternal duties"; other writers describe how a "sucklers' gang" was

---

merely to the range of then-accepted endeavors. Claude Robin, *Voyages dans L'interieur de La Louisiane . . . 1802–1806* (Paris: F. Buisson, 1807), vol. III, p. 199. "Les maitres favorisent des unions passageres qui font pour eux des enfans, source de leur richesse." Les femmes "ont la liberte de l'emploi de leur temps a condition de rapporter chaque jour le prix de leur journee; c'est ordinairement celui de leur prostitution." Robin appears to have limited his travels to an area near New Orleans, and his remarks cannot be assumed to apply more widely.

[14] Russell, *My Diary North and South,* quoted in V. Alton Moody, "Slavery on a Louisiana Sugar Plantation," *Louisiana Historical Quarterly* (April, 1924), p. 46.

[15] J. B. Thorpe (1853) quoted in Moody, *op. cit.,* p. 57; house servants on occasion included older females. It is relevant, therefore, to find the Norfleet house servants "helped the 'shufflers' pick peanuts." Guion G. Johnson, *Ante-bellum North Carolina* (1937), p. 480. But of course the elderly cook was as clearly in the labor force as the young field hand.

[16] The manual continues: "though for their own profit, for their service to the estate will be little. . . . This exemption from labor [i.e., heavy labor] will be looked upon by your negros as some indemnity for their sufferings, and the hope of those indulgencies which they are to experience if they are mothers will probably render them desirous to become so." *Practical Rules for the Management and Medical Treatment of Negro Slaves in the Sugar Colonies, by a Professional Planter* (London: J. Barfield, 1803), chap. 6, "Breeding," p. 157.

assigned work near the quarter where the infants were kept.[17] Throughout the maternity period female slaves were engaged in providing what a well-known Southern contemporary called "new accessions of young hands to . . . the original capital." [18] Jefferson, for example, valued a newborn slave infant at a sum equivalent to half the cost of maintaining an adult slave for a year, while by 1850 the estate of one of the greatest slave traders valued children aged less than 1 year at $100.[19] Female slaves, therefore, whether producing cotton, hemp, tobacco, or children, were producing goods that were marketed and had money values set upon them—a sufficient qualification for including them in the labor-force count for the period.

Changing Labor-force Rates: Supply Factors

The changing course of labor-force rates shown in Table A-11 reflects neither supply forces alone nor demand elements alone. We consider first the role of declining fertility rates in facilitating the rise in labor-force rates for females.

Fertility Change, 1830 to 1940.   To what extent did the long-term decline in fertility rates facilitate the increase in the number of working women? Available census data give us rough but useful indications of the number of children under age 5 per 1,000 white women, and we have estimated elsewhere the number of children for nonwhites.[20]

[17] D. E. Huger Smith's unpublished memoirs are quoted in Herbert R. Sass, *A Carolina Rice Plantation in the '50's* (1936), p. 71. For reference to the "sucklers' gang" see Moody, *op. cit.*, p. 46.

[18] Edmund Ruffin, "Profits of Agriculture," in *The American Farmer and Spirit of the Agricultural Journals of the Day* (Baltimore: Sands and Mills, 1849), vol. 5, new series, p. 2.

[19] Noting the importance of "breeders," Jefferson proposed the possibility of "emancipating the afterborn. . . . The estimated value of the new born infant is so low (say twelve dollars and fifty cents) that it would probably be yielded by the owner gratis." A. A. Lipscomb (ed.), *Writings* (1905), vol. XVI, p. 10. The cost of slave maintenance ran about $20 to $25 a year. Wendell Holmes Stephenson, *Isaac Franklin, Slave Trader and Planter of the Old South* (Baton Rouge: Louisiana State University Press, 1938). A Maryland Orphans Court in 1813–1815 appraised male children aged one to five as worth $90, females at $75. *American Historical Review* (1914), vol. 19, p. 817.

[20] Census data appear in Conrad Taeuber and Irene Taeuber, *The Changing Population of the United States* (1958), p. 25. Nonwhite estimates are from the author's "Population Change and Supply of Labor," in the Universities–National Bureau of Economic Research, *Conference on the Interrelations of Demographic and Economic Change* (1958), table 1a and section on Population–Labor Force Trends. That discussion concluded that fertility levels among nonwhites were more limited than some reports would suggest. It failed to note the further element of miscarriages. A Jamaica overseer found, in 1833, "physical coercion . . . necessary to the production of labour through the instrumentality of slaves"; he, "in common with many overseers to whom I have spoken on the subject" accounted for the decline in the non-

It would be hard to find a set of figures that showed a less simple relationship between long-run trends in worker rates and in fertility. For native whites, the 1830–1890 period shows a marked decline in the number of children per 1,000 women aged 20–44 and a marked rise in worker rates. So far so good. But over the succeeding 1890–1950 period the ratio of children hardly declines at all while the rise in worker rates is greater, far greater than from 1830 to 1840. For nonwhites the contrast is even more extreme. From 1830 to 1890 their worker rates fell by more than 50 percent, but the number of children hardly changed at all. From 1890 to 1950 worker rates changed very little, but the number of children declined largely. Clearly fertility declines and worker rate rises are hardly mirror images of one another. For this long sweep of time, changes in female worker rates were dominated by social and economic forces other than fertility change, facilitating though the latter may have been.

We can make a somewhat more precise analysis for the half century of change from William McKinley, Annie Besant, and "heaven will protect the working girl" to Franklin Roosevelt, Margaret Sanger, and "Rosie the Riveter." We measure the relationship between changing fertility rates and changing worker rates as follows (Table A-13).[21]

The worker rates for married women changed for a host of reasons quite apart from those linked to fertility change. To subtract out the net resultant of such other forces we define the changes for worker rates of single women as the norm, and contrast changes for married women with them. Single women constituted an enormous population sample whose worker rates changed because of the resistless movement of population from farm to city, because of an improvement of health conditions, changes in attitude toward work, and so on. We take this to give an unbiased estimate of the amount of change that would have taken place for married women apart from fertility change.[22] In the last column of Table

white population in the islands "partly to corn hole digging and to night work . . . and to the destruction of children in the womb caused by whipping." Great Britain, House of Commons, *Report from the Select Committee on the Extinction of Slavery throughout the British Dominions* (London: J. Haddon, 1833) pp. 6, 21. Since the slave population in the United States actually rose, we may assume that a milder discipline (or other causes) resulted in fewer miscarriages.

[21] Another approach appears in the multiple standardization analysis of John Durand and Edwin Goldfield. See also John Durand's study, as informative as it is succinct, "Married Women in the Labor Force," *American Journal of Sociology* (November, 1946), p. 220.

[22] An alternative method, measuring the influence of fertility change on the rate for all women regardless of marital status, appears in John Durand's fundamental study, *The Labor Force in the United States, 1890–1960* (1948), chap. 5, and in Seymour Wolfbein and A. J. Jaffe, "Demographic Factors in Labor Force Growth," *American Sociological Review* (August, 1946).

A-13 we show the excess of married worker rate change over that for single women.[23] The results are unequivocally confusing. Rates for married native white women gained less than for single women; rates for nonwhites gained more than for single women; and rates for foreign-born whites gained both more and less than for single women.

With fewer children, nonwhite married women used the time thus made available to work more outside the home. Native white women did not. It is easy to infer a simple economic relationship: White families, being already up with the Joneses, had less incentive to earn more income than did the nonwhites. Certainly cross-sectional studies show the clear inverse relationship between husband's income and worker rates for wives.[24]

The difficulty with any such simple relationship is that changes for the foreign-born did more or less parallel the native white change. Yet with immigrants working in mines and ragpicking, with foreign-born women employed in domestic service and noisome sweatshops, the influence of low and unstable income was surely at work among this group as well as among nonwhites. We hypothesize that the foreign-born whites sought to achieve prevailing goals not only with respect to income but with respect to the propriety of women's working. For nonwhites the income gap was greater; the possibility of their achieving prevailing standards was so much smaller that their already high worker rates rose still more.[25] Since 1940 (Table 2-4) the striking concomitant rise both in worker rates and in fertility is well known. The proportion of wives without little children who worked doubled, and the proportion for those with little children more than doubled. There could be few clearer demonstrations that a decline in

[23] Worker rate data from Durand, *op. cit.,* table A6. We omit data for younger age groups where "children ever born" does not measure completed fertility.

[24] See the clear-cut table 6 in *Current Population Reports,* ser. P-50, no. 81, "Family Characteristics of Working Wives: March, 1957"; the more extensive review by Paul Douglas, *The Theory of Wages,* chap. 11; and Nedra Belloc "Labor-force Participation and Employment Opportunities for Women," *Journal of the American Statistical Association* (September, 1950), p. 405. David Schwartzman, "A Note on the Supply of Female Labor," *Review of Economics and Statistics* (May, 1950), p. 161, finds a mild negative relationship. The most recent and most extensive study is Clarence Long, *The Labor Force under Changing Income and Employment* (1958).

[25] Melvin Reder, commenting on this discussion, suggests that changing employment opportunities may lie behind this differential. With opportunities in domestic service apparently open to foreign born as well as nonwhites, such changes may not be a major factor. However, more detailed study of the geographic distribution of the foreign born would be required to deny this as a major, or complementary factor.

Data in Table 2-4 from the author's "Population Change and the Supply of Labor," *op. cit.,* and Bureau of Labor Statistics, Special Labor Force Report No. 13, "Marital and Family Characteristics of Workers, March 1960," table G.

Table 2-4. Working Wives, 1940–1960
(Percent in labor force by age and by presence of young children)

	Under 65	18–24	25–34	35–44	45–64
U.S. white and nonwhite:					
Without children under 6:					
1940	16.5	26.7	26.9	17.0	9.0
1950	27.5	45.5	39.8	31.5	18.4
1954	34.4				
1957	38.2				
1960	38.7				
With children under 6:					
1940	6.1	5.8	6.5	5.6	5.5
1950	10.6	9.9	10.5	11.2	11.7
1954	14.9				
1957	17.0				
1960	18.6				
U.S. nonwhite:					
Without children under 6:					
1940	31.5	32.6	38.9	32.7	22.7
1950	37.8	36.5	46.3	43.6	27.9
1954	46.4				
1957	50.7				
1960	51.9				
With children under 6:					
1940	14.9	13.6	14.9	16.4	16.5
1950	17.3	12.8	18.2	20.6	20.0
1954	21.8				
1957	24.0				
1960	27.0				

fertility was no necessary prelude to an increase in the percent of working women.

Income Goals. For untold centuries, philosophers have demonstrated the futility of heaping up worldly possessions, a goal ever-vanishing as it is neared. And for just as many centuries, that goal has motivated much of the Western world's economic activity. A major force that accounts for the rising proportion of women working since 1830 was the desire for more income, albeit not income to the exclusion of other goals.

Success in achieving more education for children reduced the proportion of working children, and thus whittled away at family incomes. The achievement of more leisure for men (or at least less work in factory or mine) had also limited the rise in family incomes, part of the national rise in productivity being devoted to this end. Increasing privacy and comfort at home had also tended to reduce family incomes as the proportion of families with boarders and lodgers dwindled from nearly 25 percent in 1900 to a mere 5 percent by 1950.[26]

While these forces blunted the rise in family income, the opportunities for expenditure proliferated as stars from a Fourth of July rocket. The dazzling array of material goods now incorporated into the American standard of living proved to be the key incentive for increased female worker rates in recent decades. We may define this as the means to an easier life; as the desire to keep up with the Joneses (as they keep up with the Smiths); as the crass materialism characteristic of the postwar Byzantine periods in world history, etc. But, whichever of these interpretations are preferred by the specialists in these matters, the result is the same. In recent years in the United States, the consumer in "consumer durables" has proved to be the working wife.[27]

A recent study, made for quite different purposes, throws a brilliant light on one side of this problem. If we look at Table 2-5, we see a clear

Table 2-5

| Family income | Families with debts as a percent of all families (1956) | | Excess |
	With husband only working (1)	With wife and husband working (2)	(2) − (1) (3)
Under $3,000..........	57	65	+8
$3,000–$4,999..........	71	72	+1
$5,000–$7,499..........	74	78	+4
$7,500 and over........	67	74	+7

tendency at each income level for a greater proportion of families with working wives to have debts than families with only the husband working.[28] The excess for the families with working wives would be still greater if we classified the families by their husband's income alone—as is essentially done in the table for the other families—for families with working wives almost by definition have come from lower levels of income if classified by husband's income.

[26] See table 8 in the author's "Population Change and Labor Supply," *op. cit.*

[27] It does not, of course, have to follow that these causes and consequences were without parallel in other countries. The rising worker rate for women, especially married women, in other countries is discussed in UN, *Determinants* . . . , pp. 200–201.

[28] These data are based on a supplement to the Census Bureau's *Current Population Survey* for August, 1956, and appear in Federal Reserve Board, *Consumer Instalment Credit, Part I, Volume 2, Growth and Import* (1957), table D-1. Rossett's study in *Econometrica* (March, 1958), p. 326, suggests a similar conclusion.

In summary, families with working wives not merely have higher incomes, but more commonly acquire debts despite, or because of, the wife's work. It is doubtful, on the latter alternative, whether it is possible to know (or particularly useful to assert) the priority of the chicken or the egg. Work by the wife *and* the incurring of debts are interrelated means to the prompt acquisition of consumer durables.

We can proceed a bit further by examining the type of debt involved (Table 2-6).[29] A priori we might not expect any significant differences by

Table 2-6. Debtors by Type of Debt, August, 1956

Income	All debtors	Debtors for		
		Cars alone or with household equipment	Mortgages and cars	Mortgages alone or with household equipment
Under $3,000:				
Husband working..........	100	20	2	26
Wife and husband working...	100	23	2	19
		+3	0	−7
$3,000–$4,999:				
Husband working..........	100	21	7	39
Wife and husband working...	100	24	7	34
		+3	0	−5
$5,000–$7,499:				
Husband working..........	100	14	12	49
Wife and husband working...	100	23	10	36
		+9	−2	−13
$7,500 and over:				
Husband working..........	100	11	15	58
Wife and husband working...	100	18	12	47
		+7	−3	−11

type of debt, but the figures do in fact show sharp contrasts. Families with working wives, far more than those without, go into debt for cars and household equipment—at every income level. This excess does not appear where mortgage debt and car debt are both present. Where *only* mortgages are involved, or mortgages and household equipment debt, the pattern is actually reversed.[30] A steadily widening gap appears in Table 2-6 between

[29] *Ibid.,* pp. 237–238. It has been assumed that the husband worked in families reporting one paid worker and also where two or more workers were reported and the wife was working.

[30] In explaining this contrast, we must make due allowance for the role of FHA regulations and the stipulations of the capital market, not counting the income of the wife as a sufficiently solid source for buttressing mortgage loans. This element, however, does not preclude the wife's working.

families with working wives and those without, as we proceed from the figures for (1) auto purchase alone, through (2) auto purchase in combination with houses, and to (3) data for house purchase alone. Today's wife will enter the labor force to work for a car, a washing machine, a refrigerator. Such durable items can be delivered at once, and a title acquired within a finite time. They require no more than temporary labor-force participation by the wife.[31] The purchase of a home, on the other hand, is a long-range affair. Its final acquisition is necessarily obscured in the indefinite future.[32]

Changing Labor-force Rates: Demand Factors

Cost Advantage. Complementing the supply forces that pushed women into the labor market were those demand factors that drew them into jobs throughout the nation. As early as 1820, when the factory system was at its very beginning, "taylors" who were would-be emigrants to the United States were warned: Wage rates seemed high, but "their trade is much injured by the employment of women and boys who work from twenty-five to fifty percent cheaper than men." [33]

In the earliest days of the textile industry, it was discovered that women in the United States, as in Britain, were quite capable of carrying through the factory work that otherwise would have to be paid for at male rates —and quite satisfactorily too. As the early Massachusetts and New Hampshire mills began to dominate the industry in the late 1820s and early 1830s, nearly 90 percent of all employees were women.[34] When the tariff

[31] See Federal Reserve Board, *op. cit.,* p. 186, in which Murray Wernick states ". . . both the increased seeking of employment by married women and the incurrence of debt may be influenced by the desire for the ownership of additional durable goods." The "very high incidence of credit use and indebtedness among families in which the head is employed and the wife is unemployed and looking for work" suggest that "financial pressures are a factor influencing the wife to enter and remain in the labor market, when employment opportunities and incomes are at high levels."

[32] A further, but less important, influence producing this result is the tendency for house acquisition to operate as a surrogate variable for the presence of young children. However, the overall relationship between age and mortage debt is not negative, as it should be to make this factor real and substantial. The proportion with mortgage debt rises steadily by age, and the proportion with mortgage debt alone or in combination with household equipment or miscellaneous debt also shows a tendency to rise with age (Federal Reserve Board, *op. cit.,* p. 236). Most important, for present purposes, there is no inverse relationship apparent.

[33] *A Concise Geographical, Historical, Commercial and Agricultural View of the United States of America: Forming a Complete Emigrants Directory* (London: Edwards and Knibbs, 1820). Compiled by several gentlemen from a variety of original manuscripts.

[34] Payrolls for the Hamilton Manufacturing Company in July, 1831, Nashua for April, 1828, and Boston Manufacturing Company for April, 1825, all show about 90 percent. These data are summarized in the unpublished worksheets, now in the

of 1846 reduced textile prices, the farm girls of New England were replaced by farm girls from Ireland; when Southern mills began to develop, "girls from the pine forests, as green and awkward as possible to find them, soon [were found to] become skilful operatives"; when Western woolen mills developed, the initial complement of Chinamen was replaced by women.[35]

Political Changes. The hiring of women in increasing number over the decades since 1865 reflects in no mean measure the fact that they constituted a cheaper means of production than an equal number of men, children, or some other combination of factor inputs. But that ratio of advantage gained substantially as a result of political and social changes. The precedent came in 1866 when women were first introduced into machine shops, to do simple machining.[36] In World War I they became trolley-car conductors and shipyard workers, and made substantial inroads in such traditional male occupations as store clerks, telephone operators, and "typewriters." They replaced men in some insurance firms to such an extent that (at least in one) the firm's average wage bill actually declined during the war.[37] By the time of the second draft in 1918 about 110,000 more females were at work in the iron, steel, and machinery industries than the 1910 to 1920 trend would have indicated, and perhaps 40,000 extra in other industries.[38]

If we look to Table 2-7, we see that the percentage of women working in the traditional industries had changed little prior to 1920, however. They were not substituted for men to any extent over the many decades shown in this table. Apparently a rough stability had been reached, with the marginal return they produced being on a parity with that of men in these industries. Looking both to the worker rate and the employment

---

Baker Library, forming the basis of Robert Layer's substantial study, *Earnings of Cotton Mill Operatives* (1955).

[35] "Les filles de fermiers qui venaient a Lowell de tous les points de la nouvelle-angleterre pour y travailler et y amasser une dot, sont remplaces aujourdhui par des Irlandaises." ("The daughters of farmers, who came to Lowell from every point in New England to work there and accumulate a dowry, have now been replaced by Irish girls.") B. Dureau, *Les Etats Unis en 1850* (Paris: 1891), p. 400. Dureau wrote about 1851. The pine forest reference is from Thomas P. Kettell, *Southern Wealth and Northern Profits* (New York: George W. and John A. Wood, 1860), p. 63, quoting the *New York Herald.* "In 1865 80% of the woolen mill operatives in San-Francisco were Chinamen and in 1880, only 17%. In the interval probably 2,000 women had become skilful operatives . . . and they have gradually crowded out the Asiatics." John S. Hittell, *The Commerce and Industry of the Pacific Coast* (1882), p. 18.

[36] *Scientific American* (Jan. 26, 1867), p. 62.

[37] Unpublished material from one large insurance company.

[38] See Chapter 9, in which estimates are derived from *The New Position of Women in American Industry,* U.S. Women's Bureau Bulletin 12 (1920), pp. 48, 49, 86.

data, we can see a major change taking place after World War I. We attribute that shift largely to the ending of immigration. As the immense flow of low-priced labor into the country slackened and then dwindled, the spread between rates paid to male and female labor widened. The advantage of substituting female labor correspondingly rose. The next major push came during World War II, with the removal of 11 million men to the

Table 2-7. Ratio of Female Workers to Total Employees, Selected Industries and Occupations, 1830–1960

Year	Manufacturing (wage earners)						Teachers	Do-mestic servants
	Total	Cotton textiles	Woolen textiles	Boots and shoes	Clothing	Tobacco		
1830		62.6	44.6	35.9				
1850	21.6	64.0	42.2	31.3	63.7	13.9		
1860	19.2	61.4	39.9	23.2	65.5	15.9		
1870	15.8	51.4	37.3	19.8	58.0	16.3	66.2	87
1880	19.4	48.4	37.0	22.6	55.5	23.1	67.8	84
1890	18.9	48.7	42.1	29.8	55.2	29.8	70.9	84
1899	19.4	41.9	39.5	33.3	61.9	37.2	74.5	83
1909	19.7	38.7	41.3	33.3	58.4	46.5	80.2	83
1919	20.6	42.7	44.2	38.1	60.9	62.9	84.4	89
1940	25.8	37.3	40.9	45.1	73.9	66.8	75.4	93
1947	26.1	40.6	42.9	52.0	75.3	62.6	74.6*	88
1960	26.0	43.0		57.0	80.0	50.0	71.9	88

* 1950.

armed forces concurrent with an enormous rising demand by the government. These events gave entrepreneurs a choice between bidding up rates for males and changing production coefficients at a rate sufficient to dizzy the imagination, or hiring women. The rapid breaking down of traditional job patterns, the dilution of skills, and the hiring of women are matters of lively memory as well as history.

Excursus on Data

A specific issue arises with respect to the comparability between the 1890 (and possibly other censuses) with the count by later censuses of the female labor force. Jaffe has recently offered a forceful argument that the number of women in the labor force was understated in several censuses.[39] We believe that his arguments, effective though they are, have been co-

[39] A. J. Jaffe, "Trends in the Participation of Women in the Working Force," *Monthly Labor Review* (May, 1956).

gently disposed of by Sophia Cooper.[40] More recently Smuts has given a brilliant historical review to the topic of women's work, and his findings cast equal doubt on the census count.[41] Let us consider the specific "statistical indications" he offers in proof.

1. Smuts contends that the 1890 Census counted few rural farm women in the labor force: "There is simply no question that large numbers of women, probably hundreds of thousands, were counted as housewives in 1890 even though they did enough work on family farms to be counted as farm laborers in recent censuses." [42] This argument may well be correct, given one premise—but it is a premise that equally destroys all census counts of the group whatever the year, leaving unscathed only the Current Population Survey. That premise would be a general tendency for the decennial census to understate the number of working women—judging by the Census–Current Population Survey differences in 1940 and 1950, as well as by the comprehensive enumeration in 1910. Such an argument would, of course, require us to adjust not merely the 1890 but all subsequent census enumerations (except presumably the 1910 count). There are few analysts, however, so heroic as to adjust all these censuses merely on the surmise that they all undercounted. We argue, in addition, that the social judgments of each decade on what is to be called gainful work— whether by women or men—must be given preference over later a priori judgment, in the absence of specific discontinuity in the series.

Now if we examine the 1890 Census results, we find that the count for females engaged in agriculture is reasonably consistent with that for sub-

Females Aged 16 and over Gainfully Occupied in Agriculture (In thousands)

Year	White	Nonwhite
1880	459	
1890*	213	387
1900	290	440
1920	397	509
1930	345	420

* Aged 15 and over.

sequent years. Most rural Negro housewives were in fact included in the labor force. Most rural white housewives were not included in the farm

[40] See her comments in the *Monthly Labor Review* (May, 1956). The present author has considered some other objections in the same source.
[41] Robert W. Smuts, *Women and Work in America* (1959), chap. 2.
[42] "The Female Labor Force: A Case Study in the Interpretation of Historical Statistics," *Journal of the American Statistical Association* (March, 1960), pp. 75–77.

labor force then, nor in any other census enumeration of gainful workers.[43] It is quite obvious that the nonwhite population, which accounts for about 10 percent of the total population, accounts for a far greater proportion of females reported in agriculture. More important, Smuts's inference that "hundreds of thousands" were omitted in 1890, but those doing equivalent work were counted in later censuses, is hardly supported by the mild trends shown in the above figures.

2. Smuts's second major point is the excess of the Census of Manufactures over that of Population in the count for textiles, shoe, and tobacco factory employment. We must first recognize the exceptional nature of these industries. Comparison for all manufacturing industries combined gives just the opposite result: the 1890 Population Census reported about 200,000 more women in all factory and hand trades than did the Manufactures Census. Now what, specifically, about the 10,000 difference for tobacco? Reference to the census shows that it is largely accountable in terms of the number of women pieceworkers merely in New York, who rolled cigars at home. Similarly the 7,000 difference for shoe employees is readily accountable for by the pieceworkers in Massachusetts who bound shoes at home. In both instances we have little warrant for assuming that their primary status was not that of housewife: The lot of the lower-income housewife was unquestionably one of overwork, but that fact did not thereby change her labor-force status. The difference for textiles we compute at 30,000—or only 10 percent, as compared to Smuts's 50 percent.[44] The enormously greater number of women reported by the Population Census than by the Manufactures Census for the clothing industries suggests that some "operatives in lace and embroidery mills," in hat factories, or in hosiery mills, might appear under the Population Census rubric of "milliners," or operatives in "other clothing industries," or under still other headings. (Such allocation could be quite incorrect for an industry count; it would not derogate from the accuracy of the total count.)

3. Smuts lays considerable emphasis on the role of homework, and properly so.[45] Homemakers in tobacco and textiles have been allowed for above, being included in the factory totals. The major remaining group who engaged in nearly full-time paid work at home would appear to be the women who did contract work for manufacturers of men's clothing.

[43] 1900 Census, *Occupations,* pp. 10–11, 21, 25, 29, 32; 1920 Census, *Occupations,* pp. 342, 396, 405, 414, 422–438, 488, 495, 506; 1890 Census, vol. II, pp. 349, 379, 385, 391, 396; 1880 Census, *Population,* p. 745; 1930 Census, *Occupations,* pp. 138, 160, 178, 358, 364.

[44] The Population Census data we take from Alba Edwards, *Comparative Occupations Statistics, 1870–1940* (1943), p. 125, while the *Manufactures Census for 1890,* vol. VI, part 1, pp. 75 ff., gives data for industries itemized by Edwards.

[45] Smuts, "The Female Labor Force," p. 76.

Fortunately an extensive survey of that industry was made in 1910.[46] The survey showed that there were only about 5,000 women homeworkers (out of the 100,000 in the industry).[47] The noisome, miserable conditions of work have left such an indelible mark in our social history that they have tended to make us overestimate the actual numbers involved.

We conclude that a significant volume of the world's work in 1890, as in other years, was in fact done by women. But review of the numbers involved, and consideration of the classification accorded such work in prior, and subsequent, censuses both combine to suggest the proper course to achieve maximum comparability with later Population Census counts is simply to take the 1890 Census count of women workers as reported. Considerable value may nonetheless inhere in special studies that make allowance for this significant input of work—just as, for example, we could value such work for inclusion in the national income totals, which now uniformly exclude them.[48]

[46] *Report on Condition of Woman and Child Wage-earners in the United States,* 61st Cong., 2d Sess., Sen. Doc. 645 (1911), vol. II, pp. 33–35, 215. The survey covered about 30 percent of the employees in cities with two-thirds of all employees.

[47] The development of the Boston system of production since 1890 had tended to cut the amount of homework but the aggregate size of the industry had risen. We infer that the 1910 count would not seriously misstate the 1890 level.

[48] In an ancillary argument, Smuts notes the small percentage of women reporting unemployment in 1890—a fact which he sees as pointing to an underestimate. Since women's work is frequently irregular in duration, there is, however, no inconsistency between the two. Recent data indicate that with far greater numbers of jobs held during the year and far more short-time employment, the unemployment rate for women is still not much greater, and is sometimes lower than that for men. The reason is simply that women leave the labor force (rather than enter unemployment) when the work ceases.

3

THE PROCESS

WAGE DIFFERENTIALS AND LABOR MOBILITY

At half past five all were in bustle, preparing for the road. Some settling bills with the hostess; others waiting to settle; some round a long wooden trough at the pump, washing or drying themselves with their pocket handkerchiefs; some Americans drinking their morning bitters (spirits with rice, wormwood or other vegetable infusion); some women catching children who had escaped naked from bed, others packing up bed clothes or putting them into wagons; waggoners harnessing their horses. . . .

James Flint (1822)†

Behind such Breughel-like portraits of the settlement of the United States lie a number of basic forces. To understand how the labor force spread over the land since 1800, we undoubtedly ought to reckon into account the vista west from Fort Dodge; the lure of Colorado silver mines; the *gemutlichkeit* offered by Cincinnati beer parlors in the 1850s; and the spread of the boll weevil. But unless we measure area differences in total advantage tautologically—as the reciprocal of the very migration rate that we are seeking to explain—it is impossible to measure total net gains. We must be content with singling out only one component.

Procedure

We consider here one element of advantage, namely, wage-rate differentials. It is richly obvious that these ignore other economic advantages such as stability in employment, the opportunity to rise in status and be-

† James Flint, *Letters from America* (Edinburgh: W. and C. Tait, 1822), p. 44.

come an independent farmer or entrepreneur, or the verdant hope of capital gains. Moreover, the particular wage-rate measures available to us are for common labor and farm labor in the decennial census years. Unless we assume that the wage structure for the several occupations is invariant within decennial periods, we miss part of the changing influences peculiar to the many other occupations and to the other years of the period.

Yet these measures ought, even if missing more subtle gradations, to mark the coarse differences in economic advantage associated with migration shifts. Higher wage rates for a roughly equivalent grade of labor in one state than another suggest the possibility of a better combination of resources, capital, and markets in the first state. In a generally competitive labor market higher rates are not paid for the same grade of labor unless the productivity (i.e., net revenues) to be realized from that labor are expected to be higher as well. Since our measure does not encompass total advantage, we can expect to go only so far in using it. Nevertheless, it does measure economic advantage and we shall see how far it can carry us toward an understanding of interstate migration. For a measure of migration prior to 1870, we use simply percentage change in state populations— implicitly assuming equal rates of natural increase. After that date we can take advantage of Lee's estimates in the major study by Simon Kuznets and Dorothy Thomas, from which eventually our most comprehensive understanding of migration flows and forces is certain to come.[1]

To focus most closely on the problem within the range of these data, we make the following limitations. First, we study separately the migration pattern for native whites, the foreign born, and nonwhites. It is reasonable a priori, and obvious from the data here considered, that the response to wage differentials is quite different for each group. Native whites are highest on the status ladder; they have more ties of tradition; and they have greater psychic and financial investment in the state where they were born or spent their early life, than do the other groups. The foreign born, by the very fact of their first great migration to the United States, are likely to be a selected group. Their willingness to move in response to an income differential may well differ from that of native whites. All these positive differences, as well as possible further impediments, apply to the migration of Negroes. The advantage of separate consideration to each of these groups is therefore significant.

Secondly, for the years 1870ff. we limit our attention to the central group in the labor force, males aged 25–44[2] A fuller study would, of

[1] Everett Lee et al., *Population Redistribution and Economic Growth, United States, 1870–1950* (1957), vol. I, table P-1. Analysis by the estimators (pp. 74ff.) indicates these survival rates markedly differ from calculations made by the state of birth. Nevertheless, these data are far superior to any alternatives.

[2] These data can be derived from table P-1 in the Lee study, but we have had the advantage of unpublished ratios kindly provided by Dorothy Thomas.

course, consider the pattern for the other age-sex categories as well, and might even attempt to work with a more complex standardized rate for the entire population.

Findings

Before considering the pattern of change over individual decades, we may usefully note some of the more general results.

1. The data indicate that the migration flows over any decade were more largely directed toward the states with higher initial wage rates than to those with lower rates. In some decades and for some groups the linkage is very close, with increases in migration matching differences in initial rates. In nearly all decades it is apparent. Since the errors in estimating wage rates are random from decade to decade, and among the states, we may assume that the true relationship would be even more precise had our wage data been better.

2. Migrants suboptimized. Over any decade they tended to move primarily within a limited area, here approximated as a region. Neither the foreign born landing in New York nor the native white in the low-wage-rate states went at once to the highest-wage states—neither to Nebraska during the 1850s, nor to California during the 1950s. Little relationship between migration moves and wage differentials appears at any period if we view all the states together. As memoirs have indicated, migrants moved where friends, acquaintances, or nationality groups offered a focus of possibility. Moreover, as sociologists from Ravenstein to Stouffer have indicated, the frictions and costs of movement (on the one hand) and the multifarious intervening opportunities (on the other) combine to restrict migration to the more available areas. We could reckon up the costs of transport, put a valuation on the additional time for acclimatization, and combine these figures with the wage differentials. Here we take the simpler approach, however, of studying migration differentials within regions— implicitly setting these other forces as equal to zero within the region. Close relationships are evident for many periods when we deal with states within three major regions—New England and the Southern and Central regions.[3]

3. The response by white migrants to common-labor differentials is much closer than to the monthly farm-wage differentials. The job horizons

[3] We omit the Mountain and Pacific states. Common-labor wage-rate data for the bulk of the states within the Mountain region are not available before 1940, except for 1869. The farm data apply best to Negro migration, a group of little importance within this region. With only three states in the Pacific region, a study of regression relationships in that region is meaningless; we would have to include them with the Mountain states in some distance-adjusted measure. A similar consideration applies to the Middle Atlantic region, complicated further by the fact that most immigrants landed in New York. For all these regions a more comprehensive approach than our present one is requisite.

beckoning to the would-be white migrant were evidently related to non-farm work (or farm daywork?) much more closely than to farming. Such a result is certainly consistent with our earlier finding that the foreign born found work primarily in nonfarm jobs rather than in farming.

4. For Negroes we deal only with migration among the Southern states. Since 65 percent of all male Negroes in the South were in farm work in 1900 [4] (and a correspondingly higher percentage in earlier decades), we related their migration rates to farm rates. That the live alternatives open to Negro labor were in farm work, and that such labor did move in close response to wage differentials, is suggested by both our findings for periods when the mobility originated in shipment by slave owners, and for the later tide of voluntary migration. (Such alternative work as turpentine tapping, railroad construction, road building was, of course, concentrated in rural areas where wage-rate changes would have been dominated by the demands of farming. Hence we cannot conclude from a close link to farm wage rates that only labor requirements of farming were reflected.)

5. Did the migration of the foreign born link more closely to wage differentials than that of the natives? Or Negroes than whites? The data suggest a "yes" to both questions, but hardly a tub-thumping affirmative. For non-whites (in the Southern states) the migration link to wage rates is distinctly closer than for whites in any decade. On the other hand, there appears little to choose for the foreign born: Our solidest comparisons can be made for the North Central states, and without explicit identification we would not know whether the slope of relationship or closeness of correlation shown in any chart was for natives or for the foreign born in this region. We cannot conclude that true differences exist in the response pattern of native white, foreign born, or nonwhite—as for example, that Southern whites did not move within the region for economic advantage. A more precise measure of such advantage than the farm wage-rate figures may provide the basis for affirming or denying such a conclusion.

The Historical Pattern

1830 to 1840: White Population. Our first common-labor rates are for the New England states in 1832.[5] Figure 4 relates these rates to the percentage rise in the white population over the subsequent decade. The limitations of the data are, of course, severe. The use of total population gains to represent only the migration portion of that total is by definition erroneous. And the wage differentials are those maintaining at the beginning of the period (and for one grade of labor) rather than for the entire

---

[4] 1900 Census, *Occupations*, table 34.

[5] True, the three rates for the North Central states that are available fit the relationship shown here. However, these observations are too few on which to rest judgment for the region.

period. Despite such factors tending to reduce the correlation, a clear relation appears, indicating that population flowed toward the higher-wage states in the region far more than it did toward the lower-wage states.

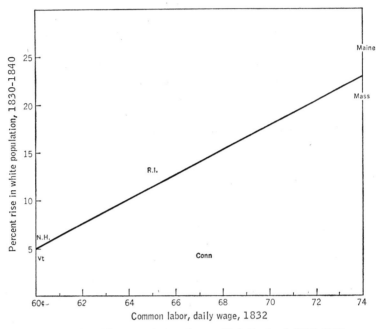

Figure 4.   White population change, New England, 1830–1840.

We lack the more relevant common-labor rates for the South. But Figure 5 reports the pattern using monthly farm-labor rates.[6] We fit the slope of relationship only to the data for the older Southern states: The signal gap that results for Alabama and Mississippi we assume to involve more than errors of estimate. White migration to these newer farming regions was closely linked to the advantages of moving slaves to new land. Such advantages involve anticipated capital gains that may not be fully recognized in hiring rates. (The point is discussed further in connection with nonwhite migration.)

1850 to 1860: White Population.   Beginning with 1850, our wage-rate data improve in quality. What does this happy advance in data produce? For New England (Figure 6) the correlation deteriorates, but not greatly. For the South (Figure 7) we again find a close fit for those states that had been closely settled by 1840. However, Arkansas and Texas have strikingly high migration rates. Again we see evidence of a new frontier that

[6] Using farm-labor rates instead of common-labor rates for New England, 1830 to 1840, gives a distinctly weaker relationship than that shown above; hence we infer that using farm-labor rates for the South, as we do, will understate the correlation.

beckoned enticingly: The admission of Texas into the union brought a greater migration flow through Arkansas than would have been suggested merely by the 1850 wage differentials. The prospective advantages to be

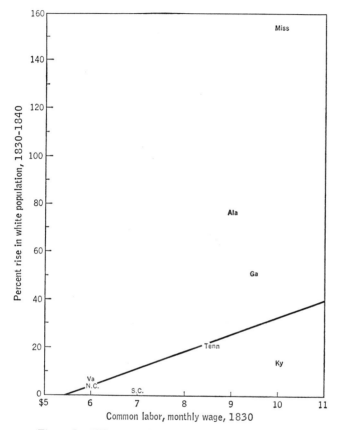

Figure 5. White population change, South, 1830–1840.

gained by settling on the frontier appear not to have been recognized in the short-term labor rates.

The most ponderous wave of migration during this decade, however, flowed into the North Central states (Figure 8). From the 18 percent rise in Ohio's population to the 2,705 percent increase for Minnesota, a variety of gains appeared. The very close relation between the differential gain and the farm-labor rates is also apparent.[7]

[7] Here we adopt farm-labor rates because the openings for migrants were primarily in farm work (unlike New England) and because the white migrants were hired as farm laborers in significant number (unlike the South). Manipulation of some wage rates would bring a closer pattern; for example, the other 1850 data (on day rates) and farm rates in all other years suggest that Ohio rates should be down to or below Indiana levels.

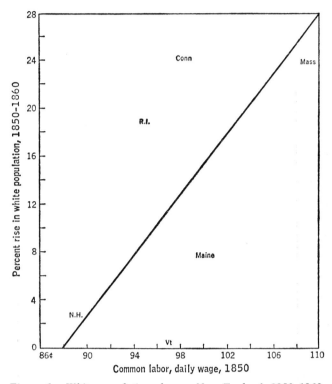

Figure 6.   White population change, New England, 1850–1860.

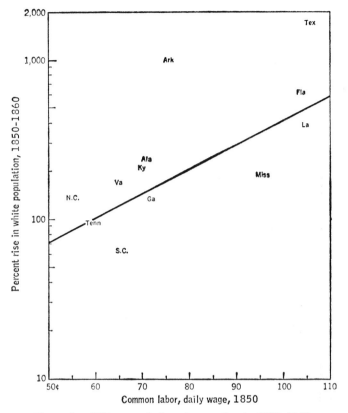

Figure 7. White population change, South, 1850–1860.

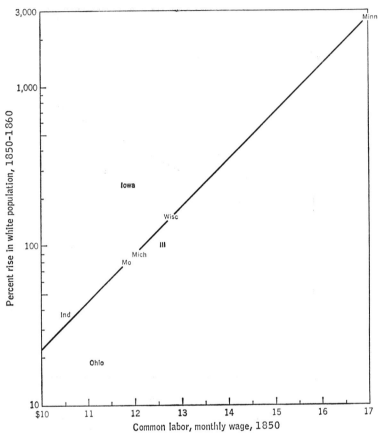

Figure 8. White population change, North Central, 1850–1860.

1820 to 1860: Slave Population. Figures 9 to 11 report the pattern of increase of the slave population of the several Southern states for 1820–1830, 1830–1840, and 1850–1860, and the farm-wage differentials at the

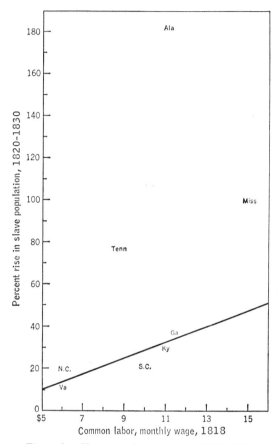

Figure 9. Slave population change, 1820–1830.

beginning of those decades. Given the persistent excess for frontier states at each date, it is clear (1) that the fairly close relationship revealed for the other states is a real one; and (2) that qualifications for errors in the data or the unbalanced age-sex composition of the population in the frontier states are not likely to explain such deviations.[8]

[8] Because of the broad age intervals shown in the early censuses, computation of survival rates is a difficult affair. A careful job might, however, determine that age-sex differences might explain a significant portion of the deviation. Slave population data from 1860 Census, *Population of the United States in 1860* (1864), p. 599ff. For Florida we use the $12 rate for hiring slaves on a road-repair job, reported at St. Augustine in December, 1829. U.S. Congress, Serial Set 208, Doc. 73, p. 55.

Alabama and Mississippi, the frontier states of 1818, had become settled areas by 1850. They then fitted into the pattern for the bulk of the
Southern states.[9] But Arkansas and Texas were now the frontier states, and

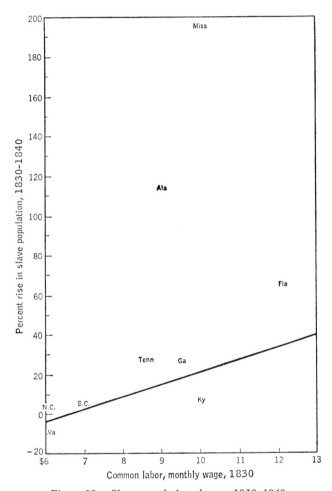

Figure 10.   Slave population change, 1830–1840.

they are fully as distant from the typical relationship as Alabama and
Mississippi once were. We suggest two primary factors in explanation.[10]

[9] The Tennessee figure we believe to be in error: Senator Holmes reports a decline
from 1818 to 1826–1830 for the other states in the region as well as Georgia and
South Carolina, reflecting the impact of the 1819 recession. His Tennessee series
shows no such decline and its 1818 value may be too low.

[10] Errors in data are always with us. Conceivably the Texas rate is too low. For
example, a $15 a month rate for hiring a Negro woman in 1855 was reported,
implying a still higher rate for male labor. Abigail Curlee, "History of a Texas
Slave Plantation, 1831–63," *Southwest Historical Quarterly* (October, 1922), p. 107.

The first is that slaves were moved in anticipation of the advantage to be gained over their entire future lifetime and not necessarily that to be achieved by hiring them out in the first year on the new plantation. Every rational calculation implied that the return on capital stock in Alabama and Mississippi when the new areas in those states were being settled, and

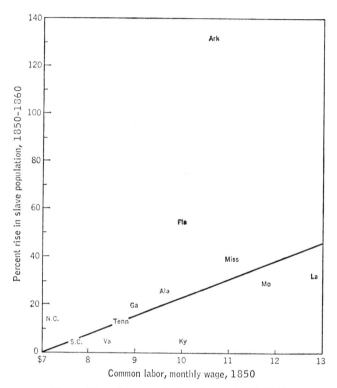

Figure 11. Slave population change, 1850–1860.

in Arkansas and Texas in later years, would reach well above the returns grasped in the older states. A visiting Englishman pointed out in 1849 that: "On the rich lands of the Mississippi one and a half to two bales of 500 pounds each per acre are not unusual, whilst in Alabama the yield does not exceed" 250 pounds. In northeast Texas the rate was somewhat under 500 pounds; in Harrison and Bowie counties, frequently 750 and in Hopkins, not over 350. A distinguished slave owner calculated that he produced 1.7 bales of cotton per hand on his efficiently run South Carolina plantation around 1850; we may contrast his return with an estimated 5 bales per hand in Louisiana (in 1846) and 7 for Texas (in 1842).[11]

[11] Edward Smith, *Account of a Journey through Northeastern Texas Undertaken in 1849 for the Purposes of Emigration* (London: 1849), p. 23. 1854: Robert F. W. Allston, *Essay on Sea Coast Crops* (Charleston: A. E. Miller, 1854), appendix.

It is not unreasonable, therefore, to find that a significant economic advantage encouraged the movement of slaves to the frontier states. But why did not the wage rates recognize this advantage? Surely slaves con-

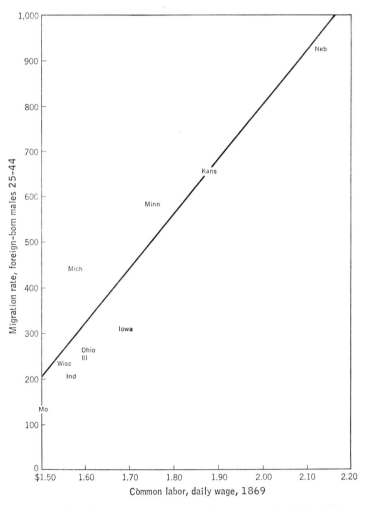

Figure 12.   Foreign-born migration, North Central, 1870–1880.

veyed into the new territories were rented out at rates that recognized their higher capitalization and the higher dollar return to be earned from them. We suggest the possibility that an imperfect market for slave rentals ex-

1846: Representative Harmonson of Louisiana, in *Congressional Globe* (June 24, 1846), p. 746. 1842: William Ballaert, "Notes on the Coast Region of the Texan Territory Taken during a Visit in 1842," *Journal of the Royal Geographic Society* (1843), vol. 13.

isted. Most slaves were brought, or bought, by owners who intended to work them on their own plantations. Without a supply of slaves accumulated from estates of widows and orphans, the volume of slaves for periodic rental would have been relatively low. In such a thin market a clear relation between slave values and hiring rates may not have existed.[12] However, until other hiring rates are used to test the reliability of the ones we have employed here (and possibly a measure of land values scrutinized as a more precise indicator of future returns), we must reserve judgment as to this or any explanation other than errors in the data.

1870 to 1920: Foreign-born Whites. Beginning with 1870 we have a far more satisfactory indication of migration than the mere change in population figures, being able to rely on the estimates from the Kuznets-Thomas study mentioned above.[13] Since a review of the different patterns for nine regions, three nativity-color groups, and four or five decennia would be far out of proportion in the current context, we review primarily the trend for the North Central block of states.

Figure 12 reports the relationship between (1) the migration rate for males aged 25–44 among the North Central states for 1870 to 1880 and (2) the common-labor rates for 1869, at the beginning of the period. (An equally close relationship applies to the shifts of native whites as well.)

The chart for 1880 to 1890 (Figure 13) reports much the same relationship. That for 1890 to 1900 (Figure 14), however, gives a much looser fit. Now the more reliable migration data for native whites shows actual out-migration from Indiana and Ohio, compared to in-migration for Illinois. Hence we infer that errors in the estimate of migration may account for part of the change. We surmise that errors in the wage rates and functional shifts in the relationship are both possible contributors, but award the palm to neither one.[14]

Our next set of rates applies to 1919 (Figure 15). The relationship continues much the same if we allow for biases tending to overstate Kansas wages and understate Michigan rates. (Only after such allowance can we speculate on the extent to which the very high rate for Michigan reflected

[12] Gary Becker, "Union Restrictions on Entry" in Philip Bradley, *The Public Stake in Union Power* (1959), p. 213, finds that "the quantity supplied to an occupation is determined by both present and future real income prospects, not by present wages alone." His model premises that unions might improve future income prospects, thus increasing the quantity supplied, without affecting current wages.

[13] Lee, *op. cit.*

[14] Our wage estimates are based on the 1890 Census of Manufactures reports on weekly wages in selected industries. Because of the high ratio of slaughtering to all factory employment for which we have weekly reports in Kansas and Nebraska, both states have higher wage rates in Table A-25 than are probably representative. Since the census rates for the several industries in Kansas are consistent with one another, we do not adjust that rate but do adjust the inconsistent Nebraska figure, using an average of $1.34 for all industries but slaughtering.

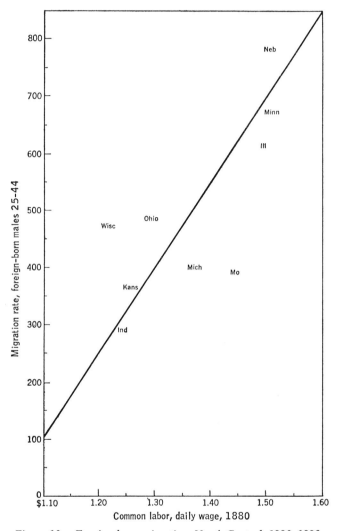

Figure 13. Foreign-born migration, North Central, 1880–1890.

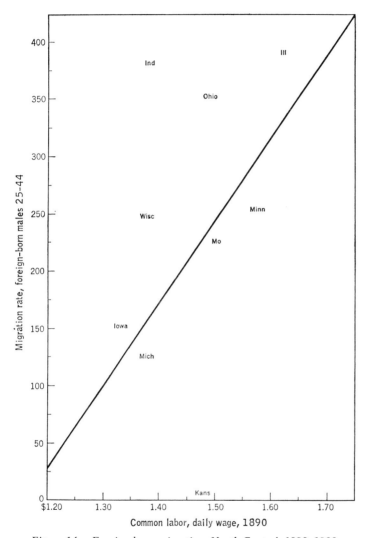

Figure 14.   *Foreign-born migration, North Central, 1890–1900.*

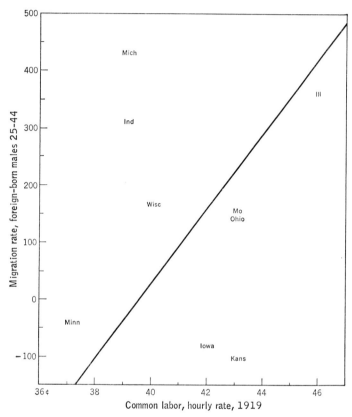

Figure 15.   Foreign-born migration, North Central, 1920–1930.

the efforts of the auto companies to attract highlanders from outside the region—from Kentucky or Tennessee.)

Negro Migration: 1870 to 1950.   Concentrations of the Negro population in sufficient numbers to permit calculating reasonably reliable migra-

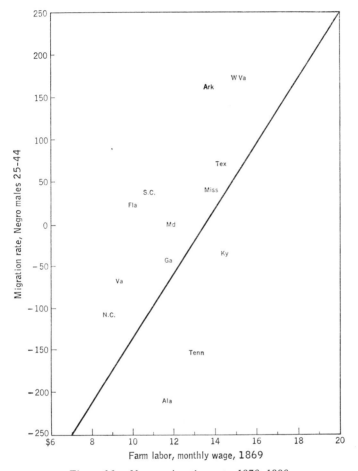

Figure 16.   Negro migration rate, 1870–1880.

tion data have existed only in the Southern states and a few individual states in the Middle Atlantic and North Central regions. For studying Negro migration within a region, we must therefore concentrate on the data for the South. These are shown in Figures 16 to 24.[15] Despite the 1870 undercount, the pattern of relationship for 1870 to 1880 migration parallels that for subsequent decades. The relationship improves in the decade before World War I and that of the depression, but otherwise does

---

[15] We take the same group of states for the entire period.

not differ strikingly.[16] In all years the influence of forces associated with wage-rate differentials is clearly linked to migration differentials. In most years Florida constitutes a distinctive exception. It is possible that the

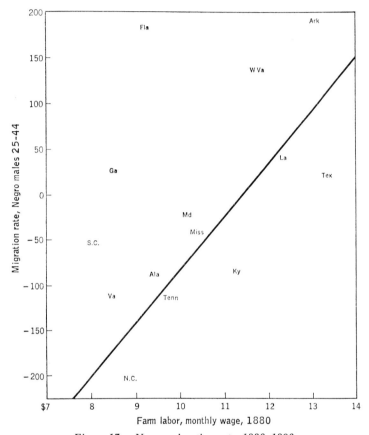

Figure 17.   Negro migration rate, 1880–1890.

plethora of palm trees constitutes an explanatory factor, but more mundane factors may be at work.[17]

[16] An obvious qualification in some years we attribute to data errors. For example, in 1900–1910, the West Virginia in-migration rate is high, even above that for Florida, and Kentucky is very low. Lee's migration estimates for all Negroes by the state-of-birth procedure (*op. cit.,* p. 91) give markedly different results than his survival rate figures.

[17] 1. Ready access to the sea meant a cheap if not free source of protein, not a trivial consideration for as low income a group as is here involved.

2. Lee's data indicate that his survival-rate estimates, which we use, are beneath the birth-residence estimates (or much the same) for these Southern states except Florida and Texas, for which they are substantially greater in nearly every decade.

Opportunities for individual farming may have been a further factor. Florida showed the highest rate of increase in number of farms for 1870 to 1880 and 1880

For the final decade, 1940–1950, we report as well the migration rates in relation to per capita personal-income differentials.[18] These income figures show forth not merely the effects of (1) differentials in wage rates,

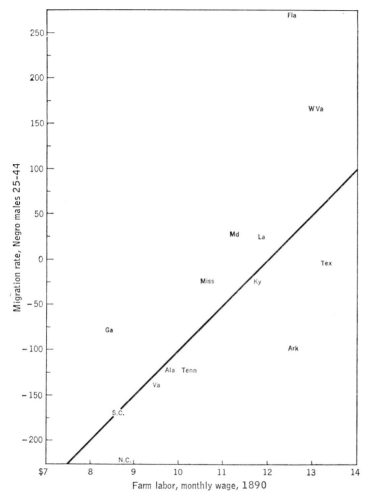

Figure 18. Negro migration rate, 1890–1900.

but of (2) steadiness of employment and of (3) the relative opportunity for higher-income work. Their relationship to the migration differentials is far more clear-cut than that of wage rates. This fact surely suggests the possibility that in earlier periods as well the link between migration differentials and income might have been tighter than the one that we con-

to 1890 (though not for 1890 to 1900) of any state on the seaboard. 1900 Census, *Agriculture,* part 1, p. lxxix.

[18] We use personal income in 1946, a year roughly midway in the period. Office of Business Economics, *Personal Income by States since 1929* (1956), p. 143.

sidered. Indeed, work by Easterlin suggests that on a regional basis net migration rates for early periods are closely correlated with his estimates

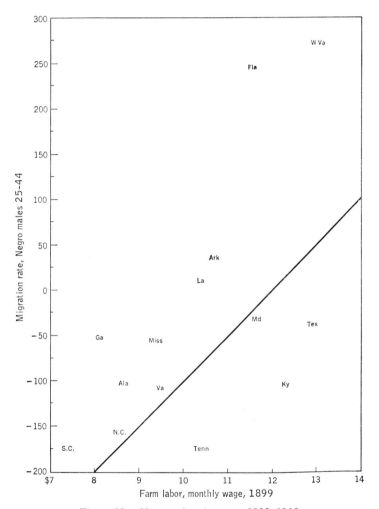

Figure 19.   Negro migration rate, 1900–1910.

of service income per worker.[19] A number of recent studies have canvassed the extent of migration from the rural farm population for 1940 to 1950.[20]

[19] See Easterlin's "Regional Growth of Income," in Simon Kuznets, Ann Miller, Richard Easterlin, *Population Redistribution and Economic Growth of the United States, 1870–1950* (1960), pp. 171–172. We use beginning-of-period differentials, whereas Easterlin is working with initial- and terminal-period averages. Using the Easterlin estimates within the regions we have considered (from Lee et al., *op. cit.,* p. 753) does not show any closer or different relation than do the wage data.

[20] Sheridan T. Maitland and Dorothy Fisher, *Area Variations in the Wages of*

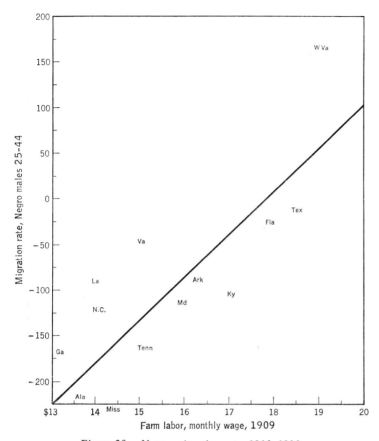

Figure 20.   Negro migration rate, 1910–1920.

Measures of general farm-income differentials were used in some of these studies. Their results, though reporting a less close relationship, are not inconsistent with the present ones.

Agricultural Labor in the United States, U.S. Department of Agriculture, Technical Bulletin 1177 (March, 1958); Charles H. Berry, *Factors Affecting the Occupational Migration of Labor from Agriculture,* Cowles Foundation Discussion Paper 103 (December, 1960); and the symposium by Hathaway, Maddox, and Johnson in the *American Economic Review, Papers and Proceedings* (May, 1960).

In a well-rounded study by Willis Weatherford, Jr., *Geographic Differentials of Agricultural Wages in the United States* (1957), net migration to farms from 1935 to 1940 and net farm income per man-hour in 1939 are correlated to give a co-efficient of +.61 (p. 76). Our focus is on the attractive forces that can be construed as causal ones because, among other things, they preceded migration.

Berry (*op. cit.*) uses a farm-operator level of living measure in 1940 as his primary income variable, working as he does with state economic area data. Un-published data kindly provided by Maitland show a —.541 correlation between the 1940 level of living index in 361 state economic areas and the rate of out-migration from the rural farm population for 1940 to 1950.

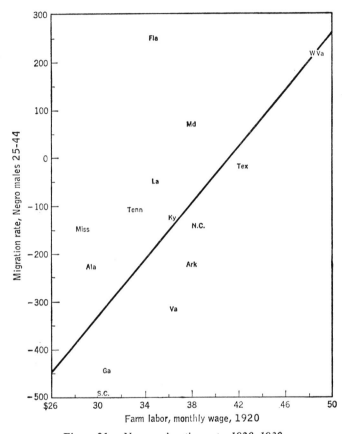

Figure 21.   Negro migration rate, 1920–1930.

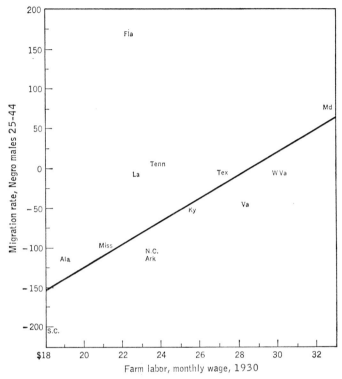

Figure 22.   Negro migration rate, 1930–1940.

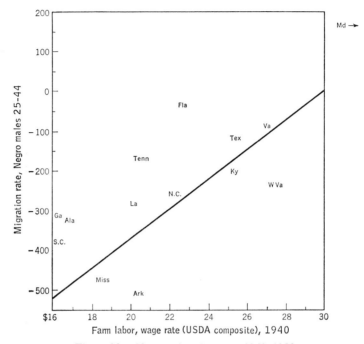

Figure 23. Negro migration rate, 1940–1950.

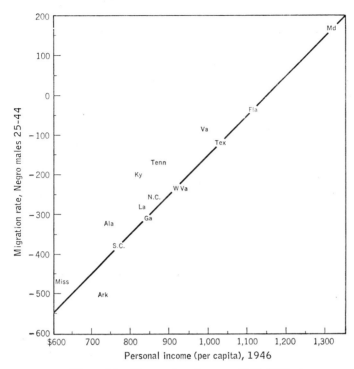

Figure 24. *Negro migration rate, 1940–1950.*

EMPLOYMENT PATTERNS IN ECONOMIC GROWTH

At least since the time of Hume, philosophers have puzzled over the question of just when a set of observed sequences becomes a demonstration of a causal relationship. Can the observer, by repeated thought and observation, raise his stature one cubit—and convert accustomed sequence into invariant law? The answer that some scientists have given is a simple one: If we have observed one example we will generalize, and go on to use that generalization until it founders, or we founder with it.

In the study of economic development it has been observed that not in one, but in many countries, as the economy matured, the share of the labor force in agriculture and other primary industries declined; the share in tertiary industries grew.[1] From this some observers have deduced a law of development: Man begins with the simple, truly productive industries that take grain from the land, fish from the sea, and minerals "digged villainously from the bowels of the earth"; he then proceeds to manufacturing and transport; and finally he turns down the sinful slope, squandering ever more and more resources on the tertiary industries. The moral overtones of physiocracy are clearly heard in the background. In the foreground is the theme of unidirectional historical development.

There is no particularly strong theoretical case for this position. What, indeed, are we to make of a rule of growth which implicitly premises that the comparative advantage of every country must always be against the primary industries as it develops—against not merely agriculture but against agriculture, mining, forestry, and fisheries severally and jointly in any combination? What are we to conclude from the corollary that every underdeveloped country is necessarily unwise to specialize in any primary product—whether cocoa, tobacco, uranium, or gold—regardless of whether there are solid continuing markets for the product and clear compara-

---

[1] The classic presentation is in Colin Clark, *The Conditions of Economic Progress* (1940), pp. 6–7. Although he attributes the observation to Sir William Petty, a more recent precursor was Alian Fisher in the *International Labour Review* (January, 1920). See too Fisher's "Tertiary Production as a Postwar International Economic Problem," *Review of Economic Statistics* (August, 1946). W. A. Lewis, *The Theory of Economic Growth* (1955), p. 230, rationalizes a decline in agriculture and a gain in manufacturing as arising from the fact that the income elasticity of demand for food is less than unity. Clark's position has recently received support in Harvey Leibenstein, *Economic Backwardness and Economic Growth* (1957), chap. 7; it was roughly handled with respect to its actual applicability to African and South American countries in P. T. Bauer and B. S. Yamey, *The Economics of Underdeveloped Countries* (1957), pp. 40–42, and their earlier studies; and is considered at greater length in Gerald Meier and Robert Baldwin, *Economic Development, Theory, History, Policy* (1957), pp. 197ff.

tive advantage in making it? Must a nation reject such specialization because the next "natural" stage is that of manufacturing—where it will need
to compete against skilled, experienced predecessors, already established
in the markets of the world? The implied answer turns largely on an appeal to actual historic experience.[2] Let us see what light the American
record may cast on the proposition.

The broad pattern of manpower use by industry changed in three massive advances during the nineteenth century—from 1800 to 1850, from
1850 to 1880, and from 1880 to the close of the century.

1800 to 1850. At the beginning of this century the nation's economy
was clearly, dominantly, and almost single-mindedly agricultural. Benjamin Rush, when given some precious mangel wurzel seeds, found it only
natural to send "the largest number of them to our great and good Virginia
farmer, General Washington." [3] Another Virginia farmer and President,
Jefferson, conducted experiments in crop rotation, while another farmer
and President from Massachusetts, Adams, delivered talks to agricultural
societies on ways to keep up soil fertility. By the end of the century, however, the farming activities of our political leaders had become mere
political adjuncts.

But this massive change took place at no regular rate. No smooth, steady
descent into urbanism appeared. Rather there was a response, varying dis-
cordantly through time as its causes varied. From 1800 to 1810 the proportion in farming rose mildly. Though well within statistical error, such a
gain may indeed have taken place, given the rush of settlers into the
Northwest Territory (where land clearing preceded supporting nonfarm
activities) and given the fervor with which slaves were imported prior to
the 1808 deadline ending such importation.

From 1810 to 1850 the proportion of the labor force at work in farming fell most decisively, from about 80 to 55 percent. While the advance
into industrial society was clear-cut, only about 1.2 million of the rise
actually went into manufacturing. Nearly twice as many flooded into trade,
service, construction, and other nonfarm pursuits. The trend, however,
was no irresistible one dominating development throughout the nation.[4] It
was, in fact, solidly localized. In the North and West a substantial shift

---

[2] A wider perspective would derive from two characteristically astute articles by
Simon Kuznets in *Economic Development and Cultural Change* (July, 1957; April,
1959).

[3] Quoted in *The Life of Robert Fulton, by his Friend Cadwallader D. Colden*
(New York: Kirk and Mercein, 1817), p. 273.

[4] For useful discussions of regional development, see two recent studies: Simon
Kuznets, Ann Miller, and Richard Easterlin, *Population Redistribution and Economic
Growth of the United States, 1870–1950* (1960); and Harvey Perloff et al., *Regions,
Resources, and Economic Growth* (1960) chap. 10, discusses regional growth
before 1870.

from agriculture to nonfarm pursuits occurred, but the South remained unwavering in its commitment.[5]

Percent of Labor Force in Agriculture

Region	1800	1850
North and West..........	68	40
South.................	82	84

Although slave labor was frequently hired out by the month or year, indifferently between steamboating and farming, manufacturing and railroad construction, canal building and turpentine farming, it remained overwhelmingly concentrated in farming.

Since the Tredegar Iron works, the Saluda and Granite mills, the Richmond tobacco factories, and a host of other firms established the competence of the South for manufacturing as early as that of the North, it would appear that comparative advantage in this region continued to favor agriculture.[6] One major labor-force shift was made within the South between 1800 and 1850, from the indigo, tobacco, and rice pattern (which continued the colonial tradition) into hemp and cane, but above all into cotton to feed the mills of England, old and new. A second, further change was the shifting of cotton labor from the Carolinas and the East Coast to the bottomlands of Mississippi and Alabama, then on to the still richer soils of Arkansas and Texas. Cotton was king in the South, and remained so until dethroned in the revolution of 1861.[7]

In the North, likewise, an equally vast move to better lands was under

[5] For 1800 we assume that the proportion of the free-labor force in agriculture —which we estimate at 68.5 percent—applied both to the North and to the South, while the proportion of the United States slave-labor force in agriculture applied to the South. We divide the free-labor force between the regions in proportion to the white population as given on p. 45 of DeBow. For 1850 we estimate the ratio for Northern and Western states from data for occupations of free males as reported in the census for that year. J. D. B. DeBow, *Statistical View of the United States . . . A Compendium of the Seventh Census* (1854), p. 128. For the South we use census state occupation data for the free population, and add our estimate of slaves in agriculture and other pursuits, described in connection with our estimates of agricultural labor force and employment in 1850.

[6] Himself the owner of two large factories in Georgia burned by General Sherman, William King, when asked in 1866 whether the South felt it ought to become a manufacturing people, replied: "No sir. Heretofore their ideas have been so perfectly absorbed with the one great thing, to make cotton, sell cotton, buy negroes, and then make more cotton, that they have never thought of anything else." *Report of the Revenue Commission,* 39th Congress, 1st Sess., January, 1866, p. 3.

[7] The Honorable John Preston, Commissioner from the State of South Carolina, in February, 1861, spoke of "that revolution that we are now enacting."

way, men from Connecticut pushing into Vermont, Vermonters heading for New York State, and men from Buffalo skirting the lake shore on their way to Michigan or Illinois.

1850 to 1880. The second massive shift in the principal pattern of manpower use occurred from 1850 to 1880, hardly interrupted at all by the war years. Over these 30 years the proportion of the labor force in agriculture remained almost frozen at just over 50 percent.[8] The remorseless engine of historical development posited by some theories had apparently been run on to a siding, meanwhile. Yet the explanation is reasonably clear, if we consider that the rate of descent on the path toward industrialization reflects chiefly the changing advantage of the nation in different pursuits. In these years American farms became the breadbasket of the world. Their efficiency for producing wheat was greater than that of the Ukraine; for cotton, than that of India; for raising meat animals, than that of Hungary and the Argentine. The magnitude of geographic labor-force movements is closely indicated by the population changes, and a look at those is revealing. The gains during each period were much the same in

Population Gains

(In millions)

Period	Northeast	North Central	South	West
1790–1820	2.4	0.8	2.4	
1820–1850	4.2	4.6	4.5	
1850–1880	5.9	12.0	7.5	1.6
1880–1910	11.1	12.5	13.0	5.1

each of the three major regions. One figure stands out as a bold exception: The rise of 12 billion for the North Central states from 1850 to 1880. One of the largest gains in any period, twice as great as the concurrent rise for the Northeast (and nearly twice as great as that for the South), this advance reflects the moving in of settlers to the central lands almost unparalleled in richness. And of the five 30-year periods since 1790, it was in that from 1850 to 1880 that the center of population moved the farthest West.[9]

1880 to 1900. Some time after 1880 two significant events occurred. First, the prices of wheat, corn, oats, and hogs, which had declined omi-

[8] This conclusion derives from the present estimates. The established Whelpton or Edwards estimates show a long-term trend of vivid regularity, reflecting their use of a parabola to relate the farm-labor force to the rural population count, and their bypassing the 1850, 1860, and 1870 census information utilized in the present estimates.

[9] *1957 Statistical Abstract*, p. 9.

nously during the decade of the 1870s, broke again in the first half of the 1880s.[10] The farmer's apparently endless horizon of high prices and bumper crops in the new states became darkened and dubious. Second, the density of population reached a new high. In the 1890 words of the civil servant: "Up to and including 1880 the country had a frontier of settle-ment, but at present the unsettled areas have been so broken into by iso-lated bodies of settlement that there can hardly be said to be a frontier line." [11] (Pared down to "the end of the frontier" by a great historian, that statement has, of course, dominated many a subsequent study of our history.)

But whether it came as a simple consequence of these events or was jointly tied to them through the forces that bring diminishing returns down upon man's worldly endeavors, the balance of manpower allocation began to shift. After 30 or more years of stability, the proportion of the labor force in nonfarm pursuits began again to increase.

1900 to 1960.   From 1900 on the pace of the shift accelerated; the absolute number in farming declined as well as the proportion. But the rate of attrition was a mild one down through to 1940 (except for a sig-nificant net loss during World War I). The really marked declines came in two brief intervals—¾ of a million down from 1944 to 1946 under the impetus of war prosperity; and about 1 million down from 1949 to 1951, again a period of sharp war preparation (in which nonfarm wages were bid up and nonfarm job opportunities burgeoned).[12]

1800 to 1960.   In summarizing this experience, what can we deduce from this mixed pattern? Essentially that the net shift away from agricul-ture was a sensitive response to the richer rewards offered in nonfarm pursuits. As far as we can tell, that shift did not stem from any faltering of American desires for food and fiber: the per capita consumption of major food products appears to have changed little since the 1830s.[13] Nor, as far

[10] Bureau of the Census, *Historical Statistics of the United States, Colonial Times to 1957,* pp. 290, 297, 298.

[11] Robert Porter, Henry Gannett, and William Hunt in 1890 Census, *Population,* vol. I, p. xxxiv.

[12] Judging from the monthly data, the net losses began to be evident late in 1949, but we require seasonally adjusted data to make a more reasonable analysis. It would also be desirable to see how much of the loss was in persons employed full time in farming, say, 35 hours or more. Judging by the January–July ratios, both groups were involved.

[13] Marvin Towne and Wayne Rasmussen, in their invaluable study, "Gross Farm Production and Gross Investment in the Nineteenth Century," a paper prepared for the 1957 Conference on Research in Income and Wealth, assume no change in per capita consumption of major items over this period. The stability since 1900 (when choices varied more and incomes rose) is indicated by U.S. Department of Agriculture, *Consumption of Food in the United States, 1909–1952,* p. 144.

as we can tell, was any differential advance of productivity in farm and nonfarm sectors a sufficient explanation of this labor shift. True, such advances were more evident at some times than at others; for example, when the shift to the prairie lands of the Midwest and the ranges of the Southwest took place, when combines, reapers, and threshers were introduced in the 1850–1880 period.

These factors, however, cannot account for the long-term decline in farming. The most effervescent, endless series of productivity advances in agriculture would cut employment in agriculture (assuming final demand patterns unchanged) only if they outpaced the concurrent advance in nonfarm industry. But it is doubtful that such was the case. A more likely explanation of the long-term fall in the ratio of farm labor to total United States labor force would refer to the shift in demand for industrial products as the growing level of United States real income permitted a rise away from mere subsistence. The per capita demand for food from farms changed little, but that for clothing, buggy whips, and welsbach mantles soared. A contributing force was the shift of our comparative advantage in international trade: In 1821, 60 percent of our imports were finished manufactures; by 1950 only 17 percent were. In 1821, 60 percent of our exports were crude materials, but by 1950 about 60 percent of our exports were finished manufactures.[14] Such differences created an upward shift in industrial as compared to farm employment.

The mere summation of random forces would be more likely to decrease than increase the proportion of the labor force in agriculture for any country that had 80 percent of its labor force in agriculture at the beginning of a period. The more important inference with respect to economic development relates not to the direction but to the causes and rate of shift. For decades during which the advantages ran in favor of agriculture, no shift of manpower out of agriculture took place. And if in an overpopulated planet, at some future date productivity advances in favor of United States agricultural production, or if changing tastes suggest that sybaritic delights derive from natural rather than machined products, a reverse tide might again occur.

A second theorem on economic development has described the inevitable cycle from rise to decline in manufacturing as the economy, and social order, matures. Table A-1 shows such data as we have been able to put together for 1810 to 1960. Rise there surely was—irregular but unequivocal, continuous if not continual. The true gain in manufacturing is probably less than shown here, for we define manufacturing as work under factory

---

[14] *Historical Statistics,* pp. 246–247; *1959 Statistical Abstract,* p. 892. The further changes by 1960, perhaps short-term in character, showed how responsive the pattern of demand could be.

conditions, measured empirically since 1850 by what the Census of Manufactures covers.[15] But men wove cloth before power looms began operating in factories. Women spun yarn at home for factory consumption some years before spinners were gathered within factory walls. This qualification, however, is not a serious one after about 1830.[16]

Our data on factory employment, in sum, report substantial rises from 1810 to 1900, yet they reveal no trend—and certainly no decline—in the ratio to the labor force since that date. Without touching upon the contentious area of the stagnation theory, enough study has been devoted to the overall rate of growth since 1900 to fortify a conclusion that the economy is no longer advancing at the long-term rate characteristic of the nineteenth century.[17] But do these data indicate any diminished share of factory in total employment? Not within the limits of the error of estimate.

Nor is there any reason in theory why it should: The concept of manufacturing employment as an area unto itself is difficult to adopt. The pattern of demands for transportation, for example, will be fixed by a combination of advertising incentives, consumer whims, public utility commission regulations, speculation in land, and the varying birth rate. In the United States these have brought a shift in demand away from transportation by business enterprise (streetcars, buses, railroads) to transportation by family enterprise (the private automobile). Since an enormously greater input of materials is required to transport persons one at a time than 70 at a time, the net result of this preference shift was a trivial 1900 to 1960 gain in transportation employment but a massive gain in factory employment to produce autos, tires, gasoline, and brochures advertising new cars.

Another example: the number of cotton farmers declined as a close result of increasing factory employment in the production of rayon, orlon, banlon, and so on.

1900 to 1960.   Since 1900 total employment has risen substantially. The detailed patterns appear in Table A-3. Because the growth was so substantial over these decades, it is difficult to disentangle the changing pattern of employment in the absolute data.

[15] For a most illuminating discussion of the meaning and changing scope of manufacturing, see Richard Easterlin, "Estimates of Manufacturing Activity," in Everett Lee et al., *Population Redistribution and Economic Growth, United States, 1870–1950* (1957), vol. I, pp. 638–646.

[16] The inclusion of homeworkers in manufacturing would, of course, have to be matched by their concurrent inclusion in the labor force, so that the net change in the percentages shown would be trivial.

[17] The major study of retardation prior to 1929 is still that of Arthur F. Burns, *Production Trends in the United States since 1870* (1934), while the recent analysis by Simon Kuznets, *Capital in the American Economy: Its Formation and Financing*, and its related studies, is the most comprehensive review since Schumpeter's landmark, *Business Cycles* (1939).

To cast some highlights on that complicated pattern we have made a number of comparisons in Tables 3-1, 3-2, and 3-3. In the first two tables we project employment from 1900 to 1958. Had the industry grown as much as the noninstitutional population, we would give it an index of 100. If it grew at double that rate its index would be 200, and so on. The

Table 3-1. All Industries: Actual Employment in 1958 as a Percent of Projected Employment

Insurance	1,947
Banking	1,922
Hospitals	1,400
Federal: defense	1,037
Armed forces	894
Cleaning and laundry	696
Amusement	667
State and local	359
Finance	342
Federal: nondefense	284
Education	222
Hotels	223
Trade	148
Clergy	146
Physicians (self-employed)	135
Service, except domestic	130
Manufacturing	106
Civilian Labor Force	102
Construction	91
Transport	72
Domestic service	57
Mining	48
Farming	22

striking range of advance, from the ideal industry of a security-conscious nation to the huge relative loss for one of the world's ancient industries, from the rise in transport (because of advancing demand) to the decline in tobacco (because of even more vigorous productivity change) is apparent. Perhaps less apparent is the fact that the rather smooth pattern of national growth is created by the complicated thrust and counterthrust of these changing forces.

In Table 3-3, instead of treating each industry on all fours with the others, we attempt to see how much in the aggregate these differences contributed to total employment. Hence had each sector risen as much as the population, we would have no sources and no uses. Weighting the indices in Table 3-1 by actual employment in 1900, we therefore derive in absolute numbers the net contribution (source) of each industry to manpower availability or its demands (use) from that pool. Where an industry declined in relative importance, it became a source of additional manpower for other industries. Where it rose relatively (as well as absolutely), it appears as a user.

Table 3-2. Manufacturing: Actual Employment in 1958 as a Percent of Projected Employment

Transport equipment	163
Petroleum	147
Rubber	145
Machinery	132
Paper	131
Chemicals	98
Metals	91
Furniture	89
Food	88
Printing	77
Beverages	59
Textiles	52
Stone, clay, glass	50
Leather	37
Wood	28
Tobacco	18

Sources. The major source was clearly *farming,* which (relative to 1900 patterns) released some 22 million people for work in other industries. The significant fall in farm family workers reflected a decline of disguised unemployment and underemployment. In addition a sizable fall took place in the amount of hired labor used. The rising price of farm labor and the shifting patterns of capital availability had replaced the man with the hoe by a tractor, and the dairymaid by a milking machine.

Three other sources together contributed about half of what farming did. (1) The rise in the *labor-force rate* reflects the volatile gains in the worker rates for women, most sharply in and after World War II. Some of this gain was a consequence of the population shift from farm to city (where nonhousehold work for women is more available) and hence dimly reflects the decline in farming. However, in substantial degree this gain reflects how intense labor demand brought new groups into the labor force. (2) The decline in urban *self-employment* reflects the replacement of the stoic, stalwart independent entrepreneur by the pedestrian hired employee. Much of this replacement took place during, and immediately after, the two world wars. We may infer no massive shift in the American status system, but rather the replacement of low-income entrepreneurs (really "disguised unemployed") by employees. (3) The substantial decline in *domestic service,* also a major source, we consider below in connection with the trend for service industries as a whole.

**Table 3-3. Sources and Uses of Labor:
1960 as Compared with 1900 Pattern
(In thousands)**

Sources:

Rise in total labor-force participation rate		3,650
Decline in farm employment		21,880
Farmers	11,390	
Family workers	5,860	
Hired workers	3,930	
Decline in nonfarm self-employment		3,000
Construction	300	
Manufacturing	560	
Trade	430	
Service	690	
Other	1,020	
Decline in domestic service		1,890
Total		29,520

Uses: Rise in:

Armed forces		2,210
Unemployment		480
Nonfarm unpaid family workers		200
Nonfarm employees		26,630
Total		29,520

Memorandum:

Rise of number of employees in nonagricultural
establishments:*

Trade		5,300
Manufacturing		3,250
Production workers	120	
Salaried personnel	3,130	
Service		2,800
State and local government		2,400
Finance		1,780
Education		1,740
Federal: defense		960
Federal: nondefense		700
Construction		0
Mining		−270
Transport and utilities		−1,620

* Not directly comparable with entries above.

Despite the steady dispersion of the population and the intricate reticulation of our network of communication, *transport and utilities* declined as an employer. This measured decline would vanish, however, if we were to combine with transport the associated and competitive industries of automobile manufacture, fueling, and repair industries—where significant, and more than compensating, gains took place (Table 3-4). The decline in *mining* evidenced a gross decline in fuel and raw materials employment— offset in part by the growth of chemical and lumber manufacturing, providing alternative materials.[18]

For *construction* little or no net change is indicated. True, nonfarm residential starts tripled over these years. But the changing pattern of houses (fewer Victorian gables, more prefabricated components) plus rising productivity offset any tendency to increasing employment. Complementary, too, was the trend toward building industrial plants with decreased building and floor-space requirements. Such continuous-process firms as those of the petroleum and chemical industry, for example, came to consist virtually all of equipment and hardly at all of physical plant.

Uses. So much for sources. Where was this labor supply of 24 million used?

Two categories led all the rest in the increasing use of labor. One was *trade.* The distribution network was already complex in McKinley's day. Yet it added about 5 million beyond the general growth increment, this despite the growth of chain stores, supermarkets, prepackaging, and all the proud advances in efficiency.[19] The search for security by military means took about 3 million—most in the armed forces, but with a civilian complement of no mean magnitude (Table 3-4).

Manufacturing production workers increased hardly at all; but the im-

---

[18] Petroleum and gas mining data from 1902 Census, *Mines and Quarries, 1902,* p. 348. Manufacturing detail from 1899 Census, *Manufactures,* vol. VII, part 1, table 2. Transportation is a component of the present estimates. State and local highway: The 1902 Census of Government data show $175 million in highway expenditures (1957 Census of Governments, *Historical Summary,* vol. IV, p. 19). Given the customary 50:50 ratio of labor costs to materials, we divide by an average wage of $500 (compared to the $593 for the construction industry in general) to get 160,-000 employees in streets and highways. The 1910 Census of Population, *Occupations,* p. 410, reports 238,000 for 1910. The 1899 Census, *Manufactures,* vol. VIII, part 1, p. 53, reports $46.4 million in paving materials. Raising this producers' value figure for transport costs and margin to $70 million, using the above 50:50 ratio and $500, gives 140,000 employment. Since the value of paving materials doubled from 1899 to 1909 (1910 Census, *Manufactures,* vol. VIII, p. 514), we assume that the 238,000 employment for 1910 is quite consistent with the 140,000 and 160,000 figures we thus derive indirectly for 1900, and we take a 150,000 average. 1958 data from Bureau of Labor Statistics, *Employment and Earnings* (February, 1959), except for state and local highway, which are from 1957 Census of Governments, *Summary of Public Employment,* vol. II, no. 1, p. 13.

[19] While employment tripled from 1900 to 1950, the volume of finished goods distributed through retail stores rose four to five times, implying a significant productivity advance. For the volume of goods, see Harold Barger's major study, *Distribution's Place in the American Economy since 1869* (1955), pp. 22–23, note g.

pressive rise in factory productivity was partially taken up by an increase in salaried employees. This rise was not sudden, nor concentrated in that 1950 to 1959 increase which alarmed so many analysts that the word Parkinson became a form of incantation. It was, in fact, the result of three

**Table 3-4. Labor Force: by Function
(In thousands)**

Function	1900	1958
Transport..............................	2,723	8,471
Transportation industry..................	2,135	2,720
Petroleum and gas mining...............	40	303
Petroleum refining......................	13	192
Tire manufacturing.....................	5	101
Transport equipment manufacturing (except air).........................	379	835
State and local: highway................	} 150	475
Construction: highway..................		256
Retail: automotive......................		1,493
Wholesale: automotive..................	} 1	158
Service: automotive.....................		488
Truck drivers and deliverymen (except transport industry).............		1,450
Defense...............................	178	4,791
Armed Forces.........................	124	2,637
Defense Department*...................	44	1,097
Veterans Administration*...............	(10)	172
Ordnance manufacturing................		127
Aircraft manufacturing.................		758
Education..............................		
Public...............................	487	2,564
Food.................................	10,328	10,634
Farming (except fiber)..................	8,400	4,707
Fishing..............................	75	68
Food manufacturing....................	428	1,476
Fertilizer, farm machinery, and can manufacturing......................	70	231
Trade (food and liquor)................	1,486	4,152

* 1900: War Department, Pension Office.

forces. One was the growth of central accounting and billing—work that other industries contracted out to accountants (who appear under the category of services) or to financial institutions (which are classified under finance). A second was the marked growth of research work—research which if contracted out would be reported under the amiable title of "engineering and other professional services n.e.c." A third contribution was indeed made by the growing forces of bureaucratization, but how great a share they offered is unknown. *Finance and education* were nearly equal claimants for additional manpower resources, while only trivial changes in service and Federal nondefense employment bring up the rear.

The vaunted rise for the major tertiary industry of *service* hardly is noticeable. The growing level of income probably was associated with a growing demand for service employment to provide creature comforts, but no corresponding supply of labor appeared. Instead, the disutilities associated with domestic service work, plus the rise in nonwhite incomes, conspired to bring great declines in domestic service—declines that substantially neutralized the gains for other service categories. Hiring domestic servants had not become unfashionable; complaints about the shortage of domestic servants abounded, while the tentative importation of servants from Copenhagen, Mexico City, and Andalusia was a further indication of the scarcity. So too was the rising consumption of domestic service when income rose, as shown in budget studies. Any "inherent tendency" in economic development, therefore, for an increased number to be employed in services, merely means—if it means anything at all—that a demand for an increase will exist. But whether such demand will be matched by a supply at a point that actually does increase employment is quite another matter. The United States record from 1900 to 1960 shows no such happy marriage of supply and demand curves.

Finally, the employment rise of that monolith, the *Federal government,* proves to be relatively slight when compared to the rise in state and local governments if we look to nondefense employment. The rise for Federal nondefense employment was about a fifth the rise for state and local government, including education.

In Table 3-4 we note briefly the net change from 1900 (or 1899) to 1958 in certain functional groupings.[20] These groupings reveal significant

---

[20] 1899: *Farm Employment* from present estimates. *Cotton Farm Employment:* Deducted from total farm, estimated as follows: 1900 *Census of Agriculture,* part 1, p. 207ff. Data on expenditure for hired labor on cotton farms were divided by a daily wage of 54 cents, derived by weighing the average daily rate in each Southern state by the number of cotton farms in each, all farm-labor expenditures divided by a United States figure of 75 cents. Wage rates are from Bureau of Agricultural Economics, *Farm Employment, Wage Rates* (1943). The ratio of one full-time employee estimate to another—10 percent—was then applied to the present estimate of 2,380,-000 hired workers in 1900. The same census volume, pp. lxxi, lxxii, lxxiii, gives the number of farms and family workers by state. The ratio computed from these data for the South Central states was applied to the census estimate of cotton farms (*Ibid,* p. 206) to give family workers at Census of Agriculture level. This figure was 30.86 percent of the Agriculture Census family worker United States count, a ratio which, when applied to the present estimate of family workers in 1900, gave the family worker estimate for cotton farms. *Wool:* Ignored, less than 25,000 farm-

labor shifts not encompassed by our traditional industrial categories. For example, the distinction between transportation of goods by a manufacturing company, using its own force-account employees, and that which it contracts out to a transportation company, is in many respects quite arbitrary. The distinction between food growing done directly by a cannery for its own use, and that done under contract to independent farmers, is also an arbitrary one in assessing manpower requirements.

We therefore propose a new, functional grouping in this table.

1. The rise in transportation, trivial, for the industry per se, proves to be enormous for the activity. Over 1 million truck drivers and deliverymen worked outside the transportation industry. About 2 million employees sold cars, parts, and gasoline. And a million in manufacturing must be supplemented with ¾ of a million in the building and maintaining of streets and highways. Allowance for policemen engaged in traffic duty, hospital employment associated with the 35,000 traffic deaths a year, plus the indirect demands on steel, coal, etc., would further raise the total measure of transportation as a generator of employment.

2. The rise for defense is second only to that of transportation. It was concentrated, moreover, in the latter third of this period. The shift from manufacturing Springfield rifles in army arsenals to missiles in aircraft plants is reflected in the Defense Department line in Table 3-4, and is allowed for in the total. (A small portion of aircraft employment not actually on government order should be excluded, but it is less important

---

ers, 1899 Census of Agriculture, p. 673, shows farms reporting fleeces averaged under $1,000 except for the Western group of 24,851 farms. *Fishing:* 1900 Census, *Occupations,* p. 8. *Manufacturing:* 1899 *Census of Manufactures,* vol. VII, p. 20ff. Total for food, liquor, baking powder, cotton oil, salt, starch, fertilizer, agricultural implements, ice, including wage earners, proprietors, salaried. *Trade:* Estimated as 40 percent of the present 1900 United States trade figure, employees plus self-employed. This ratio is that of (1) the sum of retail sales by food stores, restaurants, saloons in 1899 and 20 percent of sales of country general stores, to (2) total retail sales. Sales data from Barger, *op. cit.,* pp. 48–59, 132.

1958: Total farm from Current Population Survey. *Cotton farm:* Operators from 1954 Census of Agriculture, General Report, vol. II, p. 1292. Unpaid family workers estimated as 35 percent of operators, the ratio from Current Population Survey data. *Hired:* Estimated as 61.2 percent of reported hired cotton-farm workers (p. 1292), the ratio being that of Current Population Survey United States hired workers to the Census of Agriculture total United States hired. *Fishermen and oystermen:* 1950 Census, *Occupational Characteristics,* pp. 1B-128. *Manufacturing:* Food, fertilizer, agricultural machinery, and tin can—from BLS. Wholesale grocery and liquor, retail food—BLS 1958 average. Eating and drinking places—BLS March, 1958. Proprietors retail food, eating and drinking places: 1954 *Census of Business,* vol. I, pp. 1–5. *Truck drivers and deliverymen:* 1950 Census, *Occupation by Industry,* table 2. We increase this figure 22 percent for the change from 1950 to 1958, using the ratio of all drivers from this report to that shown in *Current Population Reports,* ser. P-50, no. 89, table 34 for 1958.

than the omission of employment on defense contracts to the motor-vehicle and shipbuilding industries.)

3. The employment gain for education was less than half as great as for defense and a third that for transportation over this period. While private education gained at a greater rate than public education, allowance for its absolute numbers would not change this order of magnitude.[21]

4. Finally, the great rise in population and increased export of food brought no increase in employment associated with providing food. The decline of about 3 million in farm workers was offset by a rise of nearly 3 million in trade and 1 million in manufacturing. Replacing the cracker barrel with cartons, the fly-specked meat store with precut and packaged hams, and substituting store-baked bread for "store-boughten flour" contributed substantially to the rise in factory employment. And fanning retail stores out all over the nation more than offset the productivity gains made when the consumer was converted from shopper to self-servant.

SOCIAL MOBILITY AND THE DIVISION OF LABOR

What can be expected of a man who has spent twenty years of his life in making heads for pins? He ultimately does his work with singular dexterity; but at the same time he loses the general faculty of applying his mind to the direction of the work . . . as the principle of the division of labor is more extensively applied, the workman becomes more weak, more narrow minded, and more dependent.

De Tocqueville, *Democracy in America,* vol. II, chap. 20.

Since Adam Smith described how production gained when the separate tasks in pinmaking were assigned to specialists, economists have been as interested as pinmakers in the spirited stimulus which the division of labor offers to productivity. But a review of the American record suggests that in practice the division of labor has two conflicting results. One is static, stimulating, and positive in its contribution to higher output. The other is dynamic, retarding, and quite possibly depressant. Before considering this static-dynamic contrast (in C), we review the extent of occupational specialization during the formative period from 1800 to 1860 (in A and B), for occupational specialization and stability of life careers are intimately linked with the real return from the division of labor. If complex jobs are broken down into simpler tasks, each then being assigned to an employee who becomes proficient in that task, it is almost inevitable that

[21] We base this judgment on data available for 1890 and 1953–1954.

such a division of labor will advance productivity. But the net advantage to any firm can only be computed after reckoning in the costs that arise from the division of labor itself. Of these the chief will be the low-productivity learning period through which the semiskilled worker (who replaces the skilled worker formerly used) passes as he learns the particular constellation of tasks required of semiskilled workers in that plant.[1] The more open the society, the greater the proportion of these workers who move on to other work before such costs are recaptured. Hence the extent of social and occupational mobility is a critical factor in determining how great the realized rewards of division of labor will actually be.

A

Let us first consider the extent to which men remained in fixed occupations during those decades when the temper and pace of American development were being established. No precise answer appears to be possible. Having said as much, let us see what the flood of anecdotes by contemporaries suggests as the direction of an answer. For the most part these do not concern manufacturing operations—the *locus classicus* in discussions of the division of labor. This may be a significant omission, but we must not overstate the potency of the factory system in forwarding our national growth. The tenor of our development had surely been set by 1860, yet as late as that year less than 15 percent of our labor force was in manufacturing. And the proportion who worked in factories of some dimensions (i.e., excluding sawmills, grain mills, and similar one-employee operations) ran closer to 10 percent. Unless we adopt the pretensions of the early "conventions of the manufacturing interest," it is difficult to argue that the division of labor in this sector, plus forward and backward linkages, produced decisive higher-order effects on the general economy.

Turning then to the inadequate, but at least random, reports of the time, what do we find? We observe that the irregularities and limitations of demand made the wide development of a class of specialists immensely difficult. Let us ignore the curiosa in which our history abounds, such as the Chief Justice of a Court of Common Pleas in 1818 who was also in active practice as a butcher, dealing out judgments and meats on the same day.[2] Or the Peoria court in 1827 that adjourned to permit jurymen and

---

[1] The skilled worker will reach maximum productivity in a new plant more quickly since his kit of abilities encompasses a wide range of skills and adaptiveness —these indeed being factors in his higher wage rate. As time goes on greater uniformity among plants develops in the tasks associated with any semiskilled occupation. The losses from substituting semiskilled for unskilled labor are, of course, not as great, but neither are the cost reductions as substantial. The direct substitution of unskilled for skilled work is feasible in principle but appears uncommon in practice.

[2] Henry Fearon, *A Narrative of a Journey* (London: Longman, Hurst, Rees, Orme, Brown, 1818), p. 318.

witnesses alike to go "bee and deer hunting, a profitable as well as necessary" business.[3]

Let us ignore, too, the more romantic occupations: Augustus Gird, a
professional guide (and perhaps as keen a one as Natty Bumpo) who
filled out his income when hunting parties were rare in Montana by making
adobe bricks (by hand) for a penny a brick.[4] And half the trappers who
constituted the roving dream of young Americans actually worked at the
dull job of keeping camp, their jobs including cooking, dressing beaver,
making leather traps, packing, and unpacking.[5]

The major task of most persons in the labor force, however, was farming. And it was among farmers that supplemental skills and other occupations developed all over the nation.[6] One reason was the fact that farmers
were ubiquitous, while mechanics and tradesmen were not. With "the first
emigrations there are no mechanics; and for many years after, but few are
found in the new settlements. The farmer, therefore, makes almost everything that he uses. Besides clearing land, building houses, and making
fences, he stocks his own plough, mends his wagon, makes his ox-yokes
and harness, and learns to supply all his wants from the forest." [7] Even
in more settled areas mechanics failed to appear where demand was too
thin to yield reasonably full employment. In Rhode Island in 1810–1811,
immediately before the textile revolution, "There were but few [carpen-
ters]. It was only at long intervals that new houses were built, and generally of small dimensions." [8] It was not the pioneering state of the nation
that was responsible but the lack of steady demand. (New York, for example, had its share of such mechanics).[9] Farmers were not merely the nation's carpenters but likewise its blacksmiths. The rudimentary division of
labor in a New Hampshire town in 1832 is indicated by an observation
that the town had seven blacksmiths: "These men are farmers as well as
mechanics, a part of their time is employed on the farm." [10]

[3] Arthur C. Baggess, *The Settlement of Illinois, 1778–1830* (1908), p. 173.

[4] George F. Weisel, *Men and Trade on the Northwest Frontier as Shown by The
Fort Owen Ledger* (1955), p. 193.

[5] Warren Angus Ferris, *Life in the Rocky Mountains, 1830–1835* (1844; reprint
1940), p. 228.

[6] The combination of trading and farming is paralleled in the able discussion of
P. T. Bauer, *Economic Analysis and Policy in Underdeveloped Countries* (1957),
pp. 69ff., where the relationship to capital accumulation in underdeveloped countries is analyzed.

[7] James Hall, *Sketches of History, Life and Manners in the West* (Philadelphia:
Harrison Hall, 1835), vol. II, p. 68.

[8] George C. Channing, *Early Recollections of Newport, Rhode Island* (Newport:
1868), p. 143.

[9] Fearon (*op. cit.,* pp. 22–23), describes the New York subcontractor and master-
carpenter operations in terms equally applicable to a much later era.

[10] Serial Set 222, *Documents on Manufactures* (1833) U.S. Congress, vol. I, p.

Many of the shipyard workers in the 1830–1840 period, particularly in Eastern areas, were "fishermen and farmers who were free from their normal trades." One doughty farmer actually built several vessels in his farmyard, then hauled them on runners to the river after winter had covered the ground with snow.[11] Men who went codfishing for the usual four-month run would return to farm work, and to cobbling shoes through the winter months.[12]

Many of the early construction contractors were actually farmers who first took contracts for building the road or canal section abutting their own land, then branched off into the business. The men who contracted to build sections of the National road were "mostly farmers of our own state who have left their farms with a view to make money, to purchase more land, etc." [13]

Many, too, of the early ministers were farmers—sometimes for a major share of their time. A biographer of one divine who entered the ministry about 1800 records matter of factly that "when Doctor Emmons came to Franklin he purchased a farm as was then common with clergymen." Textile history records the work of Reverend Greenwood, who served as an overseer in the Lowell mills.[14]

The typical retailer or wholesaler for many decades prior to 1860 would not be recognized as such by today's classifications or perceptions. The central group of wholesalers were farm or factory laborers, or seamen

756. See too Caroline Hazard (ed.), *Nailer Tom's Diary . . . 1778–1840* (1930) *passim,* and several account books circa 1810 to 1820 in the Baker Library manuscript collections.

[11] C. P. Wright, "The Origins and Early Years of the Transatlantic Packet Lines," unpublished Harvard University thesis, pp. 134, 181.

[12] U.S. Congress, Serial Set 222, vol. I, pp. 94, 234, 240. This report indicates four-, five-, and eight-month periods. George Brigham, with a 36-acre farm in wheat and corn "has earned usually in the winter $125 by shoemaking. He owns his farm. . . ." Henry Colman, *Fourth Report of the Agriculture of Massachusetts, Counties of Franklin and Middlesex* (Boston: Dutton and Wentworth, 1841), p. 414. Since farm laborers averaged $12 a month at the time, $125 was a sizable sum.

[13] *Letter from the Secretary of War: Cumberland Road,* 21st Cong., 2d Sess., Doc. 12, Dec. 17, 1830.

[14] Rev. D. S. Sherman, *Sketches of New England Divines* (New York: Carleton and Porter, 1860), p. 264. Dr. Sherman notes that Dr. Emmons's decision not to work the farm himself but to concentrate on his pastoral duties made him a signal exception. For Rev. Greenwood's history, see Charles Cowley, *Illustrated History of Lowell* (1868), p. 90.

The making of shirts for trade began in Bridgeport in 1836. "The Reverend Cyrus Silliman . . . aided in placing the work in proper hands [i.e., putting the work out] at first in his own vicinity, and afterwards conducted a separate business in which he traveled through a considerable extent of country." Orcutt, *History of Bridgeport,* quoted in Grace P. Fuller, *An Introduction to the History of Connecticut as a Manufacturing State* (1915), p. 40.

—paid off in bricks, corn, pig iron, whale oil, or whatever their employer produced. They had then to dispose of these products, partly for their own consumption, partly to other consumers, partly to storefront retailers. A significant group of retailers were primarily in the transport business. The men who poled keelboats dangerously down the Ohio or Mississippi bought and sold goods along the way.[15] Wagoners not merely controlled a six-horse team but "sometimes made a little on the side by buying some merchandise at one end and selling it at the other end of their journey." [16] Ship captains were competent not merely to sail across several oceans, but in addition to decide where and when to sell their cargo, or even their ship. "In case you can sell only part of your cargo at Bombay and it shall then appear to you to be for my interest to have you go on to Canton with a cargo of cotton, you will do that." [17]

Even the retailer of legend—pine boards, cracker barrel, potbellied stove and all—was not necessarily a lifelong retailer, developing skill and experience as he aged. The shuffling into and out of retail enterprise apparent in today's data on business births and deaths was even greater in the nineteenth century. We may give little credence to the precise numbers, but surely there is much meaning in an 1850 statement that "It is a notable fact, in the history of mercantile life in the United States, that of the number who engage in it full seven tenths fail from one to three times." [18]

The typical restaurateur was for many decades a canal contractor, forge owner, or farmer, who hired a cook or a local housewife to provide meals to his men at a fixed rate.

What occupation category brackets a man who works one day as a painter, the next as a plowman, the third as a carter, the fourth as a common laborer—receiving each day the rate of pay appropriate to the skill

[15] In winter it was "no uncommon thing to see as many as four or five hundred 'broad horns' as the flat boats were called, tied up at our landing. They averaged four men to the boat. . . . These flat boats were in active competition with the regular dealers in the city, and no good feeling at the time existed between them." H. S. Fulkerson, *Random Recollections, Early Days in Mississippi* (Vicksburg: 1888), pp. 97, 98. Fulkerson refers to the period about 1838.

[16] John Omwake, *The Conestoga Six-horse Bell Teams of Eastern Pennsylvania* (1930), p. 110. Omwake refers to the period around 1830 at Zenith.

[17] Edward Gray, *William Gray of Salem, Merchant* (1914), pp. 34–35, quoting Gray's instructions about 1811 to one of his captains. A 1787 order gave the captain leave "either [to] sell Vessel and Cargo" or cargo alone. Quoted in Margaret E. Martin, *Merchants and Trade of the Connecticut River Valley, 1750–1820* (1939), p. 47. A host of examples for the nineteenth century appear in John G. Hutchins, *The American Maritime Industries and Public Policy, 1789–1914* (1941).

[18] "The Causes of Commercial Crises," *The Bankers Magazine and Statistical Register,* July, 1850.

being called upon?[19] How are we to classify an 1813 entrepreneur who owned a tavern on the road to Pittsburgh—with a 1,300-acre farm, tanyard, flour mill, and blacksmith shop—and who was about to start a woolen mill?[20] How may we define the skills of a man who is successively a teamster, skilled mason, contractor, and farmer?[21] Or Patrick Tracy Jackson, by turns a singularly successful city subdivider, dam builder, textile mill manager, and railroad entrepreneur? Such men, whose flexibility equaled their energy, flourished in a social order that permitted them freely to shift from task to task, wherever the opportunity of gain appeared.[22]

B

To what extent can we generalize from the pattern of mobility that appears in these examples? Here we must rely largely on the uniform judgments of competent contemporary observers, who found occupational mobility in America strikingly greater, more intense, than that in Europe at the same time. What was the European frame of reference? In 1848 John Stuart Mill described one of the most open societies in Europe as typically having "hereditary distinctions of caste; each employment being chiefly recruited from the children of those already employed in it"; found the great body of laboring people excluded from the most remunerative occupations because they could acquire neither education nor training.[23] Cairnes in 1874 gave the classic exposition of the theory of noncompeting groups, describing "a series of industrial layers . . . the several strata [of which] are, for all purposes of effective competition practically isolated from each other."[24]

But wherever Europe said "No," America offered a Whitmanesque "Yes." In the early 1800s Gallatin, Swiss immigrant who had become Secretary of the Treasury, found that "every species of trade, commerce and professions and manufactures [is] equally open to all without requir-

[19] Baker Library manuscripts, Woodbridge and Backus records, "Account of Jacob Edwards," vol. 8, Bills, Labor Bills, March, 1840: 34 cents for painting, 50 cents for picking stone, 37 cents for plowing, 25 cents for carting manure.
[20] Claude G. Bowers (ed.), *The Diary of Elbridge Gerry Jr.* (1927), p. 94.
[21] *The Life of Asa G. Sheldon; Wilmington Farmer* (1862; reprint 1959).
[22] Arthur H. Cole, *Business Enterprise in Its Social Setting* (1959), pp. 193ff., gives a spirited discussion of Cochran's concept of the "general entrepreneur" that is most relevant here.
[23] John Stuart Mill, *Principles of Political Economy* (London 1848), pp. 459, 544.
[24] J. E. Cairnes, *Some Leading Principles of Political Economy Newly Expounded* (1874), part 1, chap. 3. Decades later the pattern for Europe was generally one in which the educational system "reinforced social division," the rise "from the bottom of the social pyramid to the top" being "a matter of two or three generations." Fritz Morstein Marx, *The Administrative State* (1957), p. 41.

ing any regular apprenticeship, admission or license." [25] In the 1830s Henry Carey observed that "Every man who finds business unprofitable, or employment scarce, may change his residence until he finds himself suited, without incurring the risk of being sent back to his parish as would be the case in England. . . . In the United States there are no apprentice laws and a man may change his trade as often as he thinks proper." [26] In 1868 Ezra Seaman found that men in Europe were "nearly as much fixed and confined through life . . . to the employment in which they were educated as the everlasting hills and mountains are immoveably fixed. . . . They have and understand but one employment . . . and they are compelled to work at that through life." Realistically he did not believe that America offered a complete contrast (most men remaining in the employment "to which they were bred") but that the education of the youth plus the shifting of jobs by adults provided greater mobility than Europe.[27]

Division of labor offers least advantage where occupational mobility ceaselessly subtracts persons from one occupation to another. A Swedish pioneer gives us one summary. "A person I have seen going about working as a mason served for a couple of months as an assistant in a drug store in Milwaukee, whereupon he laid aside the trowel, got himself some medical books, and assumed the title of doctor. . . . The speed with which people here change their life-calling and the slight preparation generally needed to leave one calling for another are really surprising, especially to one that has been accustomed to our Swedish guild-ordinances." [28]

A visiting British economist marked the same contrasts: "The country is so vast and the temptation to other and easier pursuits so great, that there is no constancy to certain employment as in England. The laboring population in America is not stable; it is a shifting, unsteady, improving mass." [29]

It is difficult to go through these and other materials without finding that a static analysis leads to a paradox. On the one hand, the division of

[25] Henry Carey, *Essay on the Rate of Wages* (1835), pp. 130, 132.

[26] *Ibid.*

[27] Ezra Seaman, *Essays on the Progress of Nations* (New York, 1868), p. 318. "Even among the people of our own free states (the best educated of any people in the world as a whole) perhaps not one in twenty ever attempt to change the employment to which they were bred . . . after pursuing any one 'employment' for a period of fifteen or twenty years, the mental and physical habits become so adapted to it that both mind and body . . . are unfitted for any other employment. The only way in which the proportion between . . . the different employments can be changed is by the education of the young."

[28] Nils W. Olsson (ed.), *A Pioneer in Northwest America 1841–1858: The Memoirs of Gustaf Unonius* (1950), vol. I, p. 243.

[29] James Caird, *Prairie Farming* (New York: 1859), p. 116. Paul Gates, *The Illinois Central,* discusses Caird's connection with that road, but it would hardly seem to have warped his judgment on this point.

labor in those industries where most Americans were employed from 1800 to 1860 was little more than rudimentary. (Moreover, the incessant flow of men from one occupation and one area to another meant that they were perpetually losing the skills and work habits appropriate to one task and enterprise, and having to learn new ones.) On the other hand, every story and statistic says that enormous forward gains in productivity were being achieved in these years, however we now define and measure the gains. The tradition of progress, of improvement, of changes that yield economic advantage, is reported by most visitors and by most contemporary American writers. Of course, these findings are not necessarily opposed. They may merely suggest that a still greater advance would have been achieved had the division of labor been fuller. Indeed such a conclusion is irresistible, all other things being equal. But were all other things equal during development?

We speculate that a dominant, significant force making for great productivity advance was the very absence of division of labor.[30] What, after all, is characteristic of the effective division of labor? It is that there is one preferable way and, finally, *the* approved and only right way. The procedure leads to building a vast structure of industrial habit. Knowledge is organized, procedures set up, traditions established. New entrants to the trade, the occupation, and the particular job are taught *the* best way of doing each major element in the job.

Let us assume that in fact there is a single best way at a given time. What happens when prices for various inputs change, when the requirements of those using the product shift? Surely the best way must change. To learn a new "best way" becomes a lengthy, often frustrating, process. Moreover, the gap between (1) efficiency on a particular job and (2) overall establishment profits is a great one. Years of business success and failure may be required before the newer best way is widely adopted. Meanwhile the entire force of established knowledge, well-defined ways of doing the job, works against this. Habit is first and second nature, as William James once said. But what about a new nation, with vast undiscovered resources, spirited industrialization, changing market demands? Who is to say that the best practice in June, 1819, will also yield the maximum revenue (or minimum cost) in June, 1820?

In such a situation the absence of extensive division of labor has much to commend it.[31] Instead of jobs being completed by 100,000 specialists

---

[30] A caution is due the reader in our emphasis on certain overlooked factors in our economic advance. These do not sum to a total explanation by any manner of means.

[31] Emphasizing the limitations of division of labor under uncertainty and its costs under dynamic conditions, we necessarily deal with one class of events. Under static conditions the division of labor is much more certain to be rewarding.

who chose the one "best" way—i.e., best since the eighteenth century, best by tradition—90,000 amateurs, coming from vastly different backgrounds, and 10,000 professionals tackled the work. Some, of course, botched the job horribly. Many a wise man found that American farmers were amateurs, "merely aggravating the soil a little." [32] Some did an excellent job, by traditional means. Most ambled along at less than ideal efficiency.

But a significant group took an entirely different approach to the work —because of a difference in perspective, laziness, or sheer genius. It was these who made major technological discoveries, who made substantial departures in the organization of work and enterprise.

"Tain't what we don't know that's so bad, but all the things we know that ain't so" is an old and valuable American saying. And while every nation has would-be geniuses, would-be innovators, it is only where such men are both confronted with the problem to be solved and given freedom to solve it in their own way that innovations will flourish. A most useful definition of an innovation treats it as "the setting up of a new production function." [33] Schumpeter saw heuristic value in arguing "as if every innovation . . . were embodied in a New Firm founded for the purpose. . . . Most new firms are founded with an idea and for a definite purpose. The life goes out of them when that idea or purpose has been fulfilled or has become obsolete or even if, without having become obsolete, it has ceased to be new." [34] But the frequency with which such new firms (or a flood of lesser innovations in older firms) can spring up is bounded by the nature of the social order. In the United States from 1800 to 1860 there was very little agreement on just what the wisdom of the ages had to say about how a piece of metal should be machined, or what was the preferred rotation of crops in the back forty. With inadequate division of labor there were few experts. More precisely, everyone was as expert as the next fellow. The aggressive deviant workman, as the entrepreneur, was freer to create his innovations, to put into force not only moderately new, but blindly new, procedures. For a given problem the Sicilian procedure proposed by one workman, the North Wales technique tried by another, the Baden-Baden system of a third could work very badly indeed. But one procedure, one dubious compromise, one wildly different tack, did in fact work. And out of the multitude of experiments conducted by astute men

[32] Quoted in Everett Dick, *The Sod-house Frontier, 1854–1890* (1937), p. 56. "Oh man, they're meeserable farmers. It would break your heart to see how they just scart the grun' [scarred the ground]. It's no very guid ony way, but they dinna gie't a chance." So found a man from Aberdeenshire, who had farmed near Niagara Falls for 30 years. Caird, *op. cit.*, p. 26.
[33] Joseph Schumpeter, *Business Cycles* (1939), vol. I, p. 87.
[34] *Ibid.*, p. 94.

energetically seeking success, it was inevitable that the percentages favored technical advance.

Try one innovation a decade and you stand little chance of success. Try a thousand, and some of them will certainly pay off. (The same logic is in some measure pursued by the twentieth-century corporation with directed research teams, who look down a multitude of dead-end streets but win on the percentages.) A host of novel procedures or products, having proved their worth in this ceaseless ferment of experimentation, were then adopted. Their number was inevitably greater than the count for those stolid societies where production traditions (associated with an elegantly elaborate division of labor) discourage experimentation because the best was not "to be" but long past.

Most characteristic of American workmen, wrote a distinguished French economist in the 1830s, was not better quality such as the British workmen possessed, but the fact that they had a "more general aptitude." [35] And at the beginning of the twentieth century a group of British industrialists similarly discovered that American labor revealed the "greater industry, ambition and resourcefulness of the people that emigrate. Such people, as a rule . . . cut themselves adrift from the hide-bound traditions and habits of the country where they have not realized their ideal of life. . . . [This] cannot be done without much greater effort, great readiness to meet emergencies, and a general faculty for making opportunities." [36]

What could be of more vivid value in a nation where new resource deposits and new markets were discovered daily? And with innovators free to adopt new procedures to these resources and market changes, the process of change fed upon itself, accelerated, and brought unimagined economic advance.

[35] Michel Chevalier, *Lettres sur l'Amerique du Nord* (Paris, 1836), vol. II, p. 515. "Jack of all trades—and master of none" is a characteristic description of such workmen by those steeped in long-established occupational traditions.

[36] J. Stephen Jeans, *American Industrial Conditions and Competition, Report of the Commission Appointed by the British Iron Trade Association* (London, 1902), p. 58.

ORIGINS OF THE FACTORY LABOR MARKET

I mean they lived happily ever after, though, as time went by, a factory chimney somewhat spoilt the view.

Virginia Woolf †

For liberty our fathers fought
Which their blood, they dearly bought,
The Fact'ry system sets at nought
A Slave at morn, a slave at eve
It doth my inmost feelings grieve
Hark don't you hear the factory bell
Of wit and learning 'tis the knell

"Sui Generis" (1833) ‡

Shortly after Thomas Jefferson and Aaron Burr tied for the Presidency, a number of observers began worrying about another contest, that between the traditional system of agriculture and the new factory system. With 85 gainful workers out of every 100 in agriculture and with less than 15,000 workers in all of manufacturing, the shadow was no larger than a man's hand.[1] But they felt the future of the agricultural way of life to be at stake. The unsavory working conditions in English factories, probably the worst in centuries, had been well advertised. The mingling of men and women in mines and factories away from home led to such animadversions that more than three-quarters of a century later a census report sought to prove the obvious fact that female frailty and moral lapses did not derive from, were even minimized, under the factory system.[2] The dream of America as an unspoiled new world in which the soil was cultivated by cheerful swains in honest labor could not exist alongside the vision of "dark satanic mills." Rural life is "exempt from those moral perils which exist in crowded villages; which are found in the concealment practicable in populous cities; in the indifference to the value of human life which prevails there; and especially in the corrupt associations and multiplied crimes and vices, which there inevitably abound." [3] (This from an official report of the state of Massachusetts in 1840.) And finally, the impact on labor supply and

---

† "A Talk about Memoirs," in *Granite and Rainbow.*

‡ *Picture of a Factory Village* . . . by Sui Generis: Alias Thomas Man (Providence: printed for the author, 1833). The author of this improbable effusion likewise drew "A Picture of Woonsocket."

[1] For these estimates see Table A-1.

[2] Carroll Wright, "The Factory System," 1880 *Census of Manufactures,* vol. II.

[3] Henry Colman, *Third Report of the Agriculture of Massachusetts, on Wheat and Silk* (Boston: Dutton and Wentworth, 1840), p. 56.

farm wages was widely feared. Representative Hudson of Massachusetts told the Congress in 1842 that factory operatives "were taken chiefly from the agricultural class, and when they were withdrawn wages rose." [4] This interesting example of cultural lag was uttered when his state had already staked out a major role in the new factory system.

To secure labor for factory work, therefore, the factory agents (today's "general managers") were confronted by the fact that to bid labor away from existing farm work, they must needs offer a margin large enough to overcome not merely the normal elements of labor immobility but, in addition, the fearful vision of factory work. The agents and proprietors, however, rejected any contest bidding up rates. Instead, changing their hiring preference function, they turned primarily to the use of two relatively noncompeting groups in the labor market—children and women.[5]

Cost Advantages of Female and Child Labor

"Working in factories," wrote one of the great proponents of manufacturing, "is considered disreputable in the city; and were it not for the difficulty of obtaining other employment for women and children, proprietors of factories would experience considerable difficulty in obtaining hands." [6] "Children and aged persons," added another resident thinker, "idle young men who do not earn the cigars which they smoke, and idle young women who hardly mend, much less knit, their own stockings—[all are] unproductive, produce nothing." [7]

In the plangent phrasing of the Governor of Pennsylvania in 1849: "Whatever increases profitable labor is substantially beneficial to the working classes, and affords them the means of comfort, the delights of rational enjoyment, and the opportunity of exalting their condition. . . . The manufacturer, if he be sustained in his enterprize, produces this result by

---

[4] *Congressional Globe* (1842), p. 60. In *Documents on Manufactures* (1833), U.S. Congress, Serial Set 222 (the *McLane Report*), vol. I, p. 743, Caleb Page of New Hampshire found that the manufacturing interest "has tended to depress that of the agriculturalist . . . on account of the expense of labor. . . . It is considered more respectable to be the well paid drudge of a factory, than be engaged in the service of the plain living and hard-laboring honest yeomanry of the country." See too Edward Wolcott in *Ibid.*, p. 85.

[5] The response has its later examples. Assuming "that the supply of such labor is inelastic the wage that might have to be offered would be prohibitive if all firms engaged in a wholesale wage scramble in which case to lower hiring standards might be a cheaper method of attracting workers." Brian McCormick, "Labor Hiring Policies and Monopolistic Competition Theory," *Quarterly Journal of Economics* (November, 1959), p. 608. See too Melvin Reder, "The Theory of Occupational Wage Differentials," *American Economic Review* (December, 1955), pp. 834–835.

[6] Thomas Robert Hazard, *Facts for the Labouring Man, by a Labouring Man* (Newport, R.I.: Thomas Robert Hazard, 1840), p. 107.

[7] Colman, *op. cit.*, p. 146.

opening to the laborers a new source of employment."[8] The lead was clear, and the factory system followed it.

When the "father of American manufactures" arrived in Rhode Island in 1790, he brought with him a detailed memory not merely of English machinery but of English production patterns. Samuel Slater's first table of organization called for seven boys and two girls, between the ages of seven and twelve.[9]

As late as 1833, fully 50 percent of the employees in Slater's Steam Cotton Manufacturing Company were children.[10] But child labor never became a really substantial source of labor in America—not even in farming or homework. As early as 1833 it was on the wane in the cotton textile industry, where child labor had probably been more important than in any other industry. In that year Rhode Island, with 20 percent of adult employment in cotton textiles, had some 60 percent of child workers in the industry. Massachusetts, which had already become the major textile and the major manufacturing state, filled only 10 percent of its cotton-mill jobs with children.[11]

Instead, the major source for the labor force of the rapidly growing factories came to be women. (The group at first included young girls from eight to twelve, but shortly was limited, for the most part, to those twelve and older, and even those sixteen and older.) The cost advantage was, of course, substantial. Women's pay was only a third to a quarter that of men. At the time of Quincy's 1800 visit to Slater's factory, he found the children receiving 12 to 25 cents, while women in a nearby factory received 50 cents a day.[12] This rate can be contrasted with the 75 to 90 cents paid common labor in the area.[13] But laborers in manufacturing were

[8] Governor William F. Johnson, Annual Message to the Assembly, *Pennsylvania Archives* (Harrisburg: 1902), 4th ser. vol. 7, pp. 312–313. More stimulating perhaps was the observation of the Secretary of the American Iron Association: "Home Industry is more needful and nobler than the luxuries of foreign commerce. The solution which has no centers of crystallization precipitates an amorphous, incoherent friable mass; and the government which systematically prejudices the conditions of manufacturing life against both the capital, which seeks locations and the skilled labor which asks employment, is anti-democratic, and in America is certain to be overturned." John P. Lesley, *The Iron Manufacturers Guide* (New York: John Wiley, 1859), p. 267.

[9] V. S. Clark, *History of Manufactures in the United States* (1929), vol. I, p. 397.

[10] *McLane Report,* vol. I, p. 951.

[11] Based on a summarizing of the reports for all states as shown in the *McLane Report,* vols. I and II.

[12] Quincy, *op. cit.,* p. 133, referring to a Nantucket twine factory.

[13] Baker Library manuscripts, "Israel Thorndike Collection of Business Papers," vol. 4, 1800; Aug. 9, 1800, Ship *Cyrus* account, William Leech debtor: "to one day paid a Negro man . . . 84¢"; many entries for other men appear at 5 shillings, or 90 cents. Rates of 4 shillings 6 pence for unskilled farm labor, or 50 cents, and 6 shillings for mowing (or $1) appear in Baker Library, "Captains Albert and Thomas Smith MSS 733, 1773–1814." Joseph Monro bill in 1800 "Bills, 1773–1807."

"of as high a grade as carpenters or masons, and their wages will average the same" according to one contemporary;[14] this rate should therefore perhaps be compared with the $1.25 rate paid skilled workers in the area.[15] We may, therefore, contrast the 50-cent rate for women (and the 12- to 25-cent rate for children) with a rate of more than $1.25 for males if substantial factory recruiting had pushed up rates for male labor. By 1833, as Table A-31 suggests, rates paid by the industries where most females were at work ran to about $1 for males, to about 33 cents for females.

These rate differences would be delusive indicators of the advantages of female hiring if they were offset by other costs. Here we may conclude with the succinct assurance of a Lowell: "By the erection of the boarding houses . . . putting at the head of them matrons of tried character . . . by all these precautions, they gained the confidence of the rural population, who were now no longer afraid to trust their daughters in a manufacturing town. A supply was thus obtained of respectable girls. By these means a great moral good has been obtained. Another result has followed which, if foreseen, as no doubt it was, does great credit to the sagacity of these remarkable men. The class of operatives . . . proved to be as superior in intelligence and efficiency to the degraded population elsewhere employed in manufactures, as they are in morals." [16] The rise to eminence of New England cotton manufacturing confirmed the fact that efficiency wages for women in this industry in its formative years were clearly less than those for men.

Effect of Factory System on Wages

1. The early nineteenth-century demands for factory labor, like the supply, were dispersed. Even by 1833 typical Massachusetts cotton textile factories reported 12, 15, 19, 28, 81, 221 employees. New Hampshire woolen factories reported 10, 5, 7, 14, 3, 4 employees, to take a random selection. New York cotton textile mills had 14, 60, 17, 13, 123 employees, again picking at random.[17] Such small requirements could be supplied locally without great difficulty. Among these Lilliputians the giant cotton mills stood boldly forth: The major New Hampshire firms (Great Falls Manufacturing with 1,382, New Market with 672, Cocheco with 1,075); and four mills, employing 3,036, in the single city of Lowell.[18]

Such large mills could not draw their labor force from the immediate hinterland. Employees could not report to work at 4:30 in the morning,

[14] Alvin Bronson, agent for New York State, in the *McLane Report,* vol. II, p. 6.
[15] In the Thorndike manuscripts, vol. 3, May 6, 1800, a bill by John Pickett for "work a board the Ship *Cyras*" charged 8 shillings for skilled work, or $1.25.
[16] John Amery Lowell, "Patrick Tracy Jackson," *Hunt's Merchants Magazine* (April, 1848), pp. 360–361.
[17] *McLane Report,* vol. I, *passim.*
[18] *Ibid.*

in the days when walking was the only feasible method of getting to work, if they had come from any great distance.[19] One result was the black "slaver's wagon" of New England tradition, recruiting young women to work in mill towns. Another was the distinctly higher wage rate paid by the mills in order to attract such migrants. Humanitarian inclinations and the requirements of labor supply went hand in hand. While hundreds of small plants in New York, Maine, and Rhode Island paid 30 to 33 cents a day for women to work in their cotton mills, the Lowell firms generally paid nearer to 50 cents.[20] This differential did not measure any equalizing difference in wages that arose from cost of living variations. Rates in the Massachusetts shoe factories, which were typically small, ranged from 25 to 30 cents, while rates paid for weaving palm leaf hats at home also ran 25 to 30 cents.

The concentrated demand for child labor in Rhode Island produced a similar difference. While Rhode Island paid lower rates for men in cotton textiles than any Northeastern state in 1832 and its rates for females were not above average, its rate for boys was relatively high. No state with a significant number of child employees had a higher one. A useful confirmation of how these demand forces affected both female and child rates is given by the male wage-rate figures. Since the demand for male employment was more evenly spread and more readily supplied by local labor markets, the differences among the male state averages even among the industries—cotton textiles, wool, or iron—were much less.

2. What of the level of factory earnings compared to those in nonfactory occupations? For men the interaction in the labor market makes it difficult to separate out factory wages versus nonfactory wages, since the latter were affected by demands of the former. The problem is similar to that of disentangling the influence of unions on wages by comparison of union and nonunion industry earnings for, since both derive from the same

[19] James Montgomery, superintendent of the major cotton textile factory in Maine, the Saco York factory, refers to a visit to Newport, Rhode Island, factories where operative spinners worked "from sunrise to sunset, that is from half past four o'clock in the morning to half past seven o'clock in the evening." *A Practical Detail of the Cotton Manufacture of the United States of America* (Glasgow: John Niven, 1840), p. 75. A 12½-hour workday in Massachusetts appears to have been common for the larger factories, this being exclusive, of course, of time for meals. Norman Ware, *The Industrial Worker, 1840–1860* (1924), pp. 131, 159. With merely the purchase of a horse costing half a year's wages, only the most captious would consider that a practical method of getting to work.

[20] *McLane Report, passim,* shows the 30- to 33-cent range, while Table A-31 shows the state averages. Volume I of the *McLane Report,* pp. 341–342, shows the Lowell rates, with two mills paying 50 cents, one paying 52 cents, and the major mill, Merrimac, paying 44 cents. Reference to early payroll records in the Baker Library suggests that the Merrimac average is correctly shown, but the basis for this significant difference among the Lowell factories is obscure.

labor market (or related markets), we cannot readily measure one rate free of the influence of the other.

For women a readier comparison is possible. We may contrast rates paid to domestic servants with those paid to female factory workers— factory workers being so few, even in 1832, that their influence on the rates for the widespread domestic-service group could not have been large. Referring to a variety of sources, we have the following contrasts:[21,22]

Weekly Wages of Female Employees

Region	Domestics	Cotton textile workers
1800, Massachusetts............................	$1.25	$3.00
1832, Philadelphia............................	1.25	2.50–3.00
1832, New York, New Hampshire, Delaware......	0.75	2.10

Finally, no better testimony could be offered than that of the former Secretary of the Treasury, Albert Gallatin. Free trader that he was, Gallatin would not overstate the differential. But he noted that women's factory earnings ran from $2 to $3 a week compared "to what might be earned in their usual occupations at one dollar and a half per week." [23] Since board was charged at $1.25 by the Lowell mills, we may contrast a domestic-service wage (imputed and money) of, say, $2.50 with a factory wage of $3. A 50-cent wage differential is clearly trivial by modern standards, but a 20 percent wage differential is not, and this was one major advantage of the factory wage. The other was undoubtedly the tendency of domestic service to require 7 days' work a week (compared to the factory 6-day week) and to extend over a 14-hour workday, as compared to a factory workday of 12 to 12½ hours. In real terms, therefore, wages which were the equivalent of one-third greater than those in domestic service were offered in 1800–1835 to attract labor to the confines, intensity, and discipline of factory work.

3. Once the factory system had been established, labor became available, and a market for factory labor was operative, there is some evidence that wage rates for females declined. It is perhaps not surprising that the

[21] Baker Library, Manuscripts 871, 1776–1812, p. 738. This memorandum account book reports payment to Abigail Sturtevant in 1800 at the rate of 1 shilling 2 pence per day, or about $1.25 a week. The textile figure is Quincy's 50 cent a day rate.

[22] *McLane Report,* vol. I, pp. 584, 630–631; vol. II, pp. 703, 714, 717, 720, 722. The New Hampshire textile rate is from Table A-31, while the Delaware rate is derived from a limited number of reports in the McLane volumes.

[23] Albert Gallatin, Chairman, *Memoir of the Committee Appointed by the Free Trade Convention, Philadelphia,* September–October, 1831 (New York, 1832), p. 20.

premium for factory work should disappear when it was no longer necessary, but the evidence on the point is scanty. Carroll Wright reports wages for "two of the best known factories in Massachusetts" in 1828 and in 1836—the former, the year when the major Lowell mills were being set up, the latter, a year of general prosperity. His data show declines of about a fifth in wages for the main occupational categories.[24] These rates show some falling off after 1830–1831, but this is readily accounted for, says Wright:

> When the factories of Lowell made calls to operatives, they made a bid for the best by offering wages in excess of those paid for domestic service, which ranged from 50 cents to $1 per week, including living; the women who went from house to house to spin and weave, or help in making the clothes of the family, could not earn much more than 75 cents per week. There was a widespread feeling that the factory might degrade, and thus a prejudice grew up against which it could not be removed except by wages liberal in comparison to those paid for other services.[25]

We do have two statements by the Merrimac Manufacturing Company—one covering 1824 and 1840, the other relating to 1832—which show distinct and sizable declines for the weaving group and trivial change for spinners from 1824 to 1840. Together these groups accounted for the bulk of the company's female employment.[26] Since 1840 was a recession low, we combine the 1824 figures and compare them with the 1832 McLane report, thereby confirming the decline before 1840. However, comparisons can also be made from 1828 to 1832 for a large wool factory in New York State, a sail duck factory in New Jersey, and other companies, none of these revealing any decline. We can therefore only conclude that a decline may have taken place for the very largest firms after their labor force had migrated to their immediate area.[27]

[24] Wright, *op. cit.*, folio p. 576.

[25] *Ibid.*

[26] 1880 Census, *Statistics of Wages,* p. 349, gives occupational rates for 1824 and 1840. Since rates may well have been at a temporary low because of the recession, it is necessary to refer to the 1832 average from the *McLane Report,* vol. I, p. 341.

[27] 1828 data are from Minutes of Evidence taken before the Committee on Manufactures, 20th Cong., 1st Sess., Serial Set 177, House Rep. 115, Jan. 31, 1828, pp. 77, 83, 88, 91, 100, 134. Data for the same companies can be found in the *McLane Report* (1833) vol. I, pp. 141, 213, 308, 385, 485; vol. II, p. 77.

4

SOME CONSEQUENCES

FORMATION OF A NATIONAL MARKET

The classic treatment of pure and perfect competitive markets begins by premising them, then concentrates on the question of how they are sustained, and created anew, from period to period. Such a pattern is outlined with repetitive elegance in the earliest analyses of what Bagehot called "the English school of Political Economy." [1] Recent attacks on the weaker versions of this theory have emphasized the qualifications brought by the forces of monopoly, oligopoly, and product differentiation. But a significant question is perforce ignored by these attacks: How does a competitive market develop in the first place? The most natural premise for studying an undeveloped nation may well be one of highly imperfect competition. More importantly, the course of American history suggests that the advance from imperfect labor markets to more perfect labor markets is one of the significant external economies that pace economic growth.

At the beginning of the century the typical employee heard of alternative job opportunities only by word of mouth: There were neither newspapers, employment services, union hiring halls, nor radios to inform him on the point. His information on wage differentials was even less perfect, for while word of a new factory opening might come via the roving traders or the local tavern keeper, differentials in wage rates were matters of somewhat more specialized interest. The result appears to have been occasional marked differentials in wage rates between markets. As has been reported

---

[1] No sharper description of imperfect labor markets exists than that given by Smith, or even Mill and Cairnes. We focus here on the development of more perfect from less perfect markets.

for other underdeveloped countries, a great differential in wages for identical occupations appears to have existed in nearby areas.[2]

A large-scale survey in 1832 reported wage rates for female cotton textile workers in a number of nearby New Hampshire towns:

63 cents in Peterboro
40 cents in New Ipswich
37½ cents in Winchester
42 cents in Jaffrey

These towns were all within several miles of each other, yet a 66 percent spread in rates is reported.[3] In some measure these differences may reflect the fact that one town had more productive workers than another, although we can attach no high probability to such a factor. In some measure a differentiation among the towns by type of fabric being worked on could account for the differences. But we find the range of one-third in wage rates more largely explicable in terms of the simple imperfections in the labor market of the time. Many of the female employees were married women, who clearly were not going to move from one town to another for a few cents' difference in wages. In the process of developing productive facilities at their optimum location, we would expect some localities initially to pay more than others. Where new plants were being set up we would expect them to bid higher to obtain such labor as was available. A national labor market, or a set of local markets, is the end product of economic development; it is not the initial stage.[4] When mill hours began at 4:30 in the morning, and even shoe leather was so costly that women walked to church holding their shoes until they reached the church door,[5] such differentials in wage rates could reasonably exist and be maintained for a time.

But as industrialization proceeded communication improved, commuting costs cheapened. More perfect labor markets should then have developed. The most reliable testimony to such a development would be a narrowing of wage differentials among the various areas. Several recent studies have looked to the data for recent, short periods, and sought to use differ-

[2] Differences of 33 percent for rates on identical job classifications in India as late as 1926 are noted in Morris D. Morris, "Labor Discipline, Trade Unions, and the State in India," *Journal of Political Economy* (August, 1955), p. 295.

[3] Data from the McLane Report, *Documents on Manufactures,* (1833) U.S. Congress, Serial Set 222, *passim.* Study of the reports for this and other states suggests that the variations were not errors in reporting. The similarities for different firms within the same towns suggest that differences in occupational mix were not the cause.

[4] The decline in farm laborers' wage rates in proportion to the distance from manufacturing centers in eighteenth-century England is used by Hicks as an example of such imperfect mobility. J. R. Hicks, *The Theory of Wages* (1932), p. 75.

[5] Harold Wilson, *The Hill Country of Northern New England* (1936), p. 30.

ences in manufacturing earnings as a measure of such differentials. Their results have by no means clearly demonstrated that differentials did decline.[6]

Yet if there is one thing that marginal analysis forcibly premises, it is that the endeavors of profit-making entrepreneurs in a competitive market will work to equalize marginal returns to each factor of production in its different uses. Now it does not follow, of necessity, that this tendency must be apparent in any historic period. Such a result may fail to follow in a dynamic economy: the finding of new resources, new methods for combining resources, can mantle these tendencies in obscurity. Is it possible to learn whether equalization did in fact increase in the American economy over the past century and a half? Using the method of comparative statics, we can derive some useful insights from the wage data. In section I below we shall consider an obvious source, annual factory earnings, indicating why rate data were used by preference, while in section II we shall see what conclusions follow from the wage-rate data used here.

I

A likely and available source here is the manufacturing average earnings figure, but it is afflicted by two difficulties. First, is the tendency for a shift in industrial composition to alter a state's overall factory average. This shift may lead us to delusive conclusions. For example, the Massachusetts average manufacturing earnings figure for 1850 was much the same as Kentucky, but by 1860 it was significantly lower. This change suggests that the spread among the states was increasing for any given industry. But it is far more likely that the gap reflects the increasing share of lower-wage industries in one state, of higher in the other. Such a difficulty can be reasonably well surmounted by the use of individual industry figures. A second limitation of the factory earnings figures is that transient variations will appear from time to time—a result of strikes, bad weather, failure of materials supply, tariff changes. To all these the annual average earnings figure is peculiarly sensitive; and variations going this way in one state, that way in another, will necessarily mute the trend pattern of variations among all states.

[6] Jerome L. Stein, "A Theory of Interstate Differences in the Rate of Growth of Manufacturing Employment in a Free Market Area," *International Economic Review* (May, 1960). Stein finds that differences in annual factory earnings among the states in 1939 had no association with the state rates of growth of factory employment. Martin Segal, reviewing "Regional Wage Differentials in Manufacturing in the Postwar Period," *Review of Economics and Statistics* (May, 1961), emphasizes that eliminating wage differentials among regions is a long-run process "not coming to fruition for decades." See too Harvey Perloff, Dunn, Lampard, and Muth, *Regions, Resources and Economic Growth* (1960), chap. 32, where the primary subject is differences in productivity of labor.

We can reduce such difficulties substantially if we work with data for particular occupations. Here we take common-labor and farm-labor rates as our guide. These occupations have a wide geographic spread. Common labor is not a category peculiar to nonfarm industry, while farm labor is not restricted to cotton growing, wheat, dairying, or fruit. Perfection is not available to us. The rate data are necessarily subject to the same transient factors as influence earnings, though apparently to a much smaller degree through most of the period studied. (The rigidity of wage rates, considered in other contexts, is simply a confirmation of this greater invariance.) They are subject to reporting errors, perhaps greater in some respect than the earnings figures. Moreover, the particular point in the business cycle at which they are reported must affect them—a factor not mentioned above in connection with the earnings data because it affects all our empirical material. A look at the data by state presented in Tables A-23 to A-25 for 1832 to 1940, however, suggests that such influences may not be especially distorting for these data.

II

Turning, therefore, to the wage data for common labor and for farm labor, let us see what they tell us about long-run factor cost equalization.[7] The farm wage-rate data suggest one major inference: A long-term reduction in variation, and a tendency toward equalizing factor returns for labor among the states. We know from the disappearance of great intraregional interest-rate differentials that such a tendency was strongly at work with respect to capital. These data suggest that labor, too, "of all luggage the most difficult to transport" in Adam Smith's words, was remarkably mobile. For this period it was sufficiently mobile to bring this extensive reduction of differences in rates among the states.

Studies of change over short periods have concluded that marked regional differentials in wages exist, and persist over time, in the United States farm-labor market.[8] But in a dynamic economy relatively short-term changes in production and demand forces can readily overlay any longer-run tendency toward equalization of factor returns. The short-run picture will not necessarily tell us much about the extent of longer-term adjustment.

As one empirical indication of the rapidity with which an integrated national labor market tended to develop, we compute the coefficient of

---

[7] The reader is entitled to ask: Why just these occupations? Two answers may be given. One is positive: Common labor is ubiquitous and the rates are representative. Secondly, it is quite true that these occupations are not enough; but months of work have gone into the derivation of each set of figures. Anyone is at liberty to add more occupations, particularly if he is fortunate enough to have clerical assistance.

[8] Robert J. Wolfson, "An Econometric Investigation of Regional Differentials in American Agricultural Wages," *Econometrica*, vol. 26, pp. 225–257, 1958.

variation for farm-labor rates over successive periods. (Because the number of states being compared widens over the years, the absolute level of coefficients has little meaning. Changes over paired comparison periods, however, do provide a basis for judgment.)

**Coefficients of Variation for Farm-labor
Wage Rates, 1818–1954 (Percent)**

1818	25	1880	54
1826	22	1890	31
1830	23		
		1890	30
1830	23	1899	39
1850	18		
		1899	48
1850	36	1909	40
1860	30		
		1919	33
1860	29	1929	29
1870	26		
		1940	30
1870	25	1948	35
1880	27		
		1950	28
		1954	24

These figures necessarily understate the decline as it would be reported for a constant sample of states: By beginning each comparison with a wider sample, we incorporate newer frontier states which were still actively bidding for migrants. But taking as wide a comparison as we may in each period, a persistent trend toward wiping out variations in wage rates among the states springs to the eye. Limitations in the data probably account for the irregular 1880 to 1899 trend.[9] On the other hand, the reversal from 1940 to 1948 is reliably reported and economically significant. The shift away from wartime production patterns had largely altered labor requirements, a new and stable pattern of labor supply not having yet developed. Both North Central and lower New England states were bidding more above the national farm-wage average than they had done customarily to attract labor from nonfarm pursuits, and from other regions. (No similar increase springs to the eye for either 1860 to 1870 or 1910 to 1920, suggesting the great distortion in the peacetime input patterns that World War II production had brought.)

[9] Reports for three states account for the steep 1880 to 1890 fall and subsequent rise. The 1890 to 1899 rise would change from 9 percent to 5 percent if Nevada were excluded, and would vanish altogether if Utah and California were excluded. Since reports for these states show some unreasonable year-to-year movements in the USDA series on which we rely, it is possible that a more or less regular decline occurred from 1880 to 1899. The number of states in our comparison groups was 23 for 1818 to 1830, and then, successively, 23, 34, 33, 39, 41, 48, 48.

Behind the impressive trend toward equalization, we may discern the conflicting trends in the separate states and regions. For the trend is by no means monolithic. Regions with lively, growing demands for labor offer rising wage rates; these rise faster than the national average. The gaining New England factory system is reflected in the 1832 to 1850 rise in variation for common labor in these states, despite a drawing together that the scanty data suggest for other states. As a second example, the long up-swell of prairie settlement appears in the North Central farm rates for 1860 to 1880 when homesteading, railroading, and the European grain demand attracted labor to that area. As a third example, the great variation among the new regions of cotton cultivation in 1818 to 1830—Georgia, Mississippi, and Alabama—rapidly diminishes in the next few decades.

One final note: The long-term tendency toward equalization has been necessarily understated in these figures. Since we are not concerned with the absolute level of coefficients, this fact is of no great moment. But the use of a constant sample of states, though necessary for reliable estimation, will omit (1) the states on the wilder frontiers, and (2)—for 1818 to 1909—those areas yet to become states. This must yield an underestimate. For example, Pantollio's memoir to Napoleon found that in 1800 Louisiana rates "are twice as high as in the United States." [10] But they were certainly not that much above the United States average a decade or so later. As an employee of the Texas Navy in 1836, Captain Samuel Samuels received four times the customary United States sailor's pay. And in New Mexico in 1839 American labor was not content with less than $1 (clear of expenses) according to Gregg, but Mexicans worked for two to three reales a day—or from 25 to 37 cents a day. [11] Such differentials were undoubtedly reduced after the territory had been wrested from Mexico. We conclude, therefore, that the long-term tendency toward equalization of wage rates would be somewhat more marked if we were to include not the constant sample of states used here but the entire area of the continental United States. [12]

Should we qualify this tendency toward equalization of money rates in

[10] Reprinted in Charles Gayarre, *History of Louisiana* (1885), vol. III, p. 438.

[11] Josiah Gregg, *Commerce of the Prairies* (1845; reprint 1905), p. 309. The reale was worth an eighth of a dollar, according to Theodore H. Hittell, *History of California* (1849), vol. III, p. 404. I owe the reference to Hittell to George P. Hammond, director of the Bancroft Library at the University of California.

[12] In turn, this bias is partly compensated by another. As a region began to pay higher rates and draw more workers to it, its weight necessarily increased, thus pulling the national average closer to its level. Alternatives to using a weighted national average are unsatisfactory: An unweighted average gives an odd importance to areas with few laborers, and use of a single region makes its varying level the standard.

the light of an offsetting tendency for the real value of room, board and other equalizing differences? While the evidence is scanty, we might reasonably suspect that the gaps for wage items in kind (as between the frontier and the more settled states) did narrow through time. Any such relative improvement in the frontier states would partially offset the tendency shown in wage rates. More important, however, would be the likelihood that efficiency wages need not have moved as wage rates did over this period, since the frontier states could have attracted younger, more stalwart, and more efficient workers.[13] To the extent that they did, the difference in efficiency wages at the beginning of the period would have been less than the wage-rate data suggest. However, as time passed the gap in agility and ability between workers in the newer and older states would have narrowed. Any such tendency, superimposed on the narrowing wage rate differential would have meant that efficiency wages tended to equalize even more than the wage rates did.

REAL-WAGE TRENDS: 1800 to 1960

What diff'rence does it make to ye how far ye move forward, if ivrything moves forward ahead iv ye. . . . Ye are, as Hogan would say, th' same rilitive distance fr'm a tenderline steak that ye were thin.

Mr. Dooley on Hard Times

How did real wages in the United States advance over the long term? How regularly? By how much? Answers to such questions are of concern for the study of economic growth. To provide future generations with that higher output of the material things which will yield them joy and complexity, sustenance and riot, this generation must allocate part of its own product away from consumption and into investment in capital items, including education and research. Many writers have inferred that such savings must inevitably be supplied by wage earners—either through voluntary savings arrangements, cold coercion, or other involuntary lags in the rate of wage increase behind the rate of productivity increase. Others have put special emphasis on the febrile periods of inflation that have been notably, if briefly, present in American history. They find such incidents helping to keep down real wages, thereby providing the returns to capital that become such investment for the future.[1] Either approach assumes

---

[13] I owe this suggestion to Moses Abramowitz.

[1] The recent discussion really goes back to some brief judgments in Keynes's *Economic Consequences of the Peace* (1920), chap. 2, part 3. See also Gunnar Myrdal, *Rich Lands and Poor* (1957), p. 46. Summary reviews of the well-known work by

that the path of real wages must directly reflect society's allocation between consumption and investment, and assumes that what appears to have been true historically of England, say, must likewise be true of the United States during its own salad days.

Another set of interests cluster around the welfare implications. How and at what rate did the welfare of American workers increase as measured by their real incomes? Writers such as Kuczynski have more or less argued that no gain took place over much of the nineteenth century. And our only long-term gross national product series implies that real product per capita fell during the first 40 years of the nineteenth century.[2]

How is it possible to compare the real value of incomes received by an 1800 farm laborer and a 1900 city worker (much less a 1960 employee), when each clung to different value systems, was located on a bewilderingly different preference surface? The extreme length of the period, the remoteness of its beginning, accentuate the normal index number problem. There is no answer in today's welfare economics to make precise comparison possible. True it is material, but it is irrelevant, to say that it is done all the time.[3]

However, there may be one wry consolation to those who will in any event discuss real-income trends back to World War I, or even more remote days. Consumer value systems may well suffer more change during a decade in our own time than over a cycle of Cathay. The incessant development of novelty, those irresistible urges that the salesmen and advertiser create, conspire to keep our own preference maps in continuous upheaval. There are those alive today who have switched from coal stoves to electric ones, from brooms to vacuum cleaners, from sulfur and molasses to penicillin, from buggies to airplanes; from renting a flat to owning a house; from baking bread to heating store-bought pies. It is the job of one major government agency—by underwriting mortgages—to switch consumers from renting to buying homes; of another—by Research and Marketing Act projects—to persuade consumers of the merits of cotton and wool, of the desirability of a host of farm products as against other competitors for the consumer's dollar, and so on.

Hamilton, Mitchell, and others appear in David Felix, "Profit Inflation and Economic Growth," *Quarterly Journal of Economics* (August, 1956) and, incisively, in R. A. Kessel and A. A. Alchian, "The Meaning and Validity of the Inflation-induced Lag of Wages behind Prices," *American Economic Review* (March, 1960).

[2] R. F. Martin, *National Income in the United States, 1799–1938*. See also Simon Kuznets, "Long-term Changes in the National Income of the United States of America since 1870," in International Association for Research in Income and Wealth, *Income and Wealth of the United States* (1952), pp. 221ff.

[3] See the perceptive discussion by Abramowitz in Moses Abramowitz (ed.), *The Allocation of Economic Resources: Essays in Honor of Bernard Francis Haley* (1959).

By contrast, what a pattern of stability was much of the nineteenth century. New food items came and went, it is true. But the basic dietary of pork and beef, of bread, sugar, and coffee appears to have persisted with little change. Once textiles had replaced leather clothing after the War of 1812, the significant variations were in flounces and furbelows rather than in the major materials or clothing products. The consumer durable category was trivial throughout the century, and the infrequency with which the wage earner had a piano is suggested by the intensely serious and repeated enumerations of piano and organ ownership made by the Bureau of Labor.[4] And the *dolce stile nuovo* pioneered by the houses in Pennsylvania or Minnesota mining towns did not offer much that was different from early New England or Middle Atlantic worker housing. Nonetheless we must go out the door we came in: The difficulties of long-period comparisons of real incomes inevitably exist because of changing value systems. We can take what consolation we dare from the apparent fact that making an 1800 to 1900 comparison may not really be any more lurid an endeavor than are short-period comparisons in this twentieth century of emulation, communication, salesmanship, and incessant product change.

We consider first the relationships between the trend of real wages and that of real national income, then turn to alternative approaches for measuring real-wage trends.

Real-wage–Real-income Relationships

Many of the considerations that were originally raised with respect to the growth of Great Britain, Germany, or Switzerland make little sense when directly applied to a country like the United States in the nineteenth century, or to most underdeveloped nations today. The provision of savings for investment by means of a gap between employee wages and the full value of labor's marginal product does not necessarily possess any importance in studying the major lines of United States economic growth prior to 1860. This is so for a relatively simple numerical reason. In 1800 about 90 percent of the labor force, and as late as 1850 no less than 70 percent of the labor force, were *not* employees. They were self-employed persons (farmers, mechanics, small tradesmen) or slaves. Clearly the investment that can come from marginal differences in the earnings by 10 to 30 percent of the labor force is nothing like the sum required to transform an underdeveloped nation into one of the world's leading producers. The trend in real wages need not, therefore, have reflected the trend in real incomes; unlike today, wages did not bulk so large in the total as to

[4] See the delightful, perceptive review by Lawrence Klein, "The Bell and the Bay Window," in *How American Buying Habits Change,* U.S. Department of Labor (1959).

dominate its movement. Quite the contrary. The wage trend could be up, down, or sideways while the national income total could move quite differently.

On the other hand, the operation of the labor market would in fact have tended to make real-wage and real-income trends move more or less in parallel. If the capital requirements for entry into farming or the mechanical trades were not excessive at any time, those who were employees might realistically choose between self-employment and employee status up to the point where the marginal returns in each status were equivalent for persons of equal ability and risk preference. Their doing so would in turn mean that wage and real-income trends were bound together.

We know that this was a choice unavailable to slaves. True, there was some shifting from free status into slavery (with the kidnapping of free Negro persons) and from slavery into free status (fugitive slaves and manumitted ones), but such shifts were as trivial numerically as they were significant politically. However, this was not true at all for the prospects of a laborer as a farmer, saddler, wheelwright, carpenter, or shoemaker.

In the early 1830s for example, a visitor to the famed Illinois lead mines matter of factly reported that the wages of miners were high because they "shortly become proprietors themselves." [5] Such transitions we assume were no less important when hired teamster, carpenter, or blacksmith became independent entrepreneur in those days when capital requirements were low relative to wages.

But far more important for deciding whether incomes per member of the labor force and incomes per wage earner did in fact tend to parallel each other, is the laborer-farmer shift. The flow from one status to the other proved persistent, continual. "Land," wrote one Englishman in 1849 on the advisability of a group moving to Texas, "may be procured on most easy terms. . . . The poor man may, therefore, live on his own farm with more comfort or profit" than he could as a servant, or employee. Moreover, "the settlers have usually been poor on their arrival, and could not pay for hired labour. . . . Thus no encouragement has been offered to labourers, and consequently they have become farmers themselves." [6]

In 1818 Fordham estimated that, with labor in the Illinois country at $13, it would take 2 years' work to enable a laborer to buy a quarter section, together with tools and a plow, for $305. A revealing light is cast on the extent of capital and labor mobility during this period by Fordham's

[5] Charles A. Murray, *Travels in North America during the Years 1834, 1835 and 1836* (New York: 1839), vol. II, p. 81.

[6] Edward Smith, *Account of a Journey through North-Eastern Texas Undertaken in 1849 for the Purposes of Emigration* (London: 1849), p. 38. Smith adds: "It appears that a large number of young men run over all the Western states and Texas, and hire themselves for short periods; but they cannot be depended upon."

statement that farming in the lush prairie regions would pay no more than in England: Given the availability of water communication, prices are known in both places; this affects the values in the United States; and commerce then "equalizes the profits of producing food." [7]

In 1838 James Hall found that "in any of the states west of the Ohio river, a laborer can earn 75 cents a day, and if his living is supposed to cost 25 cents, which in this plentiful country is a large estimate, he can, by the labor of one hundred days, or about four months, purchase a farm." But "as the working days in a year, excluding bad weather, might not amount to more than 200" and deductions must be made for clothing, a more realistic estimate finds that he will "be enabled to purchase a farm [of 80 acres] in six months, or a larger one in a year." [8] A more comprehensive estimate of the time found that a 40-acre field might be bought for $50, while adding in the cost of fencing, breaking up, and a cabin would run to a total of $250.[9] At going rates, 2 to 3 years' work would suffice.[10] In later years, to be sure, farm-making costs rose. By 1850 one estimate found a quarter section (160 acres) costing $200. Add in breaking up, fencing, and other costs and the total came to $920.[11] Another writer found that the big problem was "the first $500"—requiring about 4 years' work to accumulate.[12] The rush of population from East to the West nevertheless continued, raising prices and land values.

The opposition of manufacturers to free land in the West is a more than casual indication of this labor-market link. Hayne and Benton charged that New England opposed the development of the West for fear of losing labor; while Congressman Josiah Sutherland (New York) opposed the

[7] Elias Fordham, *Personal Narrative* . . . *1817–1818* (Reprinted 1906), pp. 211, 120–121.

[8] James Hall, *Notes on the Eastern States* (Philadelphia: Harrison Hall, 1838), p. 204.

[9] Anonymous, *Illinois in 1837 and 1838; A Sketch Descriptive of the Situation* . . . (Philadelphia: S. Augustus Mitchell, 1838), p. 14.

[10] The farm laborer who was a would-be farmer would himself do much of the fencing and finishing of his cabin. Hence his initial grubstake (required to take possession and raise his first crop) would run, say, $150 to $200. Hired labor at $10 a month plus food and lodging would net, say, $100 a year, deducting clothing. (Clothing averaged about $30 a year for lower-income families.) Tools averaged under $40 in this early period.

[11] Josiah T. Marshall, *The Farmers and Emigrants Hand-book* (Utica: H. H. Hawley, 1852). See also Clarence Danhof, "Farm Making Costs and the 'Safety-Valve', 1850–60," *Journal of Political Economy* (June, 1941). Danhof's discussion of the obstacles that costs presented to such mobility focuses on a somewhat later decade, relates more to Eastern wages versus Western farm-making costs, and to the total cost of a farm since not all of total cost was needed at one time. This point is not directly relatable to our present concern.

[12] *How to Get a Farm and Where to Find One*, by the author of *Ten Acres Enough* (New York: 1864), pp. 56, 55.

Homestead Bill in 1852 for the coldly explicit reason that it would take labor from the East (thereby increasing labor cost there).[13] The other side of the coin appears in the statement by Representative Hudson of Massachusetts: Operatives for the new factories of New England in the 1830s "were taken chiefly from the agricultural class, and when they were withdrawn wages rose." [14] Earlier, in the depression of 1819, Flint found "mechanics leaving the towns of the western country and becoming cultivators in the back woods." [15]

The vast growth in the number of farmers in the Midwest in the early 1820–1870 period, as in the coast states in later years, is far more than could be accounted for merely by migration of eastern farmers or those Europeans classified as "farmers" in the immigration reports. The bulk of the migrant farmers were therefore ex-laborers, ex-mechanics, youngsters coming of age. And if we consider the total self-employed group (i.e., farmers plus small tradesmen and mechanics), the same conclusion is no less likely.

But if so, the shifts from one status to another must have been frequent enough to keep the returns from farming (in which the bulk of the labor force was employed) in some consistent relationship with the returns from wage employment. (Because of the differences in the risk attached to these alternative pursuits, the conclusion is no inevitable one. We minimize this qualification, however, by showing monthly wage data for farm labor, seamen, and canal labor.) The trend in deflated earnings for these categories will, in some meaningful way, show the trend of real incomes per person in the labor force generally. It is still possible, of course, that the incomes of farmers, at equal risk and with equal ability, rose less than did those of wage earners. Farmers might quite reasonably have taken lower incomes, but banked on the capital gains that would accrue from an ever-rising price of land—a rise anticipated and understood by millions of those who moved to the West. Such gains would not appear in the real-income figures and would restrict the reasonable use of wage trends to measure real-income trends. We here speculate that time preferences then were as urgent as now, that apart from a constant allowance that would not distort trend measures, farmers sought present incomes equivalent to those of nonfarm work of equal skill and risk.

A. Real-wage Trends to 1860

Before considering in more detail the movement of selected wage-rate series, as deflated, we must note several major factors that affect the meaning of such measurements. Each of these factors would, over the period,

---

[13] Henry Nash Smith, *Virgin Land* (1950), p. 204.
[14] *Congressional Globe* for 1842, p. 60.
[15] James Flint, *Letters from America* (Edinburg: W. and C. Tait, 1822), p. 238.

have tended to produce a greater rise in the real annual income of employees than that reported by wage-rate series.

1. With the development of roads, canals (and eventually railroads); of interrelated productive markets throughout the nation; of newspapers; and of business and banking services, short-term irregularities in demand tended to diminish. It became less and less common for a firm's sales to vanish totally or for the supply of a firm's inputs to be cut off completely by the weather. Production and marketing discontinuities diminished as the economy became more integrated. The proliferation of interstitial markets and levels of distribution smoothed the disorderly process of sales and production. But as discontinuity in output diminished, so did irregularities in employment. The result was a fuller work year. Nineteenth-century producers, as twentieth-century ones, could hardly have desired to disrupt an established work force, given the costs of training and integrating a new one. But the total discontinuities of their underdeveloped economy gave them little choice.

We are so accustomed to today's high communication and easy transport that it is difficult to imagine the crudities with which elements in the productive process then meshed—or the resultant discontinuities that brought immense capital gains to some, but unemployment (hence, reduced incomes) to many others. Since provisions in the Galena silver mines were generally imported in the 1830s, an accident that kept the steamboat from arriving at St. Louis would make prices "rise frequently one or two hundred percent." [16] A still earlier example is given by the sale of 45 cords of wood in 1812. The day before the war was declared, the wood was offered at $3; the day after, it was sold at $5.[17] Since wood was available for cutting at a hundred nearby woodlots, a price response of this magnitude suggests local discontinuities in the production process equivalent to those that a later generation was to associate with transporting rubber thousands of miles from Malaya in 1941.

Perhaps our best empirical indication in labor-market data appears in the difference between daily and monthly wage rates. As a rule this difference testifies mainly to a difference in the risk attached to each. As the section on Uncertainty and Wage Rates (Chapter 5) indicates, this differential has dwindled with time. The casual laborer once received a far higher daily rate than did his fellow who compounded for a (higher) monthly income. But the difference between (*a*) 26 times the daily rate and (*b*) a steady monthly wage has diminished, until today very little difference exists. This development could not have occurred because of any major change in risk preferences: We are usually told that today's worker seeks more certainty than did his fellow a century ago. It more

[16] Murray, *loc. cit.*
[17] *Life of Asa G. Sheldon: Wilmington Farmer* (1862; reprint, 1959), p. 120.

probably reflects the fact that alternatives available to the disemployed worker today are more frequent, with less chances of lost time and a pay cut, than was true in previous (high employment) decades.

2. The agglomeration of population in larger and larger cities gave employees readier opportunity for a full work year. The worker living in open farm country, with no capital and limited ability to walk from farm to farm, was in practice limited to choice between a handful of nearby farms or forges unless he pulled up stakes altogether. If the farms were all closed to him because of the weather or short-term lack of supplies, or lack of sales, he was without work. In the cities the wage earner came within reach of many more firms, so that when one was unavailable to him he could try many others. Hence the growth of cities tended to produce the same result that the reduction in transport costs did, enabling a worker to supplement income from his regular job when temporarily interrupted, or to find a new one with less lost time and at less of a wage reduction.

3. Mark Twain was, of course, wholly incorrect when he declared that everyone talks about the weather, but no one does anything about it: Housing had been developed some time before, while heating may have been developed earlier. During the nineteenth century protection against the elements increased steadily. With each such increase came a gain in the length of the work year. As discussed in the next section (Changes in Unemployment), the proportion of the labor force in farming and in canal and road construction declined, and thereby the proportion most exposed to interruptions in income because of bad weather. In addition, the interruptions that the weather could bring to milling, iron and steel production, tanning, and the operation of road transport steadily decreased. Each such decrease may not have reduced unemployment as we measure it today, but it surely cut involuntary unemployment. With repeated contemporary assertions that 4 months' work a year was lost because of bad weather, it is clear that the lengthened work year brought a decisive addition to real incomes.

4. Real incomes rose more amply throughout the nineteenth century than is recognized in the wage-rate figures, given the decreasing practice of payment in kind rather than cash. This practice was widespread in the first half of the century. After a week or six months of work a man would find himself not with cash but with bricks, pig iron, corn, or whale oil to sell. Having finished his work as a laborer, say, he was only beginning his work as an involuntary wholesaler or jobber. It is hardly likely that the expected value of returns from such wholesaling was large, nor even necessarily positive. Had it been significantly positive the employer would presumably have performed the function, and paid in cash. Since we may assume that employees were generally less expert entrepreneurs than the employers, their return from such activity would have been even less than

the employer might have reaped. Hence reported wage rates for the early decades surely overstate real employee income relative to that in later decades.

At the beginning of the century barter was common enough. In 1804 John Holway wove some cloth, was paid "for the saim" with an otter trap. In 1809 Samuel Rodman hoed corn in exchange for a "syther, sned and tackling." In 1810 "Bashabe Cuddy worked here half a day and I paid her in corn." [18] The country storekeeper, observed one visitor to the United States in 1828, "cannot expect to be paid for his goods in cash, and is obliged to barter, if he wishes to have business." [19]

Farm laborers on many occasions earned no cash, were paid off wholly in crops.[20] With a common wage of $10 a month in the first half century and corn in the Midwest running to 33⅓ cents a bushel, this meant that at the end of a normal farm season a laborer might well have to find a buyer for some 200 bushels of corn. Thus the nineteenth-century farm laborer was even more of a sharecropper than his twentieth-century successors, for he was not merely paid off in farm products, but he (rather than the farmer) had to find a buyer for his share.

What occupation was without such payment? Ministers in the western country (i.e., Midwest) might earn $400 to $800 a year, but 80 percent of it was "paid in produce." [21] Rocky Mountain hunters were hired for so many dollars in wages, but actual payment was often made in trading goods which they then resold to the Indians.[22] One gallant mountaineer, General (to-be) Thomas James, was paid off in beaver skins for his trapping in 1810—skins he could only dispose of at $1.50, although they were selling for $6 in St. Louis.[23] An itinerant artist, whose "picturs" brought $50 in cash when available, found that, though traveling in the best society, he had to accept a silver watch for one, while a gentleman from South Carolina traded a good rifle and a large bowie knife for another.[24]

[18] Caroline Hazard (ed.), *Nailer Tom's Diary* . . . *1778–1840* (1930), pp. 238, 325, 343.

[19] *The United States of North America as They Are* (London: Simpkin and Marshall, 1828), p. 185. The anonymous author had evidently visited the United States for some months.

[20] See Noah Webster's statement quoted on p. 151. Horace Greely, *Essays Designed to Elucidate the Science of Political Economy* (1870), p. 301, asserted that laborers were commonly paid in grain in the early part of the century.

[21] *The United States of North America as They Are*, p. 143.

[22] *The Correspondence and Journals of Captain Nathaniel J. Wyeth, 1831–36*, in F. G. Young (ed.), *Sources of the History of Oregon* (1899), pp. 66, 139.

[23] General Thomas James, *Three Years among the Indians and Mexicans* (1916), p. 89. That the Missouri Fur Company charged him $12 a gallon for whisky when it was selling at 40 to 50 cents a gallon in St. Louis appeared to have disturbed him as much or more.

[24] J. F. McDermott (ed.), *Travels in Search of the Elephant: The Wanderings of*

David Crawford, working in a brickyard in Nashville for 5 long months in 1841, found his employer telling him at the end that he could give him no cash. But his own words should not be diluted. He

says to me ae morning, "Dawvit, I canna gie ye a bawbee, but I'll tell you what I'll do—I'll jist pay ye in bricks for your saxty dollars." "Weel," reported Crawford to a friend, "I took the bricks fraw him, at the rate o' sax dollars a thousand, and begoon to "mak turns" as the folk talks about hereawa'. I gaed to Mr. Leighton, the storekeeper in the toon there . . . and he gied me ten Due Bills, as he ca'd them, six dollars the piece, for my bricks. Weel I gaed down to Mr. Rae's mill o'er buye, and say I to the miller could ye gie me twa barrels o' flour? I hae naw money to pay ye, but I'll gie ye a sax dollar due Bill on Mr. Leighton's store. "Well I reckon ye may get them" (says he) saw that did me till the next Spring for makin' scones.[25]

The mere fact of payment in kind did not mean that money incomes rose with the shift to money wages. On the contrary. In the dark decades when a tradesman might discount by 2 to 10 percent the bank notes with which an employee had been paid, and when no competent businessman could operate without one of the many publications generically termed Bank Note Reporters, a bushel of corn or a bowie knife might well be preferred to a handsome engraving issued by a log-cabin bank with almost no assets. Yet over time the solidity of the banking system did increase, payment in money becoming ever more typical. By 1852 an astute writer found that "ready money is getting more plentiful than it was. . . . Wages are hardly ever, now paid in anything but cash." [26] By 1880 the census reported that one in every eight of a large sample of establishments still paid out part or all of their payroll in the form of store orders or merchandise.[27] The practice had been drastically reduced, but was still clearly extant. Payment in scrip, inferior currency, or discounting—which likewise reduced the real value of compensation—tended to decline with the passing years.[28] We cannot speak of magnitudes here, but the direction seems

---

Alfred S. Waugh . . . in 1845–56 (1951), p. 42. Waugh's transactions took place in the rising city of Independence, Mo., in 1845.

[25] Quoted in John Regan, *The Emigrants Guide* (Edinburgh: Oliver and Boyd), p. 116. Regan arrived in the United States in 1842. The second edition of his book, quoted here was apparently published ca. 1852.

[26] Regan, *op. cit.,* p. 352. Regan quotes 1852 wage rates on this page, and we assume that to be his date of reference.

[27] 1880 Census, *Report on Statistics of Wages* (1886), p. xxii.

[28] Duflot de Mafros, *Travels on the Pacific Coast* (1844; reprint 1937), vol. II, p. 86. The company "makes a profit of 25% on the wages of its employees in the Columbia River country by figuring at the rate of 5 shillings rather than 4 . . . their actual value." Mafros was a French consul in the United States.

clear enough to note this as a further influence tending to raise real earnings from the beginning to the end of the nineteenth century more than would be evidenced by earnings data.

5. A further factor making for an increase in real incomes during the nineteenth century, but not one evidenced by any wage-rate data, is the ending of the system that made the employee an involuntary part of the banking system. The greatest amount of inventory and accounts receivable financing prior to 1850 in many small enterprises (not the Lowell mills or Southern plantations) was conducted by employees. Since their wages were not usually paid until a considerable time after they had been earned, they constituted meanwhile an interest-free loan to the entrepreneur. Until 1850, wrote Francis Walker, laborers in New England were not paid off until the end of the year, advances being given them until that time.[29] As late as 1900 the French Consul General in Chicago found that in the mines: "A workman may not be paid until the last of August for work done in the first part of July." [30] The common practice in the whaling fleets and the merchant vessels of the century was similar—with short-term advances being made during the voyage (and interest charged by the whaling companies) and with the wages earned not being paid until the end of the voyage.[31] The value of such foregone interest was clearly much greater to the entrepreneur than to the employer. Given that his wage bill was equivalent to, say, half his capital, then a major share of his capital needs was provided at 0 percent rather than 10 percent for an average of 2 or 3 months (perhaps a year in whaling). Such financing may well have been a significant source of investment funds during the nineteenth century.

B. Real-wage Trends Prior to 1860

What can be said of the trend in wage rates per se, of the extent to which wages as thus measured rose meteorically, sluggishly, or not at all? **Procedure.** We begin from one basic fact. Most wage earners, in most of these years, found the most significant element in their income to be an unwavering fixed mark. They received not wages but food, lodging, and wages. This was surely true for the farm laborer, the storm-tossed seaman, the domestic servant—who together accounted for the bulk of the wage-earner group. But it was no less true of the romantic itinerants—the al-

---

[29] Francis Walker, *The Wages Question* (1876), p. 123.

[30] Quoted in Emile Levasseur, *The American Workman* (1900), p. 117.

[31] A host of examples appear in the records now in the Essex Institute. The books of account of Swift and Allen now in the Baker Library show repeated entries of advances made to sailors against wages already earned, and interest charged on such advances. Samuel Morison, in his *Maritime History of Massachusetts* (1922), alludes to interest charges upon interest charges.

ways fearless, keen-eyed trappers and scouts of the frontier, the hard-drinking keelboatmen of the Mississippi, the cowhand loping behind the cattle on a drive along the Chisholm Trail. It was true too of the thousands of laborers who dug ditches, canals, or railroad-track beds, made streets and roads, or deepened harbors; of the founders, forgemen, wood choppers, and miners who ran the Pennsylvania, Ohio, and New York forges and blast furnaces during the 1830s, 1840s, and 1850s. And it was true of the ladies who worked in Lowell mills during the hours when they were not writing poems for the *Lowell Offering.*

The system of providing board (and lodging) was a natural and ubiquitous accompaniment of the scattered population and the scanty trade and service network of the times. When the predecessors of Governor Clinton planned the big ditch, they also planned a store with provisions and liquor: How else could a host of laborers get provisions in the wilderness? [32] When the open fields near Lowell were wrested from hunters who had recently coursed over them and huge mills were established, the mill owners could have little assurance that regular meals and lodging would be available for their young ladies without sponsoring the provision of such services themselves. And even when a large force of laborers was assembled to level downtown Boston's hills into manageable lots in the 1830s, letting the men go off to victualing cellars apparently did not work. The contractor soon took over one of the doomed houses and operated it for his crew until the end.[33] The irregular provisioning arrangements that can develop when a huge labor force is assembled in some undeveloped part of a new land is best seen by the happenings in the Yuba and Feather Valleys in 1849–1850, when some miners dined on sardines and flapjacks all week, while others made 21 meals of beans. It is not on such food that steady work can be expected from wage earners. The tradition of sutlers—great, ancient, and ignoble as it was—fortunately did not commend itself beyond the army camps nor until later years.

Assessing the trend in the value of board and lodging is a fairly dubious business. It is our general conclusion that from 1800 to 1860 the real content of the board and lodging given to employees did not change materially. For deflating the total wage of employees from 1800 to 1860 we, therefore, use an index of 100 throughout for that component of the total wage. Our conclusion that the real content of board and lodging did not change rests largely on a laborious accumulation of data on the content of diets—in New Hampshire textile mills, Pennsylvania ironworks, the Massachusetts codfishing fleet, the U.S. Navy ration at various dates, and the Army ration. Differences between the ration provided for heavy work

[32] E. B. O'Callaghan, *Documentary History of the State of New York* (Albany: 1850), vol. III, p. 1101.

[33] *Life of Asa G. Sheldon: Wilmington Farmer,* p. 199.

in iron foundries and, for example, that provided to girls in the woolen mills, were great enough so that we cannot deduce a great deal from such materials. The invariance of the armed-forces diets—plus a mild rise in the amount of firewood supplied—is a substantial element in our conclusion of little change.[34]

Our major problem then is to deflate the money (or money equivalent) wage used to buy clothing, liquor, tea, coffee, soap, candles, and some lesser items. The derivation of such a price index is discussed in some detail in the section on Cost of Living, 1800 to 1860 (Chapter 8). By then dividing that price index into the money wage and weighting the resultant series with a deflated board and lodging series, we arrive at the final deflated real-wage series.

Results. Taking a preliminary sight from some of the wage rates for 1800 to 1819 (particularly Tables A-20, A-21, A-23, A-25, and Chapter 7), suggests a marked decline in wages, offset by a decline of slight magnitude in prices, to leave real-wage rates essentially unchanged. Our estimate of a money-wage decline is based upon a fall from $20 to $12.50 in earnings of able seamen; a decline in wages of female domestics from about $1.25 a week to $1; of male weavers in Rhode Island from about $20 a month in 1809 to much lower rates by 1832; and of canal labor from $10 in Massachusetts in 1800 to $8 by 1826 for the construction in Ohio and Pennsylvania. Daily rates—for boatmen, woodcutters, and common labor—do not appear to have changed greatly. Since the seamen's wage is the occupational rate with the most consistent and broadly based quotations behind it, we place special reliance on it, but the magnitude of its decline reflects in part the shift from the alarums and excursions of 1800, Napoleon and the Barbary pirates, to the quiescence of the 1819 depression. We opt for a 10 percent decline in money wages, which works out to no net change in deflated total income.

From 1819 to 1832 the money wage appears to have recovered to 1800 levels, but the decline in tea and coffee prices, and particularly the decline in textile prices as American production began breaking into the English near monopoly, brought a marked gain in deflated income.

From 1832 on, our data become much more reliable, though still weak. A 10 percent rise to 1850 reflects the marked gain in farm labor, stability for seamen, and the decline for males in the textile industry as demand

---

[34] Data on national consumption appearing in the study by Marvin Towne and Wayne Rasmussen ("Gross Farm Production and Gross Investment in the Nineteenth Century," in Conference on Research in Income and Wealth, *Trends in the American Economy in the Nineteenth Century* [1960]) provide no confirmation prior to 1840, when they had perforce to assume no change in per capita consumption rates. However, their willingness to use such as assumption and the slow change from 1840 to 1860 (derived from census data) give us some independent support.

shifted to female labor. Again textile price declines were significant, and a substantial rise in deflated income over these 18 years is stipulated.

From 1850 to 1860 a further gain in wage rates is shown, so largely offset by price rises as to produce no net gain over the decade.

In sum, these extremely preliminary figures suggest no net advance in real earnings from 1800 to 1819 (largely figuring the end-of-war inflation and the 1819 depression); a marked advance to 1850 as wages rose and clothing prices declined; and stability to 1860 (a probable rise in rates to 1856, eroded by the 1857 depression).

Even when we have much more firmly based wage data, such estimates will still be highly uncertain. We, therefore, summarize in the following section what some contemporary observers had to say during these six decades about the trend in incomes.

C. Real Wages: Contemporary Statements

Summarizing and linking the statements made during the nineteenth century that are outlined below, we arrive at the following indications of real wage and cost of living changes:

Percent Change in Wages and Cost of Living

Date	Real wages	Prices	Money wages
1789–1816	0	+100	100
1816–1828	0		
1824–1830	−33		
1833–1837	0	100	100
1835–1850	+50	−33	0
1850–1857	−36	+75	0
1855–1857			−50

We give most credence to the measures from 1789 to 1828, from 1833 to 1850. The 1824 to 1830 fall is a guess by a particularly biased writer to support his high-tariff position, while the 1850 to 1857 figure may be accurate but reflects the short term 1857 recession impact more than longer-term change.

1789 to 1816. Representative Pickering estimated, in January, 1817, "the real value of the compensation of 1789 to be double [and it was certainly more than double]" the value of the same nominal sum in 1816, referring to the fixed congressional pay scale of $6 a day.[35]

1778 to 1817. Noah Webster, on October 14, 1818, informed the New Hampshire, Franklin, and Hampden Agricultural Society that "Since

---

[35] *Annals of Congress,* January, 1817, col. 592. See also col. 667, where Representative Wendover likewise finds for a doubling.

the American revolution, money has lost nearly half its former value. In the ordinary intercourse of our citizens with each other this evil is less sensibly felt; for the prices of provisions and labor have advanced nearly in the same proportion. When the farmer gives to the laborer a bushel of rye for a days work it makes no difference to the parties whether the *nominal* value of rye and labor is fifty cents or a dollar—the *real* value is the same in both cases." [36] Webster went on to say that "a salary settled on a clergyman thirty or forty years ago . . . will purchase little more than half of the commodities . . . which it would at the time of the contract. The property of a widow or orphan invested in stock 30 years ago has already lost nearly one half its value." [37] Both statements imply a doubling of prices, while Webster indicates that nominal wages (free to rise) likewise doubled.

1816 to 1828. A free-trade group protesting the rise in tariffs found in 1828 that "so far from wages having declined, taking into consideration the fall in provisions, and all other means of living, labour was never at any period better paid than it is now." [38]

1824 to 1830. The nation's greatest pro-tariff writer contended in June, 1830, that "the value of labour in this country has depreciated full thirty-three percent since the tariff of 1824." [39] Despite his bias, his testimony is consistent with the Reverend Isaac Fidler's finding, in 1832, that New York wages "a few years ago were double of what they are now," adding that the Americans complained that emigrants have "injured them by causing redundancy of labour, increase of house rents, and prices of provisions, and depreciation of recompense of industry." [40] We infer that the 1824 to 1830 decline developed at a steady rate, that from 1828 to early 1830, therefore, being minus 15 percent in consumer prices.

1833 to 1837. In 1840 a writer on economic conditions stated that he had documents "in his possession, showing that from 1833 to 1837 provisions, house rent, fuel, etc., had advanced upon the average . . . double,

[36] Noah Webster, *An Address Delivered before the New Hampshire, Franklin and Hampden Agricultural Society, October 14, 1818.* (Northampton: Thomas W. S. Shephard Co., 1818), p. 21.

[37] *Ibid.,* p. 23.

[38] Henry Lee, *Report of a Committee of the Citizens of Boston and the Vicinity Opposed to a Further Increase of Duties on Importations* (New York: Clayton and Van Norden, 1828), p. 17. This statement appears in a discussion of complaints by woolen manufacturers about recent failures; on p. 125 Lee states that "the manufacturers assert that their goods have fallen since 1816, and their business is unprofitable," from which we take 1816 as the earlier date of reference.

[39] (Matthew Carey) Publicola, *Thirteen Essays on the Policy of Manufacturing in This Country, from the New York Morning Herald.* (Philadelphia: Clark and Roser, Jan. 29, 1830), p. 23.

[40] Reverend Isaac Fidler, *Observations on Professions, Literature, Manners and Emigration in the United States . . . in 1832* (New York: 1832), p. 113.

nay almost treble, the amount stated"; and since prices of manufacturers and tradesmen "generally speaking, kept pace with it . . . the only parties to whom this great alteration in the prices of things was seriously detrimental were the working classes. . . . For some time" their appeal to their employers "was made in vain; it then met with partial success, but it was not until the close of the year 1836 when provisions, etc., reached their maximum . . . that their demands were fully complied with." [41] Immediately previous was the author's notation that in 1835–1836 "mechanics were then working upon a scale of prices, or a settled rate of wages, which had been" agreed upon in a previous year "when every necessary of life was to say the least, thirty percent cheaper than at the time of the 'strike.' " [42]

The timing of the strikes can be fixed beginning in mid-1835 and extending into mid-1836.[43] Bezanson's data show Philadelphia wholesale prices of grain rising 50 percent from the summer of 1833 to 1837, and meat prices rising by about 10 percent.[44] The reference to 1834 being 30 percent cheaper than "at the time of the strike" is, however, consistent with the rise of grain, meat, and fish prices at wholesale in Philadelphia— these being the major components of food expenditure at the time. We can, with considerable difficulty, reconcile these data as suggesting the possibility of a strong decline in real income during the extremely sharp price rise from the beginning of 1835 to mid-1836, partially compensated for by the strike rises in 1836.[45]

The vividness of the strike impact in 1835–1836 testifies to reaction to the very earliest stages of organized labor action, but it does not automatically tell us about the real-income change. Taking prices for grain products and meat, the Philadelphia data indicate one striking fact: The 1834–1835 rise was the greatest peacetime rise since before the Revolution, and certainly the greatest ever experienced by most of those in the 1835 labor force. It is not surprising that strikes should have occurred, and that

---

[41] *The British Mechanics and Labourers Hand Book and True Guide to the United States* (London: Charles Knight, 1840), p. 191.

[42] *Ibid.*, p. 190.

[43] "The general strike for higher wages or compensation extended to the boatmen on the Schuylkill which much impeded the navigation for the first three weeks of last month." Letter of Warder Brothers of Philadelphia, Aug. 5, 1835, quoted in Anne Bezanson et al., *Wholesale Prices in Philadelphia, 1784–1861* (1936), p. 206.

[44] *Ibid.*, pp. 368–369.

[45] *The British Mechanics and Labourers Hand Book* notes that "their demands were fully complied with" by the end of 1836, but this does not indicate whether these demands were great enough to stabilize real income; on p. 205 the writer notes that carpenters earned $9 before the strike, got an advance of $1.50 as a result of it, but soon returned to the old standard.

the impression of a marked decline in real income should be deduced. To link to the material shown below with respect to 1835 to 1850, we conclude speculatively that from 1830—our previous termination—to 1835 wages did not change but a 15 percent rise in prices occurred.[46]

1835 to 1850. In October, 1850, the pride of the West, *The Western Journal and Civilian,* found that "This great decline in prices is a gain to the labouring classes who constitute the great body of consumers in every country and if, as we believe, the average money price of wages is as high now as it was in 1835, the profits of labor have increased at least fifty percent since that time." [47] (Labor in the Midwest, according to a contemporary writing about 1841–1842, "is cheaper now by 50 percent than in 1835.")[48]

1850 to 1857. In 1857 an economist found that wages had risen 25 to 50 percent after 1850, but "consequent upon the revulsion [of 1857] are again on the decline, and the still greater difficulty in getting paid, the average this spring is not greater if in reality as high as in 1850, while in many parts the cost of living has nearly doubled." [49] Given a net 10 percent rate rise and a 75 percent price rise, as his measures imply, a 42 percent fall in real wages is obtained.

1855 to 1857. Some idea of the extent to which wages had risen from 1850 to just prior to the 1857 recession is given by comparing the above surmise with one by another writer who found that in the panic the usual rates were cut in half for those still employed. Hundreds of masters, he found, got in debt to their men and failed to pay off.[50] If we take Barry's guess as implying a 42 percent decline and the no less arbitrary guess of a 50 percent fall from 1855 to 1857, we could conclude that wages did not change significantly from 1850 to 1855–1856, falling sharply under the impact of the recession. These inferences are certainly the weakest of those based on contemporary materials.

[46] The 50 percent rise from 1834 to 1836 reported by the *Hand Book* is split in half, judging from the wholesale price pattern for foods, and we reduce it arbitrarily to 15 percent to reflect the more sluggish pattern in Philadelphia prices and other areas not as sensitive as New York to that price change.

[47] Article on "Labor Saving Machinery," No. 1, p. 44. The article refers to the Secretary of the Treasury's data on prices.

[48] *Prospectus of a Railroad from Springfield the Capital of Illinois and the Principal Town in the Interior to Alton . . .* (n.d., n.p.), p. 2. (in Bureau of Railway Economics.) The pamphlet refers to the "ending of the internal improvement system" in the winter of 1840.

[49] Philip Barry, *The Theory and Practice of the International Trade of the United States and England and the Trade of the United States and Canada* (Chicago: D. B. Cooke and Company, 1858), p. 81.

[50] An English workman, *London versus New York* (London: Hosworth and Harrison, 1859), p. 77.

DETERMINANTS OF REAL-WAGE TRENDS

The long-term trend in real wages since 1800 can be summarized as follows. For 1800 to 1860 we show below a highly speculative index of real wages based on our preliminary estimates for various occupations.[1] For 1860 to 1960 we show decennial changes from 3-year averages (Tables A-17, A-19) centered on the decennial dates, rounded to the nearest $50.

Table 4-1. Percent Change in Real Wages

1800–1820	0
1820–1832	25
1832–1850	25
1850–1860	1

Dollar Change in Real Wages (Nonfarm)

1860–1870	−$100
1870–1880	0
1880–1890	100
1890–1900	50
1900–1910	$100
1910–1920	50
1920–1930	200
1930–1940	100
1940–1950	400
1950–1960	400

The moving forces behind these changes can be best seen if we note the break in the patterns of real-wage change:

Average Decennial Change

1832–1850	Marked advance
1850–1880	No rise
1880–1920	$50
1920–1930	200
1930–1940	100
1940–1960	400

This varying pattern is not instantly illuminated by reference to long-term rises in productivity, which provide the basis for real-wage advance. For the advances are by no means as regular as productivity changes would seem to have been. Nor is an adequate explanation to be found in iterative

---

[1] A considerable body of materials is available for estimating the trend prior to 1850 but is not used in these preliminary estimates.

discussion of varying trends in unionization, labor-management relations, the role of government, etc.

We note the importance of three major factors whose interaction provided the basis both for the long-term rise in real wages and for the markedly different rates of change in the decades of this long term: (1) productivity, (2) slavery, and (3) immigration.

1. Productivity

The reverberating gains in real earnings suggested above are unlikely to have occurred if not founded upon concurrent or antecedent advances in productivity. The labor market from 1832 to 1932 was, with a single qualification discussed below, as competitive as any in history. Combinations by workmen, guild traditions, or state-established wage minima were not completely absent, but by comparison with history since 1930 they were of a high order of unimportance in determining wages. Hence we find no basis for believing that the real income of labor advanced at the expense of incomes to the providers of capital or land.[2] While labor gained in unknown measure from changes in the scale of the economy, it was compensated in no mean manner from advances in productivity. We can hardly measure just how the productivity of labor per se changed. For even as the level of labor skill, application, and ingenuity shifted, massive additions were made to the volume of capital equipment with which labor worked, in the productivity of the land where it was sited, in the feverishness of entrepreneurial ability and desire. We therefore content ourselves with the sufficiently difficult task of measuring labor requirements per unit of output for selected products, and accept these trends as indicating the direction taken by labor productivity. Fortunately, the literary materials for much of the nineteenth century suggest a rising income to landowners and to investors in general, so that it is a fair inference that improved factor combinations brought about that happy prospect offered in circus shell games, where everyone wins and nobody loses.

Our estimates for the decline in manpower requirements per unit of output in selected manufacturing industries and sailing vessels, plus Department of Agriculture figures for selected crops, are shown in Table 4-2.[3]

---

[2] Per contra there is no reason in theory why the entrepreneur as a landowner could not have enjoyed lush capital gains as in fact the farmer typically appears to have done in the nineteenth century, nor why qua entrepreneur he should not have richly benefited from the tide of innovations.

[3] Our measures are cotton spindles per man, pig iron produced per man, and 1,000 tons of shipping weight per man, while the USDA figures are man-hours per bushel or bale. Martin Cooper et al., *Progress of Farm Mechanization*, USDA Misc. Publ. 630 (October, 1947), p. 3. We interpolate for 1850 between Cooper's 1840 and 1880 data. Since only limited use is made of these data here, we do not describe their derivation in any detail. It is hoped, however, to provide such derivation elsewhere.

Table 4-2. Labor Requirements per Unit of Output (1800 = 100)

	1800	1850	1900
Cotton textiles......................	100	23*	16
Pig iron.............................	100	50	4
Sailing vessels......................	100	68	45
Steam vessels........................	..	90	30
Wheat................................	100	55	29
Corn.................................	100	70	43
Cotton...............................	100	60	47
Slaves per unit of Southern crops.....	100	24*	

* 1860.

The three nonfarm series report experience for the nation as a whole. The USDA figures, however, only report changes in a given area, hence do not reflect the rise in output per man that arose from the shift to better lands. Lacking estimates for all products we do, however, attempt such a figure for the major Southern crops. These crops were cultivated almost solely by slaves (and, conversely, slaves in agriculture cultivated little but these crops).[4] We therefore relate our estimates of slaves in agriculture to the total real output of cotton, tobacco, hemp, and sugar. The resultant ratio—slaves per unit of Southern crops—appears in Table 4-2.[5]

The marked difference between figures for cotton and total Southern crops testifies primarily to the tremendous advantages of the shift in the center of cotton production from east to west. As William Elliot remarked in 1848:

> Some portion of the cotton growing country must abandon the cultivation: which must *that* be? Surely not that which can make 2,000 pounds where we make 1,200 . . . which can make a profit of 8 cents per pound where we require 10 to give an interest on our investment. . . . Why not look the difficulty in the face? It is we of the

[4] Qualification to allow for the early German settlers in Texas, for tobacco grown in Connecticut, or for corn grown on Southern plantations could hardly make much difference. One clear bias is the understatement of productivity advance: an increasing proportion of slave time was spent in land clearing as the center of production moved to the Gulf states and then westward, which more than compensates for the tendency to increased purchase of corn, clothing, sugar, machinery, and other intermediate products. Hence we tend to overestimate the 1860 number of slaves relatable to the specified crop output. A more precise estimate, therefore, would add strength to our argument for productivity advance.

[5] Gross deflated output from Marvin Towne and Wayne Rasmussen, "Farm Gross Product and Gross Investment during the Nineteenth Century," a paper prepared for the September, 1957, Conference on Research in Income and Wealth, table 10.

Atlantic states who must withdraw ourselves, with whatever regret, from a pursuit which consigns us to beggary. . . . If we would retain our laboring population within our limits, and restrict our young men from

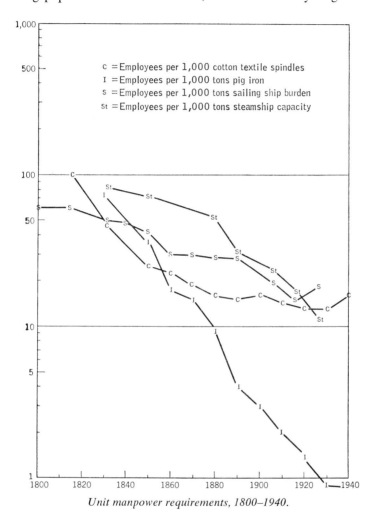

c = Employees per 1,000 cotton textile spindles
I = Employees per 1,000 tons pig iron
s = Employees per 1,000 tons sailing ship burden
St = Employees per 1,000 tons steamship capacity

Unit manpower requirements, 1800–1940.

emigration, we must find some pursuit more profitable than cotton planting.[6]

[6] Elliot continued: "The institution [i.e., slavery] is not wearing away. . . . It is merely marching southward and westward; and in that direction will continue to extend itself as surely as the Gulf stream sweeps in the opposite direction." *An Anniversary Address of the State Agricultural Society of South Carolina, Delivered in the Hall of the House of Representatives, November 30, 1848* (Charleston: Miller and Browne, 1849), pp. 31, 43.

Emigration continued in the 1850s as in the 1830s and 1840s. And the application of slave labor to better soils (plus the shift from other crops to sugar in Louisiana and from cotton to tobacco in Virginia and North Carolina) brought a massive increase in Southern output per slave. The plantation owner in 1850 found himself on a far more congenial portion of the production function because of the superior combination of land, labor, and technique that he was working with than his typical predecessor in 1820 or 1830 had.

But unfortunately for the simplest possible explanation, our data on wages extend past 1850. And while the rates of productivity advance are trivial compared to the soaring gains to 1850, they are nonetheless substantial—judged by changes in more recent decades. More important, they do not show the short-term irregularities that the wage data for the next 50 years do. We must therefore turn from the demand side of the labor market to two major supply factors where we believe the explanation to lie.

2. Slavery

The frequent opposition of Northern labor to slavery is a matter of record in congressional debates. Many a historian has concluded that "as slaves the Negroes were, in fact, more ruinous economic competitors of white labor than they were as freemen." [7] Yet a look at the economic relationships suggests that slavery contributed to keeping up the level of wages for Northern labor, while the ending of slavery contributed to depressing that wage level. We do not here attempt any overall assessment of the social context: Had slavery been absent throughout our history or ended at an earlier date, so many other forces would have been brought into play that output and real wages per employee might have differed largely from what they were.

We are, instead, focusing on Bagehot's axiom of mobility; as assumed in "English political economy," it requires that "there must be no competing system of involuntary labor limiting the number of employments or moving between them." [8] Such an axiom does not hold where half a nation consists of slaveholders and slaves. Nor do its usual corollaries with respect to the determination of wages.

In 1850 there were 1.9 million slaves, their labor provided by 347,000 slaveholders, 100,000 of them with 10 or more slaves. [9] In 1860 the 4.0 million slaves were possessed by 385,000 slave holders, with 85 percent the property of 175,000 owners. [10] The larger owners supplied blocks of

[7] The phrase is from perhaps the ablest volume we have on American slavery: Kenneth Stampp, *The Peculiar Institution* (1956), p. 426.

[8] Walter Bagehot, *Economic Studies* (1895), pp. 52–53.

[9] 1850 Census, *Compendium,* p. 95.

[10] U.S. Census, *Agriculture of the United States in 1860* (1864), p. 247.

labor to the turpentine company, the plantation owner, the steamboat line, treating as equals with the renters. On the other hand the largest number of slave owners were in no such position. We dare not, therefore, conclude that the tone of the market was set by a small group of oligopolists, other sellers sheltering under their price policies. But we can, on the other hand, take the persistent flow of rentals and sales by owners of all types as a basis for inference. Such frequency of alternatives open to slave owners, and in fact used by owners of both few and many slaves, suggests that alternative investments gave them a basis for establishing earnings on their slave property. The substantial increase in slave owners from 1790 to 1850, and from 1850 to 1860, suggests that increasing numbers of Southern entrepreneurs found ownership to be an attractive industry. Because many of them concurrently invested in local banks and railroads, borrowed money for slave purchase, they had a clear measure of alternative investment returns open to them.

What follows? The hiring rates they set for their slaves must needs have covered not merely (1) the cost of slave subsistence, but also (2) a net return on slave hiring equivalent to the net return from alternative investments. Had the slaves sold their own labor as individuals in a completely free market, their own reservation prices would have been somewhat above subsistence levels but below that achieved by their masters.[11] That gap is a measure of the difference in wage levels paid for nonwhite hiring under free and slave conditions. In the end the reservation price that the slave owner could insist on, given alternative investment opportunities, was above what the individual laborer could command.

But the slave and free labor markets were not isolated. Competition through the product markets meant that Kentucky hogs were sold in competition with hogs from Ohio, that corn from Indiana was bought by Southern plantation owners in competition with corn raised in Virginia. Free and slave labor mingled in competition in the settling of the western territories. Northern mechanics went to the South to work in the winter. And immigrants chose between working on canals in Pennsylvania and Ohio or those in Louisiana and Virginia.

Given these currents of competition in both product and factor markets, we would expect any dominant force in setting Southern hiring rates for slaves to have its decisive impact on Northern wages as well. If Northern wages were thus supported above free market levels by the way in which nonwhite labor was marketed under slavery, we would expect a sizable impact to have resulted from putting 2 million former slaves into the free labor force almost in a single year. No longer supplied by those who evaluated a return on such labor in terms of alternative investments (and

---

[11] Unlike free labor, the owners can resist a reduction in wages. Adam Hodgson, *Letters from North America* (London, 1824), p. 87.

were able to transfer its use into other areas until an adequate level of return was achieved), the rewards to nonwhite labor should have fallen relatively. And the occupations in which such labor most directly competed should have been most substantially affected. The quantity of ex-slave labor supplied and used in farming would not have changed substantially, while that in domestic service was affected in unknown measure. Hence we cannot anticipate a priori how the absolute level of Negro hiring rates would be affected. But the effect on relative wage trends in the occupations most affected can be inferred.

What, in fact, do the data show? For the decade 1860 to 1869 we have the following indications:[12]

Percent Gains in Wage Rates, 1860 to 1869

	North		South		
	New England	Middle Atlantic	Atlantic	East Central	West Central
Carpenters................	80	98	54	59	43
Iron and steel employees....	61	53	22	31	37
Common labor............	51	49	26	39	27
Domestics................	63	68	25	15	−35
Farm labor..............	34	40	−14	−9	−9

Southern wage rates for carpenters, ironworkers, and common labor rose, but far more feebly than Northern rates—largely because of the war's destruction, and the disorganization that marked the end of the slave economy. The former slaves, however, competed primarily in the market for domestics and farm laborers. The rate for domestics gained far less than for the three former occupations in the South, even declining in one region. And the rate for farm laborers actually fell in each of the three Southern regions. Such wage weakness, since cotton production was up to prewar levels, could not well have reflected any decline in the demands for labor. We infer that the decline in wage rates paid to Southern farm labor from 1860 to 1870 reflects in significant degree the inferior bargaining position of the individual farm laborer as compared with that of the slave owner.

The presence of 2 million farmer slaves in the free-labor market of the 1864–1880 period would, therefore, appear to be a major factor in accounting for the lack of any estimated real-wage gain in these years. Correspondingly, we infer that their different status in earlier years had

---

[12] Wage data are from the Appendix. For iron and steel employees we use full-time equivalent earnings.

helped bring advances in real wages greater than would have taken place if the same labor had been supplied by an equal number of individual laborers. Our measurements here are peculiarly complicated. Hiring rates for nonwhites fell. But the real incomes of nonwhites probably rose from the subsistence levels of slavery as depreciation on slave capital was no longer necessary, and as the effort exerted by free nonwhites was probably significantly greater than that by slaves.

3. Immigration

Several centuries of labor opposition to immigration indicate contemporary judgments that the inflow of migrant labor tended to keep down American wages. We have argued its dynamic advantages in our discussion of sources of American productivity. This migration induced a vast, durable increase in productivity and thereby wages. But its static, short-run effects even more clearly tended to keep wages down. Henry Carey, a supporter of unrestricted immigration and a leading economist of his time, found flatly that "the more the supply of labor the lower must certainly become its price." [13] The result was not merely the normal tendency for an increase in supply, at a given demand, to drive the wage rate down. It was, in addition, the influence deriving from lower levels of living to which Europeans were accustomed. As early as 1791 G. Cabot asserted that the wages of common labor are "much higher here" than in Europe.[14] In later years estimates that United States wages were three times as great as European levels were made. An observer in 1850, sympathetic to immigrants though he was, nonetheless found that "The wages of Dutch and Germans at home being only about 2s6d [50 cents] per week . . . they soon get themselves into employment, by working at a lower rate of wages than the Yankees, which has caused a great reduction in the price of labor. . . ." [15] And one of the earliest American labor leaders flatly denounced the employment of "outsiders" as being responsible for wage cuts.[16]

[13] Admitting the tendency but arguing the advantage, Carey went on to say: "Nevertheless . . . the growth of wages has always kept even pace with the growth of immigration." *Constitutional Convention of Pennsylvania, Report of the Committee on Industrial Interests and Labor, H. C. Carey, Chairman* (Philadelphia, 1873), p. 13.

[14] Quoted by Robert Rantoul, "The First Cotton Mill in America," *Historical Collections of the Essex Institute* (Jan.-June, 1897), p. 41.

[15] The writer continued: "They are intensely disliked by the laboring Yankees, and indeed by all except those who employ them; yet they are, notwithstanding, truly faithful and honest in their transactions." George Nettle, *A Practical Guide for Emigrants to North America* (London: 1850), p. 28.

[16] Luther Seth, *Address to Workingmen of New England* (1832), pp. 13, 16. Representative Woodbury, from the same state: "What sir! We whose revolutionary victories were won, in part by foreigners . . . by the Lafayettes, the Paul Joneses, the Kosciuskos and Steubens . . . now prate about our being inundated by the cheap laborers, as well as the cheap labor of Ireland, Germany and England . . . we whose

Many an observer felt that protection against foreign labor was warranted as much as tariff protection against foreign goods. "There is no protection for the carpenter or the bricklayer," wrote Theodore Parker, with some heat. "Yet if we cared for men more than money, and were consistent with our principles of protection, why we should exclude all foreign workmen as well as their work, and so raise the wages of native hands." [17]

We may combine the wage data shown above into major periods, and contrast it with corresponding changes in the ratio of immigrants (taken to indicate the immigrant labor-force change) to labor force.[18]

Date	Decennial change in real wages	Ratio of immigration to labor-force increase
1832–1850	+25%	53%
1850–1860	+1%	91
1860–1880	−$ 60	74
1880–1900	+ 75	60
1900–1914	+$ 90	73
1914–1930	+ 126	40

Each pair of figures relates to periods for which our wage-change estimates are from similar sources and of approximately equal quality. Nor have we any reason to feel that sharp differences in productivity advance occurred in one more than in the other member of any pair. Nevertheless, for each pair we find that the greater real-wage gain is associated with the smaller ratio of immigration to labor-force increase. The data do suggest that heavy increases in the flow of immigrants tended to depress wage increases despite rising real factor productivity.

Figure 25 summarizes the advance of real income per nonfarm employee in the century from 1860 to 1960. We note three major periods of significant change.

---

forests have been felled, whose canals dug, and railroads laid . . . will next seek to exclude from our shores this very foreign labor." *Congressional Globe*, June, 1842, appendix, p. 692. The attitude of the labor movement, treated in earlier classic studies by Commons and Ware, is graphically summarized in Arthur Schlesinger, Jr., *The Age of Jackson* (1945).

[17] Quoted in Henry Steele Commager, *Theodore Parker, Yankee Crusader* (1936) p. 184. See also similar position taken by the A. F. of L., in Philip Taft, *The A. F. of L. in the Time of Gompers* (1957), pp. 302–08.

[18] Immigration estimates for 1830 to 1870 are by Rossiter. These plus estimates for later years by Simon Kuznets and Ernest Rubin appear in the latter's *Immigration and the Foreign Born* (1954), p. 94.

1870 to 1920.   After the immediate reconstruction needs had been met, the depression of the 1870s kept real-wage rates at a dead level. Beginning in 1880 (or even in the mid-1860s) the course of wages is equable and upward on to 1920. The complex jostling of productivity advance, the varying tide of migration, and the business cycle give the fairly smooth major trend shown here, of about a $7 rise per year.

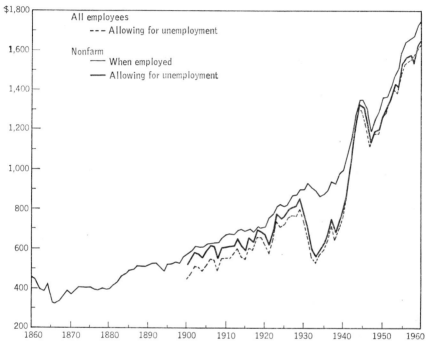

Figure 25.   Real income per employee, 1860–1960 (1914 dollars). See Tables A-16 and A-17.

1920 to 1930.   In the decade after 1920, however, this annual gain about tripled. We find it most unlikely that the rate of productivity advance or the nature of the productivity advance changed so at this point as to explain this turn.[19] Instead we find that halting the flow of millions of migrants, who entered the United States labor market with low wage horizons, offers a much more reasonable explanation of the speed-up in real-wage advance.[20] Political changes in the labor supply can be more

[19] Recent studies on total factor productivity suggest a turning point in capital-labor ratios in 1919. We find no adequate basis as yet for accepting such conclusions. If valid, they still leave the problem of causation: Did rising wages because of shortened supply bring pressures to adopt more capital intensive techniques?

[20] This explanation, which has been offered by many previous writers, is more or less accepted in the recent significant study by Albert Rees, *Real Wages Manufacturing, 1890–1914* (1961), p. 126.

effective in determining wages than even explicit attempts to fix wages. **1946 to 1960.** Perhaps the most striking part of the record describes the gains since the end of the war. After the depression declines of the 1930s and the high-pressure gains of the war years, we might have expected a return to something like the prewar rate of advance. Instead a steep gain for wages appears—steeper than in any decade since 1860, and one not much inferior to the 1938–1945 gain. Some role there must be for union bargaining, as for employer attempts to recruit a high-quality labor force. But we place major emphasis on factors associated with government intervention in both product and factor markets. In the product market the government became a massive peacetime purchaser. Buying in such overwhelming volume, emphasizing new military items (for which precise costing is difficult), and lacking the cost incentives and procedures developed by private enterprise, the government exerted feebler pressure to keep down the cost of input items required for its purchases than would entrepreneurs taking an equal volume.

Direct government actions in the factor markets were significant as well. First was the assurance that neither political party would allow another major depression to develop, plus the demonstration by both parties that action would be taken to halt cycle downturns. The traditional effect of depressions in halting real-wage gains was thus muted. Secondly, accelerated amortization and new depreciation policies speeded the introduction of new capital equipment and raised the productivity of labor, its major complementary factor. Wage rates have reflected the capturing of such advance. A precise analysis of short-period wage determination is outside our present purpose. But such analysis of the annual figures is necessary for a full understanding of how even the three tidal movements that we have outlined came to be.

CHANGES IN UNEMPLOYMENT: 1800 TO 1960 †

What, a young knave and without work? Is there not wars? Is there not employment?

King Henry IV, Part 2

Whether capitalism contained within itself the seeds of its destruction has been a question of lively interest since its earliest days. To some historians, who saw "under the aspect of eternity," the more or less inevitable decline of any social order, any economic system, was to be expected. To the

† Several pages are reprinted by kind permission of the Princeton University Press from an earlier study by the author appearing in Universities–National Bureau of Economic Research, *The Measurement and Behavior of Unemployment* (1957).

Marxists, of course, the doom of this particular order was guaranteed in a secular holy writ. To less-committed economists, as well, business cycle changes in the Western world have been a subject of keen concern both for the economic problems they pose and for the humanitarian issues they evoke. Now any long-term variation in the effectiveness with which an economy uses its resources must be intimately linked with variations in its ability to use its major perishable resource—manpower. Hence the American unemployment record will reflect any trend toward higher levels of unemployed resources. It may also cast a distant light on a substratum of attitudes that, however confused and outdated, in fact underlies the ideologies of labor and management in today's labor-market negotiations. After reviewing (A) the meaning and definition of unemployment in a free society, we consider (B) what opposing economic forces tended to drive the long-term level of unemployment away from that prevailing during the lives of the founding fathers. We then review (C) the available indications as to what the order of magnitude was in the unemployment crises since 1819; and conclude (D) with a look at the changing dimensions of unemployment in the United States since 1800.

A. Meaning of Long-period Unemployment Comparisons

Unemployment appears to have arrived in America with the white man. Want and misery had stalked among the Indians, of course, but unemployment was another matter. In 1850, for example, when the Gold Rush was tapering off, men walked the streets of San Francisco looking for work. But the nearby Digger Indians were fully employed, as had been their ancestors, gathering a dietary of grasshoppers and roots. In the Indian society, as in any composed of the self-employed (or serfs, slaves, or labor-camp inmates), no unemployment need exist. And even a society of wage earners can correctly boast that it has no unemployed if government policy forces disemployed workers into jobs regardless of their customary skills or earnings levels. But in a free nation, with a standard of living and social standards that permit an unemployed worker to remain without work while seeking a job he considers satisfactory, unemployment is to be expected. The social problem in such a society will concern how to reduce unemployment and how to shorten its duration, rather than how to abolish unemployment.

The first factor that affects long-period comparisons stems from this aspect of American society. As real incomes have risen over the decades so has the ability of the unemployed to refuse the first job available (if it is below standard), to delay until he finds "suitable" work. And as social institutions have changed (in particular, as unemployment compensation has been introduced, supplemental benefits pioneered, health services extended), this effect has been intensified.

A second factor in historical comparisons is that of changing social attitude. Not wholly independent of the first factor noted has been the growing
willingness of society to consider that unemployment does not automatically imply character deterioration. "Everybody knows that the unemployed
are the victims of their own idle, irregular courses" Arthur Young could
write years ago. "Some folks won't work" was the characteristic phrase
even in the 1920s. But after the extended experience of the Great Depression it became difficult to consider unemployment something between
personal fault and venial sin. After unemployment compensation to veterans in 1945–1946 helped create the phrase "the 52-20 club," after a national policy of working toward maximum production and employment was
first defined in 1946, the final steps were taken to demonstrate that unemployment today is considered as a social problem, requiring social as well
as individual action. Out of such experience may come better reporting of
actual unemployment today than, say, in 1900. Housewives may now be
less ashamed to admit to a Census Bureau enumerator that the family head
is without work.

A contrary force that has become particularly important since the turn
of the twentieth century is the driving tendency to put women into jobs
once considered the province of adult males. In 1900, 18 percent of our
labor was female. By 1960 the proportion was nearly twice as great. This
difference gives an unprecedented flexibility to the labor force. For while
previously one could assume that a given employment decline brought an
almost precisely commensurate unemployment rise, this is no longer true.
The most spectacular example, of course, was the transition in 1945–1946,
when, for the first time in our history, a massive decline in employment
took place without bringing an almost equally massive rise in unemployment.[1] Another recent demonstration that when women become disemployed they tend to move directly out of the labor force, rather than enter
the ranks of the unemployed, is afforded by the recession change from
December, 1948, to 1949. Millions of men and women lost their jobs, but
while half the men became unemployed only 18 percent of the women did.[2]

---

[1] The rise in unemployment insurance claims that took place does not, according
to present definitions of unemployment, indicate a rise in unemployment as measured
by direct enumeration. Although the author has opposed this position (*Review of
Economics and Statistics,* November, 1954), we must admit that a good many
women who received unemployment compensation during this period were not
looking for work with an intensity equal to that which characterizes the male unemployed in most years.

[2] U.S. Bureau of the Census, *Annual Report on the Labor Force, 1949,* ser. P-50,
no. 19, table 20. These data relate to gross changes. While subject to distinct limitations for other uses, the steadiness of the contrast between male and female rates
justifies their use here. Unfortunately we lack gross-change data for 1953. Because
of the sample revision for 1953–1954, even the absolute figures on unemployment are
in question. However, if we look to the October–December changes in unemploy-

A fourth force—the long-term improvement in morbidity and medical care—may have brought a slight reduction in unemployment rates at equivalent levels in the business cycle. We know from contemporary literature that malaria, "the agues," and "the shakes" were commonplace during the first half of the nineteenth century, whether in the Louisiana swamps or the Illinois lowlands.[3]

However, the decline in lost time since the turn of the twentieth century appears to have been less significant. Data for nonfarm male workers are available for several dates. In 1900 an average of a week was lost each year in illness; in 1915–1917, about the same; and nationwide surveys in February, 1949, and September, 1950, again report a similar figure.[4]

Since our present (Current Population Survey) series includes among the unemployed not all persons who are ill but only those who were seeking work when they became temporarily ill, we must conclude that the improvements in public health have had some measured effect in reducing unemployment, but only a minimal one.

Finally, the extensive development of paid vacations since the 1940s has tended to reduce the level of noncyclical unemployment compared to previous decades. Summer declines in demand, seasonal shutdowns, changes in models brought unemployment in earlier years. They do so today as well; but the growth in paid vacations has begun to neutralize this result. A forced vacation is one thing; going fishing while on the payroll is another. Some 4 million persons with jobs reported themselves on vacation in July, 1951, 3 million of them being on paid vacations, while millions vacationed in other months.[5]

We assume that only a fortunate few enjoyed paid vacations at any point in the nineteenth century, while a crude estimate suggests that paid vacations even as recently as 1900 were only one-tenth as common as in 1960.[6]

---

ment by sex (U.S. Bureau of the Census, *Annual Report on the Labor Force, 1954,* ser. P-50, no. 59, tables C-1 and D-1), a similar pattern is suggested.

[3] See Chap. 5.

[4] The 1900 figure is derived from the 1901 Cost of Living Survey, *Eighteenth Annual Report of the Commissioner of Labor,* U.S. Departments of Commerce and Labor (1903). The 1915–1917 figures are based on surveys made by the Metropolitan Life Insurance Company of its policyholders in seven communities. See also Ernest Bradford, *Industrial Unemployment,* Bureau of Labor Statistics Bulletin 310 (1922), p. 32, where other surveys in 1913, 1917, etc., report similar results. The 1949–1950 data appear in Theodore Woolsey, *Estimates of Disabling Illness Prevalent in the United States,* Public Health Monograph 4 (1952), and in unpublished census data.

[5] From unpublished census data. For other recent years the data suggest similar results; they cannot be used, however, because they include the effect of the Fourth of July holiday.

[6] The 1901 Cost of Living Survey of 24,402 families, found only 784 reporting vacations as a cause of nonemployment, with an average duration of 2.61

Although we shall consider below other factors that have changed the levels of unemployment since 1800, several of the foregoing social changes have affected the very meaning of comparisons of unemployment over the years. We may contend that their effects have not been great. We may even contend that they produce fewer incomparabilities than are involved in long-period deflation of dollar aggregates in a period of changing tastes and preferences. But such contentions do not contravene the limitations that afflict long-period comparisons. We are involved here in the familiar index-number problem. We must meet it, as is usual, by "looking the difficulty boldly in the face, and then passing on."

B. Opposing Forces

> *Good mechanics of almost all descriptions are much wanted in this state [Indiana]. They can here find constant and lucrative employment.*[7]

1. Since the period under concern was a booming one (in which mass migration to the Midwest was under way) and 1835–1836 was a business cycle peak, the reference not merely to lucrative but to "constant employment" is particularly suggestive. The free American labor market prior to 1860 was largely one of pure competition, but not one of perfect competition. The extent of worker and employer ignorance about short-term changes in market opportunities and requirements beyond their immediate area is hard to imagine in these days of high communication, daily newspapers, and Employment Service reports. Wages during the 1819–1820 crisis could plummet in Philadelphia, while rates in Lexington, Kentucky, were hardly affected. This could hardly occur in a perfect market.

As late as 1900 Jacob Riis could describe how, in a Long Island suburb, "work goes often begging in my sight, while men and women starve for it in the tenement house city." [8]

In part these imperfections reflect ignorance as to alternatives. In part they also reflect high costs of transport. No intercity bus lines, not even the cheap jalopies of the 1930s, existed to facilitate migration. A horse

---

weeks. *Eighteenth Annual Report of the Commissioner of Labor,* pp. 287, 291. Had the same percentage of labor-force time been spent on vacations in 1960, 110,000 would have been on vacation. The actual figure was 1,576,000, or more than ten times as great. Bureau of Labor Statistics, Special Labor Force Report No. 14, "Labor Force and Employment in 1960," tables B-1, E-1. A small number of persons reported "sickness and vacation" or "slack work and vacation" in 1901.

[7] *Steele's Western Guide Book and Emigrants Directory* (Buffalo: Oliver G. Steele, 1836), p. 76.

[8] In John P. Peters, *Labor and Capital* (1902), p. 426. "Twenty thousand harvesters are needed in Kansas. Any day New York City could turn up forty thousand men without work. How to bring them and the work together?"

cost the equivalent of 3 months' pay for the average worker in the 1830s. Even shoe leather had to be conserved, a pair of shoes costing a farm laborer more than a fourth of the money he received each month in addition to his board. With ignorance, cost, and resistance to mobility combining to create market imperfections, the fairly prompt meshing of job openings and available workers that was usual in the 1950s was atypical a century ago. The result was a tendency toward a higher level of unemployment during the many years of prosperity and business advance.[9]

2. Another factor that tended to push unemployment levels in the nineteenth century above those in the twentieth was the industrial composition of the labor force. Our major employer was the farm—but farming employment is notoriously affected by the weather. In the nineteenth century the weather's effect in shortening job duration, forcing the search for new work, was pronounced. Farming could provide only 7 or 8 months' steady work even to those employees who were considered regular workers. "A year in some farming states, such as Pennsylvania, is only of eight months' duration, four months being lost to the labourer, who is turned away as an useless animal" according to a traveler perhaps overly impressed by the 1818–1820 recession.[10]

A writer in the 1860s urged young men to work as farmhands if they would accumulate a downpayment on a farm. Such work, he admitted, would be available only for the "7 or 8 months of the busy season," but they might "teach school through the winter, or find some kind of jobwork." [11] And somewhat later Horace Greeley, telling the expectant world what he knew about farming, found that "the dearth of employment in winter for farm laborers is a great and growing evil . . . in its present magnitude it is a very modern evil. . . . Within my recollection there was timber to cut and haul to the saw mill, wood to cut . . . forest land to be cleared and fitted for future cultivation, even in New England." [12]

The best overall judgment may well be that of the serious soul who warned the potential emigrant that "unless you can obtain an engagement for 6 or 12 months, which you will probably be able to do if you are a steady and useful servant, you may very frequently be exposed to lost time in changing of places and looking about." [13] What with the sharp contrasts

---

[9] A survey of factory employees in Massachusetts (a state with better than average communications and transport) as late as 1875 reported an average of 241 days occupied. Massachusetts Bureau of Labor survey, quoted in Joseph Cook, *Labor, with Preludes on Current Events* (1880), p. 159.

[10] W. Faux, *Memorable Days in America* (1823; reprint 1905), p. 141.

[11] *How to Get a Farm and Where to Find One,* by the author of *Ten Acres Enough* (New York: 1864), p. 56.

[12] Horace Greeley, *What I Know of Farming* (1871), p. 303.

[13] Thomas Dudgeon, *A Nine Years' Residence and a Nine Months' Tour on Foot in the States of New York and Pennsylvania* (Edinburgh: Thornton and Collie, 1841), p. 19.

between Old and New World practices and the normal difference of opinion between master and employee as to what constitutes "a steady and useful servant," a succession of short-term engagements must have been relatively common in this leading American industry.

Perhaps second to farming as an employer of adult men prior to 1860 was ocean transportation—the classical home of casual employment, short-term jobs. Most employees in ocean transportation were engaged in the coasting trade. Ignoring the really short trips, providing employment for a mere month or two, what about the traditional long coasting run from New England to the West Indies? A typical round trip in 1790 took 5 months and 9 days; a typical trip in 1839 took nearly 5 months; and during the years of the Napoleonic Wars turnaround was reduced even further.[14] In later years the job durations were, if anything, somewhat shortened. The next largest group in ocean transport consisted of those on trips to Liverpool, Lubeck, Kronstadt or Havre. The average round-trip voyage in the 1812 period ran from 6 to 8 months, while in later years no great change in duration took place.[15]

Men were on the beach at the end of every such voyage until they could find another berth. Even in the palmiest days of the crimps this meant a period of unemployment. (Long-duration employment was, of course, available in whaling, but the brilliance of writers on maritime topics has shadowed the fact that only 1 or 2 percent of the labor force was in whaling.) By the twentieth century the typical transport employer was the railroad or the street railway, the stability of whose employment was notoriously greater than shipping.

3. Still another factor was the greater extent to which the nonfarm industry was subject to the weather. For the vagaries of the weather, as well as the long winter months, augmented the irregularity of employment. All outdoor operatives, in some trades, wrote George Nettle in 1850, are "suspended during the 4 or 5 winter months." Many "go into the South for employment in the winter." [16]

The largest manufacturing industry in the nation in the nineteenth cen-

---

[14] Essex Institute, Derby Papers, vol. XXVI, Ships' Papers, Portledge Bill for Schooner *Rose*; David Pingree Papers, Brig *Pactolus,* folders for seventeenth to twentieth, twenty-first to twenty-fourth voyages. For the Napoleonic period see the section on Productivity.

[15] *Report of the Committee of the House of Representatives of Massachusetts on the Subject of Impressed Seamen, with the Evidence and Documents Accompanying It, Published by Order of the House of Representatives* (Boston: Russell and Cutler, 1813), p. 52. Israel Thorndike, one of the largest shippers and one of richest men in the nation, stated that his voyages averaged 6 to 8 months. For later years, durations are given in the ships' articles cited in the section on seamen's wages (Chap. 6).

[16] George Nettle, *A Practical Guide for Emigrants to North America* (London: 1850), p. 57.

tury was constituted by country grist and oil mills. In the North and West the mills were at the mercy of the weather, and millers would be hired "only for this coming fall or so long as the Mill can run before freesing up." [17]

When iron manufacturing was becoming a major industry in the 1830s · it was common for ironworks to shut down for several months of frost and snow.[18]

The hand trades that preceded full-scale manufactures offered similarly broken periods of employment. The typical example was the Haverhill farmer or the Marblehead fisherman who turned shoemaker for part of the year. And even an idealized description of the early metalworking industry referred to "Seth Steady, the blacksmith . . . (whose) hammer is heard at the dawn of day, and the fire blazes in his shop during the evenings from the 20th of September till the 20th of March." [19]

In these many occupations that complemented farming, breaks in continuity of employment, particularly for employees, were to be expected in the shift from one to the other.

Construction, of course, provided irregular employment. Severe winter weather kept house carpenters and masons "from working for several months [out of the year]. The case is the same with the day labourer in agriculture." [20]

Transportation was even more affected. When mud ruts constituted the only links between the states, transportation employment was notably irregular. And when the great internal roadsteads—the Erie, the Pennsylvania, the Ohio, and the other canals—were opened to navigation, they had to be closed an average of 4 months every year for cold weather.[21]

4. Opposed to such influences which tended to create a level of unemployment in the nineteenth above that in the twentieth century was the fundamental difference in the class-of-worker groups in the labor force. Slaves were not unemployed. Farmers were not unemployed. Self-employed carpenters, saddlers, weavers, fishermen were not unemployed.

[17] Seymour Dunbar (ed.), *The Journals and Letters of Major John Owen, 1850–1871* (1927), p. 69.

[18] The McLane Report, *Documents on Manufactures* (1833), U.S. Congress, Serial Set 222, vol. II, pp. 303, 363, and *passim.*

[19] S. W. Cole (ed.), *New England Farmer* (Sept. 15, 1849), vol. 1, no. 20. See Caroline Hazard (ed.), *Nailer Tom's Diary . . . 1778–1840* (1930), for repeated indications of shifts from blacksmithing to farming and back again.

[20] Richard Parkinson, *A Tour in America* (London: J. Harding, 1805), vol. II, p. 593.

[21] Michel Chevalier, *Histoire et Description des Voies de Communication aux Etats Unis* (Paris: Librairie de Charles Gosselin, 1840), vol. I, p. 253. Chevalier reports the dates of opening and closing of the Erie Canal for many years, indicating an average of 75 days a year lost during the 1817–1830 period and 133 days in the 1830s because of the weather.

Taken as a whole, such categories accounted for nearly the entire labor force in 1800. By 1950 they accounted for under 10 percent. The decline in farming, the end of slavery, the growth of factories transformed the labor force from one made up of slaves and husbandmen into one of wage earners:

Percent of Total Labor Force

Date	Farmers	Slaves
1800	61	28
1850	46	24
1900	20	0
1950	7	0

The gains in the wage-earner group, of necessity, meant a rise in the proportion exposed to unemployment. The normal vicissitudes of a round-about process of production, changing patterns of consumer tastes, freedom of workers to seek better jobs, freedom of employers to seek other employees than their present ones—all these meant that a rising unemployment level would tend to be associated with the new dominance of wage earners in the labor-force total. While a slave may be unproductive, and an itinerant organ grinder may earn under a dollar a week, they are not "seeking work" and do not therefore belong with the unemployed.[22] Wage earners of equally low productivity, on the other hand, are likely to be fired, to join the ranks of the unemployed. Hence both voluntary and involuntary additions to the unemployed tend to be larger when the employee proportion of the labor force grows.

5. The steady advance of technology has brought technological unemployment in every decade since Tubal-cain. Whether the proportion of employees displaced in earlier decades of this nation was greater or less than in recent decades cannot be determined without more material than is now available. Surmise, favored with little evidence, suggests no tendency toward a decrease in unemployment from this source.[23]

C. Unemployment in Crisis Years since 1807

It was a wearily perceptive and resigned former President (if John Adams could ever have rightly been called resigned) who wrote: "I am old enough to remember the war of 1745 and its end, the war of 1755 and

[22] Current United States estimates include, in principle, anyone who says he is seeking work even if he is self-employed. The reported number in such categories is trivial. In fact we may contend that by seeking work they have changed their status to that of employees; if they can obtain work it will necessarily only be as employees.

[23] The problem is discussed at somewhat greater length by the author in 86th Cong., 2d Sess., Joint Economic Committee, Employment, Growth and Price Levels, *Hearings,* Part 3, p. 581.

its termination, the War of 1812 and its pacification. Every one of those wars has been followed by a general distress, embarrassments of commerce, destruction of manufactures, fall of the price of produce and lands." [24]

Let us consider some major periods of "general distress."

1807. Three days before Christmas, 1807, President Jefferson initiated the embargo. By February 500 ships in the port of New York had been decommissioned; not a crossing was made from New York or Boston to Liverpool in 1808, and thousands of seamen entered the British service.[25] Maritime employment, the largest nonfarm industry of the day, fell sharply, declining about 50 percent in New York, Boston, and Norfolk.[26] (However, shipping out of more southerly ports was not so affected, actually rising 50 percent in the major port of Charleston.[27]) There is little evidence that employment levels changed much in the largest industry, farming.

1812. Again in 1812 employment in shipping was slashed (by the war) as the data on tonnage entered indicate:[28]

1810	909
1811	948
1812	668
1813	238
1814	60
1815	701
1816	877

The cut imposed its gravest consequence on the large cities in the North. Unemployed seamen either made their way to Canada to ship in British boats, or remained on the town.[29] But with only 60,000 seamen out of a labor force of 2.2 million, an unemployment problem of national dimensions did not develop.[30]

1819. The first primarily commercial crisis that shook the new nation in the nineteenth century was that of 1818 to 1820. To the contagion from Europe's distress were added the effects of heavy importation of English goods as the United Kingdom attempted to wrest its former markets from

[24] *Works,* vol. X, p. 384, quoted in V. S. Clark, *History of American Manufactures* (1929), vol. I, p. 134.

[25] Works Progress Administration, *A Maritime History of New York* (1941), p. 96.

[26] *Report of the Secretary of the Treasury on Hospital Money, December 1834,* 23rd Cong., 2d Sess., Sen. Doc. 7, pp. 7, 8, 16. The report provides data on the amount of money deducted from seamen's pay for hospital support. Since a flat 20 cents a month was deducted, we may use the trend in such deductions as a measure for the employment trend.

[27] *Ibid.,* p. 25.

[28] Millions of tons, American vessels. See *Historical Statistics,* p. 216.

[29] Robert G. Albion and J. B. Pope, *Sea Lanes and Wartime* (1942), p. 96.

[30] That other problems developed is, of course, testified to by the convening of the Hartford Convention, etc.

the new American factories. "Brothers, A deep shadow has passed over our land" wrote a fraternal order of the time; "a commercial and individual gloom has created a universal stillness. In our remotest villages the hammer is not heard." [31] The Secretary of the Treasury, William Crawford, took no more optimistic view: "Few examples have occurred, of a distress so general and so severe, as that which has been exhibited in the United States." [32] And James Flint, having traveled by horse and stage through the Eastern and Midwestern states thought "that I have seen upwards of 1,500 men in quest of work within 11 months past." [33]

When, in November, 1819, *The Three Sallys* sailed from Philadelphia, 101 English workmen were aboard—men who had hopefully migrated to the United States but were now going on to Cuba in the hope of finding work.[34]

Can we combine such impressionistic material into pedestrian estimates? Hardly with ease or confidence. But we are afforded a slightly better basis of estimate from the endeavors of the contemporary National Institution. Seeking to secure higher tariffs to prevent the inflow of British-manufactured goods after the end of the Napoleonic Wars, this group developed the infant industry argument, later to be attributed to List and continental writers, and also collected a spate of numbers of employment changes in the new manufacturing centers. We can summarize from one of their reports as follows:[35]

Hands Employed in Manufacturing 1816–1819

Location	Date	Cotton goods	Woolens	Iron
Philadelphia......	1816	2,325	1,226	1,152
	1819	149	260	52
Pittsburgh........	1815	42	63	163
	1819	0	16	40
Rhode Island......	1816	15,253		
	1819	3,916		

[31] *Address of the Society of the Tammany or Columbian Order to Its Absent Members* (New York: George L. Buch and Co., 1819), p. 1.

[32] Quoted in Matthew Carey (ed.), *Cursory Views of the Liberal and Restrictive Systems of Political Economy . . . by a Citizen of Philadelphia* (Philadelphia: J. R. A. Skerrett, 1826), p. 16.

[33] James Flint, *Letters from America* (1822; reprint 1904), pp. 226–227. Flint's travels were in the period 1818–1820.

[34] Franklin D. Scott (ed.), *Baron Klinkowstrom's America, 1818–1820* (1952), p. 179.

[35] Summary estimates based on data from *Circular and Address of the National Institution for Promoting Industry in the United States, to Their Fellow Citizens* (New York: J. Seymour, 1820), pp. 21ff.

We may combine these data for the main factory centers with some for the remaining centers of any significance, to conclude that employment in cotton factories fell by about 75 percent from pre- to postpanic levels.[36]

On the other hand, the declines were less catastrophic for industries not directly exposed to British dumping and to excessive demand fluctuation. (Factory cottons, after all, were still something of a luxury in a nation where spinning wheels were a common article of household use, rather than an antique.) Thus the reports show bricklaying employment in Philadelphia declining by only 50 percent, brewery employment in Pittsburgh falling by only a third. We therefore take the 78 percent fall in employment as shown in the National Institution report for the wide range of Philadelphia industries and the 68 percent decline for a similarly wide list in Pittsburgh, to deduce that manufacturing employment in the nation generally might have fallen by about two-thirds. While the National Institution report undoubtedly concentrated on the areas hardest hit, these in fact had a major share of what was then factory employment.

But after all, few people were engaged in manufacturing. Most were in farming. And while contemporary reports suggest price declines for farm products, they do not suggest any change in the extent of farm hiring. Many persons engaged in the hand trades, those premanufacturing industries where saddles, horseshoes, flour, etc., were made. But most such persons were self-employed, and contemporary reports again give no hint of significant changes in the number of employees in these firms outside the manufacturing centers. Navigation employment was affected but little, judging from port clearance reports. The declines must have been fairly well restricted to manufacturing industries. Since these composed less than 5 percent of the labor force, a two-thirds fall in such employment would have brought a rise of, say, 3 percent in the national unemployment percentage. Given our estimate that less than 10 percent of the labor force was composed of wage earners in 1800, and allowing for some increased unemployment in the hand trades and construction, it would be hard to come to a figure much higher than 4 percent unemployment in 1819.[37] With a labor force of 3 million, this implies a maximum unemployment figure of 120,000.

[36] Spindle activity, before and after the crash, is reported in the above source for Trenton and Paterson, N.J., and Oneida County, N.Y. Taking estimates of employees per spindle from the section on Determinants of Real Wages we estimate 1,000 employees in these three areas. Combining that figure with the roughly 17,000 plus in Philadelphia, Pittsburgh, and Rhode Island suggests a 76.5 percent decline for areas that included virtually all cotton factories at this date.

[37] Even if the normal unemployment percentage for wage earners in 1817, say, had been as high as 10 percent, this would have meant only a 1 percent national unemployment rate. A two-thirds fall in employment of factory workers (estimated as 5 percent of the total labor force) would add 3.3 percent and allowance for construction, etc., would raise the total to 5 percent.

What do contemporary sources estimate? In 1822 Matthew Carey found "reason to believe that from 90,000 to 100,000 workmen were actually thrown idle and driven to labor in the country—and vast numbers on the highways" that were then being built.[38] In other publications Carey used the lower estimate of 65,000.[39] Carey's 1822 estimate leads to the same result as the present procedure, while the difference from his other estimates is surely *de minimis*.

1838. The depression that began in 1837 and scored some areas of the economy for some years evoked its quota of bitterness—and purple prose. "Our streets are filled with wandering crowds," wrote Mayor Clark of New York. "Petitions signed by hundreds asking for work are presented in vain. . . . Thousands must therefore wander to and fro on the face of the earth, filling every part of our once happy land with squalid poverty, and with profligacy." [40] In the spring of 1840 a member of the Congress, writing from Ohio, observed that "grain sells for a very low price; labor commands but little more than half the wages it did a year ago." [41] The magnitude of the wage cut suggests the sharpness, but not necessarily any shortness, of the shock.

Can we arrive at any more sufficient numerical measure? One guide is given by the relief data for New York, which double from 1837 to 1838, dropping back to precrisis levels by 1839. Such a rise is considerably greater than what the Massachusetts relief data indicate for the well-known recessions of 1857 and 1873. But because of the inherent limitations of such data (not to mention the noncomparable elements of relief criteria and procedures between New York and Massachusetts), we must also look at more indirect numerical indications. Imports of pig iron—that master material of modern industry, whose consumption rate is intimately linked with cyclical variations in employment—fell by 14 percent. Such a decline was about as great as the 1856–1857 fall. However, in 1838 imports of pig iron constituted a major source of the metal, whereas by 1857 they were much less important than domestic production. The implications we can draw for general employment levels therefore suggest that

---

[38] *An Appeal to Common Sense and Common Justice* (Philadelphia: Carey and Lea, 1822), p. 51. Carey used the National Institution data to estimate 23,725 employed in the three areas noted, then apparently multiplied by 4 or 5 for a national total.

[39] *The New Olive Branch* (1820), p. 131. More or less the same figure appears in *The Crisis: A Solemn Appeal* (1823), p. 19. Because of the order of these publications, we can infer nothing as to which figure reflected Carey's brightest illumination on the subject.

[40] Quoted in Francis Wyse, *America, Its Realities and Resources* (London: 1846), vol. I, pp. 47–49.

[41] Aaron Perry, quoted in Anthony B. Norton, *The Great Revolution of 1840, Reminiscences of the Log Cabin and Hard Cider Campaign* (Mt. Vernon, Ohio, and Dallas, Texas: A. B. Norton and Co., 1888), pp. 52, 58, 60.

the 1838 unemployment level was worse than the 1857 level. The conclusion is reinforced by what the price data report. Metals prices fell 10 percent from 1837 to 1838, but only 1 percent from 1856 to 1857. Textile prices fell by 6 percent in the earlier period and actually rose in the later. Considering the relief data, pig-iron imports, and the two price series, therefore, we conclude that the 1837–1838 recession was of greater severity than that of 1856–1857.

1858. "Not one out of five skilled workmen in the country was steadily employed" in the 1857–1861 period, according to Representative Kelley. Indeed, when a Philadelphia contractor advertised for 250 hands to be paid 60 cents a day "more than 5,000 offered, a majority of whom were skilled artisans." [42] Since the prevailing wage for skilled workers before and after the depression had been about $1.25 in Philadelphia, this cut suggests considerable weakness in the Philadelphia labor market.

Another contemporary view of the 1857 recession stated that "the seaboard cities and the manufacturing districts of the interior probably at this time contain not less than 100,000 unemployed adult persons." [43]

For the major manufacturing state of Rhode Island, we have contemporary estimates of a 68 percent fall in cotton textile jobs, 78 percent in jewelry, 43 percent in ironworks employment. [44] Such declines indicate an equally great weakness in the Rhode Island labor market. The significantly milder decline in ironworks employment than in the two other industries suggests a crisis reaction, rather than a broadly spread downturn of employment. If we were to surmise, say, a 50 percent decline in manufacturing employment but 10 percent in other nonfarm industries, we should arrive at a 10 percent unemployment figure. [45]

The national extent of the decline, however, is overemphasized by these data for the Northeast. Thus while common-labor wage rates fell by about 7 percent in New England from 1857 to 1858, the national rate fell not at all. [46] The wage-rate data, therefore, do not confirm a decline of such

[42] William D. Kelley, *Speeches, Address and Letters on Industrial and Financial Questions* (Philadelphia: H. Carey Baird, 1872), p. 257. Kelley's report on the contractor's experience has the sound of validity. His generalization about 1857–1861, however, must be treated as "not proved" because it is associated with his private war with David Wells over the effects of high tariff, the rise in real incomes after 1861, etc.

[43] *New York Herald*, quoted in D. Morier Evans, *The History of the Commercial Crisis, 1857–58* (1859), p. 111.

[44] *Transactions of the Rhode Island Society for the Encouragement of Domestic Industries in the Year 1857* (1858), p. 77, quoting the *Providence Daily Journal*.

[45] With 11.1 million in the 1860 labor force, 1.5 million in manufacturing employment, and 3.8 million in other nonfarm pursuits.

[46] This conclusion rests on state averages developed from the Weeks report, 1880 Census, *Report on the Statistics of Wages in Manufacturing Industries* (1886), weighted together by the number of nonfarm gainfully occupied as shown by the 1860 Census of Population.

severity. And the wholesale-price data, also affected by interactions in a national market, show textile prices actually rising, and metals prices falling only 1 percent. Finally, the 30 percent rise in relief in Massachusetts and the 16 percent decline in pig-iron imports suggest a level of unemployment that was serious, but by no means as serious as Representative Kelley's ominous, but retrospective, words imply. We take the serious declines in employment in Rhode Island and presumably the Philadelphia area, the significant rise in Massachusetts relief, the less substantial fall in pig-iron imports, and the inconsequential price response and common-labor–wage-rate response to imply a recession of intermediate severity, conceivably at the level of the 1875 and 1885 percentages. While similar data were used for making a crude surmise as to 1819 levels, the procedure is less satisfactory by 1857, since industry by then had become a much greater proportion of the labor force and had spread so widely through the land that we could not safely take data for the Northeast and Middle Atlantic states as suggesting national trends in nonfarm employment. We therefore do not estimate an 1858 level. He who cannot quiet his soul without such an estimate may use 6 to 8 percent.

1874.   The great crisis of 1873 brought in its wake distress throughout the country. Outdoor relief in Massachusetts shot up in 1873, continued to rise till 1876, and only declined significantly beginning in 1879.[47] In Central Kansas, John Ise reminisced years later, half the people in one county were on charity, with men going 200 miles to eastern Kansas to husk corn or cut wood or work for cash wages.[48] Frickey's estimate of manufacturing production in the nation shows the same pattern, with a total decline of 19 percent by 1876, and no significant turnaround until 1879.[49]

As of November, 1874, according to the American Iron and Steel Institute, there were "at least a million" unemployed workers.[50] The Institute felt that there were 100,000 in New York and Philadelphia alone. Since the labor force then totaled about 15 million workers (interpolating between the 1870 and 1880 totals), their figure implies a 6.7 percent unemployment rate. Given the trend in production and relief, and allowing for new entrants into the labor force, the 1875 average would have ranged from, say, 6 percent (if their estimate had been primarily a pessimistic

[47] K. D. Lumpkin and D. W. Douglas, *Child Workers in America* (1937), appendix 2.

[48] John Ise, "Pioneer Life in Western Kansas," in N. E. Himes (ed.), *Economics, Sociology and the Modern World, Essays in Honour of T. N. Carver* (1935), p. 132. Ise reported a 50-cent a day rate for summer work on farms, less than half the customary harvest rate. A grasshopper invasion helped matters further.

[49] Edwin Frickey, *Production in the United States, 1860–1914* (1947), p. 60. His series adjusted for secular trend was used.

[50] American Iron and Steel Institute, *Annual Report for 1874*, p. 7.

judgment and therefore to be discounted somewhat) to 8 percent (if they had actually been relying on reliable reports from members).

The continued decline in production and the general tendency of unemployment to accumulate after the turnaround in production suggest a higher level at the bottom point, 1876. The Silver Commission, speaking with no doubt at least the accent of politics, found that 3 million were unemployed about this time.[51] If we accept the manufacturers' figure of 1 million for 1874, then take into account Frickey's estimate of about a 20 percent decline from 1873 to 1876 in manufactures (as well as the Massachusetts relief data), a 3-million figure is not out of the question for the end of the most prolonged depression in American history.[52] We surmise that a figure of 2 million—or 13 percent of the labor force in that year—would be a reasonable figure in the light of these partial indications.[53]

1885. A contemporary estimate by the Commissioner of Labor, on the basis of field visits to factories and other checks, found that "about 5 percent" of the nation's factories, mines, etc., "were absolutely idle during the year ending July 1, 1885, and . . . perhaps 5 percent were idle a part of the time; or for a just estimate 7½ percent." [54] (This level is about the same as the 8 percent for 1875 computed from the Institute figures.) Frickey's production index shows a fall of about 16 percent from 1883 to 1885, or about the same as his 1873 to 1875 decline. However, the Massachusetts relief figures show only a mild gain from 1883 to 1884 and then decline. Frickey's data therefore appear to confirm the 1875 to 1885 similarity, while the Massachusetts relief data do not.

As another check on the Commissioner's estimate, we may refer to the report of the Industrial Commission in 1901.[55] "It is disputed whether

---

[51] 44th Cong., 2d Sess., Senate Report 703, *Silver Commission,* p. 118. The commission noted that the numbers had risen since 1873.

[52] The National Bureau of Economic Research cycle measures indicate a longer cycle downturn from 1836 to 1843. That period, however, was interrupted by a stretch of economic revival, whereas 1873ff. was one of continuous depression.

[53] In *American Business Cycles, 1865–1897* (1959), pp. 107–108, Rendig Fels questions Schumpeter's treatment of the period as one of severe depression and his reference to 3 million unemployed. Fels's doubt seems to stem primarily from the fact that production held up in these years. However, a combination of productivity advance plus the accumulation of unemployed arising in a lengthy period of pressure on family incomes (bringing new entrants to the labor force) would make the two quite consistent. The massive drop in our wage-rate series constitutes a fairly affirmative indication of heavy unemployment.

[54] First Annual Report of the Commissioner of Labor, *Industrial Depressions* (March, 1886), p. 65. The report stipulates the percentages as applying to all gainfully occupied in agriculture, trade, transportation, mining, mechanical trades, and manufactures.

[55] *Report of the Industrial Commission* (1901), vol. 14, p. xliv.

unemployment has increased on the whole, say within 20 or 30 years, but no witness supposes that it has decreased." Given the language of political controversy, we may assume that no more conclusive arguments were offered for an increase than for a decrease. If the level which prevailed during the commission's deliberations (5 percent in 1900) more or less characterized the 1870–1890 period, we would have to increase this 5 percent by at least 1 point to give, say, a 6 percent figure for the depression year of 1885.[56] Under the circumstances, the Commissioner's estimate— 7½ percent—does not appear unreasonable. Even if fancy argued for reducing it somewhat, reason offers no basis at this remove (and with such materials in evidence) for doing so.

1890 to 1899 (Table A-15). The depression of the nineties was one of the severest depressions prior to the 1930s. Available estimates of unemployment are limited to those of Paul Douglas, who relied largely on the trend in Massachusetts employment to estimate the change.[57] We derive new estimates of unemployment below, discussing in turn (1) objections to the use of the 1890 Census data on unemployment; (2) our procedures for deriving a benchmark estimate from that census; (3) our 1891–1899 estimation procedure; and (4) alternative measures.

1. Estimates of nonemployment of gainful workers in the previous year were secured in the Census of 1890.[58] These data have not been utilized in later census publications, chiefly because of doubts expressed in the volumes of the 1900 Census.[59] Because these doubts seem, on the basis of later evidence, to be overly cautious, the 1890 results are used here.

The objections of the 1900 Census reports turned chiefly on the assumption that "if the real proportions of nonemployment at the two census years (1890 and 1900) had been similar, a more thorough enumeration in 1900 than in 1890 would have resulted merely in larger figures, affecting all classes to about the same extent." [60] Since this is what seemed to have occurred, the 1890 data were rejected.

This analysis is, however, incorrect on both points. First, the level of unemployment in both years, i.e., "the real proportions of nonemployment," was almost certainly not the same. Burns and Mitchell indicate that the year preceding the 1890 Census was one of cycle expansion, while

---

[56] *The Final Report of the Industrial Commission,* p. 746, refers to an average loss of 5 weeks in unemployment according to the Seventeenth Annual Report of the Commissioner of Labor. The Commissioner's report provides the basis for the adjustment of the 1900 census reports on unemployment in the present estimates, hence really determines their 1900 level.

[57] Paul Douglas, *Real Wages in the United States, 1890–1926* (1930), pp. 435–440.

[58] 1890 *Census of Population,* vol. II, p. cxxxvii.

[59] 1900 Census, *Occupations,* p. ccxxv.

[60] *Ibid.,* pp. ccxxvii, ccxxxiii.

that before the 1900 Census was primarily one of contraction.[61] Frickey indicates that industrial and commercial production in 1889–1890 (after adjustment for secular trend) was substantially above the 1899–1900 level.[62]

Also, the change in unemployment rates did not affect "all classes to about the same extent." True, lawyers had a lower unemployment rate than glassworkers in both years, but this sort of differential has maintained to the present day. What is more important, however, is the fact that there were sharp changes in rates for occupations, for separate classes of occupations, and for the separate regions.[63]

Another consideration urged against the 1890 results was the complexity of instructions to the enumerators requesting information on secondary jobs.[64] There is strong evidence—a priori and empirical—that these instructions were largely ignored. Hence inadequate reporting on secondary employment and other complex items did take place. But the more important inference, judging from practice in later censuses, is that the enumerators probably relied chiefly on the question printed on the schedule, which was simple and direct: "months unemployed during the Census year." [65]

In addition to these negative considerations, suggesting the overcaution of the 1900 Census observers, a significant positive consideration exists. Were the 1900 Census technically a much better measure of unemploy-

[61] A. F. Burns and Wesley C. Mitchell, *Measuring Business Cycles* (1946), pp. 510–511.

[62] Frickey, *op. cit.,* p. 128.

[63] Rates for male "laborers (not specified)" rose from 33.4 to 44.3 percent; for carpenters from 31.8 to 41.4; for painters from 31.1 to 47.4. Rates for all males in manufacturing and mechanical pursuits, however, only rose from 24.3 to 28.3, while those for professional service rose from 8.6 to 13.5 (1900 Census, *Occupations,* p. ccxxviii). Regional differences are likewise apparent, the gains for the South being far greater than for the West or North (1890 Census, vol. II, table 101, and 1900 Census, *op. cit.,* p. ccxxxv).

[64] 1900 Census, *op. cit.,* p. ccxxxvii.

[65] 1900 Census, *op. cit.,* p. ccxxvi. The instructions begin "If a person having a gainful occupation was unemployed during any part of the census year it should be so stated in months and parts of months." This is direct, and likely to have been what chiefly remained in the enumerator's mind. The instructions continue: "If, as may often happen, a person was unemployed at his usual occupation for some time during the census year and yet found another temporary employment . . . this fact should be clearly stated. . . ." It is hardly surprising that few enumerators pursued this issue any distance or made many such entries. Moreover, it suggests that they simply concentrated on "months unemployed during the Census year" and hence received results not incomparable with 1900 and 1910. The complexities of the family schedule used in 1890 further suggest the unlikelihood of any detailed inquiry into secondary employment and unemployment.

ment because of lessons learned in 1890, because of closer controls, then much the same high level should have maintained in the 1910 Census, when controls were at least as good. In fact, the proportions reporting unemployment for the major occupations in 1890 were not much different from those in 1910, suggesting that the higher 1900 rate reflects primarily the cyclical change intended to be measured.[66]

2. An 1890 benchmark was derived from the unemployment data reported in the 1890 and 1900 Censuses. Data for the primary male groups in the labor force showed an unemployment percentage in 1890 that was 79.31 percent of that in 1900.[67] Applying this ratio to our 1900 unemployment rate gives an 1890 rate of 3.96 percent. This rate applied to an estimated 1890 total for labor force aged 14 and over gives our 1890 unemployment figure.[68]

3. Intercensal unemployment figures were derived by deducting an employment series from a labor-force series. For the labor-force series we interpolated between the 1890 and 1900 labor-force figures derived above. For employment we estimated 1890 and 1900 employment figures by deducting the unemployment from labor-force figures above—then interpolating by an employment series of Edward Frickey.[69] Frickey's series is based on the movement of factory employment in Massachusetts from 1890 to 1900, New Jersey, Ohio, and Pennsylvania for 1892 to 1900, and New York from 1897 to 1900. Our results appear in Table A-15.[70]

---

[66] Laborers n.o.s., the largest single occupation category, showed a 33 percent rate in 1890, 35 percent in 1910, and 44 percent in 1900. Carpenters reported 32 percent in 1890 and 30 percent in 1910; masons, 43 and 39 percent, draymen 16 and 15 percent. Sharp differences were observed for some occupations, of course. But the broad similarity for these major occupations suggests that we are no worse off in comparing 1890 and 1910 than, say, 1910 and 1930.

[67] We ignore the census data for other groups in deriving this ratio because reporting on female unemployment in the prior year is much less reliable; for farm laborers a significant undercount in 1890 occurred; while for merchants and dealers, as those in professional service, most reported "nonemployment" is not really "unemployment." Deducting these groups from the all-occupation total gave the subtotal that we used to estimate change.

[68] An adjusted 10 and over gainful worker figure for 1890 appears in the 1900 Census, *Occupations*, p. cxviii. We compute a comparable 14 and over figure by applying the 1900 ratio of the 10–13 to the 10–15 group, using data from the same source, pp. cxviii and clxii. This figure, as the 10 and over, applies only to the continental United States and was raised to an all United States figure by the 1900 ratio of continental to all United States 14 and over gainful workers.

[69] An unpublished series kindly provided by Professor Frickey some years ago, it is the basis for the chart in his *Economic Fluctuations in the U.S.,* p. 212.

[70] Other series shown were taken from the following sources: Paul Douglas, *op. cit.,* p. 440; D. P. Smelser, *Unemployment and American Trade Unions* (1919), p. 18; K. D. Lumpkin and D. W. Douglas, *loc. cit.; Historical Statistics,* vol. II, p. 409; U.S. Bureau of Labor, Bulletin 77 (July, 1908).

4. Alternative procedures are possible for this period. A U.S. Bureau of Labor series reflecting both manufacturing and construction employment is available.[71] In a broad way the series leads to a similar set of unemployment results except that it shows an improvement in the unemployment situation from 1892 to 1893, instead of a marked worsening. Such a picture, moreover, is consistent with the data on flow of finished-goods production, which rises slightly over the year.[72] We reject this trend, however, for several reasons. Real output can rise while employment is declining; marked productivity changes typically take place at cycle turns. Material bearing more directly on the level of employment does suggest a worsening of unemployment. For example, Rees's tabulation of state manufacturing data shows that average days worked in manufacturing fell by 8 percent from 1892 to 1893.[73] The Massachusetts data on persons receiving relief show a broad stability from 1889 to 1892 but rise sharply in 1893.[74]

We compute a check estimate for 1893 largely on the basis of a contemporary survey by an economist who received estimates from public officials and others in 300 cities as to the unemployment in their city.[75] For 44 cities with a population over 50,000, we can compute the percentage of male unemployed both in 1890 and 1893.[76] The 1893 rate thus computed is five times that for 1890. We apply this ratio to the 1890 rate for males in nonfarm pursuits, assuming that the rate for the male farm labor force was unchanged (Closson notes no declines in agriculture), as was that for the female labor force.[77] The result is an estimate of 13.48 percent, or 3,305,000 unemployed at the end of 1893, the period to which Closson's figures relate. This rate would refer to the entire second half of the year, the indications being that major shutdowns occurred from May to July;[78] while for the first half year we assume a rate of 4.0 percent as in the 1890 Census year, a period of generally high employment. The

---

[71] "Wages and Hours of Labor in Manufacturing Industries 1890 to 1907," U.S. Bureau of Labor, Bulletin 77 (July, 1908). Data on p. 12 show that, of 343,000 in the 1907 sample, some 85,000 were in building and street construction.

[72] William H. Shaw, *Value of Commodity Output* (1947), p. 76.

[73] Albert Rees, *Real Wages in Manufacturing, 1890 to 1914* (1961), p. 33.

[74] K. D. Lumpkin and D. W. Douglas, *loc. cit.*

[75] Carlos C. Closson, Jr., "The Unemployed in American Cities," *Quarterly Journal of Economics* (January, 1894; July, 1894), pp. 257ff., 500ff. For most of these cities Closson likewise presents estimates made by Bradstreet as well.

[76] 1890 Census, *Population,* vol. II, pp. 630ff. We take the reported distribution by period unemployed in the census year, and use as the median for each period a figure computed from the *Eighteenth Annual Report of the Commissioner of Labor,* p. 290.

[77] *Ibid.,* pp. 302, 448–449.

[78] See the comments by Closson, pp. 189, 196, 209. Frickey's quarterly employment index runs 87.5, 87.3, and then falls to 75.4 and 73.9.

annual average rate as applied to the labor-force total then gives 2,145,-000, as compared to a 2,800,000 figure derived by the general procedure used above for 1890 to 1900. Since the lower estimate is biased downward (because it premises no increase in female or farm agricultural unemployment rates), we take these contemporary materials as providing reasonable support for our 2.8 million estimate for 1893.

Our results will differ from those of Paul Douglas for two major reasons. His employment series for the period reflected changes only in Massachusetts, whereas Frickey's series allows for the trend in Ohio, Pennsylvania, and New Jersey as well (over most of the period) and for New York (at the end). Secondly, Douglas makes no use of the 1890 Census reports on unemployment to establish a benchmark in 1890, deriving his unemployment figure for that year by deducting employment from the labor force.[79]

Since 1900. For the years 1900 to 1960 a more comprehensive summary is possible. We show below the number of years in which the unemployed portion of the labor force was less than 2 percent, from 2 to 2.9 percent, and so on. The median year falls in the 4 to 4.9 percent unemployment group, as does the mode.

Percent	Number of years
Under 2	7
2–2.9	5
3–3.9	10
4–4.9	9
5–5.9	10
6–7.9	4
8–9.9	4
10–11.9	1
12–13.9	0
14–15.9	2
16 and over	8

These estimates for the years prior to 1940 are intended to measure the number of persons who are totally unemployed, having no work at all. For the 1930s this concept, however, does include one large group of persons who had both work and income from work—those on emergency work. In the United States we are concerned with measuring lack of regular work and do not minimize the total by excluding persons with made work or emergency jobs. This contrasts sharply, for example, with the

[79] A minor additional reason is that while he interpolates as we do for the native portion of the labor force, he varies the foreign-born portion according to the immigration change. However, since most of the foreign-born population was already in the United States, this procedure should be used only for the much smaller new-immigrant component. However, the net result is not largely different from our own on this account.

German practice during the 1930s when persons in the labor-force camps were classed as employed, and Soviet practice which includes employment in labor camps, if it includes it at all, as employment. While total unemployment constitutes a useful measure of the extent to which our manpower is not fully utilized, it is not a complete measure and should not be used as such. Perhaps the most important element that is excluded is partial unemployment—the involuntary idleness during split weeks or short workdays. Various predepression surveys showed from 10 to 15 percent of urban wage earners working part time—most of them presumably desirous of full-time work.[80] With the onset of the depression of the 1930s, however, the percentage increased abruptly. The immediate increase appeared to be greater than that in 1921. As one example, unemployment in Detroit about doubled from the census in the spring of 1930 to the January, 1931, special unemployment census but part-time employment increased more than 400 percent.[81] By March, 1932, according to a comprehensive survey of more than 6,000 companies with over 3 million employees, sponsored by the President's Organization on Unemployment Relief, 63 percent of all employed manufacturing workers were on part-time work.[82] No matter how this enormous percentage must be qualified, it is clear that it indicated a substantial quantity of underemployment among those with jobs. As the depression began to lift, the proportion on part time declined. In November, 1937, the proportion in manufacturing on part-time employment was about 20 percent—or substantially down from the 63 percent in early 1932.[83] By the postwar pe-

[80] In 1915 an estimated 15 percent of urban wage earners were underemployed (Paul Brissenden, "Underemployment," *Business Cycles and Unemployment*, p. 68). In 1919 a survey of manufacturing industries reported 11 percent of full time lost in idle hours (Bradford, *op. cit.*, p. 28). In April, 1930, the Census reported about 10 percent of gainful workers on part time (*Census of Unemployment, 1930*, vol. II, pp. 10, 357). King's data for 1921 give a figure of about 8 percent for factory workers in 1921 (President's Conference on Unemployment, *Business Cycles and Unemployment*, p. 95).

[81] *Census of Unemployment, 1930*, vol. II, pp. 139, 358, 482, 600.

[82] William J. Barrett, "Extent and Methods of Spreading Work," *Monthly Labor Review* (September, 1932), p. 490. These companies reported a decline in employment from 1929 to March, 1932, of 26.6 percent. The decline for all manufacturing companies was about 32 percent.

[83] The number partly unemployed as of November, 1937, is estimated in the *Census of Partial Employment, Unemployment, and Occupations*, vol. IV, *Final Report on Total and Partial Unemployment, 1937*, p. 20. Data from p. 125 of the same volume give a distribution by industry for the partly employed registrants. It was assumed that the 34 percent proportion of manufacturing employees in this registrant group (combining manufacturing industry components shown) could be applied to the p. 20 survey total. The resultant figure was then related to the current (i.e., 1963) Bureau of Labor Statistics estimate for 1937 manufacturing employment, after the latter had been adjusted to November levels by earlier BLS monthly indices.

riod the proportion was further reduced. The proportion of all persons in the labor force working part time in early 1948 was about 8 percent—and only rose to 12 percent near the peak of the 1949 recession.[84]

In summary, therefore, partial unemployment may have run to something like 10 percent for most years, while during the depth of the depression something like half of all factory workers with jobs were on part-time work.

Employment is only one dimension of the economic welfare problem. A second is the number of hours worked, or partial employment. Other dimensions of this problem are the amount of income received and the skills utilized. The general problem of underemployment, however, is still more complex, and it has received separate discussion elsewhere. It will therefore be sufficient here to emphasize that estimates of total unemployment do not include any direct allowance for this factor. The tremendous drop in the number of farmers and retail storekeepers from 1940 to 1943 is one indication of the possible magnitude of such underemployment—even after allowing for the postwar return to higher levels in trade.

With this basic qualification in mind, it may be appropriate to indicate how closely we came to achieving full employment over the past half century. Defining full employment is something like defining small business, low income, monopoly profit, or the just price. Definitions tend to be either imprecise or void of empirical reference. But if we think of the policy uses of the data, we can define full employment in the light of what we have achieved in the past. Let us arbitrarily define "workable full employment"—to adapt an admirable phrase of J. M. Clark's—as the level achieved at least one year in four during the past 60 years. If we do so the percentage of the civilian labor force totally unemployed at full employment would be less than 4 percent. (The percentage would have to be raised if our reference period were shorter, for it was achieved more frequently in the 1900–1929 period than in the 1926–1959.) It has been asserted, however, that "full employment at high wages in a private enterprise economy is undesirable and self-destroying." [85] We may therefore wish to set a figure based on the assumption that full employment is less common. If we set the goal at that which prevailed in 10 percent of the years, the ratio would run to 2 percent or less. But we may take a less pessimistic approach. High-level employment has characterized the performance of the American economy in the past half century. While even a level of 5 percent unemployed would hardly be considered to present a major eco-

---

[84] These data refer to all part-time work—only part of which, of course, was involuntary part-time work. Data from special census surveys for March, 1948, and May and August, 1949, suggest that the increase represented involuntary part-time work.

[85] R. I. Nowell in *Journal of Farm Economics* (February, 1947), p. 143.

nomic policy problem, such a level has been achieved in more than half this period.

D. Unemployment Levels since 1800

The preceding discussion of unemployment trends has had two purposes. One is to see how far some attempt at estimation might go in replacing the wonderfully graphic contemporary descriptions of panic and crisis. For our judgment on whether one or another period bred more unemployment and distress tends to turn upon the relative prose styles of those who lived at various dates. A reference to numbers, highly speculative as they may be, tends to neutralize this effect. Secondly, we have attempted estimates because of the considerable interest in early discussions of "a reserve army of the unemployed," and the putative tendency for depressions in the West to grow worse and worse.

Table 4-3. Unemployment in Years of Economic Crisis since 1800

Percent of Labor Force Unemployed	1800–1819	1820–1839	1840–1859	1860–1879	1880–1899	1900–1919	1920–1939	1940–1959
3–5	1819						1927	1949 1954 1958
6–8		1838	1858		1885	1908	1924	
9–11						1915		
12–14				1876			1921	
15 and over					1894		1930– 1940	

In Table 4-3 we have put together our best inference from the above data on unemployment in selected crisis years since 1800. From these measures the most we can conclude is that the extent of unemployment in the worst crisis years increased somewhat in the first half of the nineteenth century but has shown no trend since then. In Table 4-4 we have attempted speculative averages for entire decades since 1800—most speculatively for 1870–1880–1890. These figures, although based on less specific data than those for crisis years, are probably preferable guides to the main course of unemployment. The reason is simply that reported unemployment in the farm population, as census counts since 1890 have shown, is very small. And during most of the nineteenth century, from half to three-fourths of the labor force was in agriculture. Hence, the percentage unemployed was necessarily limited on the rise, while it could not go below zero on the decline. Even wide variances in the estimates for crisis years therefore are lost in the decade averages when we allow for the infrequency of crises and the great role of the farm-labor force.

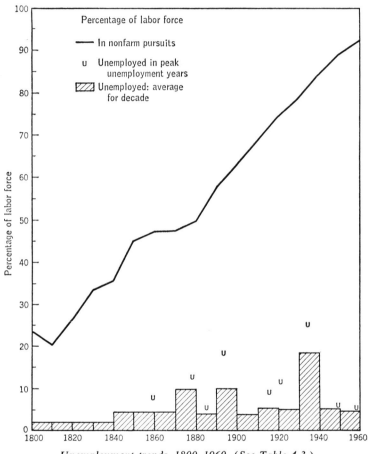

Unemployment trends, 1800–1960. (See Table 4-3.)

For the period since the Civil War no trend appears, particularly if we give credence to the 1870–1880–1890 figures. The more reliable data since 1900 emphasize the tremendous impact of the 1930s but report no discernible trend for 1900 to 1960.[86]

Direct government intervention to reduce unemployment, once a crisis had occurred, began more than a century back. In early decades there was

[86] The change in the present estimates from peak to trough business cycle year shows no trend from 1900 to 1927, nor does the 1900 to 1957 record. Geoffrey Moore (ed.), *Business Cycle Indicators* (1961), vol. I, p. 161. Moore uses an earlier version of the present estimates but one not significantly different.

a clear response by states and municipalities, starting or speeding up public works such as turnpikes. And it is, of course, impossible to ignore the extent of active government intervention in recent decades. But for at least two of these recessions we may seriously question whether government actions to reduce unemployment taken after the beginning of the crisis had any significant effect whatever on unemployment levels. (Inadvertent tax cuts do not qualify as shrewd anticyclical policy.) The problem is really part of a deeper one, reflecting the fact that government has long been enmeshed in American economic life. Its action to put a tariff on indigo and cotton under Washington, its refusal to limit immigration in the 1880s, its action to make land available under the Homestead Act, its decision to close off immigration in 1920—these and a hundred other steps shaped the structure of the economy, affected its labor market, and thereby affected the level of unemployment that developed in response to cyclical shocks.

If we look simply to the trend in unemployment averages since 1800, the evidence, such as it is, suggests a slight long-run increase in decade unemployment averages. The change from a labor force of slaves and

Table 4-4. Unemployment: 1800–1960 Decade Averages for Percent of Labor Force Unemployed

Date	Decade averages
1800–1809	
1810–1819	1–3
1820–1829	
1830–1839	
1840–1849	
1850–1859	3–6
1860–1869	
1870–1879	10 (?)
1880–1889	4 (?)
1890–1899	10
1900–1909	4
1910–1919	5
1920–1929	5
1930–1939	18
1940–1949	5
1950–1960	5

farmers to one of wage earners, plus the shift to an economy where most goods were marketed, overshadowed the many opposing forces to create this rise. This composition effect is measurable for a recent period. Thus the percent of unemployed nonfarm employees declined from 1900 to

1960 (from 12.6 to 7.1). The percent of the total labor force that was unemployed, however, actually rose because the share of self-employed fell heavily.

Yet if our concern is with the productive use of the economy's resources, or with the welfare implications of unemployment, we cannot conclude that a deterioration occurred. Present definitions of unemployment fail to include time lost because of bad weather. Moreover, we are unable to measure disguised unemployment (either of wage earners in low-skill occupations or farmers on low-productivity farms). Suppose we could allow for the increased extent to which production is carried on regularly despite bad weather. Suppose further that we could allow for the extent to which an improvement in the labor market from 1800 to 1960, plus the widening system of public education, now enables adult employees to work closer to their intellectual capacity and skill limits. We might then find that no real rise had occurred in the proportion of unemployed resources, so far as either productivity or welfare implications were concerned.

FACTOR SHARES IN THE LONG TERM †

Rational regularities pervade economic theory. But how rarely are they revealed in empirical records. And how resigned economists have become to it all, knowing full well that any constancy—whether of theory or the real world—will be hidden by the coarse irregularities of the published statistics. So well have they learned this depressing lesson, however, that they are quite unprepared on the rare occasions when a rigid constancy is reported. The share of wages in the national income seems to be such a constant, and a particularly dubious one—for it appears not only to lack a basis in theory, but even to be in conflict with it. Not surprisingly some of the most distinguished economists have been bemused by all this. Keynes with British reserve spoke of the constancy as "a bit of a miracle." Schumpeter decided that it was "a mystery," as did Joan Robinson. Solow speculates that the miracle "may be an optical illusion," but still ranks it as "an interesting problem." And Reder's recent review of the problem concludes that we are still in the dark.[1]

† This section was presented in slightly different form as a paper to the Conference on Research in Income and Wealth, and will appear in that form in the National Bureau of Economic Research, *Studies in Income and Wealth,* vol. 27.

I am deeply indebted to Bert Hickman for raising more penetrating questions on an earlier draft than are answered in this one, and to Jack Alterman for well-taken comments on an earlier version of this discussion.

[1] J. M. Keynes, "Relative Movements of Real Wages and Output," *Economic Journal* (March, 1939), p. 48. J. A. Schumpeter, *Business Cycles* (1939), vol. II, pp.

We consider here both some theoretical and statistical aspects of the question explicitly raised by Keynes: Why, over so long a period in which the relative amounts of labor and capital changed so drastically, did the share of labor and capital in the national income remain relatively so stable? Since so much of the recent discussion really originated from the observation of a striking empirical constancy, we begin with a look at some of the data involved. Part I reviews the various United States series in which constancies have been discerned. Its conclusion is that so many constancies were stipulated in the estimating process originally that the series—efficiently usable for many other purposes—are hardly a strong basis for judging the stability or instability of labor's share.

Part II focuses on a central conceptual difficulty that afflicts any review of labor's share in national income as usually measured, namely, that the economist has no conceptually solid method for disentangling what portion of entrepreneurial income is allocable to earnings on capital as distinct from earnings by entrepreneurial labor. Hence its conclusion that there is only darkling wisdom in discussions of shifts (or stability) in labor's share of national income, nonfarm income, or other totals that include sectors dominated by noncorporate activity.

Part III describes market forces that over the long term do work toward producing stability in factor shares for major United States industries. Shaping the underlying production function by their impact on the elasticity of substitution among factors, these forces will thereby shape factor share proportions.

I

What basis do we have for asserting that the share of wages in United States national income up to 1919 was in fact stable? The answer is, in brief: very little. Most of the studies in the field rely on the estimates of R. F. Martin, W. I. King, and Gale Johnson—Martin, in turn, relying largely on King for the period 1909–1919.[2] We consider each, then turn to the data since 1919.

575–576. R. M. Solow, "A Skeptical Note on the Constancy of Relative Shares," *American Economic Review* (September, 1958), pp. 618, 628. Melvin Reder, "Conflicting Views on Relative Shares," 1960 Annual Meeting of the American Economic Assn. (unpublished). We do not discuss the variety of data available for other countries. To understand the derivation of their estimates is a major project in itself. The interested reader will find a variety of comparisons for several countries, of data adjusted as best may be for comparability, in Livio Livi, *Primo Computo del Reddito Distributto al Fattori Della Produzione* (1958), chap. 11, especially p. 172. Professor Livi's data show great stability for some nations, great change for others, over the period from 1938 to about 1954.

[2] The two best-known extensive studies are by E. C. Budd, "Factor Shares, 1850–1910," Conference on Research in Income and Wealth, vol. 24, *Trends in the Amer-*

A. Martin's Estimates, 1900 to 1920

For these decades we have estimates by R. F. Martin.[3] Entrepreneurial income plus salaries and wages account for nearly 90 percent of his income totals in these years.[4] Hence to assess the constancy of factor share ratios from these data must largely require that his estimates for the two shares have been independent of one another.

Mining. Since Martin relies largely on King, the lack of notes by King means that we cannot assert too flat-footedly how the Martin estimates were derived. We believe, however, that the King-Martin procedure for these decades amounts to assuming that the trend of (1) average wage per employee was identical with that for (2) average earnings per entrepreneur.[5] Hence no matter how great the variations in the relative earnings of each, these estimates would not in consequence show any change in the ratio of entrepreneurial earnings to wages and salaries.

Manufacturing. Martin assumes the same trend from 1899 to 1919— indeed the same figures—in earnings per employee as in income per entrepreneur.[6]

Trade. Martin assumes that the trend of earnings per employee and per entrepreneur were the same for 1899 to 1919.[7]

---

ican Economy in the Nineteenth Century (1960), and D. Gale Johnson, "The Functional Distribution of Income in the United States, 1850–1952," *Review of Economics and Statistics* (May, 1954). Among the significant briefer studies is the discussion in William Fellner, *Trends and Cycles in Economic Activity* (1956), Appendix to part 3, parts 7 and 5; Simon Kuznets, *National Income: a Summary of Findings* (1946), p. 50, and Kuznets's review, more in accord with the conclusion of stability, in his "Long-term Changes in the National Income of the United States of America since 1870" in *Income and Wealth of the United States,* International Association for Research in Income and Wealth (1952), p. 85.

[3] R. F. Martin, *National Income in the United States, 1799–1938* (1939).

[4] *Ibid.,* p. 22.

[5] Martin (*ibid.*) adopts King's average entrepreneurial income, 1909–1919, and uses Douglas's earnings in coal mining to run back to 1899 (p. 119). King, of course, gives no description but his average wage in all mining (p. 93) appears to be much the same as his coal-mining wage (p. 319, weighting anthracite and bituminous together). For employees Martin uses Douglas's average earnings in coal mining also, to interpolate between 1902 and 1909 census earnings figures. But, since Douglas interpolated between census benchmarks to begin with, this means that Martin used the same average earnings trend for employees and entrepreneurs. (Martin actually uses coal plus oil mining, stipulating that oil wages varied with the value of petroleum production. But since oil wages account for 10 percent or less of the combined total, this variation makes little difference.)

[6] Martin, *op. cit.,* p. 120.

[7] *Ibid.,* p. 121. In addition Martin implicitly assumed a constant ratio of entrepreneurs to employees in the Census of Population occupation category "wholesale and retail merchants and dealers." However, in actual census reporting a varying proportion of that category were actually employees, i.e., salesmen and store managers. See Alba Edwards, *Comparative Occupation Statistics, 1870–1940* (1943), p. 110.

Construction, Transportation, Service. For each of these industries Martin uses the trend in their wage-salary bill to extrapolate that of entrepreneurial earnings—implicitly assuming (1) a constant ratio of average wage salary to average entrepreneurial earnings, and (2) a constant ratio of employees to entrepreneurs.[8]

Conclusion. For industries which (in 1910) accounted for approximately two-thirds of Martin's total for realized private production income, he estimates 1900 to 1920 trends in entrepreneurial income by assuming a constant ratio of employee earnings to earnings by entrepreneurs. In addition, for a substantial group he likewise assumes a constant ratio of employees to entrepreneurs. Hence his method of estimate forbids variation in a large area within which variations in the ratio of entrepreneurial earnings to wages and salaries—hence in the ratio of wages and salaries to national income—could occur. We conclude that the use of such data for discussing stability in the ratio of labor income to national income is a futile business, adding little to our knowledge of the subject.

B. King's Estimates for 1850 to 1900 [9]

To assess how adequate King's data are for studying factor share changes prior to 1900, we review some of the ratios and averages implicit in his figures. The result of that review is not one to encourage our use of his totals for reaching any conclusion as to the stability of factor shares. We reach this pessimistic result from a consideration of data for three sectors —agriculture, government, commerce—which together account for well over half of his income totals in these decades.[10]

Agriculture. King's figures show an unreasonably high share of farm product going to wages for 1870 and 1880 (his data imply almost 50 percent of product in wages), then decline to near 20 percent by 1910.[11] The latter ratio is reasonably close to the Department of Agriculture estimates for that year,[12] but the ratios in the early decades are startlingly high. This enormous 1870 to 1910 decline is difficult to credit for a period when the ratio of hired labor to entrepreneurs not only did not decline enormously but actually rose.

A second, no less disturbing aspect of his figures is their implication that

---

[8] Martin, *op. cit.,* pp. 120–121. The above statement must be qualified to the extent that he may have implicitly assumed a downward (or variable) trend in one set of ratios that was precisely offset by an upward (or variable) trend in the other. This seems most unlikely.

[9] I am most grateful to Elizabeth Jenks for comments on my interpretation of King's procedures and unpublished data from his "data books."

[10] W. I. King, *The Wealth and Income of the People of the United States* (1915), p. 140.

[11] *Ibid.,* pp. 138, 260.

[12] U.S. Department of Agriculture, *Major Statistical Series of the U.S. Department of Agriculture* (1957) vol. 3, p. 46.

earnings per farmer (including imputed value of food and home) were less than those per farm employee.[13] Contemporary materials, however, as well as most data for later years, suggest quite the reverse.

Commercial and Professional Services. King estimated the total product of trade, service, finance, insurance, and real estate—accounting for 30 percent of the national product in 1910—"on the basis of a constant ratio to the product of urban population and average income." [14] What is important for present purposes is not that this large sector was estimated in this quite arbitrary, if reasonable, fashion. Rather it is that the wage component is likely to have been estimated with equal (or greater) arbitrariness: King gives no information from which his procedure could be deduced. Hence we have little basis for using the trend in the factor share ratio for total national income, including as it does a large allowance for this group, to deduce yeasty conclusions about the trend in factor shares.[15]

Government. King's description of how he estimated the product total for this group reads as follows in its entirety: "The services of the government were assumed to be worth the amount paid for running the government." [16] We follow this thin lead by comparing, for example, for 1870 his $437 million for government product with the $588 million total for Federal expenditures plus state and local taxes.[17] Hence, a state and local deficit of about $150 million—more than half again as great as the $280 million of taxes raised—would therefore have had to exist if we were to reconcile King's total with these expenditure figures.

No information is given on how the wage component of his government

---

[13] King (*op. cit.,* p. 150) cites the 1900 Census, *Occupations* (p. 1) as his source for persons employed in agriculture. Referring to that volume we see, for example, that his 6 million for 1870 is identical with the reported census total for those in agricultural pursuits, farmers plus employees. We therefore divide the census 3.0 million farmers into King's entrepreneurial earnings (p. 263); then divide the residual 2.9 million (for employees) into King's wage total for farming employees (p. 260). The result is about $240 per employee, but only $190 per entrepreneur. If, however, we assume that no money wage should have been set down for unpaid family workers, this $50 gap—in the wrong direction—would have been still greater.

[14] King, *op. cit.,* p. 138.

[15] King reports money earnings per employee for all industries combined (*op. cit.,* p. 168). If we divide that average into his wage aggregates for the trade, service, and finance group (p. 260), the result shows no rise in the number of employees in this group from 1850 to 1910. In other words, his implicit trend for earnings per employee in this category would have had to decline largely over the decades, or risen significantly less than that for all employees, to give a reasonable employment trend for the group.

[16] *Ibid.,* p. 129.

[17] State and local taxes are from a census source cited in some of King's notes: 1870 Census, vol. III, *The Wealth and Industry of the People of the United States,* p. 11. Federal expenditures are from U.S. Bureau of the Census, *Historical Statistics of the United States, Colonial Times to 1957,* p. 710.

total was estimated. If we refer to the Population Census source that King cites as the basis for his employment estimates, add up the occupations shown there as associated with government employment, and divide the total into his wage bill, we get an average of $5,000 per employee in 1870.[18] This figure is over 12 times the reasonable average ($397) that he estimates for all nonfarm employees.[19] But since most government employees prior to 1900 were wage earners and lower-salaried personnel, an average of at most $500 would be more like the true figure than $5,000.

C. Johnson's Estimates, 1900ff.

In a well-known study, Gale Johnson has developed a series for factor income distribution from 1900 on. "As is generally known," he summarizes, "employee compensation has increased in relative significance since 1900—from about 53–55 percent of the total in the first two decades to about 64 percent in recent years. . . . The total share of labor [i.e., including entrepreneurial labor] increased consistently for each overlapping decade beginning in 1915. . . ." [20] The overlapping decade figures, however, overlay what the annual data show. This basic advance to a new level was largely achieved in two jumps: from 1917 to 1918, and again from 1919 to 1920. (In Table 4-5 we summarize some of Johnson's results, utilizing unpublished annual data kindly provided by him.) A look at the underlying data indicates the sources of this gain—a decline in corporate profits, a decline in entrepreneurial earnings, and a marked rise in wages.[21] How reasonable are such declines and the changing ratio that they produce?

1. For 1917–1918 Johnson relies on a series published as "Department of Commerce" but concerning whose method of estimate we have no information.[22] That series shows a 25 percent fall in nonfarm entrepreneurial income from 1917 to 1918—an almost incredible change under wartime conditions, particularly when the available estimates show no decline in the number of these entrepreneurs. King's estimates, as well as the Martin estimates based largely on them, show a mild gain over the period.[23] Until

[18] 1900 Census, *Occupations* (p. 1) checked against 1870 Census, *The Statistics of the Population of the United States* (1872), pp. 764–765. We add employees of government, clerks, officials of government, army officers, and soldiers. (Excluding the military would make matters worse.)

[19] King, *op. cit.*, p. 168.

[20] Johnson, *op. cit.*, table 1.

[21] We rely on unpublished absolute data kindly provided by Professor Johnson.

[22] The series was taken from the National Industrial Conference Board, *The Economic Almanac 1951–1952*, p. 208. Though labeled there as "Department of Commerce," it has apparently never appeared in any Department of Commerce publication and that department has no information on its source.

[23] King, *op. cit.*, p. 108; Martin, *op. cit.*, p. 39; and Kuznets, *National Income: A Summary of Findings*, p. 463.

there is some basis for knowing how this "Department of Commerce" series was derived, we find little plausibility in these particular figures. They imply a sizable decline of average entrepreneurial earnings in trade, service, and manufacturing at a time when the wage rates and annual earnings

Table 4-5. Share of Employee Compensation in National Income (Johnson)

Date	Percent
1900–1909	55.0
1910–1914	55.4
1915–1919	51.8
1920–1924	61.7
1925–1929	59.6
1915	53.5
1916	52.3
1917	46.7
1918	54.2
1919	52.6
1920	60.9
1921	66.9
1922	59.9
1923	60.4
1924	61.5

of employees in these sectors were rising significantly. It is most improbable that the earnings of self-employed carpenters were declining while those of hired carpenters were soaring, or that the incomes of store owners were falling, while those of store managers were rising. A fortiori the labor component of nonfarm entrepreneurial income should certainly not be assumed to have declined, as is implicitly done in Johnson's computation of the service share, which takes that component as a flat percentage of the total.

2. It is for 1919–1920, however, that the major problem arises, for the ratio in 1918–1919 did not differ significantly from that prevailing over the first decade of the century. The real jump—to the level for the 1920s as a whole—came from 1919 to 1920. An explanation involves several elements.

Nonfarm Entrepreneurial Income. The Kuznets total for this group (which Johnson uses without change) falls by $2.2 billion from 1919 to 1920. $1.6 billion of that decline is in trade alone. Let us see how this basic shift in level from pre-1919 to 1920 and after took place in trade.[24] Now Kuznets actually estimates a rise for the portion of earnings with-

[24] Withdrawal and savings data are from Kuznets, *National Income: A Summary of Findings,* pp. 312, 316.

drawn by trade entrepreneurs, for he assumes they gained as did the average earnings of trade employees. Hence the trade-income decline he reports derives from his estimate of a still greater decline in the net savings of trade entrepreneurs.[25] The latter is computed on the assumption that the profit rate on sales of trade entrepreneurs paralleled that of trade corporations.[26] We summarize in the following table the implicit averages from Kuznets, and our estimate of King's implicit figures:[27]

		1919	1920	1921	Change, 1919 to 1920
Average annual					
Entrepreneurial income.....	Kuznets	$4,023	$2,556	$1,420	−$1,477
	King	2,535	2,460		− 75
Wage-salary...............	Kuznets A	1,399	1,418	1,354	+ 19
	Kuznets B	1,506	1,664	1,451	+ 158

King's entrepreneurial income series declines trivially, while his wage-salary figures and both of the Kuznets wage-salary averages show rises from 1919 to 1920. Kuznets's entrepreneurial average, however, reports a marked decline. If we follow the procedure used in later years of national income estimation, we would expect a rough concordance of change between the total income of the average entrepreneur in trade and the income of the average employee. Had Kuznets followed this procedure for his trade (and manufacturing) estimate, no marked change would appear in his implicit, nor in Johnson's explicit, figures on the United States total wage share from 1919 to 1920.

Alternatively, we can do as Kuznets did and stipulate that the withdrawn portion of entrepreneurial earnings did move as the wage salary—but that,

[25] *Ibid.*, p. 724, outlines the procedure for estimating the trade withdrawals.

[26] *Ibid.*, pp. 628, 726. Kuznets outlines a more complex procedure, which we here define roughly as "profit rate on sales."

[27] Kuznets's data are from *Ibid.*, pp. 718–719, using his column 3 estimate of employees for A, and column 4 for B. The implicit King figures were derived as follows: Realized income drawn by entrepreneurs and other property owners is given in King, *op. cit.*, p. 108. From his total we deduct dividends, interest, and rent to derive his implicit entrepreneurial income. King's dividend and interest figures appear in Simon Kuznets, *National Product in Wartime* (1945), p. 141. King's rent total can be computed by deducting from his realized income total (his *National Income*, p. 94) Kuznets's estimates of the same total minus rent which appear in *National Income and Its Composition, 1919–1938* (1940), table 86. We then divided this total by King's estimate for the number of entrepreneurs (his *National Income*, p. 62). The results will differ from those appearing in Kuznets's *National Product in Wartime*, p. 141, because of adjustments made by the latter in the King data (*Ibid.*, p. 144).

in addition, net savings of the enterprise moved in relationship to sales as did the corporate profit ratio. Our only empirical evidence is from a different period: Since the middle 1930s, when independent data begin, there appears to be a rough relationship between the trend in total incomes per entrepreneur in trade and the average employee in trade.[28]

We prefer to assume that the alternative incomes that link the entrepreneurial and labor market, and that affect the flow of manpower from one to the other, are total incomes in each status, rather than assuming that one component of entrepreneurial income parallels wages while the other may pursue its separate path.

We estimate a revised figure for nonfarm entrepreneurial income (col. 2, Table 4-6) by assuming that the average income of trade entrepreneurs did not fall from 1919 to 1920, but remained unchanged while wages rose.[29]

Farm Entrepreneurial Income. For farm entrepreneurial income we use the latest Department of Agriculture estimates[30] rather than earlier ones. These figures show a greater decline than those embodied in the Kuznets figures—apparently because of a far greater fall in cotton marketings.

Corporate Profits. We take the recent estimates of Goldsmith.[31] The gain shown would be even more marked if the basic Ebersole data on corporate profits were superseded by the NBER corporate sample for these years.[32]

[28] Department of Commerce estimates prior to the Bureau of Internal Revenue figures for entrepreneurial earnings in the late 1930s cannot be considered independent evidence on this point. The two move in the same direction in the immediate postwar year of 1945–1946 as well. They do not do so for 1946 to 1948. We attribute the entrepreneurial income decline 1946 to 1948 to the rise of about 10 percent a year in the number of trade entrepreneurs, largely under the stimulus of GI loans, etc. No equal pressure on entrepreneurial earnings, however, is suggested for 1919–1920, when the count of entrepreneurs rises only 3 percent, according to King. (The cycle forces predominate in 1920–1921 and 1948–1949 and overwhelm the factors we are distinguishing here.)

[29] Kuznets (*National Income and Its Composition,* p. 718) shows a fall of $1.6 billion, with essentially no change in the count of entrepreneurs. We take 1920 as given and deduct $1.6 billion from Johnson's 1919 figure for nonfarm entrepreneurs, so that the implicit component for trade stays constant.

[30] From *USDA Agriculture Handbook* 118, vol. 3, p. 43.

[31] Raymond W. Goldsmith, *A Study of Savings,* vol. III, p. 435, for tax liability and inventory valuation adjustment; vol. I, p. 939, for net earnings.

[32] Goldsmith used the original estimates of J. F. Ebersole et al., "Income Forecasting," *Review of Economic Statistics* (August, 1929). The NBER data appear in *Historical Statistics of the United States, Colonial Times to 1957* (p. 591). Because they relate only to large corporations, it seems inappropriate to use them. However, examination of the Ebersole estimates indicates that $15.7 billion was added to the reported *Statistics of Income* figures for 1919, largely on the basis of fitting

Interest and Rent. For interest and rent we use the Johnson figures. *Employee Compensation.* For employee compensation we adopt the Kuznets figures used by Johnson with only one change. The construction sector shows a marked rise.[33] We believe a decline to be more reasonable. The reported rise reflects application to (1) United States gross construction activity totals of (2) Ohio and Pennsylvania ratios of (*a*) wages and

Table 4-6. Factor Income and Shares: 1919, 1920 (In billions)

	Johnson	Revised data
Employee compensation		
1919	$37.1	$37.7
1920	43.9	43.9
Farm entrepreneurial		
1919	8.8	9.5
1920	7.4	7.1
Nonfarm entrepreneurial		
1919	9.4	7.8
1920	7.2	7.2
Interest and rent		
1919	7.5	7.5
1920	8.2	8.2
Corporate profits		
1919	7.7	8.4
1920	5.5	9.4
National income		
1919	70.5	70.9
1920	72.1	78.1

salaries to (*b*) gross construction totals. These results are then divided by an average wage salary whose 1919–1920 change is given by that for Ohio and Pennsylvania.[34] As thus estimated the activity per person engaged falls slightly from 1919 to 1920 in current dollars. Hence a 20 percent decline in constant dollars is implied.[35] We prefer here to assume that the

trends to the number of returns, total depreciation reported, etc., for various sets of years. With an 8.7 percent profit rate implicit in the reported figures, this comes to a fairly arbitrary implicit correction of the reported figures by the addition of $1.4 billion to the 1919 net income total, leading to a greater 1919–1920 decline.

[33] For the rise, see Kuznets, *National Income and Its Composition,* p. 641.

[34] *Ibid.,* pp. 653, 646.

[35] *Ibid.,* pp. 643, 641, for gross per person engaged. The gross per employee, while not directly estimated, should, we assume, have moved the same. The implicit deflator is that derived from the constant and current price construction totals of Simon Kuznets, *Capital in the American Economy, Its Formation and Financing* (1962), vol. II, tables 4 and 5.

constant dollar volume of work per employee did not decline from 1919 to 1920.[36] Working from employment and earnings data that we have derived elsewhere, we deduce a 1919–1920 rise of $50 million instead of the $650 million rise implicit in Johnson's figures.[37]

Suppose we revise Kuznets's trade entrepreneurial totals above, adopt the latest revision of the USDA figures for farm entrepreneurial incomes rather than the earlier one available to Johnson, use corporate profits data derived from Goldsmith's recent study rather than those in the quasi "Department of Commerce" series, and make a minor change in the employee compensation figures of Kuznets that underlie Johnson's figures. We arrive at the figures in Table 4-6. What do they sum to? The share of wages in the national income as shown in Johnson's original figures and in our revised ones is given in the following table.

Percent of Wages in the National Income

	1919	1920	Gain
Johnson............	52.6	60.9	8.3
Revised............	53.2	56.2	3.0

The gain in the revised figures is less than half as great. Because Johnson links his series for the years 1900 to 1919 by a ratio link in 1919, this means that the level of these earlier years would be much closer to that of the 1920s if these revised data were used for 1919.

One further comment must be made. Take the revised figures, which reflect a marked fall in farm entrepreneurial earnings, and compute the wage share only for nonfarm income originating. What is the result?

Wage Ratio in Nonfarm Income

	1919	1920	Gain
Revised........	60.0	60.1	0.1

The gain for the nonfarm economy was trivial. Hence the massive upward shift shown in the original estimates diminishes largely in the revised fig-

[36] Our only independent evidence on the point unfortunately relates to the period since 1940, when our construction employment figures are derived independently of the volume totals. For these years a rise in the real output per employee takes place even when the rate of gain in construction is checked.

[37] We work essentially from the same activity figures as used by Kuznets, but deflate somewhat differently. Most important, however, we have an employment benchmark prior to 1929, and also interpolate between a 1900 and a 1929 benchmark for activity per employee in constant dollars.

ures. And of the gain that does appear, virtually all reflects a shift within the farm sector.

D. King's Estimates, 1909ff.

King provides annual estimates for 1909 and subsequent years that constitute the ultimate basis of most of the later work in the field.[38] They have been used by the Department of Agriculture to extrapolate national income back to 1909. They appear to be the most likely source for the "Department of Commerce" series published in the *Economic Almanac*, and used by Johnson to run his data back to 1909. And they likewise constitute the basic fund of information Martin used for extrapolating most of his components back to 1909 from 1919. Since King's figures for 1919ff. have been clearly superseded by Kuznets's work, it remains to consider only their use for 1909–1919 extrapolation.

King's results can be summarized simply—and the problem they raise noted. From 1909 to 1917 he shows little change in the ratio of wages and salaries to the national income, while for 1918 he estimates a decline.[39] Hence the rise he shows in labor's share from 1909 to 1919 derives from his estimate that a marked 1917–1918 gain took place. How does this gain arise? It comes rather simply from his estimate that entrepreneurial withdrawals rose a trivial 5 percent, while employee compensation rose by 25 percent.[40] Since he shows virtually no change in the number of entrepreneurs over this period and a decline in the number of employees, he implies an even greater discrepancy on a per earner basis. Moreover, he assumes a $2 billion rise in realized income drawn from farming. Therefore he implicitly estimates no rise (or an actual decline) in income per nonfarm entrepreneur during a period when wages were skyrocketing.[41]

Labor's share, in consequence, jumps. Such a change is wholly unreasonable. First, had such a differential developed, a substantial movement from entrepreneurial pursuits into wage work should have taken place, as in 1941–1942. But King stipulates no change in the number of entrepreneurs. Secondly, experience in World War II (when we have data rather than reasoned surmise to guide us) indicates that entrepreneurial income rose by as much as or more than wages. From 1940 to 1941, for example, wages and salaries rose by about 30 percent—or much the same as from 1917 to 1918—but income per entrepreneur income rose by

[38] W. I. King, *The National Income and Its Purchasing Power*, 1930.
[39] King's data as summarized and adjusted in Kuznets, *National Income and Its Composition*, table 94. If we relate King's employee compensation to his realized income (*Ibid.*, p. 471), we arrive at the same trend.
[40] Data summarized in *Ibid.*, table 93.
[41] King's count of entrepreneurs appears in *The National Income and Its Purchasing Power*, p. 62, while his realized income figures appear on p. 108.

nearly 40 percent.[42] If the wage worker had shifted to silk shirts in 1918 the trade entrepreneur selling them to him did not continue wearing cotton. And with construction wage rates rising (according to King) and construction booming, would the incomes of the independent construction entrepreneur have remained unchanged?

E. Estimates, 1919ff.

For the period since 1919 estimates derivable by known procedures become available. The Kuznets figures for 1919 to 1938 have already been considered in connection with Johnson's estimates. We concluded that the gain from 1919 to later years (and by extension, from 1919–1920 or 1919–1924 to later years) reflects a significant 1919–1920 rise in the estimates. After reducing this estimated rise by adopting alternative estimating techniques, we concluded that the remainder is equivalent to the decline in farm entrepreneurial earnings. Hence the share of wages in nonfarm income originating did not change for 1919 to 1929. Given the tremendous cyclical impact on the data for the 1930s, we cannot usefully use the 1930 to 1938 data in considering long-term trends.[43]

For the period since 1929, the Department of Commerce figures have been precisely and comprehensively analyzed by Denison.[44] After excluding household and government sectors—presumably because of the lack of a property income counterpart to wages for these sectors—Denison finds that a small gain in the employee percentage in the ordinary business sector took place from 1929 to 1950.[45] The well-known sizable rise of the employee share in overall national income over this period therefore proves to be primarily a reflection of changes in imputed rent on owned homes, profits on investments abroad, and other flows that are irrelevant to an interest in the substitution of one productive factor for another in the process of economic change.

We would conclude that the relevant United States data for studying factor substitution and return relate primarily to manufacturing, mining,

---

[42] U.S. Department of Commerce, *National Income,* 1954 edition, tables 14, 17, 25, 28.

[43] "The relative share of income from work in national income as a whole shows, of course, appreciable short-run variations in the course of the business cycle. . . . Consequently, when we engage in long-run analysis it is essential to select for comparison periods during which the cyclical factor may be assumed to have canceled out." Fellner, *op. cit.,* p. 264.

[44] Edward Denison, "Distribution of National Income," *Survey of Current Business* (June, 1952), pp. 16–18.

[45] Denison reports a gain of under 1 percent. If we used revised data from *U.S. Income and Output,* p. 134, the figure is 1.4 percent. Hence there seems to be no basis for a 5 percent gain that has been referred to in this connection.

the utilities, and railroads.[46] Examination of adjusted data for manufac-turing[47] show that payrolls as a percentage of value added did show a long-term stability:[48]

1889–1899	54.0
1919–1929	51.5
1947–1954	53.9

(Even the lower figure for the 1920s may reflect the inclusion of contract work in these data, unlike those for the other periods.) A more precise measurement, using direct estimates of property income (incorporating an allowance for current value depreciation) can be made from the data of Wooden and Wasson,[49] who show an approximate constancy[50] over the shorter period from 1929 to the early 1950s. But an examination of data for individual industries is really the area for investigation, and here pre-liminary study shows both striking regularity and striking variation. With the recent issuance of the long-awaited study by Creamer, Dobrovolsky, and Borenstein, together with other volumes in the broad study of capital

[46] Conceptual and empirical problems make it useless to consider long-term trends for most components of finance and transportation.

[47] 1899: 1900 *Census of Manufactures,* vol. I, p. 59, provides data from which we can adjust to exclude contract work, hand trades, and firms grossing under $500. For the 1889 to 1899 average, we compute ratios from 1954 *Census of Manufactures,* part I, pp. 2–3, then use the ratio of the 1899 average to the average of the two to raise the above adjusted 1899 estimate. (1919 to 1929 data on contract work, smaller firms are not available.) Data for later years are from 1954 Census, *loc. cit.* Data prior to 1889 were not used because of major differences in coverage of small firms.

[48] Solow (p. 627) notes a small increase after 1899 and finds it possibly due to the changing character of output. Our data show no rise. The difference may stem from the fact that procedures using unadjusted census data as reported tacitly use an 1899 figure inclusive of railroad-car construction, whereas later census figures exclude this high-wage–sales ratio industry.

[49] Donald Wooden and Robert Wasson, "Manufacturing Investment since 1929," *Survey of Current Business* (December, 1956), p. 20.

[50] An admirable, succinct study by Martin Bronfenbrenner, "A Note on Relative Shares and the Elasticity of Substitution," *Journal of Political Economy* (June, 1960) emphasizes how wide a range of substitution elasticities and changes in capital-labor ratios are compatible with what appear to be "small" changes in labor's share. His review on this ground alone throws out much discussion about long-term stability. On the other hand, suppose we credit Creamer's data on the changes in the capital-labor ratio in manufacturing from 1899 to 1919 and the reversal from 1919 to 1953. (Daniel Creamer et al., *Capital in Manufacturing and Mining: Its Formation and Financing* (1961). Then by the use of Bronfenbrenner's formula we can see that the labor-share ratios shown above imply striking changes in the elasticity of sub-stitution from one period to the next. Hence the lack of change in labor's share for manufacturing that we estimate above would appear to be of economic significance.

formation and financing, it is possible to begin such work. The prospect for an extension of Department of Commerce work on manufacturing investment gives us hope of data carefully adjusted for the complexities of recent changes in depreciation allowances. Given such materials, economists ought to be able to say something useful, if not paradoxical, about the process of long-term factor substitution in the American economy.

II

We turn now to the link between the empirical measures and the theoretical model. Suppose us the fortunate possessors of a lengthy series for national income—a series of as high quality as anyone could desire. How closely would that series bring the theoretical models to the test of reality? Many of the limitations of measured national income for this purpose have, it is fortunate, been recently canvassed by Irving Kravis, who demonstrates that varying treatment of these elements, numerous and significant though they are, would distort our reading of final results by very little.[1] However, two major factors remain, which make inappropriate any extended attention either to the statistics on labor's share in total national income, its share of income originating in agriculture, trade, and service, or any combination that includes these sectors.

A

Entrepreneurship. The problem here is that at the close of the year the entrepreneur finds in his till a sum—not always positive—reflecting the return on his personal abilities as well as the return on his invested capital. To discuss the relative return to the capital and to the labor which he uses in his activities, we must disentangle the contributions made by each. If we cannot do so, we must eschew the apparently relevant data for those industry sectors dominated by entrepreneurs. What are our dissection choices? (1) We may ask the farmer, or businessman. Without even raising the question as to whether he could give us reliable figures, we may doubt whether a rational entrepreneur would attempt to do so; what the market has joined together he will not put apart. (2) We can make some guesses from an analysis of the production function. But theory tells us nothing about how to allocate the joint product of two or more factors so as to reveal the average contributions of each factor when the market does not operate in these terms and provides us with no information.

Failing all else, most analysts have made different types of arbitrary assignments. One is to stipulate a rate of return to entrepreneurial labor.

[1] See Kravis's lucid discussion of market-nonmarket activity shifts, the role of government debt, of historical cost depreciation, etc. Irving Kravis, "Relative Income Shares in Fact and Theory," *American Economic Review* (December, 1959), pp. 926–930.

They then easily conclude that the balance of the entrepreneur's income must be the return to his capital.[2] Conversely, others have stipulated a rate of return to his capital and thence inferred the rate to his labor. One procedure, of course, gives a significantly different result than does the other—but neither one has any better theoretical justification than the other. A more thoughtful proposal allocates entrepreneurial income between capital and labor in accordance with the ratio of property to wage income in the portion of the economy outside the entrepreneurial sector, changing when that ratio changes.[3] While more precise, it does not suffice. None of these proposals deals with four basic questions.

1. How can we agree on what rate of return to stipulate for entrepreneurial capital, since stipulate we must, implicitly or explicitly? The risk may be greater, or less, than that which prevails for capital in, say, the corporate sector. Perhaps we could agree that an entrepreneur investing in his own store, or farm, must surely be more confident of earning a return than if he invested randomly in any other store or farm. (Would the typical entrepreneur go into business if he lacked such confidence?) But if so, his risks (as he perceives them) are smaller than those for investors generally in the same industry. To assume that his capital earns the full market rate of return would therefore overstate the rate for an equivalent risk as the entrepreneur himself saw it. But even if there were full agreement on this—which is doubtful—could we agree on the numerical reduction to be made in the market rate to give a truer measure of his earnings on capital?

2. Can we proceed any more successfully by intuiting the labor earnings of the entrepreneur? The massive decline of self-employment in trade, service, and agriculture during 1941–1942 suggests that crudely disguised unemployment did exist in those industries—with many a self-employed person whose capacities were below the average for employees in the same industries. The market value of the labor services of such entrepreneurs may be zero, but so long as they can pay themselves (out of capital) they will receive more than the market would offer. (Data showing a short work year for certain categories of entrepreneurs, and the high failure rate

[2] This procedure has been widely used by W. J. Spillman, the Department of Agriculture, and others. Its most recent important use is in the study by John Kendrick, *Productivity Trends in the United States* (1960). Kendrick estimates labor input by weighting man-hours in each major industry group, inclusive of those worked by proprietors and unpaid family workers, by base-period average hourly employee compensation.

[3] Kravis, *op. cit.,* p. 925. Denison suggests: "If one *must* allocate, a preferable procedure would be to assume the division between labor and property inputs and income to be the same in noncorporate as in corporate firms." Conference on Research in Income and Wealth, *Trends in the American Economy in the Nineteenth Century* (1960), vol. 24, p. 402.

for firms in trade and service suggest that this is not merely hypothetical.)[4] Conversely, there will unquestionably be many entrepreneurs whose talents reach far above the level for employees in the same industry. How do we rationally estimate the proportion in each category? Surely not by using the simple 50:50 ratio implied when we estimate their labor income as equal to the average for all employees.

3. The advantages of being one's own master surely exist and are surely positive. If they operated as other equalizing advantages do, they should work to keep down the dollar returns from self-employment. But by how much? And if some mystic with a Monte Carlo method gave us a figure, how much should we deduct from the labor share and how much from the property share? If one economist makes such an assignment, on what basis can he contend that his assignment ratio is preferable to any other?

4. But away with these qualifications. Suppose we agree on some allocation at a point in time. On what basis can we choose the true allocation for the next point in time? The shifting tide of hopefuls that enter, and failures that leave, self-employment suggests that the net returns to self-employment are ever changing relative to the returns to capital and labor elsewhere. But how much of this net change is in the return to capital and how much in the return to labor? Without light on this apparently impenetrable maze, we would only mantle in obscurity the very changes in which we are interested: namely, within industries dominated by self-employment, how do the relative returns to labor and capital change over time? Kravis's solution is surely in the right direction, for he stipulates that within self-employment the ratio of capital to labor returns will change in parallel with that outside self-employment. But our present problem still remains; the regress is apparently an infinite one. If the ratio of one to the other is assumed to vary as the outside economy, then its assumed variation over time adds nothing to our knowledge of true variation over time; we are simply iterating the changes in the nonself-employment sector.[5]

---

[4] In a typically incisive discussion of the allocation of entrepreneurial income between labor and property, Kuznets suggests different markets for entrepreneurial and other capital, as for entrepreneurial and other labor, noting that "a direct estimate of the return on the property component" for United States agriculture "leaves a return on labor that is below the going wages of hired labor; and a direct estimate of the return on labor leaves a return on property distinctly below any comparable return rate." Simon Kuznets, "Quantitative Aspects of the Economic Growth of Nations," *Economic Development and Cultural Change* (April, 1959), vol. 4, p. 26. See also Simon Rottenberg, "Note on Economic Progress and Occupational Distribution," *Review of Economics and Statistics* (May, 1953) for general comments on the level of entrepreneurial abilities in underdeveloped countries.

[5] Kravis does not suggest that the absolute level of return here adds to our knowledge, seeking only to deal with the central issue of changing relative income shares. He notes the desirability of allocation not in proportion to economy-wide shares but to those within the same industry (*op. cit.*, p. 926). But even if this were done, it would not meet the point raised above.

Given the evidence from our competitive economy of flows of men (and money) into and out of noncorporate enterprise, we have little basis for assuming that the rate of return to men (or money) in entrepreneurial pursuits is constant relative to the return in corporate enterprise, or government bonds (or enlistment in the army).[6] Moreover, we have no basis for distinguishing amid the net returns to the enterprise those belonging clearly to capital from those belonging to labor. Until we do, there is no information to be gathered from working with data inclusive of returns to self-employment.

We therefore conclude that nothing useful can be learned by dealing with relative shares for (1) the economy as a whole, (2) the nonfarm economy, or (3) agriculture, distribution, or any industry (or combination of industries) in which entrepreneurial income plays a significant part. If we stipulate an unchanged rate of return or ratio within the entrepreneurial industries, we clearly add nothing to our knowledge of the changing rate of return to each factor. If we stipulate that the returns moved parallel to that in the rest of economy or industry, we simply iterate what we know already. If we are free to stipulate a changing ratio—and in the mobile, competitive, real world changes surely take place—we can discover empirical relationships of any type, largely created by our initial arbitrary stipulation of how these changes took place. Hence we bid a regretful farewell to the limited bits of information that appear to exist even on the mere totals of entrepreneurial income, finding them of little service in our quest.

B

Government. Without descending to modern instances, there is clearly no basis for distinguishing what portion of the ancient Roman senator's salary derived from his florid oratory (labor) and what from the shining toga and elegant ivory chairs (capital) in which he reposed. Nor would we want to deduce, even with data, that the man with the larger desk received a higher income because he had a larger desk (more capital); his commanding presence alone might account for that income. Moreover, our income estimates include no allowance for the services of government capital. As estimates have been made hitherto, a rising level of government employment automatically worked to bring an increase in labor's share—whether government assets quintupled over the same period, were reduced to zero, or remained unchanged.[7]

[6] And without identical changes of capital stock-labor ratios in entrepreneurial and nonentrepreneurial sectors, we would have still not solved the problem.

[7] Solow excludes the government from his detailed analysis for this reason (p. 623). Kravis (*op. cit.,* p. 928) and Denison ("Distribution of National Income," p. 17) each note the lack of a property component in government income originating. The difficulty—if not dubiousness—of estimating the current value and return

We conclude that for measuring long-term trends in relative shares there is little to be learned about changes in relative shares resulting even from massive changes in the production functions, if we concentrate our view on changes in total national income, or income inclusive of any significant entrepreneurial components. For the United States, this leaves as industries not so dominated primarily manufacturing and individual industries in transport, communication, and mining.[8]

III

The Medusa-like fascination of the constant ratio of labor income to national income springs from an apparently glaring contrast between the classic patterns of neoclassical distribution theory and the brute statistics on distributive shares.[1] Theory begins from the reasonable definition that the respective returns to capital and labor are fixed by the relative prices and quantities of each. But since the past century has witnessed phenomenal changes in "the techniques of production, in the accumulation of capital relative to labor and in real income per head," [2] should we not expect marked changes in the ratio of labor to capital returns? Most writers at this point have gone on to contrast the statistics with this apparent implication of theory. Solow has properly raised a skeptical question, however: Can one skip so simply from one to the other? What a gulf separates the individual firm as described in neoclassical theory from the compiled numbers on factor shares for the economy. Between the two lies "a whole string of intermediate variables: elasticities of substitution, commodity demand and factor supply conditions, markets of different degrees

on government assets particularly military assets, is, of course, the reason why we have no such data.

[8] We exclude government for the reasons noted above. Construction, even without the great role of self-employment, has little reliable data on shares prior to 1939, the existing estimates being sensible reconstructions rather than relying on any independent measure.

[1] We do not consider interests beyond distribution theory. A number of authors have, however, reviewed the data with the thought that such numbers cast light on "the significance of union power . . . economic development, egalitarian movements." The quotation is from an admirable review by Paul Davidson, *Theories of Aggregate Income Distribution* (1960), p. 1. See too Allan Cartter, *Theory of Wages and Employment* (1959), chap. 11. Simon Kuznets has some concise and conclusive remarks on the limitations of the data for any such discussions in "Quantitative Aspects of the Economic Growth of Nations," *Economic Development and Cultural Change* (April, 1959), p. 56.

[2] N. Kaldor, "Alternative Theories of Distribution," *Review of Economic Studies* (February, 1956), p. 84. The recent discussion of excessive stability appears to stem from Keynes's 1939 article. In an earlier look at the same United Kingdom figures from Bowley—though not the United States figures—Hicks concluded that the capital share fell significantly from 1880 to 1913 (from 34 to 31 percent) because the elasticity of substitution fell. His frame of reference was the rise in the share from medieval times. *Theory of Wages* (1932), pp. 130–133.

of competitiveness and monopoly, far from neutral taxes" and so on.[3] Without necessarily agreeing that a look at these complicating forces leads to "an expectation of 'relative stability' if anything," [4] we take Solow's perceptive caution to mark precisely the point for initial inquiry.

A

Let us begin with a definition: The proportion of wages to property income R is a function of the price and quantity ratios for labor service W and capital service K:

$$R = f\left(\frac{P_w}{P_k}, \frac{Q_w}{Q_k}\right) \tag{1}$$

A constancy in the wage ratio must follow inexorably if every movement in the price ratio is neatly offset by a contrary change in the quantity ratio. Solow has demonstrated that such an offset is virtually assured if only we assume a reasonable figure of one-third for the elasticity of substitution.[5] Kravis finds, similarly, that a fairly constant share did appear for the United States because "under conditions of rapid expansion in production labor was relatively inelastic in supply and rising rapidly in price" while "capital was apparently much more elastic or at any rate rapidly growing in supply." [6] But we only push the question back a stage, if we thus demonstrate that a palatable figure for the elasticity of substitution will yield numbers within the bounds of our historical measures of labor's share.

Why this particular substitution rate? The elasticity of substitution that may be hypothesized—whether one-third, one-fourth, or any other figure— is surely not a new mysterious constant, given by forces outside the market economy. Why this proportion, and why this elasticity, rather than any other? [7] And why an immutably fixed one? Should we not hesitate to hazard so much on any "bright particular" number as an explanation?

[3] Solow, p. 620. Martin Bronfenbrenner, in "A Contribution to the Aggregate Theory of Wages," *Journal of Political Economy* (December, 1956), systematically reviews the most important of these factors in his study of the question of whether in recent American history wage-rate increases have added to real demand.

[4] Solow, *op. cit.*, pp. 620–621.

[5] *Ibid.*, p. 629. See too Kravis, p. 940.

[6] *Ibid.*, pp. 943–944. Weintraub finds that "either the M/A ratios [marginal to average physical product] and the Ed magnitudes [price elasticity of demand for specific products] must have remained constant or they must have operated systematically and fortuitously to neutralize each other's variation when the stock of equipment, the level of employment, and the nature of the product-mix underwent change." Sidney Weintraub, *An Approach to the Theory of Income Distribution* (1958), p. 82.

[7] Premising a constant elasticity in turn implies that the historical contract curve that relates the quantity to the price ratio must have been a straight line. But it is difficult to see why an a priori reason why the line should be straight throughout time, or why a curve would not be equally reasonable.

Kaldor premises stability as a result of a constant saving–output ratio, his corollary being that changes in the propensity to save out of profits compensate for changes in the propensity to save out of wages.[8] This question has been examined carefully by Melvin Reder, who concludes that historical data are consistent with this theory, but likewise with quite different ones.[9] In a recent telling essay on "Economic Growth and the Problem of Inflation,"[10] Kaldor stipulates that "a capitalist economy, after a certain period of adaptation, will tend to settle down to a rate of economic growth and accumulation where the growth rate of capital is the same as the growth rate of output, since at this point the . . . rate of profit on capital will be neither rising nor falling. The historical constancy of the capital output ratio, of the share of profit in income . . . in advanced capitalist economies is thus explicable in terms of forces which tend to bring these two growth rates (of capital and output) into equality with one another" (p. 223). He then goes on to state that "wages and profits form a constant proportion of output" in "any steadily growing economy where the proportion of output devoted to investment is constant" provided "the propensities to save out of profits and wages are assumed to be given" (p. 225). But why these propensities need be stable through time requires some demonstration. Indeed in later discussion of laggard growth Kaldor clearly points out that "if the savings propensities were halved, the share of profit in income would be doubled at any given ratio of investment to output," going on to discuss how "the process of accumulation and growth is periodically interrupted."[11] This surely implies that the saving propensities are not necessarily fixed.

B

We believe, however, that it is possible to seek a solution in the theory of distribution; and suggest that a market mechanism does exist which works in the direction of long-run constancy—quite apart from any specific ratio of wages to national income, or elasticity of substitution, that may seem most reasonable to us. Agreeing with the emphasis on the elasticity of substitution laid by Solow and Kravis, we go on to consider the forces that determine the level of that elasticity over long periods, constant or not.

Let us consider the quantity ratio in equation (1) above. What deter-

[8] Kaldor, *loc. cit.* Cartter (*loc. cit.*) presents a theory similar to Kaldor's in emphasizing the marginal propensities to save of laborers and capitalists, but he does not premise stability of each, nor compensating movements.

[9] "Alternative Theories of Labor's Share" in Moses Abramovitz (ed.), *The Allocation of Economic Resources* (1959).

[10] *Economica* (August, 1959).

[11] Kaldor, "Economic Growth and the Problem of Inflation, Part II," *Economica* (November, 1959), p. 290.

mines the size of this ratio? The answer, for a broadly competitive economy, is that the ratio is a function of two variables—the price ratio in the present period, and the quantity ratio in the previous period:

$$\frac{Q_w}{Q_k} = f\left(\frac{P_w}{P_k}, \frac{Q_{w_0}}{Q_{k_0}}\right) \tag{2}$$

That the price ratio in the current period is one forceful determinant we can hardly doubt: Where entrepreneurs have free access to capital and labor markets we would expect shifts in the ratio of prices to induce shifts in the quantity of each used.

However, only limited substitution possibilities can be grasped within the short term. The production coefficients are therefore destined to appear invariant to many price changes. It is for this reason that we include the quantity ratios of the prior period as a second variable, for they reflect the coefficients in being. (Thus once a bank of machines has been installed, as Johansen has recently emphasized, it will require a fixed complement of manpower throughout the life of the machines.[12] While there are some qualifications to this generalization, they do not warrant our ignoring this variable.)[13]

But of course the fixed-complement technology itself is not really a given; for the ratio of manpower to machine inputs at time zero is in turn a function of relative prices in the previous period(s)—when the machine-man ratio was adopted from a spectrum of alternatives. Substituting this earlier price ratio for the quantity ratio in the second equation gives us:

$$\frac{Q_w}{Q_k} = f\left(\frac{P_w}{P_k}, \frac{P_{w_0}}{P_{k_0}}\right) \tag{3}$$

Substituting (3) in (1), we get:

$$R = f\left(\frac{P_w}{P_k}, \frac{P_{w_0}}{P_{k_0}}\right) \tag{4}$$

The ratio of wage to property income is therefore a function of the price ratio of labor to capital in the current and preceding period—or, more precisely, preceding periods.[14]

---

[12] Lief Johansen, "Substitution versus Fixed Production Coefficients in the Theory of Economic Growth: a Synthesis," *Econometrica* (April, 1959), p. 158.

[13] Should there occur a marked variation in the ratio of the price of labor to that of capital, marginal equipment can be sold in the market and new equipment bought—and bought until a point is reached where the technical ratio has actually changed. Over a longer period technical substitution is, of course, still more likely to take place as old equipment is fully written off.

[14] Since the entrepreneurial choice is really with respect to price trends over the useful life of the capital investment under consideration, it is really the expected price ratio that is relevant. We assume that to be some function of the past and

If this sequence of price ratios could vary randomly, we would have precious little reason to anticipate any great stability of the wage–property income proportion. And if the ratios systematically rose or fell we would expect that proportion to move remorselessly up or down. Only if basic forces made for a stability in the price ratios would we anticipate a stability in the income ratio. At first sight we have no reason to expect such stability. (Indeed, if we attached the same importance to monopolistic elements as Kalecki and Mitra did when explaining the wage proportion, we would premise so solid a stability in the price trend for one factor as could only result in greater instability in the ratio of that price series to the other.)[15]

True, if we assumed a fixed elasticity of substitution all would be magically simplified. For Bronfenbrenner's analysis demonstrates that a wide choice of elasticities would all tend to give us factor shares that varied within only a narrow range. But what warrant do we have for creating any such *numerus ex machina*—a new constant, unwavering and unyielding amid all the forces of economic change? Furthermore, a look at Creamer's data for manufacturing suggests that in this major sector the capital-labor ratio went in one direction from 1899 to 1919, and in the other from 1919 to 1953. Meanwhile factor shares remained almost unchanged, according to our estimates. Hence the elasticity of substitution must have changed significantly through time. Arbitrarily positing any fixed elasticity (whether 1, 0.66, 0.50, etc.) is therefore no way to satisfactorily explain the relative constancy in the sequence of price ratios discussed above.

Let us see what can be said about the determinants of the price ratio. We simplify our problem by taking the price of labor as given in all periods. (Its determinants do not matter here; they are fixed as part of a general equilibrium solution. Here we need only deal with changes in the price of capital vis-à-vis that of labor.) What, then, fixes the price of capital used in production relative to those forces that determine the price of labor?

Demand for Capital.   Consider a manufacturing company. Its demand for capital reflects the uses to which the capital will be put—investment in machinery, or inventories, land, etc. Now while machinery, for example, is often treated as technically complementary to labor in the production of most goods (on terms set by the engineers) this relationship basically re-

present ratios. This is probably incorrect: An allowance should be made for the change in these ratios on the assumption that entrepreneurs would recognize the forces in this country making for a long-run rise in wage rates, the long-run accumulation of capital, and the decline in the risk component of capital cost. Such an allowance would lead to a bias in favor of a high capital-labor ratio. However, if steadily exercised, this bias would tend to bring back the relative price of capital.

[15] Michal Kalecki, *Theory of Economic Dynamics* (1954). Keynes speculated on the role of monopolistic elements but did not see his way to accepting them as a real force for explanation.

flects the underlying price relationship.[16] Were labor to become a free good while machinery continued to command a price, then over time we would expect a marked increase in the ratio of labor to machinery as capital-saving methods were introduced. "Technical" requirements might still forbid complete substitution. Sociological ones would certainly do so. Within the limits set by these constraints, however, there would still be ample room for wide variation determined by the relative profitability of using one factor versus the other. But that profitability would be set by the changing price ratio of one to the other—assuming an initial long-run competitive equilibrium position in which the marginal revenues from each are equal.

Supply of Capital. What about the supply side? The supply forces that work to fix the cost of capital include the interest rate and the price of a unit of capital service. Variations in the former appear to have had small consequence on the long-period share of return to capital in the national income—small not in terms of economic importance but as compared to the much greater effects of variation in the prices of machinery and plant. (Over the past 60 years prices of producers' durable equipment have risen about 300 percent, while 10-year bond yields have changed about 10 percent, from 3.2 to 2.9 percent.[17] Moreover, the ratio of interest to total costs of machinery service over the life of most equipment is relatively small. Hence variations in interest rates of high economic significance have occurred, but their contribution to changing the numbers on factor shares has been small by comparison with variations in the price of machinery and other capital items.

Let us look to the determinants of the price of these services.[18] The supply forces going to fix the unit price of machinery are those involved in

The cost of labor
The cost of materials
"Normal profits"
Rents, advertising, and other costs

---

[16] Variations in the demand for capital as a purely technical complement to labor will not tend to change the relative price of one to the other and hence can be ignored here. To simplify discussion, we convert the problem to a two-factor one, treating land costs henceforth as commutable into machinery and construction costs —and label the latter as machinery for convenience.

[17] Kuznets's implicit price index for producers' durables just about doubles from 1897–1901 to 1927–1931, and the Department of Commerce series more than doubles from 1929 to 1957. *Historical Statistics,* vol. II, pp. 142–144. Bond-yield data are from *Ibid.,* p. 657.

[18] We consider first the unit price of equipment, assuming no change in its productive capacity. In the real world, of course, the manufacturer may cheapen machinery service either by cutting price, by raising productive capacity or by a combination of the two.

In 1957 the machinery industries sold something like $26 million worth of goods, of which we may estimate that[19]

$10.0 was used for wages and salaries
$ 8.0 was used for materials purchases
$ 0.3 was used for rent and interest
$ 1.1 was used for net profit (after tax)
$ 1.7 was used for taxes

We assume that variations in rent, taxes, and corporate dividend policy are numerically unimportant in determining price variation, given their small share in total cost, a generally competitive industry, and the limited dollar range of their variation. Hence it is the fluctuating level of wage and of material costs that dominates the change of final product charges by the machinery industry. But by what are material (and component) costs determined?

On the demand side they are fixed (1) by variations in total production, but these—involving technical complementarity—do not alter the capital-labor price ratio,[20] and (2) by the buyer's option of producing in a different fashion, using a different level of fabrication as a partial substitute for raw materials or components. The use of the latter option, of course, is swayed by the supply schedules for the industries that provide materials to the components and materials industries per se, and by the wages in the latter industries. On the supply side these will reflect wage costs in steel, in hand tools, in coal, in railroads, and in the industries that directly and ultimately provide materials to the machinery industry.

Hence it is wage costs in machinery industries and in the suppliers to

[19] Data on sales, rent, interest, profit, taxes from *Statistics of Income, Corporation Income Tax Returns, 1957–58* (p. 27) for machinery except transport and electrical. For compensation of employees we use *U.S. Income and Output* (p. 200). For materials we take the Internal Revenue Service total for cost of goods sold, deduct wages, and round the figures. The major problem in this simple procedure is a possible significant change in inventory holdings. From *Business Statistics* (1959), p. 20, we see that inventory change over the taxable year was in fact quite small, assuming most tax years to end June through January.

[20] This statement is something of an exaggeration: At markedly different levels of output there could be economies of scale greater for one factor than another. (Eric Schiff, in a penetrating discussion of "Factor Substitution and the Composition of Input" for the 1958 Income Conference, has emphasized the scale effect and pointed out that production processes are not necessarily so "input homogeneous" as to permit easy substitution throughout the scale range.) We would expect that, in the long run, changes in size of production run (and possibly plant) consequent upon scale economies would be explicable for present purposes by the buyer's freedom to change production techniques. (Also, we assume that resources of one class of imports are not drastically limited while others are readily available.)

the machinery industry that substantially shape the supply price of machinery.[21]

If changes of wage costs in machinery bore no necessary relationship to changes in other industries, this would not get us forward. But in fact they do. Wage rates for common labor in the machinery industry, for example, must broadly move together with those for common labor in steel. If, for the same quality of labor, machinery industries begin paying more, then the steel industry, etc., must match the rate change or begin to lose labor.[22] The same is true for cranemen, machinists, carpenters, truck drivers, etc. And there must be a similar correspondence even for jobs that seem peculiar to one industry: Were machinery industries to double the rate paid on a simple machinery assembly operation characteristic of these industries, the steel industry and others must begin to raise their rates for broadly similar skills or see their expert semiskilled people begin moving out to jobs in machinery. In a competitive labor market over the long term, therefore, we expect to see wage rates for major occupations change similarly in the machinery industry and in its supplying industries.[23]

There remains one step. If productivity advances in the machinery industry were negatively correlated with those in its supplying industries, the broad correspondence of wage *rate* trends might be so nullified as to make each wage *cost* series take a different path. We see no reason to assume so unlikely a negative relationship. Because of the endless problems of measuring deflated output in the machinery industries, we have almost no empirical material. But if we may take such other metal-manipulating industries as transport equipment to give us a suggestion and relevant indication, we find their "labor productivity" advanced over the decades in the same direction as that for steel, coal mining, lumber manufacturing, etc.[24]

[21] I am indebted to Bert Hickman for calling my attention to the similar point made by Robert Grosse in "The Structure of Capital," in W. W. Leontief, *Studies in the Structure of the American Economy* (1953), p. 186. Grosse finds that "substitution occurs chiefly when there are technical improvements in capital goods production which result in a fall in the ratio of the price of capital goods to the price of labor. But with a given technique, there will be relatively little price substitution." Since the choice of technique itself is determined by relative prices and returns, the latter assumption leads to conclusions wide of our present concern.

[22] We are speaking here of correspondence of movement, not identity of level.

[23] We assume that the role of union and government intervention, however great, does not significantly nullify this statement. In a recent review of the considerable literature on the role of the union and an extended analysis of his own, Gregg Lewis concluded for a relatively small influence of unions on relative wages. See Lewis's paper for the Universities–National Bureau Committee for Economic Research, Conference on Labor Economics, April, 1960. A fortiori the differential effect as between industries using the same type of labor is likely to be still less.

[24] Solomon Fabricant, *Employment in Manufacturing, 1899–1939.* Harold Barger

Surely the thrust of productivity advance was at work in the machinery industry. If so, would not the price of machinery services necessarily fall in relation to wage rates? [25] The answer to this question lies in a further one: From what sources did this productivity advance derive? If it involved the use of machinery, then the machine-producing industry must needs be defined as, in this respect, a machine-using industry. In that event, however, we are promptly returned to the original question on the forces that make for the substitution between capital and labor.

Suppose the productivity advance in machinery occurred in the industry qua producer. It would then have had to result from the other modes by which the entrepreneurial function is exercised. In what direction? Highly skilled tasks would be broken down to use less skilled labor. Noncompeting groups in the labor market (immigrants, women, nonwhites) would be hired in increasing measure to replace higher-cost groups. Maintenance, standby, finishing, and clerical operations would be cut out or cut down. Each of these steps would cut wage *costs* without touching wage *rate* trends. New plants would be established in states with lower labor costs, and in areas closer to the optimum location between new market concentrations and factor sources. New control systems and revised layouts would make more efficient use of existing stocks and input flow patterns. In general this range of procedures could induce productivity advances, and in significant volume, without proportionate increases of capital or labor inputs. Many would require no increase of inputs.[26]

But each of these entrepreneurial gambits is available to the machinery-using industries as well as to machinery-producing ones. And at any time they have an equal incentive to reduce costs by adopting such alternatives. It is, of course, unnecessary and unreasonable to assume that more efficient techniques would be seized upon at precisely equal rates in machinery-using and machinery-producing industries. We do assume, however, that (apart from input increases) the long-term forces driving for

---

and Sam Schurr, *The Mining Industries, 1899–1939.* See for a few industries the dual-factor productivity measures in John Kendrick, *Productivity Trends in the United States* (1961), table D-VI.

[25] We consider here factors making for a decline in the price of machinery services. Producers may pass the decrease in their costs on either by reducing machinery prices, by improving the output capacity of machinery while keeping prices rigid, or by a combination of the two. Hence reported machinery price series without an adequate allowance for changes in machinery productivity do not measure changes in the price of machinery services.

[26] Summarizing Kendrick's data, Fabricant estimates that the physical output of the economy rose by 3.5 percent a year from 1889 to 1957, whereas man-hours and tangible capital inputs jointly rose by only 1.7 percent. Solomon Fabricant, *Basic Facts on Productivity Change* (1959), p. 19. From the numbers we infer a significant contribution by forces other than these tangible inputs, among which we give pride of place to the entrepreneurial function.

productivity advance in the machinery industries, and thereby making for lower machinery service prices, will find their parallel in similar forces that lower labor costs in the machinery-using industries. Hence the obvious fact of productivity advance in the machinery industries does not per se imply any changing ratio of capital to labor service price—that ratio whose approximate long-term stability we have inferred above as confronting the machinery-using industries.

A second component of capital costs beyond that for machinery and equipment is that for buildings. By the same line of reasoning as that used above, the bulk of building-service price variation will be determined by wage-rate variation in the building industry and those industries (cement, steel, mechanical items) that supply the construction industry, with a lesser contribution from variations in profit margins and productivity differentials.

A third component of capital costs is that for financing inventories. The price of inventories will vary with the price of the final product—in turn largely dominated by the run of wage costs in the given industry and those preceding it in the production sequence.

Finally, the decision to hold funds in working capital—whether currency deposits, securities, or receivables—must be made in terms of the opportunity cost of using such funds for actual investment in inventories or productive equipment, and hence must be relatable to the same factors as determine the cost of such investment.

A significant qualification to the above would appear to be the fact that contracts are made at one point for the acquisition of capital, their terms being constant through years to follow despite subsequent variations in the wage-cost figures. In one respect this argues for something of a distributed lag function, recognizing not merely current trends in wages but previous trends, with a diminishing distribution of weights through time. But a substantial link to current trends is still maintained for most contracts by virtue of the fact that the contracts can be broken by refinancing. The opportunity cost involved in continuing old financing is largely set by the cost of breaking old contracts and borrowing under current terms. Because of the costs and difficulties of refinancing, there will be no instant and proportionate response in contractual changes as current changes in investment opportunity occur. And the increasing reliance on internal financing for capital expansion and replacement, rather than resort to borrowing or the use of senior equity securities, tends to diminish further the scope for such response. However, such response as does occur through refinancing has a clear bias: Since it occurs at the option of the borrower, it will take place only when current costs of new capital are below those for which he has contracted. Old borrowings bring a bias to the capital-labor price ratio—old contracts being broken at the option of the borrower (i.e., via paying off and refinancing) and that option being exercised more when the price of capital is declining relative to that of labor than when the ratio is going the other way.

It must be noted that not all data on the comparative trend in the price of capital and labor in the United States would be suited to the question as we have posed it. Thus, the required measure of the price of capital is one that has meaning only for those industries where the entrepreneur can in principle substitute between his capital and labor inputs. Hence the well-known Kendrick series, which includes imputed rent of owner-occupied houses, as well as an entrepreneurial allocation of a kind not suited to our immediate concern, is unfortunately not usable here.[27] (And dealing with the price of labor service and machinery service, the reported machinery-price and wage-rate series take us only part way to the relevant measure of service price.)

The above model is intended to describe only longer-term changes in relative prices and factor shares for individual industries—or, more accurately, for those constellations of products in which sets of firms tend to specialize and, by virtue of that specialization, tend to be termed industries. The shifting boundaries of these product groups through time surely tends to blur the boundaries of what is defined as an industry. But even if a broad fixity maintains, so that individual industries continue through time as clearly delimitable, the combination of these industries into a grand total for the economy is another matter. The changing weight of products and "industries" in that greater total over the years involves a significant aggregation problem. In theory we would expect a nation to shift toward those industries that use its most abundant resources, away from those using scarcer resources, and change that specialization whenever what was once a high-cost resource becomes a low-cost one, and vice versa. The unsettled controversy over the Leontief paradox suggests, however, that empirical verification in this area still has some significant problems to solve.[28]

In summary, we define the share of national income flowing to wages

[27] Variations in the "price" of such capital, which will reflect variations in property taxation and building maintenance costs, will not cause owner-occupiers to change the proportions of labor to capital in their occupancy activity. Nor would it be true where no market measure of the capital input to the sector existed, as, for example, if it were computed by deducting an arbitrarily estimated "labor compensation" of proprietors from their total return. (The residual estimate of capital compensation to proprietors would then be divided by a capital input series to get a price of capital series.) Such a procedure does not deal with measures separately available to the proprietor, as would be necessary if his substitution between capital and labor inputs were a function of price ratios.

[28] We refer to Leontief's conclusion that the United States tends to export goods using relatively greater amounts of labor, to import those using relatively greater amounts of capital. We refer also to the extensive literature by Diab, Swerling, Hoffmeyer, and others on this proposition.

as against capital as a function of the quantity and price ratios of each factor. We find that in the long run the quantity ratio is in turn a function of the changing price ratios. Taking the price of labor service as given, we contend that the changing price of capital service must bear a constant long-term proportionality to that of labor. This proportionality derives from the fact that the supply forces working to fix the price of capital are dominantly wage costs in the capital-producing industries and those that supply them. In a competitive market these wage costs parallel wage-costs changes in capital-using industries because wage changes for identical occupations must bear a parity to one another in all employing industries, while historical experience does not suggest that productivity trends in the supplying and using industries are so negatively related as to make costs take a different course from rates.

5

SOME INFERENCES

SOURCES OF AMERICAN GROWTH

A clash of doctrines is not a disaster—it is an opportunity
Whitehead †

The population of the United States is beyond that of other countries an anxious one. All classes are either striving after wealth or endeavoring to keep up its appearance.
Benjamin McCready, 1837 ‡

What multitudinous and obscure causes stir the growth of nations, and how economic advance is initiated, "while puzzling questions, are not beyond all conjecture." A look at the ebullient history of America yields no easy answers. But the record is surely relevant. It is also a hopeful one for the world's new nations, since it highlights factors within the competence of many nations regardless of their resources, location, or economic past.

We must first consider some traditional explanations of that growth. Stalwart leader among them, surely, is the one that simply signals our incredibly rich endowment of resources—fields abundant with fertility, rivers crossing the land with easy transport facility, mines rich with ore, forests deep with timber. Economists have emphasized these factor endowments as well as historians, merely adding the qualification that the

---

† *Science and the Modern World* (1925), p. 259.
‡ Benjamin E. McCready, *On the Influence of Trades, Professions and Occupations in the United States, on the Production of Diseases* (1837; reprint, 1943), p. 123.

process of international trade can ameliorate this endowment and bring its most efficient utilization. The classic exposition in Bertil Ohlin's *Interregional and International Trade* is a brilliant expansion from premises as old as Ricardo. But the example of ancient Greece, or modern Japan, stands athwart the simple path of this exposition. Endowment is sufficient, perhaps, for growth, but hardly necessary. Nations with the most constrained budget of physical resources have nonetheless flourished as the green bay tree. And while such endowment must constitute both the support and constraint of growth, economists have increasingly come to doubt that it constitutes any harsh *sine qua non*.[1] Does the endowment of natural resources in Canada differ startlingly from that of the United States? Is not the quality of its people fully as high? Yet the growth patterns for two centuries have been dramatically different.

The "endowment of capital" is an almost meaningless phrase in an open society. Capital will flow across regional and national boundaries to those happy areas where investors see opportunity. The "endowment of labor" is almost as meaningless in any nation freely exposed to migration forces. The United States labor endowment in the nineteenth century was richly supplemented, while that of Ireland fell. Men whose quality was wasted on one side of the Atlantic became decisive contributors to economic advance on the other side. Land, resources, capital, labor—whatever the factor—it is difficult to make the "natural" endowment into a stimulus or essential for growth.[2]

A second explanation of our growth has been found in the size of the United States free-trade market. Now the most reasonable premises of economic theory do imply that the wider the market the greater the division of labor, whence flow economic efficiency and many good things, including the possibility of growth. But theory is sadly mute on the empirical question of exactly what size market is required to induce growth. The United States began its upward economic surge from 1820 to 1850. At that time the American market was tinier than that of France, no broader than that of Bavaria, Ireland, or Hungary, not one of which has been an outstanding example of economic development. Moreover, our market in this period was fractionated by natural barriers of mountain and flood.

[1] See the effective review by John H. Adler, "Changes in the Role of Resources at Different Stages of Economic Development," in *Conference on Natural Resources and Economic Growth* (1960) and the perceptive paper by Theodore Schultz for the same conference, "A General View of Natural Resources in Economic Growth."

[2] "Without changes in population or in physical supplies a country may become less well endowed or better endowed with productive resources as there occur changes in technology, in tastes, in export markets, in availability of complementary goods from abroad, or, in the case of labour, in the ratio of the labour force to population." Jacob Viner, "Stability and Progress: the Poorer Countries Problem," in Douglas Hague (ed.), *Stability and Progress in the World Economy* (1958), p. 44.

What was the largest United States submarket whose parts were linked by significant product interflows? It was one that extended no farther inland than the East Coast tidewater in some places, and not beyond the Appalachians in others. As England in the eighteenth century and Switzerland in the nineteenth had carved out through international trade a far daintier cut than that given them by nature, so America significantly widened its national market by international trade. (Even in today's restrictionist world, of course, trade continues available to any nation seeking to extend its market beyond national boundaries.)[3] Finally, it may be germane to add that we have little basis for presuming that a "large" market is required for optimum economic efficiency. Such information as we possess for our own day suggests that optimum United States plant production sizes are feasible when the market is a mere 1 of 5 percent of the United States market today—a goal within ready reach of many a nation.[4]

The central cause of our growth has been found by others to lie in the incandescent glow of American entrepreneurial ability—a rich blend of business competence and Yankee ingenuity. Not surprisingly, the most brilliant advocate of this proposition was himself an immigrant, of signal personal abilities and from the highest Old World cultural traditions. But surely Schumpeter's graceful compliment, though sincere, is too generous by half. Who have been America's entrepreneurs? American in that they resided here, yes, but what more? The entrepreneur who marked the beginning of the American factory system, Samuel Slater, was English. The aggrandizer of the fur trade, John Jacob Astor, was German. Those giants of the railroad industry—Hill of the Northern Pacific, Villard of the Union Pacific, Vanderbilt of the New York Central—were foreign-born. And the entrepreneur whose efforts marked the apogee of old-style capitalism, Andrew Carnegie, was a Scotsman. Every hallmark of technical ingenuity hammered into America's production systems recalls the ingenious immi-

---

[3] For an excellent review of the contribution of foreign trade and some penetrating arguments in favor of size and its corollaries, see Simon Kuznets, *Six Lectures on Economic Growth* (1959), Lecture 5. These issues have been most comprehensively considered in International Economic Association, *Economic Consequences of the Size of Nations* (1960).

[4] The bulk of United States farm output before 1860 appears to have come on the market from farms well under the 160-acre size. A major discussion of optimum factory plant size by industry even in our own time suggests the 1 to 5 percent range. See Joe Bain, "Economies of Scale," *American Economic Review* (March, 1954), pp. 23, 24, 27. A more obscure problem arises with respect to complementary industries—e.g., farm machinery, business services—and social overhead, all of which may only reach an optimum point with a larger market. But if we translate these efficiencies into costs to primary producers, we may assess them as differentials of a small fraction of total costs. It is hard to believe that such small ultimate differences explain anything like the massive differences in growth rates or originating forces in growth.

grant raised in a European tradition—from Du Pont a Frenchman to Ericsson a Swede, Bell a Scotsman, Marconi an Italian, Steinmetz a Czech, Tesla a Croatian.

As important as the flux of immigrant men in creating our production system has been the flux of immigrant ideas. Our borrowings from Watt and Macadam, from the Duke of Bridgewater and Stephenson, from Bessemer and Mackintosh, from Siemens and Liebig are as obvious as sunbeams on a cheerful day—and no less ubiquitous. The growth occurred in America, but its integral forces included the immigrant trained abroad, and the immigrant idea borrowed from a foreign cultural tradition. Under the circumstances it would be unrealistic, and quite ungracious, to attribute the harmony to a theme solely American.

We turn now to the first of those two forces that we believe to be central to any explanation of the driving rate of advance by the American economy. To lay claim to it may well imply a prouder boast, but it is a truer one than that made if we accept the Schumpeterian credit to our national account. That force is the wind of freedom, which blows through most of our national history. The freedom central to American economic growth was the willingness to consider new ideas; having considered, to adopt; and having adopted, vigorously and speedily to put to work. In any single sphere of free thought and action, the United States may not have been primary. France, for example, may well have outpaced eighteenth- and nineteenth-century America in adopting certain freedoms of thought and expression; England, some decisive economic freedoms; Switzerland, a forthrightness in technical work and production. But America led in all these areas by its reckless willingness to cast off tradition, to adopt new ideas whatever their provenance, and then to put them to work.

Economic growth flows from the total performance of a human society. It is not the creation of bloodless "economic men," for the stimuli to economic activity lie in the total life of the individual and the social order. It would be a decisive oddity, therefore, if while the political scientist emphasized the nature of the American state (and the historian, the nature of American society), the economist were to ignore the contribution that a free state and mobile society make in creating so many-faceted a phenomenon as economic growth.

Man, said Pascal, is a mere reed in the universe, but a thinking reed. And it is the process of thought, the application of thought, that spurs economic change. We are not speaking of the mere existence of ideas—for these do not form part of a way of life—but of the use and application of ideas in society. The major technical ideas, production schemes, of any nation have long been available to all. The finest techniques of English productive skill were equally available to Ireland. The most ingenious procedures of German technical education required only the labor of adaptation to be instituted in Spain. But the history of the economically backward areas of Europe, from Spain to Yugoslavia, from Ireland to southern Italy, suggests that economically advantageous ideas can be directly available to people of high ability, to nations that have made significant contributions to human culture, yet not be used by them. On the other hand the history of Switzerland and Japan, of a mere entrepôt such as Hong Kong, demonstrates how swiftly these ideas can be shaped to the national purpose even in countries that own only a modest complement of resources and that begin their growth with low levels of skill, industrial discipline, and technical infrastructure.

Moreover, the entrepreneur, offering deviant ideas, receptive to novelty, has apparently appeared in almost every country. Long ago Schmoller noted in how many nations the foreigner brought new products in through trade, brought new skills in via his own workmanship.[5] Petty observed that "trade is not fixed to any species of Religion as such; but rather . . . to the Heterodox part of the whole." [6]

What was decisive in America was not the presence of ideas brought in by the immigrant, by foreign letters and technical manuals. It was the unprecedented free acceptance of novel ideas. Many good economists and true have devoted high talent to demonstrating what immense power market competition offers in driving toward an optimum allocation of resources. It is surprising that so little attention has been paid to another type of competition. The competition of ideas is no less significant than that of product markets in bringing economic advance. It is probable that czarist Russia had more manufacturing enterprises competing with each other, imperial China more farmers, and Ismaili Egypt more handicraftsmen and traders all competing with each other, than did the United States throughout its whole period of rising growth. But competition conducted within the narrow boundaries of what all sensible men know to be acceptable procedures, validated by centuries of experience, does not force economic advance. Economic advance is brought by that competition which rests on a willingness to consider new ideas, to assess them in the light of today's opportunity costs rather than some prior century's—then to hazard the new. True, advance has taken place under rigorously regimented conditions where a society concentrates its supreme efforts on the construction of a pompous pyramid, a major theological effort, or a space-

---

[5] Quoted in Emile Durkheim, *Division of Labor in Society* (1933), p. 307.

[6] Stated in more general terms, adds Salin, "The capitalist entrepreneur in the same respect as the heretic was a nonconformist; both rejected tradition in seeking, with new methods, and techniques, their own ways to God and to mammon." Edgar Salin, "European Entrepreneurship," *Journal of Economic History* (Fall, 1952), p. 368.

shaking missile. But the wide and national economic growth of the United States rested on a vital competition among ideas, in which an enormous number—political, theological, social, economic, and technological—were tested and pitted against each other.

Such competition of ideas is no orchid growing gorgeously in air. It develops from social mobility and like Antaeus renews its strength each time it touches that soil. Widespread immigration, the freedom to enter any entrepreneurial pursuit without legal restraint,[7] the freedom to range across a nation rather than move mostly within parish bounds—such mobility assured the free competition of ideas that sparked American economic growth.

In this competition of thought and proposition, many ideas were tested. Most were discarded. But from the multitude of trials came the mounting probability that those combinations of resources, those techniques of production, best adapted to the demands of the national market and to the possibilities of overseas markets would be developed. Supported by the migration of men to the nation and across the land, the competition of ideas created the one economic thing needful, namely, that the factor combinations suited to one stage in development were not retained rigidly on into subsequent stages when their optimal value had been dissipated. It is to these changing combinations, and to a second decisive force in our economic growth, that we now turn.

THE PRODUCTION FUNCTION
UNDER PARTIAL CERTAINTY

> *Four phrases, like algebraic formulae, fitted every case. . . . I do not know, I cannot do it, I will have nothing to do with it, and, we shall see.*
>
> Balzac, *Eugenie Grandet*

The world of the entrepreneur is built upon doubt and compassed by uncertainty. Though his eye is on the morrow he has little to guide him beyond the evidence of the day. But how confidently dare he treat one passing day as the image of the next? In selecting today's optimum combination of productive inputs he knows that one factor is relatively ex-

---

[7] The point has been made more positively by Cochran: "In the struggle for social eminence, therefore, the businessman did not have to face strong and repressive competition from titled nobility, army, navy, government or church. . . . Compared with the businessmen of other nations, those of America have always had unusual social prestige." Thomas C. Cochran, *The American Business System* (1957), p. 3.

pensive as compared to another. But tomorrow may be different. Is he wise, therefore, to change factor proportions on the basis of recent shifts in relative prices? Uncertainty teaches him one certain moral: What is good enough for today is good enough for tomorrow.

In earlier economies, entrepreneurs lived amid the random uncertainties of political instability, irregular discovery, and inadequate information. There only the reactionary could be considered rational. From the fall of the Roman Empire to that of the British many a century passed in which the course of costs was shaped primarily by changes that the wind and the weather wrought in the price of foodstuffs, or that sudden death (by war and epidemic) imposed on the price of labor. The trend in the entrepreneur's major cost determinants was hidden in a stygian fog.

Capital costs might be known today. But tomorrow? How was he to decide when political upheaval or war (in his own or a nearby nation) would speed capital away from or to his own country, would double interest rates in a brief crisis or spin them down to secular lows? As with capital so with resources. Discovery of a mine or a new fishing ground could cut these costs sharply. If not, however, the persistent force of diminishing returns could drive resource costs upward. Today's lively opportunity for a new and happy low-cost combination of factors could become tomorrow's invincibly high-cost production scheme.

Economic analysis repeats the lessons of experience. The entrepreneur, as Fellner notes, has no basis for anticipating one change in the production function over another. "In pure competition, with no factor-rationing, the firm has no interest in seeking new knowledge of more relatively labor-saving than capital saving kinds, or vice versa." [1]

But since the entrepreneur cannot tell how to vary his procedures in shrewd anticipation of the morrow, why should he not continue to use today's? If the future is random, what rational reason for change exists? An unstable society, therefore, tends to induce a stable production function. Hence, the wise entrepreneur makes a choice that is as comfortable as it is prudent, namely, to make no change.

Now economic growth can occur under such circumstances. Production

[1] William Fellner, "Does the Market Direct the Relative Factor-saving Effects of Technological Progress?" *Conference on the Economic and Social Factors Determining the Rate and Direction of Inventive Activity* (March, 1960), p. 16. Fellner goes on (p. 27) to point out that "monposonistic awareness of factor shortages has hardly been a chronic condition in modern Western economic history," that the "increasing labor-saving slant of innovating activity . . . came after years during which" an awareness of labor shortage developed. See too J. R. Hicks, *The Theory of Wages* (1932), chap. 6, and the generally conclusive discussion with respect to invention in Gordon Bloom, "A Note on Hicks's Theory of Invention," *American Economic Review* (March, 1946), especially p. 87. The urgent economic issue would appear related not to invention, however, but to the adoption of inventions.

function changes are not actually required for growth.[2] Furthermore, the aggregate production function for an industry can be changed with no intrafirm changes, merely as a result of selective mortality among old enterprises and the entrance of new ones.

But growth without plant production function changes was not the American experience. The temper, the aspect, and (in significant measure) the very extent of our economic advance was given by the incessant change in the mode of production. What is more notorious in the American record than the avidity with which entrepreneurs have adopted new plant layouts, purchased and installed new laborsaving machines—whether or not they have commissioned them? Such a pattern of response is especially puzzling for a nation that received a vast flow of unskilled migrants decade after decade. For accepted doctrine finds that "one would not really expect entrepreneurs faced with a mass of labour coming from the land to use labour-saving devices." [3] Is our generalization wrong concerning the entrepreneur's response to uncertainty? Or is there another force at work? We believe that there was such a force during the critical century, 1819 to 1919.

Labor's Endless Horizon

> *He that loveth silver shall not be satisfied with silver, nor he that loveth abundance, with increase.*
>
> Ecclesiastes, 5:10

Social Mobility. In the new United States of America the entrepreneur had one fixed star to guide his course. Entrepreneurial planning polarized around the knowledge that America (unlike Asia or Europe) had no fixed social structure in which everyone had his place and was in it.[4] Labor in the new land was free to seek "more"—and did so. Rather than humbly pulling its forelock to its betters, labor sought to ape them, even to outstrip them. During the mightiest days of English industrial advance, Ricardo might reasonably speak of wage levels made customary by the traditions of years. But in America? True, every demand by labor for "more"

---

[2] See the fundamental studies of J. Tobin, "A Dynamic Aggregative Model," *Journal of Political Economy* (April, 1955) and Robert Solow, "A Contribution to the Theory of Economic Growth," *Quarterly Journal of Economics* (February, 1956) distinguishing models with and without such changes. An example of growth with nonspectacular innovations and limited change in investment is reviewed by R. R. Nelson, "Growth Models and the Escape from the Low-level Equilibrium Trap: the Case of Japan," *Economic Development and Cultural Change* (July, 1960), especially pp. 386ff.

[3] Brinley Thomas, in Leon Dupriez (ed.), *Economic Progress* (1955), p. 256.

[4] In *The Great Circle of Being*, Arthur Lovejoy brilliantly outlines the traditional concepts of an ordered social structure, providing a set of endless contrasts with American social attitudes and action.

could be matched by capital's insisting "no more." But in the United States neither labor nor capital could turn to a standard sanctified by the centuries, nor rely on a web of social and political restrictions. Americans came from every land, from many faiths and traditions. They differed in their cosmology, neither did they share an eschatology. Their concord of belief included only one primary article: The right to be free, in mind and market.

In the labor market this belief created incessant pressure toward higher wages. For there was no "proper" social position for an American, so there could be no "proper" wage for him. Such constraints might have complemented market forces and restrained labor's demands in the "old country," but not in the new one.[5]

Who put it better than did Ramsay Crooks (the great driving force of the American Fur Company), in the early 1800s: The French Canadian boatmen, he observed, "are indispensable to the fur trade. The American are too independent to submit quietly to a proper controul" and they "can gain anywhere a subsistence much superior to a man of the interior." [6]

Salesmanship and advertising worked to the same end, long before the settlement of Madison Avenue; worked as forcefully on the members of the labor force as anyone else. To identify income with personal accomplishment was an easy step in a social order giving high approbation to material goals.[7] It added fuel to a fire already laid, lit, and burning brightly.

Labor Mobility.   Second only to social mobility as a support for ever-rising demands by labor was the possibility of physical mobility, the vast range of alternative opportunities. "If there is good wheat land in Manitoba, the people of Minnesota and Iowa will want to go there. . . . It is not because they have not enough where they are—there is no such conception when more can be had." [8] Either the older areas raised wages or they lost labor. Furthermore, the best workers were affected most, so that a doubly potent effect on efficiency wages appeared. "Laborers in the Wisconsin and Iowa territories," wrote a visitor in 1835, "are of a more unsatisfactory description than in the east, land being so cheap that every prudent man is enabled to purchase a farm for himself in the course of a year or two." [9] Indeed a thousand cocksure thinkers concluded that this

---

[5] One visitor contrasted the similar freedom in Canada with wage fixing in connection with the English poor laws, by which "a most powerful combination, ratified by the magistracy of England, was at work to keep down husbandry labour below its proper level." Robert Gourlay, *General Introduction to Statistical Account of Upper Canada* (London: Simpkin and Marshall, 1822), vol. I, p. cvii.

[6] Quoted in H. A. Innis, *Essays on Canadian Economic History* (1956), p. 104.

[7] A succinct and illuminating discussion of the "productive atmosphere" of a society appears in J. E. Meade, *Economic Union,* p. 61.

[8] William Graham Sumner, *Earth Hunger and Other Essays* (1913), p. 47.

[9] Patrick Shureff, *A Tour through North America* (Edinburgh: 1835).

easy wealth of open land must keep wages so high that manufacturing could not develop. In 1812 Amos Stoddard assured his countrymen that "manufactures to any considerable extent can never be introduced into the United States, because we can always purchase cheaper than we can make. Our vacant lands, obtained too on moderate conditions, will continue to keep up the price of labor." [10] And that great Virginian, John Randolph, demanded whether you could expect, in that "western country where any man may get beastly drunk for three pence sterling . . . where every man can get as much meat and bread as he can consume and yet spend the best part of his days, and nights too, perhaps, on tavern benches, . . . that the people of such a country, with countless millions of wild land and wild animals besides, can be cooped up in manufacturing establishments?" [11] A hundred writers noted the connection between open land and high wages. [12]

But certainly the West attracted capital as surely as it did labor. Potent pressures should have been at work to raise capital rates, as well as labor rates. If so, how could any certainty for the entrepreneur emerge from all this? The answer (so far as the contribution of physical mobility goes) lies in two factors. Suppose we take as our standard the physical mobility possible to capital and labor either in the East during the nineteenth century or in the United States in later times. Then, relative to that standard the dangers of the nineteenth-century West were surely much greater for capital, with Indians then burning farms, pulling up railroad ties, sacking villages. Men could hide or fight back; property must inevitably lie supine. Moreover, ignorance about the West was still great enough so that such fearsome factors may well have been overly discounted in the capital market.

[10] Amos Stoddard, *Sketches, Historical and Descriptive of Louisiana* (Philadelphia: Matthew Carey, 1812), p. 261.

[11] ". . . and made to work," he continued, "16 hours a day, under the superintendence of a driver, yes, a driver, compared with whom the Southern [slave] overseer is a gentleman and a man of refinement. . . . There is no magic in this word *union.*" Annals of Congress, 18th Cong., 1st Sess. (April, 1824), col. 2363.

[12] Manufacturing was being encouraged, according to the *Knoxville Register,* by keeping "the price of public land so high that the common people cannot purchase; they will therefore be forced into the manufactories . . . [enabling] the manufacturer to employ his hands for lower wages. This is republicanism with a vengeance." Quoted in Condy Raguet, *The Free Trade Advocate* (Sept. 19, 1829), p. 186. The causation was sometimes argued the other way. Representative W. R. Smith of Alabama argued for the homestead bill that "The rapid increase of labor-saving machinery will gradually drive from the workshop the mechanic. . . . The law should look to this in advance, and provide for the change of occupation. . . . What better change can you offer to the mechanic than a farm?" *Congressional Globe,* 32nd Cong., 1st Sess. (1852), appendix p. 516.

For detailed reviews, see Helen Zahler, *Eastern Workingmen and National Land Policy, 1829–1862* (1941), and Henry N. Smith, *Virgin Land* (1950).

However, let us assume no difference for capital. One nevertheless certainly existed for labor. The composition of the American labor force was such that a much higher level of mobility was possible in response to an equivalent real-income differential in the nineteenth century than in later years.[13] First of all, much more of the labor force was foreign-born. Having only recently traveled several thousand miles across the Atlantic, they could hardly consider an additional, and shorter, trip across the United States to be a major obstacle. Secondly, the foreign born were concentrated in the most mobile ages. Even as late as 1880 (when the first comprehensive United States data became available) 94 percent of our foreign born were sixteen years or older, compared to only 60 percent for native whites.[14] Third, the small proportion of children in the foreign-born total implies, in addition, a high ratio of single males to family men.[15] And single men, of course, have always been a most mobile group. Even married males were potentially far more mobile than was the married group in decades to come. As late as 1910 fully 23 percent of married immigrants had wives living in the old country.[16] Hence the flow of labor westward during the decades of American development was facilitated by the great share of immigrants in our labor force, and by the dominance of unmarried male adults in the immigrant group itself.

Factor Substitution and Productivity.   Turn the coin of American materialism and you find the reverse side labeled American productivity. So various were the possibilities of social and physical mobility in the United States labor market that labor could, and did, steadily press for higher wages. That pressure was neither random nor transient, as it might have been in some European or Asian country after revolution had wiped out the immediate governing group or disease had struck down a large portion of the labor force. The pressure was therefore more or less steadily apparent to any entrepreneur at any time.[17] Given (1) a long-run upward pressure on wages, and (2) an uncertain future course for the price of capital, the entrepreneur's wisest choice, time and again, proved to be:

[13] Factors tending to diminish labor mobility over the decades are discussed by the writer in Joint Economic Committee, *Hearings on Employment, Growth and Price Levels* (Apr. 25–28, 1959), part 3, pp. 577–580.

[14] 1880 Census, *Statistics of the Population of the United States*, p. 549. The Immigration Reports data on age of migrants are quite inconsistent with these results. We believe the census figures rest on more reliable procedures than the *pro forma* queries of immigration officers on a statistical point of no relevance to their work.

[15] *Ibid.* Only about 3 percent of the foreign born were under ten years of age whereas about 25 percent of native whites were.

[16] U.S. Immigration Commission, *Immigration Reports*, part 23, vol. II, *Immigrants in Industry*, p. 383.

[17] It does not follow that wages actually rose in the market—a point considered below.

Adopt techniques that were not labor-intensive.[18] Land was a less satis-factory technical alternative in many instances, and no alternative at all in some. Hence the usual course was to supersede labor intensive techniques by capital-intensive ones.

Moreover, the incentive to minimize the use of labor was emphasized for the many entrepreneurs—farmers, millers, carpenters, etc.—by the fact that they themselves had immigrated from Europe: Their standard for suitable wage rates tended to be European levels. To them, especially, United States wages rates were "high" in some absolute sense. And labor costs, having so high a visibility, were surely to be minimized. "In any country, but more especially when the price of labour is high," wrote one United States observer in 1814, "there is more profit to be derived from a smaller area of land, excellently cultivated, cleared and manured" than the slovenly procedures appropriate to countries with relatively lower wages.[19] Napoleon's Consul General to the United States declared that "The object of the American farmer is not to obtain the greatest possible product out of his land but only out of the labour thereto applied, which, being in that country extremely dear, he spares by every means in his power."[20]

But the Ricardo effect is rarely inevitable. Any entrepreneur, facing the tough problems of changing the man-land or the man-machine ratio, would first seek an easier alternative. One alternative (or at least complementary)

[18] Our discussion applies only to long-run historical development. Discussion of the Ricardo effect or unionization in later periods is another matter. On recent short-run changes, see Eric Schiff, "Factor Substitution and the Composition of Input" in Conference on Research in Income and Wealth, *Output, Input and Pro-ductivity Measurement* (1961), and Gottfried Haberler in Philip D. Bradley (ed.), *The Public Stake in Union Power* (1959), p. 77. We contrast a relatively certain direction for the rates paid one factor with relative uncertainty of direction for the others. In today's world the contrast is nowhere near as great, with guarantees under-pinning both labor and capital markets and active subsidization in resource develop-ment. Hence our model does not apply here. This is so because the certainty with which today's entrepreneur can predict the main direction in the ratio of labor to capital and resource prices is nowhere near as great.

The reader is referred to the enormously stimulating book by John Habbakuk, *American and British Technology* (1962), which appeared after this study was in press. We focus on the contrast between near certainty for the trend in wage rates and uncertainty for other factor costs while Habbakuk emphasizes another mecha-nism. However, his perceptive analysis should be used for a richer understanding of these problems.

[19] Letter to the editor, *The American Weekly Messenger or Register* (Philadelphia: John Conrad, 1814), vol. I, p. 165. "I have long considered the mistaken avidity of our country folks for putting new land into cultivation as a great obstruction to agricultural improvement. . . . It is no doubt a natural passion . . . inflamed by an almost boundless extent of land easily obtainable."

[20] Felix De Beaujour, *Sketch of the United States of North America* (London: 1814), pp. 83, 86.

approach was attempted, we know. The national policy of open immigration, of course, tended to keep wage levels from rising. But that policy did not banish the problem confronting a particular entrepreneur. For he faced labor and machinery prices that were given him in the competitive market. And he kept losing workers who went West, went to the newer industries, or set themselves up as farmers.

To cope with his own incessant problem many an employer sought to import his own labor. Such attempts were widespread throughout our history. But their common result was to drive the entrepreneur to install more machinery and to seek still more efficient production methods. Let us see how this occurred. The immigrant was usually taken on at wages below the prevailing standard for "native" workmen. The employer's advantage was thus clear cut, but it was evanescent. For a time the immigrant did accept lower wages. But for how long? Glittering before him was the example of higher wages paid to native workmen on similar work —not to mention those higher wages paid for dissimilar work which he had every reason to feel he too could perform. His perception was sharpened by the efforts of native labor to keep immigrant labor from cutting the rate—pressure on the job, riots, know-nothing movements. And the migrant responded, by seeking more on the same job or by moving on.

The record is a litany of failure of employer attempts to keep wage costs down by importing labor. In 1828 the Chesapeake and Ohio Canal Company sent agents to Belfast and Cork, to the Upper Rhine, and to Liverpool. It hired workers well below prevailing rates. But a year later the company president was forced to report that while "the rise of the wages of labor was for some time controlled, and for a few months sensibly reduced by the importation of those laborers and artificers from Europe . . . difficulties of enforcing under existing laws the obligations of the emigrants and of preserving among them due subordination" made it unlikely that the company could again rely on such methods to restrict wage increases.[21]

In 1849 an Englishman warned those hopefuls who planned to bring their own mechanics with them when they emigrated to Texas: They would find them tempted away by "the high wages and abundant demand for labor"; contracts would fail to hold them since they "have so many means of escape." [22]

A third of a century later, and still farther west, the experiment yielded similar results. To build the Central Pacific Railway so great a complement of labor was required that a decision to hire native labor would

[21] *Chesapeake and Ohio Canal Company, Second Annual Report,* p. 84, U.S. National Archives.

[22] Edward Smith, *Account of a Journey through Northeastern Texas Undertaken in 1849 for the Purposes of Emigration* (London: 1849), p. 39.

surely kite up wage rates. It therefore became apparent early in the season, wrote the CPR chief engineer at the beginning of his work, "that the amount of labor likely to be required during the summer could only be supplied by the Chinese element in our population." [23]

In all, wrote one foreign contemporary, 40,000 Chinese workers were imported to California; and while they "worked very cheaply in the beginning . . . later on when they became acquainted with conditions here, they asked for higher and higher wages, and soon they worked only for as much as the white people." [24] Paid about $1 a day (as compared to native labor's $3) when they first arrived,[25] they were up to $1.25 and $1.50 by the second Cleveland administration despite a marked downward drift in the general California wage level.[26] Among those imported the turnover rate was striking. At one time the Central Pacific Railroad hired 1,000 men and transported them to help build the eastern sections of the road, but shortly thereafter found a mere 100 remaining. The rest had taken off for "the mines newly opened at Austin in Nevada." [27]

In the 1880s the Pepperell mills selected 20 women weavers in Glasgow and prepaid their fare to the United States. Others followed. "But these Scots proved an expensive experiment. Some of them left before they had repaid Pepperell the amount advanced, enticed away in several cases by other companies." [28] In the recovery beginning in 1886 a major machine-building company found that "among the second generation Irish . . . there were many who refused to endure the hardships of foundry work and who preferred to work in the shop's machining departments even at

[23] *Report of the Chief Engineer . . . of the Central Pacific Railway* (December, 1865), p. 17.

[24] Janos Xantus, "California for Hungarian Readers," *California Historical Society Quarterly* (June, 1949).

[25] The $1 rate for Chinese workmen, estimated by the Collector of the Port of San Francisco, is quoted in Henry C. Carey, *The Resources of the Union, A Lecture, December 1865* (H. C. Baird, 1866), p. 240. W. H. Martin, general agent of the California Immigrant Union, stated in 1875 that "Chinamen work willingly for 75 cents to $1 a day. We have a large supply, and they soon learn and perfect themselves in any department of business. They are a necessary evil at present, for the reason that most of the young men of our State, and new-comers generally, will not work for small wages. As soon as this is remedied by the importation of Eastern and European Labor willing to work for $1 to $1.50 per day, the employment of Chinese will gradually be diminished." Quoted in Edward Young, *Labor in Europe and America* (1875), p. 785.

[26] Hart H. North, "Chinese and Japanese Immigration to the Pacific Coast," *California Historical Quarterly* (December, 1949), p. 343. As a leader of the anti-immigration forces, North is a biased source. There seems no reason, however, to feel that his bias affects the present point.

[27] *Pacific Railroads, Argument of Creed Haymond before the Senate Committee, March 17, 1888,* p. 10.

[28] Evelyn H. Knowlton, *Pepperell's Progress* (1948), pp. 163–164.

lower pay." They therefore began in 1886 to employ "French Canadians in large numbers . . . but for every three French Canadians hired only one became a permanent employee, so rapid was the turnover." [29]

These many efforts are epitomized by the manufacturer who regretted (in 1860) that "I have brought from the country within the last fourteen months 230 girls and of these only 115 are now here." [30]

But hope failing teaches a deeper pessimism than hope never aroused. For a time entrepreneurs did reap advantage from every immigrant who worked at rates below those paid the native American. But that time—however lengthened by ignorance, fear, or lack of language facility—was not indefinite in a free nation. Men broke their contracts, quit their jobs, sought higher wages on the job. The entrepreneur who employed native labor might know that he had to pay "high wages." But the entrepreneur who used immigrant labor was perpetually made aware of demands for "higher wages." And the required marginal adjustments to such pressures had deeper impact on entrepreneurs thus disillusioned than could any general recognition of "high" United States wage rates and costs. The temporary advantages that immigrants offered in low current wage rates ended in demonstrating that future wages would be higher.

What more compelling incentive could be offered the entrepreneur to substitute machinery? If the "most important and the least docile of the productive service in an economy" [31] continually pressed for higher wages, what more obvious alternative than to reduce its role? Out of the evanescent cost advantages offered by cheap migrant labor, the entrepreneur sought to build more durable ones. Minimizing the use of labor, substituting other factors of production—most often, of course, machinery—became the entrepreneur's methods of choice for keeping down costs.[32]

Capital Costs

Persistent pressure for higher wages throughout our national history impelled entrepreneurs to find ways of cutting the role of labor in production. But the success with which these efforts were attended was largely determined by the other half of the productivity scissors—the tendency toward falling capital costs. This fall reflected one of the greatest external economies in economic growth, namely, the increasing social stability of the nation, from which came social security for capital in the form of decreasing risk.

[29] Thomas R. Navin, *The Whitin Machine Works since 1831* (1950), p. 161.

[30] Vera Shlakman, *Economic History of a Factory Town,* Smith College Studies in History (1935), p. 149.

[31] George Stigler, *The Theory of Price* (1956), p. 194.

[32] Diminishing returns in mining and agriculture would have offered a complementary incentive to install machinery. We concentrate here, however, on the contribution of rising labor rates to this result.

"From battle and murder, and from sudden death, Good Lord, deliver us" is a sentiment shared by all good men, but by none more fervently than the entrepreneur. "The first grand requisite to the growth of prudential habits," wrote a distinguished clergyman, "is the perfect security of property." [33] The maturing into stability of a political and social organization works to produce such security, for as the specter of riot, disorder, and loss diminishes so does the risk that confronts the "cautious and timid" spirit of capital. [34] And with the decline in risk, a decline in the cost of capital necessarily tends to follow. (Moreover, the equable presence of stability helps facilitate the accumulation of capital, thereby further reducing its cost.)

To prove that the risk component in the cost of capital did actually decline in the United States after 1800 is a difficult demonstration. Mere reference to the interest rate will not do; that rate reflects the net resultant of demand forces as well. We have, however, two relevant bodies of evidence on the growth of security and the decline in risk.

1. One relates to death from violence. Homicide appears to have been more common in periods, and in places, where flourished those upheavals and uncertainties that menaced the sure reward of capital. In Chaucer's England, a ratio of 2.0 homicides per accidental death is reported. [35] By T. S. Eliot's time, on the other hand, the ratio had dwindled to about .01 per accidental death. [36]

The earliest United States data are for 1860. [37] They report a ratio of two homicides to every accidental death—or triple the 1860 ratio for the more stolid, settled United Kingdom. [38] Comparison among the United States regions in 1860 suggests the gradient of political and social stability. In the New England states a rate of 1 homicide per 100,000 population was reported and much the same level prevailed in the Middle Atlantic and North Central regions. Rates three and four times as great character-

[33] Thomas Malthus, *Principles,* chap. 6, book 4.

[34] "It is well known that capitalists are cautious and timid in these times and the investments in the South are not generally sought after." *Experimental Survey of the Tennessee and Pacific Railroad from Nashville to Knoxville* (Nashville: Roberts, Waterson and Purvis, 1867), p. 72.

[35] G. C. Coulton, *Chaucer and His England,* chap. 22, p. 293. The data refer to Northumberland in 1279.

[36] UN, *Demographic Yearbook, 1957,* p. 425.

[37] 1860 Census, *Statistics of the United States* (including mortality . . .) (1866), pp. 230–232 and 1860 Census, *Population of the United States in 1860* (1864), p. 599.

[38] United Kingdom rates from 1860 Census, *Statistics of the United States,* p. 238, and 1900 data from 1959 *Statistical Abstract,* p. 66. The rise in the accident rate since then reflects the wider use of the automobile. We assume that deaths from this cause are taken as an inevitable price for glitter and progress rather than as indicating any menace to capital stability.

ized the South Atlantic and older states of the South, while a rate eight times as great is reported for the frontier Southern states of Mississippi, Louisiana, Arkansas, and Texas. For the West we would expect the highest rate, and the tales of Bret Harte and Bayard Taylor are italicized by a rate of 39. Between 1860 and 1900, the United States rate plummeted from 2 to .02 per accidental death.[39] As the country grew, the frontier states began more nearly to resemble the older ones; the prospect of a quiet life became a less random one, and the future for capital investment, more certain.

2. A more systematic indicator of declining risk to capital lies in the historical evidence on the comparative social stability of this nation and the major European ones.

After "the colonies" had become "the United States of America," the opportunities for capital in America became ever more enticing than those offered by many a European nation. Growing political stability in the United States contrasted with fever bouts of riot, revolution, and war in Europe. From 1800 to 1815, European war—on land and sea, from England to Spain through France and Austria and eastward to Russia. In the 1820s, revolution—in Greece, in Naples, Sicily, and Sardinia, and in Spain. In the 1830s, revolution in France and in Poland; and unrest in England so deep that Napier felt "revolution inevitable," while the Poet Laureate declared that "if he had money enough he would transport himself to America." [40] In the 1840s, revolution in France again, and in Austria, Hungary, Italy, Prussia, and Venice. In the 1850s, international war involving Britain, France, and Russia. Follow most of these nations through the century and their combination of actual and potential upheaval is striking. (Indeed, if economists looked more closely at the French record of revolution and seizure of political power in 1789, 1799, 1815, 1830, 1848, and 1870, they would hardly be as puzzled about the relatively slow economic advance of that country as some seem to be.)

Meanwhile, down on the United States farms, as elsewhere in the nation, neither war nor revolt of any magnitude occurred from 1814 to 1860. True, some states repudiated their debts, creating ghastly deterrents to investors, but only nine states actually defaulted.[41] Until the Kansas-

---

[39] In some wide areas even as late as the 1880s the value of guns, pistols, and dirks was greater than that of farm equipment. See *Congressional Globe,* Apr. 19, 1888, p. 3119. In 1836 the *Natchez Free Trader* found that wearing weapons "has become almost a passion throughout the whole South and Southwest." Quoted in William R. Hogan and E. E. Davis, *William Johnson's Natchez* (1951), p. 93.

[40] Quoted by Greville in Philip Morell (ed.), *Leaves from the Greville Diary,* entry for Jan. 25, 1831.

[41] It is an interesting speculation how effective were Northern agents in England during the Civil War, when they reminded English investors who sympathized with the Southern cause that Jefferson Davis had actively supported the repudiation of Mississippi's state debt in earlier years.

Nebraska Act overturned previous demarcation lines in 1854, an investor might reasonably expect that slavery would continue to exist without inducing massive upheaval.

The florid contrast we have suggested above between the prospects offered to capital in much of Europe and in most of the United States should have, and did, make "the States" a market for capital import. The addition of these foreign flows to native accumulations helped cut the rate of return to capital. Our best indication of trends appears in interest rates paid in Boston and New York on prime commercial paper, as shown in Table 5-1.[42]

It is not necessary to vouch for any given figure to see the solid and substantial decline in rates over the decades. Because of the imperfections of the money markets at the time, we are not well advised to use the rates that prevailed in 1836 for assessing the long-term fall. Excluding that single year gives a level of about 9 percent for the entire 1834–1880 period. Once the depression of the 1870s had broken interest rates from the immediate postwar levels, an average of slightly over 5 percent prevailed for peak years of the next half century. This great fall took place even as a substantial burst of investment was occurring. This new investment level was surely not below real prewar. More likely it was substantially greater. Yet in the face of such pressing forces on the demand side, interest rates concurrently fell. We can hardly explain that fall without giving pride of place to the tremendous increase in political stability as judged by native and foreign investor.

Protected from the wilder forces of uncertainty, the investor found his risks reduced in a society no longer divided over slavery. Despite the heavy demand for funds after the Civil War, the enhancement of political stability made him willing to accept far lower rates.[43] (It is more than mere happenstance that the ensuing economic advance was so lively that some historians define it as "the second American revolution.")

3. Passing on from the growth of national political stability, we must reckon in the steady growth of cities, of police and fire protection, of

[42] *Cycle peak dates:* Chronology of Burns and Mitchell, quoted in *Historical Statistics,* p. 320. *1831–1860:* rates from Erastus Bigelow, *The Tariff Question* (1862), pp. 204, 268. Roughly similar figures can be computed from the later work by Martin and the New York Federal Reserve Bank. *1857ff:* Richard Goode and Eugene Birnbaum, "The Relations between Long-term and Short-term Interest Rates in the United States," International Monetary Fund, *Staff Papers* (October, 1959), table 2. We use the Goode-Birnbaum averages for the peak stage of each cycle except that for 1873 we use the 9.6 rate, which is for the expansion stage immediately before the gold crisis. The rate for the peak, actual crisis, months was 15.1.

[43] According to the estimates of Douglas North and Matthew Simon, the net inflow of capital from abroad, never as high as $60 million before the war, ranged about $100 million or more through most of the 1860s and, after the depression of the 1870s, ran as high or higher in the eighties. *Historical Statistics,* vol. II, p. 564.

Table 5-1. Short-term Rates of Interest (Business Cycle Peaks)

I

Peak year	Percent
1836	18.7
1839	13.2
1845	6.0
1847	9.5
1853	10.2
1860	6.8

Peak stage	
1858–1861	8.3
1861–1868	8.2
1867–1871	9.2
1870–1879	9.6
1879–1885	5.4
1885–1888	5.2
1888–1891	5.2
1891–1894	5.2
1894–1897	5.0
1897–1901	3.5
1900–1904	5.5
1904–1908	5.6
1908–1912	4.8
1911–1915	5.2
1914–1919	5.9
1919–1921	6.1
1921–1924	5.1
1924–1927	4.4
1927–1933	6.1
1933–1938	1.0
1938–1945	0.8
1945–1949	1.6
1949–1954	2.8
1954–1958	3.9

II

Long-period Average of Cycle Peaks

1836–1860	11.2
1858–1880	8.8
1879–1921	5.2
1921–1933	5.2
1933–1949	1.7
1949–1958	3.3

stable living arrangements. Such stability provided a more solid basis for effective credit agencies and credit knowledge. All these forces tended to reduce the risk-premium component of capital return.

4. Working to keep down the cost of capital, as well, was the disposition of the difference between the wages that the emigrants were accustomed to receive at home and those that they did receive in the United States. The "Asiatic and European laborers can come here and cumulate wealth (or dissipate) upon wages which will supply the American laborer's family with only the bare necessities." [44] One indication is the level of immigrant remittances to relatives and others in the old country. In a period when a ditchdigger typically earned $1 a day and a domestic servant earned $1.25 a week, the average remittance made to Ireland was $28.50.[45] With 193,000 remittances in 1834–1835 through a single banking firm in one year and only 100,000 immigrants from Ireland over the previous decade, it would seem reasonable to conclude that a good many migrants could, and did, save significant amounts.[46]

5. Finally, and somewhat ironically, wage earners helped directly to finance their own replacement by capital equipment. Through most of the nineteenth century it was customary for wages to be withheld for periods of a month, six months, and even a year. Meanwhile they constituted a free line of credit available to the entrepreneur, regardless of the rate he would have had to pay if he went directly to the capital markets. In manufacturing, the practice of paying monthly or weekly seems to have developed relatively early. Cotton and iron manufacturing (the major factory trades) appear to have paid monthly in the 1830s, when the massive rise in those industries began.[47] By 1860 the rise to importance of other factory industries had significantly increased the numbers receiving weekly payments.[48] In navigation and fishing the typical payment was made at the end of the voyage—whether 3 months or 3 years.[49] (Entrepreneurs in the

[44] George Gunton, *Wealth and Progress* (1887), p. 94. Gunton observes that "the rate of wages . . . is kept up . . . by the constant pressure of the unsatisfied desires of those whose standard of living is highest in their class." p. 95. While the price of labor "tends toward the minimum cost of production, it is the minimum cost not of the cheapest but the dearest portion of the necessary supply," else the horrors of LaSalle would come true (pp. 91–92).

[45] According to a partner in the house of Abraham Sell and Company of New York, who remitted $55,000 to Ireland from January, 1834, to May, 1835. Quoted in Tyrone Power, *Impressions of America during the Years 1833, 1834, and 1835* (Philadelphia: 1836), p. 215.

[46] Matthew Simon suggests that the average reemigrant in the period from the Civil War to 1900, after staying in the United States less than 5 years, took back $160. "The United States Balance of Payments, 1861–1900," in *Trends in the American Economy in the Nineteenth Century*, pp. 688–689. Savings of, say, $40 a year matched against a common-labor annual income of about $360 for a full work year meant a saving rate of over 10 percent a year and at least 12 percent allowing for unemployment—an extraordinary rate by present standards.

[47] 1880 Census, *Report on Wages*, p. xxvi.

[48] *Ibid.*

[49] On a 3-year trip to China the ship's articles noted that "no payment of wages is

whaling industry enjoyed the use of funds at low, and possibly negative, interest rates since they charged interest upon wages paid before the end of the voyage.)[50] In agriculture much daywork was done. But the many laborers hired by the month or season apparently were paid off at the end of the period, minus advances made in the meantime. These various delays in payment, however much their importance changed over the decades, all worked uniquely in one direction—to cut the cost of capital below what present-day payment practices would have made it.

For the recent half century, we are in a position to indicate the decline in risk by contrasting the declining rate on prime commercial paper and the overall return to capital.[51] The return on capital persistently drew ahead of the return on prime paper, the gap between the indices increasing markedly, if irregularly.[52]

Return to Capital (1899 = 100)

Year	All capital	Prime commercial paper	Spread
1899	100	100	0
1919	227	98	129
1929	244	106	138
1937	159	17	142
1948	456	26	430
1957	400	69	331

Growing political stability, plus the proliferation of government guarantees in factor and final product markets, hammered down the risk elements that

---

to be made abroad unless ship goes to Canton," in which case a 2-month advance would be granted—by which time at least 7 to 10 months would have elapsed. Baker Library, Dexter Collection, vol. 145, October, 1833, ship *California.*

[50] On a 3-year voyage in the ship *Gratitude,* Miren Hemenway earned $226.12. Payment of $77 by the shipowner to H. C. Kelly and Company was noted on his account, with "interest and insurance on same @ 25 percent . . . $19.25." While this item was probably paid at the beginning of the voyage, interest was also charged on cash and slops furnished him during the voyage, not all of them likely to have been given in advance of actual earning. Baker Library, Swift and Allen manuscripts, Seamens' Accounts, V, vol. VIII, p. 21, Dec. 5, 1848. See too Samuel Eliot Morison, *The Maritime History of Massachusetts 1783–1860* (1921), pp. 319–321.

[51] The prime rate appears in *Historical Statistics,* p. 654. For capital return we utilize the average price of capital shown in table V-2 in John Kendrick's *Productivity Trends in the United States.*

[52] It is irrelevant to our present concern whether the movements over individual periods are reasonable. Some, such as the great rise from 1899 to 1919 in "all capital" and hence in the spread, seem inexplicable in the light of later gains.

dominated prime rates. The concurrent rise in opportunities for capital (keyed to population growth, the change in final demand patterns, and the increasing complement of capital per employee) brought a rise for all capital, and hence in the spread.

In an earlier section we discussed the driving impetus that freedom plus an open society gave to the advance of material productivity in the United States. In this one we have concentrated on changes in those factors shaping the production function. We have asserted that the American entrepreneur during the formative period of our development, and for many years thereafter, had a fixed element which polarized his cost calculations. Uncertain in anticipating the trends in other factor costs, he knew almost surely that wage rates in his own enterprise were likely to rise in the foreseeable future, given the endless material horizon possible for labor in an open society. This conclusion was italicized by the repeated attempts of immigrants to press for higher wages as they discovered their distance below the American standard of living. Moreover, political stability in America grew, not merely in an absolute sense but by contrast to Europe's adventures in war and revolution. Such gaining stability muted the risks confronting capital in this nation and made it increasingly attractive to foreign capital. Given the prospect of rising wage rates and this force for declining capital costs, the direction of productivity advance was fixed. Entrepreneurs increasingly superseded hand methods of production by machine methods, increasingly raised the productivity of their enterprises by other changes as well. The direct advantage that flowed from such substitution and revision was major. But it is likely that a further reward came from the frequent reconsideration of the modes of production: Fresh entrepreneurial thought must have sped productive advance more forcefully than solid but slothful entrepreneurial habit.

EXTERNAL ECONOMIES, UNCERTAINTY, AND WAGES

In assessing the external economies that accompany economic growth, economists have, in general, emphasized one major factor—education— that tended to reduce real labor costs. But a study of wage changes in the long term points to a powerful force which tended to lower wage rates and labor costs for more than a century and a half.[1] And that force is simply the decrease of uncertainty in the labor markets. As the nation grew, as its markets became more closely integrated, as communication made business response to changes more accurate, the steadiness of the work that could be offered to labor increased. Production runs lengthened,

---

[1] It did not tend to decrease annual labor incomes. If anything, it brought dynamic changes that worked to raise them.

the demands of consumers became more predictable; if sales could not be made in the local market, declining transport costs made it increasingly feasible to ship to other markets.[2] That so basic a change in the product market should be recognized by the labor market in the wage rates paid is not altogether surprising. But how great a change, and in what direction?[3]

Theorists have not always agreed whether the valuation often given to stabler employment was positive. With his sometimes incomparable lack of realism, Nassau Senior argued that wages in occupations with high uncertainty will be driven below those in comparable, more certain, occupations. Why? Because nothing "is so much disliked as steady, regular labor; and . . . the opportunities for idleness afforded by an occupation of irregular employment are so much more than an equivalent for its anxiety as to reduce the wages of such occupations below the common average."[4] On the other hand theorists of at least equal ability (including Smith and Marshall) have contended that the more irregular the employment in an occupation, the higher the wage.[5] The valuation set upon income in terms of effort is the relevant criterion; and, depending on the social order and the changing levels of income available, the empirical outcome may be one or the other. What light does American experience cast on this difference of opinion?

I

From the origins of the Republic, evidence exists that workmen in this nation did not prefer uncertainty; that higher wage rates were required to compensate, at least in part, for irregularity of employment. As the Chief Engineer of the Louisville, Cincinnati and Charleston Railroad explained in 1839: The cost of Southern railroad construction was not as much below Northern as the difference in terrain would suggest, because "whenever mechanical skill is to be brought into requisition, they (the North)

[2] R. A. Levine and R. B. Rainey, "Random Variations and Sampling Models in Production Economics," *Journal of Political Economy* (June, 1960), p. 229: "It may well be that many economies of scale are due to the random characteristics of production. Because of the workings of the law of large numbers, the larger an organization the smaller the effects of variability in optimal resource allocations."

[3] T. M. Whitin and M. H. Peston, "Random Variations, Risk, and Returns to Scale," *Quarterly Journal of Economics* (November, 1954), parts II and III, discuss scale economies in the firm that can be readily extrapolated to the nation. We assume here that labor commands a return for being exposed to such risks.

[4] *Political Economy* (1872), pp. 207–208. Almost concurrently Louis Blanc was using data on the earnings of Parisian seamstresses to argue the opposite conclusion. See Julia Poyntz, in Sidney Webb and Beatrice Webb, *The Seasonal Trades*, pp. 11–16.

[5] Adam Smith, *The Wealth of Nations*, book 1, chap. 10. Alfred Marshall, *Principles of Economics*, book VI, chap. 3, para. 6. Frederick Mills, *Contemporary Theories of Unemployment* (1917), p. 14.

having more of it, because of a more constant demand for it, can more easily command it, and at a cheaper rate." [6] As early as 1790 Benjamin Rush noted annual wages of 15 to 18 guineas for laborers, adding that "when they work by the day they receive high wages but these are seldom continued through the whole year." [7]

The gap between wage rates paid to masons and to carpenters is a historic indication of wage differences that are largely linked to differences in stability of employment. For generations masons have had less work in winter than carpenters, mortar being a more refractory material in cold weather than nails. We note below some data from 1777 (rates set by the selectmen of the town of Newburyport) through 1815 (New York) on to 1870 (New England). [8]

Date	Location	Masons	Carpenters	Ratio, %
1777	Newburyport	6s	5s 4d	110
1815	New York	$1.75	$1.50	117
1825	New England	1.62	1.45	111
1860	New England	1.64	1.40	117
1870	New England	3.50	2.97	118

Although the skill differences were greater, the allowance for stability is suggested, too, by the generally lower rates paid to the clerks of the great fur companies of the Northwest than to the trappers; to teachers than to farm laborers; to employees of government, banks, and insurance companies than to those hired by competitive enterprise.

But in all these instances it is quite possible that the supply (or demand) of one type of labor may have differed from that of another, that the skills might in fact have differed significantly. Is there some method of locating the influence of uncertainty per se?

---

[6] Broadsheet titled: *The Columbia Telescope,* Oct. 19, 1839, Letter of William Gibbes McNeil, Chief Engineer of the L. C. & C. Railroad.

[7] H. L. Butterfield (ed.), *Letters of Benjamin Rush* (1951), vol. I, p. 554: "A laborer receives annually his boarding, washing and lodging with from fifteen to eighteen guineas in the middle states." Letter of Apr. 16, 1790.

[8] *1777:* Caleb Cushing, *The History and Present State of Newburyport* (Newburyport: 1826), p. 72.

1815: A Review of the Trade and Commerce of New York from 1815 to the Present Time with an Inquiry into the Causes of the Present Distress and the Means of Obviating It, by an Observer (New York: C. S. Van Winkle, 1820).

1825: Zechariah Allen, *The Science of Mechanics* (Providence: 1839) p. 347.

1860: Aldrich Committee materials in Wesley Mitchell, *Gold, Prices and Wages* (1908), Establishments 7, 12, 35, 38, pp. 26–27.

1870: Edward Young, *Special Report on Immigration,* 42d Cong., 1st Sess., House Exec. Doc. 1 (1871) pp. 202ff.

The nineteenth-century data available for several occupations do enable us to make a more precise comparison.

Common Labor. For 1832 a variety of state data indicate that the price of common labor was from 30 to 60 percent greater when hired by the day than when hired by the month:[9]

State	Month	26 days	Margin, %
Connecticut........	$11.61	$17.41	50
Maine.............	12.43	19.56	57
New Hampshire.....	11.66	15.60	34
Georgia............	9.44	14.10	50
Indiana............	9.02	11.95	32
Missouri...........	10.15	13.52	33

Here the skills and demands of the jobs would differ little, but the prospect of constant employment was much more durable for jobs by the month than by the day.

If we add the 1850 and 1860 figures on the rates paid to labor hired by the day and to farm labor hired by the month, we arrive at similar ratios:[10]

State	Ratio		
	1832	1850	1860
Connecticut........	50	55	51
Maine.............	57	51	54
New Hampshire.....	34	35	43
Georgia............	50	44	37
Indiana............	32	36	38
Missouri...........	33	21	35

Despite the passage of the decades and the use for 1850 and 1860 of day-labor rates that must reflect demands by nonfarm as well as the dominant farm industry, few significant changes appear.[11] It is particularly worthy of note that Indiana and Missouri—then on the frontier—report ratios significantly below those for the Eastern states. Such a gap reflects an-

[9] 23rd Cong., 1st Sess., *Statistical View of the Population of the United States from 1790 to 1830*, pp. 190, 209, 214. Rates with board.
[10] J. D. B. DeBow, *Statistical View of the United States* (1854), p. 164. Eighth Census, *Statistics of the United States (including mortality, property, etc.) in 1860* (1866), p. 512.
[11] The perceptible decline for Georgia would reflect slave migration to the newer regions of Mississippi and Texas.

other dimension of the uncertainty impact. Since labor was relatively scarcer in the new (than older) regions, it would find opportunities for work there more readily. If the uncertainty gap were less, we would expect less of a premium to have been paid for short-period hiring. The lower ratios for these states are consistent with such a hypothesis.

The long-term downward trend in the differential paid for instability of employment can best be illustrated by figures for farming, our dominant industry for many decades, and a major one for so many more. For 1850 to 1866 we compare daily rates (times 26) and monthly rates, both inclusive of board, while for the subsequent period we contrast rates without board.[12]

Daily Farm Wages (times 26) as a Percentage of Monthly Rates

Date	With board	Without board
1850	146	
1866	165	151
1869		146
1880		129
1890		130
1899		129
1910		129
1915		125
1920		138
1929		114
1942		115
1950		107

Over the entire period a sharp fall—of nearly one-third—occurred in the allowance for uncertainty. If the decline reflected a change in uncertainty, then a rise in the premium for unsteady work would be expected during periods of heavy wartime demand. In fact, the differential widened significantly during 1860 to 1865, as it did again during World War I.

[12] *1850:* Rates from DeBow, *loc. cit.,* weighted by the number of males employed in agriculture as reported on p. 128.

1866–1942: United States farm wage rates, without board, per day and per month. From U.S. Department of Agriculture, *Farm Wage Rates, Farm Employment and Related Data* (January, 1943) p. 2.

1950: 1950 Census of Agriculture, *General Report,* vol. II, pp. 290–292. We adjust the reported census averages for persons paid per day and per month in order to exclude those receiving board. To the daily average we apply the ratio of (1) the median daily rate paid by farms furnishing no perquisites to (2) the median for all farms paying on a daily basis; and similarly for the monthly rates.

If this downward trend in the differential were, in fact, associated with greater labor-market stability and ease of finding work, we would expect a further consequence. Since short-run employment declines produce a generally higher level of uncertainty, the premium paid on short-duration jobs would fall as employment falls. Our data on changes in recession years, despite their limitations, confirm such a reduction:[13]

Daily Farm Wage Rates (times 26) as a Percentage of Monthly Rates

1891–1892	127
1893	120
1920	138
1921	123
1929	114
1930	112
1931	110
1932	108

Another consequence would be a higher rate for work known to be of short duration, whatever the actual hiring period. In fact rates paid for harvest labor have always been quoted above those for day labor, whether we observe the figures for Missouri in 1832, New York in 1850, or California in 1950. The bulk of this excess appears relatable only to instability. The first wave of new farm machinery during the mid-nineteenth century was in harvesting equipment, while later equipment (whether for beet topping or corn picking) tended to cut spring and fall peak labor requirements by a greater percentage than it cut needs during the rest of the year. In so doing it cut deeper into requirements for harvest and planting labor, with its high wage premium, than requirements for longer duration, lower paid workers.

Manufacturing: 1832. In later years factory labor was commonly hired for an indefinite period—usually expected to be at least a month. Hence we can deduce little about the allowance for instability from rates per se. But for 1832 there are relevant figures. In 1832 a substantial proportion of employees in nonfarm pursuits appeared to have been paid at day rates at the same time that a significant proportion were paid at monthly rates. And 26 times the day rate was typically well above the monthly figure. For example, Pennsylvania ironworks paid an average of $1.01 for those employed by the day, while the much larger number hired by the month averaged $19.24.[14] While 30 percent of the Pennsylvania

[13] From 1913 to 1914 the rate changed from 126 to 125, so mild a change that it is hardly support to the present proposition, albeit directly consonant with it.

[14] Computed from individual returns in McLane Report, *Documents on Manufactures* (1833), U.S. Congress, Serial Set 222.

employees were hired by the month, almost none are reported by the month in other states. The greater continuity of employment in Pennsylvania, which made possible hiring a larger proportion at a monthly wage, therefore resulted in a lower wage cost to the employer, given the day-month differential. Such information as is available on technology and occupational gradations does not suggest that these differences—as we would first expect—were tied to differences in either skills, arduousness, or responsibility. Higher and separate rates are quoted for forgemen, furnacemen, and carpenters; these data relate to the balance of the workmen.[15]

Seamen.   From 1800 to 1860 we have a variety of data on wages paid to able seamen, distinguishing short coastal trips from long voyages to faraway ports. Historians of the sea have found that California clippers uniformly paid less than Liverpool coasters, that rates for the long voyage to China were typically less than short coasting voyages or trips to Europe.[16] Pick up a shipping list of the period and you find, for example, wages quoted at $14 to $15 for European trips, at $11 to the East Indies.[17] We draw upon the tabulation of individual ship's articles used to prepare Table A-21 to note the comparisons shown in the following table.

These differences did not reflect differences in the labor-market situation in different ports, but primarily the stability factor. Thus data for 18 voyages from New England ports in 1833 average about $13 for able-bodied seamen hired for 1- to 3-month coasting voyages to Charleston, to Virginia ports, to Demerara—while men were being hired in the same ports at a $12 rate for the long trip to China.[18] Concurrently the Navy

[15] Throughout the McLane Report wages for labor are quoted at, for example, "75 cents a day and $12 a month." Limited individual statements about the inclusion of board suggests that board was customarily included in either instance. The small cost of lodging in the rural areas, where most ironworks, woolen and cotton mills, etc., were located, could not have accounted for much of the gap, although it may have been a factor.

[16] Robert G. Albion estimates $16 in the coasting trade as against $12 to $13 for China voyages. *Square Riggers on Schedule* (1938), p. 143. Samuel E. Morison, *The Maritime History of Massachusetts, 1783–1860* (1921), p. 353, finds a 50 percent differential, in the slack years after the war of 1812, between California and European voyages.

[17] Philadelphia shipping list for 1843, quoted in Addie C. Colman, *Captain Moses Rich Colman . . . 1807–1872* (1949), p. 5.

[18] Baker Library, Wendell Manuscripts, Boxes 5, 21, 23, using folders for the *Atlantic, Adeline, Hiram, Lavinia,* and *Enterprise,* together with listings from D. Yeaton's record book from Box 5, entitled "wages (paid seamen)." An average of $13 for 1832, of $13.35 for 1833, results.

A $14 rate paid on the brig *Hyperion* out of Baltimore is reported in U.S. Congress, Serial Set 373, House Report, 26th Cong., 1st Sess., *N. P. Trist, July 21, 1840,* 369. For the China voyage, Baker Library, Dexter manuscripts, vol. 145, contains articles for the ship *California*'s voyages beginning October, 1833, and August, 1835. These show $12 for A.B.'s and $7 for ordinary seamen.

Monthly Wages of Able Seamen

Date	Coasting trade and Europe	China and Pacific ports	U.S. Navy
1800	$20	$19	
1802	15	14	$12
1817	11	12	
1818	12	12	
1830	13	. .	12
1833	13	12	
1836	15	12	
1839	14	12	
1848–1849	15	12	
1853	15	12	
1854–1857	15	15	
1860	. .	12	15
1869	18	20	

(offering an equal hitch of steady employment) also paid relatively low rates.

Nearly a decade later Richard Henry Dana, writing his farewell to the sea, found a similar spread: "In the United States an able seaman receives twelve dollars per month. . . . In the merchant service, wages are about the same on long voyages, but on voyages to Europe, the West Indies and the Southern ports they are considerably higher, and very fluctuating." [19]

Conceivably the quality of the men hired for longer voyages differed. But (if anything) the employer would have sought higher quality for men on whom the captain must depend for three years, with dubious hope of replacement in Eastern ports. It is important to note that the $1 and $2 differences shown above were not trivial by contemporary standards. In 1837, for example, a contemporary reported: "One or two hundred sailors were marching in a body about the wharves and streets of Boston, on Wednesday 31st ult. An American flag flying, and on a board in front, 'Sailors' Rights—$15 a month.' There are but few vessels not fitting out and the small number of seamen that have been shipped for ten days past were obtained at $14 per month." [20] If $1 measured the gap between right and wrong, then clearly a $2 difference marked a significant sum.

Two final comments may be made on the wages of seamen.

1. For 1869 the table shows the total disappearance of the gap we

[19] *The Seamen's Friend* (Boston, 1841), p. 158.

[20] B. Homans (ed.), *Army and Navy Chronicle* (Washington: June 1, 1837), p. 349.

have been discussing and, in fact, a reversal. The data for laborers show a rising differential over the period, but these figures give no confirmation. The explanation, however, offers interesting insight into the role of uncertainty in keeping wage rates high. During 1860 to 1870 a critical technological change took place in the merchant marine: The substantial displacement of sail by steam. A visitor to Donald McKay's shipyard, where the greatest clipper ships had been built, found in late 1866 this "once famous shipyard was entirely deserted; not a sound was to be heard; not a single person besides Mr. McKay, himself, was there. No building materials were to be seen, no vessel was being built; nor had one been in the course of construction for over a year." McKay expressed no hope of leaving the freighting business and returning to ship construction, unless special tax relief were afforded shipbuilders.[21] Despite this ever-contemporary note, the day of the clipper ship was over. Steam was king. But as a consequence the 3-year voyage to China was a thing of the past. The ship *Herald of Morning,* leaving New York on June 14, 1870, arrived in San Francisco on November 10, or about as much time as the same ship took from Falmouth to Bremerhaven.[22] While the sailor's lot was still an uncertain one, the basis for the China (3-year) versus Europe (3-month) voyage differential had dwindled. However, where the durations continued to differ—as distinct from our use of destination as an indicator of duration—the gap remained.[23]

2. An alternative indication of the premium for instability of employment is given by the contrast in 1850 between, say, the $12 rates paid for China voyages from the East coast and the $20 to $25 paid deck crews on Mississippi River steamers at the same time; or the 1860 rates of $12 to China from the East coast, the $20 rates from San Francisco, and the $30 to $35 rates for river steamers.[24] The skills and danger associated with steamboating were certainly no greater than on the long overseas voyages. Nor is it likely that differences in tightness of the labor markets were involved. Had such forces been a sufficient explanation, we would see a parallel gap, say, between common-labor rates of the East Coast states and those through which the Mississippi flowed. But reference to Table

[21] Report by Alexander Delmar, Chief of the Treasury Bureau of Statistics, of an interview with McKay. U.S. Special Commissioner of the Revenue, *Report for 1866* (1867), pp. 207–208.

[22] Magoun Manuscript Collection 1, vol. 41. Accounts current and portage bill for the first trip; ships' articles for the April 28–Sept. 9, 1871, trip.

[23] For example, in 1875 A.B.'s on vessels leaving California ports for coasting trips were paid $40 a month, whereas deep-sea sailors, for longer voyages, were paid $26 to $30. *California Posten* (February, 1875), quoted in Kenneth Bjork's *West of the Great Divide* (1958), p. 169.

[24] Ocean-voyage data from the table above. Deck-crew rates from Louis C. Hunter, *Steamboats on the Western Rivers* (1949), p. 465.

A-24 indicates no such gap; indeed, in 1860 common-labor, carpenter, and farm-labor rates did not differ much between Middle Atlantic states and those bordering the Mississippi. As for equalizing differences, they ran the other way: board was less expensive in the valley states than in the East.[25] And the sunsets, saloons, and other amenities involved in equalizing differences were not likely to be choicer in one area than the other. We infer that the much higher rates in river steamboating reflected the shorter duration of such trips and the inconstancy of the employment they offered, as compared with the longer ocean voyages.[26]

II

A further force for lower wage costs was the declining chance of death or disablement while on the job. As the country was settled the marshy land where malaria was bred was filled in. Buildings covered the waste spaces where animal vectors could survive. And the rise in sanitation made cities with once high yellow-fever rates (and correspondingly high wages) as safe as any in the nation. Thus a mighty influence buoying up wages paid to the men building canals during the 1820s and 1830s was the danger of yellow fever and malaria. Built through marsh and swamps (in many instances) to reduce construction problems, the canals were known as killers. Captain James Alexander inspected the Ponchartrain canal being constructed near New Orleans in 1832, then summarized his views with the succinctness of a military dispatch: "Six hundred Irish perish yearly in and about New Orleans, who come in search of employment and high wages (a dollar a day) from New York and Charleston." [27] Hard on the heels of the captain came Tyrone Power. Writing of his visit with something less than equanimity, he observed that immigrants were used on such work but not slaves; the latter were "much too expensive. A good slave costs at this time two hundred pounds sterling [about $900] and to have a thousand such swept off a line of canal in one season would call for prompt consideration." [28] Where the prospect of wholesale death was less common, the rates were lower. The equally arduous work of constructing a railway line near Philadelphia at the same time paid Irish navvys reasonably well in terms of the surrounding area—three meals a day with

[25] Data on occupational wage rates and board by state in 1860 appear in the Eighth Census, *Statistics of the United States (including mortality, property, etc.) in 1860* (1866), p. 512.

[26] Indeed the Ohio, Illinois, Missouri, Kentucky, and Louisiana common-labor rates, without board, multiplied by 26, give a monthly rate closely similar to Hunter's figures for deck crew.

[27] Captain James E. Alexander, *Transatlantic Sketches* (London: 1833), vol. II, p. 29.

[28] Tyrone Power, *Impression of America during the Years 1833, 1834 and 1836*, vol. II, pp. 150–153.

coffee *and* sugar for two of them; six to eight glasses of whisky; up to 40 cents a day—but the figure was far below the $1 a day in the fever-racked swamps around New Orleans.[29]

In the construction of the James River and Kanawha Company canal $1 a day was a likely wage, but when the work approached "the heat and the dangerous area near the falls, [where] in the early part of July some fifteen or twenty of the Irishmen suddenly expired under the intensity of the heat," even a $1.30 rate found no takers, according to the company.[30]

In upstate New York in the 1830s and 1840s grown men received $10 to $12 for farm work, but thirteen-year-old boys driving an Erie canal boat through the regions where hundreds died during the cholera season were paid as much.[31] With boys customarily being paid markedly less than men, and certainly for less arduous work, the differential presumably reflected the dangers of cholera and malaria associated with being a "canawler." The allowance for unhealthy working conditions was a quite explicit part of entrepreneurial calculations. One canal company president reported wages relatively high because the canal was going through malarial land, but confidently forecast that wages would fall when the canal reached "to the healthy country about the Point of Rocks." [32] Although such wholesale death was less routine in the Northern states, the danger was present there too, in combination with the arduous work.[33]

Another dimension of the extra margin for risk and arduous work is to be found in the Hudson Bay Company rates paid to voyageurs. In 1822, for example, rates in the Red River Valley and similar territories of the company were taken as standard, the pay in the farther distant region of Athabasca then being arbitrarily set at one-third greater, with a 20 percent margin in later years.[34] Of course when the Arctic area was being ex-

[29] The Philadelphia rates are given in Michel Chevalier, *Lettres sur l'Amerique du Nord* (Paris, 1836), vol. I, p. 159. The $12 a month rate is confirmed in various works by Matthew Carey, but without data on board, etc.

[30] *Fourth Annual Report,* see also the section on Unskilled Labor: Canal Construction (chap. 7).

[31] Deacon M. Eaton, *Five Years on the Erie Canal* (Utica: Bennet, Backus and Hawley, 1845), pp. 32, 37, 75, "The reason why we have so many orphans on our canals [Eaton finds that half the drivers were orphans] is that great inducements are held out to them. Ten dollars per month has been the wages given to boys for driving." The deacon refers to a boy who left his uncle who "could only give me $5 a month." For farm wages, see Table A-24.

[32] The canal was the Chesapeake and Ohio and the quotation appears in 21st Cong., 2d Sess., House Reports of Committees, no. 31, p. 5.

[33] The results on labor supply—and presumably on wages—were similar. Charles N. Morris, "Internal Improvements in Ohio, 1825–1850," *Papers of the American Historical Association,* vol. III, p. 112.

[34] Harvey Fleming (ed.), *Minutes of Council Northern Department of Rupert Land, 1821–31* (1940), p. 305. In January, 1822, the one-third margin was set because the work "was severe and privations great."

plored a still greater margin had to be offered, nearly 100 percent.[35]

The most dangerous work regularly available was, in many respects, that of slave running; slave importations had been outlawed by many nations, while England and America maintained naval patrols to forbid the smuggling of slaves to Brazil or Cuba and thence to Texas or the United States. Since the ordinary sailor could be imprisoned as a pirate and have to find another berth, the rates of pay were higher. Thus ordinary commercial trips of 3 to 4 months' duration paid $14 in 1838, whereas men recruited for the brig *Kremlin,* to smuggle slaves from Africa, were offered $18.[36] (The men of the *Kremlin* were later offered $40 a month for that portion of the trip beginning at Havana and running thence to the Gold Coast and then to Bahia—that portion being the one where American registry no longer applied and the danger of capture was greatest.[37]) The payroll of an 1827 slave voyage notes that the men on the dangerous voyage back to Havana, with slaves aboard, received double the wages paid on the outward, safer, voyage to Africa.[38]

Needless to say, the differential for the captain was greater. In 1839 captains could contrast $40 for a safe 3-month voyage to the West Indies to $100 a month and three slaves (each worth about $350 when landed in Havana) for the dangerous slaving trip to Africa.[39]

The various examples noted above suggest that American labor has long

[35] E. E. Rich (ed.), *John Rae's Correspondence with the Hudson's Bay Company on Arctic Exploration, 1844–1855* (1953), p. 21, reports rates of 40 pounds for Orkney men, compared to 24 pounds paid ordinary engages (middlemen) in 1824. Because Canadians were usually paid less, we may assume only a doubling. Wage levels for identical categories appear to have changed little over the period.

[36] *Nathaniel P. Trist, July 21, 1840,* p. 32.

[37] *Search or Seizure of American Vessels on the Coast of Africa,* 26th Cong., 2d Sess., House Doc. 115, Mar. 3, 1841, p. 332. The $40 offer was made for them to ship aboard the *Venus.* Approximately one in six slavers were captured by the British, according to Lieutenant Bell, Commander of the United States Brig *Dolphin,* quoting the British governor of Sierra Leone. A $40 rate for slavers also appears in William L. Mathieson, *Great Britain and the Slave Trade, 1839–1865* (1929), p. 146.

[38] 1827 payroll for 18 men reported in Brantz Mayer, *Captain Canot, or Twenty Years of an African Slaver* (New York; 1854), p. 101. On a return voyage beginning the fourth of July, 1859, the crew was offered $1,500 if the trip were successful. In fact it was, slaves bought at $8 being sold in Cuba at $350. Even allowing $1,000 for captain and mate, $100 each would remain for a crew of five. George F. Dow, *Slave Ships and Slaving* (1927), pp. 325, 327, 330, 342.

[39] For the $40 figure, see the voyages of the *Hope* and *Pactolus* in Table A-22. In 1839 George Watson of the *Rebecca* was paid $280 and three slaves valued at $340 and F. A. Peterson, $100 a month and $300 "gratification." In 1839 Joseph Monroe was paid $90 a month for the voyage to Gallinas, as was a Spanish captain. In 1837 James Fox was paid $75 a month and $100 bounty when the slaves were landed. *Search or Seizure of American Vessels on the Coast of Africa,* pp. 108, 129, 145, 174, 196, 197, 215.

sought, and secured, a positive premium to compensate for instability of employment. In addition, marked allowances were made in the nineteenth century in some of the dangerous trades—whether the danger was death from cholera or malaria or the temporary interruption of work by being captured for piracy. As the economy grew in the decades after 1800, the increase in population, the contiguity of markets, the filling in of marshy land, and the growth of sanitation all worked to reduce the extent of instability in employment as well as the extent of employment in obviously dangerous trades. Since the labor market offered a premium for such instability and danger, the growth of the economy would have lowered the amount of such premium paid by employers. This reduction in real-labor costs offered a significant economy. An advantage that will not appear in any standard wage-rate series, it is nonetheless classifiable with other external economies—and quite possibly was of greater value to producers and the nation than some better-known ones.

PART **II**

COMPONENTS OF CHANGE:
NINETEENTH CENTURY

6

WAGES IN THE LONG TERM

AGRICULTURE: 1800 TO 1950
(TABLES A-23, A-24)

For most of the nineteenth century and well into the twentieth, the common method of wage payment in agriculture was monthly, with board included. Rates with board are quoted throughout the period, while comparison of the 1948 monthly rate with the representative "composite rate" of the Department of Agriculture for 1950 shows that even as late as 1948 intrastate variation is fairly well portrayed by this single rate.

Reasonably satisfactory data for individual states are available at something like decennial intervals for the entire period beginning with 1818. These figures have been supplemented with partial information to provide national estimates for the years for which this is not so—primarily 1800 and 1840—to help portray the full sweep over a century and a half.

1800. For 1800, the 1818 United States average was extrapolated primarily on the basis of Carey's assertion that agricultural wages in Pennsylvania showed little net change over the 1800–1835 period [1]—an assertion confirmed by the stability shown in earnings rates for other groups. Since Representative Troup estimated, in 1812, that agricultural wages then ran to $10 a month[2] and the Holmes data (discussed below) also averaged about $10 in 1818, the United States 1800 figure was likewise estimated at $10.[3]

---

[1] H. C. Carey, *Essay on the Rate of Wages* (Philadelphia: 1835), p. 26.
[2] *Annals of Congress*, November, 1812, col. 182.
[3] Carey's own estimate, of $9, related to Pennsylvania alone.

1818, 1826, 1830.   For these three years estimates were made in 1832 by Senator John Holmes of Maine, and reported by him in the Congressional *Register of Debates*.[4] For the key states we have, in addition, the results of a survey in 1832–1834 on 1832 farm wages made by Secretary of State Edward Livingstone, drawing on returns from many individual towns in these states— i.e., 59 of 134 towns in Connecticut, 101 of 444 in Maine, 109 of 230 in New Hampshire, etc.[5] Given the broader basis of the Secretary's survey, his figures were used to represent the 1830 average (other data indicating virtually no 1830–1832 change) with the Holmes series used to extrapolate these values to 1818 and 1826.[6]

For New Hampshire, Massachusetts, and Vermont we have, in addition, estimates by a number of local businessmen and marshals in the McLane report, all of them tending to indicate 1832 average rates of $10.[7] The McLane report data are in line with the Vermont rate, below that of New Hampshire, and above that for Massachusetts. The New Hampshire rate from the Secretary of State's report does seem high in comparison to the other New England states. But, being based on direct reports from 109 towns in that state and with a fair consistency among the reports for those towns, was left unchanged.[8] The broader basis of the State Department returns warrants their use to provide the levels for 1830, with Holmes's figures then measuring the dollar change from earlier years. For example, the State Department survey shows $9.02 for Indiana in 1832, while the Holmes data show no change for 1818–1826–1830. The $9.02 figure (rounded) was therefore used for all years. The survey shows $11.66 for New Hampshire, while Holmes data shows both 1818 and 1826 $1.50 below his 1830 figure. The present estimates therefore run $10.16, $10.16,

[4] John Holmes, in Gales and Seaton, *Register of Debates*, 22nd Cong., 1st Sess., Jan. 30, 1832, p. 218. Holmes states that "the valuation . . . is the price per month taking all seasons of the year inclusive of board and exclusive of clothing."

[5] 23rd Cong., 1st Sess., Serial Set 252, *Statistical View of the Population of the United States from 1790 to 1830 Inclusive Furnished by the Secretary of State in Accordance with the Resolution of the Senate* (Washington: Duff Green, 1835), pp. 190, 209, 214. Unpublished correspondence in the National Archives (State Department, miscellaneous letters) shows that some of these replies, though requested in the summer of 1832, were actually returned in 1834.

[6] For Maine, Rhode Island, Indiana, and Missouri, Holmes indicates no 1818 to 1830 change. For Connecticut, Georgia, and New Hampshire, the dollar value of the change reported by Holmes for 1818–1826–1830 was added to, or subtracted from, the State Department 1832 figure. Thus, the 1832 Connecticut figure was reduced $1.50 to give an 1818 figure, Holmes's 1818 estimate being that much below his 1830 figure. It is thus assumed that Holmes was referring to dollar and cents changes rather than percentage changes.

[7] U.S. Congress, Serial Set, 222, 223, *Documents Relative to the Statistics of Manufactures in the United States* (Washington: Duff Green, 1833), vols. I, II, *passim*. (Hereafter referred to as the *McLane Report*.)

[8] The individual town reports appear in U.S. Congress, Serial Set 252.

and $11.66 for these dates. For the important New England and North Central states, and for Georgia, we thus have the basis for adjusting Holmes's figures.

Because of the considerable share of employment in Massachusetts, special attention was given to estimating its rates. A $12 figure for 1830 was estimated, then extrapolated by Holmes as above. The 1830 rate was estimated by using Massachusetts Bureau of Labor rates for monthly farm labor.[9] (Since both census and Bureau of Labor reports are virtually identical for 1850, this was felt to be the soundest procedure.) There is, however, some reason to feel that the Bureau of Labor figures are too high: A variety of daily rates from the contemporary *Massachusetts Agricultural Repository* and manufacturers' statements in the McLane report would suggest an average of $10.[10] However, since a $12 rate is much more reasonable in the light of the State Department returns for the other New England states and since both the Bureau of Labor and United States Census reports for 1850 are virtually identical, a $12 rate was adopted for 1830.

What of the remaining states? For Pennsylvania, we have an 1829 estimate for a typical farm, with two hands and a boy: "The hands cost $100 or $90 a year each" [11]—$8 to $7.50, compared to Holmes's $8.50. We likewise have somewhat earlier estimates for two individual counties: $80 to $100 a year in Chester County in 1828 and $5 to $7 a month for 1832 in Bedford County, each with board.[12] For Virginia a detailed cost calculation by Edmund Ruffin of the cost in 1832 of hiring slave labor plus allowance for keep, taxes, and overhead runs to $72 for the year, plus 20 percent for "superintendence, waste, wanton thefts"—in comparison to the $6 a month estimated by Holmes.[13] For Indiana Morris Birkbeck reported meeting two widowers (with three children each) who were hired for work in Indiana at $80 a year plus house, food, and clothing for themselves and their children.[14] The figure is not unreasonably out of line with the $108

[9] Massachusetts Bureau of Labor Statistics, "Historical Review of Wages and Prices: 1752–1860," in *Sixteenth Annual Report* (1885), p. 317.

[10] *McLane Report,* vol. I, pp. 69, 70, 76, 78, 81, 86, 92, 135, 136, 146, 471, 576. The figures show daily rates first where given, then monthly by the year, as follows: $10–$12; $8; $12; 67 cents, $11; $8; $1, $12; 50 cents–$1, $9–$12; $10; $1, $12; 75 cents–$1, $12; 75 cents–$10 (three nearby towns); $1, $10–$12; and, for Suffolk County, with few laborers, $14.

[11] *Niles Register,* quoted in Condy Raguet (ed.), *The Free Trade Advocate and Journal of Political Economy* (Philadelphia: Adam Waldie, Mar. 28, 1829), p. 207.

[12] Stevenson W. Fletcher, *Pennsylvania Agriculture and Country Life, 1640–1840* (1950), pp. 307, 308.

[13] Edmund Ruffin, *An Essay on Calcareous Manures* (Petersburg: Printed for the author, 1842), p. 132.

[14] Morris Birkbeck, *Notes on a Journey in America* (London: Severn and Co., 1819), p. 43.

figure (including only his own board) for a farm laborer as estimated by Holmes.

As a crude basis of judgment for the other states, we may refer to 1818 contract prices paid by the Army for various items at different posts in the North and South Atlantic states.[15] Using the prices paid per barrel of flour (a substantial item, and one likely to have been provided locally with a minimum of transport differentials involved), we can infer the general reasonableness of the relationships among the various state rates of Holmes, except that the averages for both Pennsylvania and Maryland appear to be too high. Data on procurement prices for entire areas, e.g., "Pennsylvania East of the Alleghenies and West of the Susquehanna," "Kentucky," etc., are available for rations as of 1814.[16] These, too, suggest that Maryland and Pennsylvania rates were too high compared to the others. This indirect inference might well be rejected for Pennsylvania if most farm laborers were hired in the border areas, where rates would be higher. For Maryland, the problem is more difficult. Baltimore flour prices were only about 10 percent above Norfolk in 1818, and Maryland rations slightly above those for Virginia in 1814, yet Holmes's Maryland wage rate is far above that for Virginia. No adjustment was made, however, because substantial labor demand in Baltimore and the District of Columbia and the limited competition of slave labor would imply some excess of Maryland over Virginia rates. Moreover, it seems unwise to reduce the 1818 figure below that prevailing in 1830—a period much closer to Holmes's then current knowledge—when to do so would wipe out the 1818 to 1830 decline that Holmes presumably sought to report.

Holmes's earlier figures for 1818 cannot be tested with any degree of rigor and we must take them as simply indicating that wages in 1818 appear to have been much the same as those in 1826 to 1830, but with apparent declines in some areas as a result of the 1819 recession. With rates of about 80 cents a day, paid on a selection of individual farms in 1819, and 67 cents by 1821–1823, we have a rough confirmation of the general trend for New England in the above estimate.[17]

[15] American State Papers, *Military Affairs*, vol. I, pp. 348–350.

[16] *Letter from the Secretary of War Transmitting Statements of Contracts Made by the War Department during the Year 1814*, Feb. 9, 1815 (District of Columbia: Roger Chew Weightman, 1815).

[17] *The Massachusetts Agricultural Repository and Journal* (1821), vol. VI, p. 37, reports farm labor at 75 cents a day in Plymouth in 1819; 84 cents at Fitchburg (p. 45); and 75 cents at Fitchburg (p. 253—for harvest labor at that, normally paid above the daily average); and vol. VII, 1823—67 and 83 cents on the same farm in 1821 (pp. 53, 280); 85 cents in 1821 (p. 55); 75 cents in 1822 (p. 283). The Massachusetts Bureau of Labor Statistics (*loc. cit.*) shows daily rates falling from $1.49 (1818) to 53 cents (1819), then rising to 62 cents (1826) and 88 cents (1831). The direction is similar but the volatility improbable.

The likelihood that the Pennsylvania figure for 1818 is not in fact too high is

Adams's Vermont data, as the Holmes figures for Vermont, show little net change in daily rates from 1815 to 1832, but mark a decline after 1815.[18] An 1819 rate of 50 cents a day for New York suggests a level from which there was a marked recovery in later years, pointing to a substantial 1818–1819 drop of the kind noted in common labor for Philadelphia and in the Massachusetts Bureau of Labor day rates mentioned above.[19]

1840. A United States rate in 1840 was estimated by extrapolating the reliable 1850 rate, the latter being based on a combination of the 1850 Census reports. We outline below the state data used in deriving the 1840 to 1850 estimate of change.

For New England, Bureau of Labor Statistics data indicate a rise of $1 in monthly wages from 1840 to 1850.[20] For Maine we have a $10 to $13 rate quoted for 1841, compared to $13 from the 1850 Census.[21]

For Vermont, Adams's data show no change, consistent with the heavy out-migration from Vermont for better farm areas.[22]

Midwest. Some reliable reports for the Midwest suggest gains of $2 from 1840 to 1850 rates, while others suggest considerably less. Hall estimates $10 for 1837, while another contemporary suggests $12 to $15—both to be set against the 1850 Census figures of $12.55.[23]

G. K. Holmes's data for Ohio, Michigan, and Wisconsin taken as a

---

suggested by a much higher $14 rate for the frontier area around Pittsburgh. Henry Fearon, *Sketches of America, A Narrative of a Journey* (1818) p. 201. With few of the state's laborers in the area, its rate serves to set an upper bound and to confirm an $11 rate as not unrealistically high.

[18] T. M. Adams, *Prices Paid by Vermont Farmers* (1944), Vermont Agricultural Experiment Station, Bulletin 507, Supplementary Table 30.

[19] *Transactions of the Society for the Promotion of Useful Arts in the State of New York* (Albany, 1819), vol. 4, part 2, p. 20.

[20] Quoted by G. K. Holmes, in *Wages of Farm Labor in the United States,* U.S. Department of Agriculture, Bulletin 99. Holmes also shows a morass of data from Hoxie. The only comparable materials relate to the "summer months" of 1840 (at $12.50) and "8 month rates beginning in April" of $14.50 for 1848 and 1854. Customarily in this early period rates by the month applied to summer (4 months), winter (8 months), or the year.

[21] U.S. Industrial Commission, *Hearings* (1901), vol. XI, p. 126.

[22] Adams, *loc. cit.* See also Harold Fisher Wilson, *The Hill Country of New England,* 1790–1930 (1936), chap. 2. Adams's annual changes are most improbable; e.g., a rise from 1839 to 1841 as the recession spread—but a 3-year average shows no change.

[23] James Hall, *Notes on the Western States* (Philadelphia: Harrison Hall, 1838), p. 204. Anonymous, *Illinois in 1837: A Sketch* . . . (Philadelphia: Augustus Mitchell, 1837), pp. 70–71. G. K. Holmes (*loc. cit.*), notes a rise from about $8 in the years following 1840 to about $16 by 1860. A 50 percent rise from the 1840s to 1850 (interpolating his 1840ff. to 1860 trend) is unlikely.

whole indicate a slight rise of perhaps 50 cents a month, much the same as the Illinois figures indicate after discounting.[24]

Middle Atlantic. For the important Middle Atlantic states we have little. A series for New Jersey shows a gain from $8 to $10, with half that gain reported from 1849 to 1850. An overlapping New York series shows a $2 fall for 1840 to 1845 while the Jersey series is reporting a $2 rise.[25]

For New York we have 1842 and 1843 reports on selected farms indicating a day rate of 75 cents.[26] Such a rate could be associated with either a $10 or a $12 rate, hence affords us little basis for comparing with the $11.50 rate for 1850. We have a $12 rate for 1840 based on G. K. Holmes's compilation, and an 1844 report of $15 for 8 months in the summer and $12 in the winter, averaging $14.[27] The 1850 census rate is $11.50. The only estimate of change is but partially relevant: A Prattsville tannery reported in 1848 that its labor rates had not changed in the past 20 years.[28] Since itinerant farm workers and upstate tannery workers would be in a similar labor market, this suggests no marked change.

Finally, we have a post-Civil War estimate for 1840 made by Ezra Seaman, an expert and astute observer, who estimated a national average of $3.60 a week in the process of deriving his state and national income estimates.[29] Even assuming that Seaman included the value of board, however, since board commonly was estimated at one-third of the pay, at 4.3 weeks per month this comes to $13 a month. Such a figure is reasonable for the New England states, improbably high with reference to the 1850 data for other states and the United States. Our constellation of 1830 data, while weak, certainly makes this figure seem much too high.

We combine the above state indications into an estimate of the 1840 to

---

[24] G. K. Holmes, *op. cit.*, pp. 15–18. For Ashland County, Ohio, one series rises from $12 to $14; another series, for Butler County, rises only from $12 to $12.50; another series, for Butler County, rises only from a range of $10–$12 to $10–$13; one for Lake County shows a day rate rising from 50 cents to 50–62 cents, while his Wisconsin figures for 1840 to 1850 show a $8 to $10 range. His plethora of additional figures are useful indications of level but very hard to combine into an indication of change.

[25] Salem County, New Jersey, report from G. K. Holmes, *loc. cit.* Cortland County, New York, series from the 1846 Walker Tariff Report.

[26] *Transactions of the New York State Agricultural Society* (Albany; E. Mack, 1843), vol. II, pp. 58, 60, 61, 62, 64, 312, 321, 338. One such farm reports $1 rates.

[27] G. K. Holmes, *loc. cit.; Transactions of the New York State Agricultural Society* (1844), vol. IV, p. 80. The 1846 *Transactions,* vol. VI, p. 608, reports daily rates of $1, while the 1847 volume, p. 309, reports 5 shillings, or—given the New York shilling at 12½ cents—62½ cents.

[28] *Sixth Annual Report of the American Institution of the City of New York* (Albany: Charles van Benthuysen, 1848), p. 190.

[29] Ezra Seaman, *Essays on the Progress of Nations* (1868), p. 305.

1850 change. The Massachusetts data suggest a rise of $1 a month—attributable to the competitive textile markets in Rhode Island and Connecticut—but with no gains in Vermont or the Northern states. The Middle Atlantic data suggest a mild gain, perhaps 50 cents, in the recovery from the 1840 recession, as do the Midwestern rates. The South, if slave sales rates are any indication, showed a marked gain, and an interpolation between 1830 and 1850 rates shows a gain of above 50 cents. Putting these inadequate indications together, we reduce the 1850 figure of $10.85 to a clearly arbitrary value of $10 for 1840.

1850 to 1860.   For 1850 and 1860, special wage-rate inquiries made in connection with census reports on social statistics give monthly rates paid to farmhands (with board) and are used here.[30]

1870.   The source used for 1870 was a study made by Edward Young, Chief of the Bureau of Statistics of the Treasury Department, in which figures on wage rates in a host of occupations were collected. Because of the timing, it is possible that these data were collected in connection with the 1870 Census.[31] The data were more probably developed as the other materials in the volume were, from information secured by the assistant assessors of Internal Revenue in the various states. Their issuance, however, under the sponsorship of a competent statistician, who was experienced in data evaluation and presentation and who had worked under David A. Wells, entitles them to serious consideration.

In any event a detailed review of the Young data for each state in the light of other state wage-rate data suggested their acceptability, except for Mississippi. An estimate for the latter state was made using the special study by the Commissioner of Agriculture for 1867, the USDA estimates, and the Young nonfarm figures.[32]

For 1870, we likewise have early reports made by crop reporters to the United States Department of Agriculture.[33] No use was made of this set of statistics except as a check, since it marks a largely different measure from

[30] J. D. B. DeBow, *Statistical View of the United States* (Washington: 1854), p. 164; Eighth Census, *Statistics of the United States (including Mortality, Property, etc.)*, 1866, p. 512.

[31] Edward Young, *Special Report on Immigration* (1871), 42nd Cong., 1st Sess., Exec. Doc. 1, pp. 202ff. The 1870 Census data were collected but not published because of their inadequacy. (See Ninth Census, vol. 1, pp. xxxviii, xliii.) Since Young's data were obviously a compilation and since the basic table, including farm-wage rates, reports the occupations and modes of payment covered in the 1850 and 1860 Census enumerations of wages, this possibility exists.

[32] The Commissioner's data are quoted in G. K. Holmes *op. cit.*, p. 22. For Mississippi, a slight excess in rates above those for Alabama appears in the 1818 to 1850 estimates shown above, and in the USDA figures from 1866 on. The Commissioner's data show a great excess in 1860, markedly reduced by 1868. We have, therefore, assumed the same excess in 1870 as shown by the USDA in 1869.

[33] G. K. Holmes, *op. cit.*, p. 30.

those for other years. The earlier series tend to reflect informed judgments as to the general average—judgments by respondents in the State Department survey, by Senator John Holmes, by individual manufacturers, by the marshals (or possibly assistant marshals) for each state. The crop-reporter figures constitute a markedly different type of measure, that of particular crop reporters who were in the USDA sample *and* who were willing to report. Many of these would tend to report not on the general average but on the rates they themselves paid. Recent data indicate clearly that the crop reporter is not himself a representative farmer with respect to many characteristics; one of these is apparently the wage level he paid.[34] This problem may have been particularly acute during the early years of the reporting system. In any event, the USDA figures for 1869—the first year within the present decennial presentation—were subjected to special examination. A decision was then reached to utilize data from the Young report,[35] for three reasons: (1) Because the Young data lead to more reasonable estimates of the 1860 to 1870 change; (2) because they were reported in the context of wage rates for half a dozen nonfarm occupations so that the way they related to other rates had to make sense when subjected to contemporary examination; and (3) because the USDA figures for some states appeared to be averages not for year-round hiring but for winter season hiring—possibly reflecting the fact that the first USDA reports were made as of December. (As one example of the latter problems, we may note that the USDA showed 1866 Arkansas earnings running 25 percent above those for Texas. The 1850 and 1860 Census figures, however, as the USDA rates that begin with 1874, show them to be much the same.[36]

1880 to 1890. For these years the crop-reporter surveys of the Department of Agriculture were used to provide state but not United States estimates.[37]

[34] For data on the coefficient of variability for the wage-rate data in the several crop-reporting districts and states—running around 20 percent in most instances—as of Oct. 1, 1939, see R. F. Hale and R. L. Gastineau, *Reliability and Adequacy of Farm Wage Rate Data* (U.S. Department of Agriculture, February, 1940).

[35] The rates for ordinary labor for summer were weighted 8 (i.e., 8 months) and winter rates 4, literature of the time indicating the summer rate held for 8 months. In an earlier version of these estimates (NBER Williamstown Conference) the rates for experienced rather than ordinary farm labor were used. Analysis of farm labor–common labor wage-rate ratios in 1850, 1860, and 1880 indicated that the use of ordinary labor rates produced greater comparability.

[36] We use rates reported as "ordinary labor," giving summer rates a weight of 8 months and winter rates 4. In "Wage Trends, 1800–1900," Conference on Research in Income and Wealth, *Trends in the American Economy in the Nineteenth Century* (1960), we arrived at different results by using Young's "experienced labor" with an average of summer and winter.

[37] G. K. Holmes, *op. cit.*, p. 30, using reports for 1880–1881 and 1889–1890.

For 1880 the USDA figures for New England were adjusted upward. Examination of the year-to-year changes by state from 1869 to 1892, in the rates by the month and day, with or without board, indicates a break in comparability between the rates for "1880 or 1881" and those for "1881 or 1882" for these states. One level maintains from 1869 to 1880–1881 while another prevails for the next decade. Since the nonfarm rates, usually more sensitive, show the mildest of rises it seems unreasonable to assume that gains of 20 and 30 percent to a new level occurred in this year.

Data for the New England states were adjusted as follows: The "1881 or 1882" level was assumed satisfactory for each state, reduced 10 percent to give the 1880 level. This percentage was developed on the basis of the change over the same period of 11 percent for New York, 1 percent for New Jersey, and 4 percent for Pennsylvania.

1899. For this year the USDA survey reported not rates for men hired "by the year"—as do the reports used here for earlier periods—but "by the year or season." In examining the extent of noncomparability, we are reduced to a comparison between the two types of rates for 1909, that being the only year for which the USDA reported both types of rates. For that year major differences appear.[38] However, more detailed examination of the state-by-state trends in these rates and the daily rates suggested that this distortion was largely a reflection of the fact that the 1909 "year or season" rate appears to have been estimated by Holmes himself, but without any raw data.[39]

The 1909 Holmes estimate was therefore rejected as a basis for assessing the extent of comparability between the USDA "year-season" rates for 1891 to 1906 and the "year" rates they secured for other dates. Instead the day rates (other than harvest) were charted against the monthly rates by the year and season for the years 1891 to 1909. The scatter shows a close and simple correlation for all years but 1909—the latter the year estimated by Holmes. Given the scatter and the day rate for 1909, we can deduce a 1909 rate for the year and season that is virtually the same as the enumerated "year" rate for that date. On this basis we would simply take the year-season rate for 1899 as roughly identical with the desired year rate for that date. We secure the same result by charting the year rates for 1866 to 1890 and 1909 against the daily rate (other than harvest) and interpolating for 1899 by the daily rate. It was therefore concluded that the "year season" state rates for 1899 as actually reported could be used as satisfactory approximations of the year rates for that date.[40]

[38] G. K. Holmes, *op. cit.*, pp. 30, 33.

[39] *Ibid*, p. 23. "The present investigation has restored the old distinction between hiring by the year and by the season, and for the sake of comparison has made in the bureau a weighted combination of the two monthly rates mentioned."

[40] This implies, of course, that though farmers were asked to report monthly wages

1909 to 1954. The individual state data are from the USDA crop-reporter surveys.[41]

Regional Averages. The state data for 1818 to 1919 were combined into regional and United States averages using weights from the Population Census, and will therefore differ from the USDA regional totals in certain instances as noted below.

For 1818–1826–1830, the total persons reported by the 1820 Census as having agricultural occupations was used.[42]

For 1850, the number of free white male farmers aged fifteen and over was used for weighting, and for 1860, the number of farm laborers.[43] Examination of the ratios of farmers to farm laborers in 1860 indicated a marked degree of intrastate uniformity so that the shift from one type of weights to the other would not make a marked difference.[44]

For 1870 and 1880 the Population Census counts of agricultural laborers aged sixteen to fifty-nine were used for weights.[45] For 1890 and 1899 the census count of male agricultural laborers aged sixteen and over in 1900 was used.[46]

For 1909 and 1919 the regional estimates of the USDA were not used

---

when employed by the year and season, they continued to report the same sort of item as when asked for wages when employed by the year. Holmes's 1909 estimate implies a 49 percent rise from 1891 to 1909 in year-season rates (with board), compared to only 32 percent for day labor (in harvest) and 41 percent for day labor (other than harvest).

[41] 1909 and 1929 are from the Bureau of Agricultural Economics, *Farm Wage Rates, Farm Employment and Related Data* (January, 1943) pp. 16–19. The 1940 and 1948 data were kindly provided by Mrs. F. C. Arrowsmith of the USDA. The 1950 and 1954 composite rate data are from Sheridan T. Maitland and Dorothy A. Fisher, *Area Variations in the Wages of Agricultural Labor in the United States,* U.S. Department of Agriculture, Technical Bulletin 1177 (March, 1958), table 14.

[42] Census for 1820 (Gales and Seaton, 1821), first table.

[43] 1850 Census, p. lxx; 1860 Census, *Population of the United States in 1860* (1864), pp. 662–663.

[44] Using the 1860 regional count of farm laborers to weight the 1850 rates, thus exaggerating the noncomparability, only changed the 1850 average from $10.85 to $11.75.

[45] Data for 1870 are from the individual state tables, 1870 Census, vol. I, *Population* (1872), pp. 719ff. 1880 Census, *Statistics of the Population of the United States at the Tenth Census* (1883), p. 724. Examination of state data indicates that the only female labor included in nontrivial numbers was in the South. It is here assumed that these were in fact hired workers, and not to be excluded as unpaid family workers, a procedure followed for later years when the census coverage improved.

[46] State tables, 1900 Census, *Occupations,* pp. 220ff. For 1890 it is not possible to exclude unpaid family workers per se, nor the ten to fifteen age group as an approximation. Since this is a more sizable factor in distorting weights than would be the use of data for a decade later, the more accurate 1900 figures were used for both dates.

because they were computed using as weights the number of farms employing hired labor at any time during the year.[47] Such weights will distort the relative importance of states that characteristically hired above (or below) average proportions of migrant labor, or short-term labor. Thus while New Jersey reported roughly as many farms with hired labor in the Agricultural Census as it did hired laborers in the Population Census, North Dakota reported almost twice as many.[48] The Population Census count of farm laborers (working off-farm) was therefore used to compute regional and United States averages.[49]

For 1929 and 1940 the USDA regional figures were used, these having been weighted by the count of hired farm workers derived from the surveys themselves.

For 1948 and 1950, the 1950 Census of Agriculture count of hired farm workers was used, and for 1954, the 1954 Census of Agriculture count was used.[50]

COMMON LABOR: 1832 TO 1940 (TABLE A-25)

1832. In a haphazard way the cabinet members in 1832 seem to have been extremely busy collecting statistics. The McLane report[1] was intended to cast light on whether the tariff should be changed. How it affected Jackson's tariff policy, however, is unknown. Secretary of State Edward Livingstone was also conducting a useful inquiry, designed to cast light on another question: Whether "a republican form of government is more expensive than a monarchical." As a result of this inquiry we have a set of rates paid to common labor and to farm labor in various states in 1832 (Table A-30).[2] Several tests suggest that these rates are of sufficient quality for our use.

[47] Bureau of Agricultural Economics, *Farm Wage Rates, Farm Employment and Related Data* (January, 1943), p. 2, states that "the 1910 and 1920 Censuses of Agriculture furnish the basis for weights used for the period 1909 to 1922." Reference to the census volumes indicates that the only data that could have been used were counts of the farms reporting the use of some hired labor during the year.

[48] Illinois reported 91,000 males working off the farm as against 151,000 farms hiring labor; Idaho 14,000 compared to 25,000; New Hampshire 7,000 compared to 12,000.

[49] 1910 Census, vol. IV, table II; 1920 *Population Census,* vol. V, table 15.

[50] These data, and the rate data, by state, appear in Maitland and Fisher, *op. cit.,* table 14.

[1] *Documents Relative to the Manufactures in the United States,* 22nd Cong., 1st Sess., Exec. Doc. 308 (Washington: Duff Green, 1833), Serial Set Nos. 222, 223.

[2] *Statistical View of the Population of the United States from 1790 to 1830 inclusive,* 23rd Cong., 1st Sess., Serial Set 252 (1835), pp. 190, 209, 214. The wage data in this report appear at the end with no introduction or discussion. However,

1. Averages are reported for each town, presumably by the assessor or other town officer. The printed volume notes the number of reports received as follows: Connecticut, 59 towns reporting of 134; Maine, 101 of 444; New Hampshire, 109 of 230; Rhode Island, 16 of 31; Indiana, 28 towns: "nearly all . . . worthy of notice"; Missouri, 18 towns (not including St. Louis); Georgia, 14 towns. The volume and auspices of these reports makes them tend to confirm incidental travelers' reports, rather than vice versa. For Ohio, however, there is only a set of estimates, supplied by the Governor. His 50-cent figure for common labor, however, is confirmed (*a*) by the similarity to Indiana and Missouri rates, independently reported; (*b*) by a 50-cent estimate from the *Cincinnati Whig* for daily wages in cutting hemp in Fayette County and Springhill in February, 1833; and (*c*) by a 40-cents a day average for labor on Ohio canals in 1827, according to a report by a committee of the Chesapeake and Ohio Canal Convention.[3]

2. The internal relationships between the 1832 data in the Livingstone report are closely consistent with the same relationships in data from the 1850 Census. For example, the monthly rate paid labor in Indiana is 19.6 times the day rate in 1832. The 1850 Census data give a 19.1 ratio. For Connecticut the ratios were 17.2 and 16.7, respectively.[4]

3. The changes in day rates, and in monthly rates from 1832 to 1850, vary reasonably from state to state. Most states show gains of from 2 to 7 cents in daily rates, with Connecticut at 9 cents. Three New England states show monthly rates for farm labor gaining 50 cents to $1, while the two Midwestern states gain by $1.50—consistent with the moderate demand for farm labor in New England and the rising demand in the Midwest. The small Georgia gain is unlikely, but not impossible if only slaves were hired for monthly labor.

---

comparison of the wording and inquiry data, given on pp. 160–161 of this volume with the 1850 Census of Population (1853), p. xvii (where there is a reference to such a query) makes it almost certain that these data were derived from the Livingstone inquiry. Data for other states were either not received or perished in the Treasury fire of 1833. A search of U.S. National Archives disclosed little, only a book in the Foreign Affairs archives which refers to letters of Dec. 17, 1833, from Governor Lucas of Ohio; of Jan. 17, 1834, from Governor Lincoln of Massachusetts, etc., the letters themselves having long since disappeared. In the Treasury Archives, *Miscellaneous Series of Letter Received,* is a reply dated Sept. 27, 1833, from the Auditor's Office of Virginia, in which J. W. Meatley helpfully responds to the Livingstone request by stating merely that "labor is worth double as much in some portions of the state as it is in others."

[3] *Cincinnati Whig,* quoted in *Journal of the American Institute of New York* (F. Wakeman, 1837), vol. II, pp. 398, 401. *Proceedings* of the Chesapeake and Ohio Canal Convention, Nov. 6, 1823 . . . Dec. 6, 1826 (Washington City: Way and Gideon, 1827), p. 67.

[4] 1850 data from J. D. B. DeBow, *Statistical View of the United States* (1854), p. 164.

The one figure that is quite unreasonable is for Rhode Island day rates. It is hard to believe that the state's monthly rate was much the same as that for the two other New England states in 1832 (as well as its harvest rate and the value of construction labor), at the same time that its day rate was about 20 percent below nearby Connecticut and 30 percent below Maine rates. As a general rule we are well advised not to adjust estimates made contemporaneously, but this gap seems quite unlikely both in the abstract and by reference to male rates paid in Rhode Island's cotton and iron industries as reported in the McLane report. A revised figure was derived by charting daily against monthly rates for each state in 1832, with the least-squares slope indicating an adjusted value. (We arrive at the same result if we assume that the 1832 to 1850 percent change in Rhode Island monthly rates should have been the same as that for its daily rates, since such similarity was present for the seven other states reported.)

The Livingstone report does not provide data for Massachusetts. An average of 75 cents was estimated, using Carroll Wright's extensive summary of wages for the state. (A similar rate is indicated by various statements in the McLane report, in which manufacturers comment on the average wage of labor in their town or area.)[5] For Vermont, the New Hampshire level was used, the level for male rates in cotton, wool, and iron averaging the same in the two states in 1832. If we use the average of Ohio and Indiana rates for the East North Central, and of Missouri for the West North Central territory, our remaining concerns are the levels for the really substantial group of nonfarm labor—in the Middle Atlantic states and in the South.

The average of male rates paid in cotton textiles, wool, and iron, as a group in the Middle Atlantic states was virtually identical with that for the three New England states that were geographically close and economically competitive with them—Connecticut, Massachusetts, and Rhode Island. Therefore a weighted average of the common-labor rates for these three states was used to give the common-labor average for the Middle Atlantic region.

For the South the single Livingstone report is for Georgia. This rate cannot confidently be applied for the other Southern states. Georgia was in the midst of heavy immigration: Rates during the flush days of that state can hardly be assumed to apply to South Carolina, Virginia, and other states losing labor. For those other states, therefore, the trend in slave-hiring rates from 1830 to 1850 was used to extrapolate the 1850 Census common-labor rates.[6] For this purpose we use hiring rates in Ken-

[5] Carroll Wright, *History of Wages and Prices in Massachusetts* (1885), pp. 161–162, 167–168, using Wright's "medium rates." *McLane Report,* vol. I, pp. 92, 96, 76, 81, 88.

[6] Rates of about $100 a year in Kentucky for 1828, 1833, and 1835 appear in Elizabeth Catterall, *Judicial Cases on American Slavery* (1926–1937), vol. I, pp.

tucky, Virginia, and Maryland from Catterall's record of judicial cases; in South Carolina from Mills's extensive study of the state made in 1826; and in Alabama from Sellers' valuable study. Most free labor was to be found in Maryland, with a very marked rise; in Virginia, with perhaps a 5 percent gain; and in the Carolinas, with a slightly smaller gain. We can conclude for, say, a 5 percent gain for the South Atlantic region. What about the East South Central region? The overwhelming bulk of East South Central labor was in two states: Kentucky data indicate no change from 1828–1835 to 1850, while Tennessee slave valuations for assessment purposes declined over the period. An Alabama decline probably occurred but a rise in Mississippi population and (rates probably) took place in the other direction. We conclude by assuming no change in rates for the South as a whole.

The separate regional averages were combined into a national average, using the 1840 regional distribution of employment in mining, manufacturing, and navigation combined. (If we use the 1850 distribution of nonfarm laborers, the average differs by a penny.)[7]

1840. Since the rates with board show a decline from 1832 to 1850, the 1850 figure with board is raised by 1 cent to give a comparable 1832 figure of 88 cents. The 1840 figure is estimated as 2 cents below the 1850 rate, on the basis of the net trend shown for this period when we combine

---

320, 331, 342. (Higher rates for skilled workers, compared to $10 a year in 1850, lower for females, are shown, not relevant here. The 1850 average of $120 is from the *1850 Census Compendium*, p. 164). For Virginia, Catterall (vol. I, p. 214) gives an $8 rate for 1833, while the 1850 Census figure is $8.43. For Maryland, petitioners in a court case in 1833 offered evidence that slave hire ran from $50 to $60 a year (Catterall, *op. cit.*, vol. IV, p. 88) while the 1850 Census figure is considerably higher at $7.88. For South Carolina, Mills gives estimates by county, averaging $7.50 in 1826, compared with $7.72 in the *1850 Compendium*. Robert Mills, *Statistics of South Carolina* (Charleston: Hurburt and Lloyd, 1826), pp. 426–500. For Alabama, a $9.62 rate in 1850 can be compared with one of $15 a month offered for laborers on Muscle Shoals in 1834; even after allowing for the higher rates prevailing in canal work, a decline is indicated. James B. Sellers, *Slavery in Alabama* (1952), p. 201. Harrison Trexler (*Slavery in Missouri, 1804–1865* (1914), p. 31, reports an 1838 probate court action in which two men worth $800 were hired, one at $119 and one at $96, and one worth $600, at $90. If an $8 figure is indicated, it is to be compared with one of $11.81 from the 1850 Census, while the day rates rise from 51 to 55 cents.

[7] State averages were combined into a New England average using 1850 Census figures on gainfully occupied nonfarm laborers. 1850 Census, *The Seventh Census of the United States: 1850* (1853), p. lxxx. For weighting the regional averages, data closer to the period were desired, to minimize the impact of the migrations west and southwest. Hence the 1840 gainfully occupied in mining, manufacturing, and navigation were used. (1850 Census, *loc. cit.*)

available reports from the Weeks and Aldrich reports and from the Bureau of Labor Statistics, *History of Wages*.[8] Because figures must be estimated by some systematic procedure and the results of that procedure reported, the figures are given as they developed. No significance attaches, however, to the trivial differences in level among the three dates, 1832–1840–1850.

1850. Data were reported by the marshals of the several states in the 1850 Census.[9] Regional and United States averages were computed, using the number of nonagricultural laborers by states in 1850 as weights.[10]

For a good many of these states a few direct establishment reports were available from the Weeks study.[11] (1) Where fewer than four reports are available for a state, potentially high sampling variability suggests that we should prefer the census figure as a judicious attempt to represent wages for all laborers in the state. (2) A few additional states have about four reports. The Weeks data for these states were rejected not because of the high sampling variability, though that is present, but because they led to a trivial 1850 to 1860 rate gain. These gains are quite out of line for other states within their respective regions as shown by their Weeks data or census data. (3) The sample for New York alone is more substantial, though still based on only 10 reports. Examination indicates that four of them are from the traditionally low-paying tanneries and paper mills, while none are from the New York City area. A better-balanced sample would therefore give a higher figure and one closer to the census figure that was adopted.

1860. Data were reported by the marshals of the several states in the 1860 Census and were weighted by the number of nonagricultural laborers as tabulated in the census.[12]

What do the Weeks-Aldrich sample data show for 1860? Ignoring the states with merely a few reports, and also ignoring differences of under 5 cents as being within sampling error, we have significant differences for Massachusetts, New Hampshire, Pennsylvania, and Missouri. For the first three the sample is adopted as appearing clearly more representative, in particular putting the Massachusetts rate more in line with intraregional

---

[8] Sources and description in the author's "Wage Trends, 1800–1900," Conference on Research in Income and Wealth, *Trends in the American Economy in the Nineteenth Century* (1960).

[9] DeBow, *op. cit.,* p. 164.

[10] *The Seventh Census of the United States, 1850* (1853), p. lxxii.

[11] 1880 Census, *Report on the Statistics of Wages in Manufacturing Industries* . . . by Joseph Weeks (1886).

[12] 1860 Census, *Statistics of the United States* (1866), p. 512, and 1860 Census, *Population* (1864), pp. 658–659, 666–667.

relationships.[13] For Missouri no change is warranted; three of the five sample figures report the same $1 level as the census 98 cents.[14]

For the Colorado area we take the $2 a day figure that men in the Territory were obliged to pay if they did not work on the roads.[15] This figure is virtually identical with that given by the census for Utah and therefore is taken to be the average for the Mountain region generally. (The New Mexico rate is assumed to be relatively low for the region because of the proximity of low-paid Mexican labor.)

1870.   Data were taken from a study by the U.S. Treasury, Bureau of Statistics, the figures apparently based on reports from the assistant collectors of Internal Revenue in each state.[16]

The regional and United States averages were computed using as weights the Population Census count of the nonagricultural laborers by state.[17]

For this year the Weeks-Aldrich sample observations increase in number and reliability. For Massachusetts 31 sample reports give the same average as the Treasury study, within 1 cent. For other states a tendency for the Treasury figures to be as high as the Aldrich figures per se is apparent. Where more than five sample reports were made, their average was used instead.[18] New Hampshire, Connecticut, New York, and Ohio were thus adjusted.

[13] It is suggestive that the Aldrich component of the sample for Massachusetts and Pennsylvania gives virtually the same high average as the census, with the Weeks component nearly 10 percent lower. No obvious industry or geographic element explains this gap.

[14] A fourth, for the traditionally low-paying industry of brickmaking, shows a $1.25 figure for 1860 and a 75 cents rate for 1861—perhaps true but probably not representative. We are left with one St. Louis iron and steel firm paying $1.50, and another paying $1.

[15] "The Provisional Laws of the Jefferson Territory, 1859–60," quoted in Clifford C. Hill, "Wagon Roads in Colorado, 1858–1876," Unpublished M.A. thesis, University of Colorado, 1948, pp. 88, 90.

[16] Edward Young, *Special Report on Immigration,* 42nd Cong., 1st Sess., House Exec. Doc. 1 (1871), pp. 202ff. For three states—New Hampshire, Connecticut, and Maryland—the reported figures are out of line with relationships to their regional averages in 1850, 1860, and 1880. Adjusted estimates were made from the regression of the reported 1870 rates for common labor, by state within regions, against data also reported in the Young study on rates paid common labor in specified industries, averaging, for this purpose, reports for cotton, wool, paper, iron, hardware, etc.

[17] Ninth Census, vol. I, *The Statistics of the Population of the United States* (1872), pp. 674–675.

[18] Indiana is an exception with a 7-cent gap, for with a much larger sample in 1870, extrapolation by identical firms for 1869–1870 gives virtually the Treasury level. Wisconsin, with only one Milwaukee report (at virtually the Treasury level) out of 11, is another. Adjusting Wisconsin to the biased sample data would put it far below Michigan and Ohio, as judged both by Treasury and sample data—an unlikely state of affairs.

1880.   For this year we rely on a set of establishment reports for common-labor rates appearing in the 1880 Census. For the Northern states (barring those discussed below), the data were taken from the Weeks and Aldrich reports.[19] More than a dozen reports were available for each state, while for the states with major concentrations of common labor—Pennsylvania, Ohio, Massachusetts, and New York—50, 46, 36, and 52 reports, respectively, were available. As discussed at length below in connection with the annual estimates for 1860ff., the preferred use of such data is not to treat them as representing industry figures but simply as observations picked (perhaps at random) from a universe of common-labor wage-rate data.

For the remaining states in the North the few Weeks reports for each state were combined with data for common-labor rates in iron and steel manufacturing and in coke and stone manufacturing. The latter figures likewise were collected by the same Joseph Weeks, our universal 1880 benefactor.[20]

For the Southern states the procedures differed, depending on the data available for each state. For Kentucky and Missouri an extensive sample of Weeks reports were available, averaged, and used. For Virginia, reports from ironworks in 19 counties averaged 89 cents while the Weeks report gave 75 cents and $1 for Richmond cigar factories. The county ironworks rates were weighted by hands employed in each, thus giving greater importance to the larger works (and presumably areas of larger employment), to give a 92-cent rate. Similar procedures were used for West Virginia, Georgia, and Tennessee.[21] For the latter the railway data given in

[19] Weeks, *op. cit.*, pp. 544ff. For computational convenience the Aldrich data used were as summarized in Wesley Mitchell, *Gold Prices and Wages under the Greenback Standard* (1908).

[20] 1880 Census, *Manufactures*, Folio pp. 762ff. on the manufacture of iron and steel. 1880 Census, vol. 10, *Special Reports on Petroleum, Coke and Building Stones*, where Weeks gives wages for coke laborers, unskilled workers in limestone and other quarries. For Maine the $1.25 shown for canning, locomotive manufacture, and crystalline rock quarrying was adopted. For Vermont the $1.15 limestone quarrying rate and weighted $1.18 iron rate were averaged. For Rhode Island four textile rates, as the iron rate for Providence, average $1.17. For Minnesota an iron-manufacturing rate of $1.50, flour-mill rates of $1.15 and $1.25, and limestone rates of $1.58 were available. Flour mills being well below average, the relationship of Minnesota to Wisconsin and Missouri in both 1869 and 1890 was preserved by adopting the $1.50 rate. The $1.50 iron rate for Nebraska was adopted, ignoring the tiny sample for limestone at $1.75. For Kansas the iron and wood rates of $1.25, limestone of $1.30, and flour mill of $0.58 were transformed into a $1.25 average.

[21] For West Virginia and Georgia, the Weeks report figures proved to be much the same as weighted county averages for ironworks. The Tennessee weighted ironworks rate was 95 cents, while Fels's report gives $1 for a group primarily hired in Nashville.

Rendig Fels's valuable study offer a helpful check.[22] For the remaining Southern states, as for the West, weighted county data for ironworks rates were computed as above.

The state averages were then weighted to give regional and United States averages in proportion to the number of nonagricultural employees, in whatever industry employed, as reported by the Population Census.[23]

How does our 1880 figure of $1.23 compare with estimates from other sources? Mitchell's overall average must be ignored here because it is dominated by the New York City Public Works Department (establishment 35), while even his figures exclusive of that enterprise show a marked geographic bias. If, however, we take his 1879 figure of $1.27 for the "East" (really Northeast), we can see that it is virtually the same as the $1.28 for New England estimated here, while his $1.25 figure for the "West" (really East North Central) is similar to the present $1.30.[24] Our (U.S.) figure, therefore, will differ chiefly because it allows for wages in regions excluded from Mitchell's data.[25]

Other 1880 figures, averaged from the Weeks reports, are $1.30 (Senator McKinley), $1.34 (Edward Atkinson), $1.31 (Abbott), and $1.32 (Long).[26] Given the omission of Southern and Western reports from these figures and their lack of regional weighting, we may consider them to be in fact unweighted averages for the Northeast and, as such, reasonably consistent with the present results.

1890. For 1890 a wealth of data is available and the chief problem is its effective use. The Census of Manufactures secured data on the average weekly earnings of unskilled labor for 18 major industries, with separate reports for every state.[27]

[22] Rendig Fels, *Wages, Earnings and Employment, Nashville, Chattanooga and St. Louis Railway, 1866–1896* (1953), pp. 17, 53. Fels's figure is within a penny of that for ironworks in Hamilton County, hence the weighted average for the other counties was felt to stand reasonably well for the state.

[23] *Statistics of the Population of the United States at Tenth Census* (1883), p. 732.

[24] Mitchell, *op. cit.*, pp. 620ff. Mitchell here reports only on laborers in manufacturing establishments.

[25] This estimate therefore differs from an earlier version in the author's *"Wage Trends, 1800–1900,"* which used Mitchell's 1870 to 1880 trend, roughly adjusted to allow for the trends in the South and West, to extrapolate the 1869 figure.

[26] Fletcher W. Hewes and William McKinley, *What Are the Facts?: Protection and Reciprocity Illustrated* (1892), pp. 26–32; Edward Atkinson, *The Industrial Progress of the Nation* (1890), pp. 106–107. Similar data appear in his "Low Prices, High Wages, Small Profits; What Makes Them," *Century* (August, 1887); Edith Abbott, "The Wages of Unskilled Labor in the United States, 1850–1900," *Journal of Political Economy* (June, 1905), p. 356. Abbott weights the Aldrich and Weeks data; Clarence Long, *Wages and Earnings in the United States, 1860–1890* (1960), p. 144.

[27] *Report on Manufacturing Industries in the United States at the Eleventh Census: 1890*, part I (1895). Agricultural implements (p. 657); boots and shoes (p. 669);

For steel and for gas a less direct approach was required. Distributions of all employees by weekly wage intervals were available from the same census for these two industries.[28] Taking the median earnings in each class interval and weighting, we obtain an average weekly wage for all employees by industry and state. This wage was converted to an average weekly wage for unskilled workers by the ratio of (1) the average annual earnings of all employees to (2) those for unskilled employees, these averages being computed from census data.[29] This procedure implicitly assumes that the average weeks worked by the total group of employees was essentially the same as that of unskilled employees.[30] (Unskilled employees constituted nearly half of all employees in iron and steel.)

The resultant averages for weekly earnings of unskilled employees in these 18 major industry groups were weighted together by the census estimates for the number of unskilled employees, as reported in the same sources, to give overall averages for each state and a United States average of $1.46.

For 1890 we have the Atkinson, Abbott, and Long estimates reworking the Aldrich and other materials, giving $1.46, $1.37, and $1.51, respectively, as well as $1.50 from city data of the Department of Labor.[31] The comprehensive studies by Coombs and Hurlin, using Department of Labor figures, average $1.45 and $1.47, respectively.[32]

---

carriages and wagons, factory product (p. 677); cheese, butter (p. 689); flouring and gristmill products (p. 699); leather (p. 709); paper (p. 723); slaughtering and meat packing (p. 731). *Report on Manufacturing Industries of the United States at the Eleventh Census: 1890*, part III (1895). Wool (p. 136); cotton (p. 206); chemicals (p. 300); glass (p. 339); petroleum (p. 372); clay (p. 525); shipping (p. 573); salt (p. 589).

[28] *Report on Manufacturing Industries . . . : 1890*, part III, pp. 470, 475, 711.

[29] *Ibid.*, pp. 470–477, Blast furnaces; pp. 474–475, steel works; pp. 709–710, gas.

[30] It is to be noted that this does not imply that any given employee worked these periods but rather that the average full-time equivalent unskilled worker worked the same average as the full-time equivalent employee; in most states both worked somewhere between 44 and 49 weeks.

[31] Abbott, *op. cit.*; Long, *op. cit.*, p. 154. The Department of Labor data are conveniently presented in Long's table A-3. Edward Atkinson, "Productive Industry," in N. S. Shaler, *The United States* (1894), p. 51.

[32] Whitney Coombs, *The Wages of Unskilled Labor in the Manufacturing Industries in the United States* (1926), p. 162, appendix table A. Hurlin's estimate appears in Paul Douglas, *Real Wages in the United States, 1890–1926* (1930), pp. 165, 175.

Coombs's results were not used because state estimates were sought wherever feasible. In addition biases may be noted. His estimate for laborers in iron and steel is well above the present estimate, above the average for 1913 (*Historical Statistics of the United States*, p. 69) presumably because he intentionally included other occupations (p. 132). Limitations in the BLS data are carefully noted by Coombs. (pp. 64, 65)

1900. For 1900 a voluminous and well-nigh incredible mass of figures on wages was collected by census agents under the direction of Davis Dewey.[33] Dewey gives rates for a combined "general hands, helpers and laborers" group in most industries, both for 1890 and 1900. For 1890, the Manufactures Census is to be preferred since it does not have the biases that can creep in from sampling only firms that survived until 1900, or from the retrospective reconstruction of historical records.

What about 1900? The key problem here is that this occupation group apparently included enough "general hands" in some industries to make the level too high—or too low.[34] Given the 1890 Census levels, for which the manufacturers themselves stipulated the earnings of what they determined to be unskilled laborers, and which were based on an extensive contemporaneous survey, the preferred use of land admiral Dewey's figures is indicated. This is to employ them only for extrapolating the adequate 1890 levels to 1900. For this purpose the inclusion of a quantity of employees other than laborers is much less troublesome. Combining all of Dewey's industry data gives us an estimate of a 5 percent rise for laborers' pay from 1890 to 1900, hence $1.53 for 1900.[35]

1907 to 1919. For 1907 a moderately large-scale survey by the Bureau of Labor,[36] and for 1919 a survey covering more industries (made by the Bureau of Labor Statistics) provide us with a host of averages for individual industries.[37] Weighting these by the number of laborers in each

---

[33] Davis R. Dewey, *Employees and Wages* (1903), a volume of the 1900 Census.

[34] How high is too high? We judge here by a comparison for this category with the Census of Manufactures figures in 1890. While the Dewey figures are within 2 to 3 percent for most industries (farm implements, wagons, shipbuilding, chemicals, glass, paper, tanneries), they are markedly off for cotton, wool, shoes, and—most important—iron and steel.

[35] For the 18 industries for which Dewey shows wages in 1890 and 1900, median weekly rates were computed from the tables in his chap. 2. As weights, we used the number of laborers in each industry (1900 *Census of Manufactures,* part I) and the percentage of general hands, helpers, and laborers by industry computed from Dewey's figures in chap. 2. This procedure moderates the impact of his implicit industry weighting. Dewey's figure for "all other occupations" in iron and steel, not included, also shows a 5 percent rise (*op. cit.,* p. lxiv).

[36] Department of Commerce and Labor, *Bulletin* no. 17 of the Bureau of Labor (1908), table 1. A check estimate was made by computing percent changes in rates for identical industries 1907 to 1919. These, averaged and applied to the 1919 figure (derived below), lead to the same hourly rate, within 2 cents.

[37] *Industrial Survey in Selected Industries in the United States, 1919,* BLS Bulletin 265. The data relate largely to the fall of 1918 and the spring of 1919. The present estimate uses the rates and weights as shown by the BLS for common labor in the lengthy list of industries surveyed. The sample selection was explicitly biased but its coverage was so broad—from autos, steel, glass, leather, etc., through chemicals (fertilizers, judging from the distribution by state) and lumber—that proper weights, if available, could hardly make much difference. An 8-hour day is

industry leads to averages of 16½ and 41 cents per hour, respectively.[38] Since the 1907 survey gives data that average to a 10-hour day, and the 1919, to an 8-hour day, this gives us daily averages of $1.65 and $3.20.

1929, 1940. For these years we have the results of BLS surveys that report entrance rates of common labor in a large number of states.[39] We combine the state rates, using the employment figures from the same source.

The indefatigable statistician may enjoy comparing the data in Table A-25 that result from all the above manipulations with the fragrant potpourri of rates for laborers from 1840 to 1900 in Carroll Wright's collation of rates from early state and Bureau of Labor studies.[40] Some of the findings show a close relationship, others are cousin german at best, while others are clearly not in the family. While for the major states a good many of the decennial figures prove to be within 10 percent of the Bureau of Labor summary, the meaning of the latter is difficult to understand. Thus, in the Wright compilations Pennsylvania rates rose by more than 30 percent from 1859 to 1860, while New York and New Jersey rates hardly changed; Michigan rates in 1861 were within 4 percent of the present estimate but in 1860, some 20 percent above; Connecticut rates rose by a third from 1891 to 1892, while other New England states showed a mild change. Since any smoothing operation would conceal many of the changes in which we are interested, the reader is simply warned of the broad similarity, and the specific differences, between the present historical review and the very early studies summarized in the Bureau of Labor reports.

---

assumed. Hours data (centering around 8 hours) are given by industry in the report but show marked variability, running as low as 5.9 hours in some instances. It was assumed that because a good many schedules were collected in November–December, 1918, the effects of the armistice and subsequent turnover and reconversion were responsible for most of the figures showing less than 8 hours.

[38] The 1905 *Census of Manufactures,* part I, table 1, was used for weights of the manufacturing rates while the building labor rate was weighted by the number of laborers in building and hand trades according to the 1910 *Census of Population,* vol. IV, p. 312.

[39] *Monthly Labor Review* (October, 1929), p. 173; (January, 1941), p. 7.

[40] These are conveniently summarized in *History of Wages in the United States from Colonial Times to 1928,* BLS Bulletin 499 (1929), part 2. The early data, as noted there, come from the fifteenth and nineteenth annual reports of the Commissioner of Labor Statistics, prepared under Wright's direction. Use of these data is difficult: the data shown do not readily match those in Wright's sources. Probably direct recourse to the various state reports would be much more rewarding.

DOMESTIC SERVICE (TABLE A-26)

> *Only think of Pritchard coming to me and saying she wanted her wages raised after living with me for twenty years. I was very angry and scolded her roundly, but as she acknowledged she had been wrong, and cried and begged my pardon, I did give her two guineas a year more.*
>
> Trollope, *Last Chronicles of Barset,* chap. 15

Domestic-service wages have traditionally marked the bottom of the adult wage scale in the United States. In large part this is so because the social position of servants was associated with slavery.[1] An early visitor found service "not esteemed honorable among the Americans" and "ill paid," with only Irish immigrants and Negroes being available for such work even in New England.[2] The extent to which such reactions eventuated in higher wage levels for domestics depended in turn on the extent of immigration flows to the labor-sparse country. One "English Gentleman" who reported, with some circumspection, on the charms of the Northwest Territory in 1822, flatly observed that "A batchelor has no business in the Backwoods: for it is a wild country, where it is almost impossible to hire assistance of any kind, either male or female; a man is thrown entirely on himself." [3] Fordham declared that "respectable families from Kentucky . . . do all their domestic work except washing, with their own hands." [4] As time went on immigration increased, as did the supply of domestics. The close connection between the two in free-labor markets was noted by one Southern writer: "The dearth of servants causes always a rise in the rate of wages at the North, when immigration from any cause diminishes, as has been the case in the last few years." [5]

[1] James Fenimore Cooper wrote in 1838 that "in consequence of the domestic servants of America having once been negro slaves a prejudice has arisen among the laboring classes of the whites, who not only dislike the term servant, but have also rejected that of master . . . in lieu of the latter they have resorted to the use of the word baas, which has precisely the same meaning in Dutch." Quoted in Albert H. Marckwardt, *American English* (1958), p. 50.

[2] George Coombe, *Notes on the United States of America during a Phrenological Visit in 1838–39–40* (Philadelphia: 1841), vol. I, p. 93.

[3] Newnham Blane, *An Excursion through the United States and Canada during the Years 1822–23 by an English Gentleman* (London: Baldwin, Cradock and Joy, 1824), p. 163.

[4] Quoted in Solon J. Buck, *Illinois in 1818* (1917), p. 135. Elsewhere Fordham notes that "no white man or woman will bear being called a servant, but they will gladly do your work." Elias Fordham, *Personal Narrative . . . 1817–1818* (1818; reprinted 1906), p. 124.

[5] Thomas P. Kettell, *Southern Wealth and Northern Profits* (New York: George W. and John A. Wood, 1860), p. 102.

As a broad generalization from the data noted below (summarized in Table A-26), it would appear that domestics earned about $1 to $1.25 a week through most of the first half of the nineteenth century—higher during the Napoleonic Wars, lower during recessions; higher in such frontier areas as the Northwest during the 1815–1840 period, and in Louisiana just after Jefferson purchased it; and lowest in New York during most of the period.

1800 to 1804. For Massachusetts an old account book reports 3 shillings 6 pence for 3 days' work in June and 2 shillings 4 pence in August, 1800—a rate of $1.25 a week.[6] A $1.25 rate was likewise paid in 1801 by Stephen Girard in Philadelphia.[7] On the other hand, the Honorable S. D. Hubbard of Connecticut recorded his not so fond memory of such wages having ranged from 37 to 50 cents in that state in 1800.[8] And for a slightly earlier period, a 50-cent rate in the frontier regions of New York is also quoted.[9]

In New Orleans about 1804 a Negro woman was hired for about $12 to $15 a month or $3 to $4 a week.[10] Since the first sugar plantation had only begun operation in 1795, the level of this hiring rate would have been determined largely by domestic service. The considerable excess of Louisiana over United States wages is consistent with an 1800 statement that Louisiana wages "are twice as high as in the United States."[11] Assuming

---

[6] Baker Library, Manuscript 871, 1776–1812, p. 738.

[7] U.S. Bureau of Labor Statistics, Bulletin 499, p. 135. The same report quotes the improbable rate of only 50 cents a week from Carroll Wright's Massachusetts compilation, *History of Wages and Prices in Massachusetts* (1885), and Warden's estimated $2 to $4 a month for maid servants in Washington (BLS Bulletin 499, pp. 135–136). We find Wright's figure unreasonably low (though perhaps suggesting a figure below $1.25) and Warden's roughly consistent, given the difference of a few years. Housemaids' rates of $10 a month paid by the Pennsylvania Hospital in Philadelphia from 1801 to 1810 (*Ibid,* p. 135) are obviously inconsistent with the Girard rate. We assume that they did not include board or lodging.

[8] *Letter from S. D. Hubbard of Connecticut to His Constituents on the Alarming Crisis in the Affairs of the Country* (Washington: Mar. 13, 1846), p. 5 (Yale Library).

[9] Helen I. Cowan, *Charles Williamson,* Rochester Historical Society Publications (1941), vol. XIX, pp. 102, 103. In 1795, in Genessee County, N.Y., Williamson paid $2 a month for a maid, $130 a year for a gardener, and bought a male slave for $250. The common labor–domestic service ratio cannot be deduced from the gardener's rate: Williamson was a Scots laird with the greatest estate in the region. However, if the slave's price represents, say, 10 years' service, the maid's rate may be a reliable one.

[10] C. C. Robin, *Voyages dans L'Interieur de la Louisiane . . . 1802–1806.* (Paris: F. Buisson, 1807), vol. II, p. 113. "Une negress se loue, par mois, douze a quinze piastres."

[11] Memoir to Napoleon, quoted in Charles Gayarre, *History of Louisiana* (1885), vol. III, p. 438.

that most servants were then hired in New York City (where rates were low, it being the major port of entry), Philadelphia, Boston, Baltimore, and Charleston, we deduce a United States average of $1.

1811. Sir August Foster, his Britannic Majesty's Minister to the United States, failed to prevent the second war with Britain, but he did leave a set of notes to posterity. From these we can conclude that domestic servants earned $2 a week in Baltimore and Philadelphia during his 1811–1812 stay.[12]

1815. A 50 cent rate is recorded for this year by Carroll Wright.[13] This figure is too low to be a representative average, given (1) other data reported by Wright and (2) the fact that 1815 wage rates were at the wartime inflation peak and therefore should have at least equaled the higher figures reported for earlier years.[14]

1817 to 1819. Fearon's journey in 1817–1818 suggests that servants' rates in Philadelphia had fallen from a $2 level in the 1811–1812 period, and ranged from 75 cents to $1.50.[15] The recession of 1818–1819, of course, had a much more moderate impact on the frontier areas, if we may judge from the trends for common labor. Our first quotations for such areas are probably not particularly affected by the recession and may be considered as levels for more normal times. In the autumn of 1819 a $1.50 to $2 rate prevailed in Michigan—perhaps double the Philadelphia rate.[16] This is confirmed by a figure of $1.50 a week paid to a woman who was hired with her husband to work on an Indiana farm "and they find themselves," i.e., exclusive of board.[17] In December, 1818, female Negroes were sold for $600 in Lexington, Kentucky, and their hire was $120, or 20 percent.[18] Since most employers allowed a period of time off once a year for traveling home and visiting families, this rate may be considered for 51 weeks, or $2.35 a week. Richard Flower, visiting at about the same time, reports a rate of from $96 to $120 a year, but the same common-

[12] Richard B. Davis (ed.), *Jeffersonian America, Notes of Sir Augustus Foster* (1954), pp. 210, 271.

[13] *Massachusetts, Sixteenth Annual Report of the Bureau of Statistics of Labor,* August, 1885 (1885), p. 238.

[14] For the same year, Wright records women earning $6.50 a week as papermakers. Now since female board and lodging cost no more than $2 a week at this time, the gap in rates is clearly too great. It may be relevant that no other quotation for pay of domestic servants is given for the 1752–1860 period.

[15] Henry B. Fearon, *A Narrative of a Journey* (London: Longman, Hurst, Rees, Orme, and Browne, 1818), p. 161.

[16] Since the Philadelphia rates fell from 1818 to 1819, the Fearon figure would be reduced further: Men in 1819 were working on the Pennsylvania turnpikes for a shilling a day. The Michigan rate is from the *Detroit Gazette* (Sept. 17, 1819) quoted in George N. Fuller, *Economic and Social Beginnings of Michigan* (1916), p. 130.

[17] *Rhode Island History,* vol. I (April, 1942).

[18] James Flint, *Letters from America* (Edinburgh: W. and C. Tait, 1822), p. 114.

labor rate as Flint.[19] Hence, the rate in Lexington, Kentucky, was some-what above that in Michigan, more than double that in Philadelphia—comparing the hire of a female Negro by the year with that of a white servant customarily hired by the week or month.[20] Finally, we may note a rate of $1.50 in New York City for washing a dozen pieces.[21] Washing normally included provision of soap and hot water—no unimportant consideration in those days—and as we shall see later that the rate for a dozen pieces was the standard quotation. It appeared to be slightly below, exclusive of board, the money wage of servants. The figure is in fact slightly below the rate quoted by Cobbett for a "good woman servant," of 20 pounds sterling a year, or about $1.75 a week on Long Island.[22]

1825 to 1827. Once the crisis period of 1804 to 1819 had ended, wages appeared to be moderately stable until the early forties, and, for domestic servants, not greatly affected even then. In 1824 the American Board of Commissioners for Foreign Missions hired female slaves at $50 a year for domestic service in Brainerd, Tennessee, while other women were hired for "$1 a week in clothes." [23] For Massachusetts family account records show a servant paid $52 for a year's work both in 1820 and 1821; $1.50 for short-term help in 1822; and 65 cents a dozen for washing in 1823.[24] For 1825 Zechariah Allen, an astute manufacturer of the time, found that servant maids in the country as a whole averaged from $1 to

[19] Richard Flower, *Letters from Lexington and Illinois* (1819–1904), reprinted in Reuben G. Thwaites (ed.), *Early Western Travels* (1904–1907), vol. IX, p. 103.

[20] A Cincinnati figure of 20 shillings 3 pence to 29 shillings 3 pence—or $3.25 to $5—appears for May, 1819, in an omnibus compilation of travelers' reports entitled *A Geographical, Historical, Commercial and Agricultural View of the United States of America . . . Compiled by Several Gentlemen. . . .* (London: Edwards and Knibb, 1820), p. 521. This may be compared to a 36 shilling to 40 shilling 6 pence rate for mechanics. A rate of 75 cents was paid for a bag of wash near Nashville in October, 1820. Harlan M. Fuller and L. R. Hafen (eds.), *The Journal of Captain John R. Bell* (1957), p. 319. Without an indication of quantity, this fact is not of much help in confirming these figures.

[21] Flint, *op. cit.*, p. 7.

[22] William Cobbett, *A Years Residence in the United States of America* (New York: Clayton and Kingsland, 1819), reprinted in Thwaites, *op. cit.*, vol. II, p. 238. A range from 4 shillings 6 pence to 9 shillings a week for female servants in Philadelphia is estimated in E. Mackenzie, *An Historical, Topographical and Descriptive View of the United States of America* (Newcastle-upon-Tyne: 1819), p. 470.

[23] American Board of Commissioners for Foreign Missions, expense records, Houghton Library, Harvard University. ABC 18.3.1, vol. I, pp. 26–27. "Melinda, a mulatto woman, at 50 dollars a year, and her clothes (a slave)"; "Matilda, a black woman, $50 a year, and clothes"; "Rachel McPherson, at $1 a week and clothes," etc.

[24] Baker Library, Reuben S. Randall papers, "Labor 1808–1822." Randall's receipts include one to Mary Wentworth "To attending your family 52 weeks $52" for November, 1820–1821; and another to her, November, 1821–August, 1822, at the $1 rate; with Mary Ann English hired later at 2 shillings 6 pence a week. Abigail Blastel charged $2.44 for washing 39 pieces—relatively low perhaps, since she also provided Captain Randall with board, at $3.50 a week.

$1.50.[25] For 1827 a manufacturers' convention reported wages for girls and women running from $1.50 to $3 "in well regulated factories into which small children are not admitted." [26] We may take the lower figure as an indication of domestic-service earnings.

1830 to 1832.   Around 1830 Matthew Carey estimated servants' earnings in Philadelphia at $1.25 a week, and, if we take iteration as a demonstration of truth, his frequent repetitions of the figure give it considerable reliability.[27]

For 1832 we have a variety of McLane report data. They range from 75 cents to $1 in different counties of New York state, though New York City rates run near $1.25.[28] For New Hampshire the report agent estimates 25 cents a day for female servants in the state, while one respondent estimated 75 cents a week.[29] A Delaware estimate set girls' wages at "75¢ a week and found, or boarded at housework." [30] For Pennsylvania an estimate of $1.50 to $1.75 for the state is made by one manufacturer.[31] Patrick Shureff, a well-informed and careful traveler, puts the rate at $1 a week for servants in private families.[32] And finally, a reliable record kept by a missionary society reports $50 a year for hiring a female slave as a servant in Tennessee in 1831.[33]

1835 to 1850.   A well-informed visitor to New York at the period of the great strikes of 1835–1836 noted that the washerwomen also "took

[25] Zechariah Allen, *The Science of Mechanics* (Providence: 1829), p. 347.

[26] *General Convention of Agriculturists, and Manufacturers . . . of the Domestic Industry of the United States,* July 30, 1827 (Harrisburg), p. 32.

[27] Matthew Carey, *Letter to the Printer of the Delaware Advertiser* (n.d., n.p., probably Philadelphia, 1829), pp. 4–5, in Library of Congress Rare Book Room. Carey provides a carefully worked out set of estimates for women's earnings. In his *Remuneration for Female Labour: To the Editor of the New York Daily Sentinel* (Sentinel ed., Mar. 18, 1830) Carey estimated $1.25 as the prevailing wage for females in Philadelphia, while he is quoted to the effect that "female domestics can find abundant employment, at one dollar to one dollar and a half per week, with their board and lodging" in Condy Raguet (ed.), *The Free Trade Advocate and Journal of Political Economy* (Philadelphia: Adam Waldie), issue of Apr. 4, 1829, p. 223. We prefer Carey's contemporary judgment of the prevailing rate—and he was not inclined to overestimate wages—to the $1 Pottsville rate and a 75 cent rate somewhere near Philadelphia achieved by one family, both quoted in BLS Bulletin 499, p. 136.

[28] *Documents on Manufactures* (1833), U.S. Congress, Serial Set 222, vol. II, pp. 6, 14, 17, 20, 22, 31, 73, 77, 86. New York—i.e., New York City—rates of $4 to $5 in 1826 and $6 in 1835 are quoted in BLS Bulletin 499, p. 136—We interpolate for $5 in 1830.

[29] *McLane Report,* vol. I, pp. 584, 630–631.

[30] *Ibid.,* vol. II, p. 703.

[31] *Ibid.,* p. 440.

[32] Patrick Shureff, *A Tour through North America* (Edinburgh, 1835), p. 450.

[33] American Board of Commissioners for Foreign Missions, expense accounts.

it into their heads to include themselves among the claimants, and actually raised their charges to eight shillings, or one dollar per dozen. But many have now returned to the old rate" of 6 shillings. The same writer refers to the country more generally in a statement that adult female help received $5 to $8 a month, or $1.25 to $2.[34] In March, 1836, the *Weekly Dispatch* reported a $4 to $10 range for the country as a whole.[35] A mere 2 years later (but after the recession of 1837 had begun), Count Francesco Arese noted a sign in Warm Springs, Virginia, advertising white servants for $6 and colored servants and horses for $4 each a week.[36] (The weekly rates of $1.25 and $1 are thus closely similar to the Lexington, Kentucky, rate in 1818–1819.) In 1843 a washwoman was paid $14 a month at the Cherokee Mission, while another received $10.[37] Whether these high rates reflected frontier dangers, the generosity of a nonprofit organization, or some other factor is unknown.

Finally, linking to the census figure for 1850, we have a New York City report of washing "6 shillings a dozen, buttons replaced"—or almost precisely the $1.05 figure of the census for New York domestics.[38]

Taking the above mass of reports, we attempt a highly speculative measure of domestics' earnings at various dates. Since the bulk of free domestics prior to 1860 were employed in the coastal cities of New York, Philadelphia, Boston, and Baltimore, we give special weight to reports from those areas and adjust rates for other regions to allow for the differential between these cities and the wilder West, Tennessee, or upper New England at dates when such comparisons can be made for domestics or common labor. The result of this free-roving procedure is the following for weekly cash wages:

1800 $1
1810 $2
1819 $1.25
1832 $1.25

[34] *The British Mechanics and Labourers Handbook and True Guide to the United States* (London: Charles Knight, 1840), pp. 59, 102.

[35] Quoted in Reverend William O'Bryan, *A Narrative of Travels in the United States of America* (London: 1836), p. 344.

[36] Francesco Arese, *A Trip to the Prairies* (1934), p. 25. Originally written in 1837–1838.

[37] American Board of Commissioners of Foreign Missions, Expense accounts for the Cherokee Mission, July 11, 1843. Statement by Hitchcock of quarterly expenses. A July 16, 1844, letter notes a $13.50 rate for the washwoman.

[38] William Burns, *Life in New York In Door and Out of Doors* (New York: Bunce and Brothers, 1853). No page numbers are given. We may compare a $1.50 a week rate for needlewomen on good cotton shirts and 75 cents for flannel undershirts, from *New York in Slices: by An Experienced Carver: Being the Original Slices Published in the New York Tribune* (New York: William H. Graham, 1849), p. 51, with the $1.25 estimated by Carey for Philadelphia in 1830.

We have no data on the cost of board and lodging for domestics, normally provided in addition to cash wages, but it is possible to take some 1832 to 1835 figures as indicating $1.25 equivalent for such income in kind.[39] **1850, 1860, 1870.** For these years we have data of very different quality, data that appear to have a considerable measure of reliability. For 1850 and 1860 we have reports, for each state, by the marshals of the Population Census.[40] For 1870 we have the extensive Treasury Survey used for common-labor estimates.[41] The state data were then weighted by the number of servants in each state to give regional and United States averages.[42] **1900.** The results of a special survey made for the U.S. Industrial Commission by Gail Laughlin were used, weighted by the Population Census domestic counts to derive regional figures.[43] Where the reports received from any state related to less than 10 employees, they are shown in parentheses in the table. These data, because they relate to particular employees, may have more sampling error than the earlier figures, but they should be equally useful indications of interstate variations.

In conclusion, we may call attention to the decline from the 1832 figure of $1.25 to the $1.08 figure for 1850. We believe that this decline is a true one; it reflects the heavy influx of migrants into New York and the

[39] Female board was charged at $1.25 in 1832 at the Fitchburg Woolen Company. 1880 Census, *Report on the Statistics of Wages in Manufacturing Industries* . . . by Joseph Weeks (1886) p. 391. The same rate was charged by the Lowell Mills in 1835. Ramon de la Sagra, *Cinq Mois aux Etats-Unis de l'Amerique du Nord depuis le 29 Avril jusq'au 23 Septembre 1835* (Paris: F. G. Levrault, 1837), p. 396. De la Sagra was an early contributor to the *Journal des Economistes,* and perhaps therefore a reliable observer.

[40] J. D. B. DeBow, *Statistical View of the United States* (1854), p. 164. 1860 Census, *Statistics of the United States (including Mortality* . . . (1866), p. 512.

[41] *Special Report on Immigration,* 42nd Cong., 1st Sess., House Exec. Doc. 1 (1871), p. 216.

[42] *1850:* The reported male servant distribution was not used. Analysis of the individual state reports indicated that in that year a substantial number of servants must have been included in the "laborers" category. The 1860 distribution was therefore used instead. *1860:* No data on female servants were published in the censuses until that of 1870. A comparison between the distribution of female servants by state in 1870 and all servants in 1860 was sufficiently similar to suggest that the 1860 distribution for all servants could properly be used to weight the female servant rates in that year. *1870:* Population Census counts of female servants were used to derive regional and United States averages. 1850 Census, *Statistics of Progress,* p. lxxvii. 1860 Census, *Population of the United States in 1860* (1864), pp. 674–675. Ninth Census, *The Statistics of the Population of the United States* (1872), vol. I, pp. 686ff.

[43] Gail Laughlin, "Domestic Service," in U.S. Industrial Commission, *Reports,* vol. XIV, p. 748. (The data used relate to reports from employers concerning women in general service, excluding cooks and other higher-rated personnel.) 1900 Census, *Occupations,* pp. 114ff.

nearby states during the potato famine of the late 1840s and the continental disturbances—with the consequent effect on wage rates in the areas
where most free domestics were hired.

MANUFACTURING, BY INDUSTRY: 1832 (TABLE A-31)

Estimates of earnings for manufacturing in 1832, were computed from
an enormous study made for Louis McLane, then Secretary of the Treasury.[1] For the McLane report individual enumerators called on manufacturers all over the New England and Middle Atlantic states. It provides
estimates of earnings in thousands of firms and in hundreds of individual
towns by such hand tradesmen as house carpenters, saddlers, blacksmiths,
etc. In a real sense such comprehensive materials have not been published
since. On the other hand, no survey data can be used without consideration of their reliability; possible problems of coverage and bias are particularly to be guarded against where we know little of the conditions
under which the data were collected. In outlining below the methods followed in utilizing these data to prepare Table A-31, therefore, a reasonably full description is also given of various checks and adjustments made.

In general the rates by industry and sex of worker were computed as
weighted averages of all available reports for each state as presented in the
1,900 pages of the McLane report. A single exception was the rate for
Massachusetts shoe manufacturing: Because of the enormous number of
firms reported, the average was based on data for firms with 25 or more
employees. (Examination indicated that the averages paid by this group
—not, of course, by the very largest firms—were much the same as those
paid by the smaller ones.)

Two types of figures emerged from this process. Those of adequate reliability appear in the table without qualification. Where only a limited
number of reports were available but the coefficient of variation was small,
the results are shown in parentheses. Special procedures for individual industries are noted below.

Cotton

The rates for cotton in most states will differ somewhat from those
published in 1831 by the New York Convention.[2] For Maine the Treasury

---

[1] *Documents Relative to the Manufactures in the United States,* 22nd Cong., 1st
Sess., Exec. Doc. 308 (1833) 2 vols., Serial Sets Nos. 222 and 223, hereafter called
the McLane or Treasury Report.

[2] The New York Convention data, published in various forms, are conveniently
available in *Niles Register* (March–August, 1832), vol. 42, addendum, p. 7. Niles,

report covers more persons and includes, unlike the Convention report, the largest mill in the state—the Saco York mill which was rebuilding in 1831–1832. For Massachusetts the two reports show similar rates, and counts, for males but the Convention report shows an enormously greater number of females and a lower average than the summary of Treasury reports.[3] Since study of the latter indicates that all Lowell mills and others of any consequence (as indicated by historical materials) were included, it is difficult to see how, with no more males reported, the Convention could report nearly 50 percent more females. For Vermont, New Hampshire, Connecticut, and Rhode Island, the Treasury reports covered more employees and were therefore preferred though both give much the same results. For New York, New Jersey, and Pennsylvania, the Convention reports give slightly lower averages for both males and females and were preferred because of their much broader coverage.[4]

The general uniformity of rates among the states appears in both a summary of the Treasury reports and in the Convention statement.[5] Significant and reliable exceptions are primarily three. (1) The high male rates in Maine reflect the initial buildup of the labor force in the Saco and other mills: By James Montgomery's time the rates were in line. (2) The relatively high rate for females in Massachusetts reflects the initial stages of heavy demands in Lowell, and is confirmed by mill payroll data for Hamilton, Waltham, and Merrimac mills in the Baker Library. (3) The New Hampshire rates may also reflect an early initial buildup but since

---

as one of the Secretaries of the Convention, presumably provides as accurate a version as any, others differing in minor particulars. These appear to be the source for the 1831 data in Carroll Wright, "The Factory System," in U.S. Census Office, *Report on Manufactures of the United States at the Tenth Census* (1883), folio pp. 542–547.

[3] A possible explanation may have been an arbitrary allowance for hand weavers, which would in turn involve lowering the average wage for the females. Another contribution may have been the inclusion of both young girls and boys in the female group, since the latter were commonly paid low rates, classed with females vis-à-vis adult males.

[4] Most New York reports in the Treasury report did not distinguish between boys and adults in the data for males. (Firms that did averaged $7.14 a week for males.) The Convention average of $6 was preferred; its level is more consistent with other data, and firms that employed boys may well have differentiated the work more effectively so that the men they employed would have had above-average skills.

[5] Differences in coverage probably reflect the unwillingness of manufacturers who had recently reported to the Convention, to report again to the Treasury. (*McLane Report*, vol. II, pp. 198, 200.) The Convention report noted 3,700 hand weavers in Pennsylvania and 1,060 in New Jersey. *Journal of the Proceedings of the Friends of Domestic Industry* (Baltimore: 1831), p. 112. The gap is much greater than this, however, and the Convention figures may actually have included more. The Register of Pennsylvania in 1830 estimated 4,500 weavers in Philadelphia. *Philadelphia in 1830* (Philadelphia: Carey and Hart, 1830), p. 31.

the dominant Cocheco mill paid below New England average rates in later years, it is safest to draw no special inferences from these high rates.

Hats and Caps

The rates for Massachusetts and New Hampshire rest on reports for more than a hundred towns indicating homework on palm-leaf hats, two a day being the average product, at a shilling each.[6]

The primary problem in using the reports for these industries stemmed from the fact that Pennsylvania reports related primarily to western Pennsylvania and northeast Philadelphia.[7]

Iron

The averages shown here apply to iron manufacturing per se, exclusive of the associated work by woodchoppers, colliers, etc. Analysis of the individual reports in terms of output per man suggests that in most, but not all, of the reports manufacturers included only those closely associated with the forge. Because of productivity variations, however, it is not possible to be certain of anything more than that the great majority of quotations relate only to ironworkers. A second problem arises because Massachusetts rates are above those for Pennsylvania. The explanation proves to be the fact that virtually all the former are quoted as daily rates, while a significant proportion of the latter are quoted as monthly rates.[8] The normal differential between daily and monthly rates then produces the state differences.[9] For those paid on daily rates, the Massachusetts and

[6] Data for Connecticut relate only to one firm in New Haven and one in Hartford. Reference to the 1840 Census, however, shows most Connecticut hat employment in Tolland County and other outlying areas. The average of 38 cents paid to females in cotton manufacturing and satinet manufacturing in Tolland, slightly above other areas, was therefore used.

[7] A substantial proportion of reports for Pennsylvania covered fulling mills, with above-average rates—men at $18 a month, 84 cents a day, and $186 a year are averages deriving for each period quoted. Weighted averages come to 70 cents a day for men, while for females and boys a tiny sample gives 31 and 48 cents a day, respectively—boys doing heavier work. An average for the male and female rates was computed using the 1850 Census ratio of males to females in Pennsylvania woolen manufacture. (Since the 1850 ratio is much like the 1860, we may not be too far off in applying it still earlier.) This procedure allows for the substantial role women played in the industry, which was not reflected in the weight distribution of the reports, while the omission of a weight for the boys helps compensate for the omission of Philadelphia rates. (1850 Census, *Compendium*, p. 180; 1860 Census, *Manufactures*, p. 544.)

[8] Some 72 percent of the men for whom wage reports are given in the McLane report were paid by the month, and some 66 percent of the far fewer Connecticut employees.

[9] Typical Pennsylvania reports all indicate 12 months' work for the hands. (*McLane Report*, vol. II, pp. 266, 283, 305, 316, 393, 419, and, for New York, p. 84;

Pennsylvania rates average out within 1 cent. The differential may therefore testify to differences in ability to offer steady work.[10]

Regional Averages

To weight together the various rates into regional averages, the following procedures were used. State estimates were made by combining age-sex rates in the relative proportion shown by summarizing the McLane report figures. In turn these state figures were weighted together. For cotton the distribution of cotton-manufacturing employment by state shown in the New York Convention reports was used. For wool the distribution of employment in wool manufacturing as shown by the 1840 Census was used, while for iron the same procedure was followed. For New England shoe manufacturing the 1840 Census data on employment could not be used because they relate to numbers employed in tanneries. Instead the distribution of investment by state in leather manufactories, except tanneries, was utilized—a procedure implying a similar ratio of capital per leather-manufacturing employee among the various New England states.

All Manufacturing

If we were simply to weight together the rates available for the above industries, a figure of 75 cents would result. But it would not necessarily represent all United States manufacturing; many states have been omitted, and employment in New England textile mills would be overrepresented. For this reason a direct estimate for all manufacturing was attempted.

For approximately two-thirds of all manufacturing employment, we have more or less tolerable data. (We estimate this proportion on the basis of the distribution of employment by industry in 1840, when we first have a moderately reliable distribution by industry.) Under the heading of industries with tolerable data we include iron and metal fabricating (86 cents), cotton goods (72 cents), paper (65 cents), and New England employment in (1) hat manufacture (33 cents), (2) carriages and wagons ($1.25), and (3) shoe manufacture (70 cents). For a sixth of all employment we have symptomatic data from the McLane report and other sources that provide an individual observation here and there: Printing ($1), hats in the Middle Atlantic states (90 cents), furniture (85 cents), leather, except in New England (80 cents). For another sixth,

---

for New Jersey, p. 86.) A New York firm notes "the works are suspended by frost from manufacturing during the months of January and February." In the off months the employees customarily chopped wood for charcoal and did repair work. One Massachusetts firm, on the other hand, notes that it hired men for only 3 months; another notes only "winter work."

[10] A daily average of $1.01 and a monthly average of $19.24 for 734 and 1,866 males, respectively, is indicated by the data for Pennsylvania.

primarily brick manufacturing, liquor, and the small segments of industries outside New England (noted above), we have very little information. For the only numerically significant component of this group—brick and liquor manufacture—a $1 rate was stipulated on the basis of McLane reports for Boston, a quotation from Mrs. Royall, etc. All this weighting, of course, makes little difference in the end. It leads to an 80-cent rate for all manufacturing—5 cents above the happenstance average noted above, largely because the added employment allowed for was mostly that of males, while that included in the sample had a large proportion of females in textile factories.

WAGE TRENDS: 1860 TO 1880 (TABLE A-19)

A substantial interest attaches to the course of wage rates during and after the Civil War. How did wages change in this period of war and crisis? How did wages change during the decades when, according to many accounts, the foundations of today's industrial system were being laid? And how did wage adjustment work out in a largely free-enterprise economy, with little in the way of government intervention, monopolies, or unions as compared to today's economy?

For answering these questions we have two sets of data, collected in the 1880–1890 period. One, customarily termed the Aldrich report, was based on reports collected by the Commissioner of Labor in the early nineties; the other, collected as part of the 1880 Census, is termed the Weeks report.[1] These both provide a haphazard collection of wage data that need analysis, allowance for bias, and careful weighting before they can be utilized. The major study in the field was made by Wesley Mitchell in a now-neglected work of indefatigable endeavor and broad economic insight.[2] A variety of other studies have been made, from Faulkner's original compilation of the Aldrich committee material, through to the recent study by Clarence Long.[3]

---

[1] *Report on Wholesale Prices, on Wages and on Transportation,* 52d Cong., 2d Sess. (1893): 1880 Census, *Report on the Statistics of Wages in Manufacturing Industries* (1886).

[2] *Gold Prices and Wages under the Greenback Standard* (1908).

[3] Clarence Long, *Wages and Earnings in the United States, 1860–1890* (1960). In a thoughtful review of "The Course of Wage-rates in Five Countries, 1860–1939," *Oxford Economic Papers* (June, 1950), E. H. Phelps Brown and Sheila V. Hopkins use the Aldrich data, as did Mitchell, to develop an 1860–1890 index, although they differ somewhat in the weights used for combining industry series. Hence the limitations in the Aldrich data discussed below will apply to their index as well. Their perceptive discussion of long-term trends, however, is not distorted by this fact.

I

We discuss first the Aldrich material and its four limitations, all four present in the original estimates by Faulkner, one removed by Mitchell, one by Long.

1. Faulkner gave equal weight to all occupational quotations within each industry. Thus, when establishment 43 reported one wage series for a single overseer and one for 115 weavers, he implicitly gave equal weight to each series. Extended to all the reports, his procedure ended up in an extreme overweighting for the rates paid to the limited group of overseers and foremen, for whom a phenomenal number of wage quotations were secured, and a massive underweighting of wages for semiskilled and unskilled employees. Since the wage trends for the two groups differed, the result was a biased wage index. Faulkner's procedures were raked fore and aft by Warren Waite and Mitchell, but his data have been widely reproduced and form a basis for many estimates.[4]

2. Mitchell utilized the occupational employment data (available in the Aldrich reports but bypassed by Faulkner) to give each occupational quotation its proper weight in deriving industry employment totals. He then, implicitly, weighted each establishment by its reported employment and each industry by its reported employment, to derive an overall wage-trend series. As a consequence even careful studies, such as those of Phelps Brown, that rely on Mitchell's overall index—the least important part of his work—rely on an index that reflects the happenstance of establishment and industry sampling in the work of the Commissioner of Labor. The most graphic example of its limitations is the fact that the New York City Department of Public Works accounted for one-third of all employment in the sample at its beginning point, January, 1860.[5] Hence overall industry estimates based on these reports have their trend given by one basic factor: 60 percent of all employees in the Aldrich sample worked in two New York City firms and three Massachusetts ones.[6]

[4] Faulkner's series appears in *Historical Statistics of the United States,* p. 66. According to information kindly communicated by Witt Bowden, it is also the basis for the BLS series back to 1840, that appears in the BLS *History of Wages,* in early issues of the *Monthly Labor Review,* and elsewhere—the Faulkner daily rates merely being adjusted for changes in hours per day.

[5] Mitchell, *op. cit.,* p. 98, shows 5,638 total male and females, while the sum of occupational data for establishment no. 35 (city public works, New York) on pp. 448–450 is 1,885.

[6] Total employment from Mitchell, *op. cit.,* 154, for July, 1860, with data for establishments 35, 38, 39, 43, and 47 from his Appendix. Use is commonly made of his basic tables 33 and 37, which are subject to this limitation. In his analysis of wage-price–gold-price relationships, however, Mitchell notes that excluding the "city public works industry" will provide "a fairer index of the course of wages"; he does so in his tables 65 to 68, as on p. 145, n. 3, and p. 167, n. 6.

3. Long, noting the industry bias that remains in Mitchell's series, adjusted for it by returning to Faulkner's procedure of using census weights. Long's series differs significantly from Mitchell's implicit manufacturing wage series only because of this difference in weights.[7]

Since Long uses census weights, his decennial changes will differ from the census primarily for one reason—differences between the Aldrich and census trend for wages within particular industries.[8] Hence judgment on whether the Long-Aldrich series is to be preferred to the census for measuring decennial changes turns on how well the Aldrich sample does for these particular industries. We seek to cast some light on this by the tabulation in Table 6-1.[9]

The industries shown in block I are those where the Aldrich sample covers less than 75 employees in each industry, and where the states involved accounted for no more than 15 percent of United States employment in the industry.[10] For these industries we choose the census trend

[7] Long apparently used the Census of Manufactures weights while Faulkner, covering more than manufacturing, used Census of Population weights. Long (*op. cit.* table 5, p. 22) provides a helpful analysis indicating that his use of different weights produces differences from 8 to 20 points from Mitchell (depending on the year) whereas only 1- to 3-point differences occur because he also computed dollar averages directly rather than from relatives.

[8] Minor differences arise from other factors. (1) Long includes in his manufacturing total the mysterious Aldrich "stone" industry. However, this is really a mining industry if we may judge from its occupational composition (quarrymen, laborers). (2) Long uses only a selection of manufacturing industries to represent all manufacturing. However, he demonstrates carefully that the resultant difference is unimportant. (3) Unemployment during the year and other conceptual differences between Aldrich and census data are discussed by Long, pp. 46–49. However, study of individual industries shows differences so extreme and irregular that they cannot reasonably be associated with such factors. Long's own analysis implies that less unemployment existed in 1880, after the longest and deepest depression to that date, than in 1870 (p. 48). Such an unlikely report indicates that other factors at work were more important. We suggest below that the errors in the Aldrich data constitute these factors.

[9] *1860–1870 percentage change:* Long, *op. cit.,* tables A-1 and A-9, with the following exceptions. For census lumber we use total lumber, not sawn lumber as shown by Long. (The comparison would be worse, in fact, if sawn lumber were used.) For Long's implicit state data, we benefited from unpublished material provided by Margaret Chen and Professor Long; for census state data we compute from the 1870 Census, *Industry and Wealth,* pp. 399ff. *Employment:* Census data from 1870 Census, *loc. cit.* For the Aldrich "ale, beer, porter" industry we use malt liquors; for "white lead," paints, lead, and zinc; for "metals," cast iron; for "stone," stone quarrying. It is not clear from Long's study which industries he used as equivalent. The major question arises with respect to metals; analysis of the Aldrich occupational data indicates that they included few if any plants making pig iron. Hence castings (plus the tiny forging group) would be most comparable.

[10] We infer that one of the two firms constituting the Long-Aldrich lumber manufacturing industry (the New York firm) was actually a distributor: Of its 11 em-

Table 6-1. 1860–1870 Wage Trend: Long-Aldrich and Census

	Percent change in wages, 1860–1870			Number of wage earners, 1870			Number of establishments, 1870	
	Census	Long-Aldrich	Aldrich sample	Census	States with Aldrich sample establishments	Aldrich sample	Census
I							
Agricultural implements	41	50	21	25,249	477	1	2,076
Carriages and wagons..	7	86	22	54,928	8,784	1	11,847
Leather..............	32	53	61	35,243	5,553	2	7,569
Lumber..............	44	61	34	159,111	19,999	2	26,945
II							
Ale, beer, porter.......	52	58	43	12,443	2,942	1	1,972
Paper...............	57	39	33	18,779	4,566	1	684
White lead..........		52	10	1,932	561	1	75
III							
Books and newspapers.	62	61	120	12,263	3,156	3	1,239
Illuminating gas.......	84	102	394	8,723	3,863	4	390
Metals..............	46	52	1,094	51,305	31,723	19	2,328
Stone...............		91	488	6,719	15,117	6	1,120
Woolen..............	45	59	283	34,189	77,870	3	1,938
Cotton..............	47	72	1,422	129,442	50,364	5	956
Massachusetts......	55	72		43,512	43,512	4	191
New York..........	57	55		9,144	9,144	1	81
Rest of United States	36	72		82,713	0	0	684
Woolen..............	45	59	283	80,053	77,870	3	1,938
Massachusetts......	53	78		20,550	20,550		
Connecticut........	55	50		7,297	7,297		
Rhode Island.......	38	39		6,363	6,363		
Rest of United States	39	59		45,843	0		

over the Aldrich sample. We do so because one does not customarily prefer a sample consisting of one establishment to a sample of 12,000 establishments, nor a sample covering 15 percent of all employees to one with 100 percent of all employees, merely because the former defines wages slightly more precisely than the latter. The fact that the tiny sample (as

ployees 9 were yard hands, 2 teamsters, and 1 a salesman—an odd force with which to manufacture lumber. (Occupational data from Mitchell, *op. cit.*, p. 477). Moreover, the yard hands were paid $1.04 a day in 1860—or as high as laborers' wages in New York City public works (*Ibid.*, p. 449), not a likely level in a lumber factory (most of which are outside cities) and three times the lumber laborer's rate for New Hampshire.

in agricultural implements) may show nearly the same results is a pleasant coincidence, just as the enormous gap for carriages and wagons is an unpleasant reminder of the dangers of using a very small sample.

Similarly we find that for the industries in block II, in which the Aldrich sample consists of a single establishment per industry, and that with less than 50 employees, there is no warrant for preferring the Aldrich reports to the census benchmark estimates of change.

The block III industries include those offering better odds that the Aldrich sample can provide more information than sampling error. For the one industry where the Aldrich sample has widest geographical coverage and the largest number of reporting firms—metals—the results are surprisingly similar to the census change estimates. And for all block III industries except cotton and woolen, the differences are at least not enormous.

What about cotton goods? The very sizable difference for cotton goods reflects two forces at work. (1) A major factor is Long's implicit assumption that the weighted average of change in one New York and four Massachusetts reports will properly represent the change for the 70 percent of the cotton textile industry that is outside those states. The census data, however, clearly suggest that this assumption is open to question; the gain for the rest of the United States was in fact nowhere near as great as for these two. (2) The other factor at work must be differences for the two Aldrich states. However, the New York State change is 55 percent in Aldrich and 57 percent in census. Hence there must be a massive difference for Massachusetts—where the Aldrich sample unquestionably had substantial, even impressive, coverage. Is the answer here simply the difference in concept and definition carefully explored by Long?[11]

We think not, and suggest instead a simple, outstanding bias in the Aldrich data. The table below gives the number reported in each selected occupation for the five textile firms covered in the Aldrich reports:[12]

Number of	Plant number				
	38	39	40	41	43
Machinists	8	24	17	1	6
Weaving overseers	4	1	2		1
Weavers	0	19	20	53	200
Spinning overseers	2	1	1		2
Frame spinners	0	28	0		19

[11] See Long's discussion, *op. cit.,* pp. 44ff.
[12] The data are from the Aldrich report. They modify slightly a similar table in the author's "Wage Trends, 1800–1900," Conference on Research in Income and Wealth, *Trends in the American Economy in the Nineteenth Century* (1960).

These data point to some remarkably significant omissions in the Aldrich material. Would firm 38 have four weaving supervisors and no weavers? Or two spinning supervisors and no frame spinners? If firm 41 had 53 weavers but no spinners, how representative is it in an industry where a substantial volume of activity in 1860 customarily involved spinning, with weaving only as a supplemental activity? Can we imagine that firm 39, with 24 times as many machinists as firm 41, had fewer employees in spinning and weaving, the core activities of textile mills? The problem created by this distortion is that the Aldrich reports gave trivial representation to occupations with perhaps 90 percent of the work force. The overrepresented group is known from other evidence to have much greater wage increases than the 90 percent group.

We can get some idea of the resultant bias by referring to contemporary reports not included within the Aldrich-Faulkner universe.

A contemporary study made by David A. Wells as Special Commissioner of the Revenue obtained reports from major United States firms. One was a reply from the Merrimac Manufacturing Company, the largest textile firm in Massachusetts and the United States. The firm reported gains from 1860 to the end of 1868 of 52 percent in the spinning department, 53 percent in weaving, 60 percent in carding, and 75 percent in dressing—all underweighted in Aldrich—and 63 percent for the over-weighted mechanics group.[13] If we weight these, we arrive at an estimate of 57 percent for the company as a whole, compared to 64 percent in the Aldrich data for Massachusetts.[14] For the longer period from 1860 to mid-1870, the census reports a 55 percent rise. This compares closely with figures we compute for the Nashua Mill (60 percent), the Lawrence (76 percent), and the Hamilton (58 percent), all leading mills in Massachusetts and the country.[15] The Aldrich data, however, report a 70 percent rise.[16] Again the Aldrich data prove to be on the high side—presumably because of their gross underrepresentation of spinners and weavers, departments where wages rose less than in the overrepresented mechanics group.[17]

A final limitation of these figures is that one of the five reports gives

[13] David A. Wells letter, Washington, March, 1869: *The Working Classes, Their Condition Past and Present; Wages and Prices.* A newspaper clipping reprint—this letter is in the W. G. Sumner collection in the Sterling Library at Yale.

[14] For weights we use the four department distributions of the Nashua, Lawrence, and Hamilton mills in January, 1860, as shown in the payroll transcription work sheets of Robert Layer's textile study, in the manuscript room of the Baker Library, Harvard Business School. The Wells letter reports a 36 percent gain for overseers. With a somewhat greater weighting for overseers than for mechanics, the four-department figure of 57 percent should probably be reduced.

[15] We compute these from data in Layer's work sheets, as above.

[16] The census data are for the years ending June, 1860, and June, 1870. We use the Aldrich averages for January and July, 1860, July, 1869, and July, 1870.

[17] Carding and dressing departments appear to be represented in proportion.

only piece rates for the important weavers category, thus missing the effect on earnings of the known rise in productivity.[18]

For the woolen industry we find both Aldrich and census changes remarkably alike for Connecticut and Rhode Island, while the Massachusetts Aldrich figure is markedly above the census. Because of Long's weighting procedure, this in turn means that the implicit figure for the rest of the United States is far above that from the census.

II

In conclusion, we find the following with respect to the adequacy of the Aldrich sample, used by Faulkner, Mitchell, and Long, when compared to the census for measurement of decennial change.

1. For seven industries the Aldrich sample is absurdly small, typically one firm, and that with fewer than 50 employees. We find no warrant for preferring such reports to the comprehensive census reports from thousands of firms.

2. For four industries the Aldrich sample has somewhat greater substance, particularly for metals. For these industries the Aldrich change for 1860 to 1870 proves to be within hailing distance, or better, of the census change.

3. For cotton and woolen textiles we break the Aldrich sample down to individual states. We then find that both sources for individual states indicate much the same 1860 to 1870 change, except for Massachusetts. Here we argue, from an analysis of the occupational composition of the Aldrich reports for cotton, that a clear bias in occupational reporting is present, with overrepresentation of the groups that showed the highest wage gains. Moreover, the procedure used by Long attributes to the substantial textile industry outside the states with Aldrich reports a rate of gain markedly out of line with census figures, and with no exposition of why this change should be assumed.

We conclude that the Aldrich data for most industries are clearly inferior to the census trends shown for individual states, and markedly inferior as an indication of the trend in the states for which no Aldrich reports were received. For some few industries the Aldrich reports afford a reasonably representative sample, and for these industries they show the same changes as the census. We, therefore, find that the census data are clearly to be preferred to the inadequate and biased Aldrich reports.

III

The present estimates for all nonfarm employees are wider in coverage than the manufacturing series of Long, or even the wider estimates by Mitchell. More important, however, is the difference in method. We reject

---

[18] The New York City firm 41 was omitted by Mitchell, presumably because of this fact, but was used by Long and others.

the Aldrich reports with their geographic, industrial, and occupational biases. Instead, we rely on the Weeks reports, which have an enormously broader scope because they come from many more establishments, in more states, without the obvious occupational biases in some of the key Aldrich reports. We use the Weeks reports, however, primarily for interpolating between benchmarks derived from the Population Census and other reports. Finally, we check the movement of the series thus derived against an extensive set of contemporary investigations made by David A. Wells and not used in previous studies.

The obviously wider scope of the Weeks reports have made them attractive to previous investigators. Their lack of use reflects the fact that although many wage series are reported, no occupational weights are attached to them. A simple averaging of such wage reports for an establishment, or for an industry, will produce a series that is both insensitive in cyclical response and unrealistic in its measure of decadal changes because of an inevitable overweighting of the higher occupational grades.[19]

It is possible, however, to develop reasonable weights for the Weeks materials from the Population Census data on gainful workers by occupation. To do so we utilize these occupational wage series to measure the trend of wages within a given occupation, and not as a mere intermediate measure for developing a trend within an industry. Thus, we use a report for the trend of earnings by common labor in Pennsylvania and combine it with other Weeks reports on common-labor rate trends in Pennsylvania machine shops, blast furnaces, rolling mills, hardware, paper, tanneries, furniture, etc. We treat each of these as random observations of the trend for wages of that group. We then combine these series to interpolate between benchmark estimates for common labor in Pennsylvania. The benchmarks for 1850 and 1860 are from the Population Census reports for those years; for 1870 from the Treasury *Report on Immigration;* and for 1880 from the census data on rates paid in iron and steel, coke, stone, and other industries. (The derivation of the benchmark data is discussed at length in Chapter 6 in the section of the present study on common labor rates.) Similar combinations and interpolations are made for common labor in the other states.[20]

---

[19] Mitchell's discussion of the limitations of the Faulkner reports applies, almost without change, to the use of unweighted occupational figures from the Weeks reports. Mitchell does use such series, on p. 175 in his study, for a contrast of East and West, one industry versus another, where such limitations are least important. Long averages Weeks reports in tables 1, 7, and A-3 of his study, and analyzes their 1860 to 1890 trends in his chap. 3.

[20] We combine the state series, using the count of nonfarm laborers as estimated in the 1870 Population Census, since the 1860 Census does not distinguish separately farm from nonfarm. On the basis of parallelism of benchmark change, we attribute the Iowa weight to the Indiana series, the Minnesota weight to Wisconsin.

Employees in other nonfarm occupations are all allocated to 1860 wage intervals (by procedures outlined below) and the trend in the Weeks data for these wage intervals is used as the trend series for these groups.[21] This amounts to saying that the trend of earnings for machinists, wheelwrights, carpenters, painters, and others reported by Weeks, who are classifiable in the $1.50 to $1.99 wage interval in 1860, should be similar to the trend for all other workmen in that interval. To justify this assumption, the Weeks reports should be both numerous and widely spread geographically. The evidence of the hundreds of series reported, and the states and industries represented, suggests that it is true in some absolute sense and is far truer of the Weeks than the Aldrich data. It is also necessary for us to have a reasonable basis for classifying all nonfarm gainfully occupied in 1860, and the procedures outlined below suggest that this can be accomplished by reasonable means from contemporary data. (If we were to apply the same procedure to the Aldrich reports, the result would suffer from (1) the geographic bias in those reports and (2) the higher sampling error resultant from using, say, the 49 reports that Long finds acceptable in the Aldrich manufacturing data,[22] rather than the 600 reports in Weeks.) The parallelism of wage movement for individual occupations within a wage-rate interval can be verified by study of the trend for individual occupations, such trends being apparent in the raw data and also in the excellently summarized occupational data of Mitchell.[23]

Before outlining the detailed procedure, we summarize below the key figures involved:[24]

1860 Census
(In thousands)

Total nonfarm employees	2,983
Laborers	972
Miners, boatmen, and others earning $1.00 to $1.49	453
Carpenters, blacksmiths and others earning $1.50 to $1.99	744
Domestic servants	566
All others	248

The 13 states thus represented had 0.7 out of 1.0 million nonfarm laborers (n.o.s.) and thus provide a comprehensive measure for interpolating the United States averages derived in the benchmark calculation.

[21] This procedure is preliminary and subject to revision when one similar to the laboriously detailed laborers' procedure can be adopted for these too. However, the linkage to the laborers series as described below should make it a fair approximation of the final result.

[22] Long, *op. cit.,* table A-1.

[23] Mitchell provides a variety of occupational series based on both the Aldrich and the Weeks reports. Comparison among those with similar starting-date wage figures is readily made.

[24] Of 8.2 million gainfully occupied (excluding students and nuns), some 3.3 million were in agriculture and 1.2 million in such occupations as merchants, bankers,

If we can develop series for the first four categories, it is clear that we can do fairly well for the variety of occupations in the last category: The weight given the first four categories is so great that their sum will largely determine the trend in the overall series. We turn to a consideration of the procedure for each group.

Laborers (972).[25] We utilize the 452 laborers' reports that Weeks collected for this group (as compared to the 20 from Aldrich, or even the 78 from Weeks's firms where reports were available for the full period), averaging them to compute individual state series and then weighting each state series as outlined above. These are then used to interpolate between the United States benchmarks for the group.

Table 6-2. Common Labor: Daily Wage Rates, 1860–1880

	Present estimate	Abbott-Weeks	McKinley-Weeks	Long-Weeks	Long-Aldrich
1860	$1.06	$1.03	$1.01	$1.03	$0.98
1861	1.08	1.03	1.06	1.04	0.97
1862	1.12	1.07	1.12	1.08	0.97
1863	1.28	1.21	1.21	1.20	1.11
1864	1.46	1.43	1.35	1.39	1.30
1865	1.54	1.47	1.45	1.48	1.48
1866	1.54	1.52	1.48	1.53	1.52
1867	1.54	1.63	1.47	1.53	1.53
1868	1.55	1.49	1.47	1.51	1.54
1869	1.55	1.52	1.45	1.53	1.56
1870	1.51	1.48	1.45	1.52	1.56
1871	1.50	1.49	1.44	1.50	1.57
1872	1.51	1.51	1.47	1.52	1.59
1873	1.44	1.51	1.46	1.52	1.59
1874	1.39	1.43	1.37	1.43	1.58
1875	1.32	1.39	1.34	1.39	1.54
1876	1.25	1.35	1.30	1.33	1.49
1877	1.21	1.26	1.27	1.28	1.42
1878	1.18	1.24	1.26	1.26	1.37
1879	1.16	1.25	1.26	1.27	1.35
1880	1.23	1.31	1.30	1.32	1.35

In Table 6-2 we compare the resultant series with that prepared by Edith Abbott from the Weeks materials; the Mitchell series for the group;

milliners, tailors, shoemakers, and other occupations that were dominantly self-employed. To allow for the limited number in this latter set that were employees, we have included all construction tradesmen—carpenters, painters, etc.—on the assumption that such overinclusion will roughly compensate.

[25] The number in each occupation (in thousands) is shown in parentheses after its title.

the two Long series, one derived from 20 Aldrich establishments and the other from 78 Weeks establishments; and the interesting series, also based on Weeks, prepared by President (then Senator) McKinley.[26]

Miners (158). We class this group in the $1.00 to $1.49 interval on the basis of the following information. In January, 1867, Representative Kerr of Pennsylvania stated that miners were paid $2 a day, wages having risen about 100 percent since the war began.[27] Carroll Wright's Bureau of Labor tabulations of state reports show wage rates in Pennsylvania coal ($1.16) and Michigan and New York iron mines (of $1 to $1.35) in 1860.[28] The 1860 Census shows average annual earnings of $275 in coal mining and $284 in iron-ore mining—figures consistent, after allowance for unemployment, with a $1 daily rate.[29] David A. Wells estimated copper-mining wages to have risen 100 percent from 1860 to 1866—a rate identical with Kerr's estimate of the percentage gain to the $2 rate in 1866.[30] Weeks gives a $1.25 rate for stone quarrying in Ohio, an 80-cent rate for Pennsylvania mining, and an 85-cent rate for New Jersey mining.[31] (See also Table A-20.)

Carpenters, Painters, Plumbers, Plasterers, Mechanics (365). By combining the Aldrich and Weeks reports, we have 56 quotations for the earnings of carpenters in a wide range of states and industries, averaging $1.52 per day in 1860. Analysis of the more limited range of quotations for painters, plumbers, roofers, and plasterers available from these same sources suggests that the average for the larger group would be the same. Contemporary estimates for New York City skilled workers also show the same figures for carpenters as painters.[32]

Blacksmiths (114). Combining 45 Aldrich and Weeks quotations gives an average of $1.69 for blacksmiths.

Machinists (44). Combining 65 Aldrich and Weeks quotations gives an average of $1.64 for this group.

Teamsters (78). Combining both Aldrich and Weeks reports, we have only 10 quotations for teamsters rates. Since these reports ranged over a wide range of industries, we minimize sampling variability by using the reports only to compute ratios of teamster to common-labor rates in the same establishments. The average of these ratios, 126 percent, was then applied to the United States common-laborer rate as derived in detail above, to give a teamster average of $1.34.

[26] The reasons for difference between the present series and those of Abbott and Mitchell are discussed in the author's paper "Wage Trends, 1800–1900."

[27] *Congressional Globe* (Jan. 1, 1867), appendix p. 135.

[28] *BLS Bulletin 499,* p. 330.

[29] 1860 Census, *Manufactures,* pp. 735, 737.

[30] U.S. Special Commissioner of the Revenue, *Report* (January, 1867).

[31] Weeks, *op. cit.,* pp. 114, 242ff.

[32] Erastus Bigelow, *The Tariff Question* (1862), appendix 115.

Boatmen, Steamboatmen (102). This group is assumed to have the equivalent of a daily income in the $1.00 to $1.49 class for the reasons noted below, though normally paid by the month. Individual voyages in 1860–1861 indicate customary rates of the immediate prewar years. Thus in May, 1861, the ship *Sooloo* sailed from Boston to San Francisco, shipping her A.B.'s at $12 a month.[33] And in 1860 the ship *Herald of Morning* sailed from Boston to San Francisco, shipping men at $12 a month.[34] In May, 1861, the *Electric Spark* sailed from Boston to Havre, with men signed at $14, $15, and $18.[35] Given the normal differential between China voyages and those to nearer ports, we can take $14 as the rate for voyages of equivalent duration and stability. In turn, the 1860 Census figures on earnings of farm laborers show $13.70 for a monthly rate—or virtually the same, while wages of $1 a day for short-term hiring of farm laborers in harvest suggest the basis for conversion. We, therefore, take an average of $14 a month for sailors to be equivalent to $1 a day rates and put this group in with the $1 to $1.49 interval.[36]

Railroad Men (37). The small number of gainfully occupied reported under this rubric suggests that trackwalkers and other unskilled labor were not included, but only such characteristic occupations as conductors, trainmen, and engineers. We have two bits of evidence for assigning the weight of this group to the proper wage interval. The Aldrich reports give data for individual occupations on a Massachusetts railroad. Weighting these by the number employed gives an average of $1.80, compared to a $1.30 rate for carpenters in the same company, and $1.43 for painters. Averaging the latter two, we derive a ratio of 140 percent for rail to mechanical rates and this ratio times the previous carpenter estimate of $1.52 gives a figure of $2.13. The median for the class interval into which this figure falls shows an 1860 to 1869 rise of 38 percent using the Weeks data.[37] This may be compared with the estimate of a 50 to 66 percent rise for the Vermont Central Railroad according to Wells.[38] Since the latter would be substantially affected by the rise for common labor, the two are not grossly inconsistent.

Clerks (185). Approximately 50,000 of the 185,000 clerks reported by the 1860 Population Census were in New York. *Hunt's Merchants Magazine* for 1860 estimated that New York City grocers' clerks and drug

---

[33] Essex Institute Manuscripts, George Allen, Shipping Accounts 1841–1866, ship's article for voyage.

[34] Baker Library, Manuscripts collection, Magoun Papers, Collection no. 1, vol. 38. Portage bill paid by Scott, Curtis and Co. of San Francisco.

[35] *Ibid.*, vol. 44.

[36] Rates of $30 to $35 a month for deck crews in the interior of the United States appear in Louis C. Hunter, *Steamboats in the Western Rivers* (1949), p. 465.

[37] Mitchell, *op. cit.*, pp. 187ff.

[38] David A. Wells, letter to Representative Kelly, *loc. cit.*

clerks averaged $9 a week, dry goods clerks $10.50—compared to $9 for carpenters and $11 for machinists.[39] Assuming that most clerks outside New York would have been in general stores, that the gap between their earnings and those of common labor would have been less because they could offer only the untutored talents of, say, a Lincoln rather than the expert assistance of a big city salesman, we conclude for a $9 average for the nation, or $1.50 a day.

Foremen (38). This numerically unimportant group is well represented in the Aldrich and Weeks reports, and an averaging of the 85 quotations in these sources gives $2.40.[40]

Masons (63). From a limited number of Aldrich reports, we compute masons' earnings at 117 percent of carpenters', giving, when applied to the carpenter average computed above, a figure of $1.78.[41]

Selected Skilled Trades (101). *Molders (17)* in eight Aldrich establishments earned an average of 98 percent of machinists, while in 11 Weeks establishments they earned 169 percent of laborers' rates. Applying these ratios to the machinist and laborer averages above and averaging gives greater weight to the Northeast reports in both sources, where employment was concentrated, and an average of $1.70. *Cabinetmakers (30)* were similarly estimated from laborers, at $1.67. *Wheelwrights (33)* were similarly estimated from laborers at $1.53. *Coopers (44)* were estimated to receive $1.52, the same as carpenters, with the New York City rates for each being the same in 1860; and BLS Bulletin 499 reported closely similar rates for each at various dates. *Millwrights (9)* earned the same as machinists in the New York City report and about three times the labor rate in three Weeks reports. We take the similarity of work to be great enough so that we use the United States machinists' average of $1.64. *Tinsmiths (17)* and *other metal workers (12)* are assumed at the blacksmith rate of $1.69. (A single Weeks report for tinsmiths is $1.75.) *Printers (24)* are estimated at $1.64, the scanty Aldrich material and the New York City report suggesting that compositors plus pressmen would together make such an average. *Weavers (36)* were estimated at 80 cents. We can compute a 68 percent ratio to labor rates in nine New England mills from Carroll Wright's report on the factory system; of 72 percent from the New England cotton mills reported by Weeks; and of 86 percent from Weeks's New England woolen mill data.[42] With an apparently higher

---

[39] Quoted in Bigelow, *loc. cit.*

[40] The Aldrich average is $2.27; the Weeks daily rates, $2.71; and the Weeks monthly rates, $62 or—assuming a 26-day work month—$2.38.

[41] Aldrich establishments 7, 12, 35, and 38. A ratio of 122 percent can be derived for 1870 from reports for individual cities covered by Department of Labor Bulletin 18, pp. 678ff.

[42] Carroll Wright, in 1880 Census, *Report on Manufactures,* p. 578. Weeks's data for two mills in Illinois, one in Ohio, and one in Philadelphia indicate rates of 100

302 Components of Change: Nineteenth Century

ratio in Weeks data for a few mid-Western mills (where we assume the
division of labor and use of females to have been less extensive) we take
a 75 percent ratio to laborers' rates for male plus female employees, in
cotton and wool factories.

Servants (566). For this sizable group, we have state by state data
from the Population Census which, when weighted by the state distribution of servants, yield a United States average of $1.34 a week.

Teachers (110). For teachers a monthly average of $17 for women
and $27 for men was estimated on the basis of rates paid in the state sys-
tems of four New England, three Middle Atlantic, and six Midwestern
states.[43] These rates were extrapolated by series for teachers' salaries in
three cities and two country districts collected by the Aldrich Committee.[44]

Coachmakers (19); Harness Makers (25). We stipulate the blacksmith's rate, the rates being similar in 1832.

Apprentices (55). The median of 11 apprentice rates quoted in the
Weeks reports, 50 cents, was used.

Lumbermen (16). Of the two Aldrich reports for lumbering, one is
clearly not for lumbering, while a single New Hampshire report indicates
50 cents for lumbermen.[45] A New Jersey report for woodchoppers is at
85 cents.[46] However, data for lumbering in Oregon and Washington in the
1876–1886 period suggests that sawmills and logging combined averaged
about the same as common labor, and on this basis we use the common-
labor rate for this group.[47]

Other Nonfarm Employees (123). For *factory hands not specified
(88)* we assume a generally low level of skill, since the skilled occupations normally have preference in occupational reporting to census enumerators. For *tanners (16)* we likewise assume low rates of pay, given
later data and eight Aldrich reports for rates paid to teamsters in tanneries. We, therefore, estimate the common-labor rate for both groups.

Given the above distribution of employees by average daily earnings in
1860, we utilize the Weeks data as follows. Mitchell has combined the
hundreds of quotations into wage-interval groups and computed indices of

---

percent and better. Two Aldrich rates imply unreasonably low rates of 36 and 54
percent; for a third mill, the Aldrich rates are useless as they are piece rates. For
the fourth Aldrich mill, the rate is about half the carpenter rate, implying something
like two-thirds the laborer rate.

[43] Reported in T. W. Higginson and Lucy Stone, *The Women's Rights Almanac for
1858,* pp. 20–21, and Daniel Wilder, *The Annals of Kansas* (1875), p. 673.

[44] Mitchell, *op. cit.,* table 63. The series were weighted 1 and 2, respectively, given
the proportion of male to female teachers from the 1880 Census, *Population,* p. 742.

[45] One firm in New York reports employment of one salesman and two teamsters
—suggesting that it was a lumber distributor.

[46] Weeks, *op. cit.,* p. 114.

[47] Kenneth O. Bjork, *West of the Great Divide* (1958), pp. 339, 340.

medians for each interval—e.g., 25–99 cents $1–$1.49, etc., for 1860 to 1880.[48] We weight these indices by the 1860 employment distribution shown above and compute an index for all nonfarm employees. We then compute for each year the ratio of the resultant median to that shown by Mitchell as the median for the $1–$1.49 interval. For example, by 1870 the overall median had risen 57.7 percent whereas the $1–$1.49 interval had risen by 67 percent, which yields a ratio of 94.4 percent.

We then apply this ratio to the series for laborers as previously derived to give an overall average. In this way we use the full detail, weighted state by state for laborers, to establish the year-to-year trend in average earnings over the 1860–1880 period, but modified to reflect the difference between the trend for laborers and all employees by a set of ratios computed from the medians. Because the trend in medians per se would be hardly satisfactory as a measure of the trend in averages, we do not use the median data for anything but deriving adjustment ratios with which to step down the laborers trend to an all-employees trend.

IV

The difference between the resultant series (Table A-19 and column 1 in Table 6-2) and prior series (Table 6-2) derives from several sources.

1. A major one is the reliance on the Weeks data, which report trends in many states in addition to the Northeastern bloc which dominates the Aldrich reports—and thence the Mitchell, Phelps Brown, and Long estimates. Mitchell has well analyzed the difference between trends in what he terms Western states (included by Weeks) and the Eastern states (primarily Northeastern), showing that Western rates climbed less over the two decades than did the Eastern, and Long summarizes the Bureau of Labor data for 1870 to 1880, showing a smaller decline in Western than Eastern cities.[49]

2. The wide differences between the Aldrich and census data where the Aldrich samples are small, and the occupational distributions they report are truncated, suggest a further cause of difference. For every industry but one in Table 6-1, we see that the Aldrich materials point to much greater gains than do the census figures. Taking groups I and II, we find that in these industries, for any one of which the Aldrich reports have data for only one or two firms, the Aldrich data lead to a 62 percent estimate of the 1860–1870 wage-rate increase, whereas the broader census data show a 37 percent gain.[50] And for cotton and woolen wage changes outside the

[48] Mitchell, *op. cit.*, pp. 187ff.
[49] Mitchell compares Western and Eastern medians, *op. cit.*, p. 192.
[50] We use the census weights to combine first the Long-Aldrich and then the census percent change figures for agricultural implements, carriages, leather, lumber, ale, and paper.

states shown in Table 6-2, the Census shows a 37 percent gain compared to 67 percent in the Aldrich data. If we combine these two categories, we cover roughly 430,000 out of the 884,000 in manufacturing in 1860, finding that for this large group the Aldrich materials imply about a 65 percent wage rise compared to the 37 percent indicated by Census.[51]

[51] The 1860 manufacturing total employment figure is the one used by Long, *op. cit.,* vol. III, p. 6.

7

OCCUPATIONAL EARNINGS:

1800 TO 1860

SEAMEN (TABLES A-21, A-22)

The estimates for earnings of seamen during the nineteenth century are based on an extended review of ships' articles and other records pertaining to individual voyages. The primary sources were ships' articles and portage bills in the collections of the Baker Library at the Harvard Business School (summarized in Table A-22A) and at the Essex Institute in Salem (summarized in Table A-22B). To these we have added some figures for individual voyages as reported in local histories, memoirs, and articles on particular ships. Our final series represents an attempt to make the best estimate for each year of earnings by able seamen in coasting or European voyages, or to China and the Pacific ports. Since the number of observations for individual years is limited, we cannot lay great stress on year-to-year changes. (They are nonetheless indicated to give some indication of the sensitivity of wages in this widely competitive and major labor market.)

I

Since primary reliance for the derivation of these tables is placed on the unpublished materials, a brief description of their character is desirable.

1. Commonest of these are the ships' articles. Signed by all members of the crew, these articles give the date signed aboard, the ship's destination, the monthly wages and occupation (or "quality") of each man. Frequently they also provide information on the total elapsed period of the voyage, the

term for which the men agreed to serve, as well as money advanced, etc. Although probably 95 percent of the articles used were standard printed forms, some were hand made but followed the usual format. (In a few instances, duration of voyage plus total wages reported for one man enabled translation of the total pay of others into monthly rates. Since desertions were common, however, such a translation could be used only rarely, and then when the amount of advances was clearly excluded.)

2. Next in frequency to the ships' articles was the portage (or portledge) bill, in which the crew members acknowledged the amount paid to them at the end of the voyages, this bill commonly reporting their monthly rate as well as the total due. (Where only the latter was reported, the portage bill could not be used since advances, deductions for clothing from the slop chest, etc., might have been made.)

3. In a number of instances the owners' records include bills submitted by shipping masters who assembled crews for them. Where the bills did not report the monthly rate but merely the advances made to each man, it was usually possible to go by the standard 2-month advance to deduce a monthly rate—checking, however, to see whether the result was consistent with other figures for the period.

4. A kaleidoscope of other records appear in the papers of owners and companies assembled in the Baker Library, which were of use on occasion. For example, a memorandum of account of the ship *Herald of Morning* with Captain William Winsor provides a figure for his salary circa 1870. Other materials include memoranda by captains of disbursements made by them, bills of advances, a statement filed with the United States Consul of the rates paid to deserters (to make possible the hiring of foreign sailors), etc.

II

The sources used for the individual figures in Table A-22 are listed below. For convenience the following letters will be used to indicate unpublished material from the Baker Library manuscript collection:

C   Captain Albert and Thomas Smith MSS 733, 1773–1814
D   Dexter collection
H   Hancock papers
I   Israel Thorndike papers
J   Brig *Jason* papers: MSS 766
L   Nathan Lord: shipping, 1788–1811
Ma   MSS 766: Ship *Marmion,* Accounts current
M   Magoun collection
MM   MSS 733: Miscellaneous
MN   MSS 733: Papers, Captain Nathaniel Adams
MS   MSS 733: Seamen's Wages

P   Perry and Sherman papers
PA   Ebenezer and Gorham Parsons, Shipping Papers, 1779 to 1829
T   Thomas E. Oliver papers
W   Wendell papers

The volume number of a group of papers is added directly after the above letters. Thus M2 indicates the second volume of the Magoun collection, D145 indicates the 145th volume of the Dexter collection, etc. Since each volume in turn has many file folders included, the folder is next briefly indicated wherever the name of the ship and date of voyage as given in the table are not sufficient to indicate which folder was used. For published volumes and articles a brief citation is given.

1795 to 1826. *Sch. Industry:*   H41 (For 1795 C also reports the ship *Argo* with three sailors receiving 7.4.0 and one, at 6.0.0. Such figures may be, but are not surely pounds, shillings, and pence or dollars per month. Conceivably they are dollars per week; the master's rate of 10.0.0 would compare with the $40 on the *industry*—but weekly rates are quoted nowhere else in the lengthy record.)

Brig Hitty: L.

Essex: Charles C. Bassett, "The Career of the Frigate Essex," *Essex Institute Historical Collections,* January, 1951.

Wonolancet: W. Ship *Wonolancet* Box Sch. *Betsey.*

Sch. Silvius: MN (The boys' rate of $8 argues that the handmade form used is a record of monthly wages, with the three seamen at $30 being A.B.'s and the two at $15, ordinary.)

Brig Jason: J. *Ship Horace, Brig Rover:* Edward Gray, *William Grey of Salem, Merchant* (1914), p. 63. (On the *Horace* one-half the seamen were listed at $20, one-half at $16. The captain's privilege was 5 tons of cargo, the mate's 30 cwt, the second mate's 20 cwt.)

Boat Jefferson: W. V-IIg-1, Ledger, 1810–1818, p. 36. Samuel Muchemore received "$33.15 for 2 m 11 wages on board." On page 42 Benjamin Randall is reported as a fisherman with a $20 rate, but Randall is elsewhere reported as captain.

Brig Henry: W. Jacob Wendell, Miscellaneous Ships, 1814–1864.

Sch. Favourite: MM.

Brig Nancy: MS. *Brig Lucy:* W. Brig *Lucy,* 1814–1836. *Brig Martha and Jane:* W.

Sch. McDonough: W. Jacob Wendell, Miscellaneous Ships, 1814–1864.

Ship Marmion: Ma. *Hodgson:* Adam Hodgson, *Letters from North America* (London, 1824) p. 87. Hodgson's rate is for Negro slaves hired out of Norfolk.

Sch. Olive Branch: T1. *Alling:* Elizabeth L. Alling, *The Sea Made Men, Memoirs of Captain Gorham Low* (1938), p. 29. Low also shipped in 1823 for $12 a month—presumably as an A.B., having turned down a second mate's position (p. 47). In 1826–1828 he sailed around the world as chief mate of a brig, receiving $28.

Brig Brutus: W. Jacob Wendell, Miscellaneous Ships, 1814–1864.

1827 to 1841. *Sch. Hope:* T1. *Meteor:* MS. *Yeaton:* W Box 5, Account Book: Wages (Paid Seamen), D. Yeaton Book.

Sch. Hiram, Adeline, Enterprise, Brig Lavinia: W. Box 23. U.S. Congress, Serial Set 373, 26th Cong., 1st Sess., House Report, *N.P. Trist, July 21, 1840,* p. 369: Pay of Seaman Boyce on Brig *Hyperion* out of Baltimore.

Brig Atlantic: W. Box 21, Brig *Atlantic,* Miscellaneous.

Ship California: D145. *Sch. Paramount:* T2. *Ship Timoleon:* M, Mss. 1819–1885 Ships, vol. 34. *Sch. Edward:* T2. *Ship Archimedes:* M2-3 (Memorandum Captain Gershom Winsor, Oct. 2, 1836). *Sch. Amelia:* T4. *Sch. Red Robin:* T2. *Sch. Equator:* T5. *Sch. Frances:* T3. *Sch. Miriam:* T3. *Sch. Armida:* T3. (In September, 1841, all crew members but the cook were share fishing.)

1842 to 1875. *Ship Medford 1842:* M34. "Philadelphia Shipping List," quoted in Addie C. Colman, *Captain Moses Rich Colman . . . 1807–1872* (1949), p. 5. September rates: $11 East Indies; $12 to $13 West Indies; $13 to $14 Coasting, and $14 to $15 Europe. *Sch. Governor, Albion, Kanawha:* T6. *Sch. Sarah:* P15. *Ship Jacob Perkins:* M2-4. *Brig Albert Perkins:* T7. *Sch. General Warren:* T7. *Ship Medford* 1850: Magoun Mss 1816–1879, vol. 2. *Ship Timoleon:* M35. *Ship Medford* (1851–1852): M2-2. *Ashbridge:* Market Report, J. H. Ashbridge, May 21, 1853, New Orleans, in MS. *Ship Medford* (October, 1853; November, 1854): M37. *Ship Herald of Morning* (1854): M2-5. (June, 1855): M38. (November, 1856; June, 1860): M38. (March, 1862–1865): M39. *Ship Electric Spark:* M34. *New York Post,* quoted in Addie C. Colman, *Captain Moses Rich Colman . . . 1807–1872* (1949), p. 105. New York to Liverpool, Havre, North Europe, $20; Mediterranean and South America, $16; West Indies, $18; East Indies and California, $15; Coasting, $20. *Ship Electric Spark* (1861ff): M44. *Ship Swallow* (1863): M2. (1864): M46. (1872): M47. *Ship Herald of Morning* (1866–1869): M40. (1870–1871): M41. (1872–1873): M42. (1874–1875): M43.

III

The data in Table A-22B are based on manuscript materials in the Essex Institute. In virtually all instances they were taken from the original ships' articles. In a few they derive from portage bills and other sources. The collections, and the ships for whose wages they were the source, were as follows: *Benjamin Pickman Papers,* vol. III: Coromandel, Derby; vol. IV: Hannah William, Henry; vol. V, Martha, John, Katy; vol. VI, Three Friends, Trader, Texel. *Kimball Papers,* Reward, Susannah, Mary. *Pingree Papers,* Hope, Pactolus, Rolla, William and Henry, Shawmut. *Derby Papers,* Peggy, Rose, Three Sisters. *Ship Borneo Accounts, John Gardner Ledger,* Moses, Talbot. *George H. Allen, Shipping Accounts,* Sooloo, Derby, Mindoro, Syren, Eliza Ann, Ocean Rover, Augustine Heard.

UNSKILLED LABOR: CANAL CONSTRUCTION

Two aspects of the rates quoted for canal construction must be noted initially. First, a margin over ordinary unskilled labor has long existed for labor where the work is particularly heavy and arduous. Canals were commonly put through marsh and swamp. Illness or death from malaria was a common hazard, anticipated by the men and recognized in the wage rate. Whisky was considered a specific for malaria and was provided in addition to money pay, but it hardly affected the death rate. Secondly, the figures quoted below are for both daily and monthly rates. As usual, the daily rates come to considerably more than 26 times the monthly rate. The causes are discussed in the section on uncertainty in the labor market (Chapter 5), but suffice it to state here that the difference recognized the greater instability of employment involved in jobs for brief periods rather than where a full 6- or 8-month stretch of work could be anticipated. (This qualification, of course, does not apply where the data relate to contractors' costs.)

1791. Though outside our period of review, we may note the 50-cent rate specified for laborers in planning the predecessor of the Erie Canal, in 1791.[1]

1790. For this year we have the rate paid during the construction of the first canal in the United States, the Middlesex Canal in Massachusetts. Laborers were paid $8 a month in 1790, and from $8 to $10 over the period of construction.[2]

---

[1] "The Report of a Committee Appointed to Explore the Western Waters in the State of New York," 1792. In E. B. O'Callaghan, *Documentary History of the State of New York* (Albany: Weeks, Parsons, and Co., 1850), vol. III, p. 1095. A 4-shilling rate is quoted. The New York shilling then ran eight to a dollar.

[2] Young, in *A Treatise on Internal Navigation* (Ballston Spa: U. F. Doubleday, 1817), p. 147, states that when the canal was begun in 1790 "the price of labor by the month was $8." In 1821, John L. Sullivan, then superintendent of the canal, wrote to DeWitt Clinton stating that in the construction of the canal, "labor at that time was low. Common men had from $8 to $10 a month." Quoted in *Public Documents Relating to the New York Canals . . . Printed under the Direction of the New York Corresponding Association for the Promotion of Internal Improvements* (New York: William A. Mercein, 1821), p. 230.

1800 to 1804.   We are fortunate in having actual payroll records of the Middlesex Canal construction for this period,[3] showing the following figures:

1800		$10
1801		10
1802		10
1803	Jan–May	10
	June	13
	July–Dec	14
1804		14

The most interesting aspect of these figures is the stability for more than 3 years and the sharp break in May, 1803, when continental power politics affected American wages as England and France renewed their war.

1806.   For this year a laborer hired to work on the Amoskeag Canal in Massachusetts received $14 for his work. "Boarding himself," he also received the value of board (and presumably lodging) at $12.80 a month.[4]

1817.   A pair of single-minded citizens, waiting for neither state nor Federal assistance, built a canal in Genessee County, New York, in 1816. The cost of labor, for four equivalent man-years, ran to 62½ cents a day, plus "subsistence for men at 16 shillings per week, the common price for boarding," i.e., 33⅓ cents per working day.[5]

1826.   The end of wartime prosperity appears in the decline in wages from the $14 paid on the Middlesex Canal to the rates paid on the Pennsylvania Canal in 1826. Thomas Encock states that "our contracts on the western section of the Pennsylvania Canal" provide for laborers, per month of 26 working days, deducting lost time by reason of bad weather, at from $7 to $8 per month.[6] A. Lacock, building a canal on the Allegheny at this time, stated that he was paying $8.50 and "found." [7] The basis on which

[3] Theophilus Manning, *Middlesex Canal Accounts, Payrolls, 1799–1810,* in Baker Library Manuscripts, file folder, Water Transport.

[4] Loamni Baldwin Papers, vol. 16, "Amoskeag Canal, Wage Receipts, 1804–1805." Baker Library Manuscripts, "Receipts to Proprietors of the Blodget Canal at Amoskeag Falls, Joshua Baldwin, September 1806." "Board" for 18 days, $7.68.

[5] Letter of Matthew and Francis Brown, Jan. 1, 1817, in *The Official Reports of the Canal Commissioners of the State of New York and the Acts of the Legislature* (New York: T. and W. Mercein, 1817). "Teams labour" is specified at 50 cents. Subsistence for teams at 16 shillings is noted in the letter reprint in New York State, *Report of the Board of Commissioners on the Northern Champlain Canal* (1817), p. 28.

[6] Letter of Nov. 30, 1826, printed in *Proceedings of the Chesapeake and Ohio Canal Convention, November 6, 1823 . . . December 6, 1826* (Washington City: Way and Gideon, 1827), p. 90. The Encock letter is reprinted directly and is assumed to be more reliable than a letter referred to on p. 93 stating that on the Western Pennsylvania Canal common day labor received $15 a month.

[7] *Ibid.,* p. 89.

the Canal Convention, summarizing all this material, concluded that labor on the Ohio and on the Pennsylvania Canals was being paid 40 cents a day is presumably the addition of food at the common rate of 50 percent of pay, making $8.50 pay and $12 total wages.[8] Finally, we must note the beginnings of the impact on wages that the growing number of canals under construction was having, in the form of higher wages on one of the newest canals, the Chesapeake and Ohio: Committees sent by the Convention "along the route of the Chesapeake and Ohio Canal . . . during the last summer" found prevailing rates to be 50 cents or, at 26 days, $13 a month.[9]

Two sources unconnected with the report quoted above may also be noted for this year. The *Ohio Civil Engineer and Herald* of August, 1828, cited Ohio canal rates for 1826 at $8 a month.[10] And Matthew Carey refers to "Irish laborers in canals and turnpikes" in Pennsylvania receiving 75 cents a day, with their board coming to $2 a week.[11]

1827. A plan prepared by the United States Engineers in 1827 for a canal to connect the Mississippi with Lake Ponchartrain estimated laborers' wages at $1.25 a day, apparently exclusive of board.[12]

1828. A contemporary report on the Ohio states that "50,000 hands are said to be employed on the Pennsylvania Canal; and more laborers are in demand at from $12 to $15 per month." [13]

1829. Nathan Roberts, well-known engineer of the Second Division of the Chesapeake and Ohio Canal, estimated in September of this year labor "for digging tunnels where required" to run $1 a day, with 50 cents for board and other subsistence.[14]

A no less authoritative source is to be found in a letter from the President of the Chesapeake and Ohio Canal Company to his emigration agent

---

[8] *Ibid.*, p. 67.

[9] *Ibid.*, p. 67.

[10] Quoted in E. L. Bogart, *Internal Improvements and the State Debt in Ohio* (1924), pp. 24–25.

[11] Matthew Carey, *Reflections on the Subject of Emigration from Europe* (Philadelphia: 1826), p. 22. Carey contrasts this rate with the 75-cent to $1 rate paid to country laborers.

[12] U.S. National Archives, War Department Archives, in R.G. 77, Office of the Chief of Engineers, 1818–1831, *Report: Plan and Estimate of a Canal Destined to Connect the Mississippi with Lake Ponchartrain* (Mar. 1, 1827). This report to General Bernard does not specify cost of subsistence separately, while those noted below for 1829–1830 all do. It is therefore assumed that the cost of subsistence is included in the $1.25.

[13] John Kilbourn, *Public Documents concerning the Ohio Canals* (Columbus: I. N. Whiting, 1832), p. 129, reprinting the *Ohio Civil Engineer and Herald* for Aug. 16, 1828.

[14] *Chesapeake and Ohio Canal*, 22nd Cong., 1st Sess., House Doc. 18 (Dec. 19, 1831).

in Europe, wherein he states: "I wish to reduce the price of labor on the Canal to $10 per month of 26 working days. It is now $12 and $13 a month." [15]

1830. For 1829–1830 we benefit from surveys by the U.S. Board of Internal Improvements giving the cost of harbor improvements desired by various localities. They indicate for February, 1829, a rate for dredging the Roanoke Inlet of $12 to $15 a month; $12 for work near Cape Fear in North Carolina, for November of that year; and $15 for deepening the harbor at Pensacola, at the same date.[16] A similar estimate for work on Sag Harbor, New York, in February, 1830, sets a $12 figure.[17] The money-wage figures estimated for common labor, and the corresponding subsistence rates, were as follows:

Location	Wages	Subsistence
Sag Harbor.........	$12	$6
Roanoke...........	12, 15	6
Cape Fear.........	12	8
Pensacola.........	15	8

1831. Joseph McIlvaine, Secretary to the Pennsylvania Board of Canal Commissioners, queried by the indefatigable, ubiquitous student of the period, Matthew Carey, wrote to him in February, 1831. In the wintertime canal labor might, he said, expect to receive $5 a month and food, sometimes only food. In the busier periods a $10 to $12 average might be expected. "Contractors in making their calculations set down 70 to 75 cents a day for each man employed, including wages and food. This would give $12 a month as average wages." [18] If we take a 26-day working month and deduct, say, 2 days for bad weather, a 72½-cent rate gives $17.40. In other words, a rate of about $12 for wages and $6 for food and liquor was envisaged.

[15] U.S. National Archives, *Letterbook of the Chesapeake and Ohio Canal Company*, p. 84, Mercer to Richards, July 8, 1829. A somewhat lower figure—of $10 to $12—is estimated for November, 1828, in the excellent study of the canal company by Walter Sanderlin, *The Great National Project* (1946), p. 71.

[16] U.S. National Archives, War Department Archives, Board of Internal Improvements, Topographical Engineers Reports, Dec. 1, 1827 to June 9, 1831. *Report on the Survey of Roanoke Inlet and Sound* (Feb. 12, 1829). Four hands at $15 and six at $12 were indicated. *Report: Examination of Cape Fear below Wilmington* (Nov. 7, 1829); *Report: Deepening the Water over the Bar at the Entrance of the Harbour of Pensacola* (Dec. 6, 1829).

[17] U.S. National Archives, War Department Archives, in RG 77, Office of the Chief of Engineers, 1818–1831. *Report of the Survey of Sag Harbor* by Hartman Bache, Captain Topographical Engineers.

[18] Quoted in Matthew Carey, *Appeal to the Wealthy of the Land* (Philadelphia: L. Johnson, 1833), p. 9. The same source is utilized in Thomas Brothers, *The United States of North America as They Are* (London: 1840), p. 387.

1833. Abdy quotes a newspaper advertisement of May 24, 1833, by contractors seeking laborers to work on the Muscle Shoals Canal for $15 a month, the contractors alternatively being willing to hire Negroes by the year.[19]

1839. As the national canal fever was abating, work began on the James River and Kanawha Company Canal. The company offered contractors $1.30 a day in July, 1839, for men to work "in the heat and dangerous area near the falls." None were willing to accept the offer because "in the early part of July some fifteen or twenty of the Irishmen suddenly expired under the intensity of the heat." [20] It is obvious that the figure offered must have been well above the customary one. By how much? One indication lies in the study in which the chief engineer of the company anticipated much that was to make Cournot famous at a later date. In that study Ellet, estimating the costs of operation of a railway line to be used for transshipment from the canal, suggests that the line would require 80 men at $1 a day.[21]

1800 to 1850. Can we summarize the above data to indicate the major changes in rates paid for labor on canal construction? As a rough indication, let us consider the following, given the realization that the locus of canal construction was shifting ever south and westward from its start in Massachusetts and New York.

For 1790 an $8 rate is indicated, this (as other rates to be quoted below) exclusive of board except where specified. From the same Massachusetts data a rate of $10 from 1800 through mid-1803 appears, with a rise to $14 from 1804 to 1806. For 1826 we have a monthly rate of $8 (Ohio), $7 to $8 and $8.50 (Pennsylvania). The value of board is indicated at $3.50 for Pennsylvania, if we deduct the $8.50 rate from the 40-cent daily average times 24 days. For the Chesapeake and Ohio Canal a similar derivation from a 50-cent rate suggests perhaps a higher $9 rate required in securing manpower for the newest canal to be put under construction.

For 1829 to 1831 a $12 to $13 rate prevailed for the Chesapeake and Ohio (Mercer's letter), for the Pennsylvania canals (McIlvaine's letter), and for New York and North Carolina dredging (Board of Internal Improvements Reports). Associated with these rates was board valued at about $6. As a parallel indication of rates of change, we may take the daily rates, which rose from 62½ cents (33⅓ cents for board) for New York in 1817, to 75 cents (33 cents for board) cost per working day for the

[19] E. S. Abdy, *Journal of a Residence and Tour in the United States of North America from April 1833 to October 1834* (London: 1835), vol. II, p. 109.

[20] *Fourth Annual Report of the President to the Stockholders of the James River and Kanawha Company* (Richmond: Shepherd and Colin, Printers, 1839), p. 33.

[21] Charles Ellet, Jr., *An Essay on the Laws of Trade* (Richmond: P. D. Bernard, 1839), p. 261.

Pennsylvania canals in 1826, to $1 (50 cents for board) for the Chesapeake and Ohio canal in 1829. The historian of this period in Pennsylvania reports rates rising from 75 cents in 1833 to 80 cents in 1836, and to $1 in 1837 and 1840.[22]

Despite the self-seeking aspects of Chesapeake and Ohio's President Mercer's justifications, we may take as a helpful confirmation his reference to "competitions for labor, by which its costs to the contractors was augmented, after the first contracts, in 1828, more than 30 percent." [23]

MINERS (TABLE A-20)

From 1800 to 1860, and particularly in the decades before 1840, American miners were typically entrepreneurs or contractors, who dug the ore and paid the mineowners a fixed share of their ore or returns. Therefore the importance of mining wages in an overall wage series is trivial. At the same time the trend in earnings open to men in such pursuits should be a useful measure of alternative wage opportunities available to the wage earner. We have something like a reliable benchmark for 1832, and yearly full-time equivalent earnings beginning with the Census of 1860. From the scanty materials outlined below, we have derived in Table 7-1 the suggestive measure of wage trends in the mining industries to link with census data from 1860 on:

Table 7-1. Preliminary Estimates of Mining Wages, 1811–1860

Year	United States	Pennsylvania	Region
1811	$12 monthly		Missouri lead mines
1817		$1.20 daily	Pennsylvania mines
1822	15 monthly		Chicago coal mines
1832	0.85 daily		U.S. average
1840		1 daily, 16 monthly	Pennsylvania coal
	0.85 daily		U.S. average
1850		0.87 daily	Pennsylvania coal
	1.20 daily		U.S. average
1860		1.25 daily	Pennsylvania coal
	1 daily, $275 full-time equivalent		U.S. average

[22] William A. Sullivan, *The Industrial Worker in Pennsylvania, 1800–1840* (1955), p. 73. In addition to these rates, intended as comparable, Sullivan reports other data on pages 30, 33, 152, etc., for other dates in the decade, confirming the general level but difficult to use in establishing a trend.

[23] *Chesapeake and Ohio Canal Company,* 22d Cong., 2d Sess., Serial Set 234, Doc. 93 (Jan. 14, 1833).

Allowing for the growth and concentration of the industry, a speculative United States average from these very unsatisfactory materials would be:

Table 7-2.

Year	Monthly	Daily
1811	$12	$0.90
1817		1.20
1822	15	
1832	15	0.85
1840		0.85
1850		1.20
1860		1.00

The trend shown is an attempt to reflect (1) the initial growth in wages with the growth of the industry; (2) a following decline in daily (but not monthly) rates as steadier work began to be available from the larger industry; (3) a net stability for 1832 to 1840 (a rise in the early years and a decline after the recession of 1837); (4) the feverish rise in 1849–1850 with the discovery of gold; and (5) the decline back to less antic levels by 1860.

1811.   A highly speculative estimate can be hazarded for this date from some figures in Brackenridge's contemporary study.[1] Given his figure of $40 to $50 a ton of ore, Schoolcraft's hundredweight a day average per miner, and several figures of a 40 percent share to miners, we compute a daily return of, say, $1.60 to $2 for lead miners near St. Louis.[2]

1816.   From a reliable contemporary review, in *American State Papers,* we have a report for the largest mine in the St. Louis area, then paying a woodchopper at $15 a month and log furnacemen at $22—with a miner's income more likely to be similar to the former than the latter figure.[3]

1817.   Fearon reports miners in Pennsylvania making from $1.13 to $1.32 in October, 1817.[4]

[1] H. M. Brackenridge, *Views of Louisiana* (Baltimore: Schaeffer and Maund, 1817), p. 125, describes lead production in 1811, by the mines at the Ouisconsing on the Mississippi above Prairie du Chien. We assume that his later discussion of the mines at St. Genevieve is for the same date.

[2] Brackenridge's ore price is from his p. 261. Schoolcraft's figure is from *American State Papers, Public Lands,* vol. III, p. 663, and vol. IV, p. 558. That the miner received 800 pounds of lead for each ton of ore is indicated in *Ibid.,* vol. III, p. 700; vol. IV, p. 557. From Brackenridge, *op. cit.,* p. 267, we can compute only 4,333 pounds a man-year but nothing like a full year was worked, part of the year being devoted to farming.

[3] *American State Papers, Public Lands,* vol. III, p. 703.

[4] Henry Fearon, *Narrative of a Journey* (1818), p. 203. We convert his estimate from shillings by the ratio of $14 = 63 shillings on his p. 172. Because of the variety

1822. In connection with the operation of one of its Indian factories in Chicago, the Federal government hired a collier at $15, or the same rate as it paid a laborer in Fort Wayne.[5]

1826. Lead miners earned about $1.60 a day in the center of the industry near St. Louis. We deduce this from contemporary reports on output per miner, and the miner's share.[6]

1832. Because of the concentration of the mining industry of the time in Pennsylvania, as an adjunct to iron manufacturing, we have a tolerable basis for estimate by taking the various data from the McLane report that indicate what manufacturers paid colliers. These figures clearly suggest a $1 a day average.[7] The figure is the same as the $1 a day for 1831 recorded in the Congress (by Representative Ramsey) and in the depths of Pottsville, Pennsylvania, by the associate editor of the *Miner's Journal*.[8] A $1 a day was also reported for the Pennsylvania and Delaware Coal Company in 1832 by Representative Chapman of Maryland.[9]

For marble and copper mining in Vermont, rates of 60 cents a day and board, or an equivalent of 75 cents, are indicated.[10] For Southern gold

---

of exchange rates in use, we are interested not in a "true" rate, but in the one he apparently used.

[5] *American State Papers, Indian Affairs,* vol. II, p. 403.

[6] *General Operations and History of Lead Mines in Missouri,* 19th Cong., 1st Sess., Doc. 501 (1826). Lieutenant Thomas, in charge of mining leases for the United States, agrees with Schoolcraft's figure of miners raising a hundredweight of ore per day throughout the year on an average (p. 558). He notes that miners are paid to the value of 800 pounds of lead for each ton of ore delivered (p. 557) and finds, therefore, "this would be $2.25" a day (i.e., 40 pounds times the prevailing 5- to 5¼-cent rate). Then he adds: but let us estimate $1 a day "throughout the year." From *American State Papers, Public Lands,* vol. III, p. 700, we have an 1822 figure of 4 cents a pound, leading to $1.60. New York pig-lead prices were pretty much unchanged for 1819 to 1826. *Historical Statistics,* vol. II, p. 370. We take 4 cents times 40 pounds to give $1.60—a compromise between Lieutenant Thomas's high and low.

[7] *Documents Relative to the Manufactures in the United States,* 22d Cong., 1st Sess., Exec. Doc. 308 (1833). Colliers' rates from vol. I include New York, "near $1" (p. 108); Pennsylvania, $1 (p. 479); and $1 to $1.50 (p. 493) paid colliers for saltworks and $16 a month, consistent with a daily rate of $1 (p. 528). Three New Jersey reports for all employees in two ironworks explicitly relate to all employees inclusive of colliers and woodchoppers (pp. 186, 190, 192). One is $1 a day and the other 8 shillings (presumably New York shillings at 12½ cents). An all-employee average for such firms would reflect primarily the miner and woodchopper rate, since usually one-third or less of the employees were forgemen or skilled hands.

[8] *Congressional Globe,* appendix, June 19, 1846; Ele Bowen, *The Coal Regions of Pennsylvania* (Pottsville: E. N. Carvalho, 1848), p. 60.

[9] Representative Chapman in *Register of Debates,* Aug. 1, 1846.

[10] *McLane Report,* vol. I, pp. 879, 889, 893, 895. Annual earnings of $180, $180, and $192 to $216 suggest a daily rate computed from multiplying 300 days by 60 cents. A $5 a week board valuation is explicitly added to the earnings figure for the copper mines.

mines at the time a daily average of $1.75 can be surmised on the basis of a contemporary report for South Carolina.[11] And a 75 cent rate for New Jersey iron mining is likewise reported.[12]

We take the concentration of $1 rates in Pennsylvania as applying to mining in that state in general, while a 75 cent figure is used for mining in other states. Given the distribution of mining employees by state in 1840, we conclude for a United States average of 85 cents.[13]

1840.   The Pennsylvania miners' rate may have risen somewhat prior to the 1837 recession. In 1837 it was estimated that miners could take out from 100 to 120 bushels a day, at 1 cent a bushel, in a Frostburg mine.[14] The scanty band of gold miners in North Carolina in 1837 included slaves and white miners—the latter receiving 50 cents a day and maintaining themselves.[15] But by 1840 the coal miners' rate was down to 87½ cents in Pennsylvania.[16] We assume a United States rate of 85 cents—implicitly stipulating some rise in the regions outside Pennsylvania as mining developed there in growing competition with Pennsylvania.

1850.   By this year the range of wages paid to miners had widened greatly. By mid-1850 the typical gold miner in California had come down from gold-rush levels to $4 to $6 a day, while laborers on the Sacramento levee, doing work of similar character, were receiving $75 a month and board.[17]

Iron mining, on the shores of Lake Superior, was presumed to cost $1.60 a day for miners.[18] A New Jersey coal mine reported a rise of 20 percent

[11] *Assay Offices, Gold Districts of North Carolina and Georgia,* U.S. Congress, Serial Set 210, Report 82, p. 29, quotes a letter by James Blair, Feb. 2, 1831, from the capital with respect to a mine in Chesterfield where the hands "realize from $1½ to $3 each day," their share being "two-thirds or three-fourths." On p. 24, $2.50 a day raised per hand in Georgia is estimated.

[12] 1880 Census, *Statistics of Wages,* p. 114.

[13] Employees reported as in iron, lead, gold mines, coal, granite, marble, and stone, 1840 Census, *Compendium* (1841), pp. 358–359.

[14] *Report of the Examination and Survey of the Coal Fields and Iron Ore Belonging to the Boston and New York Coal Company at Frostburg, Maryland* (New York: B. Clayton, 1837), p. 18.

[15] G. W. Featherstonhaugh, *A Canal Voyage up the Minnay Sotor* (London, 1847), vol. II, p. 332.

[16] Bowen, *loc. cit.* A $1 rate is quoted by Representative Ramsey, of Pennsylvania, in *Congressional Globe,* appendix (June 19, 1846). Both Ramsey and Bowen estimate 87 cents for 1842. We assume that a decline under the impact of the 1837–1839 recession was more likely than not. Perhaps, too, Bowen was a better witness, closer to the source.

[17] For the day rate, see John Hale, *California as It Is* (reprint, 1954) p. 260; *The Shirley Letters,* p. 34; Lorenzo Sawyer, Chief Justice of the Supreme Court of California, *Way Sketches* (1926), p. 113; Kenneth Bjork, *West of the Great Divide* (1958), pp. 56, 62; Ulla S. Fawkes (ed.), *The Journal of Walter Griffith Pigman* (1942), p. 37.

[18] *Report of the Directors and Superintendent of the Albion Mining Company*

from 1840 to 1850 (from 70 to 85 cents).[19] Our best overall figure, however, must derive from the Census of 1850, which gives a full-time equivalent figure of $269 for coal mining.[20] Assuming that most gold miners were
self-employed, the largest bulk of wage earners in mining would then have
been employed in coal mines or in nearby labor-market areas. Now since
the United States coal-mining average in 1860 was virtually identical—at
$264—we assume the same proportion of the year employed in both
years, from which we derive a $1.20 daily rate.[21] This rate is roughly con-
firmed by the $1.25 paid in 1846 and 1847 in Pennsylvania coal mines,
according to Bowen.[22] It is also virtually the same as the daily rate paid
to the small group employed in Michigan copper mines.[23]

1860.   For the coal-mining industry a United States full-time equivalent
figure of $264 can be derived from the census.[24] We associate this with a
daily rate of $1, based on some scanty reports.[25] The implicit 9½ months'
work is not an unreasonable figure.

The census gives a full-time equivalent figure of $352 for copper mining,
of $284 for iron.[26] Much of total copper and iron mining was centered in
Michigan and nearby states. Some 70 percent of copper miners were employed in Michigan alone.[27] We have a single daily-rate figure of $1.35
for Michigan iron mining in 1860, and 75 cents for New Jersey.[28] With

---

(New York: Van Orden and Amerman, 1853), p. 8. The report projects the cost
of mine operation, 36 miners 1 year for $18,000. We assume an implicit work year
of about 300 days.

[19] 1880 Census, *Report on the Statistics of Wages in Manufacturing Industries . . .*
by Joseph Weeks (1886), p. 114.

[20] 1902 *Census of Mineral Industries,* p. 665.

[21] BLS Bulletin 449, p. 330, gives a $1.16 figure for coal in Pennsylvania coal
mining, which was divided into the United States $264 to give time worked.

[22] Bowen (*op. cit.*) gives a $1 rate for 1848. We assume that the discovery of
California gold brought miners' rates in the East back up from 1848 to at least 1847
levels.

[23] A monthly rate of $30 in 1845 and $33 in 1853, derived from contemporary
materials, is estimated by William G. Gates, Jr., *Michigan Copper and Boston Dollars* (1951), p. 101. At 26 working days, a $1.20 figure for 1850 is likely.

[24] 1902 Census, *Mines and Quarries,* p. 665.

[25] The *Weeks Report* gives rates of 80 cents for miners in Hokendaqua, Pennsylvania (p. 254), and 85 cents in New Jersey (p. 114). On the other hand, BLS Bulletin 499 (p. 330) reports $1.16 for the state in general. Instead of the near 90-cent
average of these three nonrandom reports, we rely on a statement by Representative
Kerr of Pennsylvania (*Congressional Globe,* appendix, Nov. 1, 1867, p. 135) that
miners earned $2 in 1867 and wages had risen about 100 percent during the war.

[26] 1902 Census, *Mines and Quarries,* pp. 469, 395. David A. Wells, in *Report of
the Special Commissioner of Internal Revenue for 1868,* 40th Cong., 3d Sess., House
Exec. Doc. 16 (1868–1869), p. 13, reports copper-mining wages up 100 percent for
1860 to 1866; or the same as Kerr reported for miners in general.

[27] 1902 Census, *Mines and Quarries,* pp. 469, 483.

[28] BLS Bulletin 499, p. 330, for Michigan, and *Weeks Report,* p. 114, for New
Jersey.

iron mining having the same annual figure as coal, can we credit the BLS Michigan daily rate 35 percent above the coal rate? Since the BLS data are questionable where they can be checked, it is desirable to test this report. We do so by deriving an estimate of monthly mining rates of $27 in Michigan at the time.[29] Such a monthly rate would give the more reasonable figure of about $1 a day.[30]

1866 to 1867.   Just past the peak point of war-inflated wages, we have reports on mining wages from a number of contemporaries. Lake Superior copper mining, wrote one on the basis of his "25 years experience," offered miners' wages of $2 a day in 1866–1867.[31] Since the major Quincy mine in that area was then paying $53 a month and a 26-day month was typical, we find the two quite consistent.[32] In November, 1867, Representative Kerr of Pennsylvania stated that miners then earned $2 a day, wages having doubled since 1860.[33] On the other hand, iron miners outside the main centers appear to have earned markedly less.[34] For coal miners in 1866 in Pennsylvania the BLS report also quotes $2—with a drastic fall in 1867 to $1.79 (presumably under the impact of the new tariff on Nova Scotia coal) rising to $2.50 in 1868, and to $2.59 by 1870.[35] As with other BLS data, the level of these figures seems somewhat high.[36]

Coal-mining Wages (Table A-20)

Annual.   For 1850ff. the census provides employment and wage figures, these being used to compute annual earnings figures except for 1902, when the census data are useless for this purpose.[37]

[29] Wells (*loc. cit.*) reports copper wages up 100 percent from 1860 to 1866. (The gain is the same as the 1860 to 1867 rise reported by Representative Kerr.) Since copper mining was then centered in Michigan, we may take this as an estimate of the change in Michigan iron wages and apply it to an 1866 Michigan copper average of $53. The latter is for the Quincy Mining Company as reported in the 1902 Census, *Mines and Quarries*, p. 484.

[30] The same BLS citation gives a $2.25 rate for 1870, as contrasted with a $46 monthly figure for a major Michigan producer in that year. (1902 Census, *Mines and Quarries*.)

[31] Ovando J. Hollister, *The Mines of Colorado* (Springfield: Samuel Bowles, 1867), pp. 343–344. Hollister outlines the present costs of mining, using for reference his experience with the copper mines.

[32] The Quincy rates are quoted in Horace J. Stevens, *The Copper Handbook* (1903), vol. III, p. 459.

[33] Kerr, *loc. cit.*

[34] The Weeks Report, pp. 114, 254, gives figures of $1.50 for mines in Pennsylvania and New Jersey. Both firms, however, reported a near doubling since 1860.

[35] BLS Bulletin 499, p. 330.

[36] Weeks, *op. cit.* p. 239, reports authoritatively on wages paid by month from 1869 to 1880, and his 1870 average is $11.46 a week, or $2.

[37] Data in 1902 Census, *Mines and Quarries*, p. 395. The 1902 Census did not publish actual employment figures but only a synthetic employee total—for 300-day equivalent employees. Hence, division of wages by employment simply gives the daily rate times 300. *Ibid.*, p. 1122.

Daily. Daily rates for 1889 and 1902 are from the census.[38] For 1870 and 1880 we have the weekly data from the Weeks report.[39] We extrapolate the 1870 figure to 1860 by a regression of the series for the labor cost of coal per ton of pig iron on daily wages, since the two series are closely related over the years from 1869 to 1880.[40] For 1850 we rely on a combination of contemporary estimates.[41] For 1840 we use a near-contemporary estimate.[42] For 1830 we take the $1 figure estimated by three writers in the 1840s.[43] For 1817 we take the midpoint of Fearon's contemporary range.[44]

Iron-mining Wages (Table A-20)

Annual. Annual earnings data for 1850ff. are available from the census.[45] For 1840 we estimate a level 10 percent below 1850 on the basis of daily-rate figures for iron mining in New Jersey and New York, and coal mining in Pennsylvania, which was then the leading iron-mining state.[46]

Daily. Daily rates for 1889 and 1902 are from the census.[47] For 1880 we have a figure of $2 for Lake Superior—then the center of the industry —adjusted to United States levels by the 1889 ratio of one rate to the other.[48]

[38] 1890 Census, p. 350. 1902 Census, pp. 673, 679.

[39] *Weeks Report*, p. 239, divided by 6.

[40] Cost data pertain to anthracite pig iron at a furnace in eastern Pennsylvania; they appear on p. 111 in the Weeks report, while the wage data are from p. 239.

[41] A series in BLS Bulletin 499, p. 330, reports $1.16 for Pennsylvania coal mining in 1845 and 1850. For 1846 we have two estimates of $1.25 for Pennsylvania miners: Ramsey, *op. cit.*, p. 710. Bowen, *op. cit.*, p. 60. We combine these to average $1.20.

[42] We take Ramsey's estimate (made in 1846) rather than Bowen's, for Ramsey's series shows an 1840 to 1842 decline, as do anthracite prices, whereas Bowen's series does not.

[43] Ramsey, *op. cit.* Bowen, *op. cit.* Representative Chapman of Maryland, *op. cit.*, reported a $1 rate for the Delaware and Hudson Coal Company miners.

[44] Fearon (*loc. cit.*) gives a range of 31 shillings 6 pence to 36 shillings per week; we take the midpoint and convert by $14 equals 63 shillings, from his p. 172.

[45] 1902 Census, *Mines and Quarries,* p. 395.

[46] New Jersey rates appear in the *Weeks Report,* p. 114, and BLS Bulletin 499, pp. 333–334, the latter including a New York series as well. For Pennsylvania, see the previous discussion on coal mining.

[47] 1902 Census, pp. 402, 679, 673. 1890 Census, vol. VII, *Report on Mineral Industries,* p. 17.

[48] *Report of the Tariff Commission,* 47th Cong., 2d Sess., House Misc. Doc. 6, part 1, pp. 122–123, quotes payroll data for the 788 employees of the Lake Superior Iron Company and the Republic Iron Company in 1882. This was raised 10 percent to an 1880 level (by the ratio of pig-iron prices) and adjusted by the ratio of the Michigan to the United States iron-miners' wage rate, the latter from the 1890 Census, p. 18.

Copper-mining Wages (Table A-20)

Annual. Decennial census reports for annual earnings are available from 1860 on. In 1850, at the very beginning of the industry, Michigan produced 88 percent of all copper.[49] Because of the close links between mining and manufacturing, we take wages in Michigan copper mining as equal to those in Michigan copper manufacturing—$375. (The two are within 2 percent of each other in 1870.)[50] The result is close to 12 times Gates's 1853 figure.

Monthly. We have monthly earnings figures from 1864 on for the major Quincy mine in the Lake Superior area.[51] The representativeness of the latter series for showing trends prior, say, to 1890 is suggested by two bits of evidence. For 1889 the daily rate for mines in Michigan according to the census is $1.90, which comes to $49.40 for a 26-day month.[52] The Quincy average is $49.15. For 1890, however, the United States average is higher, because of the growing importance of Montana and other Western states. In 1867 an experienced mining writer estimated $2 a day in the Lake Superior copper mines; at 26 days this comes to $52, compared to the Quincy figure of $53.16.[53] For 1860 we use an estimate derived by William Gates of $33, which, compared to the annual average of $352, implies an 11-month work year.[54] For 1850 we have a monthly estimate for the North American Mine.[55] As the richness of the area became apparent, mining expanded rapidly and higher wages were paid, apparently reaching the 1860 level by 1853.[56]

---

[49] For comparative production figures, see Charles Van Hise and C. K. Leith, *The Geology of the Lake Superior Region,* U.S. Geological Survey Monographs (1911), p. 30.

[50] 1850 *Abstract of Manufactures,* p. 42. 1870 Census, *Industry and Trade,* pp. 429, 762.

[51] Horace J. Stevens, *The Copper Handbook* (1903), vol. III, pp. 458–459.

[52] 1890 Census, *Mineral Industries,* p. 156.

[53] The $2 rate is from Hollister, *op. cit.,* p. 343. We assume his rate applies to the prior year, though the 1866 figure is similar.

[54] Gates, *loc. cit.*

[55] J. W. Foster and J. D. Whitney, *Report on the Geology, and Topography of a Portion of the Lake Superior Land District,* 31st Cong., 1st Sess., House Doc. 69, p. 132. We weight their figures for miners at $24 and surface men at $20.

[56] In the year ending May, 1854, the North West Company paid surface hands and mechanics $21.12 a month, clear, while miners received $30.46. *The Mining Journal* (October, 1854), p. 426. The same source shows the Copper Falls Co. paying miners $34.58 in the prior year and notes current rates of $26 to $28 for ordinary surface labor. The issue for September, 1853 (p. 293), quotes the *Detroit Advertiser* as finding surface men receiving $1 a day on the average when employed by the month, with contract miners paid so as to average "about $35 per month," from which, of course, fuses, powder, and similar costs had to be deducted.

Lead-mining Wages (Table A-20)

Annual. Annual earnings for lead miners are taken from the censuses for 1870, 1880, 1902.[57]

Daily. For 1811 a daily rate of $1.60 to $2 was computed on the basis of Brackenridge's contemporary ore price of $20 to $25 for 1,000 pounds.[58] Relying on an independent estimate of 4 cents a pound as the price of lead for the 1800–1820 period generally, we estimate a mining-wage figure of $1.60.[59] With the same price and proportion maintaining in 1826, we arrive at the same $1.60. For 1816 we take the $15 a month rate paid to a woodchopper at the largest mine in St. Louis, although the miners' rate is likely to have been somewhat greater.[60]

For 1870ff. data are available for the St. Joseph Lead Company, a key producer in the Missouri area where the industry was centered for so long.[61]

BOATMEN

Boatmen were not readily distinguishable in their character, attainments, or skills from common labor. Their wage rates do not therefore report trends in a noncompeting market. However, the duration of their employment and its limited character enables us to be somewhat clearer about what it is that is being paid for than if we deal merely with quotations for common labor.

1795. Michaux quotes a $1 a day rate for boatmen to ascend the Cheraquis in Tennessee—perhaps the earliest example we shall report of that ubiquitous $1 quotation for day labor that runs through much of the nineteenth century.[1]

---

[57] These data are summarized in the 1902 Census, p. 445. No figures are available for 1890.

[58] Brackenridge, *op. cit.,* Schoolcraft, *op. cit.,* and *American State Papers, Public Lands.*

[59] Arthur Winslow, *Lead and Zinc Deposits,* Missouri Geological Survey (1894), vol. VI, p. 276, estimates a 4-cent price, with 2 cents to the diggers. He does not give his source, but on p. 279 refers to Schoolcraft's $2.25 a day and Lieutenant Thomas's "fair average" for the year of $1.

[60] For details on the 1816 figures, see *American State Papers, Public Lands,* vol. III, p. 703. For 1826, see footnote 6 above.

[61] These appear in Walter Renton Ingalls, *Lead and Zinc in the United States* (1908), p. 236. We use Ingalls's figures for back hands as being comparable to the earlier rates, since his figure for 1890 to 1893 is identical with the all-employees daily rate as given in the 1890 Census, *Mineral Industries,* p. 167, though above the census reports a $1.13 rate for miners alone.

[1] F. A. Michaux, *Travels* (1805; reprint 1904), Reuben G. Thwaites (ed.), *Early Western Travels,* vol. III, p. 74.

1805.   In his travels in Louisiana, M. Claude Robin noted that the French Canadian "engages" hired as boatmen, received, on the average, $1, including the value of their food.[2]

Collot, Governor of Guadeloupe, traveling through Louisiana at a slightly later date, also reports a $1 figure.[3]

1806.   Following the traditional course of seeking help from the government, the Chesapeake and Delaware Canal Company petitioned the Commonwealth of Pennsylvania in 1806. In the process it estimated the advantages of their proposed canal, finding that the costs of carrying coal by boat involved horse hire at $1 a day, and the hire of a man, also at $1 a day.[4]

1808.   Basing his calculations on experience with the Lancaster Turnpike, Robert Fulton estimated that the proposed canal from Philadelphia to Columbia might be operated with canal men paid $1 a day—each boat requiring one man, one horse (likewise $1), and one boy (at 50 cents.)[5]

1824 to 1825.   Comparing alternative costs of transportation, the Pennsylvania Canal Commissioners in 1824 use a figure of $1 a day per man.[6]

We likewise have an estimate for Maryland in 1825 by Hollins, suggesting a $10 monthly rate. The rate is identical with that estimated for Maryland farm laborers in 1826 by Senator Holmes (see section on Agricultural Wages, above).[7]

1826.   De Witt Clinton, Jr., surveying the route of the Altamah and Savannah Canal, gave it as his opinion in February, 1826, that the canal could operate with boats manned by two men, at $20 a month each, and one boy at $10.[8] Assuming that Clinton adopted Southern terminology in

---

[2] Claude Robin, *Voyages dans l'Interieur de la Louisiane . . . 1802–1806* (Paris: F. Buisson, 1807), vol. II, p. 216. "Le prix moyen pour chaque homme, y compris sa nourriture, revient a une piastre par jour." Since Robin had covered other countries after his trip began in 1802, we may assume his period in Louisiana was about 1804–1805.

[3] Victor Collot, *A Journey in North America* (1826; reprint 1924), vol. I, p. 140.

[4] *The Memorial and Petition of the President and Directors of the Chesapeake and Delaware Canal Company to the Honorable, the Senate and House of Representatives of the Commonwealth of Pennsylvania* (Dec. 24, 1806), p. 7.

[5] Quoted in *Report of the Secretary of the Treasury on Public Roads and Canals*, Apr. 12, 1808 (Washington: R. C. Weightman, 1808), pp. 111, 120. See also Young, *A Treatise on Internal Navigation* (Ballston Spa: U. F. Doubleday, 1817), pp. 103, 111.

[6] Pennsylvania, Board of Canal Commissioners, *Report of the Commission for Promoting the Internal Improvement of the State* (1824), pp. 28–29.

[7] William Hollins, *Views on the Subject of Internal Improvements between the Atlantic and Western States and Navigating the River Susquehanna with Steamboats 1825* (Baltimore: William Woody, 1825), p. 10. Hollins, estimating 35 cents a day per man as the cost of operation, must be dividing a $10 figure by 30 days.

[8] His report was printed in the *Savannah Republican*, Feb. 15, 1826, and in other papers. He estimated that one horse could move 30 tons; that the average boat's expense would be $110 a month, with two horses at $30.

referring to a boy, his figures are consistent with those of Robert Mills of South Carolina who, in 1826, noted Charleston rates of $2 a day for white workmen; "black or colored $1, and colored labor by the month, $10–$12." [9]

1832. Hall, in a detailed estimate of the cost of operating a steamboat in the Midwest, uses an implicit $1 a day figure for employees. [10] This is comparable with the $20 a month offered Wyeth to act as a fireman aboard a steamboat from New Orleans to St. Louis, lacking as he was in any previous experience. [11]

1834. Basing their figures on the experience of the Pennsylvania Canal, sponsors of Internal Improvements estimated that the C and O Canal could hire boatmen at $1, and boys and horses at 75 cents alike. [12]

1836 to 1839. For these years we have reports by the Pennsylvania Canal Commissioners of the rates paid watermen and firemen both on the canal and employed on the Columbia and Philadelphia Railway, ranging from 75 cents to $1 for the same men at different periods over the years. [13]

1842. John Regan quotes a $12 a month rate offered a seventeen-year-old boy to "work his ark down the river" from Canton, Illinois to New Orleans, taking 6 to 8 weeks to do so, and we have no reason to presume that this is below an adult rate. [14]

1845. The 5,000 boys employed on Erie Canal boats customarily received $10 a month—for 7 months of the year. [15] Stepping this up for the gap between pay for boys and men, we may conclude that this figure is reasonably consistent with, say, a $12 to $13 a month rate for men.

1850 to 1865. Louis Hunter has estimated rates paid deck hands on

[9] Robert Mills, *Statistics of South Carolina* (Charleston: Hurlburt and Lloyd, 1826), p. 427.

[10] James Hall, *Notes on the Western States* (Philadelphia: Harrison Hall, 1838), pp. 237, 247, estimates $1,671,840 as wages paid on steamboats and 4,800 as their crews, giving a full-time equivalent figure of $346. This is sufficiently close to $1 a day to suggest that Hall began with $1.

[11] John B. Wyeth, *Oregon* (1833; reprint 1905), p. 93.

[12] *Journal of the Internal Improvement Convention, which assembled in the city of Baltimore on the 18th day of December, 1834* (Baltimore: Sands and Neilson, 1835), p. 49. The convention estimates two men and one boy per boat.

[13] *Report of the Canal Commissioners of Pennsylvania*, 1836 (Harrisburg; Packer, Barret, and Parke, 1837), p. 78; *Annual Report of the Canal Commissioners for 1839* (Harrisburg: Holbrook, Henlock and Bratton, 1841), pp. 81ff.

[14] John Regan, *The Emigrants Guide*, 2d ed. (Edinburgh: Oliver and Boyd, 1852), p. 66. Regan himself was offered $12 a month somewhat earlier in New Orleans as a sign painter (p. 31).

[15] Deacon M. Eaton, *Five Years on the Erie Canal* (Utica: Bennett, Backhaus and Hawley, 1845), p. 32.

steamers on the Mississippi and its tributaries.[16] His figures run as follows, starting well above Regan's contemporary figure for 1852, and tracing an unusually irregular course:

1850	$20–25	1859	$40 plus
1854	40	1860	30–35
1855	15	1861	15–20
1856	30	1862	40
1857	40	1865	60
1858	20	later 1860s	20–35

1852. For this year John Regan reports rates on the Peoria area, with canal men receiving $14 to $18, or much the same as the $14 to $16 he indicates for farm servants.[17] Regan quotes a rate for farmhands in harvest work of $1 a day for 1850.[18] Since harvest rates were normally above the regular monthly hiring rates, we may consider his canal rate as equivalent to $1 a day.

1795 to 1860. The above rates fall into two groups. For daily rates a flat $1 a day appears throughout this long period, and along the Eastern seaboard as well as inland. Response to varying labor requirements and supply appears not at all in the daily rates, which seem to be arbitrary and unchanging, but rather in monthly rates. A $10 rate for the settled state of Maryland in 1826, a $20 rate for South Carolina in the same year, where white workmen were scarce and relatively well paid, and a $20 rate offered Wyeth for the traditionally high-wage New Orleans area suggest this variation.

After the crash of 1839 and the doldrums of the early 1840s, we have a $12 rate for Illinois in 1842, perhaps a $12 to $13 rate for New York canals in 1845, a $14 to $18 rate for canals in Illinois in 1852. Hunter's rates for the Western rivers suggest rises to 1857, a drop of marked but brief magnitude to 1858, a decline at the beginning of the Civil War, and the wartime rise beginning in 1862.

1873. An indication of the long-run stability of the rate for canal men is given by an estimate made in 1873 of the proposed cost of operating power canal boats on the New York State canals, in place of the traditional horse-drawn ones; the estimate of men on both the horse boat and the power boat is $1,[19] identical with the Fulton figure of 1808.

---

[16] Louis Hunter, *Steamboats on the Western Rivers* (1949), p. 465.

[17] Regan, *op. cit.*, p. 352.

[18] *Ibid.*, p. 223.

[19] New York State, *Commission on Steam or Other Power on Canal Boats: Steam on Canals, Second Annual Report* (Albany 1873), p. 111. For a horse boat, one captain at $2 and one man at $1; for a steamer, an engineer at $3, a captain at $2, two men at $1 each, and a cook at 40 cents.

WOODCUTTERS

The exhortation to spare that tree—like most hortatory comment—came after the fact: Woodsmen roamed the continent during its period of settlement and transformation. Since the job of the woodchopper was virtually identical wherever it appeared—Tennessee, Illinois, Oregon—it provides us with material on differences in basic wage rates both over time and space, with none of the usual problems of comparability in skill. In general, if we assume a stint of two cords of wood per day, the woodchopper could expect to earn $1 a day through most of the period from 1800 to 1850 in the East and Midwest.

1800. An advertisement for woodcutters in the *Tennessee Gazette* for June, 1800, promised 50 cents a cord, "payable in salt, castings or bar iron" 6 months later.[1]

We have a confirmation of the woodchoppers' rate as equivalent (at two cords a day) to the daily common-labor rate in the $1 a day figure for men paid to ascend the rivers of the Cheraquis, in Tennessee in 1795.[2]

1815 to 1817. In 1815 M. Bonnet observed, presumably of the Midwest, that a workman on log cabins "gagne quarante sols par jour," while for 1817 Fordham, visiting the Illinois territory, reports that men could earn $1 a day splitting rails for their neighbors.[3] In 1820 a Massachusetts shipowner paid 75 cents a cord for splitting and sawing wood—the high rate presumably reflecting the use of men from the ship.[4]

1828. In this year Jerry Church found that in upper New York state "many woods-boys . . . are bound to work for 25 cents per day," having neither capital nor credit.[5] Church's figure is unusually low, however, and his "woods boys" may be merely upstate farm laborers earning $7.50 a month. In fact, a few years later, Subaltern Coke quotes cordwood selling

---

[1] Quoted in John B. McMaster, *A History of the People of the United States* (1893), vol. III, p. 484.

[2] F. A. Michaux, *Travels* (1805; reprint 1904), Reuben G. Thwaites (ed.), *Early Western Travels,* vol. III, p. 74. The extent of the inflationary rise since the war is indicated by Mann Butler's statement that in 1775 near Boonseborough, Transylvania, "ordinary labor credited at 33 ⅓ cents. . . . Fifty cents per day was paid for ranging, hunting and working on the roads." Quoted in Theodore Roosevelt, *The Winning of the West* (1926), chap. 10, p. 221.

[3] M. E. Bonnet, *Tableau des Etats-Unis de l'Amerique* (Paris: 1816), p. 119. Elias Fordham, *Personal Narrative . . . 1817–1818* (reprint 1906), p. 211.

[4] Essex Institute, Pickman Manuscripts, vol. VI, Jan. 20, 1820, Brig *Texcel,* 5 shillings for each of four cords.

[5] *Journal of Travels, Adventures and Remarks of Jerry Church* (1845; reprint 1933), p. 43. Church gives no place or date, but on p. 9 refers to Olean Point, N.Y. ca. 1828, and his narrative appears to continue from there.

at $1.25 in Geneva, New York.[6] Given a seller's markup, Coke's figure implies no less than 80 cents to $1 for chopping.

1832.   A variety of statements by manufacturers in the McLane report indicate 37½ cents a cord in New Jersey, 40 cents in Pennsylvania, and, for New Hampshire, lumber manufacturing, 75 cents a day.[7]

1837 to 1843.   For Illinois in 1837, James Hall estimated 50 cents a cord for cutting wood, while Regan also stipulates a rate of 50 cents for the 1830–1840 period.[8] The dean of American woodchoppers gives a 50 cents a cord rate for 1842.[9] For the work of hewing a frame house about 1840, carrying through from free chopping to cutting out the sills, Regan quotes this colloquy: "What are your terms? Wal, they *used* to allow me a dollar a day; but I guess seventy-five cents will be enough *these* hard times." [10] A recovery in wages to 1843 is indicated by an estimate of $1 a day for the cost of cutting and logging timber for a frame house in Illinois in 1843, and $1 a day paid in Randolph County, Illinois, for building a rail fence.[11]

1847 to 1852.   We have an interesting measure of the effect which the discovery of gold in California had on labor demand on the coast in the form of figures for Oregon in 1847 and 1851. In 1847 chopping a cord of wood was worth 75 cents to $1, and cutting and splitting rails, $1.25 a thousand.[12] In 1851 cutting reputedly ran to $6 a cord.[13] A contemporary report for 1850 put both common labor in a coal mine and chopping wood at $6 a day in Sacramento, the heart of the recent gold-rush territory.[14]

---

[6] E. T. Coke, *A Subaltern's Furlough* (New York: 1833), vol. II, p. 16.

[7] U.S. Congress, Serial Set 222, *Documents Relative to the Statistics of Manufactures in the United States* (Washington: Duff Green, 1833) vol. II, pp. 183, 287, 331, vol. I, p. 683.

[8] James Hall, *Notes on the Western States* (Philadelphia: Harrison Hall, 1838), p. 145. John Regan, *The Emigrants Guide,* 2d ed. (Edinburgh: Oliver and Boyd, 1852), p. 89.

[9] Henry Thoreau, "Sunday," *A Week on the Concord and Merrimac Rivers.*

[10] *Op. cit.,* p. 85.

[11] William Oliver, *Eight Months in Illinois, with Information to Immigrants* (Newcastle-upon-Tyne: 1843; reprint 1924), pp. 243–244.

[12] Ulla S. Fowkes (ed.), *The Journal of Walter Griffith Pigman* (1942), p. 37. Pigman's notes refer to Aug. 4, 1850. In Josiah T. Marshall, *The Farmers and Emigrants Hand-Book* (Utica: H. H. Hawley, 1852), an estimate of the cost of clearing prairie land and building a house is made, with a 50-cent a day rate set for cutting timber, raising the house, etc. This figure seems unreasonably low: it may reflect casual attention by Marshall in putting together an estimate in which other aspects were of major concern, or it may reveal an attempt to minimize the costs of settlement.

[13] Joel Palmer, *Journal of Travels over the Rocky Mountains* (1847, reprint, 1906), pp. 218–228.

[14] Hubert H. Bancroft, *Chronicles of the Builders of the Commonwealth* (1891), p. 603, quotes William Sargent Ladd, New Hampshire resident who moved to the Coast, retrospectively describing what he expected to make there, "I can do better

For New York State in 1848 there is a 50-cent estimate for cutting wood in Rockland County.[15] Finally, for 1858 a rate of 25 cents a cord in Wisconsin is reported—this very low level for the frontier area presumably reflecting the effects of the 1857–1858 depression on wage rates and labor demand.[16]

What does this congeries of data indicate? Assuming two cords of wood a day, we may say the following. The Tennessee rate of $1 a day was payable in kind and with a 6 months' delay—surely a discounting aspect. We can conclude that payment in usual terms meant an 80-cents a day rate in 1800 (Tennessee), in 1815–1817 (Illinois), and in 1832 (New Jersey, Pennsylvania). Spreading settlement in the Midwest was associated with a $1 rate in 1837 to 1847 (Illinois, New York, Oregon). And in turn the very lively rate of settlement in Oregon during and after the gold rush brought a tripling (or quadrupling?) of wages for this work on the coast.

TEAMSTERS

An 1818 volume on the advantages of the new mode of transportation stated wagoners wages at $20 a month, basing its estimate on the experience near Baltimore of Messrs. Ellicott, Cheston, and others, who had for many years been in the business of grinding and transporting wheat.[1] For 1826 a canal builder on the Allegheny paid $15 to $16 a month for a man and team of two horses, "all found." [2] Allowing for the value of found— i.e., food—the rate on this area, which was then frontier, probably ran to well above $20.

1832. A wagoner in a Pennsylvania glass works was paid $16 a month, or the same rate as the firm paid coal miners.[3] (A figure of $8 to $10 for wagoners (exclusive of teams) on the national turnpike has been estimated by a modern writer.[4]) And a New Jersey cotton factory paid its

than work here [in a responsible railroad job in New Hampshire] at $20 a month when they are paying six dollars a cord for chopping wood over there and I can cut two cords a day."

[15] *Sixth Annual Report of the American Institution of the City of New York* (Albany: Charles van Benthuysen, 1848), p. 128.

[16] George William Rankin, *William Dempster Hoard* (W. D. Hoard and Sons, 1925), pp. 18–19.

[1] John B. Howard, Jr., *Remarks on the Intercourse of Baltimore with the Western Country* (Joseph Robinson, 1818), p. 15.

[2] A. Lacock of Pittsburgh, Letter of November, 1826, quoted in *Proceedings of the Chesapeake and Ohio Canal Convention, November 6, 1823 . . . December 6, 1826* (Washington City: Way and Gideon, 1827), p. 90.

[3] *Documents Relative to the Statistics of Manufactures in the United States* (Washington: Duff Green, 1833), vol. II, p. 528.

[4] John Omwake, *The Conestoga Six-horse Bell Teams of Eastern Pennsylvania* (1930), p. 110.

"horse drivers" 87½ cents a day—compared to $1.37 for the rest of its male employees, and a general average for males in the state.[5]

1840.   A modern historian states that stagecoach drivers earned $14 a month around 1840, while the *Wheeling Times and Advertiser* for June 2, 1845, estimating the cost of a relay system, figured drivers at $20 a month.[6]

An 1848 report for New York State gives the same $20 figure for men with teams, an $11 rate for men without.[7] Such a monthly rate may be contrasted with a daily rate of $2 at about the same time and place[8]— presumably $1 for the driver and $1 for his horse and wagon, a 50:50 division being commonly used. For the period around 1830 we have a Pennsylvania figure of $8 to $10 a month for wagoners without their own teams.[9]

In 1848 the hire of teamsters any place along the Atlantic Coast was estimated by the Quartermaster General to cost the Army about $16 a month (including the cost of food), plus clothing and fuel.[10]

We take these various figures as suggesting that wagoners (without teams) were paid $10 a month for 1818 to 1848 along the east coast.

PHYSICIANS

While a systematic estimate for physicians could undoubtedly be suggested by using the records of institutions as a guide, we note below merely those figures that happened to turn up in the materials surveyed for the present review of earnings of wage earners.

1814.   In 1814 Navy surgeons (i.e., physicians) received $50 a month plus two rations a day. The latter were "never drawn in kind, but in their value in money, that is, 40 cents per day." [1] This estimate, by a Navy

[5] *McLane Report,* vol. II, p. 162. The $1 state average for males in ironworks is from p. 194.

[6] Philip D. Jordan, *The National Road* (1948), p. 185. Jordan quotes the *Wheeling Times* on p. 226, estimating 78 drivers at an annual cost of $18,720 and 12 laborers at $3,600. It is to be noted that the laborers are assumed at a higher rate, probably reflecting the use of a $1 a day rate.

[7] *Sixth Annual Report of the American Institution of the City of New York* (Albany: Charles van Benthuysen, 1848), pp. 128, 190. One figure is for "teamsters"; the other is for teamsters employed by a Prattsville tannery, the horses presumably supplied by the tannery.

[8] New York State, Senate Documents, 1844, quoted by Martin D. Lewis, "The Chenango," vol. V, *Explorations in Entrepreneurial History* (1952–1953), p. 105.

[9] John Omwake, *loc. cit.*

[10] *Alabama, Florida and Georgia Railroad,* 30th Cong., 1st Sess., House Doc. (Feb. 18, 1848). He estimates $186.75 plus $30.71 for clothing and equipage, $9.50 for fuel, $1.32 for straw.

[1] William P. C. Barton, *A Treatise Containing a Plan for the Internal Organization and Government of Marine Hospitals* (Philadelphia: 1814), p. 208.

surgeon, may be set alongside his figures of $300 a year for physicians to outpatients in the Pennsylvania Hospital, of $1.33 a week to nurses in the hospital, and of annual rates to laborers of $144.[2] Against a $12 rate for laborers (quite typical of the times) we therefore have a $65 figure for navy physicians—allowing a small sum for lodging, candles, etc.—and perhaps $35 for civilian physicians.

1848. By 1848, Navy surgeons were receiving $1,000 a year. We may presume the figure to be well above that for civilian physicians from the comment made by Navy Surgeon Ruschenberger: "$1,000 is an ample bid, for the competition is so great that it commands not only medical, but in some instances also political party services in the bargain. . . . What gentleman would give his time and labour to any institution for $1,000 yearly if he could command more for his services in private or other practice?" [3]

In 1832 Secretary of War Lewis Gas contracted for the vaccination of Indians against smallpox, the disease that had wiped out whole tribes of Indians and was the true scourge of the plains. His contracts called for $6 a day: "The vaccination of 100 Indians will be considered equal to a days service by a physician." [4] The same $6 a day also measured earnings in 1853–1854 by an illiterate physician treating smallpox in the West.[5]

These figures seem quite low in terms of the rates paid per visit as reported by some travelers. In June, 1817, for example, Fordham consulted a Pittsburgh physician, paying $6 for an office visit.[6] And the charges in gold-rush days were notorious; one forty-niner said $10 for a visit (but common labor in San Francisco then received $10 a day) while another, in 1850, paid $16 a visit.[7] However, rates in more settled areas were far lower.[8]

Moreover, the difference reflects the gap between unit charges and annual income. High physicians' rates encouraged the continuation of self-

[2] *Ibid.*, pp. 128–129. For "medicines administered and medical attendance to his family . . . April 23–May 29, 1822," a wealthy New Englander paid $2.63. Essex Institute, Benjamin Pickman Manuscripts, Ships, vol. VIII, receipt from E. A. Holyoke.

[3] William S. W. Ruschenberger, *Remarks on the Condition of the Marine Hospital Fund . . . by a Surgeon U.S. Navy* (Philadelphia: Lindsay and Blakiston, 1848), p. 4.

[4] 22nd Cong., 2d Sess., Serial Set 234, No. 82.

[5] Kenneth Bjork, *West of the Great Divide* (1958), p. 68.

[6] Elias Fordham, *Personal Narrative . . . 1817–1818* (reprint 1906), p. 71.

[7] Richard I. Hale, in Carolyn R. Hale (ed.), *The Log of a Forty-Niner* (1923), pp. 65, 70. John Hale, *California As It Is* (1954), p. 34.

[8] A Salem physician charged 42 cents a visit prior to 1836; 50 cents from 1836 through 1863; and $1 beginning in 1864. Deborah B. Zobel, "Doctor Despite Himself," *Essex Institute Historical Collections* (July, 1959), p. 236.

medication and of untrained healers, with physicians' annual incomes probably being nowhere equal to what unit charges might suggest.

MINISTERS

> *A domestic chaplain "might be had for his board, a small garret and 10 pounds a year, and might not only perform his own professional functions, might not only be always ready in fine weather for bowls and in rainy weather for shovel board, but might also save the expense of a gardener or groom."*
>
> Macaulay, *History of England,* chap. 3

The conditions of life of the American clergy, and their salaries as well as their eschatology differed in significant respects from the English tradition. Through the first half of the nineteenth century many of the clergy, as the American people, were country folk. The salaries paid in the great cities were therefore above the general average.

Because of the difficulty of determining that general average, we can most usefully work backward from some figures for the 1850–1860 decade. In 1856 Francis Bowen, leading economist of the eastern seaboard north of New York, found that in Ohio and presumably in most of the Western states, "the salaries of the clergymen are not equal to the wages of a good journeyman blacksmith, the former do not receive on the average of more than $500 a year." [1] This figure receives good confirmation from the $600 figure for the salary and perquisites of the Albany clergy as reported in the New York State Census for that year,[2] for we would expect city salaries to be greater. For 1860 the average salary of preachers in the Pittsburgh Conference of the Methodist Church, covering the edge of what was then the West, was $426.[3]

For 1840 Reverend Bristol, then preaching in Franklin, Ohio, received a salary of $400.[4]

For 1832 a figure of $400 again seems most typical. This year was an *annus mirabilis* for all those who desire to estimate clerical salaries prior to 1900, if such there be. An extremely helpful guide is given by a Treasury

[1] Francis Bowen, *The Principles of Political Economy* (Boston, 1856), p. 218.
[2] 1854 New York State Census, reporting 88 clergymen, $53,206 in salaries and perquisites. This volume is in the Library of Congress.
[3] Wallace G. Smeltzer, *Methodism on the Headwaters of the Ohio* (1951), p. 206.
[4] Reverend Sherlock Bristol, *The Pioneer Preacher, An Autobiography* (1887), p. 115. Reverend Bristol adds that he should have, but did not, receive an additional $200 from the home missionary society.

survey made in that year. Its data lead to an average of $423 for 378 clergymen in Connecticut and $255 for 759 clergymen in Ohio, wages in the frontier areas being typically lower than the eastern seaboard where most of the clergy resided.[5] An attaché of Her Britannic Majesty's government, at Washington, devoting considerable attention to the earnings of clergy in the states, estimated a general average of $400; $300 for the Methodists; and $600 as a good average "in a county of some importance." The 100-pound average he estimated for New York was, he thought, above the general average.[6] In the same year the Reverend Isaac Fidler concluded that the country clergy in the raw United States received from 30 to 150 pounds, i.e., from about $135 to $665 a year.[7] Yet a third British traveler—Lieutenant Coke of the 45th Regiment—notes that in upstate New York the clergy received a salary of $1,000 in small towns.[8] And finally, for the same period, Abdy reports from Auburn, New York, clergymen receiving about $500 in that part of the country. He notes as an exception the $700 paid an independent minister near Hartford, the elders of the congregation objecting to "so large a sum." [9] We take Reverend Fidler's low figure of $135 and Subaltern Coke's high one of $1,000 as suggesting something of the range that prevailed outside the big cities. As a general average, however, we adopt a figure of $400, relying heavily on Ouseley, who devoted two chapters of attention to the subject.

For the 1820s a somewhat lower level appears. Peter Cartwright, one of the most famous pioneer preachers, was paid $40 a month in 1824–1825 and $60 in 1825–1826, or $480 to $720 annually, and thought it good pay.[10] And indeed by customary standards so it was. In 1823 a Methodist bishop received $300 a year, while in 1821–1822 a circuit rider possessed of a wife and seven children found his total receipts running to $76, plus "little pay worth mentioning." [11]

---

[5] *Statistical View of the Population of the United States from 1790 to 1830, Inclusive,* 23rd Cong., 1st Sess., Serial Set 252 (Washington: Duff Green, 1835), pp. 190, 209. In this survey returns were made by the mayors and chief officers of hundreds of towns throughout the country. Data are likewise given for Maine and Rhode Island (averaging $148 and $266, respectively) but here ignored as obviously being too low. A few reports for Indiana and Missouri were ignored as well; averages of $65 and $42 are below the Methodist allowance for preachers in 1800 and must reflect either errors, part-time ministers, or both.

[6] William G. Ouseley, *Remarks on the Statistics and Political Institutions of the United States* (Philadelphia: Carey and Lea, 1832), pp. 148–149.

[7] Reverend Isaac Fidler, *Observations on the Professions, Literature, Manners and Emigrants in the United States . . . in 1832* (New York, 1832), p. 30.

[8] E. T. Coke, *A Subaltern's Furlough* (New York, 1833), vol. I, p. 217.

[9] E. S. Abdy, *Journal of a Residence and Tour in the United States of North America from April 1833 to October 1834* (London: 1835), vol. I, pp. 248, 276.

[10] Arthur C. Baggess, *The Settlement of Illinois, 1778–1830* (1908), p. 175.

[11] William W. Sweet, *Circuit Rider Days in Indiana* (1916), p. 35.

Finally, for the earlier period we may refer to the "allowance of preach-ers" in the Methodist Church, which was $80 a year in 1800, rising to $100 in 1816, and remaining there until 1860. For married men the 1816–1860 allowance was $200, plus $16 each for children under seven and $24 for those aged seven to fourteen.[12]

What may we conclude for the trend in ministerial salaries over the 1800–1860 period? Upper limits can be set from several figures. (1) The $426 paid in 1860 to Pittsburgh Conference preachers would have been at least as great as the salary in earlier times. (2) The $600 figure for Albany clergy in 1854, and the $600 figure for clergy "in a city of importance" in 1832, according to Ouseley, must likewise have been above the general average. (3) The $300 paid an Indiana bishop in 1823 must likewise have been above that customary for the regular frontier clergy. As a single figure for the period 1820–1860 we may take a $400 salary—recognizing that clergy in the West (circuit riders and established alike) earned closer to $200 to $300, while clergymen in the larger cities received closer to $600 in pay and perquisites. Judging from the allowances of the Methodist Church, the average for 1800 to 1820 may have run closer to $350.

[12] David Sherman, *History of the Methodist Church,* quoted in Smeltzer, *op. cit.,* p. 205. Smeltzer notes that in 1846 the allowances in the Pittsburgh Conference ran to $27,000 a year, while table expense and travel equaled $11,000. We may assume that much of the latter item was for travel.

8

LONG-TERM TRENDS

IN LIVING COSTS, LABOR FORCE,

AND EMPLOYMENT

COST OF LIVING: 1800 TO 1860 (TABLE A-32)

As outlined in the discussion of real-wage trends, major items of real income (food, lodging) do not enter into the money-income figures subject to deflation by usual procedures. We are here estimating an index of selected retail prices only for those items customarily bought for cash by employees (and others) in this period. We select textiles, shoes, rum, tea, and coffee both as commodities that accounted for the largest share of such expenditures and as items whose price trend is closely related to the trend for all items bought at retail, if properly weighted by expenditures.

For our price data, one obvious source would appear to be the index of prices paid by farmers in Vermont, developed by Professor T. M. Adams and already used as an indication of "cost of living in the United States." [1] One obstacle to such use of the index, as noted by Ethel Hoover, is that we are uncertain "as to the similarity of price changes for Vermont farmers and the rest of the Nation." A more serious problem lies in the fact that Adams's index intentionally applies only to items bought by farmers.

[1] Adams's series appears in *Prices Paid by Vermont Farmers* . . . , Vermont Agricultural Experiment Station, Bulletin 5-7 (February, 1944), p. 32. It is used as a United States index in Joint Economic Committee, *Hearings on Employment, Growth and Price Levels* (Apr. 7–10, 1959), part 2, pp. 384ff. (testimony of Ethel D. Hoover).

334

While 80 percent of wage-earner (and probably United States) food expenditures from 1800 to 1850 were for meat, bread, and flour, Adams's index makes no allowance for these items prior to 1845, and no allowance for meat or bread after that date. Conversely, 60 percent of his food group weight was for tea, butter, and fish—items that actually account for only a small portion of wage-earner diets in 1800–1860.

Present Procedure

In a set of imperfect markets such as the United States was from 1800 to 1860, with considerable short period difficulty in communications and in maintaining a steady organized market, it is desirable to get as wide geographic representation of price trends as possible. We do so—for individual items—by using Adams's retail prices for Vermont, Wright's retail prices for Massachusetts, and wholesale price indices for Philadelphia and New York.[2] If each of these sets of data were sufficient measures of retail price trends in their state or region, we would weight by the number employed in that area. Since they are not, we prefer simply to average them, treating each as another indication of price trend on the East Coast, where most of the free population lived. Now it is well known that wholesale price movements are identical neither in amplitude nor timing to those of retail prices. How is it possible to combine these two types of materials in a meaningful index? We begin from the assumption that broad geographic representation is necessary; with the bulk of wage earners in the New York, New Jersey, Philadelphia, Delaware area, for which New York and Philadelphia price trends should be relevant, it should be helpful to combine the erratic up-country Vermont data with data more relevant to trends where wage earners actually lived.

We are able to do so if we do not attempt year-to-year measures, but only those for decade-to-decade change. In a period such as that from 1800 to 1860, there was a wide-open labor market and considerable intermediate and long-term mobility of labor and capital. There were few legal limitations on either retailing or wholesaling, and none on entrance into either. In such a market we assume it most unlikely that over decennial intervals a marked difference between retail and wholesale margins would develop. If retailers began making high profits compared to wholesalers, more of the new entrants to trade would enter the high-profit area, thus driving margins down to closer equivalence with wholesaling. Nor do we have reason to believe that the comparative risks and skills demanded in retailing, as against wholesaling, changed so distinctly over the period

---

[2] Carroll Wright, *History of Wages and Prices in Massachusetts, 1752–1883* (1885). Arthur H. Cole, *Wholesale Commodity Prices in the United States, 1760–1861* (1938). Anne Bezanson, Robert Gray, and Miriam Hussey, *Wholesale Prices in Philadelphia 1784–1861* (1937), vol. II.

as to produce a greater return in one than the other because of such factors. If, therefore, we make our periods of sufficient length and do not begin (or end) in a year that appears particularly disadvantageous to one level of distribution as against another, we may use wholesale trends for some states as a helpful complement to our retail data for others.

Prices.   We show in Table A-32 the price trends for textiles, shoes, whisky, tea, and coffee.

Textiles.   For textiles we find the differences between the states explicable in terms of local trends rather than retail-wholesale differentials.[3] For 1810 to 1840 we find no clear difference among the quotations that would testify to more than sampling variation, and therefore average the four area averages. For 1800 to 1810 the declines in sheeting and cloth shown for Massachusetts by Wright seem less reasonable than the series of year-to-year quotations in the Philadelphia area that show an upward course, and we use the latter. For 1840 to 1860 the decline for Vermont seems incredible, but it is dimly matched by the Massachusetts data, and if we assume that the trend for the bulk of the population declined far less, but in fact more than the wholesale price data show, the average of the four again provides a rough indication.

Shoes.   Our wholesale price quotations relate only to leather, and therefore comparisons are seriously affected by the development of production under the factory system and by the changing cost of labor. However, the leather price trends are helpful confirmation of the shoe-price changes with two exceptions. (1) The 1800 to 1810 leather-price rise for Philadelphia is directly contrary to the stability for Vermont and the marked decline for Massachusetts. However, the 1799 to 1810 change for Massachusetts shoes is virtually identical with that for Philadelphia leather. From 1800 to 1810 Vermont shoe prices remain unchanged, Massachusetts shoe prices fall markedly, while Philadelphia leather prices rise somewhat. Since the same pattern appears if we take 3-year averages, because the adjoining years are similar, we assume these to be real contrasts. We assume the Vermont price indicates up-country price stability in the face of mild raw-material price rises, but marked declines in retail prices in the population centers as war demand ended and the shoe industry began to move from its putting-out stage into something closer to factory production. We average the Massachusetts and Vermont indices to extrapolate an 1810 average to 1800. (2) For 1820 to 1830, each

[3] For Massachusetts we average indices computed using the Wright figures for cloth, flannel, sheeting, shirting, ticking, and calico. For Vermont: cotton cloth, gingham, and calico. For Philadelphia and New York: sheeting. The sharpest change for any of the components is for Massachusetts sheeting, with an 1810 figure 5.5 times that for 1840. This is confirmed by a 5.8 ratio for Rhode Island (1811 compared to 1840) using data given in Thomas R. Hazard, *Facts for a Laboring Man by a Laboring Man* (Newport: James Atkinson, Printer, 1840), pp. 16–17.

series goes its separate way. However, since Massachusetts shoe prices show no change and since Vermont prices for 1820 to 1829 likewise show no change, we assume no United States change from 1820 to 1830. (3) For 1810 to 1819, 1820 we take an average of the Massachusetts and Vermont price changes. (4) For 1830 to 1850 both retail series show similar declines, but one reports the 1850 level being reached by 1839, the other, by 1842. In this instance we assume that Massachusetts prices were buoyed up through the recession of 1837 by the rising tide of industrialization, declining only with the textile declines of the early 1840s. Hence the Vermont trend is assumed to be more generally representative for 1830, 1840, 1850. (For 1850 to 1860, we average Massachusetts and Vermont.)

Spirits. Massachusetts retail prices and Philadelphia wholesale prices for New England rum trace an almost identical course over the decades. The Vermont series shows nothing like the same decline from 1810 to 1820 but falls far more from 1820 to 1830. Whether this testifies to price rigidity in the further reaches of the country in the early decades, with prices falling when roads began to be opened up, or to mere shifts in the group of stores covered at different periods, we have no way of knowing. On neither basis is there any reason for using these data as representative. We average Massachusetts and Philadelphia price indices for the trend prior to 1830, while for 1830 to 1860 we average the Philadelphia rum and rye whisky indices, the growing consumption of the latter thus being allowed for.

The various individual price series were combined with 1830 expenditure weights. The weights were derived from data on clothing expenditures at various years from 1804 through 1863, and estimates of the physical volume of beverage consumption at various dates from 1804 through 1850 multiplied by price data.[4]

COST OF LIVING: 1860 TO 1880 (TABLE A-33)

For these years estimates of the trend in the cost of living have been made by Wesley Mitchell and Ethel D. Hoover, while David A. Wells, in 1869, computed the change from 1860 to 1868.[1] Mitchell's estimates

---

[4] It is hoped that the materials on consumption patterns will be published in detail at some later date.

[1] Wesley Mitchell, *Gold, Prices and Wages under the Greenback Standard* (1908), p. 91. Ethel D. Hoover, "Prices in the United States in the Nineteenth Century," in Conference on Research in Income and Wealth, *Trends in the American Economy in the Nineteenth Century* (1960). David A. Wells, *Report of the Special Commissioner of the Revenue for the Year 1868,* 40th Cong., 3d Sess., Serial Set 1372, House Exec. Doc. 16 (1868–1869).

for certain categories are still the most satisfactory available; for others the Hoover estimates mark a real advance. Neither series is satisfactory for the important rent category because of inadequacies in the underlying Weeks materials used by both. We review below these earlier estimates (I) and then describe our own procedure (II). The latter draws upon Mitchell, Hoover, and Wells data and, for rents, a quite different independent computation.

I. Mitchell, Hoover Estimates

The classic source on trends in living costs over this period is Wesley Mitchell's study noted above. More recently Hoover has gone back to the original tabulation of price data made by Weeks, from which Mitchell worked, to make a new cost of living series for 1850 to 1880.[2]

Three major differences in approach were adopted by Ethel Hoover.

1. One is the use of a different weighting pattern.[3] The explicit allocation of weights that results from this approach is clearly preferable in principle. In practice, however, it creates only a small amount of difference between her results and those of Mitchell. For example, both rise 40 percent in the first flush of wartime inflation from 1860 to 1863, while the decline from 1866 to 1880 is 28 percent in one series and 35 percent in the other.[4] Had the weights been a major factor in producing differences, such similarities would be most unlikely.

2. The key difference between the Mitchell and Hoover series apparently results from Hoover's extensive use of a class of price quotations not included by Mitchell, namely, those which Weeks obtained for a single date in the year (e.g., June 1) or without any date being specified. Mitchell put aside these reports, restricting himself to those specifically shown by Weeks as being annual averages.[5] It is this choice that creates the most decisive difference between the Mitchell and Hoover series.

However, the wisdom of Mitchell's exclusion of June 1 and nonspecified series is suggested by an examination of the detailed price quotations. White potato prices for 1865–1866, for example, offer a clear indication

---

[2] 1880 Census, Joseph Weeks, *Report on the Average Retail Prices of Necessaries of Life in the United States* (*1886*).

[3] While thoroughly described by Hoover, the differences essentially reflect the use of an 1875 expenditure survey for a few hundred Massachusetts laborers' families, and the explicit allocation of weights to certain expenditure categories, instead of Mitchell's reliance on the 1901 Cost of Living Survey (plus an 1890–1891 smaller survey for some details) and an implicit allocation to certain categories.

[4] Data from Hoover, *op. cit.*, table 5.

[5] In addition, Mitchell excluded those annual average series, a limited group, "not approximately complete for the whole period, 1860 to 1880," Mitchell, *op. cit.*, p. 65.

of the basis for his distrust. We show below, from Weeks, prices in selected areas:

Region	1865	1866	Change, %
Connecticut			
Year–New Haven...............	$2.00	$2.00	0
June–Danielson................	1.00	0.90	−10
June–Danielson................	0.80	0.60	−25
Ohio			
Year–Springfield...............	0.85	1.00	+18
Year–Zanesville................	1.00	1.00	0
June–Columbus................	0.80	1.50	+87
? –Hamilton................	1.00	1.00	0
Pennsylvania			
Year–Philadelphia..............	0.90	1.00	+11
June–Norristown...............	2.00	2.00	0
June–Sharon..................	0.50	1.00	+100
New York			
June–Amsterdam...............	0.40	1.00	+150
June–Cohoes.................	1.00	0.80	−20

In the light of trends for other cities within the same states and the general pattern of mild change in annual average figures throughout the country, the June rates that purport to show a doubling for Columbus, Sharon, and Amsterdam are in striking contrast. It is not to be assumed that year-to-year price trends in these cities were in fact at such striking variance with trends in nearby cities, but rather that these figures reflect the potent seasonal variation of prices. (Such variation is commonly evident in the prices for vegetables, eggs, and other seasonal items in more recent years.) But if we seek to measure year-to-year change, we can have little hope that the "June 1" and "no date" prices will report primarily such change. In fact if we consider the reports for the various vegetable items and even meat items in relationship to changes for nearby cities (annual averages), we might well conclude that these price reports tell us more about seasonal variation than year-to-year change.

3. Another force distinguishing the Hoover from the Mitchell results is the fact that for certain foods within the food group Mitchell gives equal weight to individual price indices while Hoover uses differential weights based on the 1875 Massachusetts expenditure study. Thus Mitchell implicitly gives equal weights to beef soup pieces and beef roasting pieces in establishing his beef price index, while Hoover gives much greater weight to one than the other. This contrasting procedure, while making a slight difference in textiles, and in other groups, creates a substantial

difference in the food index. We discuss the point in greater detail in connection with our own food estimate below.

Fortunately, we are able to test the Mitchell and Hoover indices against a contemporary study of substantial worth. For three successive years, 1868, 1869, and 1870, David A. Wells, as Special Commissioner of Revenue, made an annual report in which, based on reports received from an extensive list of companies, he estimated wages and the change in prices for detailed components of the cost of living.[6] We rely largely on his findings because of his extensive contacts, his known abilities, and the considerable discussion of his reports in the Congress—in which his conclusions as to tariff and revenue policy were impugned but his statistical findings (printed with those conclusions) were not really challenged.[7] In an interchange with Representative Kelley, Wells took occasion to list some of the companies from whom he had received wage reports, and that list proves to have quite extensive industrial and spatial coverage for the North.[8] No data were given on his price sources, however, beyond the indication in his statement that he did not report a greater rent rise because many New England manufacturing corporations owned their own tenements and did not advance their rent as much as did commercial sources.[9]

We note below Wells's figures on the change from 1860 to 1867–1868, with parallel figures from Mitchell and Hoover.[10]

Food.   The table suggests some sharp differences. The Wells and Mitchell series show similar changes, while Hoover (adding the June 1 series to the ones used by Mitchell) shows strikingly smaller gains.

Fuel.   The Wells and Mitchell indices are very similar, while all of the components of the Hoover fuel index except coal oil show much the same change as the Mitchell components. The Hoover series differs in showing a marked 1860 to 1862 decline (Mitchell shows a constancy), with limited recovery by 1867–1868. The source of this difference is presumably the inclusion of a handful of noncontinuous series, although very few series are available at all. For example, a series for coal oil in Watertown,

---

[6] Wells, *op. cit.*

[7] See H. R. Ferleger, *David A. Wells and the American Revenue System* (1942).

[8] David A. Wells's letter, Washington, March, 1869, *The Working Classes, Their Condition, Past and Present: Wages and Prices.* Newspaper clipping in the Sterling Library, Yale University.

[9] Wells, *Report of the Special Commissioner of the Revenue for the Year 1868,* p. 14. The similarity of towns suggested that at least some of his price data were provided by company stores.

[10] Mitchell's group indices above were computed using his indices for 1867–1868 averaged (p. 67) and his weights (p. 84). The Hoover indices are from her table 1, and her weights are from her appendix table 1. The Hoover component indices and weights as above were used to estimate her implicit meat, flour, bread indices.

New York, shows an improbable 1861–1862 decline from $1.12 to $0.50.[11]

Clothing. The Wells and Hoover indices are broadly similar. The Mitchell index, if it used the same group expenditure weights as the Hoover index, would be somewhat higher, estimating an 88 percent gain rather than the Hoover 66 percent.[12] The use of June 1 prices appears to

Item	1867–1868 Index (1860 = 100)			Percent of difference	
	Wells	Mitchell	Hoover	Wells-Mitchell	Wells-Hoover
Food.................	88	82	67	− 8	−21
Flour and bread........	92	104	99	+12	+ 7
Butter...............	91	112	49	+21	−42
Milk.................	61	55	34	− 6	−27
Meats...............	86	72	60	−14	−26
Fuel..................	57	55	40	− 2	−17
Clothing..............	75	102	66	+27	− 9
Rent..................	65	36	35	−29	−30
Cost of living...........					
Using Hoover weights...	80	75	56	− 5	−24
Reported.............	75	69	56	− 6	−19

have less effect here than in food, and since the seasonal variation in food prices is so much greater than that in clothing, the result is not surprising. Hoover's addition of a considerable number of quotations to those used by Mitchell provides a result closer to the Wells index.

Rent. Wells shows a startlingly greater gain than Mitchell or Hoover. The latter two agree, there being here no issue of June 1 series or differences in weights within the group. Wells's contemporary report has some preference, but how can we explain so wide a divergence on a major item? The answer appears to involve two biases in the Weeks reports, and hence in any series that utilizes them.

1. Weeks's quotations show a stability of rents for the war years and the postwar cycle that is well-nigh incredible to anyone who considers the trend of rents vis-à-vis other prices during World War I and even during the price-control period of World War II. A basic element here seems to

[11] Weeks, *op. cit.*, p. 103.

[12] Using Mitchell's weights, from his p. 84, gives a 102 percent gain as compared to an 88 percent gain using the Hoover weights. In addition to the use of June 1 price series, the Hoover index probably differs because Mitchell did not weight *within* the textile group—using prices for sheeting, ticking, etc., as equal indications of the trend in textile prices—whereas Hoover weighted each series. Bleached shirtings and sheetings are given a much higher than average weight in this way, and for these items the use of June 1 prices creates a substantial Mitchell-Hoover difference.

be excessive representation of rents charged by companies to their own employees. Our evidence appears in the materials of the Weeks report itself. In the wage section[13] for example, Weeks reports wages for the Thomas Iron Company of Hokendauqua, Pennsylvania, noting that "very low rent is charged to those employees living in the company's houses." In the later section on prices[14] he gives a rent series for a four-room house in Hokendauqua—used by Mitchell and Hoover—showing a constant figure from 1864 through 1880. In the wage section[15] he reports for the Pilot Knob Iron Company of Pilot Knob, Missouri: "employees are given house-rent, garden . . . ," while his price series[16] gives rents for a four-room house in Pilot Knob, with stable figures for 1864 to 1870 and 1871 to 1878. Because of the unusual place names involved, we have a fair indication that the rent data were secured from the same firms that provided the wage data. But other reports likewise indicate the provision of tenements at low rents,[17] and it seems not unreasonable that Weeks should have sought to secure rent data from the same firms that he was contacting for wage data.[18]

2. Another consideration arguing against the representativeness of the Weeks rent data is the trend in the price of construction inputs. The trend of wholesale prices for pine boards and for bricks is reported in Mitchell's study.[19] And we use our present estimate of nonfarm earnings as an indication of labor-cost trends. From 1860–1861 to the first quarter of 1868 the gains were as follows:

> Pine boards. 75%
> Bricks. 159%
> Labor. 46%

Assuming a 75 percent rise for materials (far more wood than brick construction being common) and a 46 percent rise for labor, and giving the two equal weights (as 1900 and more recent data suggest) yields a rise of, say, 61 percent for construction. (This contrasts with the 35 to 36 percent rises estimated by Hoover and Mitchell.) Ignoring a possible productivity gain, which would reduce the excess, the figure is not at all out of line with Wells's overall figure of a 65 percent gain in rents.[20]

[13] Weeks, *op. cit.,* p. 254.

[14] *Ibid.,* p. 106.

[15] *Ibid.,* p. 130.

[16] *Ibid.,* p. 104.

[17] *Ibid.,* pp. 267, 277, 287.

[18] Weeks notes (*Ibid.,* p. 2): "The effort was made to have these returns on the necessaries of life cover . . . the towns from which schedules of wages were secured."

[19] See, for example, *Ibid.,* pp. 340, 356, 442ff.

[20] Wells, *Report of the Special Commissioner of the Revenue for the Year 1868,* p. 14.

For individual areas he shows the following:

Smaller towns in Pennsylvania................	81%
New Jersey.................................	111%
New York, Philadelphia, Newark, Pittsburgh...	90–100%

Elsewhere Wells quotes a leading contemporary economist, Amasa Walker, to the effect that rents in North Brookfield, Massachusetts, had risen "not less than about sixty five percent," and a letter from a real estate agent that rents in Pennsylvania's Fourth Congressional District had risen by 131%.[21] Wells's overall 65 percent is lower than these components because, he explicitly notes, New England manufacturing corporations had not advanced rents as much in the tenements they provided their own workers, as the general advance.

In the light of the construction-cost data suggesting a 61 percent rise in new construction, the direct rent reports suggesting rises from 80 to 100 percent, and Wells's combined rent estimate of 65 percent, the 35 percent gain suggested by the Weeks data used by Mitchell and Hoover seems quite unreasonable. We attribute the difference to a marked concentration of Weeks's reports from small Midwestern towns, a region where only a small share of wage earners were employed, and to the possibility that a disproportionate share of Weeks's rent returns were provided by the companies to whom he likewise sent wage schedules.

3. A final difficulty arises not from Weeks's rent data per se but the simple combination of them, unweighted, into a United States average. If we take advantage of the regional series computed by Mitchell, we find a rise over the period of 46 percent for the East and 32 percent for the West.[22] Unlike the markets for more portable products, there is no reason to assume that variations in the supply-demand situation for housing in the Midwestern states should be essentially the same as those in the Eastern states. Only a limited transfer of resources could take place within a 7- to 8-year period, particularly during the war years. If we adopt all the Weeks reports as used by Mitchell and Hoover but weight each state average by the number of nonfarm gainfully occupied in 1860, we arrive at a weighted change of 42 percent.[23] This, of course, is 6 percent greater than the Mitchell change.

---

[21] *Letter on the Working Classes*. Wells also quotes a letter from a New York worker whose rent had risen from $10 (for three rooms) in 1860 to $15 for one room by 1868, in the same house.

[22] Mitchell, *op. cit.*, p. 90.

[23] 1860 *Population Census*, p. 680. State data for the gainfully occupied, farmers, farm labor, were added to give regional estimates for the Northeast and the North Central regions, giving 2.6 and 1.1 million, respectively.

II. Present Estimates

The best estimate of cost of living changes from 1860 to 1880 must draw upon all the materials discussed above—the Weeks data as processed by Mitchell and by Hoover and the Wells benchmark figures for 1860 to 1868. No one source is uniformly preferable, and we outline below the combination of weights and price series used.

Weights. For major group weights, i.e., food, clothing, etc., we adopt the weights from the 1875 survey of Massachusetts earners likewise used by Ethel Hoover.[24] Within the food group, however, we rely on the distribution of expenditures by item as estimated in 1868 by Wells on the basis of budget reports for employees in various New England and Middle Atlantic states.[25] We agree with Hoover in eschewing the 1901 weights used by Mitchell—first because the survey was 40 years after the fact, and secondly because it relates to high-income families. (The bias in that survey can be seen by comparing its earnings averages with those to be derived from the Census of Manufactures and other sources used in deriving the present earnings series for 1900ff.) We do not follow Hoover in the use of the 1875 survey for food details, preferring the more contemporary and geographically spread data provided by Wells.[26]

Wells does not provide detailed weights within the meat group, and we distribute his total as between beef and pork, using overall United States data on the consumption of each as indicated in the Department of Agriculture data.[27] These national data show beef consumption at 60 percent of pork—sharply different from the expenditure data for Massachusetts, which imply a ratio closer to 300 percent.[28]

Neither source provided weights within the fuel group. From Barger's estimates we can derive a figure in 1869 of three times as much spent for wood as for coal.[29] And from Shaw's figures we can find that the mine

[24] These are conveniently summarized in her appendix table 1. We adjust these weights to 1860 levels by using our group price indices developed below.

[25] *Report of the Special Commissioner of the Revenue for the Year 1868,* p. 122. See also pp. 15, 16, 118ff. for the geographic spread of reports.

[26] Wells's major group weights were not used, largely because they give a much greater total for "other" expenditures than does any later survey, at the expense of clothing and rent weights. Actually the choice between the Wells group weight and the 1875 weights makes no great difference in the final series.

[27] Marvin Towne and Wayne Rasmussen, "Farm Gross Product and Gross Investment during the 19th Century," in Conference on Research in Income and Wealth, *Trends in the American Economy in the Nineteenth Century* (1960), table 7, pp. 283–284.

[28] Hoover, *op. cit.,* appendix table 1. This is another indication of the specialized high-income character of the Massachusetts sample.

[29] Harold Barger, *Distribution's Place in the American Economy since 1869* (1955). From pp. 130–131 we compute nonmanufactured fuel at producers' prices (before freight) at 197, of which 147 (total of 587 from p. 128 times 25 percent

value of anthracite coal used by consumers in 1869 was over 10 times as great as that for bituminous.[30] Our weights within the fuel group are therefore 75 percent for wood, 23 percent for anthracite, and 2 percent for bituminous, as compared to Hoover's 25 percent each for pinewood, hardwood, anthracite, and bituminous.

For lighting, the Hoover figures use a coal-oil price series. The 1860 Census data imply at least as great an expenditure for candles[31] and whale oil as for coal oil. The Philadelphia wholesale price data indicate as much of a percentage rise in candle prices from 1860 to 1868 as petroleum prices fell.[32] However, Wells's study shows, for each state covered, marked declines in family expenditures for lighting. We, therefore, give the lighting weight to the price series that showed approximately this decline, namely, that for coal oil.

Food Price Series.   For individual food items we use the Mitchell price indices in preference to those of Hoover. We do so for three reasons.

Seasonality.   While the inclusion of part-period series by Hoover is a definite improvement in principle, its empirical advantage is outweighed by the concurrent inclusion of the June 1 prices. This procedure appears to introduce a major seasonal factor that produces year-to-year changes reflecting neither trend nor cycle changes but merely differences dependent upon which month of the year was priced.

For flour and bread, seasonality is limited. Here the Wells figure of 92 percent, the Mitchell of 104 percent, and the Hoover 99 percent prove to be much the same. For milk the seasonal variation in prices is greater; while the Wells and Mitchell figures are similar, the Hoover index is significantly different. So it is for meats. For butter the seasonal factor is still greater, and the Hoover index gains only 49 percent as compared to 91 percent and 112 percent for Wells and Mitchell. (It does so because of remarkable year-to-year movements in some constituent series.)[33]

---

from p. 129) was firewood. To the extent that coal was shipped farther than wood, the freight margins would have differed somewhat from this 3 to 1 margin.

[30] William H. Shaw, *Value of Commodity Output since 1869* (1947), p. 262.

[31] 1870 Census, *Industry and Wealth,* table VII (B), reporting $4.3 million in coal-oil products and $1.1 million for candles. The latter, however, encompasses reports from a mere five establishments; the establishment size cutoff of $500 undoubtedly excluded much production throughout the nation, not to mention the $6 million reported for whale oil.

[32] Anne Bezanson et al., *Wholesale Prices in Philadelphia, 1852–1896* (1954), pp. 87, 92, 42, 237. Whale-oil prices rose between 50 and 70 percent, candles (adamantine) 33 percent, but petroleum fell 38 percent.

[33] With so few reports, each has a relatively great weight. Three June 1 reports are shown for New York cities. Amsterdam: 15 cents (1860), 40 cents (1866), 28 cents (1867), 42 cents (1868). Cohoes: 25 cents (1860), 16 cents (1861). Homer: 16 cents (1860), 28 cents (1866), 40 cents (1867), 30 cents (1868). Such short-term changes are most unlikely indications of year-to-year shifts, as would be necessary for their proper use in a measure of annual changes.

Internal Weighting. Mitchell's procedure does not allow for greater weight to one item within a food group than to another, for example, to "beef soup pieces" than to "beef roasting pieces." [34] In principle the Hoover procedure of giving separate weights to each item within a group should be preferable. But because of the nature of the price reports, with apparently great sampling variability present, Mitchell's inadvertent averaging provides a better measure of price trend.

We take as one example the Weeks price data used by both Mitchell and Hoover for pork products in Zanesville, Ohio. The Weeks data show for 1860–1861 no change for bacon, a rise of 9 percent for ham and 64 percent for salt pork. For mutton they report no change for forequarters and a 30 percent price decline for chops.[35] Experience in more recent years surely indicates that within a group such as fresh beef, fresh pork, etc., price trends for the individual items are much more similar than such differences would suggest. Consumer tastes are more adaptable and the windfall possibilities inherent in switching to greater consumption of the items gaining least within the same group do not long remain unexplored. With Weeks's prices of Yellow B sugar and Yellow C sugar tracing a similar course in Cedar Rapids from 1860 to 1865, is it likely that one would then rise 27 percent for 1865–1866 while the other rose by a mere 4 percent? [36] The answer must surely be that such a discordant movement is possible, but unlikely.

We therefore follow Mitchell on his internal group weights for food, averaging rather than weighting. In so doing we assume, for example, that the reported price trend for bacon, salt pork, ham, and sausage all are indications of the trend in prices of preserved pork products, no one to be given a higher weight than the others because we do not know one to be more representative of the price trend for that group than the others. Not knowing which is more representative, we take them all as observations of the group price trend and weight equally. (This weighting, be it noted, is simply *within* such categories as fresh beef, corned beef, fresh pork, etc.)

Group Weights. We find that the 1892 survey of expenditures by 232 families in the Aldrich report,[37] used by Hoover in making estimates for individual item and subgroup weights, is not satisfactory for food items. That survey, as noted above, leads to a beef weight more than three times as great as that for pork, whereas the Department of Agriculture estimates

[34] Mitchell, *op. cit.,* p. 66: "The series for closely related commodities were grouped together and an average struck for these groups"; on p. 84 he shows a weight for fresh beef as a single item, with no further detail.

[35] Data from *Ibid.,* table 4.

[36] *Ibid.,* p. 431.

[37] *Report on Wholesale Prices, on Wages and on Transportation,* 52nd Cong., 2d Sess. (1893).

lead to a ⅔ ratio.[38] With the farm value of eggs only 7 percent of the pork total, can we trust the findings in the Aldrich report, which asserts that the proportion was not 7 percent but 100 percent? For our item weights within the food group, therefore, we rely instead on the Wells data, which are both contemporary and much closer to what the comprehensive Agriculture Department data indicate.

Clothing Prices.   The 75 percent rise shown by Wells and the 66 percent rise of Hoover are much the same, both well below Mitchell's 102 percent. Using Hoover's expenditure weights and Mitchell's price series reduces his gain to 88 percent, but it is still above Hoover's. The seasonal factor in the prices for textiles is much smaller than that for food, while the number of textile prices added by Hoover is very substantial (unlike the number added for food groups). We therefore adopt the Hoover series for this category.[39]

Fuel Prices.   The Wells 57 percent gain and the Mitchell 55 percent are similar, while Hoover shows 40 percent. The major difference between Mitchell and Hoover is the result of Hoover's addition of a few noncontinuous series for coal oil to the limited number of series used by Mitchell. The Weeks coal prices, used by both Mitchell and Hoover, largely relate only to the Midwest. Indeed, Midwestern reports are the only ones available for bituminous coal (which has half the coal weight) during the peak period of war inflation. Their reliability is hard to establish; for example, Weeks gives three Ohio reports for 1862 to 1864. One rises 100 percent and another 75 percent, while a third showed no change whatever.[40] The much greater gain for anthracite than bituminous shown by Mitchell and Hoover over the entire period from 1860 to 1870, and the continued gap from 1870 to 1880 shown by Hoover, seem hard to credit. As Wells pointed out in 1867, "Anthracite and bituminous coals may be grouped together. The price of one to a great degree regulates the price of the other, because . . . either will be used indifferently according to the cheapness of its cost." [41] His data show a rise of 96 percent from 1859–1862

[38] Reference to the price data in Wells indicates that aggregate expenditures would be similarly proportioned.

[39] The problem of internal weights exists here, too, though to a lesser degree. Thus the 1891 family survey used by Hoover gives cotton flannel a weight equivalent to that of cotton prints, the two together getting nearly a third of the total weight. But the 1870 Census (*Industry and Wealth*, p. 597) reported an output of 490 million yards of print cloth, as against only 8 million of flannel.

[40] The level of prices shown for anthracite in Boston is well above that shown for other areas, particularly Philadelphia. However, invoices for at least one Boston purchaser suggest no such difference. See Baker Library, Perry and Sherman papers, vol. 18, "Ellis Perry Invoices, 1864–71," indicating similar levels.

[41] The quotation is from U.S. Special Commissioner of the Revenue, *Report* (January 1867), p. 189. From data he gives on p. 66, we estimate the October annual average ratio which, applied to his retail figure from p. 189, gives 95.5 percent.

to 1866, as compared with a gain of 92 percent for anthracite in Mitchell and Hoover. We therefore take the Hoover anthracite coal index (virtually identical with Mitchell) to represent the trend for all coal, eschewing the bituminous index, whose largely different movement presumably reflects its geographic (and possibly other) biases.[42]

We adopt the Hoover series for anthracite coal, hardwood, pinewood, and coal oil, but give them the weights noted above in deriving a fuel and lighting series. While the Hoover additions to the price series used by Mitchell make little difference for three of these categories and the addition of more observations is in principle preferable, they substantially affect the coal oil series. Here we prefer the Hoover series to Mitchell largely for a single reason: The series shows somewhat better conformity with the trends and the net 1860 to 1870 change shown for refined petroleum at wholesale.[43]

Rent. For a rent series we first establish a benchmark change from 1860 to 1868 of plus 58 percent, relying on Wells's estimate of that change and the supporting detail he provides. (This compares with the 31 to 32 percent rise shown by both Mitchell and Hoover for four rooms, and the 46 to 49 percent they show for six to seven rooms. These two, when weighted together, give their rent indices.) We then compute the change in construction materials and labor over the same period, indicating a 67 percent rise.[44] On this basis we adopt Wells's implicit index of 100 for 1860 and 158 for 1868, interpolating and then extrapolating to 1880 by the index of construction materials and labor thus computed.

Our preference for this procedure over the Weeks data (and hence the Mitchell and Hoover series that rely on them) rests on several grounds.

1. The empirical result of the procedure for 1860 to 1868 gives us a result closely similar to that derived by Wells early in 1869 on the basis of contemporary quotations from dwelling units in various parts of the

[42] Weeks's wage reports now and then note that fuel is provided to employees "at cost." While trivial as an element in national earnings, this may have affected prices from areas with mining and iron industries such as Weeks shows—prices reported in some instances from company stores.

[43] For the latter, see Bezanson, *op. cit.*, p. 237.

[44] For materials we use pine boards, the common building material of the time. With mechanical components limited largely to plumbing and flues, the use of a pine-board series may not be as dubious as it would be in later times. The brick series that is also available rises even more; we exclude it because such inventory data as exist suggest limited use of bricks for constructing houses. For labor we use the present estimate of daily wages of nonfarm employees. A weighted average of unskilled and skilled labor similar to that used for more recent periods would give results very similar to the nonfarm series we use. We weight materials and labor equally, an equal weight being indicated by the 1899, 1929, and 1939 Census construction data used elsewhere in the section on employment for 1900–1960 (chap. 9).

New England, Middle Atlantic, and North Central states, where the bulk of wage earners lived.

2. In general we would not expect the tremendous gap between construction costs for new properties and rents paid on old properties in a free market to develop to the extent that is indicated if we compare the Mitchell and Hoover rent indices with construction-cost trends. If new construction went on, those who sponsored it must have made at least a modest profit. To do so they would have had to charge rents well above the levels associated with costs embodied in existing housing. Under the circumstances, it is hard to believe that landlords of existing properties did not change the rents on them to reflect this market situation, did not raise them enough to bring a rough conformity of change between the two. Because of the sluggishness of rents under existing contracts, we would not a priori expect an immediate, proportionate, nor precise response. However, the empirical result of our 1860 to 1868 comparison is enough to suggest that the response was sufficiently proportionate.

3. During the war years (when there were the largest differences between the present and the Mitchell and Hoover indices) population shifted toward the big cities. Hence even if construction costs and rents for each property remained unchanged, rents paid by nonfarm employees would have risen.[45]

4. The basic Weeks materials have a definite geographic bias, applying more to the Midwest and to small towns than the actual distribution of the employee population would require.[46]

5. The Weeks materials were additionally biased because of Weeks's attempt to get reports from employers, so that an undue proportion of reports of subsidized rents and unduly stable rents appear.

Overall Index.   Comparisons of the present cost of living series with earlier estimates reveal, of course, differences. The present series reports a 23 percent gain from 1860 to 1880, compared to Mitchell's 28 percent and Hoover's 10 percent. It shows an 1865 peak and a marked 1864–1865 rise, as does Mitchell, while Hoover shows both 1864 and 1865 at the same peak level. Its peak, in 1865, is greater than Hoover's because of higher food, rent, and fuel levels, while the greater 1860 to 1880 gain

---

[45] This opposed factor helps compensate for any tendency for construction productivity to have advanced during the war, and thereby reduced costs and selling prices below what our price per unit components indicate.

[46] For the 1862 to 1869 change, where the present estimates differ most markedly from Mitchell and Hoover, the underlying Weeks series relate almost solely to the Midwest. In 1865, for example, New England is represented by one small Connecticut town and Boston (7 reports); the entire Middle Atlantic by two reports from Camden and two from Philadelphia; but there were 28 reports from Indiana, Ohio, Illinois, Iowa, and Missouri.

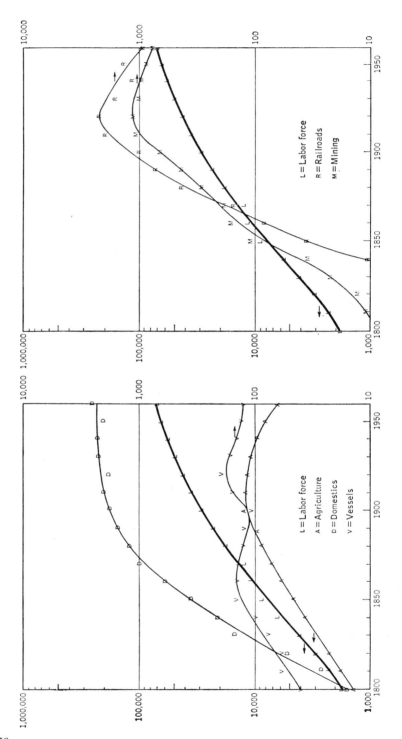

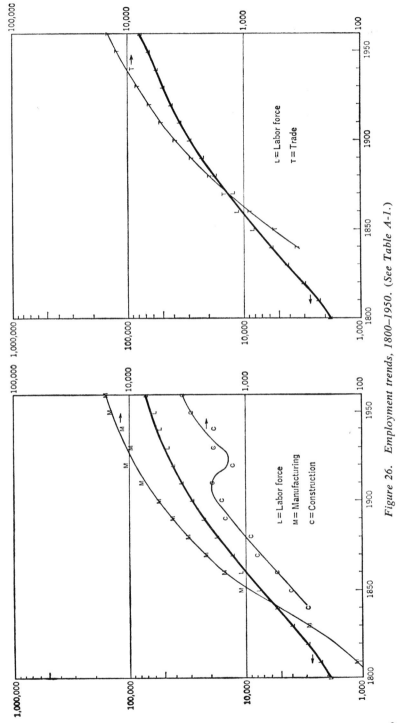

Figure 26. Employment trends, 1800–1950. (See Table A-1.)

L = Labor force
T = Trade

L = Labor force
M = Manufacturing
c = Construction

351

is largely a result of the differences between the food series used by Hoover and the present one.

LABOR FORCE AND EMPLOYMENT: 1800 to 1960 (TABLES A-1, A-2)

The individual series on labor force and employment for 1800 to 1960 which appear in Appendix Tables A-1, A-2, A-10, A-12, A-13, and A-15 were derived in extensive detail by a variety of methods differing from series to series. A full description of the procedures used for most series will appear in a paper for the 1963 meetings of the Conference on Research in Income and Wealth, and will be published in the proceedings of that conference in *Studies in Income and Wealth*, vol. 29.[1]

---

[1] Nearly 150 pages of typescript were required to provide this derivation, and were cut from the present text to shorten it. Since only limited use is made of these data in the textual analysis, it is hoped that users will not be inconvenienced. It is expected that materials not covered by the conference paper will be published elsewhere.

PART III

METHODS OF ESTIMATE:

ANNUAL SERIES,

1900 to 1960

Negative Capability, that is when a man is capable of being in uncertainties, mysteries, doubts, without any irritable reaching after fact and reason.

Letters of Keats, December 21, 1817

9

LABOR FORCE, EMPLOYMENT,

AND UNEMPLOYMENT

In this and the next chapter we outline the procedures used for estimating the several hundred component series on employment and labor force that were derived in the present study. This chapter is devoted to the derivation of the basic series on employment, unemployment, and labor force that appear in Tables A-3, A-4, A-5, A-6, A-7, and A-8. (Chapter 10 is devoted to detail on employees in nonagricultural establishments.)

We briefly contrast the present series for labor force, unemployment, and total employment with the major alternative series, and then outline the contrast for the employees in nonagricultural establishments. After this *coup d'oeil* we make a more detailed comparison for labor force, unemployment, and employment.

The specific details on present procedures begin with a description of the estimates for the self-employed, domestics, and unpaid family workers for 1930 to 1940 that appear in Table A-9 (full industrial detail but not comparable with aggregates) and Table A-4 (comparable with other labor-force components). The procedures for the earlier decades, 1900 to 1930, and the final results for 1900 to 1940 are then summarized.

We move on to the estimates of labor force next. Benchmark estimates of gainful workers and an explanation of the annual series for 1900 to 1930 are provided. An excursus on the problem of a 1918 benchmark and the extent of "extra workers" in World War I is presented. How these gainful worker estimates are linked to the figures for 1940ff., and the

355

general problem of the relationship between gainful worker and labor force series is also treated.

The discussion then turns to unemployment in benchmark years and to the relation between our 1929 to 1939 figures and earlier Bureau of Labor Statistics and other series. For the other intercensal years, of course, we compute unemployment as the difference between our labor-force and total employment series (inclusive of self-employed, unpaid family workers, domestic service employees, and employees in nonfarm enterprise), the derivation of these components being given above. A relatively extended review is then given to the meaning of the unemployment measures, how they contrast with earlier series, and what they tell us as compared with other measures of economic change.

Having thus surveyed the data for 1900 to 1940, we discuss the figures for 1940 to 1960. Although the bulk of these numbers are the official Current Population Survey findings, we have had to make supplemental estimates for detail lacking in certain years from 1940 to 1946, and to give detail on self-employed by industry for the entire 1940–1960 period. It is not that we lack for a variety of government series under that general rubric for 1940–1960 but that we lack series directly comparable with the Current Population Survey totals. Since the latter form the basic material for current labor-force analysis, we have thus supplemented them.

The remaining estimates of employment relate to employees in individual nonagricultural industries—series comparable with the BLS series for employees in nonagricultural establishments and therefore not comparable with the Current Population Survey figures. We have derived a considerable volume of such series, as well as a total for each year from 1900 to 1928 that is comparable with the official BLS series since that date (Tables A-5, A-6). These are discussed in detail in the following chapter, as is the derivation of the self-employed totals for certain of those industries from 1900 to 1940.

RELATIONSHIP TO CURRENT SERIES AND PRIOR ESTIMATES

Current Series

A primary purpose in developing the present estimates was to provide series that would be as closely comparable as possible with the various official series that begin in the past few decades. Such comparability should facilitate the comparison of recent and prior cycles, as well as offer a firmer foundation for measuring long-term trends in national income, manpower input, and real earnings.

For total labor force, total employment, farm employment, nonfarm employment, self-employment, domestic employment, and unemployment, the present estimates (in Tables A-3, A-4, A-6, A-7) are designed to be comparable with those of the Current Population Survey. That survey (conducted by the Census Bureau, with its labor-force data presented by the Bureau of Labor Statistics) provides the continuing official source of reliable data on these subjects. Hence we seek to link to the levels it provides for the years since 1940, when it began. However, the Survey estimates are not wholly consistent with the decennial census levels for 1940, 1950, and 1960. Our present estimates, in consequence, will be at variance with studies tied to decennial census figures.[1] Because the Survey estimates are not consistent with the farm-employment series of the Department of Agriculture, nor with the employees in nonagricultural establishment series of the Department of Labor, neither will the present series be consistent with the latter.[2] Because the Survey estimates are not comparable with the estimates for persons engaged, proprietors, or business firms as issued by the Office of Business Economics, the present estimates will not be comparable with the latter either.[3]

[1] We therefore will differ from the fundamental study by John Durand, *The Labor Force in the United States, 1890–1960* (1948) p. 208 and *passim,* for he benchmarks to the 1940 Census; and from the review by Clarence Long, in *The Labor Force under Changing Income and Employment* (1958), appendix A, for he adopts the 1940 and 1950 Census levels rather than survey levels. Similarly the massive summary of decennial census materials by David L. Kaplan and M. Claire Casey, *Occupational Trends in the United States 1900 to 1950,* Bureau of the Census Working Paper no. 5 (1958), will differ since it is intentionally based on the decennial census results. As a minor point it should be noted that our 1940 and 1950 Current Population Survey levels differ from those as originally published in the Census P-50 series as they include an allowance for armed forces overseas. For revised CPS figures: Bureau of the Census, *Historical Statistics of the U.S.,* vol. II, pp. 70–71.

[2] For 1930 to 1939 the labor force, farm employment, and total nonfarm employment series will also differ slightly from those estimated for the Bureau of Labor Statistics in 1948. The latter estimates appear in the author's "Labor Force, Employment and Unemployment, 1929–39: Estimating Methods," *Monthly Labor Review* (July, 1948) table 1, and have been reprinted in the *Handbook of Labor Statistics, Historical Statistics* and a wide variety of other publications. To maintain comparability as much as possible, the present absolute unemployment series has been kept the same as the original BLS estimates. Differences between the present revised employment series and the original BLS series have been taken up in the labor-force estimates, thus producing minor differences in the total labor force, civilian labor force, and percent unemployed series.

[3] The National Income Division estimates of persons engaged include an estimate for active proprietors of unincorporated enterprises devoting the major portion of their time to the business. See Office of Business Economics, *U.S. Income and Output, 1958,* table VI-16. This estimate is not adjusted to Survey levels. The present series, as the OBE proprietors' count, will likewise differ from the OBE count of business firms. See, for example, Betty Churchill, "Rise in the Business Population," *Survey of Current Business* (May, 1959).

The detailed industry employee estimates in the present series (Tables A-5 and A-8) are intended to be comparable with the corresponding components of the BLS series for employees in manufacturing, mining, and other nonagricultural establishments. The latter constitute a widely used comprehensive body of data, available monthly for the study of changing employment conditions. They differ in some respects from the National Income Division estimates for employees.[4]

Historical Series

The present estimates have benefited from, and differ from, a variety of historical estimates of labor force, employment, and unemployment. Although various detailed references are made in the sections on methodology, some general comments may be made here on the data for 1900 to 1960. (On the earlier years see above.)

Labor Force. The basic decennial census data on gainful workers for the years prior to 1940 have been worked over by a number of estimators. In general we differ from earlier investigators (1) in our attempt to make the historical series comparable with the present Current Population Survey (CPS) results, (2) in the principles followed in evaluating the decennial census gainful-worker benchmarks, (3) in the detail in which intercensal interpolations were made, (4) in the study given to the effects of "extra workers" during the depression, and (5) in adjustment for women entering the labor force during World War I and the irregular effects of immigration between 1900 and 1914.

Kaplan and Casey have summarized the census data most recently and carefully, adopting the adjustments made by their predecessor in census occupational analysis, Alba Edwards.[5] Aside from our excluding the 10–13 age group from the 1900ff. annual estimates (to provide easier comparability with the CPS series beginning in 1940) our major difference from these estimates lies in their adoption of Edwards's adjustments of the 1910 and 1920 Census, and his adjustment of the 1900 count for "laborers not specified." [6] We differ from Edwards's 1910 adjustment because he arbitrarily assumes that ratios which maintained in 1900 must have maintained in the subsequent census. We prefer instead a systematic procedure that relates labor-force components to more reliably measured

---

[4] In part because of differences in the rate at which either agency adjusts current data to Social Security benchmarks. But in addition there will be differences reflecting the use of the Standard Industrial Classification. For example, the BLS includes automotive repair with services whereas the OBE series classifies such repair under trade.

[5] Kaplan and Casey, *op. cit.*

[6] Alba Edwards, *Comparative Occupation Statistics in the United States, 1870 to 1940* (1943), constitutes the central systematic work in the field by a man with years of experience in developing the census occupation data.

contemporary census data. We differ from his 1920 adjustment because (1) it was made largely on a priori grounds, and (2) the experience of World War II now suggests that the change from 1910 to 1920 labor-force rates could readily have been accounted for by war and prosperity rather than by differences in enumeration date.

As noted above, we differ from the major study by John Durand chiefly because his 1900, 1920, and 1930 Census data figures are designed to be comparable with the 1940 Census levels, whereas our estimates tie in to the markedly different level of the Current Population Survey since 1940.[7] Moreover, he provides no 1910 figure.

We differ from the decennial estimates of Clarence Long for two major reasons.[8] The first is his adjustment for the 1910 overcount. He assumes that the worker rates for females aged 14–24 and 45–64 were reported incorrectly by the census, but that this general tendency to overcount females somehow missed the central 25–44 group; that the worker rate for women 45–64 was simply an average of the 1900 and 1920 rates; that the rate for boys 14–19 not in school and for unmarried girls not in school was an average of 1900 and 1920 rates. We find no explanation of why the general tendency to overcount, following from the 1910 enumerator instructions and approach, missed this single group of females 25–44; we find no rationale given for an averaging of 1900 and 1920 rates (the latter clearly affected by World War I). A priori stipulation could as well set the 1910 worker rates for females and children above 1900 rates, at 1900 levels, or between 1900 and 1920 rates. Secondly, his 1940 and 1950 figures, from the decennial censuses, are treated as directly comparable with the gainful-worker counts from earlier censuses. For 1940 and 1950, however, we use the higher (annual average) levels from the Current Population Survey, finding that it is the broader coverage by that survey —but not the decennial census—that yields figures most comparable with the gainful-worker enumerations in earlier decades.

We likewise differ from the National Industrial Conference Board series, which are tied to the original, unadjusted, census data and interpolated by using population series less carefully developed than the recently issued census annual population figures relied upon in the present procedures.[9]

---

[7] Durand, *op. cit.* We conclude that the gainful worker–labor force difference analyzed by Durand (and the earlier study by Durand and Goldfield) is neutralized by the revisions in Current Population Survey approach developed in 1945 and later years.

[8] Long, *op. cit.,* supplementary appendix g, mimeographed. We differ in addition because Long makes minor adjustments in the 1900 Census (a census which no other expert has challenged) and that for 1890 (for which we follow the revisions given in the 1900 Census, *Occupations*).

[9] National Industrial Conference Board, "Employment and Unemployment of the Labor Force, 1900 to 1940," *Conference Board Economic Record* (Mar. 20, 1940); reprinted in subsequent issues of *The Economic Almanac.*

Our difference from the pioneering work by Daniel Carson, as from the Fabricant estimates which utilize his figures, arises from Carson's 1910 and 1920 adjustment, discussed in more detail in connection with the labor-force methodology.[10]

Our present labor-force series differs in level from that of the original BLS estimates for the 1930s largely because we assert (1) that the April gainful-worker rate is in fact the best estimate of the annual labor-force worker rate; and (2) that in the light of the many revisions in the Current Population Survey since 1940, there is no warrant for adjusting the original census rate seasonally. (Original and revised figures alike allow for population change.)

Unemployment. The unemployment estimates in the present study differ from prior series (e.g., of the National Industrial Conference Board, of Paul Douglas for unemployment in selected industries, and of other estimators) for a variety of reasons discussed in some detail elsewhere.[11] One major reason is that the present estimates rely on benchmark estimates derived from 1910 Census materials (the latter published only in 1948), with adjustments based on the more comprehensive materials of the 1901 Cost of Living Survey and an extensive survey by the 1910 Immigration Commission. Most prior estimates either used no benchmark or used the census data without adjusting for obvious undercoverage. A second source of variance is the difference between the labor-force series and the employment series used for intercensal interpolation.

Differences from earlier unemployment estimates by the author[12] reflect selective improvements in the basic data.[13] The higher level for 1920, for example, reflects the addition to the labor force of armed forces overseas in 1920, omitted in earlier estimates. The higher level for 1918 reflects the adjustment of the 1918 labor force for extra workers rather than stipulating the 1918 unemployment percentage by analogy from World War II. The higher 1901 figure reflects the use of Frickey's sample of state

[10] Daniel Carson, "Changes in the Industrial Composition of Manpower since the Civil War," in *Studies in Income and Wealth* (1949), vol. XI. Solomon Fabricant, "The Changing Industrial Distribution of Gainful Workers," in *Ibid.* Carson's data are used by Simon Kuznets, *National Product since 1869* (1946), p. 120, and "Long Term Changes in the National Income of the United States of America since 1870," in *Income and Wealth*, series II (1952).

[11] Differences for the 1930s are discussed in the *Monthly Labor Review* (July, 1948); for earlier decades, in the section on unemployment methodology.

[12] Appearing in Universities—National Bureau of Economic Research, *The Measurement and Behavior of Unemployment* (1957), p. 215; Joint Economic Committee, *Productivity, Prices, and Incomes* (1957), p. 87; *Historical Statistics*, vol. II, p. 73.

[13] Differences from NICB and other estimates are discussed in detail in the later section in this chapter on unemployment estimates.

factory reports (plus those of Berridge and Jerome) for intercensal interpolation, rather than the prior procedure of relying on the flow of non-agicultural finished commodities. Lower levels for the 1920s reflect a more precise handling of trade employment: employment in 11 kinds of business was related to the separate flows of goods rather than the earlier simple linking of two aggregate series.

Employment.   It is impossible to detail the various causes of difference in employment estimates, for they arise from differences between the 60 or 70 employment series estimated for the present series and the corresponding (explicit or implicit) estimates of other estimators. We merely note a few broad contrasts.

For farm employment the customary source used by prior estimators is that of the United States Department of Agriculture.[14] The USDA series differs in concept from the farm-employment series that we are attempting to extend, that of the Current Population Survey. Our estimates differ, in addition, because we rely on Population Census benchmarks instead of the inferior Census of Agriculture benchmarks; because we find the use of the Shaw-Hopkins series for interpolating farm wage-earner employment unsatisfactory; and because the new USDA series has a pattern of change for the 1930s contradictory to that shown in the basic crop-reporter data on which all series for that period eventually rest.

Major differences from earlier series appear in the categories of finance, service, trade, and construction.[15] Besides decennial estimates for trade and those by Stigler for domestic service, the major sources for these components are King (for 1909 to 1919) and Kuznets (for 1919 to 1929).[16] King's estimates for finance, trade, and service are estimated en bloc and are not worth particular attention.[17] The Kuznets estimates are a major

[14] Harold Barger and Hans Landsberg, *American Agriculture, 1899–1939* (1942), p. 251, rely on earlier Bureau of Agricultural Economics series and on census benchmarks. John Kendrick, *Productivity Trends in the United States* (1961), Appendix B, uses the USDA series for his employment estimates, 1919ff. For prior years he uses Census of Population data (as we do), though these are not comparable with the Census of Agriculture benchmarks embodied in the USDA series.

[15] This is least true of the Kendrick estimates, which rely largely on a 1951 version of the present series.

[16] Harold Barger, *Distribution's Place in the American Economy since 1869* (1955), p. 4. Barger relies on Carson's estimates. George Stigler, *Domestic Servants in the United States 1900–1940* (1946). Willford I. King, *The National Income and Its Purchasing Power* (1930); Simon Kuznets, *National Income and Its Composition* (1941); and Paul Douglas, *Real Wages in the United States, 1890–1926* (1930), p. 455, give estimates for construction.

[17] King presents virtually no description of his methodology (see his p. 50 notes); hence we must rely on the somewhat less scanty record in his earlier study, in Wesley Mitchell (ed.), *Income in the United States, Its Amount and Distribution 1909–1919* (1922).

source of careful workmanship. We differ from his trade-employee estimates because we develop a benchmark for 1920 and 1930 and because we interpolate by a series for United States manpower requirements in trade (based on Shaw's flow of finished commodities) rather than rely on the use of employment data for two to four states.[18] We differ from his construction estimate because we develop an employment benchmark for 1899, while he uses none prior to 1929; because our interpolation procedure is done in somewhat more detail than his; and because we rely on the basic series of William Shaw on construction-materials output rather than on the less satisfactory Chawner estimates of construction activity. For finance and service the Kuznets estimates are clearly superior to those of the NICB. We nonetheless differ for a variety of reasons—chiefly reliance on additional detailed sources (e.g., Bureau of Internal Revenue reports on bowling-alley licenses; a count of motion-picture licensees in 1920; Census of Benevolent Institutions reports on nursing employment); corrections in others (e.g., the AMA series for physicians); and so on.

For manufacturing and mining, the census benchmarks have been commonly used. For mining, we follow essentially the interpolation of Barger and Schurr, differing thereby somewhat from Kuznets and Douglas.[19] For manufacturing, differences occur primarily for 1900 to 1909, where we combine unpublished estimates of Frickey for selected states with those of Jerome and Berridge for other states; and for 1909 to 1919, where we interpolate by Shaw's finished commodities, adjusted for inventory change. For utilities and transport, differences from Barger, Gould, Douglas, and Kuznets reflect variations in the treatment of water transport and of livery-stable employment; the use of the American Gas Association series on gas employment; and the use of unpublished Western Union data.[20]

For the Federal government, we use the recently revised Civil Service Commission figures in place of the earlier CSC figures used by Fabricant and Kuznets.[21] For state government, we develop a variety of benchmark estimates and interpolate by national data. King uses New York State, Fabricant the New York and Massachusetts series, while Kuznets's series

[18] We describe the series used for his income estimates. Kuznets also provides a second estimate for 1919 to 1929 similar in approach to ours, differing largely in that we use the flow of finished commodities, by type, to interpolate 1920 and 1930 employment figures by type of store, instead of using the entire total for finished commodities as he does.

[19] Harold Barger and Sam Schurr, *The Mining Industries, 1899–1939* (1944).

[20] Harold Barger, *The Transportation Industries, 1899–1946* (1951); Jacob M. Gould, *Output and Productivity in the Electric and Gas Utilities, 1899–1942* (1946).

[21] Solomon Fabricant, *The Trend of Government Activity in the United States since 1900* (1952).

are substantially affected by the inclusion of Ohio and Iowa soldiers' pensions in his wage totals for 1919–1923. For local government from 1900 to 1919, we develop United States 1900, 1905, 1910, and 1920 benchmarks whereas Fabricant relies largely on New York and Chicago employment trends prior to 1919. For 1919ff. we follow Fabricant, who differs slightly from Kuznets's series.[22]

For the industrial groups where self-employment was numerically great —construction, trade, transport, service—detailed benchmark estimates were derived by computing self-employed–employee ratios from the 1910, 1930, and 1940 Population Censuses and using various methods of interpolation. Particularly for the 1930s, the method of interpolating varied the ratios to reflect the changing tide of the business cycle, thus producing a series stabler than the corresponding series for employees in the same industry. This last is a major factor in producing differences between the present estimates and the National Income Division estimates of active proprietors for the 1930s.

Differences from the BLS series for employees in nonagricultural establishments for 1919 to 1929[23] stem from a variety of reasons. For mining and manufacturing, the BLS procedures were similar to those used in the present estimates except that BLS use of regression relationships to the Barger-Schurr data and the Fabricant data produced some erroneous results. For construction, the BLS procedures adopt a less accurate procedure for handling force-account construction. For state and local government, the BLS extrapolated 1929 employment by Kuznets's series. The BLS trade-employment series was extrapolated by a regression against Kuznets's deflated consumption expenditures. Thus it was not tied to any employment benchmark and did not allow as precisely as do the present estimates for the difference in volume of employment produced by a $1 million rise in food store sales as against an equivalent rise in department store sales. For banking, a regression against bank loans was used by BLS, whereas the present series are tied, via employee-bank ratios, to the reliable series for number of banks. For the balance of finance and service, regressions against Kuznets's series were used by BLS.[24]

---

[22] Minor revisions bring differences from earlier estimates by the author used in Council of State Governments, *A State Department of Administration* (1957), appendix A.

[23] Appearing in BLS Bulletin 1312, *Employment and Earnings Statistics for the United States, 1909–60* (1961); in *Historical Statistics,* vol. II; and other sources.

[24] BLS series are described in an unpublished memorandum of December, 1948, by John Wymer, and reflect (except for trade, finance, service) earlier estimates by the present author.

NONFARM SELF-EMPLOYED BY DETAILED INDUSTRY: 1930 TO 1940 (TABLE A-9)

The following section outlines in some detail the methods used to estimate changes of detailed components of this group, the results being summarized in Table A-9. In deriving Table A-4 aggregates for the self-employed, however, as well as for unpaid family workers and domestics, the series thus derived were benchmarked to 1940 Current Population Survey averages.

I

The series for self-employed persons operates only as a set of registration totals. Many more persons than appear in the figures of this series were self-employed at one time or other during any year. Thus, thousands of persons attempted to strike out on their own during the depression as grocery retailers, insurance salesmen, filling-station operators, or truckers. But at the same time that many were trying to find a minimum of income in entrepreneurship, thousands of entrepreneurs were going out of business. It is only the net balancing of entrances and exits which shows up in this series. It is particularly important to note that the drop in self-employment between 1929 and 1933, being a net decline, does not contradict the frequently made statement that many persons opened stores during the depression because they could find no other method of making a living.[1]

---

[1] The present series is considerably higher than previous estimates by Woytinsky et al. for 1930, and hence for later years. This occurs because it is tied to a higher base-year estimate: The 1940 Census included many own-account and self-employed workers who were not included in the restricted occupation categories used by estimates based on the 1930 classifications. (These estimates customarily included only owners, operators, and proprietors, building contractors, and a few very small groupings.)

A direct indication of the shortcoming in these series can be gotten from the addition to 1930 totals for BLS employees and for agriculture these alternate self-employed estimates. The resultant totals are either below or quite close to the census employment estimate. The obvious inference would be that the BLS duplicating component of near 1.5 million in 1940 had grown from next to nothing in 1930—a most unlikely eventuality.

The single exception is the National Research Project series, which is higher than the current series by reason of some overgenerous allocations. Thus it assumes that all "owners, proprietors, managers and officials" in manufacturing and retail trade were self-employed. The actual proportions shown in the 1940 Census were not 100 and 100 percent but 36 and 81 percent. This series assumes 75 percent of clergymen were self-employed, the 1940 Census showing only 1 percent. This series assumes 7.5

A further fact to be noted is the apparent influence of employment and business activity on the level of self-employment. It will be noted from Table A-4 that the depression low for the self-employed (other than domestics) was 1933 while the low year for nonagricultural employees was 1932. This lag was not fortuitous. Over the entire 1930–1940 period the number of self-employed other than domestics tended, by and large, to vary with the number of employees a half year before (with an allowance necessary for a downward trend in the self-employed). As the depression deepened, employment fell off; payrolls, retail sales, and business profits dropped; and, eventually, business failures mounted. The same train of events occurred in reverse on the upswing. Employees were hired, and payrolls rose in manufacturing and related fields. Potential trade and service entrepreneurs then ordered goods, rented and repaired stores, and, some time after payrolls had first risen, the business population finally increased in number.[2]

II

The procedures employed in deriving the present estimates are so essential a departure from techniques previously employed that a fairly detailed description of procedure is given in part IV. A general comparison, however, can be made between the present methods and earlier techniques.

1. The self-employed may be estimated by assuming that their number varied directly and proportionately with the number of employees. This, by and large, is the procedure utilized in the estimates of the National Industrial Conference Board.

2. The self-employed may be estimated by a combination of methods— such as carrying groups as a constant between Industrial Census dates, extrapolating totals by business-failure estimates, and alternate methods. In general such procedures have been employed by Daniel Carson and Henrietta Liebman, by Simon Kuznets, and in prior estimates of the Bureau of Labor Statistics.

3. The self-employed may be estimated by working out the changing ratios of self-employed to employees in major industry groups, applying

---

percent of "public school teachers" were self-employed, while the 1940 Census indicates only 1 percent of "teachers n.e.c." were self-employed. Taking account of merely these four categories, the difference can be cut down by nearly ¾ of a million.

[2] The correlation of nonagricultural self-employed other than domestics with (1) nonagricultural employees in the previous year, (2) nonagricultural employees in the given year, and (3) time, was extremely high. The values estimated from these relationships were within 3 percent of the true values. Similar results were derived by using deflated gross national product instead of employment. The gross product values were those presented by J. L. Mosak, *Econometrica* (January, 1945), and by the present author, *American Economic Review* (March, 1945).

the ratios to the BLS employees series, and thus arriving at a series for self-employed persons in the specified industry groups. That, in essence, is the procedure used in the present estimates.

The 1945–1947 revisions in the BLS series on nonagricultural employees make it one of the strongest available for measuring economic activity over the period. If the changing relationships between employees and self-employed can be precisely ascertained, then the self-employed can be estimated from the movement of this series, on whose nature and characteristics we are reasonably well informed.

The chief problem, therefore, becomes one of computing the ratios of employees to self-employed in each industrial division.[3] The computation is facilitated by several factors. First, the ratios change at a moderate rate and in accordance with certain ascertainable rules. It is a surer matter to interpolate between ratios than between decennial figures on self-employment, or even figures on employees—as is done by those estimators who seek to number the self-employed more or less directly. Further facilitating the computation of ratios is the fact that noncomparable employment data can be used in checking them. Although the absolute levels of Population and Industrial Census data may not be comparable, ratios taken from them may reasonably be compared in many cases.

It was found, in general, that the ratios tended to vary with the level of employment in each industry group. In poor times there are fewer employees per proprietor than in better years. In years of high-level activity, employees are hired at a faster rate than businesses are organized. This general pattern of relationship had to be modified for some industries because of the considerable importance of long-term trends. Thus, in the bituminous coal industry the steady progress of mechanization was a major factor, and in retail trade the growing concentration of employment in chain stores was of substantial importance.

By way of summary, it may be said that this changing ratio procedure was employed for estimating just over 70 percent of the self-employed (excluding domestic) group.[4] About 10 percent of the total was derived from a more or less direct count. For several groups which were not very important numerically, a constant ratio was assumed. The figures for domestics were based on semiannual surveys by the National Bureau of Economic Research and the Department of Commerce during the period covered.

The self-employed series developed by applying ratios so derived suf-

---

[3] Ratios could be computed from the 1929, 1933, 1935, and 1939 Census of Distribution and Business, the biennial Census of Manufactures, and the 1919, 1929, and 1939 Census of Mineral Industries. In some cases comparative data were computed from the 1930 and 1940 Census of Population.

[4] As of 1940.

fered from one inevitable shortcoming: Most of its constituent series are open-end series. While base data from the Census of Population in 1940 are available in considerable detail, no comparable detail is available for earlier years. The figures cannot be tied to 1930 Census data: The difference between the comprehensive 1940 totals for self-employed and own-account workers on the one hand, and the much thinner 1930 totals for "owners, operators and proprietors" (plus builders and a few other trivial groupings) on the other, is too great.

The same shortcoming has, of course, handicapped all previous estimates. In addition, the paucity of data available to previous estimators has been a hindrance, for previous estimates all start from the 1930 Census totals, proceeding indefinitely from that year without check or *terminus ad quem*.[5] The present series, however, could begin with the far more comprehensive and detailed data of the 1940 Census.

Lacking any direct check on the net movement of the series, we have nevertheless, a partial and indirect one, for when it is added to the estimates of total employees the indicated gain in total employment over the decade is 5 percent. The quite independent Census of Population figures, adjusted to an annual average basis, rose by 7.8 percent. The implied Bureau of Labor Statistics duplication component in the present estimates runs from 1.1 million in 1930 (or 3.9 percent) to 1.3 million in 1940 (or 4.2 percent). These figures suggest a gratifying, if not conclusive, similarity of movement. The estimates of self-employed persons—secured though they are through open-end methods and by a considerable and novel variety of techniques—have at the very least not distorted the movement of total employment. Inferentially, the movement of self-employment is confirmed.

III

There are currently available perhaps five comprehensive attempts to estimate the self-employed for most or all of the period between the end of the boom and the beginning of World War II.[6] In addition to these

---

[5] In addition, most of these series rely on some base figure such as that derived by Woytinsky, adding "owners, operators and proprietors," plus a few minor groups. W. S. Woytinsky, *Labor in the United States* (1938). Such a total, necessarily restricted by the 1930 classifications, could not give as satisfactory a picture as the data later available.

[6] Bureau of Labor Statistics, estimates of total nonagricultural employment (release of January, 1940). Bureau of Foreign and Domestic Commerce, *National Income in the United States, 1929–1935* (1937). Simon Kuznets, *National Income and Its Composition, 1919–1938* (1941). National Industrial Conference Board, "Employment and Unemployment of the Labor Force, 1900–1940," *The Conference Board Economic Record* (Mar. 20, 1940). Daniel Carson and Henrietta Liebman,

estimates there have been those implicitly made by Robert Nathan, the CIO, the AFL and the Alexander Hamilton Institute in the process of deriving unemployment estimates.[7] Since a description of the procedure employed by the carefully constructed Kuznets and NICB series is given below for each component set of estimates, a general discussion of these alternate series may suffice.

1. The Bureau of Labor Statistics series on nonagricultural employment—now withdrawn—estimated the self-employed for major industrial groupings, relying primarily on interpolation between Industrial Census totals to get at movement, but to some extent using wage-earner employment to get some components and carrying other figures forward as a constant to get other component series. Problems of comparability between reported census figures and the shortcomings of linear interpolation as an estimating procedure make this series unsatisfactory for present purposes.

2. The Department of Commerce has prepared estimates of the self-employed for the 1929–1935 period as a step in its derivation of national income totals. Since many of the techniques utilized proved to be unsatisfactory and since the method of computation for national income estimates has changed, this series was not continued beyond 1935. The shortcomings of the procedures were, in most instances, similar to those noted above and to those noted in other series. For a number of significant groupings, however—primarily domestic and professional service—that agency still computes estimates of self-employed and own-account workers. These estimates were examined through the courtesy of members of the National Income Division and, in certain instances, their procedure adopted.

3. Daniel Carson and Henrietta Liebman prepared a series on the self-employed covering the 1930–1937 period. Relying on a 1930 base, as do all the other estimates previously made, they divided the base figure into two sections: One covered by Dun and Bradstreet reporting; the other, not so covered. For the former group a movement series was based from the annual number of concerns reported by Dun and Bradstreet in the appropriate industrial categories. For the second group—which included professional workers, insurance agents, and others totaling a third of all

---

Labor Supply and Employment (Works Progress Administration, mimeograph, November, 1939).

Mention might also be made of a series constructed by E. E. Lincoln. This series, intended to be a balancing item, fails to include unpaid family workers or wage and salaried domestics. Linearly interpolated between 1930 and 1940 and held as a constant between 1938 and 1940, the series hardly requires separate analysis.

[7] In none of these series are separate estimates of the self-employed computed, their totals being allocated to employment totals under the assumption that the movement of the self-employed is identical with that of employees.

the self-employed—the 1930 total was run at a constant over the 7-year period. Wage-earner domestic employment in private families was computed using the movement of total employment in manufacturing, trade, transportation, and communication. Since so large a portion of the total is merely carried as a constant or imputed by the total movement of employment; since Dun and Bradstreet coverage is at best rather low (and there is no assurance that the coverage is equally great from year to year, as is the implicit assumption); since the procedure takes no account of data from the various industrial censuses or relevant employment series, this procedure was felt to be unsatisfactory.

4. The estimates of the National Industrial Conference Board, like most of those made in connection with unemployment estimates, tend to assume in all cases that the level of self-employment varies with that of all other employment in any particular industry. This is so for their estimates for forestry, fishing, mining, construction, transportation, utilities, finances, miscellaneous, and other groupings. For professional and domestic service groupings, the Conference Board utilized National Income Division estimates. For manufacturing, the Board interpolated linearly between census data, while for trade a similar procedure was employed. The basic total employed figure was, as in the other series, the 1930 gainfully occupied value.

The chief assumption—that the self-employed varied with the employed in most industries—requires the ratio of self-employed to employees in the respective industries to have remained constant over the period. This assumption is not borne out by Industrial Census data. Furthermore, their interpolation between census data in trade apparently does not adjust for incomparabilities between reported census totals, while for both trade and manufacturing the interpolation procedure gives inadequate allowance to the effects of changing business conditions.

5. The most careful series covering the entire period is undoubtedly that constructed by Kuznets. However, the unavailability of the 1940 Population Census and the 1939 Industrial Census data, together with various qualifications noted below where details are discussed, made this careful series a stimulating and useful reference point, but one unacceptable for present purposes.

IV

We discuss below the estimates for each of the self-employed categories, from those in forestry through "not elsewhere classified."

Forestry

The 1,900 odd self-employed and own-account workers in the forestry group in 1940 were primarily those engaged in the gathering of barks and gums.[8] Their number was therefore estimated by the movement of a series of proprietors engaged in gathering gums.[9,10]

Fisheries

In the absence of reliable data on proprietors in the fishing industry for any year but 1940,[11] it was assumed that the movement of the self-employed group over the period was identical with that of the employed.[12] A series on fisheries employment was derived from annual estimates which the Bureau of Fisheries has published for various fishing regions in the United States,[13] and applied directly to the 1940 figure of 36,015 to secure a series on the self-employed.[14]

[8] Most of the persons in timber management and fire control are employees of governmental agencies and hence not in the self-employed group.

[9] The NICB used the movement of the BLS sawmill employment index. Kuznets includes forestry in the miscellaneous group and uses for movement a combination of motor transportation, miscellaneous banking and brokerage, air transportation, and fisheries. The National Income Division currently uses for movement a series on the volume of production of naval stores. But inasmuch as curtailment programs for the industry were initiated in 1934, 1936, and 1939–1940, changes in production in those years probably do not parallel changes in the number of entrepreneurs.

[10] Estimates of proprietors who tapped their own trees were supplied by Jay Ward of the Forest Service.

[11] The 1930 gainfully employed and the 1940 labor-force values cannot be satisfactorily compared. See Alba Edwards, *Comparative Occupation Statistics, 1870–1940* (1943), p. 33.

[12] The NICB used agricultural employment changes to determine the changes in the self-employed group in fisheries. The Department of Commerce previously applied a ratio of proprietors per fisheries employee (based on a 1934 NRA study) to employment estimates of the Bureau of Fisheries, a procedure followed by Kuznets. For the 1930s that agency relies on Bureau of Fisheries totals for 1932, 1937, and 1938, with straight-line extrapolation and interpolation for the remaining years in the 1932–1940 period. Then by relating and adjusting gainfully employed total for 1930 to the labor force in 1940, it secures a 1930 estimate. The year 1931 is then interpolated between 1930 and 1932.

[13] These estimates appear in that agency's annual publication, *Fishery Statistics in the United States*. Figures are given for seven regions in the United States. Estimates for the Mississippi region are available only for 1931 and hence could not be used in deriving a series. Estimates for two regions, New England and Middle Atlantic, are available annually except for 1934 and 1936. Data for the South Atlantic and Great Lakes areas are available for all years but 1933 and 1935. The missing data for these four regions were derived simply by linear interpolation, and the final component series added to give one on total fisheries employment. (Interpolation or direct use of a series on fisheries production or on employment in the Chesapeake and Pacific regions—for both of which continuous series are available—was found to give results inconsistent with the annual data that are available.)

[14] The basic 1940 total for "forestry, except logging, and fishery" was split by the ratio of own-account fisherman to own-account fisherman plus foresters as estimated in the 1940 Census, *Industrial Characteristics*, pp. 65, 67.

Bituminous Coal

Self-employed and own-account workers in bituminous coal—totaling under 10,000 in 1940—were estimated by securing a regression of the ratio of wage earners to proprietors on time, deriving interpolated ratios, and applying the interpolated ratios to the BLS employment series for bituminous coal.[15],[16] Although the relationship between the ratios and employment and the number of small mines was considered, apparently the trend of mechanization was by far the most important determinant since an almost perfect fit of the ratios on time was obtained.[17] (The ratio changed from 154 in 1929 to 109 in 1935 to 80 in 1939.)

Anthracite Coal

The self-employed and own-account workers in the Pennsylvania anthracite industry were estimated by applying to the basic 1940 figure of 1,953 the movement of a series on anthracite coal establishments in Pennsylvania.[18],[19]

[15] The NICB apparently carried the 1929 proprietor total forward by the BLS employment series, without checking into the 1935 or 1939 census figures. Since the number of proprietors did not in fact vary with employment, this procedure is quite inappropriate. Kuznets used census totals for 1929 and 1935, interpolating by the number of class 5 mines in operation. This procedure is likewise inadequate since the 1935 total is not at all comparable with the 1929 total and since the series for proprietors moves more neatly with time than with the number of class 5 mines.

[16] The data for 1929 and 1939 are available from the 1939 Census of Mineral Industries. The 1935 data as published are not comparable with these years, inasmuch as the proprietors of 2,023 "local mines" were included not with proprietors but with wage earners in that year. As a result the ratio of all proprietors to class 5 mines is 1.2 in 1929 and 1.4 in 1939, but only 0.4 in the intermediate year of 1935. According to Mrs. McMillan of the National Coal Association, who worked on the 1935 Census, the 2,023 "local" mines, which are not defined in census reports, mined between 1,000 and 5,000 tons. It was therefore assumed that the number of proprietors per mine of this size in 1939 (using data from Miss Spencer of the Bureau of the Census) was the same as the number in 1935. That ratio was applied to the 2,023 mines figure, and new proprietor and ratio estimates were derived. These final estimates were then utilized in the fashion described above.

[17] It should be noted that this series is probably of little value for determining the trend of bituminous proprietors per se, inasmuch as a considerable if not total undercoverage of illegal mines characterized the census.

[18] Kuznets's procedure for 1930 to 1934 is similar, although based on a different series (annual reports of Pennsylvania on *Productive Industries*). Following 1935, however, he holds the entrepreneurial figure as a constant. The NICB implicitly used the movement of anthracite employment.

[19] The basic 1940 total was divided between bituminous and anthracite by the proportion of wage earners in each industry, as given in the 1939 Census of Mineral Industries.

The movement series was based simply on linear interpolation between the 1929 and the 1939 reported totals of collieries, washeries, and dredges. The 1935 total is

Metal Mining

Bureau of Mines estimates of the number of gold and silver mines in the continental United States were used to extrapolate the basic 1940 total of 13,009. Census of Mineral Industries figures for 1939, as well as 1929, indicated that a substantial majority of the covered proprietors were in gold and silver mining. Inasmuch as the proprietors missed by the Mineral Industry Census but included by the Population Census were also likely to have been small gold or silver miners, it was felt that the series on number of mines would suffice for interpolation.[20,21]

Other Mining

An additional 4,900 self-employed and own-account workers were, in 1940, engaged in mining other than metal mining. For the stone and quarrying group, several industrial subgroups were combined to derive ratios of wage earners per proprietor in 1929 and 1939. The ratios were interpolated linearly and applied to the BLS employees series, thus deriving a set of estimates for self-employed in the other mining group.[22,23]

---

somewhat above this line but inasmuch as the usual $2,500 minimum was ignored that year, no minimum having been set, this excess was ignored as being probably due to that fact. The statistics for establishments reported in the annual Pennsylvania *Report on Productive Industries, Public Utilities and Miscellaneous Statistics* were examined but the obvious undercoverage (in 1929 the establishments reported by the census being more than twice as numerous as those tabulated in the Pennsylvania report) and the very great stability in the number there reported (the report showing a decline of 8 establishments from 1929 to 1935, while the census shows a gain of 47) tended to make simple extrapolation preferable to any combination of census data and intermediate data from the report.

[20] For movement, Kuznets used the series on metal-mine active operators as reported in *Metal-mine Accidents*. The series on employment derived from the same source and presented in the study by Harold Barger and Sam Schurr, *The Mining Industry 1899–1939* (1944), shows unexplained divergences of movement from the BLS series for metallic mining. In the absence of justification, the BLS series was used. The NICB implicitly assumed that the movement of proprietors varies directly with that of employees.

[21] Census data were taken from the 1939 *Census of Mineral Industries*. The industry groups used—groups which include most of the proprietors—were copper, lead and zinc, gold lode and placer, silver, and mercury. As of 1939, there were no proprietors in iron mining and a negligible number in metals other than those specified.

[22] The procedures employed by the NICB and Kuznets are similar to those they employed for metal mining.

[23] The constituent industry groups used were limestone, granite, basalt, slate, sandstone, sand, and gravel. With the exception of the clay-products groups, for which 1929 figures comparable with the expanded 1939 definition of the industry are not available, these industry groups included the great bulk of proprietors in the industry. Census data were from the 1939 *Census of Mineral Industries*. The employment series used was the revised BLS quarrying and nonmetallic series.

Oil and Gas

Estimates of the self-employed and own-account group in crude petroleum and natural gas mining are based on the assumption implicit in the
calculations for most other industry groups: The bulk of the self-employed
are to be found in the proprietor category. The basic 1940 total of 9,964
is therefore taken back by the movement of a series on proprietors—a
series derived by applying ratios of wage earners per proprietor to the
BLS wage-earner series.[24,25]

Construction

The self-employed and own-account workers in the construction industry were divided into two sections, each of which was estimated independently.[26] (The two groups together totaled 481,000 in 1940.)

The first group, including the persons reported in the Censuses of Construction, was estimated by a regression of ratios of construction employees
to proprietors on (1) annual estimates of construction employment and
(2) time.[27]

[24] Kuznets carries as a constant the figure for owners, managers, and proprietors
in the oil and gas group as reported in the 1930 Population Census. The NICB
uses the movement of BLS employment in crude petroleum production.

[25] Ratios for 1930 and 1940 were computed from the Population Censuses. For
1930, the sum of owners, operators, and proprietors was used to equal proprietors
while the remainder of the oil and gas group, excepting only builders and building
contractors, was defined as employees.

It should be noted that the ratios computed from the Census of Population data
are in line with those which can be derived for 1919 and 1929 from the Census of
Mineral Industries. The 1919 ratio is intelligibly in line with the 1930 and 1940
ratios when charted against time, while the 1940 Population Census ratio is not far
distant from the 1939 Mineral Census ratio.

[26] The NICB estimates are for the movement of construction employment, based
in turn on estimates of construction volume. Since the ratio of proprietors to employees changed materially over the period, rising from 4.40 in 1929 to 5.91 in
1935 and dropping back to 4.73 in 1939, this procedure—which assumes a constant
ratio—is inadequate. Kuznets used the movement of construction establishments in
Ohio for 1930 to 1935, while for 1936 to 1938 he carries the 1935 figure as a
constant.

[27] The basic series on construction employment was provided from unpublished
estimates of the National Income Division through the courtesy of Charles Schwartz.

The basic data on proprietors and employees for census years were taken from the
following sources: 1939, Census of Business, *Construction,* p. 28; 1935, Census of
Business, *Construction,* vol. III, p. 28; 1929, *Census of Construction,* pp. 32, 66, 88.
The 1939 totals were taken back to 1929 by the movement of establishments grossing $25,000 or more. These establishments are tabulated separately for 1929 and
1939. This latter procedure is satisfactory if the relative importance of the $25,000
plus group in the total does not change greatly over the period. In point of fact, the
group does not materially shift in importance during the years between 1935 and
1939, the only ones for which data are available. It constitutes 48.8 percent of

The second group, composed of those persons not reported in the Census of Construction but reporting themselves as members of the construction industry in Population Census data, was estimated simply by the movement of total construction employment.[28]

Manufacturing

The self-employed and own-account workers in manufacturing—totaling 267,560 in 1940—were estimated in three groups.[29,30]

---

general contractors and builders in 1935 and 42.2 in 1939; 9.1 percent of special trade contractors in 1935 and 8.2 in 1939.

From these basic data, ratios of employees to proprietors were constructed for census years. The ratios were then correlated with construction employment and time to derive interpolated values for the ratios. The interpolated values applied to construction employment gave a series on proprietors. This series (weighted by the number of male proprietors in construction n.e.c. from the Census of Population 1940, *Occupational Characteristics,* table 6) was added to the series whose computation is described in footnote 26 (which in turn was weighted by the number of male own-account and self-employed workers other than proprietors)—the total constituting a series on self-employed and own-account workers in construction over the entire period.

[28] It is assumed that the persons who have reported themselves as part of the construction industry in the Census of Population, but who are not included in the Census of Construction, are primarily small contractors and others on the margins of the construction industry. The difference between the 480,000 which the Population Census reports and the 226,000 which the construction census reports can be found primarily in a few groups: 175,000 of the difference can be found merely in the three categories of carpenters, painters, and masons. Although some of those reporting in these groups do so because they either have no trade of their own or no expectation of resuming their old, nonetheless it would appear that a majority of those we are concerned with are the odd-job, small operators. A small number may appear in manufacturing force-account data but the number of self-employed in this group is bound to be small and is, in any event, indeterminable in size. It seems not unreasonable, therefore, to vary their number with that of total employment in the construction industry.

[29] The NICB interpolated between census proprietor figures, a procedure which makes insufficient allowance for considerable changes in activity between census periods. The Department of Commerce previously employed volume of production estimates for intercensal interpolation. Kuznets interpolated for eight manufacturing groups by the movement of failures reported to Dun and Bradstreet, assuming that a change in entrepreneurs from one census year to another is proportional to a change in the failures. However, a comparison for recent years between the Dun and Bradstreet figures and those of the Old-Age and Survivors Insurance system suggest that the former do not take correct account of the movement of failures. In addition, it is doubtful if they hold a constant relationship to the *net* change in entrepreneurships, as is required by Kuznets's procedure.

[30] In summary form, the derivation of the three group totals may be indicated as follows:

Self-employed and own-account workers 267,560
    (Population Census, total count)

The first group, covering the 124,385 proprietors reported in the Census of Manufactures, was computed by deriving ratios of proprietors to wage earners from the biennial census data, interpolating between those ratios, and applying the ratios to the BLS employment series.[31]

The second group, comprising those 27,795 manufacturing proprietors reported in the Population Census but not in the Census of Manufactures, was taken back by the movement of proprietors in business, repair, and personal service—a group which does not differ substantially in its movement from the hand trades and small manufacturing proprietors.[32]

The third group, composed of own-account workers in manufacturing other than proprietors, was taken back by the movement of BLS estimates for manufacturing employees other than wage earners.[33]

Taxicabs

Self-employed and own-account workers in the taxicab industry were estimated by taking the basic 1940 total (19,487) back by a series on the

---

Self-employed and own-account "proprietors, managers, and officials"	152,180
(Population Census, sample statistics)	
Self-employed proprietors in industrial census	124,385
(Census of Manufactures)	
Other self-employed proprietors (152,180 less 124,385)	27,795
Self-employed and own-account workers other than proprietors, managers, and officials (267,560 less 152,180)	115,380

It is to be emphasized that these totals were derived merely to weight the component movement series in arriving at the final movement series. The level of that series is fixed by the controlling 1940 Population Census total of 267,560.

[31] The data are reported in the 1939 Census of Manufactures, with the exception of an estimate of proprietors for 1931. To estimate 1931, ratios of proprietors per establishment were computed and charted against time. The indicated curve gave an interpolated ratio for 1931, and hence an estimated proprietor value. The ratio of wage earners per proprietor could then be computed for each census year and interpolated for intercensal years. To estimate 1940, the number of proprietors in 1939 was brought forward by the movement of employing organizations in manufacturing reporting to the Bureau of Old-Age and Survivors Insurance, utilizing data supplied by Benjamin Mandel of that organization.

[32] The service proprietors series was that developed for use in this memorandum, which is described in the section on Services below. The base total is computed as the difference between 152,180 total self-employed and own-account "proprietors, managers and officials n.e.c." in manufacturing as reported in the 1940 Census, *Occupational Characteristics,* table 6, and the number of proprietors reported in the 1939 Census of Manufactures, 124,385—or a residuum of 27,795.

[33] The base total is equal to 267,560 self-employed and own-account workers in manufacturing—as reported in *The Labor Force,* vol. III—less the 152,180 own-account "proprietors, managers and officials n.e.c." from *Occupational Characteristics.* (The comparability between the direct tabulations and the sample statistics is suggested by the fact that for manufacturing the total own-account group in the sample data—*Industrial Characteristics,* table 7—amounted to 269,140 as compared to 267,560 in the direct tabulation.)

number of cabs in operation.[34] The series is based on estimates made by the Cab Research Bureau, an industry organization.[35]

Trucking

The number of self-employed and own-account workers in the trucking industry was estimated by applying to motor-truck registration data a series of ratios of vehicles per operator, using the resultant movement series to carry back the 1940 total of 154,314.[36,37] This procedure evades certain difficulties evident in previous estimates, but still is less than satisfactory because of the faulty reporting and insufficient data characteristic of the trucking field.

---

[34] Both the NICB and Kuznets use the procedures of the National Income Division for this group. The Division estimates cab drivers by the movement of a series on cabs using estimates of the BLS for 1929 to 1933, the American Transit Association for 1934, and the Cab Research Bureau for 1940. This series shows steady declines from 1929 through 1939, with a sudden increase of more than 7,000 between 1939 and 1940. In place of any attempt to adjust that series it was decided to use the procedure outlined in footnote 35.

[35] Estimates for 1932, 1934, and 1940 are given in the Cab Research Bureau's *Taxicabs as a Factor in Urban Transportation* (1942), p. 6. To secure a 1929 value, the 1932 figure was taken back by the movement of the series on entrepreneurs in the industry, which appears in *National Income in the United States, 1929–35* (1936), p. 146. These figures were linearly interpolated for intervening years. The resultant series shows a downward trend over the period and is therefore in line with the progressive application of *numerus clausus* regulations by city Public Utility Commissions.

The basic 1940 total was secured by splitting the total for self-employed in "transportation, communication and other public utilities" by the detailed industry data appearing in the 1940 Census of Population, *Industrial Characteristics*.

[36] Kuznets uses the procedure formerly employed by the Department of Commerce, as the NICB apparently does. This procedure applies a constant ratio, based on 1934 data, of proprietors per truck to truck registrations.

[37] The ratio of vehicles per carrier for 1944, both intercity and local, was provided through the courtesy of James Riley of the Office of Defense Transportation and based on certificates of necessity filed with that agency. For 1934 it was computed from a study made by the Federal Coordinator of Transportation. The intercity ratios were interpolated and extrapolated by a freehand curve. The local ratio for 1944 was carried as a constant. (The Federal coordinator's estimated ratio for 1934 was not below 1944 as it should have been, given the increasing concentration in the industry, the effect of the draft, manpower, and parts shortages. It could not, therefore, be sensibly used.) The relative proportion of for-hire trucks to total trucks registered, and of for-hire intercity trucks to total for-hire trucks, was computed for 1944 and 1932, 1934, respectively. The latter proportions changed so little between these dates that little error arises from the assumption implicit in the present estimate that these proportions remained constant.

The series for motor-truck registrations was provided through the courtesy of the Bureau of Public Roads; it excludes public vehicles.

The basic 1940 total was derived in the same fashion as that for taxicabs.

Other Transportation and Utilities

The number of self-employed workers in this grouping was estimated by taking the basic 1940 total of 15,280 back by the movement of the self-employed group in trucking.[38],[39]

Wholesale Trade

The self-employed in wholesale trade—roughly 182,000 in 1940—were computed as a constant percentage of total employment in that industry since the ratio of employees to proprietors in 1933, 1935, and 1939 was virtually identical.[40] An average of those three ratios could therefore be applied to the latest BLS wholesale trade series to derive a movement series for use with the 1940 self-employed and own-account total.[41],[42] What is known about the general stability of relationships and procedures in wholesale trade would seem to substantiate the validity of this procedure.

Retail Trade

Second only to agriculture and domestic service, retail trade has the largest group of self-employed and own-account workers—primarily proprietors.[43] The basic total of more than 1.75 million is available from the

---

[38] Kuznets follows the older Department of Commerce procedure in simply using the movement of employment in water transportation for that grouping. For electric light and power he used the number of unincorporated firms in 1927, 1932, and 1937, interpolating linearly between these totals. The NICB followed the Department of Commerce in using the movement of employment in finance, advertising agencies, and public warehousing.

[39] Since half of this group appears in warehousing and bus lines, it was felt that the series on trucking entrepreneurs was a not unreasonable series to employ for movement.

[40] The procedure employed by the NICB, by Kuznets, and previously by the Department of Commerce was straight-line interpolation of reported Census of Service totals.

[41] The three ratios for 1933, 1935, and 1939 were 12.94, 13.25, and 13.54. The ratio for 1929 is considerably higher, 16.73—a divergence which in all likelihood arises from the fact that in that census, unlike the later ones, a limitation to proprietors devoting "all or practically all of their time to the business" was made. In later years enumerators were to report those who devoted "a major portion of their time" or merely "active" proprietors. The relative underenumeration of proprietors in 1929 naturally resulted in a greater number of employees per proprietor.

[42] Certain minor adjustments were made in reported data. Proprietor and employee totals for 1939 were reduced to exclude commission bulk petroleum stations, coffee roasters and spice grinders, and cream stations. Cream stations were also deducted from the 1935 totals. No data for 1933 were available, while the 1929 data included a trivial number of cream stations and chain-store warehouses—facts which almost certainly are without significant effect on the ratios computed.

[43] The NICB estimates of proprietors are "based on the Census of American Business for 1929, 1933, and 1935." Apparently no adjustment was made for the lack of

1940 Population Census.[44] This total was taken back by the procedure we used for many of the other industry groups. Ratios of employees to proprietors in the retail trade census years of 1929, 1933, 1935, and 1939 were computed. These ratios were related by a regression to the BLS series on retail-trade employment. The regression gives interpolated values of the ratios for the intercensal years in the 1929–1940 period—values which when applied to the BLS retail-trade employment series gave a movement series. This series was then used to extrapolate the basic 1940 total.

The procedures and adjustments utilized for this important group differ noticeably from those of the NICB and Kuznets, and therefore will be discussed at greater length. The 1929 and 1935 Census of Services data were adjusted to deduct for service garages, which were not included in 1933 or 1939.[45] The 1939 data were taken directly from the census figures. The 1933 figures required considerable manipulation to allow for an overcount which apparently occurred in that year.[46]

The measure of the 1933 overcount was secured by charting the ratio of proprietors per independent store over the period.[47,48] A downward trend is

comparability between the definition of proprietors in the 1933 and other censuses. Kuznets employed the same procedure but utilized old BLS estimates of entrepreneurs in retail trade for 1936 to 1938.

[44] For retail trade, the total for automobile storage, rental, and repair was added to that for retail trade in order to secure a total which could be added to BLS estimates for employees in trade.

[45] The proprietor and employee data used were taken from the following sources: 1929 *Census of Retail Distribution*, part I, p. 68; 1933 *Census of Retail Distribution*, vol. I, pp. A-3, A-12; 1935 *Retail Distribution*, vol. IV, p. 13; 1939 *Retail Trade*, p. 57.

[46] The 1929 schedule required those "devoting all or practically all of their time to the business"; the 1935 and 1939 schedules sought active proprietors and firm members "devoting the major portion of their time to the operation of the business"; while the 1933 schedule required only "number of proprietors and firm members," with a fine-print exclusion of salaried officers of corporations and inactive partners.

[47] The ratio of proprietors per store could not be used, since changing proportions of independent and chain stores from year to year would in themselves change the ratio of proprietors per store.

[48] For 1929 the independent group total was secured by adding the totals for single store, two-store, and three-store independents plus the total for roadside markets, curbside markets, itinerant vendors, rolling stores, retailers and wholesalers, and retailers-country buyers. In terms of size, the only substantial addition is the country-buyer group, the others amounting to very little in the aggregate.

For 1933 additions also had to be made to the independent category to arrive at a comprehensive total for independents. This was done by taking 93.91 percent of the "other types" category and adding the resultant figure to the independent total. The percentage was based on the comparable percentage from the 1929 data.

For 1935 the proper inclusion of country buyers with independents allowed the

very evident in the data, but the 1933 ratio is far above the trend line. It was assumed that the true value for 1933 was that indicated by the trend, and the adjusted ratio was used to derive a new proprietor estimate for 1933. This estimate in turn provided a new employee-proprietor ratio in that year.[49] The new ratio gave considerably more intelligible results when charted against the BLS retail-trade-employment series in order to arrive at interpolated ratios for the period.[50] These ratios applied to employment estimates yielded a movement series which, applied to the basic 1940 total, gave a series on the self-employed.

Banking and Other Finance

The basic 1940 total for this group (23,835) was taken back by the movement of the BLS series on bank and security brokerage employment.[51,52]

---

arbitrary proposition that no independents were to be found outside the group specified as such. However, it should be noted that there is some likelihood that in 1933 and in 1935 country buyers were to a large extent missed. The 1933 total, for example, which purports to include country buyers in the "other types" classification, is about 21,000, although the single component of country buyers in 1929 aggregated over 73,000. An additional point to be made is that no adjustment could be made for service garages in 1929 or 1935; but it is hardly likely that this would throw off the ratio of proprietors per store, which is all that is sought here. For 1939 the "independents" total was used as is.

[49] A memorandum of the BLS Employment Statistics Division titled, "Retail Trade Proprietors—1934 and Later Years" (no date or author, circa 1938), proposes to define the overcount as the number of proprietors of stores whose sales were under $1,000, since such stores "could not in 1933 support the draft of a full-time wage by the proprietor" (p. 9). But since the percent of all stores with sales $1,000 or less was negligibly different between 1933—when there was an overcount—and 1935—when there was not an overcount—this measurement seems inappropriate. The percent in 1935 (based on data for 10 states, as reported in *Domestic Commerce* and used in the Employment Statistics memo) is 11.94. The percent in 1935 (based on statistics for 72.6 percent of all establishments reporting activity in that year) was 13.07 (1935 *Census of Retail Distribution,* vol. 6, tables 4A and 4C). This measurement of the overcount was, therefore, felt to be unacceptable.

[50] When retail sales reach upward, the staff of existing enterprise expands at a faster rate than that at which new enterprises are organized—it being considerably easier to take on a new clerk than to open a new enterprise—and vice versa when sales decline. Thus the employee-proprietor ratio changes when retail sales (and hence retail employment) changes.

[51] Kuznets implicitly uses the movement of various bank employment series. NICB implicitly uses employment in finance, advertising agencies, and public warehousing, as estimated by the Department of Commerce.

[52] For 1939 and 1940, special employment estimates based on totals for banking and trust company employment by state were used in order to obtain a more logical movement.

Real Estate

The basic 1940 total was extrapolated by the movement of the BLS series for real estate, inclusive of building service.[53]

Insurance

For insurance the basic 1940 total was extrapolated by the movement of the BLS series on insurance agents and carriers. This procedure suffers from the shortcoming that it may represent the movement of insurance agents but will not necessarily reveal that of self-employed agents.[54] It is, however, preferable to procedures hitherto employed.[55] Insurance and real estate together include about 165,000 self-employed persons.

Service: Business, Repair (except Automotive), Personal, and Amusement

Estimates of the self-employed and own-account workers attached to the service industry were derived by the application to a series on employment in service[56] of a series of employee-proprietor ratios taken from the

[53] Kuznets employs the movement of Nathan's index of employment in banking, brokerage, insurance and real estate, and domestic and personal service. NICB follows the same procedure for real estate as for banking.

[54] The coverage of the BLS series includes all employed persons, excluding such groups as office solicitors. It can be noted, however, that the ratio of insurance agents to total insurance employees is 50.6 in 1930 (using gainfully employed data from the Census of Population), 45.1 in 1935 (using the total for office solicitors, direct-selling agents, and proprietors of agencies and brokerage offices as compared with the total reported for all groups on the 1935 Census of Business), and 45.8 in 1940 (using sample statistics data). This constancy suggests that relatively little change occurred over the period in these ratios.

[55] Kuznets uses for movement between 1929 and 1935 a series on number of agents reported for 61 companies by the Association of Life Insurance Presidents, and for 1936–1938, BLS employment indices. The series on agents is quite unsatisfactory: While the number of insurance proprietors, managers and officials n.e.c.—the closest series conceptually to self-employed and own-account agents—increased by nearly 6,000 over the period (Alba Edwards, *Comparative Occupation Statistics, 1870–1940* (1943), table 2) and while the BLS indices show a similar growth, the series for the 61 companies' agents indicates a steady, remorseless decline from 1931 through 1936. To show the same net change between 1930 and 1940 as indicated by Edwards's figures, the series would have had to rise by a third between 1936 and 1940—from 176,362 to 233,395.

The NICB uses for movement the estimates of the Department of Commerce for employment in finance, advertising agencies, and public warehousing.

[56] The employment series was computed as the sum of various movement series weighted in proportion to the number of private wage and salary workers reported for the specified industry group in the 1940 Population Census. For hotels, laundries, dry cleaning, motion pictures, other recreation and amusement, and miscellaneous personal service, the BLS series for those groupings was employed. For business services, a series on full-time equivalent employees prepared by Edward Denison of the Commerce Department was used. This series has a highly unsatisfactory year-to-

1933, 1935, and 1939 censuses.[57] This procedure yielded a series whose movement, when applied to the 1940 total of 804,000, gave estimates of self-employed and own-account workers for the 1929–1940 period.[58] The rationale is identical with that behind the estimate of self-employed in retail trade.

Service: Medical and Other Health

For the bulk of this group—physicians, dentists, osteopaths, trained nurses, chiropodists, chiropractors, and veterinarians—the series of the National Income Division were used for movement. "Healers n.e.c." were extrapolated by the movement of a subtotal of the specified groups, and the final series was derived by combining these two into a single movement series for extrapolating the basic 1940 value of 260,864.[59]

Service: Legal, Engineering, and Miscellaneous Professional

Self-employed and own-account workers in this group were estimated by taking the basic 1940 figure of 192,523 back by a combination of

---

year movement but is apparently satisfactory for general movement over the decade. Since no reasonable method of smoothing it existed, it was used as is.

[57] Proprietor and employee data from the census were treated in three sections: (1) hotels and lodging places, (2) amusements, recreation, and related services, and (3) business and repair services, laundering, cleaning, and dry cleaning, miscellaneous personal services.

1. Hotel data for 1939 were secured from Census of Services, 1939. These figures were taken back to 1933 and 1935 by data for year-round hotels.

2. Amusement totals were those for the sum of five groups—billiard, bowling, dance, skating, and theaters—directly as reported in the 1933, 1935, and 1939 censuses.

3. For the remaining service group, 1939 totals were secured from the Census of Services in that year; 1935 totals were kindly supplied by William Ruff of the Bureau of the Census; 1933 figures, not comparable, are from the *Census of Business, Services, Amusements and Hotels,* vol. 1, p. 1.

The resultant set of data was used to compute ratios of employees to proprietors in services for the specified census years. These ratios were charted against the employment series, and ratios for intervening years were interpolated by geometric construction. No special allowance was made for the movement of such own-account workers in the amusement group as artists, authors, actors, dancers, showmen, athletes, or musicians since no information on their movement or that of the hand-trade component is available.

[58] The NICB computed no separate series for entrepreneurial employment— implicitly, therefore, assuming that it moved directly with total employment in services and that the ratio remained unchanged over the period. In point of fact, the ratio rose from 1.56 in 1933 to 2.31 in 1939. Kuznets extrapolates adjusted Census of Service totals by the movement of employment in retail trade, by linear interpolation, and by holding totals constant, *inter alia.*

[59] The NICB utilizes "appropriate series compiled by the National Income Section of the Department of Commerce," while Kuznets, though relying heavily on these series, appears to have made special adjustments of his own.

movement series computed by the National Income Division of the Department of Commerce for self-employed persons in these groups. The series for the largest component of the group, lawyers, was computed by the Division from listings in legal directories and other sources.[60]

Charitable, Religious, and Membership Organizations

Somewhat under 3,000 persons were reported in this group as self-employed and own-account workers. Inasmuch as a very substantial portion of the total in the group was probably misclassified and should have been returned as employees, the entire group has been excluded from the estimate of the self-employed.[61,62]

Educational Services

Given the very scanty information available on this field and some general indications of lack of change in their number, it was decided to carry the basic 1940 total of 54,681 back to 1929 as a constant.[63,64]

Domestics

Domestic employment was calculated by taking back the basic 1940 total for private wage and salary plus self-employed domestics (2,365,-000), using the movement of the National Income Division series for that group.[65] This latter series is based on periodic surveys of employment

[60] Both Kuznets and NICB rely largely on the series of the National Income Division.

[61] For this group Kuznets implicitly uses the movement of employees in trade, service, and a group of "miscellaneous" categories. NICB used the movement of all employment other than its miscellaneous group.

[62] Apparently the chief component classifications that were correctly made were those for a handful of persons who were itinerant evangelists, proprietors of private orphan asylums, or persons who had contracts from county poorhouses.

[63] Data from Edwards (*op. cit.,* p. 49) suggest a gain in the numbers of artists and art teachers, musicians and music teachers over the period. Inasmuch as these data cannot be adequately broken as between employees and self-employed, this change gives no information on the movement of the self-employed over the period.

A tabulation of teachers of music and dancing listed in 1931 city directories, made by Edward Denison of the Commerce Department, yielded totals reasonably close to those indicated in the 1940 Census. This similarity suggests that for the major self-employed group in the educational services category—teachers of music and art —the net change over the period was negligible. Series on correspondence and commercial schools from 1929 to 1937, supplied by Denison, also suggested the absence of any notable change.

[64] The movement of Kuznets's series is given primarily by the combined movement of physicians, dentists, lawyers, engineers, and clergymen in practice, although some use is made of the Department of Commerce data mentioned in note 63. The NICB employs "appropriate series" from the same source.

[65] Both the NICB and Kuznets use the estimates of the National Income Division for movement.

agencies made by the Division and provides the most reliable movement series for the period.[66]

Industry Not Reported

The basic 1940 total of 39,323 was taken back by the movement of all self-employed workers other than those in agriculture.[67]

Nonagricultural Unpaid Family Workers

Unpaid family workers in nonagricultural pursuits—278,000 in 1940—were assumed to vary in number with the movement of proprietors in service, trade, and construction—industries in which the majority of unpaid family workers were employed.[68]

NONFARM SELF-EMPLOYED AND UNPAID FAMILY WORKERS: 1900 TO 1940 (TABLE A-7)

No Current Population Survey estimate for this group being available for 1940, we approximated its level as follows. The CPS figure for nonfarm self-employed plus unpaid family workers was split between these two groups in the ratio of each in the decennial census.[1] The self-employed

[66] The basic 1940 total included all domestic-service workers but unpaid family workers, on the assumption that the latter group was on the whole incorrectly entered in the labor force. The April, 1930, total is based on the labor-force figure given by Edwards (*op. cit.*), reduced because of apparently overgenerous allocations to this group in Edwards's revision, with a deduction for unemployment, the final total being converted to an annual average basis by the movement of the Department of Commerce estimates. The 1940 figure, as the movement series, is that of the National Income Division.

[67] It was assumed that no sizable bias in nonreporting occurred within these industry groups; that the majority of schedules returned for agriculture would, by virtue of the entry on occupation or class of worker, have been correctly allocated to agriculture.

[68] The base total was that given in the 1940 Population Census, less the number of unpaid family workers reported in domestic service (on the assumption that all these had been misclassified as unpaid family workers), plus an estimated 5,000 to allow for omitted entries in this group. The movement series used was a combination of three series, each of which was weighted by the number of unpaid family workers in the appropriate industry, with the balance of the group fluctuated by the trade component. The series used for construction was one for construction employees, on the assumption that the unpaid workers in this industry were attached to small concerns whose number moved closely with general construction employment. For service and for the balance group including trade, the estimates of proprietors in service and trade which had already been computed were utilized.

[1] 1940 Census, *Population,* vol. III, table 78.

total was then split by industry in the proportions shown for 1940 in Table A-9, based again on decennial census results.

The 1940 estimates for each component were then extrapolated to 1930 on the basis of the data in Table A-9, as derived in the previous pages. These 1930 estimates for the self-employed were summed into five sector totals—construction, manufacturing, trade, service, and other—these totals then being extrapolated to 1900 by sector estimates derived in Chapter 10. The 1930 total for unpaid family workers was similarly extrapolated.

GAINFUL WORKERS: 1900 TO 1930

As a preliminary to deriving annual estimates of labor force for 1900 to 1930, we compute benchmark estimates for gainful workers decennially.

1900: Gainful Workers

We adopt the 1900 Census of Population figures, with minor adjustment to derive data for age 14 and over. (See the section, 1900–1930, Annual Estimates: Gainful Workers, below.) Edwards, Kaplan and Casey, Durand, Carson, and Miller have accepted the basic figures, and we do the same, not adopting rather speculative changes recently made in the estimates by Long.

1910: Gainful Workers

Beginning with the original publications of the 1910 Census of Population, the Census Bureau has noted an overcount in the number of women and children reported as gainful workers in 1910. Alba Edwards provided one measure of the overcount in the 1910 Census report on *Occupations,* and one in his 1940 Census report, the latter adopted in the authoritative Kaplan-Casey monograph published by the census in 1958.[1]

The lack of comparability was immediate, clear cut and substantial. Ex post it became clear that the change in the enumerator instructions from 1900 to 1910 was responsible.[2] But instructions are always changing,

---

[1] 1910 Census, *Population,* vol. IV, pp. 26–29, where Edwards estimates a 468,100 overcount of females; 1940 Census, *Comparative Occupation Statistics,* p. 138, where Edwards estimates 630,985 for females and 165,557 for boys. David L. Kaplan and M. Claire Casey, *Occupational Trends in the United States 1900 to 1950* (1958), pp. 1, 9, adopt Edwards's adjustments.

[2] The 1900 instruction began coolly: "This question applies to every person 10 years of age and over who is at work. . . ." The 1910 instruction began with direct urgency: "An entry should be made in this column for every person enumerated." The subsequent exhortation that "it must never be taken for granted" without in-

enumerator performance is always varying, and the basis for questioning and adjusting the figures lay not in a consideration of the instructions but in the numbers. In a careful, shrewd discussion, Edwards pointed out in the 1910 Census the improbability that female farm labor rose 135 percent from 1900 to 1910, since it had risen only 23 percent in the prior decade; that women were reported as 25.3 percent of all farm laborers in 1910 compared to 15.1 percent a decade earlier, etc.[3] Reference to state data makes the point even more graphically. In Mississippi, for example, females in agriculture ran to 128,000, 133,000, and 142,000 in 1900, 1920, and 1930—but were reported at 241,000 in 1910.

Adjusting the 1910 Data

Three critical premises determine our method of adjusting the 1910 data and the resultant differences from other estimators.

1. In a changing economy such as that of the United States from 1890 to 1930, we cannot simply take the ratio of farm laborers to another category, or any other ratio, and assume that because it maintained at one date it must apply equally well in 1910.

2. We cannot develop a function for the trend in gainful worker totals for any category, or for worker rates for any group, and simply interpolate for 1910, for unless there are reference points external to the series being considered, no check on the adequacy of such interpolation process is possible. He who wishes may interpolate, say, to make 1910 below 1920, above, or precisely equal. The point of inflection is decisive, and it is tacitly stipulated by the estimator unless he is restrained by working to some external check point or ratio.

3. The census in general should not be adjusted except where it is clearly in error as judged by long-time relationships or external data. Relying on our knowledge that variations in enumerator performance in these decades produced most erroneous counts in the South (the 1870, 1890 undercounts) and in that region primarily for females, we begin our adjustment for that group, and continue only insofar as clearly required.

Female Agricultural Labor. We estimate the adjustment required for this group as 610,000. For check estimates we use three other procedures —giving figures of 560,000, 615,000, and 685,000, respectively. Our estimate is within 5 percent of Edwards, well above that of Carson, well below that of Long. We describe first the three check estimates.

1. *560,000.* One procedure was to relate the number of females aged

---

quiry, "that a woman or child has no occupation" merely added fuel to the fire. One result, noted on p. 16 of the 1910 Census, was the "tendency among the enumerators to return a gainful occupation for every negro, especially every negro woman and child" in the South.

[3] Edwards, *Comparative Occupation Statistics,* p. 27.

10 and over gainfully occupied in agriculture in every state to the number of farms in that state from 1880 to 1930.[4] In this way we use the number of farms, a more accurately enumerated figure, and the trend over a number of decades as the control. For South Carolina, for example, the figures run as follows:

**Females Aged 10 and Over in Farming
in South Carolina**

Year	Total (000)	Ratio to farms, %
1880	86	91
1890	97	84
1900	115	74
1910	191	108
1920	127	
1930	89	56

For most states the downward trend in ratios is quite obvious. Because of the fact that the 1890 figure was adjusted by census, we relied primarily on the 1880 to 1900 change in the few instances where there was any difference between the 1880–1900 and the 1880–1890–1900 extrapolation.[5]

2. *615,000.* An alternative estimate was made relating the number of females in farming to the number of males.[6] The number of males in farming includes unpaid family workers and hired hands as well as farmers, but trends for this group will be necessarily not far different from that for farmers alone, as indicated in the prior estimate, and it is not surprising that these data indicate an adjustment within 10 percent of the prior method.

3. *685,000.* Females in agriculture related to the number of farm families gives a similar estimate.[7] While the relationship thus derived for

[4] Farms: 1940 Census, *Agriculture,* vol. III, p. 58. Gainful workers: 1900 Census, *Occupations,* p. xcii, for 1880, 1890, and 1900. 1910 Census, vol. V, p. 48; 1920 Census, vol. IV, p. 54; 1930 Census, vol. V, p. 60.

[5] For Georgia, 102,000 were reported for 1880, 100,000 for 1900, and 100,000 were estimated for 1910. For Florida the prewar years ran to 12,000 to 13,000, and 1920 to 15,000—compared to the 1910 Census figure of 26,000. We estimate 13,000 for 1910.

[6] We use the convenient summary of the census data, adjusted for laborers not specified, in Everett Lee et al., *Population Redistribution and Economic Growth, 1870–1950* (1957), table L-4. Since these figures do not include an allowance for the 1890 undercount, however, we increase them for that year by the census estimates of that undercount as given in 1900 Census, *Occupations,* p. lxxi.

[7] Data on farms from 1920 *Census of Agriculture,* vol. V, p. 38, and 1940 *Census*

the South Central states is unequivocal, that for the South Atlantic states leaves too much to the judgment of the analyst; this procedure is therefore considered the least reliable of those used here.

4. *608,000.* After having bounded the general dimensions of the adjustment by previous procedures, we come to the one actually used here. Beginning with 1900, the census reports distinguish between those females in agriculture who worked on family farms and those who were wage earners. It is assumed that the overenumeration in 1910 affected the wage-earner counts very little, was concentrated in the family-worker group: This was the key marginal area on which census instructions laid emphasis, the area most subject to enumerator judgment as to inclusion or exclusion. For 1900 to 1930 we compute the following ratios:[8]

Female Family Workers in Agriculture as a Proportion of Farmers

1900	7.78
1910	19.10
1920	9.00
1930	7.90

These data indicate that the ratio for 1900 was virtually identical with that for 1930. Equally important, however, is the 1920 figure, for it suggests that, after the war shortages of manpower had increased the relative number of female family workers on farms, the ratio went no higher than 9 percent. Our estimate of the true value for 1910 then should not be above 9 percent. It may more reasonably be set at the 1900 value, however, particularly with the confirmation of a similar ratio in 1930. Given this 30-year trend, we could well assume that the 1900 rate of female home family workers to farmers applied in 1910. Instead of using this estimate generally, however, we make separate estimates for each Southern state.[9]

---

of Agriculture, vol. III, p. 38. Number of farm families from 1910 *Census of Population,* vol. I, p. 1302, and 1930 *Census of Population,* vol. VI, p. 35. Number of families in 1920 were estimated from the regression against farms over the period in each region. The resultant 1920 data that appear in the 1930 Census, vol. VI, p. 11 and 1940 Census, *Families, General Characteristics,* p. 4, are, according to Dr. Leon Truesdell, belated tabulations of the 1920 results. These data show a 600,000 rise in farm families over a period during which the rural farm population fell about 450,-000 (Truesdell, *Farm Population in the United States,* p. 45) and the number of farms 10 acres and over rose by only 132,000. Moreover, 1910–1920–1930 changes for many states seem improbable; e.g., Georgia's 277,000, 335,000, and 387,000 (data from 1930 Census, vol. VI, table 2).

[8] 1900 Census, *Occupations,* p. 7; 1930 Census, vol. V, p. 40.

[9] 1900 *Occupations,* table 33; 1910 Census, table VII. As one example, in Florida an 11 percent gain in both the number of farmers and male family workers occurred, while female family workers more than doubled. For Mississippi, a 20 percent rise

Male Agricultural Labor. For male family workers we adopt the same procedures outlined above in (4) for female family workers, and arrive at an estimate of 75,000 for an adjustment.

Previous Estimates. A number of substantial attempts have been made previously to estimate the 1910 overcount. The work of Edwards must be given special note as done by a man involved in the 1910 Census and with immense experience in the intricacies of census procedure. His estimate for females proves to be within 2 percent of the present one. The major reason why his procedures were not adopted in the first place is that they cannot be defended per se but only on the basis of his long experience. For women he assumes that the 1900 and 1910 ratios of rural population to females in farming must have been identical, without testing how the two were in fact related over a number of censuses. For girls he simply posits no 1900 to 1910 change, while for boys he does the same. The only rationale he offers for the latter is that since the total number of boys, as the total rural male population, increased, it is unlikely that the number of boys in farming decreased "as some estimates indicate . . . therefore it has been assumed that the number was the same in 1910 as in 1900." [10]

Carson's estimate of the undercount was not adopted for two reasons. He bases his estimate on "the observation that there is a close and inverse relation between changes in worker rates of children and the percentage attending school." [11] He cites as proof relevant to estimating the 1900 to 1910 change, data on 1920 to 1930 relationships, data for females for 1900 to 1920 that clearly contradict his assumption, and data for males aged 10–15 for 1900 to 1920 that appear to support it. Apparently, how-ever, he did not take into account a fundamental change in the definition of school attendance used beginning with the 1910 Census—a change that makes it impossible to use the 1900 to 1910 and 1900 to 1920 data as he does.[12] For girls aged 16–19 he assumes that the 1900 to 1910 change in worker rates was the same as the 1890 to 1900 one—reasonable enough

---

for farmers and male family workers occurred, as against a 56 percent reported gain for female family workers.

Adjustment by state made it possible to see whether the wage-earner data showed untoward changes as well as the family workers. While gains did appear for the former, they were not unreasonable in the light of the changes in the number of farms. If an overcount did occur for this group, it cannot be discerned amid the vagaries of reporting and the volatility of 1900 to 1930 changes. This consideration applies equally to the family worker count in Northern and Western states.

[10] Edwards, *Comparative Occupation Statistics,* p. 138.

[11] Daniel Carson, "Industrial Composition of Manpower in the United States, 1870–1940," *Studies in Income and Wealth* (1949), vol. 11, p. 83.

[12] Carson, *op. cit.,* refers to his invaluable and unfortunately unpublished study for the WPA. Reference to that study (table 36, p. 116) indicates he is referring to 1920 to 1930 data. His 1900 to 1920 data appear on p. 85. For males a 12 percent rise in school attendance and a 15 percent fall in worker rates is shown; for females, an 11.5 percent rise in school attendance and a 4.6 percent fall in worker rates.

if (1) we were certain of the 1890 rate, and (2) if we did not examine the resultant unlikely figure, which implies a more than 100 percent overcount for this group. For women over 19 years of age he simply stipulates no adjustment. We do not rely on his estimates, ingenious as they are, because his estimates rest on the use of 1900 to 1920 school-attendance data as published, despite the basic change in 1910 in the definition of school attendance.[13] Moreover, we question the probability of a 100 percent overcount for females aged 16–19, particularly when this estimate was derived by a relatively arbitrary procedure.[14]

A detailed estimate by Clarence Long is not used for two major reasons.[15] (1) He implicitly assumes that census enumerators substantially overreported labor-force participation by females under 25, and those over 44—but correctly reported for the 25–44 group. But we find no explanation of why the general tendency to overcount (following from the emphasis of the 1910 enumerator instructions on including all work done by women) should have spared this single group. Many later efforts to improve the measurement of female labor-force participation commonly demonstrate that the erroneous counting of work done by housewives 25–44 is a significant factor in erroneous labor-force enumeration. (2) He assumes that the correct labor-force rate in 1910 was a simple average of 1900 and 1920 rates for three groups—women 45–64; boys 14–19 not in school; and unmarried girls not in school. Since the 1920 rates for such marginal groups were substantially affected by the wartime experience, we find little basis for this averaging procedure.[16] It is necessary to link to some contemporary data and work with contemporary relationships to minimize the role of the estimator's fiat.

1920: Gainful Workers

The number of gainful workers as reported in the 1920 Census is accepted without adjustment except to raise this January figure to an annual average.[17]

[13] 1910 Census, vol. I, p. 1104. Some indication of trend might be derived from the 1890 and 1900 Censuses for those attending 6 months of school or more, but extrapolation even over this decade is a dubious matter.

[14] Carson (1949, p. 85) estimates a 244,191 overcount for girls 16–19 while the census reported 340,820 for the larger 16–20 group.

[15] Clarence Long, *The Labor Force under Changing Income and Employment* (1958), appendix G.

[16] Long reduces the 1900 Census count of the number of children in the labor force by 224,000. For boys 14–19, for example, he does so by assuming that an average of 1920 and 1930 labor-force rates applied in 1900. We prefer the results of the 1900 Census as reported. It was one of the most competently conducted we have ever had, with no evidence of bias, and has been accepted by Edwards, Kaplan, Durand, Miller, and others.

[17] 1920 *Census of Population* vol. IV, pp. 35, 476 to give a total for 14 and older. The 1920–1921 change in the preliminary labor-force series interpolated between

In adopting the census figures as reported, we do not follow Edwards's procedure of adjusting for a presumed undercount in 1920,[18] for these reasons: There is no unequivocal evidence that any adjustment is in fact necessary; there is no direct method of making one; and the maximum possible adjustment would be well within the limits of error customary in such historical data.

A

The assumption that an underestimate occurred in the Census of 1920 was first made in the original 1920 Census reports. It has since been repeated in other census volumes. It rests on a twofold premise.

1. "The change of the Census date from April 15 in 1910 to January 1 in 1920 doubtless had a pronounced effect on the number of workers returned as pursuing those occupations which are seasonal or largely seasonal."

2. Enumerators' schedules reported "large numbers of children and young persons living on farms . . ." having no occupations; a considerable proportion of these were returned as neither at school nor at work.[19]

B

How adequate are these contentions? So far as the seasonal effect is concerned there are three basic objections.

1. Seasonal variations in the family worker labor force—at least since 1925, when data become available—have been greatest in the South.[20] Hence any undercount in 1920 should have been proportionately more severe in the South than other regions. As data in Table 9-1 indicate,[21] however, the percentage decline from 1900 to 1920 among the group aged

---

reported 1920 and 1930 Census figures was 743,000, half of which was added to the January, 1920, figure to give the 1920 benchmark.

[18] 1920 Census, vol. IV, pp. 22–23; *Comparative Occupation Statistics*, p. 138. See too the report by Kaplan and Casey, *op. cit.*, in which these experts adopt Edwards's adjustments in a census study that "constitutes primarily an up-dating of the material in " Edwards. John Durand, *The Labor Force in the United States, 1890–1960* (1948), p. 194, Carson (*op. cit.*, pp. 85–87), and Long, *The Labor Force in Wartime America* (1944), p. 9, adopt the published census figures without revision. Carson's arguments on this point are particularly cogent.

[19] 1920 Census, vol. IV, pp. 22–23.

[20] Taking April 1 as 98 for 1925–1936 (the annual average being 100), the United States January 1 figure is 84. For the South the rates are 96 (100) and 77. Eldon E. Shaw and John A. Hopkins, *Trends in Employment in Agriculture, 1909–1936* (November 1938). Computed from tables on seasonal variation, *passim*.

[21] Edwards assumes, with minor qualifications, that children 10–15 in agriculture "formed the same proportion of the farm population in 1920 as of the estimated farm population in 1910" (*op. cit.*, p. 138). Given the heavy 1910 to 1920 immigration of adults, the wartime migration to cities, and the residual uncertainty concerning even the level of farm population in 1910, there is little basis for assuming this lack of change.

Table 9-1. Percent of Population Aged 10–15 Gainfully Occupied

Region	Male		Female	
	1900	1920	1900	1920
United States............	26.1	11.3	10.2	5.6
New England...........	13.3	9.0	8.9	6.5
Middle Atlantic.........	18.3	6.4	9.8	4.6
East North Central.......	15.3	6.2	5.6	2.5
West North Central.......	19.5	6.1	4.0	1.6
South Atlantic..........	41.6	18.9	18.5	9.7
East South Central.......	47.3	23.7	17.9	11.1
West South Central.......	37.5	17.2	12.1	8.2
Mountain...............	12.9	6.3	2.9	1.6
Pacific.................	9.4	5.0	2.5	1.2

10–15 (the group most likely to have been enumerated incorrectly) was not more severe in the South than the North.[22] The most precipitous decline actually took place in the Middle Atlantic region.

2. Moreover, the putative undercount should have been at least as evident in data for girls as for boys. However, there was actually a greater proportion of rural white girls employed in agriculture in 1920 than in 1900.[23] This rise, which is contrary to Edwards's thesis of an overcount, probably points to extra work by women and girls on family farms during a period of farm-labor shortage. The decline in the numbers of boys and of nonwhite girls probably arose because of the effect of prosperity on worker rates—an effect also apparent during and after World War II, an analogy not available to Edwards.

3. Finally, the trend in the ratio of females 16 and over gainfully occupied in agriculture—a group that was substantially affected by the 1910 undercount—to rural female population 16 and over does not suggest any undercount in 1920:[24]

	1900	1920	1930	1940
Rural population...............	13,327,000	15,108,000	16,315,000	18,618,000
Gainfully occupied in agriculture..	770,000	896,000	784,000	489,000
Ratio.......................	5.8%	5.9%	4.8%	2.6%

[22] 1910 Census, vol. IV, p. 75; 1920 Census, vol. IV, p. 514.

[23] The number rose from 58,000 to 79,000. Data for children gainfully occupied in agriculture: 1900 Census, *Occupations* pp. 20, 24, 26; 1920 Census, vol. IV, pp. 408, 506, 594; 1920 Census, vol. V, p. 358. Data for rural population aged 10–14 in 1900 are estimated by extrapolating 1910 Census figures (1940 Census, vol. II, p. 22) by the percentage change in the population aged 5–14 in cities under 2,500 and rural districts (1910 Census, vol. I, pp. 425, 427, 432). Population figures for other years are from 1940 Census, vol. II, pp. 18-19, 23.

[24] Unpublished estimates of the rural female population, comparable with 1940,

C

Edwards's contention as to the large number of children without occupations presents a major difficulty: How considerable was his "considerable proportion"? Lacking any tabulation for 1920 or earlier years, it was not possible for him at the time the census volumes were originally published to determine whether the percentage was abnormally high or low. There is no way of knowing, for example, that it was not at least as great as that for 1930 or 1940. Possibly if it could be compared with the 1930 figures (5.2 percent of the boys and 7.1 percent of the girls were neither in school nor at work), or with data for 1940, the percentages would seem quite reasonable.[25]

D

It is possible to make a maximum estimate of a possible undercount in 1920, and from this demonstrate that such an adjustment is less than the margin of error which must be accepted in these early Census figures. An inverse relation between the worker rate for children and the percent in school is logically and empirically evident. Taking the school attendance rates for 1910, 1920, and 1930 as reported and the worker rates for 1910 and 1930, we can interpolate for the trend ratio of worker rate to school-attendance rate in 1920. The resultant estimate then would imply an undercount of 228,000—or say 10 percent—for the 10–15 group, perhaps the gainful worker group most affected by seasonal change. However, the 1910 figure thus used is clearly an overestimate, which maximizes this 1920 undercount figure. Since we cannot extend even this worker rate–school attendance relationship to years beyond the 1910–1930 period and since worker rates for children have proved particularly susceptible to the effects of war and prosperity, it seems doubtful that an error of, say, 3 to 5 percent in estimating their number for 1920 could be detected—or measured accurately if detected. These considerations apply a fortiori to any adjustment for older workers and male workers.[26] So many considera-

were kindly provided by the Bureau of the Census. The number of females in agriculture is reported in 1920 Census Report S-1 (Hill) p. 19; 1930 Census Report, vol. V, p. 116; 1940 Census Report A-3, pp. 199-200.

[25] 1930 Census, vol. II, p. 1182; Data for ages 14–15 in 1940 Census, vol. IV, pp. 94, 95, are somewhat above those for 1930. The rate for ages 14–17 fell from roughly 13 percent in April, 1940, to 9 percent by 1947 (Census Release ser. P-20, no. 12).

[26] Durand also denies the need for a 1920 adjustment, but does so by interpolating for a 1920 value between the 1880 and 1930 Census results. (Durand, *op. cit.,* p. 194). Such a procedure is reasonable since most of the intermediate censuses require adjustment. However, it does not possess sufficient precision. (1) Interpolation between estimates of two censuses that are separated by 50 years can hardly produce very certain results. (2) This procedure implicitly assumes that the trend in

tions are at work, so many incomparabilities exist, therefore, that there is no basis for making a reasonable adjustment in the published census data. Hence, they are adopted without change.[27]

1930: Gainful Workers

The number of gainful workers as reported in the April Census is adopted, raised to an annual average.[28]

1900–1930, Annual Estimates: Gainful Workers (Table A-3)

Preliminary annual gainful-worker estimates were derived by interpolating between detailed worker rates in the census years, and applying the resultant series to unpublished census estimates of population annually from 1900 to 1930.

1. For 1900, 1910, 1920, and 1930 we compute worker rates separately for males and females in each of three nativity groups—native white, foreign-born white, and Negro—and within each group for the separate age intervals (10–13, 14–19, 20–24, 25–44, 45–64, 65 and over). For 1920 and 1930, we use the census data without adjustment.[29] For 1900, minor adjustment is required in the reported data to develop estimates for the 10–13, 14–19, and 20–24 groups.[30] For 1910 we use a preliminary set of rates roughly consistent with our adjusted United States estimate.[31]

---

worker rates was downward after 1880. Because of the uncertainty of census results following that year, we do not know this to be so; the downward trend may in fact have begun only after 1900 or 1910.

[27] Male rates were, of course, substantially affected by conscription, war production, and war prosperity—so substantially that no adjustment for seasonal influences could be considered unless there were the clearest evidence that such adjustment was required. The female data demonstrate the contrary.

[28] 1930 *Census of Population,* vol. V, p. 115. This figure was raised to an annual average by adding one-third of the annual gain from the 1930 to the 1940 labor-force figures shown in *Monthly Labor Review* (July, 1948).

[29] 1920 Census, *Occupations,* p. 377. 1930 Census, *Occupations,* p. 117. The reported data were combined into the desired age intervals.

[30] 1900 Census, *Occupations,* p. cxviii. From the same source, p. clxii, and the 1900 Census, *Population,* vol. II, p. 2, we can compute worker rates for boys 10–13. By applying the ratios of these rates to the rates for boys 10–15 (within the separate nativity groups), we derive the needed 10–13 rates. A similar procedure was used for girls 10–13. By subtraction, we then get data for the 14–15 group. To add 20-year-olds to the reported 21–24 figures, we assumed that the worker rates for each category were the same, the two sets of rates being much the same in 1940. (1940 Census, *Population,* vol. IV, p. 90.)

[31] The detailed interpolations were made on the basis of an earlier overall adjustment. Since we make annual interpolations merely to reflect the changing age-sex-nativity composition of the labor force, the difference in implicit adjustment used for the intercensal trend of the interpolating series is not important.

The worker rates used for 1900, 1920, and 1930 necessarily differ from the well-known estimates of Durand, as the latter are all adjusted to be comparable with the 1940 Census totals, whereas the present series is comparable with the *Current Population Survey* estimates for 1940ff.[32]

2. The worker rates for each age-sex-nativity group were interpolated to give annual estimates for 1900 to 1930, then applied to unpublished census data on population. Two adjustments were made in the data thus derived. Armed forces overseas, excluded from the census series, were added to the preliminary labor-force series for 1917 to 1919.[33] Secondly, the census estimates were based largely on school-attendance figures and other series not particularly sensitive to the in-migration of adult workers. We, therefore, compute a direct estimate for 1900 to 1914 of immigrant worker arrivals, and use that series as a measure of 1900 to 1914 labor-force trends among the foreign born.[34]

3. The preliminary 1900 to 1930 gainful-worker trend series thus derived for persons aged 14 and over was used to interpolate between gainful-worker figures for 1900, 1910, 1920, and 1930. The decennial rates of gain were used to adjust from reported census date figures to annual averages.[35] In addition, the reported 1910 figure was adjusted upward to allow for the overcount of that year. (This adjustment for all persons aged 10 and over is described earlier in this chapter.) We estimate the adjustment for males 14 and over as for females, on the assumption that the overcounted group included only home farm workers, having the same age distribution as reported home farm workers.[36]

---

[32] Durand, *op. cit.*, table A-6, p. 208. For the same reason they will differ from those of Clarence Long.

[33] Unpublished data kindly provided by the Bureau of the Census indicate as of July, 1917, some 148,000; July, 1918, 1,347,000; July, 1919, 551,000.

[34] Harry Jerome, *Migration and Business Cycles* (1926), p. 50, gives fiscal-year net alien arrivals for 1900 to 1908. We convert these to alien worker arrival estimates by the ratio, in each year, of immigrants with occupation to all immigrants. (The latter data are from the *Reports* of the Immigration Commission, vol. III, p. 178.) For 1909 to 1914 we use fiscal-year data from Jerome (p. 52). These were all then converted to calendar-year data, using the ratio of (1) the male immigrant arrivals calendar-year estimate of Jerome (p. 246) to (2) fiscal-year totals (*Historical Statistics,* p. 36). Cumulated arrivals from 1900 to 1910 were roughly double the parallel change in the estimated foreign-born labor force, and the annual data were stepped down by the 44.7 percent ratio and used for interpolating between 1900 and 1910 foreign-born labor-force figures, the same ratio being used for 1910 to 1914. No adjustment was made after 1914.

[35] Reported totals from 1900 Census, *Occupations,* pp. 7, 40; 1910 Census, *Occupations,* p. 91; 1920 Census, *Occupations,* pp. 35, 478; 1930 Census, *Occupations,* p. 115. For example, the intercensal estimates show a 1920 to 1921 gain of 743,000 in gainful workers, and half that was estimated as the gain from the January enumeration date to the annual average level.

[36] Age distribution data from 1910 Census, *Occupations,* p. 302.

1918: Gainful Workers

One of the most difficult problems in estimating intercensal trends in the labor force from 1900 to 1930 is the impact of World War I. Did it bring a substantial volume of extra workers into the labor market—as occurred in World War II? Or was the number relatively small—just as the impact of World War I on the economy was relatively small compared to the impact of World War II? The question is not whether the war had an impact on the labor market. It obviously did. And substantial declines in the large groups of servants and laundresses, an increase of better than 300,000 in semiskilled operatives in manufacturing between 1910 and 1920 are allowed for by intercensal interpolation. The question is rather to what extent extra workers had been brought into the 1917–1918 labor market who had left by January, 1920 (when the census was taken). In section A we discuss the number of "extra" female workers in 1918 not already allowed for by our interpolation procedure. Section B outlines our overall adjustment for 1918.

A

We may take as a point of departure the experience in World War II. The data indicate that increases in the female labor force closely paralleled increases in manufacturing employment.[37] For World War II, it is clear that declines in trade, finance, service, and most industry groups except manufacturing occurred. Hence the pattern of change in manufacturing is likely to suggest the maximum number of extra workers in the female labor force. The procedure used was the following.

For iron, steel, and machinery products, and for other detailed industry groups we have census counts of total and female wage earners in 1914 and 1919. Employment for intercensal years was interpolated by Shaw's series for output of producers durables (in constant prices).[38] We can estimate the ratio of female to total wage earners in 1918 from data secured in a Women's Bureau study covering firms that employed about 2.5 million workers in 1918.[39] Applying the ratio to the total number of wage earners yields an estimate of 300,000 female wage earners in these industries after the second draft in 1918—i.e., at peak employment.

As against this direct estimate, the present labor-force estimates im-

[37] BLS data for manufacturing, Current Population Survey data for labor force. Allowance for a 6-month lag in response would make the relationship even more precise.

[38] William H. Shaw, *Value of Commodity Output since 1869* (1947), p. 77.

[39] *The New Position of Women in American Industry,* Women's Bureau Bulletin 12 (1920), pp. 48, 49, 86. This study enables us to compute the proportion of female to total wage earners in 1916, after the first draft in 1918, after the second draft in 1918, and in 1919.

plicitly interpolate between census totals. If therefore we simply interpolate between the 1909 and 1919 Census of Manufactures totals for female wage earners, we secure an estimate of 190,000. Subtracting this figure from the estimated 300,000 actually employed gives an estimate of 110,000 extra female workers in this industry at the peak of war production.[40] We can make similar estimates for lumber, stone, clay, and glass products as well as for textiles, apparel, food, and tobacco. Because most female manufacturing workers were employed in the latter groups and because the proportions of females employed in those groups changed not at all under the influence of peak war production, the result of these estimates is to add only 40,000 extra workers to the 110,000 extra in metals.[41] By making similar estimates for these industries in the earlier part of 1918—after the first draft—then computing an average for the year and making similar estimates for 1914, 1916, and 1919, we can reach a significant conclusion.

The maximum number of additional female workers in manufacturing industry for any year in World War I was about 100,000. The achievement of this maximum must in part have been at the expense of declines in domestic service, in trade, and in other industries. Hence the maximum number of additional female workers in the labor force in any war year must have been less than that figure; in years except 1918, far less. It has therefore seemed both unwise and unnecessary to make any adjustment in the preliminary labor-force figures arrived at by interpolating between 1910 and 1920 rates. This influence is consistent with the statement that thousands and even hundreds of thousands of women entered war work in World War I who had not previously been in such work. It is simply that some of these women were recruited from nonwar industries, the total impact of World War I on the labor market was much less than World War II, and much of what effect the war did have was still present in the labor force rates for 1920—and hence allowed for by our procedure of interpolating between 1910 and 1920 rates.

B

The gainful worker estimate for 1918 is derived by adjusting the preliminary 1918 value secured by applying age-sex worker rates interpolated between 1910 and 1920 to the population detail. The adjustment is the

---

[40] This, of course, exaggerates the limitations of the interpolation procedure. Interpolation is fully consistent, say, with declines in domestic service, agriculture, and trade and offsetting gains in manufacturing—which is roughly what actually occurred.

[41] The proportions of females in the food and fiber groups are available only for the periods after the first and the second draft in 1918. However, the metals data indicate that the major changes from 1914 to 1919 were concentrated in the period between the two 1918 drafts. A fortiori, if there were no changes for this period in these food and fiber industries, we are safe in assuming no substantial changes in the other periods.

difference between two employment estimates for this year. One was arrived at by applying interpolated ratios for the duplicating item to the total employment figures secured by summing employees plus self-employed from the individual series in Tables A-5, A-6, and A-7. The other was secured by computing ratios of duplicated employment plus armed forces in 1910 and in 1919, interpolating for 1911 to 1917 by the changes in the duplicating ratios computed above, then interpolating for the ratio in 1918. The basis of this procedure is simply that by interpolating for the usual duplicating item, we assume that the ratio of jobs per persons moved steadily between 1910 and 1919, whereas the sudden growth of the armed forces in 1918 undoubtedly had its impact in changing that ratio. The alternative ratio for 1918 indicates an unduplicated employment figure of 835,000 greater than the ratio, ignoring the armed forces. We take this difference as a measure of the additional workers entering the labor force in 1918 because of armed force demands (as well as prosperity) and add it to the gainful worker total.[42]

A partial indication of the reasonableness of the computation is given by the unemployment figures that result. In the spring of 1919 Secretary of Labor Wilson reported 350,000 unemployed "at the places which we are getting reports" from, deduced 700,000 for the year.[43] Given the improvement later in the year, his figure is tolerably consistent with our 540,000.

1930 to 1940 (Table A-3)

Interpolation between 1930 and 1940 benchmark totals was by means of the BLS total labor force series.[44] The BLS series was derived by applying annual worker rates for age-sex groups to census population data for the corresponding groups. The worker rates were interpolations between estimated 1930 labor-force rates and those shown for 1940 by the Current

---

[42] The NICB's negative unemployment of 3 million in 1918 implies a much more substantial complement of "extra workers." Clarence Long, *The Labor Force in Wartime America* (1944), part 7, estimates that no especially large 1917–1918 gain in the labor force took place.

[43] *Monthly Labor Review* (April, 1919), p. 72.

[44] From the author's "Labor Force, Employment and Unemployment, 1929–39: Estimating methods," *Monthly Labor Review* (July, 1948), table 1.

For benchmark totals we use the 1930 gainful-worker total from the Population Census (*Occupations,* vol. V, p. 115), adjust for armed forces overseas (130,000 according to a BLS estimate) and adjust for April to July growth in gainful workers by taking an aliquot share of the 1930 to 1940 labor-force change as reported in the above-cited article. For 1940 we take the figure from Census series P-50, no. 2, *Labor Force, Employment and Unemployment in the United States, 1940 to 1946,* p. 11, with an addition of 150,000 for armed forces overseas. For the propriety of thus linking gainful-worker and labor-force figures, see the discussion immediately following.

Population Survey.[45] The resultant series reflects changing proportions among the various age-sex groups, and these changes are therefore reflected in the present series.

GAINFUL WORKER–LABOR FORCE DIFFERENCES

For many decades the Census Bureau data on the economically occupied measured the number of gainful workers, but beginning in 1940 the Bureau shifted to the labor-force concept.[1] An initial review of the differences in approach and intent that separated the 1930 from the 1940 Census technique led to the well-known Durand-Goldfield set of adjustment factors for translating the 1930 gainful-worker data into figures that would be more closely comparable with those of the 1940 Census.[2] In turn these factors have been utilized to adjust earlier census data to the 1940 labor-force concept.[3]

Beginning in 1945, however, a basic revision was made in the Current Population Survey interviewing procedure for securing labor-force data— a revision which added a substantial number of student and female seasonal workers to the number reported by the labor-force approach of the Current Population Survey from 1940 to 1945.[4] So significant were the effects of the new procedure that it appears to have offset almost precisely the adjustments originally made for the gainful worker–labor force conceptual difference.

In column 1 below we show the original factors developed by the Cen-

[45] The 1940 figures appear in Census Bureau, Current Population Reports, *Labor Force, Employment and Unemployment in the United States, 1940 to 1946*, ser. P-50, no. 2. The BLS 1930 rates rest, in the first instance, on the Durand-Goldfield revisions in the reported census data, to convert gainful-worker to 1940 labor-force comparable figures; secondly, on an adjustment to annual average; thirdly, on adjustment of the rates thus derived by the same percentage adjustments as were made on the original 1940 labor-force figures as a result of the 1945 revisions. On the latter, see pp. 5ff. in ser. P-50, no. 2, noted above.

[1] The basic discussions of the subject appear in three comprehensive works by most expert students: Louis J. Ducoff and Margaret Jarman Hagood, *Labor Force Definition and Measurement* (1947), chap. 2, and appendix A by John Durand; John D. Durand, *The Labor Force in the United States, 1890 to 1960* (1948); and Gertrude Bancroft, *The American Labor Force: Its Growth and Changing Composition* (1958).

[2] See the 1940 Census study by John Durand and Edwin Goldfield, *Estimates of Labor Force, Employment, and Unemployment in the United States, 1940 and 1930* (1944).

[3] Durand, *op. cit.*, appendix A.

[4] Census Bureau, *Current Population Reports*, ser. P-50, no. 2. Although the labor-force concept was not changed, the enumerative approach was, and the labor-force totals were significantly affected.

sus Bureau to adjust gainful-worker data to a labor-force basis, while column 2 shows the factors developed by the Census Bureau to make comparable the labor-force figures secured by the 1940 approach to those secured by the 1945 approach.[5] In column 3 we give the cross product of the two.

	(1)	(2)	(3)
Male...........	97.61	101.53	99.10
Female.........	97.35	106.33	103.51
Total...........	97.55	102.72	100.20

A net decrease for males and a net increase for females give a total comparable labor-force figure for 1945 which is within two-tenths of 1 percent of the gainful-worker level. The most detailed and thoughtful adjustment of the 1930 data for the gainful worker–labor force conceptual difference yields an adjustment ratio virtually identical with the opposite adjustment that resulted when the same labor-force concept was used, not with the 1940 questionnaire approach, but with the 1945 approach. The adjustments, in sum, simply cancel each other.

These conflicting elements are implicit in the BLS labor-force benchmark for 1930. Starting from the census April, 1930, figure of 48,595,000, the BLS reduced it to 47,404,000 by following the original census procedure for translating gainful workers to labor force, then raised it back to 48,-766,000 by the 1945 adjustment.[6] Next a revision from the April (Census date) to a July worker rate raised the figure to 48,949,000; the addition of armed forces outside the United States (omitted by Census) gave 49,079,000; and a seasonal adjustment to an annual average yielded the published figure of 50,080,000.

We conclude from the above that the original adjustment developed by the Census Bureau in 1943 for translating gainful-worker into labor-force estimate was effectively nullified by later changes in Current Population Survey enumerative practice.

It is desirable, however, to consider whether the wealth of information on the labor force collected since 1940 provides any more light on whether an adjustment is needed. A few summary judgments may be made.

1. In the 1944 Census report two upward adjustments (for omitted entries and new workers) just about balanced two downward adjustments

[5] Column 1 is derived from data in Durand and Goldfield, *op. cit.,* table 10. Column 2 is based on data from Current Population Reports, ser. P-50, no. 2, table IV.

[6] These and other figures are from unpublished BLS work sheets behind the estimates of the *Labor Review* (July, 1948).

(for the institutional population and the retired, disabled group).[7] We have no basis for changing these adjustments, nor for surmising that they would not essentially sum to zero for earlier decades.[8]

2. The net census adjustment in gainful-worker estimates for 1930 therefore is just about identical with the single adjustment for seasonal workers ($-1,191,000$ compared to $-1,156,000$).

About half the seasonal adjustment was made for the participation of student workers in the labor force; this comes from the assumption that the percentages in 1930 should have been no greater in 1930 than in 1940.[9] This assumption was the only reasonable one at the time that the original adjustment was made. Since then, however, the census has provided a wealth of additional data on the relationship between school attendance and labor participation. These data challenge the assumption made in 1944. While, for example, 4.4 percent of the children aged 14–17 and enrolled in school also worked in 1940, the proportion in the 10 years from 1947 through 1957 ranged from 17 to 24 percent.[10] Given this sizable rise from 4.4 percent even to the lowest postwar figure of 17 percent, it is now possible to conclude that the much smaller excess of 1930 over 1940 rates reflected economic circumstances and not—as the census report concluded—enumerative changes.[11] The worker rates in 1940 were unusually low, not because of a change in survey concept but because of the difficulty young persons had in getting jobs after years of depression. The 1930 rates differ from the 1940 rates—as do the postwar rates—less because of changes in concepts of the economically active population than

[7] Census Bureau, *Estimates of Labor Force, 1940 and 1930,* p. 7.

[8] The rate of omitted entries might have tended to be greater in earlier enumerations, with less adequate background of Census Bureau experience. On the other hand, the pay scale of census enumerators would have provided a relatively greater reward under wage levels of earlier days, so that we cannot conclude for any clear direction of omission rates. The percent retired would probably have been somewhat less in 1900 to 1920, with less retirement customary than in the years preceding the 1930 Census. The rising number of prisoners and mental-institution commitments, in relation to the number of males 14 and over, likewise suggests a relatively greater percentage adjustment in 1930 than warranted for earlier decades (1925 *Statistical Abstract,* p. 70; 1935 *Abstract,* p. 70). On the other hand, a tendency for children to enter the labor force earlier in the first decades of the century would imply a greater proportion of new workers than in 1930, hence a greater proportionate adjustment required. Assuming, therefore, no distinct change for omitted entries; a rise in the inmate, retired ratio; and a decline in the new-worker ratio, we conclude that a zero adjustment for these four groups in earlier decades would be about as reasonable as for 1930.

[9] *Estimates of Labor Force,* table 13.

[10] Census Bureau, *Current Population Reports, Employment of Students and Other Young Persons: 1957,* ser. P-50, no. 83, table A.

[11] The 1930 rate for the 14–19 group was 8.0; the 1940 rate, 4.4 (computed from *Estimates of Labor Force,* table 13).

because they are more typical of the active labor markets of 1900, 1910, 1920, and 1929 (carried over into early 1930) than is the depression-affected measure of 1940.

We come, therefore, to the difficult category of adult seasonal workers. Our question here is really this: Under 1930 Census conditions how many adult seasonal workers, not then in the labor force, would nonetheless have been included in the gainful-worker count? For this purpose the original census adjustment factor is less satisfactory than recent data. That factor relied on the most up-to-date measure then available—the excess of the maximum month in 1940–1941 over April levels. But clearly such a measure suffers from two defects. First, it reflects not merely seasonal factors but the tremendous upsurge in labor-force participation that occurred in these first years of World War II. Second, it uses the sensitive measuring instrument of the monthly Current Population Survey, rather than the blunter measure of the decennial census. We can avoid both difficulties, with only a limited offset, by drawing upon experience in the 1950 Census. Here we have an enumeration under census conditions, and here we have a much closer measure of the seasonal component.

For males not in the census data labor force, we have data on weeks worked in the prior year.[12] We exclude the inmates of institutions, those unable to work and keeping house, and those under 19 and over 65 years of age because they have been covered in the other adjustments. Of the balance, 325,000 worked 40 weeks or more in the prior year. A similar calculation for females gives a figure of 117,000.[13] If we adjust the census total for seasonal workers on this basis our adjustment comes to seven-tenths of 1 percent, or only about one-third of that made in the Census Bureau 1943 study.[14]

Hence the downward adjustment for adult seasonal workers, based on data less affected by the circumstances of the depression and more comparable with the 1930 Census results (because likewise derived from a census, rather than the more probing Current Population Survey), suggests an adjustment for adult seasonal workers of only a third the proportion in the original census adjustment.[15]

[12] 1950 Census, *Employment and Personal Characteristics,* table 16.

[13] We exclude those keeping house for reasons clearly set out by Durand and Goldfield (*op. cit.*) and assume that those not reporting weeks worked had less than 40 weeks.

[14] We relate the 1950 data to the total labor force. The absolute adjustment number is less than half of that in the census study, while the labor force by 1950—however defined—was at least 20 percent greater.

[15] A similar order of magnitude is suggested, however, by the *Current Population Survey.* See, for example, *Current Population Reports, Work Experience of the Population in 1955,* ser. P-50, no. 68, table 7.

Conclusions on Gainful-Worker–Labor Force Differences

The basic measure of the difference between the gainful-worker and labor-force concepts is that made by the Census Bureau for 1930 in a comprehensive study conducted during the mid-1940s.[16]

1. That study turned up a variety of lesser adjustments which, taken as a whole, canceled each other. We contend that for these items in the Censuses of 1900, 1910, and 1920 there would similarly be no net adjustment.

2. The study's significant adjustment for student seasonal workers proves, in the light of data developed by Census in later years, to be unwarranted.

3. The study's other significant adjustment (for adult seasonal workers) proves to be substantially smaller than that estimated in the census study if we draw upon the array of data that has become available since the time of the original adjustment.

4. A definite seasonal adjustment is still required to translate the gainful-worker into labor-force figures. We are fortunate, however, in the practical inferences from this fact. For our concern is not to derive a labor force as of April 1930, January 1920, etc., but a labor force at annual average levels for the census years. However, the difference between the April, 1930 figure and the 1930 annual average is precisely this seasonal group, included by the gainful-worker approach. This group, which must be excluded to provide labor-force comparable data, must be included back to derive an annual average.

5. We conclude, therefore, that the worker rates shown by the census for April 1930, are adequate measures of the annual average labor-force participation rates for 1930. Instead of making a double adjustment for seasonal workers, we simply adopt the published census figures as giving our best measure of the annual average labor force. The practical difference that this produces between the present estimates and the BLS estimates is that we do not exclude 1.1 million seasonal workers from the April, 1930, gainful-worker total, add back some of them implicitly when the adjustment for comparability with the 1945 results is made, and then add 1.0 million to convert an April figure to an annual average. We eschew all three adjustments and take the census April, 1930, gainful-worker total as the best estimate of the annual labor-force total, including seasonal workers. And we follow the same procedure, for the same reasons, for the 1900, 1910, and 1920 Censuses. (Other adjustments—for population growth from the census date to the annual average, for off-continent armed forces—are discussed in connection with the decennial estimates.)

As a terminal note, the comment may be ventured that the course of experience with the Current Population Survey since 1940 has led to

[16] *Estimates of the Labor Force.*

repeated changes in sample design, control of enumerator performance, schedule design and even, to a degree, concept. In this process the labor-force survey began to enumerate ever more short-time workers, seasonal workers, and female workers. Comparisons with the 1940, 1950, and 1960 Census results show that the more reliable enumerative performance of the Current Population Survey puts more persons into the labor-force total than does the census. Hence, the difference at a single point of time between good enumerative performance and inferior performance creates a greater numerical difference than do all the putative differences between the gainful-worker and labor-force concept put together. Moreover, the steady tendency toward more comprehensive totals under the current survey program suggests that so far as the mere aggregate totals are concerned we are working our way back to the gainful-worker levels.[17]

UNEMPLOYMENT: 1900 TO 1940 (TABLE A-3)

The unemployment series for 1900 to 1930 was derived by making direct benchmark estimates of unemployment in 1900, 1910, and 1930, using the Population Census data on unemployment in those years. Intercensal estimates were then obtained by estimating civilian labor force and employment for the half century and deducting one series from the other.

Benchmark Estimates

1900. The estimate of unemployment in 1900 was based on data collected in two enumerations. One was the 1900 Census of Population, which secured information on nonemployment during the year preceding the taking of the census. The second was an extensive survey made by the Commissioner of Labor of family income and expenditures that secured detailed information for about 25,000 families on cause and duration of unemployment during 1900–1901.

The starting point is the distribution of unemployment as shown in the 1900 Census of Population.[1] From the total shown there, teachers, self-employed in agriculture, and others in occupations characteristically domi-

---

[17] It would be a wry, but not wholly unjustified conclusion, that the 1910 overcount really enumerated a total that is closer to what our present procedures produce than any other figure for that year. Our present estimates adjust the 1910 total, however, so that the movement from 1900 to 1910 to 1920 may be more in accord with the facts as we know them, rather than making much more hypothetical adjustments in the 1900, 1920, 1930, and 1940 census results as well as Current Population Survey results for at least the 1940–1945 period.

[1] *Occupations,* tables 1, 25.

nated by self-employment were excluded—to exclude periods of "nonemployment" that were really periods "not in the labor force." [2]

The distribution of male nonfarm employees by duration of unemployment derived in this fashion was adjusted to take account of the information provided by the 1901 Cost of Living Survey.[3] That survey reported for male heads of urban families in the wage-earner group the level and duration of unemployment by cause of unemployment.[4] Two adjustments were made on the basis of these data. First, an estimate was derived of the percent of persons who should be excluded from each duration group because the causes of their idleness—e.g., no work wanted, drunkenness, old age, strike, vacation—would not currently be considered as justifying the classification of unemployment.[5] Secondly, it was assumed that the higher level of unemployment shown in the Cost of Living Survey, based as it was on a detailed reckoning of the families' employment, income, and expenditure experience over the year, was likely to be more precise than the necessarily brief enumeration in a survey made only every 10 years. The proportion unemployed shown in this survey was therefore first adjusted to allow for unemployment of nonfarm workers not covered by the survey— primarily those not heads of families[6]—and then the differences between that proportion and the rate indicated by the census was used to adjust the census total unemployment figure upward. The adjustment was distributed into the various duration groups in the same way as the reported duration data of the Cost of Living Survey indicate, which in fact implies that three-quarters of census omissions were in the lowest-duration group—a reasonable implication since Census Bureau enumerators were likely to miss less of the hard-core unemployment.

The average duration of unemployment in each duration group was computed from the very detailed interval data in the cost of living survey. Multiplying the number in each group by average duration and dividing by 50

[2] Such occupations include dentists, lawyers, boardinghouse keepers, saloon keepers, etc.

[3] *Eighteenth Annual Report of the Commissioner of Labor,* 1903.

[4] *Ibid.,* pp. 290–291.

[5] The sickness and accident groups were also excluded on the assumption that most persons reporting sickness should be classed as not in the labor force. On the other hand, those for whom any of these causes was reported in combination with another cause were included. This was done because current procedures undoubtedly include some workers as unemployed who report these causes, particularly those who had been seeking work when they became temporarily ill.

[6] The ratio of employment rates among nonfarm gainful workers who were and were not family heads was estimated on the basis of 1930 relationships. These indicated the rate for singles was one-third greater (*Census of Population,* 1930, vol. II, p. 848, and *Census of Unemployment,* 1930, vol. II, p. 336). Adjustment for the relatively small portion of all nonfarm employees who were not within the scope of the survey was not attempted; it would make little difference in the results.

to get estimated full-time unemployment gives a benchmark figure for male nonfarm workers in 1900.

For female workers the census data were reduced to exclude data for teachers, agricultural pursuits, and other occupations, multiplied by average duration data (the same average within each duration group was used as above), and then converted to full time unemployment.

For male farm laborers the reported census total included unemployment of family workers. An estimate for wage earners alone was made as follows: In 1910, the unemployment percentage for male laborers not elsewhere specified, building and hand trades, was 34.8 compared to 11.5 for farm wage-earner laborers. The ratio of one to the other was applied to the laborer (domestic and personal service) rate of 44.3 in 1900 to give an estimate of 14.7 for male farm laborers (wage earners). A similar procedure was used for females. These were then distributed by duration as reported farm laborers.

1910.   Although the Census of 1910 secured data on unemployment of wage earners in the previous year, these data were not tabulated until 1948.

The 1910 data on unemployment are in the form of distributions for unemployed wage earners 16 years and over by duration of unemployment.[7] By applying the distribution to the total for wage earners 16 years and over, and deducting estimates made similarly for teachers and home-farm laborers (wage earners) we secure a preliminary estimate for the number of unemployed wage earners by duration group. The resultant distribution was reduced to exclude unemployment that would not be counted by current definitions. We use the same proportions within each group as indicated in the 1901 Cost of Living Survey—multiplying by the same average duration figures, within each group, as used for 1900, and computing man-years of unemployment.

The resultant total was adjusted upward for underenumeration. This adjustment was derived as follows: A large-scale survey on the employment and income of wage earners in selected industries in 1910 was conducted by the Immigration Commission. The survey provided data on duration of employment for 220,000 male wage earners (aged 18 and over) in a broad range of industries.[8] Because the Commission was concerned with the foreign born, the sample overrepresented foreign-born workers and those in certain industries. The separate distributions—e.g., males, native born of native father; white, employed in the agricultural implements industry; foreign born in bituminous coal mining, etc.—were therefore reweighted in accordance with the census gainful-worker totals[9] to

---

[7] These data were reproduced by the Census Bureau in a set of lithoprinted sheets, in 1948.

[8] *Reports,* Immigration Commission (1911), vol. 23, table 27.

[9] *Census of Population, 1910,* vol. IV, table VI.

derive distributions for each industry of the male employees by employment duration. The resultant distributions, while covering all major mining and manufacturing industries (coal, cotton goods, furniture, meat packing, etc.) could not in themselves be taken as an adequate sample for a direct estimate of employment levels. They constitute, however, a very large sample with which to adjust the reported census unemployment data for the same industries. The ratio of adjusted to unadjusted totals for the sum of these industries was then used to adjust the grand total census figures estimated above.[10] There are two reasons for using the Immigration Commission survey to adjust the census reports. First, a detailed inquiry into family economic status was being made, with opportunity for a much more careful consideration of employment status during the previous year than would normally occur during the brief census interview. Second, the instructions in the Immigration Survey specifically required an explanation of lost time or low earnings, presumably leading to a more careful estimation of employment duration than the more general census interview where short duration figures would not be questioned.[11] The result of these differing procedures is apparent in the data. Thus the census report shows 82 to 86 percent of male employees in cotton goods with no unemployment in the previous year, whereas the Immigration Commission data show only 63 percent.[12] For coal mining the census shows 32 percent of the operatives with a full year's employment while the Immigration Commission shows 15 percent—a figure much more consistent with data on mine activity.[13] To the adjusted census data for unemployment among wage earners was added an allowance for unemployment among those classified as self-employed on the census day but who had periods in the labor-force year during which they sought work as employees. The sum of the two figures then gives the 1910 unemployment benchmark.[14]

[10] One example may be given. The Immigration Commission data indicate an average duration of employment in iron and steel manufacturing of 9.2 months for native white males of native parentage, 8.5 for native whites of foreign parentage, 7.9 for foreign born, and 10.8 for Negro. Weighting these by the census gainful-worker distributions gives an estimate of 8.5 for the industry—or 3.5 months unemployed. The census data for males in iron and steel indicate 9.1 weeks of unemployment for laborers and 8.4 for semiskilled workers or, a weighted average of 9.0 weeks. Since these data relate to wage earners in mining and manufacturing in 1910, it is reasonably safe to equate periods of nonemployment with periods of unemployment, vacations being infrequent and periods of sickness being deducted in the earlier adjustment.

[11] *Reports,* Immigration Commission (1911), vol. 2, p. 703.

[12] Census data are not available for the industry but are shown for laborers, beamers, bobbin boys, spinners, and other occupations in cotton goods.

[13] *Mineral Resources of the U.S., 1911,* Geological Survey, part 2, pp. 45, 52. These data suggest the number of active days per year ran to about 200, roughly 29 days being lost in strikes in 1909.

[14] This procedure implicitly assumes the same unemployment rate among the wage

1930. An annual average benchmark for this year was estimated as follows. From the Durand-Goldfield estimates we find that 5.17 percent of the gainfully occupied total for April were unemployed according to present definitions.[15] This ratio, applied to the census gainful-worker total for April, gives an April unemployment figure and, by subtraction, an employment figure.[16] The annual average employment was estimated at 97.02 percent of the April level, using ratios for its agricultural, manufacturing, and other components.[17] Adding armed forces overseas to this figure and subtracting from the annual average gainful-worker total gives us an unemployment figure for 1930.[18]

1929 to 1939. Following the procedure used for the original BLS estimates, but adopting a variety of revisions in the labor force and the component employment series, gives unemployment estimates for this decade that differ in trivial amount from those in the published BLS series except for 1929, which is approximately 20 percent different.[19] Because of the widespread use of the BLS figures and because the differences are well within the error involved in the computation of the duplicating item,

---

earners as the self-employed. Such an assumption is consistent with census practice in 1890 and 1910, and allows for the fact that not only are some self-employed indistinguishable from wage earners—e.g., carpenters—but that some bona fide self-employed were wage earners for some period in the census year. For example, the unemployment rate for seamstresses and dressmakers was about the same in 1890 and 1910. If there were no unemployment among the self-employed in 1910, then the implicit rate of unemployment for wage earners was nearly double that for 1890 —hardly a likely state of affairs.

[15] John Durand and Edwin Goldfield, *Estimates of Labor Force, Employment and Unemployment in the United States, 1940 and 1930* (1944), p. 13. We implicitly assume the same rate for seasonal workers largely because we have little warrant for an alternative, because the total group constitutes less than 3 percent of the gainful-worker total, and because Durand and Goldfield have already included a substantial portion of the seasonal group Class A and Class B unemployed.

[16] Census figures for aged 14 and over are from 1930 Census, *Occupations,* p. 115.

[17] For agriculture we use the ratio of 101.89—the implicit ratio of the census figures as adjusted to the BLS 1930 annual average shown in *Monthly Labor Review* (July, 1948). For manufacturing the ratio of 90.19 is derived from monthly BLS production-worker indices from a BLS lithoprinted sheet giving data for 1919 to 1943, adjusted to second quarter, 1942, social security benchmarks. We estimate 1930 employment for other employees as 96.27 percent of 1929; for manufacturing as 89.24 percent; and for unpaid family workers and domestics and self-employed as 97.08 percent. We then compute the ratio of each to that for manufacturing; applying these latter ratios to the 90.19 for manufacturing gives us 97.23 for other employees and 98.10 for the nonfarm self-employed.

[18] The census April total for gainful workers was increased by 203,000 to an annual average, plus 130,000 for armed forces overseas. This 4,180,000 figure compares with the 4,340,000 in the BLS estimates.

[19] Beginning with 1929, the figures run as follows (000): 1,315; 4,180; 7,933; 11,996; 12,717; 11,194; 10,614; 9,000; 7,625; 10,408; 9,555.

we adopt the BLS figures for 1930ff. as our unemployment totals, then subtract these from the labor-force totals to give our employment series.[20]

UNEMPLOYMENT AND RELATED SERIES

Comparison with Other Unemployment Estimates

How does the pattern of economic change indicated by the present unemployment series compare with that indicated by other series and other measures of economic change?

The comparative change in the present and other unemployment series is indicated in Table 9-2.[1] The broad picture shows no startling changes in the way we are accustomed to considering this period: 1921 is still a year of major recession; 1908, 1914, 1924, 1927 are still years of recession. But the general magnitude of unemployment as measured by the present series nevertheless differs significantly from that reported by earlier series. (So too does the ranking of individual years with respect to the severity of their unemployment.) Thus the present unemployment figures exceed the National Industrial Conference Board estimates for the three decades in the 1900–1930 period—by 40 percent in the first decade, 900 percent in the second (because the NICB shows negative unemployment for 1917–1919), and 10 percent in the third. Since Lord Beveridge used the NICB series in framing his post-World War II full-employment goal, this difference in levels is of some interest.

[20] In 1930 the total employment figure from the census as estimated here is 94.39 percent of the sum of the individual series for nonfarm employees, self-employed, etc., while the ratio for 1940 is 95.29. Interpolating between these ratios for the intermediate years, as was done in the preliminary BLS estimates, gives us the employment figures that yield the unemployment estimates noted above. These ratios reflect incomparabilities between the two series, with their differing original sources of information, and, in large measure, the fact that an employee who moves from one job to another during a payroll period will be reported twice by payroll reports from each establishment. The movement of this duplicating item is sufficiently irregular in recent years so that the implied trend for it if we use the BLS unemployment series for the 1930s is not at all unreasonable.

[1] Column 1, Table A-3; column 2, *Economic Almanac, 1953–1954,* National Industrial Conference Board (1953), pp. 422–423; column 3, Paul Douglas, *Real Wages in the United States, 1890–1926* (New York: Houghton Mifflin, 1930), p. 460; column 4, Daniel Carson, "Labor Supply and Employment," WPA, unpublished study (1939), p. 357; column 5, Meredith Givens, in *Recent Economic Changes in the United States,* National Bureau of Economic Research (1929) vol. II, p. 478; column 6, Brookmire Service, quoted in *ibid.,* p. 468; column 7, Hornell Hart, *Fluctuations in Employment in Cities of the United States, 1902 to 1917,* Trounstine Foundation (1919), p. 48; column 8, David Weintraub, *Technological Trends and National Policy,* National Resources Committee (1937), p. 70.

Table 9-2. Selected Estimates of Unemployment, 1900 to 1930 (In thousands)

Year	Present esti- mates (1)	NICB (2)	Douglas* (3)	Carson† (4)	Givens‡ (5)	Brook- mire Eco- nomic Service (6)	Hart§ (per- cent) (7)	Wein- traub (per- cent)¶ (8)
1900	1,420	1,647	755					
1901	1,205	1,721	584					
1902	1,097	500	569				14.1	
1903	1,204	1,523	609				9.3	
1904	1,691	1,430	883				11.5	
1905	1,381	621	622				9.3	
1906	574	−143	577				5.5	
1907	945	756	695				6.0	
1908	2,780	2,296	1,654				14.8	
1909	1,824	719	925				8.6	
1910	2,150	553	774			0	6.5	
1911	2,518	1,571	1,025			496	10.8	
1912	1,759	920	775			0	9.6	
1913	1,671	1,018	936			267	9.3	
1914	3,120	2,214	1,899			2,027	15.8	
1915	3,377	2,355	1,822			1,479	16.0	
1916	2,043	187	774			112	7.1	
1917	1,848	−1,933	774			0	4.7	
1918	536	−3,099	719			58		
1919	546	−870	880			75		
1920	2,132	558	938	2,695	1,401	0		6
1921	4,918	4,754	2,913	6,085	4,270	3,653		25
1922	2,859	2,917	2,338	4,595	3,441	2,567		22
1923	1,049	749	1,010	2,880	1,532	0		11
1924	2,190	2,034	1,506	3,665	2,315	1,390		13
1925	1,453	817	1,120	2,855	1,775	387		13
1926	801	464	962	2,080	1,669	0		11
1927	1,519	1,620		2,380	2,055	1,466		12
1928	1,982	1,857		2,575				13
1929	1,550	429		1,910				10
1930	4,340	2,896		4,825				19

* Unemployment in manufacturing, transportation, building, and mining.
† Unemployment of wage and salary workers.
‡ Minimum unemployment.
§ Unemployment as a percentage of nonagricultural workers.
¶ Unemployment as a percentage of labor supply.

Looking at the periods of rising unemployment, we may note that the present series shows larger gains during the recessions before World War I but distinctly smaller rises during the recessions after that war. The difference in the postwar estimates reflects a difference in the sensitivity of the two series. The NICB *unemployment* series is necessarily more variable because the NICB *employment* series is more variable—and that for two reasons:

1. NICB estimates of employees in trade and service rest more largely on the use of manufacturing employment as an extrapolator—and manufacturing employment is one of the most sensitive employment series. The present estimates for these segments rest on more stable series.

2. NICB series for self-employed persons and domestic servants generally are estimated to fluctuate with the number of employees in those groups. Present procedures rest on the assumption—made in the light of changes reported from population census to census, and data on annual changes since 1930—that the self-employment series is far less sensitive than that for employees. Douglas's estimates, being limited to unemployment in four major industry groups, will naturally show smaller absolute changes in unemployment. With a smaller absolute base they can, and do, show much greater variations in percentage change.

A second point may be made. Not only is the present series generally less volatile, but the order of depression years in terms of severity is somewhat different. Thus the present estimates indicate the 1937–1938 unemployment rise to have been about as severe as 1929–1930—rather than substantially more severe, as the NICB data indicate. Also they indicate that the 1920–1921 rise in unemployment was clearly less than the 1930–1931 rise—rather than slightly more.

In addition to these general conclusions we may consider three specific examples of difference: 1920–1921, 1916–1917, and 1900–1901.

One of the most significant differences between the year-to-year trends shown by the NICB series and the present estimates is that for 1920–1921, when the NICB shows unemployment rising by 1.4 million more than the present estimates do.

1. The difference arises chiefly because the NICB estimates a greater decline in trade and service employment to have occurred than the present series does.

2. The NICB decline for these groups is considerably larger than that indicated in a special survey conducted during 1923 for the National Bureau of Economic Research by Willford I. King.[2]

The present estimates show a mild gain, reflecting the fact that the constant dollar volume of goods available for distribution in 1921 was

[2] Willford I. King, *Business Cycles and Unemployment,* National Bureau of Economic Research (1923).

about the same as in 1920.[3] The NICB figures, on the other hand, reflect the sharp drop in current dollar sales.[4] We assume that trade-employment trends should more closely parallel trends in the real volume of goods than money sales.

The present estimates show a rise in domestic service and self-employment in service—both substantial groups in the service total. The NICB figures were derived from an estimating series dominated by manufacturing employment, and the latter fell by 25 percent in this period.[5] Experience in the past quarter century, when we have reasonably reliable direct-employment measures, indicates that total service employment in this category (and particularly self-employment) does not respond markedly to short-run cycle fluctuations, and shows little parallelism with the change in manufacturing employment.

For the 1920–1921 change in trade and service employment, and indeed in employment as a whole, we can refer to the estimates secured by King from direct employer reports.[6] While these data have limitations, they represent direct reports from a surprisingly large sample of employers. King's data indicate changes in the trade and service groups which are much more modest than the NICB data. His estimate of total employment shows a 1920–1921 drop of 3.2 million, almost equal to the present estimate of 2.8 million for the 1920–1921 rise in unemployment. (It is unlikely that ¾ of a million additional workers entered the labor market during this period above and beyond the normal labor-force growth—as would be necessary to make the NICB unemployment change consistent with King's employment change.)

For 1916–1917, NICB shows a far sharper fall in unemployment than the present estimates, and one which would a priori seem more likely in the light of the growth of war production. The difference arises chiefly because the NICB data for manufacturing employment (based on "a sample comprising 64 percent of the total manufacturing employment in 1919") rose by 1.2 million,[7] while the present estimates report little gain

[3] The volume data used for the present estimates were those of William Howard Shaw, *Value of Commodity Output since 1869*, National Bureau of Economic Research (1947).

[4] The NICB used "the appropriate NY Federal Reserve Bank Index of distribution to extrapolate trade employment." The New York Bank index as reported by Norris Johnson in "New Indexes of Production and Trade," *Journal of the American Statistical Association* (June, 1938), is composed of less-than-carload lot carloadings data, department store sales, chain grocery sales, other chain sales, mail order sales, etc.

[5] NICB and present figures for service components other than domestic and personal would not differ greatly in the amount of change. It is the domestic and personal group which would account for differences in change.

[6] *Op. cit.*, p. 88.

[7] Because the NICB used manufacturing employment in estimating trade employ-

since the deflated volume of manufacturing production as reported in Shaw's data shows only a small rise.[8] Douglas's direct-employment series for manufacturing (based on BLS and New York State) shows a gain of 537,000, much closer to the present 200,000 than to the NICB 1.2 million.[9]

As a final comparison we may take the 1900–1901 change. Here the present estimates show a clear decline in unemployment while the NICB figures actually rise slightly. The difference occurs because of estimated differences in the trend of trade and service. The NICB series uses the combined movement of agricultural, mining, and manufacturing employment. The very substantial stability in agricultural employment over many decades and the lack of change in manufacturing employment during this year amount to positing no change in the trade and service group.[10] The present series, on the other hand, reports a growth in employment assumed as resulting from (1) an increase of roughly 12 percent in the volume of finished commodities (except producer durables) to be handled through the distribution system, and (2) the long-term upward trend of self-employment in these industries.

Unemployment and Other Measures of Economic Change

How do variations in unemployment as measured by the present estimates relate to variations in other measures of economic change? The question is as difficult to answer as it is interesting. The reason for the difficulty is simple. The present estimates were developed on the premise that the best possible employment and unemployment estimates were desired. This meant that the soundest procedure was to take advantage of the major advances in our knowledge of this period which are associated with the names of Shaw, Fabricant, Kuznets, and others who have laboriously developed basic production series for the National Bureau. Hence while a vast variety of other sources were used, together with quite independent

---

ment—and via trade, for service employment—the estimate for manufacturing becomes basic in determining this change. For a simple comparison between present and NICB estimates, we should also note that NICB includes the armed forces under the service total.

[8] Shaw shows a mild rise for total finished goods, and a drop in manufactured food, clothing, furniture, floor coverings, and miscellaneous housefurnishings (*Op. cit.,* pp. 70, 72, 73). These latter data are used in the present procedure to estimate the trend for employment in trade and such service categories as dressmakers, etc.

[9] Douglas, *op. cit.,* p. 439. Douglas's sample covers some 15 per cent of manufacturing employment in 1914 and Berridge's combination of state data covered not much more as of 1914 or 1919. No information appears to be available concerning the sample used for the NICB estimates.

[10] Douglas shows a change similar to NICB, but since his data do not attempt to reflect trends in trade and service they are not inconsistent with present estimates.

data from censuses of prisons, reports of the Collector of Internal Revenue, lists of securities dealers, etc., substantial reliance was placed on these studies which worked the basic Census of Manufactures data into consistent detailed series. Similarly the employment estimates for construction rest on detailed estimates of deflated activity developed for the purpose at hand. Year-to-year changes in unemployment will closely reflect changes in employment. Individual employment series for key industries will in turn tend to reflect changes in production because of the method of estimate. However, the frequency of benchmark counts—quinquennial censuses of manufacturing before the war and biennial after it—means fairly frequent checks on the combined productivity and hours factor interpolated between these dates. Hence even for these series changes from one benchmark year to the next are independent of the production data.

While the relationship to production series therefore presents problems, the relationship to the national income estimates is less troublesome. This is because the Kuznets estimates that were used for 1919 to 1929 are derived chiefly by totaling the factor shares. Interest, rent, profits—these are certainly independent of the data used for the present estimates. And payrolls, the largest single component, are derived in most instances by applying ratios of pay to gross income, sales, or total outlays of the industry concerned. While for manufacturing, for example, the payroll data come from the same source, indeed the same reports, as do the employment data, so that there is likely to be a built-in consistency, the estimating process does not rest on the use of payroll estimates. For the 1930–1940 period, the interrelationship of estimates is far less: Beginning with 1936, reliance on the payroll totals from the independent body of tax reports filed under the social security system achieves a satisfactory degree of independence. For the 1940–1960 period, the estimates are essentially independent in provenance. Deflated income data, however, are not available. Data on changes in deflated product were therefore used. The extremely close similarity between year-to-year changes in undeflated income and product justified such a step.[11]

With these qualifications we may review the pattern shown in Figure 27, where year-to-year changes in unemployment are matched against corresponding changes in deflated gross national product.[12] The relationship in-

[11] The trend in employment is used in developing the trend in payrolls for domestic service, but aside from this limited group there is nothing of note.

[12] Unemployment: present estimates. GNP from *U.S. Income and Output,* pp. 126–127, 138–139 and *Survey of Current Business* (July, 1961). Deflated military pay was deducted, being estimated by multiplying the OBE estimates of military employment from these sources by the average military pay implied in the OBE 1954 revision of the income estimates.

Since this discussion was first written, an elegant review of unemployment and GNP change relationships has been provided by Arthur Okun in the Annual Report

dicated is remarkably close. On the one hand we have estimates derived for the 1920–1940 period as a residual between labor force and employment totals. As such they are subject to the net resultant of errors in each

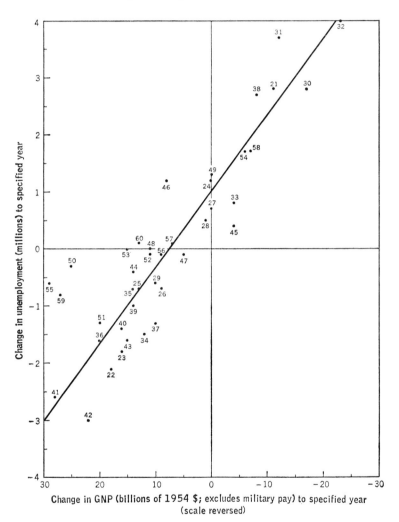

Figure 27.   Changes in unemployment and deflated gross national product, 1920–1960. Note: GNP excludes military pay.

series, with differences then calculated from these residuals. For the 1940–1960 period, the series rests on reports from a continuously changing

of the Council of Economic Advisers and in his "Potential GNP: Its Measurement and Significance" in American Statistical Association, *Proceedings* of the Business and Economic Statistics Section (1962).

sample, consisting primarily of housewives reporting on the employment status of members of their family. On the other hand, the GNP totals represent the sum of a mass of component estimates developed from a

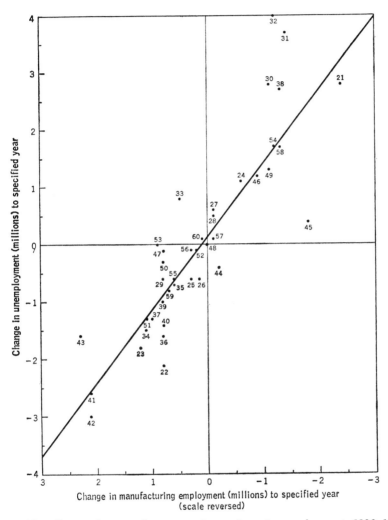

Figure 28. Changes in unemployment and manufacturing employment, 1920–1960.

hundred different sources, then deflated by a host of price data reported primarily by a vast sample of retailers. Reporting errors of necessity exist in the production, the margin, and the price data, while conceptual differences separate some of the data (particularly the price data) from those which are required for consistent estimating.

The relationship is nevertheless extremely close. The fact that it is so reflects three factors.

1. Year-to-year changes in unemployment tend to be mirror images of changes in employment. To judge from the 1940 to 1960 data, the stability in the labor-force totals from year to year is very great.[13] Despite sharp changes in worker rates for females and particular age groups, the fact that most adult males are in the labor force year in and year out gives a considerable stability to the labor-force totals.

2. Year-to-year changes in the employment estimates, though derived from a broad variety of sources, are dominated by variations in manufacturing employment (Figure 28). Of necessity annual changes in employment are sensibly linked to changes in payrolls, in sales, and—with some stability in the distributive margin estimate—in final product values.

3. The GNP estimates were adjusted to exclude changes in military pay —an item which pretty well accounts for most of the changes in gross government product during the war years. This was done because variations in military payrolls had little current impact on the domestic productive economy.[14]

The sharp exceptions to this relationship have their own interest. For the early years we might confidently refer to limitations of the unemployment estimates. And for 1946 we might emphasize the problems in accurately translating a $50-billion decline in government expenditures into a constant dollar decline of 90 billions, and the unprecedented withdrawal of female workers from the labor force. But for 1950, 1955, and 1959 we have no such solutions. In these years the results are directly from the Current Population Survey, and unemployment would have had to decline to absolute zero to fit the regression indicated. Since each of these was a year of recovery, a massive turnaround in inventories was reported, but even the widest variation in inventory valuation procedures would hardly bring a close fit.

Figure 28 emphasizes how closely changes in factory employment and unemployment parallel each other. Figure 27 indicates that unemployment tends to rise even with no decline in GNP; presumably this occurs because of the advance of productivity. Figure 28 suggests that if factory employment does not slump, neither will the other forces that combine to create additional unemployment. Other demands are so sensitively keyed to those of manufacturing, and supply of labor is so responsive to the totality, that as factory employment goes so goes unemployment (in reverse). Excess

---

[13] Because the estimates before 1940 are interpolations, they cast no direct light on this point.

[14] Data from *National Income Supplement, 1954.* Variations in government purchases, including those of food and clothing for the armed forces, are, of course, not excluded by this procedure.

entries of women in 1943 to the labor force, and withdrawals from war jobs in 1945, create two striking exceptions to this generalization. And the 1931 and 1932 figures, however inadequate, are probably true reflections of additions to unemployment flowing from even the stablest industries as the economy reached its nadir.

How, it may be asked, do the variations in unemployment correspond with variations in business conditions if we use not a single aggregate measure such as GNP but the broad summary measure of products prices, financial transactions, etc., implicit in the NBER reference cycles? In the table below, the years are classified into two groups, namely, those in which the Burns and Mitchell chronology reports more months of cyclical expansion than decline, and vice versa.[15] Each of these is then divided between those in which the percentage of the labor force employed, as measured by the current series, rose or fell.

Years in which NBER reported more months of:	Years in which percentage of labor force employed:			
	Rose		Declined	
Expansion than decline..........	1901	1919	1908	
	1902	1922	1915	
	1905	1925	1924	
	1906	1926	1928	
	1909	1934	1933	
	1912	1935	1938	
	1916	1936		
	1917	1939		
	1918	1940		
Decline than expansion..........	1913		1903	1920
	1923		1904	1921
	1929		1907	1927
	1937		1910	1930
			1911	1931
			1914	1932

[15] Arthur F. Burns and Wesley C. Mitchell, *Measuring Business Cycles*, National Bureau of Economic Research (1946), appendix A.

Concentrating on years with 8 months or more in expansion or contraction gives us the following array:

Years with 8 months (or more):	Years in which percentage of labor force employed:	
	Rose	Declined
Expansion...................	1901 1925	1915
	1905 1926	1928
	1906 1934	1933
	1909 1935	
	1912 1936	
	1916 1939	
	1922 1940	
Decline.....................	1913	1903 1921
		1910 1927
		1911 1930
		1914 1931
		1920 1932

Four years of all those in the period do not fall into the main diagonal. Of these the unemployment change for two (1913, 1915) is so small as to be well within the margin of error. For 1928 and 1933, in which the mass of cycle indicators point to change in one direction while the unemployment series moves in the opposite direction, no single explanation is possible. It will, however, be recognized that these were years of weak expansion; that relatively long series tend to conform less well to the cyclical indexes than short series; and that for the pre-World War I years, the dating may not be finally established.[16]

LABOR FORCE, EMPLOYMENT, UNEMPLOYMENT: 1940 TO 1960 (TABLES A-3, A-4, A-5, A-6, A-7)

Beginning with 1940, we turn to two sets of official series on labor-force components and industry employment, supplementing them for certain omissions as outlined below.

---

[16] Wesley Mitchell, *What Happens during Business Cycles,* National Bureau of Economic Research (1951), p. 281. There must be few bits of testimony to inherent nobility of scholarship that equal Mitchell's labeling of the reference dates, after more than a quarter century of work, as "tentative."

Labor Force, Total Employment, Unemployment (Tables A3, A-4, A-6)

We adopt the Census Bureau's Current Population Survey reports for these series as well as for figures on total farm and total nonfarm employment, and domestic service.[1]

Nonfarm Self-employed and Unpaid Family Workers; 1940 to 1960 (Tables A-4, A-7)

CPS totals for these two groups from 1947 to 1960 were used.[2] No official breakdown is available for 1941 to 1946. Since unpaid family workers in CPS estimates during 1947 to 1951 ranged from 396,000 to 427,000, we assumed a flat 400,000 for 1943 to 1945, then interpolated between the 1940 and 1943 figures for 1941 and 1942 counts. The self-employed totals were then computed by subtraction from the larger total.

Industry detail for the self-employed from 1947 to 1960 was provided by the BLS from unpublished CPS data. For 1941 to 1946, detail was derived as follows: For 1950 we used the decennial census count of self-employed in each industry to split the 1950 CPS total for the year, just as we had done for 1940.[3] We then interpolated between 1940 and 1950 benchmarks by the OBE estimates of the business population by industry.[4]

Domestic Service: 1940 to 1960 (Table A-4)

This activity is not included in the BLS series for employees in non-agricultural establishments nor in our series for employees in nonfarm enterprise. For 1941 to 1946 unpublished CPS data, and for 1947 to 1960

---

[1] The data appear in the Census Bureau's *Current Population Survey,* ser. P-50 reports, and, beginning in 1958, in monthly issues of the Bureau of Labor Statistics, *Employment and Earnings.*

[2] Census Bureau, *Current Population Reports,* ser. P-50, nos. 2, 13, 19, 31, 40, 45, 59, 67, 72, 85, 89.

[3] The 1950 CPS total (P-50, no. 31) is 6,069,000, while the corresponding census total is 5,236,000, including only those reporting industry. Industrial detail for the latter appears in the 1950 Census, vol. II, part 1, *U.S. Summary,* table 133.

[4] Betty Churchill, "Recent Business Population Movements," *Survey of Current Business* (January, 1954), table 1. These data relate to firms in operation, annual average, through 1950. Data for firms in operation on Jan. 1 in subsequent years appear in Betty Churchill, "Rise in the Business Population," *Survey of Current Business* (May, 1959) table 2, and unpublished data for 1960. Because there are estimating as well as conceptual differences between the two sources of data, if we were to apply this same procedure to each industrial category, the sum of figures based on the OBE series would not equal that of the CPS. Instead of distributing such a difference by industry, the "other" group—combining a mixture of transport, finance, real estate, etc.—was omitted as being of little analytic value.

Because the interpolated values for trade and manufacturing were within 1 percent of the CPS figures in 1947, and 3 percent for construction and service, we assumed the series to be directly comparable.

published CPS data, were used. For 1940 the ratio of domestic service to all nonfarm employees was computed from decennial census materials and applied to the CPS level for nonfarm employees. The result checks closely with an estimate built up from the CPS domestic data available for 8 months in 1940.[5] The National Income Division figures will differ slightly because they are benchmarked directly to 1940 decennial census levels, albeit using CPS for trend.[6]

Employment by Nonfarm Industry (Table A-5)

The most widely used series to measure trends of employment in individual nonfarm industry is that of the Bureau of Labor Statistics on "employees in nonagricultural establishments." We use these figures for individual industries for 1929ff. Our industry detail for earlier years is intended as comparable with these figures.[7] (We differ from the BLS figures for 1919 to 1928,[8] which utilized an earlier version of the present estimates.)

[5] Direct use of decennial data is improper since for all other components they differ from CPS levels, to which we adhere. From 1940 Census, Vol. III, table 78, we compute an estimate that 7.27 percent of nonfarm employees there reported were in domestic service. Applying that ratio to the CPS nonfarm employee average (in series P-50, no. 2) gives 2,350,000. Taking the CPS unpublished average for the last 8 months of 1940, assuming that a continuous rate of decline from 1940 to 1941 took place (to derive the first 4 months) gives 2,285,000.

[6] Our 2,300,000 for 1940 is virtually identical with the original Denison estimate for the NID (given in NID mimeographed notes). The July, 1947, *National Income Supplement* (p. 40) changed that figure to 2,120,000; the *1951 Supplement* to 2,365,000 (p. 182); and the *1954 Supplement* to 2,454,000 (p. 198). The original BLS estimates, as implicit in presently published BLS labor-force and unemployment figures for the 1930s, benchmark to decennial census data with minor adjustment for "unpaid workers" reported in domestic service.

[7] Bureau of Labor Statistics, Bulletin 1312, *Employment ana Earnings Statistics for the United States, 1909–1960* (1961). Because of minor errors in the government employment figures published in this volume, we use corrected figures kindly provided by the BLS from unpublished data.

[8] *Ibid.*

10

EMPLOYEES, BY INDUSTRY:
1900 TO 1960 (TABLES A-5, A-6) †

COMPARISONS WITH PRIOR
EMPLOYEE ESTIMATES

Although specific comparisons are made throughout the discussion of estimating procedures, we note here a general comparison between present results and earlier estimates for 1919 to 1929 (or 1920 to 1930). This period is of special interest and one for which we have detailed estimates by Kuznets, NICB, and various NBER studies, as well as the decennial figures of Carson.

Agriculture

Differences between present estimates of agricultural employment and those of Shaw and Hopkins for the National Research Project and Barger and Landsberg (discussed below in detail) arise because the present estimates accept the 1920 Population Census count without adjustment, assuming that its low level compared to 1910 and 1930 can be sufficiently explained by the same kind of off-the-farm movement which we experienced during World War II, and therefore we are not justified in adjusting this apparently low figure for a putative seasonal undercount.

Differences from the present U.S. Department of Agriculture Series (adopted for this period in the estimates of Knowles and Kendrick) largely

† The description below relates only to the estimates for 1900 to 1928. These estimates link directly to the BLS figures for 1929ff., which appear in BLS Bulletin 1312, *Employment and Earnings Statistics for the United States, 1909–60* (1961).

reflect the fact that the USDA series are benchmarked to decennial Census of Agriculture rather than Census of Population estimates. We find that the Census of Agriculture count of farms for this period is a weaker guide for manpower estimation. A second cause of difference from these various estimates is that they relate to persons aged 10 and over. Our series, for persons aged 14 and over, necessarily does not reflect the sharp declines in the 10–13 age group.

Construction

BLS and other prior estimates (e.g., Carson, Whelpton, Kendrick, NICB) will differ from present estimates because their benchmarks, if any, were Population Census benchmarks prior to 1929.[1] The present series uses an 1899 benchmark derived from the Census of Manufactures survey of 69,000 construction firms in that year. Carson, in addition, differs significantly in level because he includes (in 1920) the construction occupations in shipbuilding.[2] (His 1920 to 1930 percent change of 40 percent, however, compares closely to the present 41 percent for employees plus self-employed.) The NICB increase is substantially greater and apparently derives from its use of the Population Census occupation group— "building, general and not specified laborers"—a large and changing proportion of whom were not in construction. Kuznets has no employment benchmark prior to 1930, estimating employment in 1920 by the 1920 to 1930 trend in the ratio of employment to construction volume in two states, Ohio and Pennsylvania.

Manufacturing

The present estimates for employees are identical with (and for self-employed, very close to) the preliminary BLS figures. These two series (as those of Fabricant, Kuznets, and others) use basic BLS series based on Census of Manufactures data interpolated by BLS reports. Carson, however, uses Population Census benchmarks, as does the NICB. Such data appear to be less comparable over time than do Census of Manufactures totals but do not differ markedly.[3]

---

[1] Preliminary BLS figures for this and other industries appear in the BLS *Handbook of Labor Statistics, 1950,* and in BLS Bulletin 1312. Simon Kuznets, *National Income and Its Composition, 1919–1938* (1941). National Industrial Conference Board, *Economic Record* (1940).

[2] Carson, using selected occupations, shows a gain of 861,000. Daniel Carson, "Changes in the Industrial Composition of Manpower since the Civil War," *Studies in Income and Wealth,* vol. 11 (1949). The laborers group gained 425,000. The sum of the two shows a gain of 1,286,000, compared to an NICB gain of 1,260,000.

[3] Solomon Fabricant, *Employment in Manufacturing, 1899 to 1939* (1942). NICB uses for interpolation BLS annual data (as of September, 1938), which have since been revised.

Transport and Utilities

The present estimates and BLS, Kuznets, and other National Bureau studies by Barger and Gould in this area differ little in 1919 to 1929 movement except for a single category, inasmuch as they all rely on industry censuses and similar sources. BLS, being estimated by correlation with Kuznets, implicitly adopts his procedure of estimating waterways employment by extrapolating the 1916 Water Transportation Census total by using tonnage cleared through United States ports. This series includes vessels—and hence employment—of foreign countries as well as the United States. The present estimates use data for the tonnage of documented United States vessels only—and within that group, for steam and motor vessels. The result is to show a decline from the 1919 postwar reconstruction period to 1929 instead of the Kuznets report of no change.

The NICB figures show much the same decade change for public utilities; they differ in transport chiefly, it is believed, because they extrapolate highway transport employment by motor-vehicle registration. The present estimates allocate part of that growth to passenger vehicles and in addition allow for a decline of employment on horse-drawn vehicles.

Carson's change for utilities and transport differs again because the present estimates rely on industrial censuses for major components of this group whereas Carson uses Population Census totals. (For example, ICC data indicate a decline of 500,000 in steam-railroad employment but Carson's railroad totals decline by only 125,000.)

Trade

BLS estimates of employees in trade were estimated from Kuznets's change. The two differ from the present series chiefly because the present estimates allow (1) for the change in the number of employees classified in the "retail dealer" group in the Population Census as well as (2) for the change in the number of cooks and bartenders in retail trade—a sizable group included in service by the Population Census, and hence by Kuznets, but here (consistent with the Standard Industria' Classification) included in trade. The recent release of 1910 Census data and the studies of Gladys Palmer make it possible to estimate this latter group.

The 1920 to 1930 gain for employees plus self-employed in the present estimates is 2.2 million—compared with 2.0 million for Carson, the difference arising chiefly because of the cook and bartender group. NICB includes trade with finance, but—using Population Census data—should implicitly have much the same movement.

Finance, Insurance, and Real Estate

BLS estimates were based on a regression from Kuznets's series. Although the differences between these two series and the present one are not great, they do arise because Kuznets assumes that the entire gain in the number of charwomen, janitors, and porters between 1920 and 1930 occurred in real estate. Since as of 1940 only 20 percent of this group was employed in real estate, the present estimates do not allocate all the increase of about 125,000 in this group to this industry.

Carson shows a 1920 to 1930 gain of 625,000 compared to the present 545,000 gain, the difference arising because the present estimates for banking are not tied wholly to Population Census benchmarks but are estimated instead so that there is a consistency with Comptroller of the Currency data on employees per bank.

NICB estimates are combined with those for trade, but—being benchmarked to Population Census data—should have roughly the same characteristics as Carson's.[4]

Service

Substantial differences exist between the present estimates on the one hand and the preliminary BLS figures and those of Kuznets on the other hand.[5] (The BLS service was estimated by a regression from Kuznets's estimates.)

1. Kuznets includes restaurants and garages, greasing stations, etc., in service. The present estimates follow the Standard Industrial Classification and include these under trade.

2. Kuznets includes in the employee group self-employed persons in automotive service.

3. Kuznets does not include employees of dressmakers, tailors, and blacksmiths in the selected occupations used to establish 1920 and 1930 benchmarks.

4. Kuznets estimates hospital employment by multiplying the number of hospital beds for each year by the average salary per hospital bed in New York, then dividing by the average salary per hospital employee in Ohio. The present estimates use 1910, 1923, and 1935 Census of Hospitals data on employees.

NICB combines service with government and domestic service. The combined group rises by 2.4 million compared to the present series of gain of 1.8 million. The present series uses Industrial Census and similar benchmarks—considered more comparable over time—for such groups as private education, hospital employment, and government, whereas NICB

---

[4] Carson's trade plus finance plus hotel and restaurant group (not including automotive service) rise by 3 million, whereas the apparently comparable NICB group rises by 2.2 million. Part of the difference may be in the NICB allowance for unemployment.

[5] Kuznets's procedure for restaurants from p. 765, for automotive service from p. 789, for hospitals from pp. 778, 795. Preliminary BLS estimates used Kuznets's professional plus miscellaneous plus personal service for movement.

uses Population Census benchmarks. Similar comments apply to Carson's figures, particularly for government and professional service where his figures can be compared with benchmarks other than the Population Census.

Government

The present estimates will differ from the Stigler estimates of employment in education because direct estimates for nonacademic personnel from 1900 to 1919 were made, using contemporary figures from the Census, *Statistics of Cities*. For state nonschool employment, we use national benchmark figures, whereas Fabricant relies largely on data for New York and Massachusetts; we use procedures similar to Kuznets for the 1920s (and thereby BLS, which follows Kuznets) but adjust to exclude veterans' pensions from the payroll series Kuznets uses for interpolation. For local nonschool employment, we follow Fabricant for the 1920s (thereby differing somewhat from Kuznets) but for the earlier decades rely on national data rather than, as Fabricant, on figures for New York and Chicago. For the Federal government, we rely on the latest revisions of the Civil Service Commission rather than the earlier ones used by prior estimators.

AGRICULTURE (TABLE A-6)

Farmers

For decennial census years we use the Population Census count of farmers, after adjustment to exclude managers and after subsequent adjustment to annual average levels.[1] For intercensal years 1920 to 1930, we interpolate by the number of farms.[2] In doing so we must allow for the likelihood that the number of part-time farms decreased during World War I and its immediate aftermath.[3] For 1901 to 1909 we interpolate

[1] Totals for farmers plus managers appear in David L. Kaplan and Claire M. Casey, *Occupational Trends in the United States 1900 to 1950,* Bureau of the Census Working Paper 5 (1958), p. 6. They include not merely farmers but such exotic specialists as apiarists, stock raisers, etc. For 1920 and 1930 these figures do not include managers. For 1910 the Kaplan-Casey estimate does include them, and we deduct, using data from the 1910 Census, p. 302. For 1900 we assume 37,000 managers, as compared to the 47,000 for 1910. The annual average adjustment is the ratio of April to annual average total agricultural employment in 1930. This ratio, between the reported census and the BLS *Monthly Labor Review* (March, 1948) estimate, rests on a seasonal factor estimated by Louis Ducoff.

[2] Agricultural Marketing Service, *Number of Farms, by States, 1910–56* (November, 1957), pp. 5–7.

[3] In 1910 and 1930 the number of farms was roughly 5 percent greater than the number of farmers, whereas no excess appeared in 1920. We take a ratio of 100 percent for the years from 1918 (when the number of farms first falls markedly) through 1922 (the last year before the number of farms again resumes a peacetime declining trend).

linearly, basing such stability on the steady, equally invariant, changes in the number of farms over the subsequent 1910–1916 period. For 1911 to 1916 we extrapolate the 1910 level by the 1900 to 1910 rate of change, while for 1917 to 1919 we interpolate between 1916 and 1920.

Unpaid Family Workers

For the decennial census years we utilize reported census figures after adjustment to annual average, by the same procedure as for farm operators, and after two other adjustments. (1) For 1900 an estimate of agricultural laborers included in the "laborers not otherwise specified" group was made in connection with the adjusted census gainful-worker estimate for that year.[4] (2) For 1910 we exclude that portion of the overcount (discussed in connection with the gainful-worker estimate for that year) that represents unpaid family workers.[5]

Interpolation for 1901 to 1909 was linear; for 1911 to 1919 by the trend in farm population.[6] For 1925 to 1930 the 1930 average was extrapolated by the USDA series for family-farm workers—a series based on direct reports that begins with 1925.[7] For 1921 to 1924 interpolation was by the number of farms.[8]

Hired Workers

Decennial census figures were converted to annual average levels in the same way as the data for farm operators were, while the adjustment for the 1900 Census inclusion of some farm hired workers in the "laborers not specified" group and for the 1910 overcount of this group were done by procedures described above for family workers.[9] Interpolation for 1931

---

[4] In that estimate we computed the ratio of "laborers not specified" to total population in a 58-city sample, applied this to the total urban population, and deducted the result from the total laborers n.o.s. group to get a rural group. Using the reported age distribution for this group, we excluded those aged 10–13 and distributed the balance between hired and unpaid workers by the census proportions. This procedure is fully outlined in the description to be published on the estimates for 1800ff.

[5] We assumed that the 73,000 males and the 608,000 females in the overcount were all home-farm workers and distributed them by age interval, as were home-farm workers reported in the census. (1910 Census, *Occupations,* p. 302.) Hence 553,000 was taken as the overcount of family-farm workers aged 14 and over.

[6] Farm population data from *Major Statistical Series of the United States Department of Agriculture,* vol. 7, *Farm Population,* USDA, Agricultural Marketing Service, Handbook 118 (1957), p. 7.

[7] The USDA series appears in *Ibid.,* p. 9.

[8] *Number of Farms by States, 1910–56.*

[9] Unemployed farm workers were estimated (from unpublished 1910 Census data

to 1939 and extrapolation for 1925 to 1929 were by the USDA series for hired workers.[10] Intercensal estimates for 1900 to 1920 and for 1921 to 1924 were estimated by deducting family labor from total farm employment.

Total Farm Employment

For 1925ff., total farm employment was estimated as the sum of employment of the self-employed, family workers, and hired workers. For 1900, 1910, and 1920, benchmarks were derived for each of these same components (as described above) and their sum gave the total farm employment for those years. Intercensal employment between these dates was estimated by means of the USDA series for man-hours used for farm work.[11] The series essentially moves as a measure of the quantity of man-hours demanded. Its use here amounts to assuming that the difference between the trend in man-hours demanded (adjusted to actual employment benchmarks) and the number of family workers (estimated from other sources) is taken up by changes in the number of wage earners. Hence this relationship provides the basis for the present estimate of wage earners in the years prior to 1925. While requiring some adjustment for this use, this broadly based series represents, it is believed, the most reliable and objective indication of changing employment in the years before the direct field surveys of the USDA begin.[12]

Relation to USDA Series.   The above estimates will differ from those of the U.S. Department of Agriculture for two main reasons.[13] (1) The present series is designed to be consistent with the Current Population

---

and published data for other years) in connection with the unemployment estimate and deducted from the gainful-worker totals.

[10] *USDA Handbook 118,* vol. 7, p. 9.

[11] *Changes in Farm Production and Efficiency,* USDA Statistical Bulletin 233 (1959), p. 19. This series was extrapolated to 1900 by the ideal output index of Frederic Strauss and Louis Bean, *Gross Farm Income and Indices of Farm Production and Prices in the United States, 1869–1937* (1940), p. 126. This series reflects the changing demand for labor as indicated by applying labor requirements coefficients to actual data on acres and units of livestock, with allowance for chores and overhead labor not so directly related.

[12] Enormous variations in cotton-crop yield have a marked effect on the series. Since for these early years a major portion of the cotton crop was cultivated by family workers and sharecroppers, we exclude cotton man-hour requirements from the labor requirements series, using weights from Reuben W. Hecht and Glen T. Barton. *Gains in the Productivity of Farm Labor,* USDA Technical Bulletin 1020 (1950), p. 89. John Kendrick, *Productivity Trends in the United States* (1961) follows our 1951 procedure of using these estimates for interpolation; hence he does not adjust as we do here for cotton man-hour requirements.

[13] *USDA Handbook 118,* vol. 7, p. 9. Though benefiting from much earlier work by Shaw and Hopkins, these figures are largely the work of Paul Wallrabenstein.

Survey series and is therefore basically benchmarked to the decennial Censuses of Population rather than, as the USDA series, to the much higher levels of the decennial Censuses of Agriculture. (2) The present series relies on procedures for intercensal interpolation that give a more variable series for hired labor than does the USDA procedure. We may examine each of these differences in somewhat more detail.

Benchmark Differences. *Unpaid Family Workers.* The gross significant differences between the present estimates and the USDA series involve primarily the count of unpaid family workers. For these the Census of Agriculture reports almost twice as many as does the Census of Population in 1920, 1930, and 1940, and even more in 1950.[14] Preference between the Agriculture and the Population Census counts cannot turn on differences in coverage, enumerator efficiency, etc., for in these censuses the same enumerator filled out both the Agriculture and Population Census schedules for a given farm.

1. Part of the difference may be accounted for by the inclusion in the Agriculture Census of children below the Population Census age limitation—under 10 prior to 1940, and under 14 in that year.[15] However, Wallrabenstein's USDA adjustment of the 1940 Census figures for the 10–13 age group still leaves nearly twice as many in his figure derived from the Agriculture Census as from the Population Census.

2. Part of the difference involves persons with primary jobs in nonfarm occupations who, in a given period, also worked at farm jobs.[16] However, only a small portion of these dual-job holders were unpaid family workers, and no greater ratio would have maintained at earlier censuses.

3. Both the above factors likewise apply, though not as forcefully, to the hired-worker count, where both censuses give results within 10 percent of each other.

We must, therefore, seek a third factor capable of producing these 100 percent differences. A pointer to that factor is to be found in the great similarity from state to state in the ratio of unpaid family workers per farm as reported by the 1940 Census of Agriculture. The census data

[14] Comparisons are conveniently made in the unpublished USDA study by Paul P. Wallrabenstein, "Revision of BAE Farm Employment Series" (April, 1953), table 3. In 1950 the Agriculture Census count is almost triple that of the Population Census; it is double in 1920, 1930, and 1940; however, in 1910, the Population Census overcount brings a transient equality.

[15] An unpublished census survey estimated 738,000 children aged 6–13 working at farm jobs in August, 1951—somewhat more than 10 percent of wage earners and somewhat less than one-third of unpaid family workers. The ratios for those aged 6–9, relevant to the 1900–1930 Census, would presumably be lower.

[16] The August, 1951, survey estimated about 800,000 persons in this category. This harvest date figure would presumably be somewhat less than for the spring date of the census.

imply the following ratios of unpaid family workers to farm operators in 1940:[17]

Region	Population census	Agriculture census
Northeast..........	16	55
North Central.......	18	52
South.............	29	62
West.............	12	45

When the enumerators filled in the Population Census schedule, they sought the number of family workers who had worked only 1 hour or more—coming up with data giving the ratios from 12 to 29 percent. When they filled in the Census of Agriculture schedule, with its narrower requirement of those who worked at least 2 days or more, they came up not with fewer persons but with so many more that the ratios run from 45 to 62 percent. A second paradox is the marked difference between the Population Census ratios for the South as against the West and North—differences of much milder dimension in Agriculture figures than in the Population Census.

A look at the schedule confronting the enumerator when he collected the farm-labor portion of the Agriculture Census suggests a simple answer: Ignoring the fine-print limitation of "two days or more," he simply reported what the schedule called for, the number of operators and unpaid family members, and the number of hired laborers.[18] The Agriculture Census therefore tended to give a larger, and less realistic, measure of the number of unpaid persons connected with the farm, rather than the number actually gainfully occupied on it.

Operators. Benchmark differences for groups other than unpaid family workers are much smaller. The USDA estimates for farm operators will differ because of their assumption that the number of working operators per farm changed much less from 1930 to 1940 than the Population Census data imply.[19] However, there is no reason for great stability in this ratio; for the period for which the Population Census data are questioned, the argument is not a strong one. The stability in the Agriculture Census count of farm operators arises as the net resultant of (1) a marked decline in tenants and (2) a distinct rise in the number of owners aged 65

[17] 1940 Census, *The Labor Force,* vol. III, table 58. 1940 Census, *Agriculture, General Report,* vol. III, chap. 6, table 13. We assume one operator per farm reporting and deduct from the family labor count to give a count of unpaid family workers.

[18] 1940 Census, *Agriculture, General Report,* vol. III, p. 3.

[19] Wallrabenstein, *op. cit.,* p. 4.

and over.[20] The Population Census reports a decline for all farmers and a decline for the older groups.[21] Is it unreasonable to surmise that there was a marked growth in the number of farms operated part time by persons who were really retired, so that the number of farm operators (measuring in terms of activity in the labor force) did in fact decline?[22]

Differences for earlier census years reflect the implicit USDA assumption that the percent of all farmers working 250 days or more a year off the farm was the same in those years as in 1940, a conclusion we find dubious, given the growing trend toward off-farm work.[23]

Hired Workers. Differences between the two sources for hired workers are trivial compared to the above differences. For 1940 and 1950 the difference is less than 10 percent; for earlier years the USDA precludes difference by simply adopting the Population Census data directly. Hence the great conceptual differences between Population Census (gainful workers at any time during the year) and the Agriculture Census (those actually employed 2 days or more in the census week, etc.) prove to be unimportant empirically.

Interpolation Procedure Differences. *Since 1925.* Both series use the monthly crop-reporter series of the USDA for interpolation, as did the earlier Shaw-Hopkins estimates.[24] However, the USDA 1953 estimates show a significant difference for the early 1930s. They report not the downward trend shown in the Shaw-Hopkins (and present) estimates but a rise from 1930 to 1934, deriving from a much more marked rise in the family-worker count. Since the revised USDA series shows a much greater net decline over the 1930–1940 period than did Shaw-Hopkins, this is particularly surprising. We assume here that no improved data on the 1930 to 1940 year-to-year change in fact became available to the USDA after the Shaw-Hopkins work, and we therefore continue with the crop-reporter trends as summarized by Shaw and Hopkins.

Prior to 1925. The procedures for farmers and unpaid family workers

[20] 1950 *Census of Agriculture*, vol. II, p. 814. The gain was almost solely in the age 55 and over category.

[21] 1930 *Census of Population*, vol. V, pp. 118–119; 1940 *Census of Population*, vol. III, pp. 98, 100.

[22] The detailed study by the Departments of Agriculture and Commerce, *Farms and Farm People* (1953), p. 61, uses the 1950 Census to demonstrate the substantial number of farms operated by persons who considered their major occupation to be not in farming but in nonfarm pursuits.

[23] Wallrabenstein, *loc. cit.*, uses a procedure which implies that the number who worked 250 days and more off the farm in 1940 formed the same proportion of all farmers in 1930 as in 1940—and, by extrapolating to earlier years, that this was so for them as well.

[24] Eldon E. Shaw and John A. Hopkins, *Trends in Employment in Agriculture, 1909–1936*, Works Progress Administration, National Research Project Report A-8 (1938).

are similar and the results more or less similar.[25] But for the hired workers, the present series rejects the Shaw-Hopkins procedure, hence differs
significantly from the present USDA series, which uses Shaw-Hopkins for
interpolation. The Shaw-Hopkins series is based on some combination of
population trends, number of farm trends, and trend in production. Since
no description is available of just how these factors were put together to
derive an estimate, we can only look at the final results.[26] Doing so reveals obvious inconsistencies. For example, the series for the three Southern regions shows stability from 1920 to 1921 in the number of hired
workers. Yet the harvested acreage of cotton fell by 15 percent over this
period, while that for tobacco fell by 32 percent.[27] Is it likely that, given
this immense fall in labor requirements, farmers continued to hire workers
at the same rate, merely because farm-population counts and numbers of
farms did not change? As another indication we may take the direction
of change from year to year in the labor requirements and in the hired
labor series. For the period 1910–1925, when the USDA series rely on
the Shaw-Hopkins movement, the USDA labor-requirements series and
hired-workers series differ in direction of year-to-year change for 11 out
of the 16 years. On the other hand, for the most recent 16 years (1941
to 1956), when the Bureau of Agricultural Economics crop-reporter sample was used and that sample was at its historic best, the two series differed in direction for only 6 years—or half as much.[28]

It is unnecessary to discuss at any length the series of Shaw and Hopkins and the earlier USDA series appearing in *Historical Statistics of the
United States;* both were USDA series now superseded by the USDA, and
clearly unsatisfactory in a number of critical respects.[29] Key limitations in
the Shaw and Hopkins procedures are: (1) No adjustment for the overcount of women in 1910. (2) Adjustment for overcount of children in
1910 on the simple assumption that 1910 was midway between 1900 and

[25] The data we use are better, but not significantly better. Thus we rely on a farm-
operators series of the USDA issued in 1957, whereas the USDA employment series
used the operator series available when the employment estimates were made in
1953. For unpaid family workers, the USDA series relied on "revised BAE farm
population estimates and a series of population estimates for earlier years prepared
as a WPA study," while we rely on the USDA farm population series available and
revised as of 1957, with, however, the same movement for earlier decades.

[26] Limited descriptive material appears in Shaw and Hopkins, *op. cit.,* p. 92, and in
Thomas C. M. Robinson and Paul P. Wallrabenstein, "Estimates of Agricultural
Employment and Wage Rates," *Journal of Farm Economics* (May, 1949).

[27] *Agricultural Statistics 1942,* pp. 100, 456. There is no indication that preharvest
work took a different path.

[28] USDA *Handbook 118,* vol. 7, p. 9; vol. 2, p. 12. We contrast three categories
—rise, decline, no change. More complex measures, which allow for degrees of
difference, would emphasize a few very large deviations for the earlier decade.

[29] Shaw and Hopkins, *op. cit.,* pp. 11, 127; *Historical Statistics,* p. 97.

1920—despite the fact that the latter was probably low because of wartime influences. (3) Intercensal interpolation procedures for 1909 to 1924, discussed below.

Another historically important series was developed by Barger and Landsberg as part of their impressive study of agriculture.[30] That series uses the Edwards decennial series estimates from the Population Census—thereby implicitly adjusting the 1920 Census total for an undercount, unlike the present estimates, and adjusting the 1910 Census for a different undercount than the present series does. Intercensal interpolation in the Barger-Landsberg series is by the Shaw-Hopkins estimates.[31]

The weakest part of the Shaw-Hopkins series is their interpolating procedure, relying as it does "on the basis of relationships between employment computed on the basis of . . . farm population, number of farms, and the trend in agricultural population . . . and that determined from crop reports for the years 1925–36." [32] The resultant interpolation for critical periods is quite unsatisfactory. The movement during the war years, for example, reflects the trend in population since Shaw and Hopkins used a number of farms series estimated by simple interpolation, and a production index that was remarkably steady. Here we find little warrant for their estimate of a 1917 to 1919 decline of 500,000 in unpaid family workers—a decline that was considerably greater, relative to population, than that occurring under the more pressing forces in World War II.[33]

The intercensal movement of the Shaw-Hopkins series, however, is less evident in the final Barger-Landsberg series since the latter interpolates between benchmarks that are much closer to one another in level than those of Shaw and Hopkins. Thus the Shaw-Hopkins rise in employment from 1920 to 1921 becomes, because of the interpolation procedure, an estimate of no change.[34] In the present estimates we rely on the marked decline in crops in that year as reflected in the decline in man-hour requirements to suggest that the number of hired hands, and therefore of employment, must have declined.

The most recent estimates of agricultural employment made in the National Bureau of Economic Research appear in a study by Solomon Fabri-

---

[30] Harold Barger and Hans Landsberg, *American Agriculture, 1899–1939* (1942), p. 251.

[31] *Ibid.,* pp. 242, 251.

[32] Shaw and Hopkins, *op. cit.,* p. 92.

[33] The family-worker count is from *Ibid.,* p. 11, from which their count of the number of farms, p. 113, is deducted. Their farm-population estimates, which are not shown, appear to be based on a memorandum of Madeleine Jaffe, giving farm-population changes similar to those shown in USDA *Income Parity for Agriculture,* part V, sec. II, which is itself based on changes in estimated farm employment, etc.

[34] Barger and Landsberg, *op. cit.,* pp. 242, 251.

cant, and form the basis for estimates of the Joint Economic Committee.[35] These estimates, prepared by John Kendrick and Maud Pech, adopt the USDA series for employment since 1910 and a USDA 1900 figure based on Edwards's data, and interpolate linearly for 1901 to 1909.[36] The man-hours series presented in the same report is derived by the USDA from quite unrelated sources, namely, agricultural output series to which ratios of requirements per acre of different types of crop, etc., had been applied by the Department of Agriculture.[37] Not being tied to census employment benchmarks, its broad changes are significantly different. For example, the USDA employment series used by Kendrick and Peck shows little net change from 1910 to 1920 (and a marked 1910 to 1919 decline), while the man-hours requirements series of Kendrick and Peck shows a substantial rise over these periods.[38] The differences between the USDA employment series that they adopt and the present series have been considered above.

The man-hours series that Kendrick and Peck use do not link to actual employment benchmarks available from either the Census of Population or the Census of Agriculture, while its intercensal movement has the great volatility that properly reflects variations in man-hour requirement, but not so well variations in actual employment in an industry that has been the traditional home of "disguised unemployment." It will therefore differ in level and movement from the sample employment data from the USDA employment reports since 1925, and the actual employment (and man-hours) data of the Current Population Survey since 1940.

MINING

Mining employment was estimated by developing benchmark figures for man-days of mining employment in 1900, 1910, 1920, and 1929; interpolating between the 1900 and 1910 figures by estimates of adjusted man-days in coal mining; interpolating between 1910, 1920, and 1929 by adjusted man-days in total mining; and then using the resultant series to extrapolate the 1929 BLS employment total.

[35] Solomon Fabricant, *Basic Facts on Productivity Change,* National Bureau of Economic Research, Occasional Paper 63 (1959), tables A and B. James W. Knowles, *The Potential Economic Growth in the United States,* Study Paper 20 for the Joint Economic Committee (1960), pp. 26, 51.

[36] Kendrick, *op. cit.,* appendix B.

[37] It is this series, with adjustment, that is used in the present estimates to interpolate the wage-earner series between census dates.

[38] In first presenting this man-hours series, Hecht and Barton (*op. cit.,* pp. 4–5) carefully outlined the differences between man-hour requirements and actual employment.

1. Comparable benchmark figures for man-days of employment in mining (except gas and oil wells) were estimated for 1902, 1909, and 1929 from the Barger-Schurr data.[1] Parallel estimates were made for 1900 and 1910.[2] To these data were added separate estimates of man-days in oil and gas wells.[3]

2. Man-days of employment in mining, 1911 to 1919, 1921 to 1928, were estimated by interpolating between the 1910, 1920, and 1929 benchmark estimates by the sum of separate series for man-days in (a) oil and gas wells and (b) all other mining. The oil and gas well figures were estimated by dividing output figures by interpolated values for output per man-day.[4] Man-days in mining (except oil and gas) were taken from Barger and Schurr.[5]

3. For 1901 to 1909, man-days in mining were interpolated between the 1900 and 1910 benchmarks by the movement of man-days in coal mining.[6] A study of the relationship between the two series for the years

[1] Harold Barger and Sam H. Schurr, *The Mining Industries, 1899–1939* (1944) represents the basic study in this field. Barger and Schurr give estimates for all mining except gas and oil wells as of these three dates. The 1902 estimate was adjusted by the ratio to be computed between two 1911 figures given by Barger and Schurr, one comparable with earlier and one with later years.

[2] The percentage change (1) from 1902 to 1900 and (2) from 1902 to 1911 of man-days in coal mining was computed. The ratio of one to the other was then applied to the percent change of man-days in all mining (except oil and gas) from 1902 to 1911 to provide an estimate of the 1902–1900 change. (This procedure allows for the differential rate of growth between coal mining and all other mining except gas and oil.) For 1910 the 1911 total for mining (except oil and gas) was extrapolated by the comparable output series, output per man-day being assumed the same in both years.

[3] The Barger and Schurr 1902 man-hours total for oil and gas wells (*op. cit.*, p. 311), divided by 10, gave a 1902 total for 10-hour man-days. (The average day implied in their 1902 data for all mining was 9.1.) This was extrapolated to 1900 by the 1900–1902 percent change in man-hours. A 1900 total for man-hours was estimated by dividing the 1900 output totals by an estimated output per man-hour, the latter having been extrapolated to 1900 from the 1902–1929 trend in output per man-hour.

A 1910 man-days total was extrapolated from the Barger-Schurr 1902 man-hours figure on the basis of the annual percent change shown in the 1902–1909 man-hours estimates in O. E. Kiessling et al., *Petroleum and Natural Gas Production* (1939), p. 327. A 1920 man-days figure was estimated by interpolation between the 1919 and 1929 Kiessling figures.

[4] Production data from Barger and Schurr, *op. cit.*, p. 348; man-days in oil and gas in 1910 and 1920, as estimated above; linear interpolation between the ratios of one to the other (1910: 72.1; 1920: 71.7; 1929: 51.6) gave the output per man-day series. The procedure is similar to that used in Vivian Spencer, *Production, Employment and Productivity in the Mineral Extractive Industries, 1880–1938* (1940), p. 62.

[5] Barger and Schurr, *op. cit.*, p. 310.

[6] *Ibid.*, p. 312.

1900 and 1910 to 1920 showed it to be extremely close (with a correlation well over .90). This occurred in part because coal mining accounted for so large a share of man-days in this period (almost precisely two-thirds), in part because of parallel growth in the output of each group. (Man-days in coal mining rose by 67.5 percent between 1900 and 1910, while man-days in all mining rose 67.8 percent.)

4. The man-days series thus estimated was used to extrapolate the 1929 BLS total for employment in mining.

The resultant series is more volatile than one conceptually akin in the Bureau of Mines active-period employment, as can be seen by comparing the man-days and active-period employment series for bituminous coal mining.[7] The present series is thus, both in level and movement, more closely comparable to series for other industrial groups than one based on active period employment. Moreover, it is to be noted that the use of man-days for extrapolation provides estimates which are within 10 percent of direct Census of Mineral Industries employment totals for 1902, 1909, 1919, and 1929.[8]

Self-employment in Mining

Self-employment at census dates was estimated as follows. For 1910 the census total, and for 1930 the BLS estimate were used. A 1920 total was estimated by the 1910 to 1920 change in the total gainfully occupied in three occupation groups.[9] These groups together accounted for 90 percent of the self-employed persons in 1910. Moreover, the 1910 to 1930 decline for this group was 31 percent—virtually the same as the 29 percent decline for the self-employed. Given these facts, the sum of the three occupation totals was used to interpolate for 1920. For 1900, the 1910 total was extrapolated by the sum of gold and silver miners and officials and operators of mining companies.

Intercensal estimates were made by the change in the number of gold and silver mines.[10]

[7] *Ibid.*, p. 312 and their informative discussion on pp. 273–275.

[8] 1939 *Census of Mineral Industries,* vol. I, pp. 22–23. Because of incomparabilities in the coverage of the 1929 Census and the treatment of employment returns in 1902, the difference can be estimated only approximately. Carson's totals are about 20 percent above the 1900–1902 level, somewhat less than 10 percent above the 1909, 1919, and 1929 figures. Daniel Carson, "Changes in the Industrial Composition of Manpower since the Civil War," in *Studies in Income and Wealth* (1949), vol. XI.

[9] Operators, extraction of minerals; gold and silver mine operatives; operatives in other and not specified mines except lead and zinc.

[10] Data on the number of mines appear in *Mineral Resources of the United States,* 1920, part I, p. 531; 1929, part I, p. 888. It is probably fortuitous, but the number of mines showed almost precisely the same 1910 to 1920 and 1920 to 1930 change as the number of self-employed.

MANUFACTURING

For the census years, recently revised figures are available from the Bureau of the Census.[1]

Intercensal interpolations for 1899 to 1909 were made by an index of employment in selected states.[2] That index is based on employment in states having 50 percent of all manufacturing employment as of 1904, the midpoint in the period. The component estimates are those of Berridge (for Massachusetts), Jerome (for New Jersey), and extensive work by Frickey for Ohio, Pennsylvania, and New York.[3] These indices were combined, using as weights the 1904 distribution of manufacturing employment.[4] Taking 1899 as 100.0, the index for five-state employment was 117.5 in 1904 and 144.1 in 1909—virtually identical with indices of 117.0 and 144.6, respectively, obtained for the entire country from census data.[5] Because it is possible to take advantage of Frickey's basic research, the present series may be more representative than earlier series based on data for fewer states.

For 1909 to 1919, the sample of available states is sharply restricted and the estimates were therefore made by another procedure. William H. Shaw's data on the trend (in constant dollars) of the output of finished

[1] *Historical Statistics of the United States,* p. 179.

[2] Some of the most careful estimates made with state data include William A. Berridge, "What the Present Statistics of Employment Show," in National Bureau of Economic Research, *Business Cycles and Unemployment* (1923); Paul Douglas, *Real Wages in the United States, 1890–1926* (1930), chap. 24; Edwin Frickey, *Economic Fluctuations in the United States* (1942), chap. 9; Hornell Hart, *Fluctuations in Unemployment in Cities of the United States, 1902 to 1917* (1921). Both Douglas and Hart used data in addition to those from state reports. Harry Jerome, *Migration and Business Cycles* (1926), pp. 69–75; Paul F. Brissenden, *Earnings of Factory Workers 1899 to 1927* (1929), chap. 15; W. I. King in National Bureau of Economic Research, *Income in the United States, Its Amount and Distribution, 1909–1919* (1922), p. 90. Solomon Fabricant, *Employment in Manufacturing, 1899–1939* (1942), p. 331, follows Douglas, who uses state estimates for interpolation.

[3] Unpublished data were kindly provided by Professor Frickey for the separate states.

[4] U.S. Bureau of the Census, *Manufactures, 1905,* table 6. Frickey's estimates for Pennsylvania end with 1905. An estimate for 1906 was made by correlating 1892–1905 and 1909 manufacturing employment in that state with the production of pig iron. Data for five states therefore were used for 1899 to 1906 and four states for 1906 to 1909.

[5] The five-state sample included 50 percent of all employment, with relative overrepresentation of iron and nondurables, relative underrepresentation of metalworking, transportation equipment, tobacco, etc. The inclusion of Pennsylvania in the group apparently produces a fairly acceptable balance.

goods were used.[6] More specifically, a series was computed as the sum of the output of finished goods, plus that for construction materials, minus the output of nonmanufactured foods. The estimation for the war years is a particularly chancy one and consideration was given to using the BLS indices on which Douglas relied.[7] However, that series seems less than satisfactory for these early years.[8]

Consideration was also given to the use of alternative output series such as Kuznets's and Fabricant's. The valuable Kuznets series on gross national product was not used chiefly because its movement derives basically from the Shaw estimates, and these latter could be used directly.[9] Fabricant's series for output in manufacturing has much to commend it: In addition to being carefully developed it is affected by changes in the production of intermediate output, just as total employment would be. However, its movement actually is much the same as that of the adjusted Shaw series, and furthermore, like the Frickey series, it is available for only part of the period.

Manufacturing Employees: 1919 to 1929

Fabricant's carefully adjusted estimates were used for this period.[10] Since he gives total employees' figures only for census years, intercensal

[6] William H. Shaw, *Value of Commodity Output since 1869* (1947), pp. 70, 71, 76, 77. They were combined into a series for making a regression estimate.

[7] Douglas, *op. cit.,* p. 439.

[8] Douglas arbitrarily weights the BLS series 3 and a New York State index 1 to compute a movement series. The resultant series gains 15.4 percent between 1914 and 1919. Census, however, shows a gain of 27.6 percent, while the output series gains 22.4 percent. (Moreover, the Douglas series declined from 1917 to 1918 and then to 1919. Such declines are contrary to other information.) See also the comments by Isadore Lubin on the BLS series even after many later improvements, in *Unemployment in the United States,* 70th Cong., 2d Sess., Sen. Rep. 2072 (1929), pp. 507–508.

[9] Simon Kuznets, *National Product since 1869* (1946). Basically Kuznets estimated gross product by adding to Shaw's figures (1) a fairly constant proportion for distributive margins (a constant proportion within each major product group) and (2) an allowance for services to consumers.

(1) While the constancy of margins is only mildly contradicted by recent estimates of Harold Barger, *Distribution's Place in the American Economy since 1869* (1955), p. 57, the area is one of doubt. (2) The service estimates are useful for a multitude of purposes but are derived from consumer-survey data and are therefore not very likely to be consistent with data from establishment sources. (A discussion of limitations in even the much more satisfactory recent survey data appears in a paper given by the author before the American Statistical Association in December, 1949.)

[10] Fabricant, *loc. cit.* The identical movement for the census years 1919–1929 is given in Simon Kuznets, *National Income and Its Composition,* vol. II, p. 597, and by the BLS indices presented in a BLS lithoprint (n.d.). Fabricant uses the BLS for intercensal estimates.

estimates were secured from a regression of his wage-earner figures on his employee estimates. These indices were then converted to BLS comparable figures by a ratio splice in 1929.[11]

Because of the extremely heavy fall in employment from 1920 to 1921 —a drop of 23 percent as compared with a 1929–1930 decline of only 13 percent—a special effort was made to check on the validity of the 1920 estimate. A review of the original Thomas-Berridge worksheets in the Federal Reserve Board files (on which the present BLS indices for the period are based) indicated that satisfactory study of the procedures used in getting these estimates was impossible in any relatively short time. What was done by way of check was to work from data collected by the National Bureau of Economic Research in 1922 covering the 1920 to 1922 employment shift.[12] Weights for four industry groups by three size-of-firm categories were derived from the 1919 Census of Manufactures[13] and applied to movement series based on the data reported to the NBER. The final series indicated a 1920–1921 movement from 100.0 to 79.0 contrasting to the Fabricant–BLS movement from 100.0 to 76.6. Because of the trivial difference, it was felt desirable to adhere to that shown in the published BLS estimates.

Manufacturing: Self-employed

The BLS 1930 total for self-employed persons in manufacturing was extrapolated by a series for proprietors and firm members in manufacturing establishments. The series was developed in five steps.

1. For 1899 the number of proprietors was estimated from the number of census establishments.[14]

2. Census totals for 1904 and 1909 were adjusted as not being comparable with other years. For 1904, 14,000 was added to allow for custom flour and gristmills not canvassed in that year.[15] On the other hand, the

---

[11] The Fabricant 1919 to 1929 and the BLS 1929 to 1940 movement being directly comparable, there is no particular problem of the relationship of levels.

[12] Willford King, *Employment Hours and Earnings in Prosperity and Depression* (1923), pp. 32, 34.

[13] 1919 *Census of Manufactures,* vol. VIII, table 19. The groups were combined into industry groups as indicated on p. 30 of the NBER report. The NBER data were reweighted because no explanation is given of the reason for the departure from 1919 Census weights. It may, of course, actually be that the 1919 weights had been brought up to 1920 levels.

[14] The ratio of proprietors and firm members to establishments—103 percent in 1909 and 105.5 percent in 1904—was assumed to be 105 percent in 1899. Census data from *Historical Statistics,* p. 179.

[15] 1910 Census, vol. VIII, p. 384, notes that custom mills were not canvassed in 1904. These mills, numbering 16,000 in 1899 and 12,000 in 1909, were assumed at 14,000 for 1904. Comparison of the unadjusted 1904 total of 216,180 establishments (1909 Census, vol. VIII, p. 32) with the figure shown in *Historical Statistics,* p. 179, indicates that no adjustment for custom mills was made in the latter revision.

1909 total was unduly high because of changing practices in the enumeration of sawmills. The total for that year was reduced by 14,000 establishments.[16]

Although there is fairly specific reason for these adjustments, a further consideration is the fact that the census schedules for 1909 were not edited.[17]

3. The census 1914 and 1919 totals were adopted without change.[18]

4. For 1921 to 1929, the reported census totals were increased to allow for proprietors of small firms. The percentage of establishments in the $500 to $5,000 group for 1921 to 1929 was estimated by extrapolating their 1919 percentage to total by the ratio which the $5,000 to $20,000 establishments constituted of all establishments in subsequent census years. (This procedure allows for the differential growth of small firms and for changing price levels.)[19]

5. For intercensal years estimates were made by interpolating from the curve fitting the ten census figures, except that 1920 was assumed to remain at the 1919 level.[20]

CONSTRUCTION

We describe below the methods used for estimating construction employment from 1900 to 1939.[1] Broadly put, the procedure was to develop

---

[16] Sawmills are always enumerated with difficulty, and even in recent years comparability is hard to achieve. The jump from 19,000 to 33,000 sawmills between 1904 and 1909 seems entirely unreasonable, as it is seven times as great an increase as in any previous period and gives a 1909 total greater than the 1914 total for the still larger group, lumber and timber products. With lumber and timber products having essentially the same number of establishments in 1904 and 1914—25,000 and 27,000, respectively (1910 Census, vol. VIII, pp. 422–423; 1920 Census, vol. VIII, p. 165), it was assumed that the 1909 total for sawmills would have been essentially unchanged, at the 1904 level of 19,000 instead of the reported 33,000.

[17] Shaw, *op. cit.*, p. 80.

[18] The 1939 *Census of Manufactures* and *Historical Statistics* alike give a 1919 total—249,881—for establishments with products of $5,000 or more. This figure, however, actually relates to establishments with products of $500 or more, and was used as such. (Discussion with Miss White of the Census Bureau indicated that the original 1919 figure of 269,137 was reduced by 19,256 to exclude certain industry groups but no exclusion was made for 59,975 proprietors of firms in the $500 to $5,000 group. An exclusion was made, however, for their establishments in the Census of 1939 revision.)

[19] 1925 *Census of Manufactures*, p. 1221; 1930 *Census*, vol. I, p. 63.

[20] Kuznets secures almost identical intercensal changes for 1921 to 1929 by using Dun and Bradstreet data on business failures. The 1919–1920 decline which the failure data indicate, however, is unreasonable in the light of the fact that the number of employees did not decline: a fortiori the number of self-employed, being a stabler series, would not have declined substantially.

[1] A description of the procedures used in making the BLS 1929 to 1939 estimates

benchmark estimates for 1899, 1929, 1935, and 1939 by adjusting the Census of Construction data in those years, then interpolating by a series for deflated contract construction activity.

1899. For this year the Census of Manufactures provided data on materials consumption, employment, and product of 69,000 construction firms.[2]

We reduce the product total to exclude work contracted out, and we adjust the materials consumption total to producers' prices by excluding the value of transportation and distribution costs embodied in that total.[3]

We then compute the ratio of (1) materials consumption (at producers prices) to (2) final product of contract construction (excluding work contracted out) for the census universe. By applying this ratio to Shaw's comprehensive estimates of materials consumption (at producers prices), we develop an estimate for total United States construction activity.[4]

We then derive an employment total associated with that activity figure as follows: The 1899 Census reports construction employment and construction activity totals for the 209 largest cities in the United States and for the remaining areas covered by the census.[5] We take the reported estimate of employment for these 209 cities. For employment in the rest of the United States, we deduct construction activity reported in these cities from our estimate for the United States, dividing the resultant activity figure by employment per $1 million of activity in the rest of the United States—the latter ratio being from the census.[6]

---

has not been published; it is therefore incorporated here since the procedures are closely similar for the earlier period.

[2] 1900 *Census of Manufactures,* part 1, pp. 124–126, 298–301, 332–337, 354–361. We include carpentering, masonry, plastering, plumbing, painting, and paperhanging.

[3] From *Ibid.,* p. 53, contract work in specified trades can be computed as 10 percent of the value of the product reported. We estimate that 15 percent of the materials expenditure by construction firms reflects freight, and wholesale and retail margin. This estimate rests on a 9 percent freight cost implicit in Harold Barger, *Distribution's Place in the American Economy since 1869* (1955), pp. 130–131; on Barger's figures on retail and wholesale margins and the proportion flowing through each channel (*Ibid.,* tables 24, 25, B-5); and on a comparison with Shaw's data to derive the amount of direct sales to contractors.

[4] William H. Shaw, *Value of Commodity Output since 1869* (1947), p. 77. The activity figures were deflated by the procedure outlined in note 7 below. Shaw's data were already deflated.

[5] 1900 *Census of Manufactures,* part 1, p. ccxlvi.

[6] Activity per person engaged (after adjustment to exclude contract work) was $1,812 in the 209 cities, $1,465 in the rest of the United States. We measure persons engaged as equal to the number of employees plus the number of establishments, since the detailed census data by industry (p. 53) indicate that the number of establishments constitutes a close measure of the number of proprietors.

The activity figure derived above for 1899 was deflated by a combined materials price index and average earnings series.[7]

1929, 1935, 1938–1940. Employment in 1929, 1935, and 1939 was derived from the Construction Censuses for those years. The procedure adopted for each census was to compute activity per employee by type of contractor. These figures were adjusted to apply to all firms, including those omitted by census, using the raising ratios implicit in the 1939 data for larger firms versus that for all firms, by type. The resultant figures for activity per employee were then divided into a series for contract construction activity. The activity series was derived much as the 1900 to 1928 one described below, except that it was raised to adjust for the undercount of contract employees in 1939 as indicated by Unemployment Compensation and Old-Age and Survivors Insurance data and as estimated from such data by the National Income Division. For 1938–1940, the estimates of that Division were used.

1920 to 1938. For 1899 and 1929 we can derive estimates of activity per employee as noted above. The trend in this ratio through to 1935 and 1939, when we have Construction Censuses, reports a reasonable advance in productivity per man and hence the ratios were linearly interpolated for intervening years. These were then applied to a series for deflated construction activity. The activity series, resting primarily on the trend in William Shaw's estimates of construction materials, was derived as follows. For 1920 to 1938 we take the estimates of the Department of Commerce, in current dollars, excluding public utility construction because variations in that component have little impact on variations in contract construction employment.[8] We deflate these estimates by a combined materials price and wage-rate index.

The materials price index is a geometrically weighted average of the BLS buildings-materials price index (which is a variable weighted index) and a fixed weighted index—the latter computed from the BLS data using 1919–1921 weights for the 1919–1929 period, and 1929–1931 weights for the later years.[9]

[7] For the materials price index, we use Shaw's estimate (*op. cit.,* pp. 294–295). For wages we use the trend in average annual earnings estimated elsewhere in this study. The two were weighted together by materials and labor outlays of construction firms reporting in the 1900 Census. Payrolls prove to be 37.6 percent of payrolls plus materials—as compared with the 1930 Census figure of 41.6 percent. 1930 Census, *Construction Industry,* p. 20.

[8] Activity data from BLS Bulletin 1146, *Construction during 5 Decades* (1953), table 7.

[9] Price series from BLS, *Weighted Index Numbers of Wholesale Price by Groups and Subgroups of Commodities* (n.d.). Quantity weights from BLS *Quantity Weighting Factors Used in Calculating Index Numbers, 1890–1934* (1935). Since the 1929 estimate was virtually the same in either fixed-weight series, the two were merely spliced in that year.

For wage rates we use the trend in union-wage rates, in part because there is no alternative, in part because average earnings in building construction do parallel the trend in union-wage rates over the period 1934–1941, however much the level differs.[10] We do not use the existing series for union-wage rates, which combines individual craft rates with union membership figures for weights, but derive weights from the number of gainfully occupied persons as indicated by the Population Census data.[11]

This series for wage rates was taken as a crude measure of labor cost trends, comparison of employment and deflated activity figures previously computed for 1929 to 1940 having shown no tangible productivity increase after an hours adjustment had been made.

We combine the wage-rate and materials index by a series of changing ratios. These ratios were based on the ratio of materials to labor costs in each of the four major types of construction, each ratio being weighted in each year by the volume of activity in that type in that year.[12]

Applying the deflator thus derived to the contract activity series gives us a series for deflated contract activity. Before using this series as an interpolator, we adjust it for changes in average weekly hours, for which we have some measure of data for the 1930s and for which we assume no change prior to 1929.[13] (The constancy assumption is acceptable be-

[10] A comparison can be made from data in BLS Bulletin 786, *The Construction Industry in the United States* (1944), p. 46.

[11] BLS Bulletin 815, *Union Wages and Hours in the Building Trades* (1945), pp. 5–7. The average of gainfully occupied in 1920 and 1930 was here used for the 1919 to 1929 rates, and of 1930 and 1940 for the 1929 to 1940 rates. The occupation data are those from the respective Population Censuses, except that for combining stonemason and stonecutter rates, as plasterers and cement finishers, we used the count of wage and salary workers from the 1940 Census, *The Labor Force*, vol. III, p. 77. The laborers series was combined with a series for the journeymen trades as thus computed, using the ratio of one group to the other as indicated in the 1930 Population Census data.

[12] The ratios were derived from the 1939 Construction Census materials. Comparison of ratios for the larger contractors with those implicit in the 1929 Census showed great similarity; plumbing, for example, was 32.9 in 1929 and 34.5 in 1939; painting and decorating, 71.2 and 70.8, etc. The resultant ratios were 38.7 for residential, 39.9 for nonresidential, 41.0 for highway, and 45.2 for heavy construction. For military and naval activity, a BLS tabulation for the war year 1943 (*Engineering News Record,* Apr. 20, 1944, p. 154) was used. Public utility construction was excluded in all years as being primarily force account.

[13] Data on union hours, while available, are too inflexible for this purpose. During 1935 to 1941 we have reported data on average weekly hours in building construction. (Private construction hours are from BLS Bulletin 786, p. 46; public construction hours from the BLS Division of Construction and Public Employment. The two were weighted by employment in each category.) A regression of this series against total deflated contract construction activity was used to extrapolate for 1932 to 1934. A 1929 figure was estimated in consultation with BLS construction specialists, taking into account the absolute level of private building hours in

cause we are using this series for interpolation—consistent with an implicit long-term decline in hours or any other linear trend.)

The resultant deflator has certain advantages in principle over deflators developed since the 1929 to 1939 estimates were first prepared in 1945, but in practice there are only a few significant differences.[14]

1900 to 1920.   Official estimates of construction activity reach back to 1915 but they seem unsatisfactory for the 1915–1918 period.[15] This judgment rests largely on the very odd relationship between materials inputs (Shaw's data) and construction activity in these years as compared with all other years.

We therefore estimate deflated construction activity for the entire 1900–1918 period by using Shaw's deflated construction materials series for interpolating between construction activity in 1899 and 1919.[16]

1900 to 1930.   The total number engaged in the industry was split between self-employed and employee, using data from the Censuses of

---

the late 1930s and the regression relationship with activity. For 1930–1931 we interpolated between 1929 and 1932.

[14] The recent Department of Commerce Composite Index (*Business Statistics,* 1959 edition) is a weighted average of various private indices. It follows Kuznets's procedure in his *Commodity Flow and Capital Formation,* p. 379, and *Value of Product since 1869,* p. 41, as does the implicit deflator used in deriving the National Income Division activity—estimates used in turn for computing employment figures for the 1930s. These series rely on the American Appraisal index for residential construction, which excludes the important mechanical items of plumbing, heating, and electrical work; and on the Aberthaw series for nonresidential construction, which prices one reinforced-concrete building erected in Connecticut in 1914. The BLS deflator (*Monthly Labor Review,* February, 1945) rests largely on ENR indices, these reflecting a rather simple weighting of skilled labor, steel, lumber, and cement (*Engineering News Record,* Apr. 20, 1944, p. 105). Leo Grebler et al., *Capital Formation in Residential Real Estate* (1956), p. 342, relies on the Boeckh index back to 1914.

[15] These estimates are reprinted in the BLS Bulletin 1146, table 7, and are presumably a reworking of the original estimates of Lowell Chawner, *Construction Activity in the United States, 1915–1937* (1938). Grebler, *op. cit.,* pp. 335, 338, reports figures significantly different for the pre-1921 period than those he reprints on p. 436 from the Department of Commerce estimates. Presumably these revisions by David Blank reflect dissatisfaction with the Commerce revisions of Chawner's figures for these years.

[16] The 1899 and 1919 figures were derived above. Shaw's figures are from *op. cit.,* p. 77. We adopt the Commerce figures for 1919–1920 despite Blank's revisions in residential construction because they are official and are not unreasonably out of line with the materials totals. Ratios of deflated activity to employment in 1899 and 1929 were derived previously, interpolated, and applied to this activity series to give the number of persons engaged in the contract construction industry. Public utility construction was excluded from the series initially used for all years 1919ff., while for earlier years the 16.8 percent ratio of such construction to total construction implicit in the Commerce 1915 figures was used.

Manufactures and Population. The Censuses of Manufactures and Construction indicate much the same proportion of self-employed to total persons in 1899 and in 1939.[17] We therefore apply the 1929 ratio in earlier years, on the assumption that the pattern for the entire industry was reasonably close to constancy.[18]

UTILITIES

For electric light and power employment, Census of Electric Light and Power reports are available quinquennially beginning in 1902.[1] For intercensal years prior to 1917, interpolations were made from the growth curve clearly portrayed by the data. For years subsequent to 1917, Kuznets's data on employment in private plants are available.[2]

For employment in manufactured gas, Census of Manufactures data are available from 1899; for intercensal years they were interpolated by a regression against the output series appearing in Gould's basic study.[3] (Gould does provide intercensal employment estimates for the 1919–1939 period, based on American Gas Association data. However, these were not used because there are major inconsistencies of movement between the census and the AGA series.)[4]

[17] 1899 *Census of Manufactures*, part I, pp. 51–52, ratio of proprietors to proprietors plus salaried and wage earners. 1939 *Construction Census*, p. 28. Comparison with the 1929 *Construction Census*, pp. 32, 88, can only be for the much less meaningful group of large contractors, the ratio for which changed slightly for 1929 to 1939.

[18] The 1929 ratio is derived from the BLS series for self-employed and for employees. It rests ultimately on the 1940 Census proportion of one to the other, the two series, however, being independently extrapolated back to 1929 utilizing Construction Census materials. The unpublished 1910 Census materials on class of worker imply 16.5 percent self-employed among specified crafts, as against the 27.2 percent used here. We rely on comparison of the 1899 and 1939 Construction Census to indicate no change, hence do not choose to show an upward trend from 1910 to 1929. We assume that the 1940 Census, comprehending all workers in construction, is more useful for estimating level than the 1910 Census, the latter including only certain crafts, and, for these crafts, including workers in other industries as well as those merely in construction.

[1] Summarized in Jacob M. Gould, *Output and Productivity in the Electric and Gas Utilities, 1899–1942* (1946), table 21.

[2] In Gould, *loc. cit.*

[3] Census employment data are summarized in Gould, *op. cit.*, table 36; the output data, in his table A13.

[4] See *Ibid.*, table 37, for Gould's employment estimates based on AGA. The census series declines 16 percent between 1919 and 1921 whereas the AGA series rises. Similarly the census series declines 13 percent between 1927 and 1929 whereas the AGA series falls a tenth of a point. Hence it has been assumed that the AGA series is not properly comparable for use in interpolating over this period.

It is to be noted that the present estimate differs from Gould's in the base year

For employment in natural gas, no accurate estimates are possible, but the growth trend is so marked that it was felt proper to give it some weight in total utilities employment, which was done, following Gould, by interpolating between the 1899 and 1929 estimates which he provides.[5]

For pipelines, ICC data are available beginning with 1921; they were extrapolated by the movement of oil- and gas-well employment, each series having gained at essentially the same rates over the 1920–1929 period.[6]

For telephone company employment, an American Telephone and Telegraph series was used.[7]

For telegraph employment, estimates of the Federal Communications Commission, based on reports to the ICC for 1926 to 1929, were used to extrapolate the BLS figures. The 1926 figure was extrapolated to 1917 by unpublished data supplied by the Western Union Company on employment in Western Union and Postal Telegraph (except cable), with extrapolation to earlier years on the basis of the telegraph employment reported in the Census of Electrical Industries.[8]

LAND TRANSPORT

For the industry which in this period employed the great majority of all transport workers, steam railways, we possess excellent estimates from the ICC. These data need only be shifted from a fiscal- to a calendar-year

---

1929 because the present series is based on census data for all years whereas Gould (table 42) is apparently at the census level prior to 1929 and at the higher AGA level afterward.

[5] Gould, *op. cit.* Comparison between his tables 42 and 37 indicates Gould's procedure. His 1899 figure appears on p. 125 and the 1929 AGA figure on p. 123.

[6] ICC data summarized in Harold Barger, *The Transportation Industries, 1889–1946* (1951), p. 251. For 1910 to 1920, the man-days in oil- and gas-well employment computed for the present estimates were used. The 1920 figure of 7,000 was carried as a constant prior to 1920.

[7] Indices based on the American Telephone and Telegraph series appear in Solomon Fabricant, *Labor Savings in American Industry, 1899–1939* (1945), p. 49. These were used to extrapolate the 1929 BLS total for the industry.

[8] Federal Communications Commission, *Statistics of the Communication Industry in the United States* (1948), p. 131; information secured directly from Western Union; Census of Electrical Industries data summarized in *Statistical Abstract*, 1949, p. 503. The Census of Electrical Industries totals for 1917 and 1927 are 10 percent below the comparable figures of the BLS; for 1922, they are 8 percent below. It was therefore assumed that the census figures for 1907 and 1912 were likewise 10 percent low. Interpolations between 1907, 1912, and 1917 and extrapolations for 1907 to 1900 were made from the growth curve fitted to the estimates for census dates.

basis to make them suitable for present purposes.[1] (This adjustment has the incidental advantage of making the data more suitable for cycle analysis: 1907 is now below 1906 instead of above it as in the fiscal-year data, and the 1913–1914 drop is now considerably more severe than the 1914–1915 decline.)

For pullman, express, and switching company employment there are ICC data for the 1920s. For earlier years it is fortunate that total employment in this group amounted to less than 10 percent of steam-railway employment, since contradictory trends shown in available data forced the arbitrary procedure of carrying the 1920 estimate back with a slight decline to 1910 and as a constant from then to 1900.[2]

For electric railways the BLS 1929 estimate was extrapolated to 1890, 1902, 1907, 1912, and 1917 by employment data from the Census of Street Railways, with a minor adjustment.[3] We interpolate for 1900 to 1916 by Douglas's series for a sample of those states whose employment dominated the group, while the 1917 figure was extrapolated to 1929 by Barger's series.[4]

For highway transport the procedure followed by NICB was to extrapolate a 1929 total by the movement of motor-truck registrations. This procedure produces a sharp steady gain in employment—a large share of which, however, truly arises from increased use of trucks by farmers, construction firms, and retail businesses rather than by over-the-road truckers. The procedure followed by Kuznets was to establish Census of Population benchmarks, then interpolate by employment in all other industries. However, these benchmarks—for the total number of chauffeurs, draymen, and a few other occupations—are similarly affected by the fact that many truck drivers are not employed in trucking. (In 1930 only about a third of all chauffeurs and draymen were employed in truck, transfer, and cab companies.)

If, therefore, we restrict our estimates to the persons in these occupa-

---

[1] The ICC data are summarized in *Historical Statistics,* p. 206. For years prior to 1916, the data relate to years ending in June; these were interpolated to provide annual figures approximately comparable with later data. The ICC data are also summarized in Harold Barger, *The Transportation Industries, 1889–1946* (1951).

[2] Alba Edwards, *Comparative Occupation Statistics in the United States, 1870 to 1940* (1943), p. 109, shows yardmen declining from 9,600 in 1910 to 7,100 by 1920, while switchmen rose from 73,400 to 101,900. Barger provides additional data on pullman employment.

[3] Interstate Commerce Commission, *Electric Railway Statistics, 1890–1934* (1935), p. 15. We adjust the census figures for 1912 and 1917 to annual figures.

[4] Paul Douglas, *Real Wages in the United States, 1890–1926* (Boston: Houghton Mifflin, 1930), p. 440; Barger, *op. cit.,* p. 216. The contradictions between establishment and Population Census materials are emphasized by the fact that the number of conductors plus motormen was 61,400 according to the 1900 Population Census and 80,000 according to the 1902 Electrical Industries Census.

tions who are engaged in the motor-trucking industry, it appears that only a slight increase occurred in the numbers from 1910 to 1930.[5] More to the point, the number of employees in road transport appears to have changed not at all between these two dates.[6] This remarkable stability in census results was produced by a decline of livery-stable employment from 106,000 to 8,000 at the same time that truck, transfer, and cab employment rose from 355,000 to 453,000—one gain neutralizing the other loss. Unlikely as it first seems, therefore, the soundest procedure is to carry this group as a constant over the period, thus assuming that the trend growth of one and the decline of the other were the major factors behind employment changes in this industry, and that one essentially counteracted the other in its impact on employment totals.

WATERWAYS

Employment in waterways was estimated in two segments. For employment on vessels other than fishing, census results for 1906, 1916, and 1926 are available.[1] (Because of presumed inadequacies in the original census for 1889, a comparable employment figure for that year was estimated from the clear relationship in later census years between vessel employment except fishing and employment on steam and motor vessels.)[2] For employment on land associated with vessel employment, estimates are available from the Transportation Censuses for 1906 and 1916 and can be extrapolated for other census years from Population Census returns for longshoremen and stevedores, totals for the latter group having a surprisingly similar trend in both sources.[3] For intercensal years, employment was estimated from changes in the tonnage of United States documented

[5] Industry information is not available for 1900 and 1920. The 1910 total of 317,000 relate to chauffeurs and draymen in truck, transfer, and cab companies, to carriage and hack drivers in livery stables. The 1930 total of 370,000 relates merely to the former occupations.

[6] The decennial census number of employees of livery stables plus truck, transfer, and cab companies (exclusive of owners and proprietors) was 461,000 in both 1910 and 1930.

[1] U.S. Bureau of the Census, *Transportation by Water, 1916* (1920), p. 20. U.S. Bureau of the Census, *Water Transportation, 1926* (1929), p. 8.

[2] The 1889 results do not look particularly dubious for employment, despite rude denigration in later census volumes (1906 Census, pp. 3–4). Data for the relationship used were taken from the sources specified above.

[3] *Transportation by Water, 1916,* p. 59. By interpolating between Population Census figures for longshoremen and stevedores (Edwards, *op. cit.,* p. 109, and 1900 Census, *Occupations* p. 8), we secure an estimate of 50,000 for 1906 (compared to the Transportation Census figure of 47,400 for all offshore employees) and similarly 80,000 (compared to 83,600 in the Transportation Census).

steam and motor vessels—data which yield figures for census years virtually the same as those reported by census.[4]

Employees of fishing vessels are reported by the Transportation Censuses for 1916 and 1926 and can be estimated from Population Census data for other years.[5] The figures appear to be almost directly comparable, given reported variations in the fishing catch:

1890	22.2
1916	26.1
1920	19.6
1926	27.7
1930	27.2

Intercensal years were estimated by interpolation.[6]

BANKING

For banking employment the starting point is the Comptroller of Currency series for the number of banks.[1] If it is possible to estimate employment per bank, a simple combination of the two series would give employment estimates. National banks constituted about a third of all banks throughout the period, and it appears that the trend of employment per bank in these banks is sufficiently indicative of the trend in employment per bank for all banks.[2] Data from the Comptroller of the Currency at various dates—1910, 1916, 1918, 1936, and 1940—enable us to extrap-

[4] Tonnage data from *Historical Statistics,* p. 207. Both Simon Kuznets, in *National Income and Its Composition, 1919–1938* (1941), p. 711, and Harold Barger, *The Transportation Industries, 1889–1946* (1951), p. 263 use tonnage cleared for their estimates. However, comparisons for the 1930s and 1940s, where we possess independent estimates of employment, suggest that documented tonnage of steam and motor vessels is preferable to tonnage cleared or number of vessels—the latter used by NICB. (Barger uses a gross tonnage figure per employee for estimating 1920.) By excluding foreign tonnage, we achieve more comparable results.

[5] Transportation Census data in *Water Transportation, 1926,* p. 8. Population Census data for 1910 (lithoprinted tables, 1948) and for 1940 (sixteenth Census, *Occupational Characteristics,* table 6) give ratios of wage earners to total occupied— 37.2 and 36.5 percent, respectively. Interpolating and applying to total occupied figures given by Edwards (*op. cit.,* p. 104) gives wage-earner estimates.

[6] Data on fishing catch do not appear to be of such quality that using them to interpolate would improve the employment estimates. *Historical Statistics,* p. 128; A. F. Burns, *Production Trends in the United States since 1870* (1934), pp. 288, 348, 352.

[1] *Historical Statistics,* p. 262. This series counts each branch bank as a bank. For use in combination with employment per bank, this series is preferable to alternative Federal Reserve bank estimates.

[2] For the only prewar period over which comparisons can be directly made—1936 to 1940—the gain in employees per bank was 10 percent for national banks and 11 percent for all banks.

olate the employment per bank in all banks after some adjustment.[3] The resultant time series showed a very clear linear trend and was interpolated on this basis. The final series, when multiplied by the number of banks, gives employment in banks.

These estimates differ substantially from those of King and Kuznets. The King benchmark figure for 1918—and hence figures for other years— is substantially lower because he fails to adjust for an obvious error in the Comptroller's employment figure for that year.[4] Kuznets's level is nearly twice that of King. His 1920 to 1930 change is 15 percent, as compared to 48 percent in the present estimates and 61 percent implied in the Population Census data for banking and brokerage.[5] While consiliency with the Population Census data is not necessarily a requirement, the limitations of the procedure used by Kuznets (and Carson) derive from their assumption that the trend in full-time equivalent earnings in the 12 Federal Reserve banks parallels that in all banks.[6] This procedure is tied to no employment benchmark prior to 1934 and any change in the 1934 ratio of average salary in the 12 banks to that in all 16,000 banks will distort the employment series.[7] (Employment in these banks is heavily concentrated

[3] For 1910 employees per national bank were estimated from the trend in deposit accounts per national bank, as shown in the relationship of 1916, 1918, and 1936. Account data are from the *Reports* of the Comptroller of Currency: 1917, vol. I, p. 14; 1918, vol. I, p. 161; and from the *Annual Report* of the Federal Deposit Insurance Corporation, 1934, p. 187.

Employment in national banks is taken from the *Reports* of the Comptroller of the Currency: 1916, vol. I, p. 157; 1918, vol. I, pp. 16, 81, 106; 1936, pp. 5, 618; 1940, pp. 147, 149. The reported data for 1918 indicate a gain over 1916 of 20,000 employees although the number of banks and deposit accounts increased only slightly. After consultation with the Comptroller's Office, it was decided that the 1918 report included under the heading of employees the reported "employees in military service," which group was therefore deducted from the total. For 1900 the 1910 employees per bank figure was reduced less than extrapolation of the 1910 to 1940 trend in national bank employment per bank would indicate, in order to allow for the declining proportion of national to total banks in this decade.

[4] See note 3 above. W. I. King, *National Income and Its Purchasing Power* (1930).

[5] Census data for 1910 (vol. V, p. 418) indicate that bankers, brokers, and lenders constituted 50 percent of gainful workers in banking and brokerage. Census data for 1930 indicate a ratio of 36 percent (vol. V, p. 360). Interpolating for the 1920 ratio and applying to the number of bankers, brokers, and lenders (Edwards, *op. cit.,* p. 69) indicates a 1920–1930 gain for the industry of 61 percent.

[6] Kuznets, *op. cit.,* p. 755; Daniel Carson and Henrietta Liebman, *Labor Supply and Employment* (Works Progress Administration, 1939), pp. 213ff.

[7] Because Kuznets's procedure is tied eventually to estimates of loans and deposits, it is particularly sensitive to any changes in that total. Kuznets's employment in commercial banks showed a 1919–1920 gain twice as great as that in any of his subsequent years—including 1928–1929. This gain of 35,000 (while the number of banks increased by only 1,000) derives basically from the great gain in loans and deposits between 1919 and 1920.

in New York, Chicago, and Cleveland. Thus there was no 1929 to 1933 decline in average salaries for this group, but there was almost certainly a decline in the industry as a whole.)

OTHER FINANCE

Employees

For employees, the 1929 total of the National Income Division was extrapolated by the sum of two series—one for employees of building and loan associations and one for employees of brokers.

1. For building and loan association employment, estimates of the number of associations were multiplied by a series for the number of employees per association, the latter being available for 1935 and extrapolated by the trend in employees per bank.[1]

2. For brokers, a series for self-employed brokers (see below) was multiplied by a series for employees per broker. The number of employees per broker in 1910 would be estimated at 3.2 by deducting the employment in banks from the total shown by the Population Census for banking and brokerage that year. However, we use the figure of 3.9 (as for employees per bank) because the former is a residual estimate. For 1930 the number of employees per self-employed broker is assumed to be the same as that indicated by the 1935 Census.[2] Hence the present estimates indicate that between 1910 and 1930 employment per bank rose from 3.9 to 15.6 while employment per self-employed person in other finance rose from 3.9 to 11.9. The intercensal ratios were interpolated.

Self-employed

For self-employed persons in banking and brokerage, the sum of two series was used to extrapolate the 1930 total.[3] For stockbrokers, the census totals for 1920 and 1930 were interpolated by the number of stock-

[1] The number of associations appears in *Statistical Abstract,* 1924, p. 261, and in *Historical Statistics,* p. 175. The number of employees per association indicated by the 1935 Census was assumed to apply to 1930. Employees per bank doubled every decade. Employees per association, being less subject to this growth trend, were assumed to have doubled over the 1900–1930 period.

[2] 1935 Census of Business, *Financial Institutions Other than Banks.* The ratio is that for total number of employees per active proprietor and firm member for all institutions except building and loan associations. Employees per bank rose about 10 percent over this quinquennium. It was assumed that no growth occurred for brokerage houses, etc.

[3] The 1930 total was estimated as 40 percent of the 1930 Population Census total for commercial, loan, stock, and other brokers. The percentage is based on the 1910 and 1940 data for similar groups.

brokers as indicated by annual issues of *Security Dealers of North America*.[4] For 1910 to 1920 the census totals were interpolated. The assumption of steady growth for 1910 to 1920 is suggested, although not confirmed, by the number of stockbrokers paying occupational taxes to the Bureau of Internal Revenue in 1900, 1902, and 1915.[5] For the 1900–1910 period, the growth in banking employment could alone account for the entire growth shown by the census category of banking and brokerage.[6] Hence no gain in brokerage can be posited, and the 1910 brokerage figure was carried as a constant, 1900–1910.

For brokers except stockbrokers, similar procedures were used to estimate the 1900 to 1920 figures. Data for 1921 to 1929 were interpolated by applying to the annual estimates of stockbrokers trend estimates for the ratio of stockbrokers to other brokers. (Other brokers constituted 258 percent of stockbrokers in 1910, 167 percent in 1920, and 80 percent in 1930—or a drop of about 90 points in each decade.)

INSURANCE

Gainful workers in insurance equaled 170 percent of insurance agents in 1910, 197 percent in 1930, and 220 percent in 1940.[1] Extrapolating for 1900 and 1920 gave census date totals which were used to extrapolate the 1930 employee total of the National Income Division. Intercensal interpolation was by means of the number of life insurance policies.[2]

---

[4] Counts of offices for several years were kindly supplied by Herbert D. Seibert and Co., publishers of *Security Dealers of North America*. For intervening years the number of pages in the annual issues of that directory were used for interpolation. To extrapolate their 1922 count of number of offices to 1920, the 1916, 1920, and 1925 issues of *Investment Bankers and Brokers of America* were used.

[5] Data for BIR are from issues of the *Annual Report* of the Commissioner for these years. The figures show so little 1900 to 1915 growth that they cannot be considered a very reliable guide.

[6] The total number of "bankers and brokers" plus "bank officials and cashiers" rose from roughly 88,000 to 105,000 between 1900 and 1910. Since the number of banks rose by 13,000 over this decade, a very substantial share of the 17,000 gain would be accounted for merely by banking employment. In later decades the rise in bankers and officials was 17,000 and 19,000 greater than the rise in the number of banks; hence to assume a rise in their number equal to the number of banks is to make a minimum likely estimate.

[1] Data on agents for 1910 to 1940 from Edwards, *op. cit.*, pp. 69, 51. Data on employment from 1910 Census, vol. V, p. 420; 1930, vol. V, p. 564; 1940, *The Labor Force*, vol. III, pp. 76, 180. The number of agents in 1900 was estimated at 36 percent of the reported census total of real estate and insurance agents in 1900—the percentages in 1910, 1920, and 1930 being 41, 45, and 52.

[2] *Life Insurance Fact Book*, 1951, p. 12.

The number of self-employed persons in insurance was estimated as a percentage of wage earners, using census data for 1910 and 1940.[3]

REAL ESTATE

Estimates of gainful workers in real estate at the decennial census dates were made by utilizing the census data on real estate agents. In 1910 agents and officials were 82 percent of gainful workers in the industry; in 1930, they were 83 percent.[1] Assuming that these percentages applied to the immediately preceding censuses, we can estimate the number of gainful workers in each Census. These totals were adjusted to the 1929 total for the industry as shown by the National Income Division. For intercensal interpolation, use was made of the close relationship between the number of gainful workers at census dates and the number of available nonfarm housing units—agents being primarily concerned with marketing and renting such units.[2]

Self-employed persons in real estate were estimated by applying to the total for gainful workers the percentage of self-employed persons in each year, these percentages being secured by interpolating and extrapolating the 1910 percent of 20.5 and the 1940 figure of 15.[3]

TRADE

Employees in Trade

Estimates of employment in trade, as those for tertiary industry generally, are of a different quality than those for manufacturing and steam railroads, for example. This difficulty arises chiefly because there are no reliable data from establishment sources for the period prior to 1929.[1]

---

[3] Self-employed agents constituted 9.1 percent of wage and salary workers in insurance in the 1940 Population Census data, 4.1 percent in 1910. (Census of Business data for 1935 give a ratio of 12.5 percent). Interpolating and extrapolating these percentages and applying to the employees series give total self-employed.

[1] 1910 Census, vol. IV, p. 240; 1930 Census, vol. V, p. 564.

[2] Gainful workers per 1,000 units rose from 98 in 1900 to 118 in 1910, declined to 108 in 1920 and rose again to 127 in 1930 (*Historical Statistics,* p. 173). It was assumed that the 1910 rate maintained through 1916, and then fell to the 1920 figure under the influence of alternative employments and war prosperity.

[3] It was assumed that the 1940 percentage applied equally in 1930, thus allowing somewhat for the impact of the depression in slowing the relative decline in self-employment.

[1] The first national Census of Business covered the year 1929. A trial census made in 11 cities in 1926 by the Chamber of Commerce is here rejected for two reasons. First, any pioneering effort in such an area is likely to produce results which are not

However, we can estimate employment in trade for census dates reasonably well from the Censuses of Population. The 1930 BLS total for employees in trade was therefore extrapolated to 1900, 1910, and 1920 by the sum of estimates for five other groups: (1) Gainful workers in specified trade occupations, such as salesmen and saleswomen, clerks in stores, etc.;[2] (2) employees included under the census "retail dealers" occupation category;[3] (3) cooks and bartenders in trade, estimated by a somewhat complex procedure;[4] (4) estimated "laborers not otherwise specified," who were actually in trade;[5] (5) less the number unemployed in trade.[6]

Given the decennial benchmarks, our next task is to interpolate between them. The NICB interpolated by total employment in agriculture, mining, and manufacturing. This procedure, however, produces too volatile a series: Reference to the 1929 to 1940 data indicates quite clearly that employment in trade is distinctly more stable than in agriculture, mining, and manufacturing. Kuznets uses employment in three states which provide

---

comparable with later censuses. Moreover, the inadequacies of the 1929 and 1939 Census of Business suggest, a fortiori, that the 1926 effort must have been still more dubious. Secondly, the accuracy with which trends in employment in 11 cities can indicate trends in the nation is open to doubt.

[2] We include total decennial census employment in trade as shown by Edwards except dealers and except Edwards's summary group, "all other occupations." (Edwards, *op. cit.*, p. 110.) By far the largest share of this latter group were not engaged in trade.

[3] The number of self-employed dealers—estimated below in the section on Trade: Self-employed—was deducted from Edwards's figures for total dealers, exporters, and importers.

[4] For (1) the number of cooks not in homes, see the estimation procedure for Domestic Service (p. 476). The proportion of this subgroup in trade was taken from unpublished data for 1910 which were used for Gladys Palmer and Ann Ratner, *Industrial and Occupational Trends in National Employment* (1949), and were kindly supplied by Gladys Palmer. For 1900 it was assumed that the 1910 proportion of (cooks) to (bartenders plus waiters) applied. For (2) bartenders and waiters, the 1910 proportion in trade as shown by the Palmer data was applied to 1900 and 1920. Census data are available for 1930.

[5] This adjustment is required only for 1900. Laborers in trade for 1900 were estimated as a proportion to dealers by extrapolating the 1910 to 1930 trend in the ratio of laborers to dealers. The result is strikingly different from Edwards's total. Because Edwards estimates this group by an indirect, residual method, he has no control over this ratio. As a result he implicitly estimates that there were 40 laborers per 100 dealers in trade in 1900, despite the fact that every subsequent census reports between 15 and 18 per 100.

[6] The proportion of trade workers unemployed can be calculated for 1930 and for 1910 from census data. The ratios between (1) these unemployment percentages and (2) the total percent of gainful workers except farmers that were unemployed, were calculated for the same years, extrapolated, and applied to the percent of gainful workers (except farmers) that were unemployed in 1900.

data for varying portions of the period. However, changes of employment in these states do not parallel those for the country over a period for which we do possess data—1929 to 1940. (For example, employment in these three states showed no change from 1929 to 1933, but the national total fell by 21 percent.)[7] Moreover, data for only one state, Ohio, are available for the full period.

Preference has therefore been given to an alternative procedure. Our estimates for employees in trade at census dates were interpolated by a series for estimated labor requirements in trade. This series was secured as follows.

Estimates of the number of retail dealers in the major lines of trade—food, drug, furniture, hardware, etc.—were compiled from decennial census data.[8] Preliminary estimates of employees in each line of trade for census dates were then secured by multiplying these estimates of dealers by ratios of employees per dealer in each industry line.[9] The number of employees was interpolated between these census dates by the relevant Shaw series on the value of finished commodities destined for domestic consumption, in constant dollars.[10] Thus the series for food and kindred products was used to interpolate employment in grocery, provision, produce, related stores, etc.[11]

The sum of the preliminary series thus computed was used to interpo-

---

[7] The Wisconsin and Pennsylvania data actually show increases from 1929 to 1933. The Wisconsin data were taken from successive issues of *The Wisconsin Labor Market*. Ohio data are from Bulletin 29 of the Division of Labor Statistics, *Rates of Wages, Fluctuation of Employment . . . 1930 to 1937*. The Pennsylvania data are from *Annual Report on Employment and Payrolls in Pennsylvania* (Pennsylvania: Department of Labor and Industry, 1938). The three indices were weighted by employment as reported in the 1939 Census. (Data from the 1933 and 1935 Censuses were too incomplete to be used for this purpose.)

[8] 1910 Census, *Occupations,* pp. 420, 422 and Edwards, *op. cit.,* p. 69. For 1900 the 1910 industry distribution of dealers was applied to the 1900 total.

[9] The ratios were computed from the *1948 Census of Business,* vol. I, *Retail Trade,* using data for full work week paid employees and active proprietors of unincorporated businesses in 1948. Test use was made of ratios for other census dates but little difference resulted in the intercensal movement. Since this movement is the only subject of concern here, it was felt desirable to use the results of the best Census of Distribution prior to the date at which this estimate was made.

[10] William H. Shaw, *Value of Commodity Output since 1869* (1947), pp. 70ff.

[11] Data for drug, toilet, and household preparations were used for drugstores; magazines, etc., for book and stationery stores; nonmanufactured fuel for coal, wood, and ice; semidurables except tires and tubes for drygoods, etc., and for trade not separately computed; furniture for furniture stores; heating and cooking apparatus and household appliances (including electrical) for hardware; lumber for lumber and building materials stores. For restaurants census totals were interpolated linearly. Employment in saloons was interpolated by the number of saloon keepers estimated above.

late between the census date employee totals previously estimated.[12] It will be seen that this procedure is closely related to that used by Kuznets and Carson, who relied on changes in commodity-flow totals. The present procedure, however, differs in that it adjusts those data to allow for the differing increases that a billion-dollar rise in the commodity-flow totals will produce in trade employment depending on whether that increase is in food, apparel, drug products, etc.

Shaw's commodity output data were used in preference to deflated commodity purchases because the deflated estimates for earlier years are little more than the addition of arbitrary and, more important, constant margins to Shaw's data. Moreover, their use to estimate employment in the 1920–1930 period results in changes contrary to what other measures indicate.[13]

Trade: Self-employed

For census dates the number of self-employed persons in trade was estimated as follows:

1. The number of retail dealers is reported by census.[14]

2. The number of wholesale dealers is reported by census except for 1900, for which an estimate was made.[15]

---

[12] The ratio of the preliminary employee series to that shown by the census was the same in 1900 as in 1910 and was therefore assumed the same for the intercensal years. For 1911 to 1916 it was assumed the same as 1910, with 1917 to 1919 interpolated between the 1916 and 1920 ratio. This procedure allows for the impact of World War I on trade employment. The year 1916 was selected as a turning point because output declined in 1918 and the number of proprietors declined in 1917. During 1929 to 1940, the number of proprietors declined approximately one-half year after the number of employees changed.

[13] For the years prior to 1919, Kuznets's data are only available on a decade basis. These represent Shaw's data plus constant markup percentages for perishables, semidurables, and durables. Simon Kuznets, *National Product since 1869* (1946). The combination of these percentages yields margins 34.7 percent of retail price in 1894 to 1903, 35.0 percent in 1904 to 1913, and 35.2 percent for 1914 to 1923. Equally moderate changes are indicated by Barger's figures for 1899, 1919, and 1929: 39.8, 39.6 and 41.7 percent. Harold Barger, *Distribution's Place in the American Economy since 1869* (1955), p. 57.

Kuznets's data could, of course, be used for the 1920s alone. However, their use leads to estimated employment gains from 1920 to 1921, from 1923 to 1924, and from 1926 to 1927. Such gains are contrary to King's survey results for 1920 to 1922, and contrary to experiences in later recessions. Since the margins even for the 1920s are difficult estimates, it was not felt that they had to be used in the face of such anfractuosities.

[14] Edwards, *op. cit.,* table 8.

[15] *Ibid.* For 1900 an estimate was made by extrapolating the 1910 to 1930 trend in ratios of wholesale dealers to the combined group of wholesale dealers and proprietors of grain elevators.

3. The number of employees included in the dealer group was estimated and deducted from the sum of (1) and (2).[16]

4. The number of restaurant keepers, bakers, milliners, and other self-employed persons in trade but not defined as retail dealers by census was estimated from census data and from unpublished material kindly provided by Gladys Palmer.[17]

5. The number of saloon keepers, available from the Census for 1900, 1910, and 1920, was assumed as zero in 1930.[18]

Intercensal estimates for self-employed in trade were computed to be consistent with those for employees in trade. Ratios of self-employed to employees were derived from the Population Census data, interpolated for the intercensal years.[19] These ratios, applied to the present series for employees, gave the number of self-employed at each date.

The estimates thus computed relate to self-employed persons except saloon keepers. For the latter category the census figures were interpolated on the basis of the number of actual special taxpayers holding Federal retail liquor licenses—a series consistent with the census data.[20]

The sum of self-employed persons except saloon keepers plus saloon keepers was used to extrapolate the basic 1930 total and thus compute the final series for self-employed in trade.

SERVICE

The number of self-employed persons in service was computed as the sum of those in (1) professional and (2) other service.

[16] The number of wage earners in the retail dealer group for 1910 is given in the 1948 lithoprinted census release; for 1940 the proportion of wage earners in the category of proprietors, managers, and officials in trade is given in *Occupational Characteristics*, table 6. The 1940 proportion was extrapolated to 1930 so as to yield figures consistent with earlier estimates of self-employment in trade for 1930 to 1940. Estimates for 1900 and 1920 were linearly extrapolated and interpolated.

[17] For restaurant keepers and commercial brokers, Edwards's tables 4 and 8 were used. For tailors, bakers, and milliners the proportion in trade was generally taken as that used for 1910 in Palmer and Ratner, *op. cit.*

[18] 1900 Census, *Occupations,* table 1; 1910 Census, vol. V, p. 302; 1920 Census, vol. V, p. 394.

[19] Population Census data as above. These were checked against Business Census data as adjusted for use in preparing the 1930 to 1940 estimates and 1948 Census of Business, *Retail Trade, U.S. Summary,* table 1.

[20] Data are from the Annual Reports of the Commissioner of Internal Revenue, and relate to the number holding licenses for retail spirits. The number of licensees in 1900 and 1910 is extremely close to the total number of liquor and wine dealers, hotel keepers, plus restaurant and saloon keepers as reported by census. Reported for 1900, 1910, and 1930 by the census, we assumed their number in 1920 as zero.

For professional service estimates were secured as the sum of series for physicians, dentists, lawyers, trained nurses, midwives, and untrained nurses. The derivation of these series is described below.

For other service the estimates used were the sum of separate series for self-employed barbers, shoemakers, blacksmiths, dressmakers, tailors, and millinery dealers, jewelers, musicians, hotel and lodging-place keepers, theatre owners, billiard-parlor and bowling-alley owners, laundry cleaning and dyeing establishment owners. The derivation of these series is described below.

Because the BLS 1929 to 1940 estimates of the self-employed in this group were computed without using a 1930 Census population benchmark, independent benchmark estimates for 1930 were derived, from a variety of sources as noted below. The resultant estimate for 1930 was within 10 percent of the total service figure previously derived. Since this is well within the margin of error which would result from combining benchmark data from a variety of sources, the BLS total for 1930 was taken as given and the series computed herewith were used simply to extrapolate that total.

The number of employees in professional and in other service was estimated by similar procedures, the derivation of which is described below.

PHYSICIANS

For census dates the number of physicians and surgeons as reported by the census was used.[1] *AMA Directory* totals were used to interpolate for selected intercensal years after adjustment for incomparability in these totals.[2] The census-level totals were then split between self-employed and salaried physicians on the basis of census data for 1910 and 1940, an estimate by Maurice Leven for 1930, and an OBE survey for 1949.[3] The

[1] Edwards, *op. cit.*, table 8. It was assumed that the number of osteopaths to be deducted from the 1900 and 1910 totals was 4,000—compared to a 5,000 total in 1920. For 1900 an estimated 4,000 faith healers were also deducted.

[2] The AMA uses *Polk's Medical Register* to 1906, the *AMA Directory* from then on (*Historical Statistics*, pp. 42, 50). The AMA reports a decline in the number of physicians from 1906 to 1909, despite the fact that 15,000 persons graduated from medical schools during the period. This decline presumably reflects incomparabilities between these sources. Lewis Mayers and Leonard V. Harrison, *The Distribution of Physicians in the United States* (1924), p. 160, contrasts the Directory total for 1906 of 122,028 with the Polk Register figure of 134,688, noting that "the increase shown in earlier editions of the directory are . . . in part due to the listing of names previously omitted." The 1909 figure was assumed to be the same as that for 1906. By interpolating ratios of Directory to census totals, census-comparable totals were estimated for Directory years, with the remaining years interpolated.

[3] The percentage self-employed in 1910 was 91; for 1940 it was 74. For 1929 it

1910 to 1940 trend in the ratio of hospital beds to salaried physicians was used to interpolate for the 1920 percentage since a substantial proportion of salaried physicians are employed in hospitals.[4] Intercensal percentages were then interpolated to compute the number of self-employed and salaried physicians.

The gainful worker self-employed estimates were then reduced to exclude physicians not in the labor force.[5]

The AMA series for number of physicians was not used for several reasons.

1. It seeks to measure the number of physicians rather than the number of active physicians in the labor force.

2. Despite the aftermath of the Flexner report and the decline in medical-school graduates, it shows a marked 1910 to 1920 gain. This presumably reflects the increasing membership in, and importance of, the AMA rather than the changed number of physicians.[6]

3. It shows an obvious break in comparability between the 1900 to 1906 estimates, based on *Polk's Register,* and the post-1909 estimates, based on the *AMA Directory.*

DENTISTS

Census date totals for dentists are given by the Population Census.[1] The proportion of self-employed, 90 percent in 1910 and 95 percent in

---

was estimated at 78 by Maurice Leven, *The Incomes of Physicians* (1932). For 1949 the percent (based on major source of medical income) was 78 (*Survey of Current Business,* July, 1951).

[4] There were approximately 30 hospital beds per salaried physician in 1910 and 1940; 25 in 1930. It was assumed that the 1920 figure was 27, which, in turn, makes the 1920 percentage self-employed 81. With 1910 at 91 percent, the 1900 percent was assumed at 95.

[5] The number of physicians over 65 was 11,000 in 1900 and 1920, and 13,000 in 1930. The number of retired physicians was estimated by the AMA at 9,000 in 1928 (Allen Peebles, *A Survey of Statistical Data on Medical Facilities in the United States* (1929), p. 55) and 9,700 in 1950 (*1950 AMA Directory,* pp. 9, 11). For 1940 the AMA total (including nonpracticing physicians) was 10,000 greater than the census labor-force total. On the basis of these figures, a flat 10,000 was deducted each year for physicians not in the labor force.

[6] The adjusted census figures indicate a slight drop in number of physicians between 1910 and 1920; AMA, a gain of 10,000. On the face of it, the census absolute decline in the face of 52,000 graduates during the previous decade is unreasonable. However, analysis by age level indicates the trend to be reasonable. Thus the number aged under 45 in 1910 minus osteopaths, less those aged 35–44, allowing for deaths, plus the number of graduates, less deaths among graduates, gives an estimated 76,000 physicians under age 45 in 1920. The reported census figure is 72,000.

[1] Edwards, *op. cit.,* table 8.

1940, was assumed as 90 percent throughout the period.[2] Intercensal estimates of the self-employed were made by adding to the census totals the number of graduates each year less the number of deaths in the profession. Comprehensive data on graduation are available for each year and death rates were assumed to be the same as those tabulated for physicians.[3]

LAWYERS

The number of lawyers at census dates is available from the census.[1] In 1910 the number of self-employed lawyers constituted 82 percent of the total.[2] In 1930 we can estimate the ratio at 78 percent, by assuming that the self-employed lawyers constituted the same proportion of lawyers in the professional service industry as in 1940.[3] The proportion for 1940 was 73 percent and for 1951—from a different source—86 percent.[4] Applying the 1910 percentage to earlier years and interpolating between the other percentages gives the estimated number of self-employed in each census year. The number in intercensal years was estimated by interpolation after consideration of the movement in the number of listings shown in Martindale's *American Law Directory.*[5]

[2] 1910 data from lithoprint; 1940 from *Occupational Characteristics,* table 6.

[3] Graduation data from *Historical Statistics,* p. 50. The number of physicians' deaths were estimated from a name count of AMA Directory lists by Mayers and Harrison, *op. cit.,* p. 160. The ratio of these deaths to the number of physicians as estimated above gave the death rates used. In actual fact the changes in graduations were small enough so that the use of the death rates made little difference in the trend of the final results.

[1] Edwards, *op. cit.,* table 8.

[2] Census lithoprinted tables.

[3] In 1940 (*Occupational Characteristics,* tables 6 and 19), self-employed lawyers equaled 90.2 percent of lawyers in professional service. Applying this proportion to the 1930 total for lawyers in professional service gives 126,000, or 78 percent of the total. The National Income Division estimate (1951 *National Income Supplement*) derives from an assumption (*National Income in the US 1929–35,* p. 292) that the Population Census would have allocated all wage-earning lawyers in the professional service industry to that industry. This is probably incorrect, giving as it does a ratio of 108 self-employed lawyers to 161 total, or 67 percent—well below that recorded for other dates.

[4] 1940 data from *Occupational Characteristics;* Martindale-Hubbell, *Survey of the Legal Profession,* 1952 ed., p. 2.

[5] The number of pages in the directory provides some reasonable indication of trend between census dates if allowances are made for changes in procedure, i.e., size of type, etc. Since census totals changed by less than 5 percent over the 1900–1910 and 1910–1920 decades, there is little problem of interpolation for these decades. For 1920–1930, the Martindale listings suggest that straight interpolation is satisfactory.

NURSES

Estimates were computed separately for trained and untrained nurses.

1. The Population Census volumes refer to a confusion by enumerators and coders between trained and untrained nurses. The census date benchmarks were therefore examined to see whether adjustment was required. The reported 1900 total for trained nurses was adjusted because the census shows the same 1900 to 1910 gain for this group as that between 1910 and 1920—despite a substantially greater number of graduations in the second decade. (Since trained nurses were separately distinguished from untrained nurses in the census for the first time in 1900, and 1900 was a generally excellent census, it is not unreasonable to assume that overly great caution should have been used in classifying nurses as trained.) The basis of adjustment was a computation of the ratio between the numbers of native white nurses and of trained nurses. The ratio—63, 64, and 69 percent in 1910, 1920 and 1930—was estimated at 63 percent in 1900, in place of the 17 percent implicit in the reported figures.[1,2]

The number of trained nurses at each census date that were self-employed was estimated as equal to the number of private-duty nurses. (The reported census figures on self-employment are quite low when a comparison is made between the nurses reported in the Census of Hospitals and the total shown in the Population Census.)[3] The total number of nurses and the number of private-duty nurses were estimated for 1947 by the Bureau of Labor Statistics, and that ratio was carried back to earlier years by the data on self-employment shown in the Population Census.[4,5] De-

[1] 1900 Census, *Occupations,* pp. 1, 10; 1910 Census, vol. IV, p. 431; 1920 Census, vol. IV, pp. 356–358; 1930 Census, vol. V, p. 582.

[2] Carson adjusts 1900 by extrapolating the trend in the ratio of trained to total nurses. This is a reasonable procedure, unduly affected, however, by the changing impact of economic conditions, particularly in 1920, on the number of midwives and untrained nurses.

[3] In 1930, for example, 294,189 trained nurses were reported by the Population Census. By increasing to 13 percent the 1940 self-employment percentage of 10 percent (the 1910 percentage was 17), we estimate 38,000. With at most 160,000 nurses in hospitals (the 1935 Census of Hospitals reported 156,000 and the number of patients and beds changed very little over the period), the residual of 100,000 for nurses employed in other pursuits is unreasonably great. A similar problem arises in 1923 if we adjust the 1923 census totals to include all hospitals.

[4] Data kindly provided by Lily Mary David of BLS indicate that there were approximately 250,000 nurses in 1947—59,000 of whom were private duty, according to the American Nursing Association. (The percentage is close to that shown in an ANA survey for 1949.) Census percentages for 1940 and for 1950 (from unpublished data kindly provided by the Census Bureau) were interpolated for 1947, the ratio between this and the BLS percentage being applied to the interpolated census percentages for earlier decades.

[5] The self-employment percentages were applied to census totals for trained nurses

cennial totals were interpolated by numbers of graduates from nursing schools.[6]

The level of the final series will differ from that developed by Kuznets and the National Income Division since both utilize an estimate of self-employed developed in a study by Burgess.[7] The Burgess figures rest on a survey with a high nonresponse rate and cannot be considered very reliable.

2. The number of midwives and untrained nurses in 1900 was revised in accordance with the revision for trained nurses, census totals being accepted for other dates. Intercensal interpolation for 1920 to 1930 was by the number of nonwhite births.[8] For 1910 to 1920, the number of white births was used.[9] From 1900 to 1910 the ratio of nonwhite children under five to all children under five—and by implication the number of births—was essentially unchanged.[10] Hence the intercensal years were interpolated directly. Since midwives and untrained nurses were concentrated in rural areas and among nonwhite groups, the nonwhite birth series was used where available. With nonwhite births a reasonably constant proportion of total births for the 1920s, the number of births was taken as a trend indicator for 1910 to 1920. It was assumed that all persons in the midwife and untrained-nurse group were self-employed.[11]

HOSPITALS

Hospital employment for 1909 to 1930 was estimated as the product of the number of hospital beds and the number of employees per bed. Esti-

---

aged 20 and over, on the assumption that student nurses are excluded from these totals reasonably well by excluding nurses under 20 years of age.

[6] Data from the *Biennial Survey of Education 1910* and later issues, and data for 420 nursing schools reported in May Ayres Burgess, *Nurses, Patients and Pocketbooks* (1928), p. 51.

[7] Burgess, *op. cit.*, p. 239. Kuznets and NID use data from Allen Peebles—who, however, merely reproduces the Burgess estimates. Burgess provides a series on number of nurses in the profession for 1920 to 1927 based on a mail survey. The 1920 to 1927 change shown differs sharply from what the census 1920 to 1930 figures would suggest.

[8] P. K. Whelpton, *Birth and Birth Rates in the Entire United States, 1909–1948,* National Office of Vital Statistics, Special Reports, vol. 33, no. 8.

[9] *Ibid.*

[10] W. S. Thompson and P. K. Whelpton, *Population Trends in the United States* (1933), p. 263. The Whelpton adjustments for underenumeration and deaths differ in this study from those in his NOVS study, but, because of the procedure used, the relationship of 1900 to 1910 would not differ more than trivially.

[11] Census data indicate 21 percent self-employed in 1910 and 17 percent in 1940. However these persons, albeit working for others, have employment relationships more characteristic of domestics and other self-employed persons.

mates of hospital beds for most of these years are available from the annual Census of Hospitals conducted by the American Medical Association since 1920, from the American Medical Directory prior to that date.[1] The number of employees per hospital is given in the 1935 Census of Hospitals conducted by the Public Health Service.[2] For 1923 the Census of Hospitals gives numbers of nurses and beds for 4,978 hospitals.[3] For these hospitals it was assumed that the ratio of employees to nurses shown in the 1935 Census also maintained in 1923. It was assumed that 1,800 hospitals reported by the AMA but not covered by the census were proprietary hospitals. Employment in these hospitals was estimated on the basis of the 1923 data and 1935 ratios.[4]

For 1910, data on the number of nurses in nonprofit hospitals are available from the Census of Benevolent Institutions.[5] Adjusting these by the 1935 ratio to give number of employees per bed and allowing for employment in other hospitals gives total employment in 1910.[6]

A 1900 total-employment figure was estimated by extrapolating the 1910 total by the change in the number of nurses, except those in private-duty work.[7]

For intercensal years the employment per bed was interpolated and total employment estimated.

[1] *Historical Statistics*, p. 51.

[2] E. H. Pennell et al., *Business Census of Hospitals, 1935, General Report*, Supplement 154 to Public Health Reports, tables 23, 25.

[3] U.S. Bureau of the Census, *Hospitals and Dispensaries, 1923* (1925).

[4] The number of employees per hospital bed in proprietary hospitals in 1910 was estimated at 0.37 (see below). For 1935 it was 0.59. The 1923 rate was therefore interpolated at 0.48. This ratio combined with that for reported hospitals gives an aggregate ratio of 0.682 which, applied to the number of hospital beds, gives total employment.

[5] U.S. Bureau of the Census, *Benevolent Institutions, 1910* (1914), p. 48.

[6] It was assumed that the 1,918 benevolent institutions reported by the census constituted all the nonprofit institutions, the balance of all hospitals being profit making. The 1935 Census indicated (Pennell, *op. cit.,* table 23) that employment per hospital bed in proprietary institutions was 54 percent of that in nonprofit institutions. Applying this ratio to the employment per bed shown in the 1910 Census and weighting by the respective numbers of institutions gives total employment in 1910.

[7] The number of all nurses and private-duty nurses was estimated as described in the section on nursing. Applying this same procedure to 1910 gives a figure for the number of nurses close to that estimated above from the Census of Benevolent Institutions. J. P. Ferrell and P. A. Mead, *History of County Health Organizations in the United States, 1908–33,* USPHS Bulletin 222, indicate no such organizations prior to 1908. It is reasonably safe to assume that virtually all wage-earner nurses before 1910 were employed in hospitals.

HOTELS

Self-employed persons in hotels and lodging houses at census dates were estimated by extrapolating a 1930 total for hotel keepers and boarding- and lodging-housekeepers. The 1930 total for hotel keepers was taken directly from census; that for boarding- and lodging-housekeepers, from census after reducing the 1930 total to exclude housewives improperly included under that heading.[1] For extrapolation to census dates, the 1900 and 1920 Census totals for these groups were used. The 1910 total for boarding- and lodging-housekeepers was rejected. Census estimates for that group are in error in 1910, presumably as a result of the same factors which produced an overcount in agricultural employment. An adjustment was made based on the historical ratios of the number of boarding- and lodging-housekeepers to female housekeepers.[2]

Annual estimates for 1900 to 1920 were interpolated, presumably being less affected by short-term business-cycle movements than by the steadier changes in number of migrants—both from rural to urban areas and from other countries to the United States—and the marriage rate. For 1920 to 1930 interpolation was by the number of hotels.[3]

The number of wage earners in 1930 was estimated as follows.

From the 1930 Population Census total for all gainful workers in hotels, boarding and lodging houses, and restaurants, we deducted the number of hotel and other keepers. Employment in restaurants as reported in the Census of Distribution for 1929 was then deducted from the residual after the latter was adjusted for omissions in coverage.[4] The resultant total of 435,000 for employees in hotels and lodging places may be compared with a rough estimate from the Census of Hotels in 1930. The latter reports 291,000 employees, and an adjustment for omissions brings the total up

---

[1] 1930 data from Edwards, *op. cit.*, table 8. A special tabulation of 1930 schedules made by Edwards in 1940 indicated that 26.8 percent of boarding- and lodging-housekeepers in large cities were presumably not in the labor force (*op. cit.*, p. 30). This percentage was assumed to apply to the United States total.

[2] The ratios were 50, 50, 65, and 60 percent for 1890, 1900, 1920, and 1930. For 1910, however, the reported data give a ratio of 95 percent. Since the trend in the number of female housekeepers was reasonable over the decades, boarding- and lodging-housekeepers were computed as 60 percent of the 1910 figure for that occupation.

[3] *Hotel Management* estimates given in M. M. Willey and S. A. Rice, *Communication Agencies and Social Life* (1933), p. 70.

[4] 1929 Census of Distribution, *Food Retailing* (1934), p. 24, reports 478,000 employees, and 149,000 proprietors and firm members. Since the Population Census shows not 149,000 but 165,000 restaurant, lunchroom, and cafe keepers, it was assumed that this group—and along with them one employee per proprietor—had been omitted from the Census of Distribution count.

to 351,000.[5] If we assume one employee per boarding- and lodging-house proprietor,[6] this makes a grand total of 458,000—compared to the 478,-000 estimated above.

Estimates of Kuznets and the National Income Division are substantially lower, chiefly because they adjust the 1929 Census of Hotels figure to include employment in small hotels on the basis of relationship from the 1933 Census of Hotels. That census, however, implies that there were 22 employees per proprietor in small hotels (i.e., except year-round hotels with 25 or more rooms) as compared with 2, 3, and 4 in the censuses of 1948, 1939, and 1935. It is therefore believed unsatisfactory for present use.[7]

For 1920 to 1929 the number of wage earners was interpolated by the number of hotel rooms occupied.[8] For 1920 and prior years, the 1929 ratio of self-employed persons per proprietor in hotels was extrapolated by the similar ratios for retail trade, computed above. (It was assumed that there were no employees in boarding and lodging houses not already included under the census rubric of keepers.) This procedure allows for growth in the size of hotels and for variations over the decades in the ratio of self-employed to employee.[9]

AMUSEMENTS

The 1910 Population Census total for gainful workers in the amusement industry for 1930, less persons in specified occupations, was taken to equal the number of employees in the industry.[1] The total was extrapolated to

[5] In 1939 the Service Census reported 24,000 proprietors, compared to 43,000 male proprietors, managers, and officials "not elsewhere counted" in hotels and lodging places, or 39,000 male employers and own-account workers in hotels and lodging places. At a rough estimate we may assume 20,000 omitted proprietors in 1929, in addition to 14,000 reported, and three employees per proprietor. The number of employees per proprietor in hotels other than year-round ones with 25 and over rooms was 3 in 1939; 4 in 1946; and 22—probably erroneous—in 1933.

[6] It will be remembered that the reported number in this group was reduced to exclude persons not in the labor force.

[7] The procedure used in *National Income in the United States, 1929–35* adds 30,000 entrepreneurs—or even more than appear to have been present in 1940 Population Census totals—but adds only 60,000 employment for these entrepreneurs and the hundred-odd-thousand boarding- and lodging-housekeepers.

[8] W. I. Hamilton, *Promoting New Hotels* (1930), p. 131.

[9] No use was made of Population Census counts of waiters, cooks, and other servants; the majority of these persons were occupied in industries other than hotels and lodging places, and use of data for this group would add only a spurious accuracy to the estimates.

[1] These occupations included showmen, keepers of pleasure resorts, theater owners, proprietors of billiard halls and bowling alleys, plus an estimate for self-employed musicians.

1910 by the number of employees in movie theaters, billiard parlors, and bowling alleys and by the number of musicians.

1. For employment in theaters, estimates of the number of theaters and employees per theater were used.[2] The 1910 figure was extrapolated to 1900 by the percentage change over this decade in the Population Census count of actors, showmen, keepers of resorts, and theater owners.

2. For billiard parlors and bowling alleys the procedure was similar.[3]

3. The number of musicians and music teachers, as reported by the Population Census, was interpolated for intercensal years by an estimate of the inventory of musical instruments.[4] The proportion of this group that was self-employed was 54 percent in 1910 and 40 percent in 1940: Interpolation and extrapolation of these percentages for other years was considered reasonably safe except for 1920 to 1930, when the advent of sound in motion pictures requires special adjustment.[5]

For self-employment in the amusement group, the 1930 total was extrapolated by the number of self-employed musicians, proprietors of bowling alleys and billiard halls, and motion picture theater owners.[6]

[2] General Film was organized about 1910; it started with 10,000 exhibitors and eventually covered 12,000 licensees. Benjamin Hampton, *History of the Movies* (1931), pp. 66, 69, 71. Since this was a strong patent monopoly, its total licensees were taken as equivalent to the total number of theaters. For 1920 a direct count from WID's Yearbook is given in Elizabeth D. Johns, *Final Report on Community Facilities in the Urban Community* (National Resources Committee, 1937, typescript). Figures for 1926 to 1930 are based on a direct listing of names from the *Yearbook of Motion Pictures* and were kindly supplied by Mr. Golden of the National Production Authority, Motion Picture-Photographic Products Division. The number of employees per theater in 1930 was assumed at eight (between the census average for 1935 and 1939), taken at one in 1910, and interpolated between those dates.

[3] Edwards, *op. cit.,* table 8 gives census data for proprietors, owners, and managers in 1910, 1920, and 1930. A 1900 total was estimated by the percentage change in the number of billiard and pool tables and bowling alleys over the 1900 to 1910 decade. Data on this item for 1900 and 1917 are available from the *Reports of the Commissioner of Internal Revenue* for these years. Employees per proprietor, as reported by the Census of Business, were 1.5 in 1933, 1.8 in 1935, and 2.5 in 1939. A figure of 2 was assumed for 1930 and ½ for 1900, the other years then being interpolated.

[4] Production of musical goods in 1913 prices is given in W. H. Shaw, *Value of Commodity Output since 1869* (1947), p. 73, and inventory was taken as the cumulated sum of output since 1890. The relationship between the two sets of data is surprisingly close.

[5] Unpublished census data for 1910; *Occupational Characteristics,* table 6, for 1940. The percent for 1920 and 1930 was assumed at 48 to allow for the impact of World War I and the depression, respectively, while 1900 was estimated from 1910 on the basis of the 30-year rate of change. For 1920 to 1926 the 1900 to 1910 annual change in employees was assumed to apply. (The 1910 to 1920 change was downward.) The 1927 to 1929 figures were then interpolated.

[6] The number of theater owners is taken as equal to the number of theaters, an

LAUNDRIES, DRY CLEANING

Data for employees in laundries are reported in the 1909, 1914, 1919, 1925, 1927, and 1929 Census of Manufactures.[1] For 1900 the total was computed by applying to the 1909 figure the percent change indicated by figures estimated from the Population Census.[2]

For employees in cleaning and dyeing establishments, Census of Manufactures data for 1919, 1925, 1927, and 1929 are available.[3] For 1909 the 1919 total was extrapolated by Population Census totals for cleaning, dyeing, and pressing-shop workers.[4] The 1900 total was estimated from the regression of laundry employment against cleaning and dyeing employment in census years.

The number of employees in laundries and cleaning and dyeing in 1900, 1909, 1919, 1925, 1927, 1929, and 1939 was charted against employment in trade.[5] Given the extremely close fit, this correlation was used to estimate total employment in this group for intercensal years.

OTHER PERSONAL SERVICES

The classification "other service employees" includes total employment in a variety of industries.

1. The number of employees in dressmaking, tailoring, and millinery shops was estimated as follows: For 1910, 1920, and 1930 the total for gainful workers classed as dressmakers, milliners, or tailors is available from the Population Census.[1] For 1900, however, the number of dressmakers and tailors in factories was combined by the census with the total for those not in factories. The number in factories was therefore estimated, using the trend of employment in the relevant industry group shown by

---

erroneous assumption (particularly for the late 1920s) but not likely to mean a difference of more than 5,000 to 10,000 out of 300-odd thousand.

[1] 1919, vol. X, p. 887; 1914, vol. II, p. 847; 1920, vol. X, p. 1027; 1925, p. 1266; 1927, pp. 1292, 1298; 1929, pp. 1393, 1397.

[2] Population Census totals are within a few percent of the Census of Manufactures totals for 1909, 1919, and 1929, hence it was felt safe to use them directly. For 1900 the number of laundry operatives was estimated as 80 percent of the reported group—laundry operatives, owners, etc., and launderers not in laundry—the ratio in subsequent years being 80, 80, and 60 percent.

[3] 1920, vol. X, p. 1050; 1925, p. 1269; 1927, p. 1306; 1929, pp. 1403, 1408.

[4] Edwards, *op. cit.,* table 8. The 1919 and 1920 figures from the respective sources are almost identical.

[5] 1939 data from *Service Establishments* (1939), pp. 443, 468. Trade employment as estimated above.

[1] Edwards, *op. cit.,* table 8. Data relate to persons not in factories.

the Census of Manufactures.[2] This total, deducted from the larger group total, gave the requisite estimate. The number of milliners in 1900 is available direct from the Population Census.

Population Census data indicate that 46 percent of these persons were self-employed in 1910 and 47 percent in 1940, and 46 percent was assumed for other census years.[3]

Intercensal interpolation for self-employed persons was linear for 1900 to 1910 and 1920 to 1930. The annual change from 1910 to 1916 was assumed at half the annual rate of gain during 1900 to 1910. Given the rise in clothing output which Shaw's data indicate beginning in 1916, it was assumed that the decline in self-employment between 1910 and 1920 begin in 1916, as employment opportunities in the factories rose.

Intercensal interpolation for wage earners was by means of the movement of trade employees.

2. Census totals for a hand-trade group were arrived at as follows:

a. The number of barbers, hairdressers, and manicurists is taken from the Population Census.

b. The number of shoemakers not in factories is available from the Census for 1910, 1920, and 1930 and is estimated for 1900 by splitting the total for shoemakers (in and not in factories) by Census of Manufactures data.[4]

c. The number of jewelers not in factories was estimated in a similar fashion.

d. The number of blacksmiths is taken from the Population Census.

e. For the sum of the four previous occupational categories, the proportion of self-employed is 46 percent in 1910, 49 percent in 1940, and is assumed at 46 percent for the other census years covered.[5]

f. Intercensal interpolation for the self-employed was linear except for 1910 to 1920. It was felt that the 1910 to 1920 decline did not begin in 1910, as would be implied with any direct interpolation procedure. Hence

---

[2] The number of wage earners in outerwear, men's clothing, women's clothing n.e.c., and millinery industries appears in Fabricant, *Employment in Manufacturing, 1899 to 1939* (1942), pp. 186–187. The number of operatives and laborers in other clothing and suit, coat, and overall factories as reported in the Population Census was equal to 61 percent of wage earners in these groups for 1929, 55 percent in 1919, and 51 percent in 1909; it was assumed at 49 percent for 1899–1900.

[3] For 1910, data for dressmakers not in factories, milliners (and apprentices), and tailors not in factories were used. For 1940 data for female dressmakers and male tailors were used.

[4] The ratio of (*a*) Population Census totals for operatives and laborers in shoe factories to (*b*) wage earners in shoe factories as shown by Fabricant, was 111 percent in 1929–1930, 106.5 percent in 1919–1920, and 101.4 percent in 1909–1910; it was assumed at 100 percent for 1899–1900.

[5] 1910 data are from census lithoprinted data; 1940, from *Occupational Characteristics*.

1910 to 1914 was assumed to gain at half the per annum gain during 1910 to 1920, with 1915 to 1919 then interpolated.

LOCAL GOVERNMENT (TABLES A-5, A-8)

1. Municipal nonschool employment benchmark data for 1900, 1905, and 1910 were estimated on the basis of the close relationship between trends in the employment of firemen and policemen and all municipal nonschool employment—the ratio of one to the other ranging from 26.1 in 1920 and 26.3 in 1950 to 23.5 in the end-of-depression year 1940 and 24.6 in 1930.[1,2]

For interpolation between benchmark years 1900 to 1920, two methods were considered initially and a third used. In the first, the constancy in the ratio of the number of urban teachers to firemen and policemen over the half century suggested using the number of urban teachers for interpolation.[3] In the second, the operating expense data for cities of 30,000 and over were deflated by an average salary series.[4] Both the resultant series were so similar to direct linear interpolation that the latter procedure was in fact used.[5]

[1] The data for firemen and policemen are from 1900 Census, *Occupations* p. 7; 1910, vol. IV, p. 930; 1920, vol. IV, pp. 410–411; 1930, vol. V, p. 200; 1940, vol. III, p. 79; 1950, vol. II, part I, pp. 1–266. Municipal nonschool employment for these years are from Solomon Fabricant, *The Trend of Government Activity in the United States since 1900* (1952), p. 190, and U.S. Bureau of the Census, *Government Employment.*

[2] For 1905 the number of firemen and policemen in cities with 30,000 population and over—a group accounting for the great bulk of such employment—was reported in Census, *Statistics of Cities Having a Population over 30,000: 1905,* pp. 156, 157, 318, 330. (Data for 1907 are also available but apparently include special policemen without pay.) The figure of 60,000 for this group was inflated to a United States figure by the 1903 ratio of (1) operation and maintenance expenses, "protection of person and property," for cities in this size group (Census, *Financial Statistics of Cities: 1930* (1932), p. 51) to (2) public safety expenditures, operation, by all local governments. Census, *Historical Review of State and Local Government Finances,* Special Studies 25 (June, 1948), p. 17. The ratio was much the same in 1913.

[3] Urban-teacher data were kindly provided by Emery Foster of the Office of Education for the earlier years, with *Biennial Survey* data used for 1930, 1940, and 1950. The ratio of one to the other was also charted against the ratio of protective to school operating expenses in cities 30,000 and over.

[4] Operating expenses for protection of person and property (Census, *Historical Review, loc. cit.*) were deflated by the average salary of urban teachers, the latter data from the Office of Education.

[5] This was preferred since the separate series used above each have particular reporting problems. Thus, the Office of Education coverage of cities varied slightly

2. In estimating nonmunicipal nonschool government employment, we come close to relying on nondata. But the task is not impossible. Most expenditures in this group are made by counties, and data on county expenditures, nonschool operating, are available for 1903, 1913, 1932, and 1942.[6] On the basis of property receipts by counties and state aid data for 1922, a parallel estimate for 1922 can be made.[7] Dividing these operation data by the average nonschool operation cost per employee in cities gives an index used to extrapolate the 1929 employment total for this group as derived from the State County and Municipal Survey data.[8]

For the years 1920 to 1930, the estimates of Fabricant were used.[9] Because the present estimates for 1900 and 1910 are similar to those of Fabricant, it is believed that this produces a reasonably consistent set of figures.[10]

3. Alternative series have been estimated by Fabricant and Kuznets. The Kuznets data (for the 1920s) were not used since the direct-employment reports used by Fabricant are likely to be preferable to Kuznets's indirect procedure of dividing payrolls by an average wage.[11] The Fabricant data for the 1920s are consistent with other data. Moreover, they are based on a sample of cities accounting for a large share of municipal employment.

For the years prior to 1920, however, the Fabricant data were not adopted because, in overwhelming measure, they simply reflect trends in

from year to year, with more marked changes when the use of field agents replaced that of mail questionnaires. Moreover, the expense data are available only biennially, and then not for the complete period.

[6] Census, *Historical Review*, p. 17, and Census, *Financial Statistics of State and Local Governments: 1932*, p. 28.

[7] Property tax data from *Historical Review*, and Census, *Financial Statistics of Counties: 1941, Final Report* (1943), p. 3. State-aid data to counties is from *Historical Review* for all years but 1922. For 1922 it was estimated to equal 78 percent of total state-aid payments, on the basis of the ratio of such payments to aid received by counties from other governments in 1902, 1913, and 1942.

[8] Cost data for cities 30,000 and over from Census, *Financial Statistics of Cities: 1931*, p. 47, and municipal employment as estimated above. Because a substantial volume of county employment is in urban counties—e.g., Wayne, Cook, Cuyahoga —it is assumed that the trend of cost per employee in cities is most applicable for this purpose. Since Fabricant uses such data for cities plus states (and the states show a much more marked rise in cost per employee), his results show a much smaller 1900 to 1930 gain in number of employees.

[9] Fabricant, *op. cit.*, p. 190, shows a 1928–1929 drop in employment. This seems unreasonable both a priori and in the light of the data on government operations costs for 1928, 1929, and 1930.

[10] The present estimates were within 5 percent of Fabricant's for 1900 and 1910.

[11] The wage procedure, for example, leads to an estimated 1920 to 1921 drop in local employment—a shift that hardly seems likely.

New York—and to a lesser extent, Chicago—rather than in the nation.[12] Thus, employment per capita shows virtually no 1910 to 1920 change in the Fabricant sample of cities,[13] whereas the rise for all municipalities was probably about 20 percent.[14] As an indicator of trend we prefer United States totals for firemen and policemen, who constitute so large a segment of employment in this group.

STATE GOVERNMENT (TABLES A-5, A-8)

State nonschool employment was estimated by extrapolating the 1929 State-County-Municipal Survey total[1] by a series for full-time state nonschool employment. The latter series was estimated as follows.

1. For 1919 to 1929, employment was estimated by multiplying (*a*) state operating expenses of general departments except "pensions and gratuities to soldiers and sailors, other relief," education, and highway apportionment, by (*b*) the ratio of wages and salaries to such expenses, and then dividing by an average salary.[2]

[12] "Population-weighted average city nonschool employment per capita" (Fabricant, *op. cit.* p. 190) means that, given the size of New York and Chicago, their averages will fairly well dominate any limited sample. Yet both of these, with developed standards of municipal service for some time, show employment trends strikingly different from the country as a whole.

[13] *Ibid.,* p. 191.

[14] Because Fabricant uses population weights, his sample shows a per capita employment trend identical with that for Chicago and New York. However, the number of policemen and firemen per capita (using Occupation Census data) rose by 3 percent in Chicago and declined by 5 percent in New York over the 1910–1920 period, whereas the national total rose 19 percent. The differences in trend for this group suggest similar differences in data for other municipal employees. Moreover, because of the importance of Chicago in the earlier period estimate, Fabricant's inclusion of school employment in measuring nonschool employment trends in that city makes the data additionally less appropriate.

[1] From Carol Brainerd, "Public Employment and Pay Rolls in the United States, 1929–39, and Post War Implications," *Monthly Labor Review* (February, 1945), p. 250.

[2] Data on expenses of departments for operation, for education operations, for highway apportionment, and for soldiers' and sailors' relief for 1919 and 1923 to 1930 were secured from table 11 in the issues of Bureau of the Census, *Financial Statistics of States,* for the respective years. For 1922, item detail is available only for 30 states. The 1922 ratio of (1) total cost payments less miscellaneous payments in these 30 states to (2) such payments for all states was used to estimate a 1921 comparable total. The 1920 total was estimated as two-thirds of the way between 1919 and 1921 on the basis of Kuznets's data for selected states, from which Ohio data were excluded because of the pension movement. Data on wages and operating costs for eight states were kindly provided by Lillian Epstein of the National Bureau of Economic Research. The resultant wage-cost ratio was essentially unchanged

2. For 1910 employment was estimated by computing the change of state employment in mental hospitals,[3] prisons,[4] education,[5] and general operations.[6] Indexes of employment changes in each of these categories were weighted by estimated wages paid in the appropriate expenditure groups as tabulated by the census—hospitals and institutions for the handicapped, correction, schools, and general control—to give an index of 1910 to 1923 employment change.[7]

3. For 1900 employment was estimated by dividing state operating nonschool expenses by the average expense per employee. The expense data were derived as a ratio to school revenue from state sources. This ratio which was 2.44 in 1902, 2.37 in 1910, and 2.43 in 1915, was assumed at 2.44 in 1900.[8] The average expense per employee in 1910 was extrap-

---

from 1919 to 1929. Average salary data are from Simon Kuznets, *National Income and Its Composition, 1919–1938* (1941), pp. 812, 814.

[3] The number of nurses per bed in 1910 was computed from Bureau of the Census, *Benevolent Institutions, 1910* (1914), p. 48; the number in 1923 was computed from Bureau of the Census, *Hospitals and Dispensaries, 1923* (1925), p. 814; the number in 1935 was computed from Elliott H. Pennell et al., *Business Census of Hospitals, 1935, General Report,* Supplement 154 to the Public Health Reports, pp. 13, 32. (The 1935 census data used relate to nonmilitary Federal, plus other government, plus nonprofit hospitals—the group most closely approximating the coverage indicated in table I of the 1910 Census.) These ratios were then applied to the number of patients in state mental hospitals and institutions for the feebleminded as reported in the *Statistical Abstract, 1932,* p. 70, and *1953,* p. 86. The resultant index was used to extrapolate hospital employment for the specified types of hospital as reported in Pennell, *op. cit.,* p. 32.

[4] Employment in state prisons in 1923 as reported in Bureau of the Census, *Prisoners: 1923* (1926), p. 188, was reduced slightly for 1910, given the small change in number of prisoners in prisons and reformatories indicated on p. 23 of the same report.

[5] The percent change in state educational employment was taken to equal that for public higher education as estimated above.

[6] For general administration, the percent change shown in the Population Census listing for "officers and inspectors, state" was used, with interpolation for 1923. 1910 Census, vol. IV, p. 93; 1920 Census, vol. IV, p. 42; 1930 Census, vol. V, p. 572.

[7] The operation expenditure data reported in Census, *Historical Review,* p. 21, were reduced to wage data on the basis of the ratios of wage to total operation expense data from the prison report noted above and state school system expense data from the *Biennial Survey.* (The use of these weights leads an estimate of 1923 as 52 percent above 1910. The direct use of the expenditure data leads to the very similar figure of 47 percent.)

[8] School revenue from state sources is reported in the *Annual Reports of the Commissioner of Education* and the *Biennial Survey.* Operating expense data for 1902 and 1915 are from Bureau of the Census, *Historical Review,* pp. 17, 21. For 1910 and 1915 estimates of expenditures (including interest and outlays) were derived from individual state reports in Mabel Newcomer, *Financial Statistics of Public Education in the United States, 1910–20,* Educational Finance Inquiry Commis-

olated to 1910 by the average nonschool expense per employee in the selected states for which Fabricant reports employment.[9]

An alternative estimate for 1900 was made by taking the percent change for 1900 to 1910 shown in the Population Census category for "state officials and inspectors."[10] The result is identical.

4. The 1900 to 1910 rise in employment is 62,000, while the 1910 to 1920 gain is much the same, 54,000. In the light of these figures and the change in state nonschool expenses for selected years over the period, it was assumed that employment in this group rose steadily between the decennial dates, and the figures were therefore interpolated.

The estimates of state nonschool employment which were made for many of these years in the recent basic study by Fabricant were not used.[11] The chief reason for not doing so is the fact that two states with developed standards of state service—New York and Massachusetts—dominate Fabricant's 1910 to 1920 change estimate. These states developed many state services earlier than did the country as a whole. State expenditures per capita rose by 37 percent from 1902 to 1913 in the states used by Fabricant, whereas the gain for all states was 21 percent. (For 1919 to 1929, conversely, the sample states showed a gain of 70 percent, as compared with 94 percent for all states.)[12] We cannot assume these differences in expenditure trends to be wholly absent in employment trends. Hence,

sion (1924), p. 11. Deducting highways and education from this total to remove education and some outlays and apportionments, the ratio of the resultant figure to the expense figure was 125 percent. This percentage, applied to the Newcomer figure for 1910, gave an appropriate 1910 expense figure.

[9] The 1910 figure was estimated by dividing the employment previously estimated into the 1910 expense total, whose derivation is noted above. The Fabricant data (*op. cit.,* p. 189) on employees per capita were interpolated and combined with 1902 and 1913 Census of Wealth data on total payments for general expenses (minus education) for the three specified states and with population data to derive payments per employee. The resultant figure for 1902 was virtually identical with the 1913 one. It is assumed to be safer to extrapolate wage rate, or expense per employee, trends from a small sample than trends in services per capita demanded.

[10] 1900, *Occupations,* p. 7; 1910, vol. IV, p. 93; 1920, vol. IV, p. 42. The representativeness of this very small group is suggested by the fact that the 1910 to 1923 percent employment change it showed is the same as that for hospital, prison, and higher education employment as a group for the same period, as indicated above.

[11] *Op. cit.,* p. 188.

[12] Fabricant's employment per capita data for selected states in 1900, 1910, 1920, and 1929 (*Ibid.,* p. 189) were interpolated for 1902 and 1913. Population data from Census, *Vital Statistics in the United States, 1900–1940,* pp. 824ff. Expenditure data from Census, *Wealth, Debt and Taxation* (1907), pp. 998, 1000—total payments for general expenditures less education. Data on expenditures for general departments minus schools and minus apportionments from Census, *National and State Revenues and Expenditures 1913 and 1903 and Public Properties of the States, 1913* (1914), pp. 32–33.

while the estimates are sound for many purposes, they are not used for the present purpose of developing a continuous annual employment series.

The procedures used here for 1900 to 1919 are similar to those employed for the well-known estimates of Simon Kuznets for 1919 to 1938. Because, however, the Kuznets estimates showed no gain in employment immediately after World War I (the 1920 figure being slightly above the 1923 total), despite a substantial rise in governmental costs, and because they show a 1925–1926 decline, not likely to have characterized state employment during this period, they were reviewed in some detail. Examination of work-sheet data kindly provided by Lillian Epstein of the National Bureau of Economic Research indicated that the inclusion of soldiers' pensions, which were large in some years and trivial in others, was responsible. By deducting such pensions, as well as highway apportionments (neither of which result in direct state employment), but using the same procedure, we secure more stable figures for these years.[13] (In addition, of course, it is to be noted that the Kuznets data were necessarily not benchmarked at any point to a direct employment estimate. The present figures take advantage of the benchmark figures which derive from the State, County and Municipal Survey of the BLS covering 1938.)

King's estimates for 1909 to 1918 essentially use the trend in New York State salaries to divide into a series for wages, using the ratio of New York State wages and salaries to total expenses in developing the latter.[14] While the results are not unreasonable, an average wage-salary figure based on national data is preferable to one based on the single state of New York. In addition, changing rates of pay in New York would have an undue effect on the ratio of wages to operating expenses in such a procedure.[15]

PUBLIC EDUCATION (TABLES A-5, A-8)

Public education was estimated by extrapolating the 1929 BLS estimate to 1919 by Kuznets's estimate and to 1900 by the sum of series for primary and secondary education, for higher education, and for special state schools.

Primary and secondary education employment was estimated as the sum of (1) teachers (as reported in the Commissioner Reports and the

---

[13] The Kuznets data show a marked decline in the ratio of wages and salaries to operating expenditures from 1919 to 1923. This decline originates because two of the states included in the Kuznets sample, Ohio and Iowa, paid no bonuses in 1919–1920 but paid a large bonus in 1923.

[14] W. I. King, *Income in the United States, Its Amount and Distribution, 1909–1919* (1922), pp. 210–213.

[15] The differences are not spectacular; King, for example, shows just under a 50 percent employment gain from 1910 to 1918; the present estimate rises 40 percent.

Biennial Survey) together with (2) estimates for nonacademic employees.[1]

For nonacademic employees, trends during the late 1920s through to 1950 indicate that the ratio of (1) the number in this group to (2) the number of teachers varied as did the ratio of city to total teachers.[2] (This implies a relatively constant ratio of auxiliary personnel to teachers both in cities and in rural areas, with the shift in population weights accounting for the change in the overall ratio.) On this basis, it was possible to extrapolate the ratios to 1900.[3] These ratios, applied to the number of teachers, gave the estimated number of nonacademic personnel for 1900 to 1919.[4,5]

For public higher education from 1900 to 1919, the number of professors and instructors was derived from various Office of Education publications for quinquennial dates.[6] The proportion of these in public employment was extrapolated from 1920 to 1900, 1905, 1910, and 1915 by the

[1] The estimated number of teachers was kindly provided by Emery Foster of the Office of Education, the data being taken from the national summary tables in the successive *Reports* of the Commissioner and the *Biennial Survey*. These figures, for the number of different teachers employed, ran between 2 and 4 percent above the number of teaching positions during the 1920s. Hence only a trivial error is involved in using this series for extrapolation instead of the conceptually preferable, but nonexistent, series for teaching positions.

[2] The ratio of other employees to teachers estimated for 1925 and later years by Kuznets was kindly made available by Lillian Epstein. (Prior to 1925, Kuznets carried this ratio as a constant.) For 1950 it was estimated from the *Biennial Survey for 1949–50*, chap. 2, pp. 36, 38. The number of teachers in state systems and in cities with populations of 8,000 (or 10,000) and over was computed from the Commissioners *Reports* for 1905, vol. I, pp. 408, 430; for 1910, vol. II, pp. xiv, 691; and from *Biennial Surveys* for 1916, vol. II, pp. 29, 51–53; 1918–1920, vol. II, pp. 45, 110; 1924–1926, vol. II, pp. 574, 625; 1928–1930, pp. 40, 105; 1949–1950, chap. 2, p. 28; chap. 3, p. 19.

[3] The ratio of urban to total teachers rose by approximately as much from 1900 to 1925 as from 1925 to 1950, and the ratio of other employees to teachers was assumed to have risen from 1900 to 1925 as it did from 1925 to 1950.

[4] The reports in the Census series, *Statistics of Cities Having a Population of over 30,000* for 1910 (pp. 254, 300) and 1912 (p. 354), show such employees running at about 10 percent of academic employment. Data on payrolls for 1902 to 1905 (1905 report, p. 186) lead to the same inference. Now since teachers in cities of this size ran to about 20 percent of all teachers and the ratio in rural districts must have been much lower, the national percentage could not be much over 5 percent, giving a 1910 figure about 20,000 lower than the one used here for consistency with Kuznets.

[5] Even at this level the figures are well below those suggested in George Stigler, *Employment and Compensation in Education* (1950), p. 67, which, in the light of the direct employment figures in the 1902 to 1912 city reports, are too high.

[6] *Annual Report of the Commissioner of Education, 1905*, vol. II, pp. 550, 561, 564, 567, 721; and *1916*, vol. II, pp. 245, 353—summing figures for colleges for men and both sexes, for women, Divisions A and B, technological and professional schools, and deducting professional departments where included under professional schools; *Biennial Survey of Education, 1928–30*, vol. II, p. 338.

proportion of students in public colleges, the two ratios moving closely together over the 1922–1950 period.[7] These ratios, applied to totals for professors and instructors, gave quinquennial totals. Estimates for intervening years were made by direct interpolation. This series was used to extrapolate the Kuznets 1920 estimate for all employees in higher education.

For special schools, the trend in number of teachers was used to extrapolate the Kuznets estimates.[8]

FEDERAL GOVERNMENT (TABLES A-5, A-8)

1900 to 1928. We adopt the estimates of the Civil Service Commission for these years.[1] These estimates include a small number of government employees outside the United States—56,000 as of 1929. For the convenience of having data comparable with the more detailed figures shown by the Commission for individual agencies, we adopt its totals and link directly with the BLS figures for 1929 following, although the latter exclude this small group.

1929ff. We adopt the BLS–Civil Service Commission figures for these years, these constituting the Federal civilian component of the BLS series for employees in nonagricultural establishments.[2]

[7] Biennial Survey data for biennia ending in 1922, 1924, 1926, 1928, and 1950 indicate the proportion of all teachers in public colleges ran about 1.5 percentage points below the proportion of students. Data on students and teachers from the Commissioners *Reports* for 1905, vol. I, p. 545; 1910, vol. II, pp. 850–851; 1916, vol. II, pp. 242–243; *Biennial Surveys* for 1922, pp. 323–324, 328–329; for 1922–1924, pp. 598–599, 603–604; for 1924–1926, pp. 825–826, 830–831; for 1926–1928, pp. 720–721, 726–727; for 1928–1930, pp. 341–343, 345–347; for 1949–1950, chap. 4, sec. 1, pp. 11, 15. For comparability with earlier years, professional departments are excluded from the 1918–1920 data.

[8] *1905 Report of the Commissioner of Education*, vol. 2, pp. 1330, 1948, 1949, indicated a figure of 2,779 teachers, compared with Kuznets's 1919 figure of 3,281 and a 1925 estimate of 3,778. Total employment in this group, constituting less than 1 percent of total employment in education, was therefore taken for 1905 as much below 1919 as that was below 1925.

[1] *Historical Statistics of the United States*, vol. II. These data are more comparable with the 1929ff. series of the BLS than are the estimates of Solomon Fabricant in his basic study, *The Trend of Government Activity in the United States since 1900* (1952), or Kuznets (*op. cit.*), both of whom rely on earlier estimates made by the Civil Service Commission.

[2] This series differs in some respects from the Federal series appearing in the National Income accounts.

DOMESTIC SERVICE (TABLE A-4)

The 1930 BLS figure for employment in domestic service was extrapolated to 1920 and 1910 by the total number of private family domestics in four occupations: cooks, launderers and laundresses, nurses and midwives, and other servants.[1] Since the total for the gainful workers in these occupations includes hotel cooks, laundry workers in hospitals, and various other domestics employed outside private homes, it was necessary to exclude such gainful workers from the total. For this purpose Stigler has assumed that the 1930 ratio of such workers to the total for these four occupations applied equally well to earlier census dates.[2] In view of the many factors which might have changed the ratio, however, it was felt preferable to adopt an alternative procedure.[3] The one actually followed rests on the observation that most domestics in private homes are in certain sex and nationality groups. Three-quarters of all cooks in private homes, in 1930, for example, were Negro females; conversely, 86 percent of all Negro female cooks were employed in private homes.[4] Hence the number of cooks in private homes in 1930 was extrapolated to 1910 and 1920 by the number of female Negro cooks.[5]

For "other servants," the 1930 data show that nearly 90 percent of this group consisted of females employed in private homes, hence the group total was used to extrapolate the 1930 total for "other servants in private homes." [6] For launderers and laundresses, as for nurses and midwives, the census data for females were used for extrapolation.[7,8]

For 1900 even less occupational information is available. However, it

[1] Alba Edwards, *Comparative Occupation Statistics in the United States, 1870 to 1940* (1943), table 8, as adjusted below.

[2] George Stigler, *Domestic Servants in the United States, 1900–1940* (1946), pp. 38, 39.

[3] Less than half of all cooks in 1930, for example, were in private homes. The use of a series for all cooks, therefore, might conceivably be unsatisfactory as an indicator of trend for a component of this relative size. Some check on the adequacy of this procedure from outside data is required.

[4] 1930 Census, vol. V, pp. 85, 582.

[5] 1910 Census, vol. IV, p. 431. 1920 Census, vol. V, p. 359. 1930 Census, vol. V, pp. 85, 582.

[6] *Ibid.*

[7] Edwards, *op. cit.,* table 10.

[8] Gladys Palmer and Ann Ratner, *Industrial and Occupational Trends in National Employment* (1949), utilize unpublished census estimates in allocating 179,500 persons from the combined cooks, housekeeper, steward, and other servant group to industries outside domestic service. The census allocation was essentially an arbitrary one. The present estimates allocate 580,000 cooks and other servants alone— an estimate implicit in the direct estimate of persons in domestic service as compared to the total in these occupations.

is known that the servant group in that period was composed primarily of Negro and foreign-born women. For each census date from 1910 to 1930, therefore, we computed the ratio of the four occupational group total to the total for (Negro females in domestic and personal service) plus (foreign-born female servants and waitresses). This ratio was 69 percent in 1910, 77 percent in 1920, and 76 percent in 1930.[9] We assumed that a trend rate of growth existed, speeded up by the war, and a figure of 65 percent was therefore used in estimating the 1900 total.

As a rough confirmation of the general procedures followed, an independent estimate of the number of cooks in hotels and other businesses was made by extrapolating the 1930 figure by the total number of white male cooks. (Most white male cooks worked outside private homes. Conversely, most male cooks outside those in private homes were white.) The total for cooks except in private homes as thus estimated, when added to that estimated above for those in private homes, came within 13 percent of the total for all cooks in 1910.

Two further points concerning the census data should be mentioned.

1. No use was made of the data for housekeepers for extrapolation, chiefly because the reported number varied almost precisely with the number of boarding and lodging housekeepers over the 1890–1940 period. Such covariance suggests that this occupation title included not so much domestic servants as employees in personal service.

2. The census results for 1920 are accepted despite Stigler's doubts as to their adequacy.[10] The number of females in domestic and personal service shows a steady gain in both the North Atlantic and North Central regions, with a sharp 1920 drop in the South Atlantic and South Central regions.[11] Such a differential is quite in accord with World War II experience. The January, 1920, enumeration indicated a domestic-service total about 25 percent below the 1890 to 1930 trend. The January, 1947, figure —the month bears the same relationship to the end of World War II as January, 1920, does to World War I—was likewise about 25 percent below trend.[12] It therefore appears reasonable to believe that in both wars the impact of prosperity, an expanding labor market, and increased internal

[9] 1900 Census, *Occupations,* p. cxv; 1910 Census, vol. V, pp. 431, 433; 1920 Census, vol. IV, pp. 358, 359; 1930 Census, vol. V, p. 85.

[10] Stigler, *op. cit.,* p. 39.

[11] 1900 Census, *Occupations,* p. xcii; 1910 Census, vol. IV, p. 49; 1920 Census, vol. IV, p. 54; 1930 Census, vol. V, p. 60.

[12] The 1890 to 1930 data are from Edwards, *op. cit.,* p. 129. The 1940 figure is from *Ibid.,* table 7; the 1947 from the Bureau of the Census, *Annual Report of the Labor Force, 1948,* table 13; and the 1950 from the *Annual Report of the Labor Force, 1950,* table 14. It is to be noted that the 1940 total is probably below trend because of the impact of the depression. Hence 1947, though a quarter below the 1940 to 1950 trend, would be even more below a longer-term trend.

migration all conspired to reduce the size of the Southern domestic labor force. On this assumption the reported 1920 total is not open to special question.

Interpolation of domestic-service employment between census dates is a doubtful enterprise. Able investigators such as Stigler have simply omitted intercensal estimates, while Carson and others have interpolated by the movement of employment in all other industries. Hardly any more satisfactory characteristics attach to the present estimate. If we compute figures for the number of domestic servants per family for the period 1890–1950, the sharp impact of both wars on the employment of domestics is apparent.[13] As a working hypothesis it is assumed that for the years except 1915 to 1920 the trend in the number of employed domestic servants for 1900 to 1929 can be estimated by interpolating between census dates. This procedure assumes that domestic employment does not depart significantly from its trend rate of growth during a period of prosperity and brief recessions such as occurred from 1900 to 1929. It does not rise as sharply as all other employment because much of the employment (in the South, in well-to-do families in the North) is more a matter of custom and family composition than a function of short-term economic changes. For the same reasons domestic employment does not drop as sharply in a short-term recession. What does occur is an increase in unemployment within employment. However, the Current Population Survey concepts, to which we are adhering, define persons as employed if they do 1 hour or more of work a week. Such a definition is obviously elastic enough so that a reduction in domestic employment from 5 days a week to 3, or from 3 days to 1 will still have no effect on total numbers employed.

While the quantity demanded is thus fairly stable, the supply is seriously affected by a prosperity labor market such as attends war production, rising wages, and—most important—a substantial short-term rise in the number of job openings accessible to unskilled workers. Hence for the 1910–1920 period it is assumed (following World War II experience) that employment was essentially unchanged from 1910 through 1914 and then fell steadily to the 1920 level by 1918.

[13] Data from table A-10.

11

FULL-TIME EQUIVALENT EARNINGS

In this chapter we outline the derivation of the estimates of full-time equivalent earnings for employees in individual industries and in two weighted totals from these component series, one for the nonfarm employee group and the other for all employees combined. The earnings figures were computed to link to those of the U.S. Department of Commerce national income accounts for 1929ff. In most instances we extrapolated the Commerce full-time earnings figure back, while in others independent estimates were made and ratio linked at 1929. Substantial use was made of a wide variety of sources, including the massive studies by Kuznets and Douglas. We describe the differences of estimate between our findings and those of these authorities as well as such other major contributors as Rees, Barger, Stigler, Fabricant, and King. The order of exposition is first a discussion of our weighted averages, and the accompanying estimates of income loss from unemployment and income after unemployment, followed then by a description of procedures for each individual industry series.

ALL EMPLOYEES, NONFARM EMPLOYEES
(TABLES A-16, A-17)

Full-time earnings series for these combined groups were computed as weighted averages of the series for individual industries as derived below. The weights were the numbers employed by industry as given in Table A-5. (Other series in Tables A-16 and A-17 were derived by procedures outlined elsewhere.)[1] Briefly summarized, the income loss from unemploy-

[1] See the author's "Earnings of Nonfarm Employees in the United States, 1890–1946," *Journal of the American Statistical Association* (March, 1948).

ment was estimated by applying to the full-time earnings figure computed above the relevant unemployment percentage—for civilian labor force or nonfarm employees—as given in Table A-3. This income loss, when subtracted from the full-time earnings (i.e., "when employed"), gave the earnings after deduction for unemployment. Both these series were deflated by the consumer price index to yield real earnings when employed and after deduction for unemployment. The price index was the BLS index 1913–1960 extrapolated by Albert Rees to 1900.[2]

EMPLOYEES, BY INDUSTRY (TABLE A-18)
AGRICULTURE

For 1910 to 1929, average earnings were computed, as are the Department of Agriculture figures since 1929, from estimates of wages of hired labor (including the value of perquisites) and the average employment of such labor.[1]

1899. Total cost of hired labor as reported in the Agriculture Census and total employment of hired labor as reported in the Population Census were used for computing earnings figures.[2]

1902, 1906, 1909. Figures for these years were interpolated between 1899 and 1910 averages by the average monthly farm wage rates as derived from the surveys of the USDA.[3]

Other Years. Analysis by Louis Ducoff indicates the close relationship over the entire 1910–1943 period between farm wage-rate changes and prices received by farmers.[4] We therefore use the BLS wholesale price index component for farm prices for interpolating between the above estimates.[5]

MINING: TOTAL, COAL, COPPER, OIL

The estimates for all mining were computed as the weighted sum of series for anthracite, bituminous, metal, and oil mining for 1902, 1909, and

[2] Albert Rees, *Real Wages in Manufacturing, 1890 to 1914* (1961).

[1] USDA, Agricultural Handbook 118, *Major Statistical Series of the United States Department of Agriculture,* vol. 3, p. 39, and vol. 7, p. 9.

[2] 1900 Census, *Agriculture,* part I, p. 143; 1900 Census, *Occupations,* p. 7. The USDA payrolls figures for 1910ff. are similarly benchmarked to the Agriculture Census; its employment figures, to the Population Census.

[3] Wage-rate index from the Bureau of Agricultural Economics, *Farm Wage Rates, Farm Employment and Related Data* (January, 1943). This is the composite monthly index whose movement can be linked to the current composite hourly series.

[4] Louis Ducoff, *Wages of Agricultural Labor in the United States,* USDA Technical Bulletin 895 (July, 1945), p. 55.

[5] As printed in *Historical Statistics,* p. 233.

the years 1914 to 1929. For the remaining years in the 1900–1913 period, total mining was estimated from the trend in coal mining, the ratio of one average to the other being much the same in 1902, 1909, and 1914.[1]

Anthracite and Bituminous Coal

Separate estimates were computed for each industry for the years 1900 to 1929. For 1919 to 1929, the averages can be readily derived from Kuznets's estimates.[2] For earlier years, the census data have been interpolated by Paul Douglas on the basis of the relevant state series and his figures were used for extrapolation after some adjustments.[3] For both the anthracite coal strike of 1902 and the bituminous one of 1919 we follow Douglas in showing a decline in earnings, relating total payrolls to the average number customarily employed in the nonstrike months. Since this decline is also reflected in our employment data, the two may not be multiplied together for these years to give total payrolls.

Metal Mining

For metal mining we interpolate between census benchmark data by the weighted trend of earnings in copper and iron mining. Because the precious metals, lead, and zinc, were mined primarily in the West during this period, we give the employment weight for these industries to the series for copper, which is primarily one for the Mountain states.[4]

Copper Mining

For this industry in 1902, 1909, 1919, and 1929, the Census of Mineral Industries provides wage and salary data.[5] The 1919 average was extrapolated to 1918 by data provided by the Anaconda Copper Company, this

---

[1] All mining earnings were 108.5 percent of coal mining in 1914 and 107.8 percent in 1909. For 1902 they were 11.3 percent, a difference explained by the anthracite strike of that year. The 1909 ratio was therefore used for 1900 to 1913.

[2] Simon Kuznets, *National Income and Its Composition 1919 to 1938* (1941), pp. 553, 557. As usual, the average was benchmarked to the NID 1929 estimate.

[3] Paul Douglas, *Real Wages in the United States 1890 to 1926* (1930), p. 350. Douglas does not give anthracite data for 1900 or 1901. For 1901 we use the *Report of the Anthracite Coal Commission* as reprinted in Bulletin 46 of the U.S. Department of Labor (May, 1903), p. 482. For 1900 we extrapolate 1901 by the number of days worked times average hourly earnings. Days worked are from *Mineral Resources of the United States, 1911,* part 2, p. 47; hourly rates are from Douglas, *op. cit.,* p. 161.

[4] The data from the Censuses of 1902, 1909, 1919 and 1929 are conveniently summarized in the 1929 Census, p. 33, and the 1902 Census, p. 36.

[5] 1920 Census, *Mines and Quarries, 1919,* vol. XI, p. 364; 1930 Census, *Mines and Quarries: 1929,* p. 44.

1918 figure then being extrapolated to 1913 to 1918 by average wages paid machine miners in the major copper-mining states.[6]
For 1921, 1923, 1925, and 1927, estimates were computed from the trend for earnings in copper refining and smelting.[7] Since copper mining and smelting are closely related industries, both geographically and in their labor markets, the separation of the data for the respective productive units is always a difficult problem in census enumeration. Moreover, the similarity in the ratio of earnings in mining to that in smelting for 1919 and 1929 (107 percent and 106 percent, respectively) warrants interpolation of the ratio for the intermediate census years. (Use of this procedure for 1914 gives an estimate within 3 percent of that derived above by wage-rate data.)[8] For 1922, the 1921 and 1923 rates were interpolated by rates paid to machine miners in Butte.[9]
Interpolation for 1924, 1926, and 1928 was by the price of copper, the two series being closely related over this decade.[10] For 1900, the 1902 figure was used.

Iron Mining

Benchmarks were established for iron-mining earnings in 1902, 1909, and 1919 from the Census of Mineral Industries.[11] For 1899, earnings were estimated as 115 percent of the state average from the Biennial Report of the Minnesota Bureau of Labor Statistics.[12] (The percentage is the United States–Minnesota ratio indicated for 1902 in the census data.)[13]

---

[6] W. C. Roney, chief statistician of The Anaconda Copper Company, kindly provided an index of common-labor rates paid by the company for 1913 to 1919. The 1913 to 1918 data for copper-mining machinemen are from a report by the Engineer of the California Metal Producers Association, quoted in the *Monthly Labor Review* (April, 1918), pp. 177–178. The rates shown for Montana, Arizona, and Utah were combined, using 1919 copper-mining employment in each state.

[7] 1929 *Census of Manufactures,* vol. II, p. 1085.

[8] The 1909 ratio was applied to the 1914 smelting average.

[9] *Monthly Labor Review* (October, 1938). Since most of the industry was in the West, the Michigan data shown in this source were ignored, though broadly similar in trend.

[10] Price data are from Harold Barger and Sam Schurr, *The Mining Industries, 1899–1939* (1944), p. 280. They note that these data are really Bureau of Mines "value" data.

[11] Census Bureau, *Mines and Quarries, 1902* (1905). This census converted reported employment into 300-day equivalents. N. Yaworski et al., *Technology, Employment and Output per Man in Iron Mining* (WPA, 1940), p. 206, estimates a 260-day year. This estimate is adopted by Barger and Schurr, *op. cit.,* p. 320. We divide Yaworski's man-shift total by 260, add to other employees, and divide into the census wage and salary total he gives. 1920 Census, *Mines and Quarries,* p. 335.

[12] *Biennial Report* for 1899–1900, pp. 276–277.

[13] Census Bureau, *Mines and Quarries, 1902* (1905), pp. 400, 401. Medians were computed from distributions shown in this source.

The 1902 figure was extrapolated to 1903 and 1904 by data for Minnesota mining.[14]

For other prewar years, we rely largely on data for Minnesota iron-mining rates, since Minnesota accounted for nearly half the iron ore mined in this period, while the Lake Superior region accounted for about three-quarters of the United States total.[15] The basic estimates were derived by the trend in earnings of iron miners in the major center, Itasca County, Minnesota.[16] These averages were then checked against more limited data for St. Louis County in the same state, the results proving closely similar.[17]

Interpolation for 1920 to 1928 is by the average daily wage in Itasca County.[18]

Oil and Gas Mining

Census of Mineral Industries data give us the basis for computing 1902, 1909, and 1919 averages,[19] while BLS data are used by NID for 1929. For 1914, 1924, and 1926, we estimate averages from rates for selected occupations as reported in an American Petroleum Industry survey.[20] For the other years in the 1920s, we interpolate by the trend of earnings in petroleum refining.[21]

[14] The *Biennial Reports* for 1903–1904, p. 373, and for 1906, p. 444, show contract miners' rates falling from $2.291 in December, 1902, to $2.265 in December, 1903; they show all miners' rates at $1.885 in 1904—compared to $1.91 to be computed for Minnesota from the 1902 Census. The 1 percent decline from December, 1902 to December, 1903, as that from 1902 to 1904, was taken to indicate no significant United States change for 1902–1903–1904.

[15] See 1909 Census, vol. XI, p. 240.

[16] Minnesota Department of Labor and Industry, *Biennial Report, 1931–32*, summarizing the 1909 to 1931 record. For earlier years the fiscal-year reports were converted to calendar-year averages.

[17] Data for all miners, or contract miners, appear in Minnesota *Biennial Report of the Bureau of Labor, 1911–12*, p. 379; *1913–14*, p. 145; *1915–16*, p. 148; *1917–19*, pp. 55, 129; *1919–20*, p. 85.

[18] Minnesota Department of Labor and Industry, *loc. cit.* Kuznets, *op. cit.*, p. 553, interpolates metal-mining wages between 1919 and 1929 by the average daily wage in Itasca County.

[19] 1919 Census, p. 311. No canvass of the industry was made in 1929. The 1929 average of BLS-NID seems unreasonably high in the light of the long-term relation between average earnings in metal mining and in oil and gas. Adjustment to this level explains the fairly unreasonable 1919 to 1929 gains.

[20] Reported in the Temporary National Economic Commission, *Hearings*, part 16, p. 273. We average the rates shown there for driller, pumper, and roustabout. The resultant series shows very little change from 1919 to 1924–1926–1929. The gain shown here arises from adjustment to the 1919 and the much higher 1929 NID averages.

[21] Kuznets, *op. cit.*, pp. 581, 599. Kuznets shows a slightly different trend, as he uses the refining data for all years from 1920 to 1928.

MANUFACTURING

For manufacturing employees, we rely on the Census of Manufactures series for census years, interpolating for the pre-1919 years by the state data as combined by Paul Douglas, and for the post-1919 years by similar data as combined by Simon Kuznets.[1] For 1900 to 1914, we do not use the recent estimates of Albert Rees. They mark a significant advance for the measurement of hourly earnings, which was his primary objective, but are less suitable for measuring annual earnings.[2]

CONSTRUCTION

The 1929 NID average was extrapolated to 1919 by the implicit full-time earnings figures in the Kuznets estimates.[1] We then extrapolated to 1900 by an adjusted index of weekly earnings, using Douglas's series for building tradesmen and for unskilled laborers, and weighting these together by Population Census weights.[2] To adjust this series for the varying volume of employment from year to year, we multiplied by an adjustment ratio— computed as the ratio of an index of weekly to one of annual earnings in manufacturing.[3]

We then computed check estimates for 1899 and 1908. For 1899 we utilized the wage bill reported for 331,000 construction employees in the 1900 Census—the census in that year still covering a sizable volume of hand trades.[4] This check estimate of $576 compared favorably with our preliminary $593. For 1908, we take average daily rates paid to males in

[1] Census figures, revised to exclude hand and neighborhood industries, appear in *Historical Statistics,* p. 179. Douglas, *op. cit.,* p. 246. Douglas's series relates to wage earners and is revised for 1910 by Rees's data, as discussed below. Kuznets, *op. cit.,* pp. 578, 602. Kuznets's series relates to wage and salary workers.

[2] Rees, *op. cit.,* p. 32, note 16, comments that he seeks "annual earnings only as a means of estimating daily earnings" and therefore rejects information for states covered by Douglas which do not conduce to that end. For our present concern, we prefer to derive the intercensal movement from the Douglas series, relying as it does on data for eight states, rather than from the Rees series, which uses data for only three of the eight states (*op. cit.,* p. 31). Rees (p. 32) amends a $14 arithmetic error in Douglas's 1910 estimate, and we reduce our 1910 figure by $14. (Rees is $6 below Douglas in most years and is $20 below in 1910.)

[1] Kuznets, *op. cit.,* p. 641.

[2] Douglas, *op. cit.,* pp. 137, 177. The 1910 *Census of Population* indicates "laborers, building and specified" ran to about 25 percent of specified trades, and the 1930 Census, to about 31 percent. We use a 3 to 1 ratio.

[3] Indices were based on data from Douglas, *op. cit.,* pp. 130, 246.

[4] 1900 Census, vol. VII, *Manufactures,* part I, p. 52.

building and hand trades as reported to the Immigration Commission.[5] For a 313-day full-time year, they lead to an average of $691, as compared to our preliminary $721. Since these differences are minor, we use our preliminary series, as it was computed by a uniform procedure, which should yield maximum year-to-year comparability.

TRANSPORT, UTILITIES

The group average, as those for utilities and for communications, is a weighted average of earnings in individual industry sectors. The weights used were the employment estimates derived above. The average earnings were in general the NID 1929 figure extrapolated to 1919 by Kuznets's series, and to 1900 by Douglas's series.[1] There were three partial exceptions to this primary procedure.

1. For gas and electricity, we make alternative estimates of the 1900 to 1904 trend because Douglas's figures, based on Wisconsin reports, show an unreasonable trend.[2]

2. For telephone and telegraph, we extrapolate the 1902 estimate to 1900 by the trend for street-railway earnings, the two showing similar trends in immediately subsequent years.[3]

3. For water transport, we take the 1900 to 1918 trend of average weekly earnings of seamen, adjusting to the trend for annual earnings by the ratios of weekly to annual series for earnings on steam railroads.[4]

TRADE

Existing data for earnings in trade are scanty. Douglas omitted the group entirely; King refers to "a study of 166 average wage records, some more or less fragmentary" for all of trade and service; while Knauth used the general average for all persons in other industries earning under $2,000.[1]

[5] *Reports of the Immigration Commission* (1911), part 23, vol. I, p. 222. The rates given here for individual nativity groups were weighted by the number of each in this occupation as shown by the 1910 Census, *Population,* vol. IV, p. 312.

[1] Kuznets, *op. cit.,* pp. 663–676. Douglas, *op. cit.,* pp. 330–334.

[2] Census of Industry figures show a rise for average earnings in gas from 1899 to 1904, in light and power from 1902 to 1907. The Douglas estimates for 1900 to 1904 decline. As a result, while the average for this group is within $8 of the factory-earnings average in 1904 and 1905, his figure is $140 greater in 1900. We rely instead on the street-railway trend, an industry using similar urban personnel.

[3] Douglas, *op. cit.,* p. 334.

[4] *Ibid.,* pp. 168, 173, 325.

[1] W. I. King *et al., Income in the United States: Its Amount and Distribution* (1922), vol. II, pp. 223, 285.

The only two series are Kuznets's estimates for 1919ff. and a recent study by Harold Barger giving hourly rates for decennial dates 1899ff., based on a survey of state reports.[2] The latter rates are so well above earnings in other industry groups in 1899 and 1909 as to be questionable in the light of relationships in later years when we have sounder data.

Direct estimates for trade were therefore made, using as basic sources a variety of direct studies of earnings made in this period. In broad outline, the procedure detailed below was as follows. Benchmark estimates were made for 1900 using the 1901 Cost of Living Survey (of 24,000 families), an 1895–1896 study by the Commissioner of Labor on earnings in the various industries of 30 states, and the 1899 Census of Manufactures.[3] Benchmark estimates for 1909 and 1919 were developed from censuses of manufactures, laundries, and the telephone industry, from a massive 1909 Bureau of Labor study of women's earnings, and from a 1921 study by the National Bureau of Economic Research and the Census Bureau. Interpolations were then made between these benchmark averages.

1901.   The basic estimate for earnings in 1901 was derived as the weighted sum of separate estimates for males and for females. From the 1901 Cost of Living Survey we can derive an average of $625 for the earnings of male heads of families engaged in trade.[4] This figure, however, cannot be used directly. While the survey was comprehensive, it was not designed as a sample of all male employees but of wage earners who headed more or less normal families. Single men and heads of broken families were excluded, and while "some" nonwhite families were included there are no data to indicate that an adequate number were. Moreover, even within the family head group, a bias is apparent when we note that more than a third of the families covered paid union dues—a percentage that was certain to be much higher than the average even for urban wage earners.[5]

However, the relationships among the several industry averages may be utilized for our purpose if we apply them to reliable direct estimates of earnings. Average earnings for each of the several industry groups reported in the 1899 Census of Manufactures were therefore computed.[6] These were charted against those to be derived from the Cost of Living Survey. (Separate allowance was made for the Commissioner's survey having an

[2] Harold Barger, *Distribution's Place in the American Economy since 1869* (1955), p. 109.

[3] *18th Annual Report of the Commissioner of Labor* (1904) reports the earnings of male heads of families by occupation and industry for 1901. Earnings data were secured for 2,254 trade employees in 32 states (p. 263).

[4] *Ibid.*, p. 285.

[5] *Ibid.*, p. 507.

[6] Census data for males 16 and over were used, as reported in the 1900 *Census of Manufactures*, vol. VII, part 1, pp. 22ff.

excessive number of skilled workers in the printing and in the clay and glass group.)[7]

The relationship thus shown was sufficiently clear and strong to serve as a basis for converting the 1901 survey average for (1) trade employees who were heads of families into one for (2) all male employees in trade. However, this could not be done directly because the 1901 survey figures for all trade would reflect that survey's underrepresentation of the percentage of salesmen to the total.[8] (Presumably this occurred because the survey was concentrated in cities, where the use of cashboys, clerks, etc., was much more common than in the typical country store where the salesman handled all other chores.) Averages were therefore computed from the survey data for salesmen ($692) and for other employees ($592)—these then being reweighted by the 1910 Census proportions to give an average of $660 for all male employees in trade. Taking this adjusted survey figure for male heads of families in trade, we can utilize the relationship shown in the chart to arrive at an estimate of $530 for all male employees in trade.

The validity of this figure was approximately checked as follows. Occupational wage rates in 1895–1896 are available for males employed by 89 establishments in states that accounted for 90 percent of the employment of salesmen and saleswomen in 1900.[9] These reports were weighted together, giving an average of $10.78 per week or $539 for a 50-week year— or within 1 percent of the above estimate. Assuming some rise in wage rates for 1895–1896 to 1899, the two figures are still gratifyingly similar.

[7] The 1901 *Cost of Living Survey* (p. 273) shows 31 percent of the stone, clay and glass employees sample as stonecutters, instead of 10 percent as shown by the 1910 Census, vol. IV, table VI. Adjustment here reduces the $685 average to $643. The report also shows 491 employees in paper and printing, with virtually all of these in printing, and 168 of these as compositors. The 1910 Census, however, shows not 34 percent of printing employees as compositors but 21 percent. However, the 1901 average of $758 is only reduced to $749 even if all compositors were excluded. Finally, review of the occupations reported in the survey for the liquor industry shows that the data relate primarily to breweries, and therefore census data for malt liquors were used for comparison.

[8] The 1901 survey (p. 280) shows 36 percent of the trade employees as salesmen, agents, and clerks as compared to the 75 percent indicated in the 1910 Census.

[9] *11th Annual Report of the Commissioner of Labor, 1895–96, Work and Wages of Men, Women and Children* (1897), pp. 485–507. Data were given for 119 establishments, but for consistency and convenience only the 89 dry goods and general merchandise reports were used. All male earnings rates were used, weighted by the occupational distribution reported for each individual establishment. The states covered included 75 percent of all salespersons in 1900 (1900 Census, *Occupations*, table 33). The weighted average for New York, Pennsylvania, Massachusetts, and Connecticut was assumed to apply to New Jersey, and that for Michigan, Illinois, Iowa, and Missouri to apply to Ohio and Wisconsin—thus covering 90 percent of all salespersons.

The average earnings of females in trade were estimated as a percentage of the earnings of males. The percentage was based on the extensive 1895–1896 survey noted above, with occupational earnings data for females weighted just as those for males have been and the ratio of the final average for females to that for males computed. The ratio—70.5 percent—is reasonable in the light of other data, such as state Bureau of Labor Reports for 1900, and those of King for 1920.[10]

The resultant estimate—$373—looks reasonable in the light of wages paid to substantial groups in the labor market that would have been competitive with the trade employee group. Thus, in 1899, all female clerks in manufacturing averaged $414, clerks in millinery stores $340,[11] and female salesmen in trade $402.[12] The average for females was then weighted with that for males to give an average of $510 for all trade employees in 1901.[13]

1909.   A benchmark estimate for this year was made by using the 1901 to 1909 20 percent rise in earnings of clerks in manufacturing. In addition to the general labor interrelationship between clerical employees in the two groups, the fact that over the 1901–1919 period the trade employee figure rose 110 percent while that for manufacturing clerks rose by much the same percentage—92 percent—appeared to warrant this procedure.[14]

[10] Earnings data for dry-goods clerks in eight states, derived from annual reports of the individual states, appear in the *Ninth Biennial Report of the Bureau of Labor Statistics of the State of California for 1899–1900* (1900). W. I. King, *Employment, Hours and Earnings in Prosperity and Depression, United States, 1920–1922* (1923), p. 111. King's data imply a ratio of 64 percent in data he developed for 96 individual employee records.

[11] 1900 *Census of Manufactures*, pp. 51, 59, reports data on the number and payroll for female clerks, officials, and other salaried employees. When separately designated in subsequent censuses, the female clerks group may be seen to have constituted virtually all of this broader category.

[12] The ratio of female to total salespersons and clerks in 1910 (28.6) was 9 points above that for all employees except dealers (19.8). 1910 Census, vol. IV, pp. 420, 422. The cross classification of industry by occupation is, of course, not available for 1900. It was therefore assumed that the 1900 ratio for salespersons, 19.8 (1900 Census, *Occupations*, p. 7) when stepped down 9 points could be used for weighting.

[13] Salesmen, as reported in the 1901 survey, averaged $692. Utilizing the chart scatter, this figure implies an average for all salesmen, including those not heads of families, of $570. Applying the ratio of female to male earnings of 70.5 used above, we arrive at an average of $402. Since other occupations than salesmen were covered in deriving this ratio, it is undoubtedly somewhat high; given the distribution of weights among the occupations, however, it is probably not very much too high.

[14] Data for all female salaried personnel are available for 1899 (1900 Census, vol. VII, part 1, p. 59) and for 1904 (1904 *Census of Manufactures*, part 1, p. 69). We assume that this average relates to female clerks. The 1899 to 1909 gain for this group, $61, is virtually identical with the $58 gain over the same period for all salaried personnel. Hence we use the all salaried average percent gain from 1901 to 1919 as estimated by Douglas (*op. cit.*, p. 361).

1. As one check on this benchmark figure, we compute the earnings of laundry clerks. This group earned within 6 percent of the trade average for 1919, and their 1909 average proves to be within 2 percent of our trade estimate for 1909.[15]

2. Another indication of the reasonableness of the 1909 benchmark is the fact that telephone clerks, a related occupational group, averaged $620 in 1907—compared to $580 for trade employees in that year and $609 in 1909.[16]

3. For 1907 to 1909, a massive study of woman and child wage earners made by the U.S. Bureau of Labor provides data on earnings of female trade employees in five cities.[17] Although these cities are not in fact unrepresentative of the United States average—judging from data on manufacturing and laundry earnings—the average weekly earnings for trade employees are puzzlingly low, ranging from $6.11 in New York to $7.25 in Chicago.[18] Analysis of the data indicates that one factor was the great predominance of young workers in the sample; for example, 70 percent of those reported as working in stores in New York were 20 years of age or less, as compared with the 37 percent indicated by census data for 1910.[19] Reweighting by the census age distribution, assuming a 50-week year, and averaging the five city reports gives an average of $383 for females in trade for 1907 to 1909.[20] This figure is still likely to be low because the proportion of ancillary workers—cash girls, messengers, etc.—in large cities was higher than that for the country; hence, the average would be lower. Excluding the age group under 20 gives a figure of $423. Therefore, this survey's results are probably within 10 percent of the present estimate of $453 for females in 1909. There is additional contemporary material arguing for a $300 to $400 range over the 1909–1913 period.[21]

[15] 1914 *Census of Manufactures,* vol. II, p. 847; 1920 *Census of Manufactures,* vol. X, p. 1027. Whether salesmen were included with clerks is unclear (1920 Census, vol. VIII, p. 524, instruction no. 71 versus no. 72).

[16] For 1902 likewise, the telephone average is within 3 percent of the trade estimate. Special Reports of the Census, *Telephone and Telegraphs, 1902* (1906), pp. 84–85; *Telephones: 1907,* p. 111. The data used relate only to commercial systems. Excluding New York City, of major importance in the early period, brings the averages even closer together.

[17] U.S. Bureau of Labor, *Report on Condition of Woman and Child Wage Earners in the United States* (1910), vol. V, chaps. 4–9 and appendix table II.

[18] Data from *Ibid.,* appendix table II are combined with the weights there given, with medians for the open-end group based on data in table I.

[19] Study data from *Ibid.* Census data for 1910 from vol. IV, table VIII.

[20] Aside from Chicago, at $404, the other cities run from $365 to $374. The New York weekly figure of $7.29 is well above the direct average of $6.07 but still below that of $7.93 reported by 12 department stores. U.S. Bureau of Labor, *op. cit.,* p. 146.

[21] Elizabeth B. Butler, *Women and the Trades, Pittsburgh, 1907–1908* (1911), pp.

1920. For this year use was made of the direct reports on earnings collected in a nationwide survey for the President's Conference on Unemployment.[22] Utilizing the hours and hourly earnings data reported in this survey, we get an average of $1,270 for 1920. (A figure of $1,230 is secured by applying, in 1920, the 1929 ratio of earnings in trade to earnings in food and drink manufacturing.[23] Wages for these two industry groups moved similarly over other periods, while 1929 was both the first year we had a national census of trade and was at the end of the decade of postwar prosperity that began in 1919.)

The 1920 figure of $1,270, moreover, is very similar to the Ohio trade earnings figure of $1,212 (as the two are similar in the 1929 Census).[24] The present estimate for 1920 implies a substantial rise from the 1920 to the 1929 level reported in the latter census—a rise in line with the 1920 to 1929 gains indicated for other industries with relatively low average wages in 1920, such as telephones and local transport. It is also in line with the general trend over these decades for lower-wage occupations to gain proportionately more than higher ones.[25]

Other Years. For interpolation, the earnings of salaried employees in manufacturing were used.[26] As indicated earlier, the trend for all salaried

---

304, 338, gives data which, when weighted, average $5.08 per week or $290 a year. Illinois Bureau of Labor Statistics, *Biennial Report, 1908* (1910), p. 413 reports $6.98 in Chicago and $5.68 downstate. Thomas H. Russell, *The Girls Fight for a Living* (1913), reports employer testimony before an Illinois legislative committee with wages in Hellmans, Montgomery Ward, Sears, Siegel Carson, Marshall Field, and Carson Pirie—to pick only the leaders—averaging $9.35. The U.S. *Commission on Industrial Relations* (1916) reports an inquiry in 17 New York stores leading to an average of $8.70 for all employees. L. M. Bosworthy, "The Living Wage of Women Workers," *Annals of the American Academy of Political and Social Science* (May, 1911), supplement, p. 16, reports interviews with 450 women workers in Boston, with sales personnel averaging $357, factory $382, clerical $500. Given interstate and intertemporal differences, a $300 to $400 range in 1909 might be supported by these surveys.

[22] Willford I. King, *Employment, Hours and Earnings in Prosperity and Depression, United States, 1920–1922* (1923), pp. 113, 187. The possibility of an overrepresentation of large stores, characteristic of certain small-scale surveys, is unimportant since King's averages for both large and small stores are virtually identical.

[23] The ratio of full-time earnings in 1929 was computed from data in the 1954 edition of the *National Income Supplement,* table 27. The 1920 earnings figure for food and drink manufacturing is derived from data in Kuznets, *op. cit.,* pp. 579, 598.

[24] The Ohio figure appears in F. C. Croxton, "Average Wage and Salary Payments in Wholesale and Retail Trade in Ohio, 1916 to 1932," *Monthly Labor Review* (May, 1934), p. 1039.

[25] On the trend in rates over the first half of the century, see the author's "Wage Structures," *Review of Economics and Statistics* (November, 1947) and later work by Mansfield, Keat, etc.

[26] Census estimates as interpolated by Douglas (*op. cit.,* p. 361) were used for

employees appears to parallel that for female clerks from 1899 to 1909 and the series was therefore used for interpolation between the 1899, 1909, and 1919 figures.[27]

Prior Estimates

Neither Douglas nor King made estimates for this group; the only prior estimates of consequence are those of Kuznets for 1919ff. and Harold Barger for 1899, 1909, and 1919. The Kuznets figures were of course of real value as guides but were not finally used for two reasons. First, their 1919 to 1929 gain is a mere 10 percent over a decade in which the census data for laundries, telephones, and telegraphs show rises of between 40 and 50 percent. Moreover, such high-wage industries as manufacturing, construction, rail transport, and electric power all show much larger percentage gains than that implied for trade. Secondly, Kuznets makes no direct estimates of average earnings in trade, being concerned only with employment and wages. He is therefore in a position to use completely independent estimates for employment (based on an extrapolation to 1919 by employment trends in four states) and wages (based on the application to sales totals of wage-sales ratios that were derived from a variety of operating cost studies), even though the implicit ratio of one to the other—average earnings—may not be wholly reasonable.[28] It seemed preferable, therefore, to work to directly estimated earnings figures for benchmark dates.

The 1926 trial Census of Business was likewise rejected, primarily because it leads to an unreasonable 1926 to 1929 decline in earnings, and also because of certain internal inconsistencies in its figures.[29]

1900 to 1919, and as interpolated by Kuznets (*op. cit.*, pp. 723–727) for 1920 to 1929.

[27] The 1920 average computed above was extrapolated to 1919 by the earnings of salaried personnel in manufacturing. A similar figure would have resulted from using average trade earnings for Ohio.

[28] The ratio of wages and salaries to sales is 10.4 in 1929, 10.7 in 1939, and 10.4 in 1948, according to the Censuses of Distribution for those years. In contrast to such stability, Kuznets's data imply a rise from 5.6 percent in 1920 to 6.4 percent in 1921. Behind these figures is an implied estimate that trade wages fell by 14.6 percent, whereas King's direct reports on wages indicate a fall of only 3 percent from 1920 to 1921, *Employment . . . 1920–1922* (p. 104).

[29] Taking the 12 cities surveyed in 1926 and the corresponding 12 in 1929, we find an implied decline in earnings from 1926 to 1929—a decline without particular warrant. Chamber of Commerce of the United States, *Retail and Wholesale Trade of Eleven Cities* (May, 1928), p. 26; 1930 *Census of Distribution*, vol. I, part 2. It may be noted that in 1926 the implied ratio of payrolls to sales in retail trade was 12.9 percent (*Retail and Wholesale Trade of Eleven Cities*, p. 28) or well above the 10.4 and 10.7 reported in 1929, 1939, and 1948 (1948 *Census of Business, Retail Trade*, vol. I, p. 0.04). Moreover, the average earnings figures in all

Barger's extensive study of distribution provides alternative estimates for 1899 and 1909, derived from "an extensive survey of state reports." [30] They were not used because they are as high (1899) or higher (1909) than manufacturing earnings, a relationship that is improbable given the sex distribution of employment in both categories and the direct earnings reports for the period. The state reports have serious problems of representativeness, and the fact that Barger's 1899 figure for all employees in trade is above that reported for male salesmen in the 1901 survey, even with its upward bias, makes their use unsuitable for present purposes.[31]

FINANCE, INSURANCE, AND REAL ESTATE

Prior to 1919, when Kuznets's data begin, we have few guidelines for this group, neither King nor Douglas attempting any explicit estimate. We here compute earnings as the weighted sum of earnings in the two major occupational categories present in the industry—agents and clerical personnel.

Agents. In connection with the employment series, estimates were made from the Population Census data of the number of agents who were employees. Average earnings in 1900, 1905, 1910, and 1920 were available for Metropolitan Life Insurance company agents, the largest company in the field.[1] Interpolation for 1901 to 1904 and 1910 to 1920 was by the movement of earnings in trade.[2] For 1906 to 1909, a linear trend was used

---

retail trade to be derived for each city in 1926 are well above those for department stores alone, whereas the 1929 data show department store earnings to be at about the average for all stores.

[30] Harold Barger, *op. cit.,* p. 109. Barger derives a 1919 figure from King in much the same fashion as the present estimates. He makes no interdecade estimates.

[31] Barger's 1899 average is much the same as that reported for salesmen in the Michigan state report of the time—but female store clerks in Michigan earned half that amount. Michigan, *Eighteenth Annual Report of the Bureau of Labor* (1901), pp. 212, 222. If we use data shown in this source, which relate to 238 male and 25 female store clerks, we derive an average well above that secured by using census weights, which report a higher proportion of female employment in the industry. The New Jersey Bureau *Report for 1901* (1902), pp. 254–258, reports lower figures for males alone than Barger's United States male plus female average.

[1] 1900: Louis Dublin, *A Family of Thirty Million* (1943), p. 271. 1905: Armstrong investigation data, as summarized in Louis Brandeis, *Wage Earners' Life Insurance* (1906), p. 14. 1910 and 1920: Marquis James, *The Metropolitan Life* (1947), pp. 178, 345.

[2] Earnings of life insurance agents and all trade employees in 1900 were virtually identical, but the growth for agents, particularly after the Armstrong investigation, appears to have been much greater.

to reflect the readjustment of agents' earnings after the Armstrong investigation, leading to a much greater 1905 to 1910 growth than appears in trade earnings.

Clerical Employees.   Unpublished figures on earnings of salaried employees in one of the five largest insurance companies were used for the years 1909 and 1914 to 1919. These were extrapolated to 1900 and interpolated for 1910 to 1913 by the trend in earnings of salaried personnel in manufacturing.[3]

The two series thus estimated were combined with employment weights derived from the 1910 Census, giving a trend series for 1900 to 1919.[4] This series was used to extrapolate the 1919 to 1929 figures derived from Kuznets's estimates.[5]

Among the few independent bits of evidence for the early period is an average for insurance solicitors in the 1901 Cost of Living Survey, which comes to nearly $900. Another estimate is the contemporary report by no less a person than Lucien V. La Taste, President of the Traveling Men's Protective Association, who asserted that men who travel over "a very limited territory, say 100 to 150 miles from home for local houses in lines that do not pay a large profit" could earn as a minimum "about $900 per year plus their expenses." [6] As against the 15 or so employees in the BLS sample, the comprehensiveness of the Metropolitan Life figure is clearly to be preferred. As against the figure paid to traveling salesmen in the heady days of Jim Brady, a figure as low as $500 for stay-at-home drudges may not be unrealistically low—especially in the light of the substantial gains after 1905. The data available for commissions and expense from the Spectator Yearbooks are helpful guides, but the changing number of policies per agent and changing rates of commission make this a less secure guide for interpolation than earnings of related groups in the labor market.[7]

[3] Census of Manufactures data interpolated by Paul Douglas, *op. cit.*, p. 361.

[4] 1910 Census, *Occupations*, pp. 419–420, groups all employees in finance, insurance, and real estate. Most could be classified as agents, clerks, or persons whose earnings would have a trend similar to that for clerks. Few service personnel were employed at this period.

[5] Kuznets, *op. cit.*, pp. 733, 737. The movement of Kuznets's series is largely determined by a series on average earnings of employees in 61 life insurance companies.

[6] U.S. Industrial Commission, *Hearings*, vol. XIII, p. 30.

[7] Commissions per policy show little gain from 1908 to 1918 though salaries are here estimated to have gained sizably. Clerical earnings are estimated to have changed little over the same period, but clerical costs per policy fell markedly in two large companies: Eugene Benge, *Cutting Clerical Costs* (1931). The implied productivity gain is not at all unreasonable.

PERSONAL SERVICES

The first step in developing this series was to make a benchmark earnings estimate for 1900. This was done by estimating averages for key occupations and industries, then weighting them together by the number of employees in each. (Consistent weights are available from the special class-of-worker tabulations from the 1910 Census.)[1]

1. For employees in cleaning and dyeing and in dressmaking, earnings data were available from the Census of Manufactures.[2]

2. For male employees in the main personal-service occupations—barbers, bartenders, janitors, cooks, waiters, etc.—earnings were reported by the 1901 Cost of Living Survey.[3]

3. For female housekeepers, charwomen, laundresses not in factories, housekeepers, and midwives and untrained nurses as a group, the earnings average was estimated at a third above that for domestic servants. This margin is that indicated in data for both 1939 and 1949, as well as in figures for four major cities surveyed in 1894.[4]

4. For laundry operatives the 1909 Census of Manufactures average[5] for that group was extrapolated to 1900 by the changes in trade earnings over the same period, giving a figure of $358, or very close to the $418 estimated for cleaning and dyeing.

The four earnings figures thus estimated range from a low of $210 for female laundresses and housekeepers through $280 for dressmakers, $418

[1] Lithoprinted sheets issued by the Census Bureau in 1948.

[2] 1900 Census, *Manufactures,* vol. VII, part I, p. 52. For dressmaking the weighted average wage of females in (1) clothing, men's custom work and repair; and (2) clothing and women's dressmaking was computed.

[3] U.S. Commissioner of Labor, 18th Annual Report, *Cost of Living and Retail Prices of Food* (1903), pp. 264–283. These data for male heads of families were converted to estimates for all males by the regression procedure outlined above for the trade group. In addition, the survey data on earnings of janitors were used for representing earnings of "cleaners"; of coachmen, for "other servants"; of laborers in domestic service, for "porters." (The occupations in quotation marks are those specified in the 1910 Census.) For porters the rate reported for laborers was used directly, it being clear that the wage scale for male heads in the 1901 survey sample did not differ from that for all males in this low-paid occupation. (The average for all manufacturing laborers ran to $1.48 a day, according to the Abbott data, or $450 a year, so that the reported average of $374 for laborers in domestic service was already reasonably below that for manufacturing.)

[4] The 1939 and 1949 figures for full-time "service workers n.e.c." appear in Herman Miller, *Income of the American People* (1955), tables C-2, C-4. The 1894 data are from the Seventh Special Report of the Commissioner of Labor, *The Slums of Baltimore, Chicago, New York and Philadelphia* (1894), table XVIII.

[5] 1910 Census, *Manufactures,* vol. X, pp. 898–899.

for cleaning and dyeing, to $434 for male barbers, bartenders, etc. The weighted average for the entire group—$329—reflects the substantial number of females in this industry and their low wage rates.

Since neither King, Douglas, nor any other recent investigator has estimated earnings in service for these early years, it is particularly necessary to try conclusions in judging the reliability of this 1900 benchmark figure. One indication can be found by comparing this figure with the corresponding earnings figure for cleaning and dyeing as reported by the 1900 Census of Manufactures. The ratio of one to the other is 77 percent—or virtually identical with the ratio of 75 percent for 1919 when we have quite independent survey data for personal service and census data for cleaning and dyeing.[6]

For 1920 and 1921 the results of a Census–National Bureau of Economic Research nationwide survey for the President's Conference on Unemployment were used, giving averages of $940 and $938.[7] Although the survey secured direct reports from employers, the responses related only to 146 reporting units with some 20,000 employees.[8] As an indication of the validity of these findings, however, we may note that they indicate a ratio of personal service to trade earnings of 74 percent—or virtually identical with the 71, 67, and 73 percent to be deduced from the National Income Division figures for the years in which we have had a Census of Business, namely, 1929, 1939, and 1948.[9]

The personal-service earnings figures thus derived for 1900 and 1920, as well as that for 1929 shown in the National Income Division estimates, are virtually identical with the average earnings in laundries at these dates, even after making allowance for the inclusion of the laundry group figure in the broader total. Therefore, the Census of Manufactures data on laundry earnings in 1909, 1914, 1919, 1925, and 1927 were used to extrapolate the 1919 service earnings figure to these additional years.[10]

---

[6] The ratio of 77 percent was computed after excluding from the personal service average the average for cleaning and dyeing included within it. Since the latter group constitutes a mere 1 percent of employment in personal service in 1900, however, the adjustment is, in fact, trivial.

[7] W. I. King, *Employment, Hours and Earnings in Prosperity and Depression* (1923), pp. 113, 187.

[8] *Ibid*, p. 20.

[9] 1954 ed., *National Income Supplement*, tables 15 and 25, combining data for hotels and personal service. The National Income Division adjusted census data in both trade and service for undercoverage, using different adjustment factors for each. This fact helps account for some of the variations among these percentages.

[10] 1909, *Manufactures*, vol. X, pp. 898–899; 1914, *Manufactures*, vol. II, pp. 859–860; 1920, *Manufactures*, vol. X, p. 1048; 1925, *Manufactures*, pp. 1266–1267; 1927, *Manufactures*, p. 1299.

We are now in a position to compute the ratio of personal service earnings to those for another segment for which yearly estimates have already been made and which draws upon a labor market similar in certain key respects to that of service, namely, trade. The ratios were as follows:

1900	65
1909	69
1914	67
1921	73
1925	69
1927	70

The relationship appears to be quite reasonable and steady, even to the extent of indicating a relatively greater rise for the lower-paid industry than the higher during World War I and after—a phenomenon apparent in other series based on very solid annual or biennial reports. These ratios were, therefore, interpolated and applied to the trade series to give the estimates of earnings in personal service.

It would have been desirable to utilize the Kuznets series for 1920 to 1929, based as it is on reports from several states. One reason this was not done is the lack of consiliency between the source data used by Kuznets and the national census data. Thus Kuznets used Ohio data for extrapolating laundry earnings, but the Ohio figures rise by 70 percent from 1920 to 1925 whereas the census average increases by only 35 percent.[11] On the other hand, the earnings in Ohio barbershops—used by Kuznets to estimate the trends for all personal service except laundries and hotels—rose by 20 percent over the same period, and Ohio hotel earnings rose by only 13 percent.[12] While the reason for the sharply different trends in Ohio and the United States are not clear, it appears that a sampling bias may have been at work since the coverage in the annual reporting sample of firms in Ohio increased very sharply over the period. (If the initial group covered were the larger firms in the industry—as is true of many of the early state surveys—the expanded coverage would have drawn disproportionately heavily from the smaller, less well-paying firms and thus tended to understate the rise of earnings over the period.) A second reason for not using the series even for interpolation lies in the unusual year-to-year trends— with a decline in earnings reported from 1925 to the prosperity year of 1926, and from 1928 to 1929, as well as a rise from 1920 to the depression year of 1921. A priori these changes are unreasonable and they seem to be associated with the marked changes in the number of reporting firms between these pairs of years. In the absence of any special warrant, therefore, these data could not be used.

[11] Kuznets, *op. cit.,* p. 781. U.S. Bureau of Labor Statistics Bulletin 613, p. 171.
[12] *Ibid.*

LOCAL GOVERNMENT

An initial benchmark for local government earnings in 1905 was established as follows:

1. For policemen and firemen—the largest single group—earnings data are available for cities of 30,000 and over in population in 1905.[1] These averages for the large cities were adjusted to apply to all cities on the basis of the ratio of teachers' earnings in larger and smaller cities.[2] The resultant figure, of $860 for all firemen and policemen, is remarkably similar to that of $912 to be derived from the Cost of Living Survey made in selected cities in 1901.

2. For the next largest occupation group, city labor, the 1905 Census data for employees of street-cleaning departments were used, after an adjustment similar to that noted above to make the figures apply to the United States as a whole.

3. For city officials and other city employees, the average for policemen and firemen was used.

4. For state and county officials, the Office of Education data on average earnings of teachers were used since the two were very similar in level during stable periods in the 1920s.[3]

5. In addition to the employees shown by the Population Census under the heading of government service, there was a substantial number of government employees in hospital service. An estimate of the number employed in state mental hospitals and institutions for the feebleminded was

[1] Bureau of the Census, *Statistics of Cities Having a Population of over 30,000: 1905*, tables 5, 35, 39, and 40. Census reports give payroll totals for other years but, except in 1907, not for the number of employees as well. The 1907 report was not used because special policemen without pay were apparently included in the employment count for that year. The data taken from the 1905 report relate to regular employees of the police department, and to regulars and "other employees" of the fire department.

[2] From unpublished summaries of published Office of Education reports, kindly provided by that office, averages were computed for teachers and supervisors in cities of 4,000 population and over. From the above-mentioned census report, an average was computed for teachers and supervisors in cities of 30,000 and over. The implicit average for the smaller cities was used to compute a ratio of smaller to larger city earnings. This ratio was then applied to the census data for firemen and policemen. Using Census of Population total counts (1910 Census, vol. IV, p. 93), weights were derived for earnings in each size of city group and weighted averages were then computed for all policemen and firemen.

[3] This generalization does not apply during the postwar years 1921 to 1923, when teachers' salaries were belatedly catching up, nor during the later 1930s when teachers' salaries lost ground. It does seem to describe a customary relationship in stable times during the predepression decades.

prepared as part of the employment estimates.[4] The average salary for this group was assumed the same as that for all hospitals, computed above as part of the estimates for service.

These five earnings averages were then weighted together by the occupation data for local government in 1910 as shown by the Census of Population.

For 1919 to 1929, we have the careful etimates of Kuznets based on a review of available reports for individual cities and states.[5] The 1905–1919–1929 data show a close similarity of trend to that for the earnings of urban teachers, suggesting that the latter could be used for interpolation.[6] It is, however, clear that in the critical overlap period of 1919 to 1921 the rate of change in teachers' salaries was not proportionate to that for other state employees, salaries of the former lagging behind increases previously granted to other local employees and, in addition, reflecting the impact of heavy postwar enrollments. The procedure used, therefore, was to extrapolate the 1919 estimate to 1916 by the movement of earnings for policemen and firemen in selected cities as estimated by W. I. King.[7] The resultant estimate of local government earnings in 1916 was 91 percent of the average salary of urban teachers, a ratio almost identical with the 88 percent implicit in the 1905 figures estimated earlier. By extrapolating and interpolating these percentages and those for 1905 and 1919 and applying them to the urban teachers' salary estimates, the final series for local government was derived.

PUBLIC EDUCATION

For public education the long-established set of surveys by the Office of Education provides the basic raw materials. These have been developed into consistent estimates by Paul Douglas and Simon Kuznets and their series were used to extrapolate the 1929 NID benchmark.[1]

[4] Essentially the number was estimated by computing the number of hospital nurses per bed in nonprofit institutions (from the 1910 *Census of Benevolent Institutions*). This ratio times the number of patients in state mental hospitals gave an employment index which was used to extrapolate total employment in 1923 in "other government" mental hospitals to 1910.

[5] Kuznets, *op. cit.,* pp. 812, 814, 834–835.

[6] Earnings of teachers are from unpublished summaries of Office of Education reports.

[7] W. I. King, *The National Income and Its Purchasing Power* (1930), p. 365. King's procedure is outlined in *Income in the United States* (1922), pp. 212–213. For extrapolation the average of the 1919 ratio—63.4 percent—and the 1920 ratio—63.3 percent—was used.

[1] Douglas, *op. cit.,* p. 382 was used for 1900 to 1918, and Kuznets, *op. cit.,* pp. 812, 814, for 1919 to 1928.

FEDERAL GOVERNMENT

Separate earnings series were derived for postal and for nonpostal civilian employees of the Federal government, the two series being weighted together and then used to interpolate between benchmark estimates for 1899 and 1929. The derivation of the component movement series is discussed below. The 1899 benchmark was derived by sampling the complete list of Federal employees and their salaries as recorded in the United States Official Register for 1899. The separate benchmarks for postal and nonpostal employees are described below. For 1929, the NID data were used.[1]

POSTAL SERVICE

A benchmark estimate for 1899 earnings in postal service was computed by sampling from the Official Register for that year, with interpolation between that figure and the implicit NID 1929 average by a series for all postal employees. The details of this procedure were as follows:

1899 Benchmark

The *Official Register* of United States government employees for this year listed in alphabetical order the names and salary rates of all employees in the postal service, barring certain temporary employees. Separate listings for each major occupation category—postmasters, city carriers, rural carriers, railway mail clerks, post office clerks—are given in the *Register*. Averages for each group were computed from this listing. In sampling we took two successive samples from the alphabetical list provided by the register, the names being quite clearly randomly distributed within each occupation category. The double-sampling procedure was adopted to make certain that the first sample provided a stable average. Further samples were unnecessary because the second averages in all cases were within a

---

[1] The 1954 *National Income Supplement,* p. 200, reports an average of $1,933 for Federal general government—civilian except work relief, and $1,903 for Federal government enterprises. Unpublished NID data indicate the latter group comprised only the Post Office at this date. The two averages were therefore weighted together by the amount of employment in each. It differs slightly from the implicit BLS average in *Historical Statistics of the United States,* p. 295. The component movement series were weighted together by Fabricant's estimates of full-time employment in each category. (Solomon Fabricant, *The Trend of Government Activity in the United States since 1900* (1952), pp. 176, 182). Fabricant's estimates differ from those developed in the present study but the differences are not significant for their use as weights here.

few dollars of the first.[1] Since the *Register* does not distinguish between class of office, we take the Postmaster General's count of 71,000 fourth-class post offices and 4,000 first- to third-class offices as a basis for assuming that the lowest 71/75ths of the distribution derived from the *Register* were fourth-class postmasters. An average of $149 for fourth-class offices and $1,662 for first- through third-class was thus derived. (As a check on the direct average for the small latter group, we compute a confirmatory $1,612 by an indirect procedure from total expenditure data.)[2] A similar problem of part-time workers applies to post office clerks. From the distribution we derive for the clerks we determined a $600 minimum for full-time clerks and computed an average of $161 for part time, of $828 for full time.[3] The averages estimated in similar fashion for regular employees ranged narrowly from $1,031 for railway mail clerks, $904 for city carriers, to $828 for clerks, while the $400 for rural carriers indicates it is an average for part-time employees. These were weighted by the number of full-time equivalent employees in each occupation to give a $955 figure for all full-time employees in fiscal 1899. An approximate check for some occupations, made possible by the use of the annual report of the Postmaster General, gives closely similar findings.[4]

[1] *Official Register of the United States* (1899), vol. II. The six names at the head of each column (two per page for most occupations) were taken from every tenth page, beginning with p. 5, to give an estimate for postmasters. For other occupations the top six names were taken from every fifth or tenth page, depending on the size of the group. The second sample was taken in the same fashion, beginning at p. 7 for postmasters, with a similar lag for other occupations. The coverage of the *Register* is quite adequate. For example, it had 407 pages listing postmasters with an average of 185 names on a number of sampled pages—implying a 75,295 total. This compares with the 75,000 reported for 1899 in the *Report of the Postmaster General, 1905.*

[2] From the *Report of the Postmaster General* we take the compensation of all postmasters and deduct $149 times 71,000 (for fourth-class offices), to get an implicit $1,612 for first- to third-class offices.

[3] We imply that 63 percent of all clerks were part time, whereas about 90 percent of clerks were in the smaller third- and fourth-class offices. We pick a $600 minimum on three grounds:

1. Salaries for city letter carriers begin at $600, excluding the $1 temporaries.

2. Railway mail clerks' salaries likewise begin at $600, as judged from our tabulation.

3. The clerk sample showed a clear break at the $600 to $699 interval, with many in the below-$200 groups, very few in the intervals up to $600, and a marked increase in the $600 to $699 group.

[4] *Annual Reports of the Post Office Department, Fiscal Year 1899* (1899), pp. 133, 124. The distribution shown in this source gives an average of $862 for clerks with incomes $600 and greater, as compared to the $828 computed here. For all free-delivery carriers in the estimates for the next fiscal year, an average of $915 is indicated, as against the $904 shown here for city carriers.

Interpolating Series

From various official reports we summarize postal salaries for occupations accounting for virtually all postal salaries, then divide by employment in those occupations.[5] This procedure gives an average for 1899 of $967—virtually identical with our $955 benchmark figure—and very similar results for 1929. The resultant series was shifted to a calendar-year basis and used to interpolate between our 1899 and 1929 benchmark averages.

FEDERAL GOVERNMENT (NONPOSTAL)

Benchmark average for all Federal employees outside the postal service were computed for 1899 and 1919, by sampling from the complete list of employees shown in the *Official Register* for those years. The procedure was identical with that used for postal employees.[1] Interpolation from 1899 to 1919 was by the trend of salaries of government employees in the District of Columbia.[2] For 1920 to 1929 we interpolate between the 1919 figure above and Kuznets's 1929 figure.[3]

The relationship to prior estimates can be briefly summarized. (1) Douglas's series for postal employees is very similar. Differences arise largely because his series for 1900 to 1905 applies only to city letter carriers, and from 1906 on relates only to city carriers plus clerks in first-

---

[5] 1900–1905: *Preliminary Report of the Joint Committee on Business Methods of Post Office Department and Postal Service* (1908), 60th Cong., 1st Sess. Rep. 201. 1906–1910: *Report of the Postmaster General, 1915* (1916), pp. 57–58; 1911–1920: *Report of the Postmaster General, 1920* (1920), p. 134; 1921–1930: *Report of the Postmaster General, 1930* (1930), p. 89. Salaries of postmasters, and of clerks; city delivery service costs, rural delivery service costs; railway mail service. Comparison of these totals against the details of expenditures shows that these items were overwhelmingly salary items and, in turn, account for most salaries. They were divided by the sum of employment in postal occupations, as conveniently presented in Solomon Fabricant, *op. cit.,* pp. 176–177, exclusive, however, of fourth-class postmasters and third- and fourth-class clerks.

[1] Except that day rate, monthly, and hourly employees were converted to year equivalent rates.

[2] Averages, exclusive of the bonus, for District of Columbia employees appear in Mary Conyngton, "The Government's Wage Policy during the Last Quarter Century," *Monthly Labor Review* (June, 1920), p. 1327. Ratios of the estimates based on *The Official Register* data (likewise exclusive of the bonus) to the Conyngton data were computed. These ratios were interpolated and applied to Paul Douglas's estimates (*op. cit.,* p. 375) which are for the calendar year and which allow for the bonuses, thus adjusting his series for District of Columbia employees to one for all employees.

[3] The 1929 figure, based on the budget data for that year, was kindly provided from unpublished material by Elizabeth Jenks.

and second-class offices. The present series applies to all employees and allows for the higher incomes of postmasters and railway mail clerks. The present series for nonpostal employees differs from Douglas's nonpostal data because it includes not merely District of Columbia employees (as he does) but also the large, and changing, proportion of employees in the field services. (2) Kuznets's figures for nonpostal employees implicitly show an 85 percent rise from 1919 to 1929, as compared to the present 11 percent figure. The difference appears to lie in an unduly low level for the earlier years.[4] (3) King's estimates for 1900 to 1918 are similar for nonpostal employees, half as great for postal.[5] His cryptic description provides no basis for understanding, but we may surmise that his average really relates to all employees and not merely to full-time ones.

DOMESTIC SERVICE

The most difficult estimate to make for any significant industry group is unquestionably that for domestic service, for even currently we have neither reliable nor consistent figures on earnings for this group. The primary estimate developed below was therefore checked by three alternative procedures.

1. The most direct source of data appears to be a survey conducted for the Industrial Commission, in which a scattering of reports were secured from women's club members in each of 39 states.[1] George Stigler has weighted the rates for some 33 states by "the number of domestic servants of each type in each state in 1910," to arrive at a weekly average of $3.16.[2] Because of obvious biases that may afflict a survey of this character, all emphasized by Stigler, alternative estimates were made as a check.

2. The procedure we actually used in making the final estimate relied

---

[4] Elizabeth Jenks was kind enough to provide work-sheet data on the Kuznets procedures, indicating that the employment series was much the same as the present one, as was the 1929 earnings average. Apparently the low 1919 figure (and subsequent ones) arises from the method of using "a continuous total of listed executive civil service salaries" from the budget statement.

[5] Willford I. King et al., *Income in the United States, Its Amount and Distribution 1909–1919* (1922), vol. II, p. 214. Comparison of his employment and salary totals from this source (pp. 212, 213) for all government with those in his *The National Income and Its Purchasing Power* (1930), pp. 60, 138, suggests no marked change in procedure in the latter study, but the absence of detail makes this a mere guess.

[1] U.S. Industrial Commission, *Reports.* Vol. XIV (1901), p. 748. Data by occupation for the individual states appear in this report.

[2] George Stigler, *Domestic Servants in the United States, 1900–1940* (1946), pp. 12, 42–43.

on occupational wage-rate data from a special canvass made by Davis Dewey as part of the 1900 Census.[3]

The lowest occupational wage rate reported by Dewey as paid to a substantial number of females was taken as equivalent to that paid to servants in each major section of the country. For the South, the $3 average paid stemmers in tobacco (and for all employees in cotton) was used; for New England, the $4 average for bobbin hands; and for the Central (and likewise the Middle) region, the $3 average for all candy-factory employees.[4] Weighting these figures by the number of servants and laundresses in the respective regions gives a national average of $3.12 per week—within 4 cents of the figure derived from the Industrial Commission data.[5]

3. Earnings distributions for servants in four major cities—Baltimore, Chicago, New York, and Philadelphia—are available as of 1894. These data, as reported in a special survey of the slums in these cities, made by the Commissioner of Labor, indicate weekly median earnings of $3 for both New York and Philadelphia, $2.50 for Baltimore, and $5 for Chicago.[6] For each of these cities ratios were then computed of the earnings of female servants as a percentage of earnings of male laborers in the same cities (from the same source). The average of these ratios as applied to an independent United States figure on earnings of male laborers leads to a figure of $3.21 for domestics, or within 5 cents of the Industrial Commission average.[7]

4. A fourth procedure rests upon the observation that domestic servants' wages averaged 38 percent of those for janitors in 1949 and 40 per-

[3] Twelfth Census, Special Reports, *Employees and Wages*, by Davis R. Dewey (1903), chap. 2.

[4] In all regions there were several industries paying the same lowest rate. For the Pacific Coast, the rate was computed as double the rate for the South, since "general hands, helpers and laborers" in all industries surveyed by Dewey were paid 10 cents per hour in the median Southern industry group (and the modal) whereas the median for the Pacific was 20 cents.

As a variant procedure, an average was computed from the percentage change from 1899 to 1939 in the average for all female factory wage earners. This indicated an 1899 figure of $110 but was ignored because it reflects marked changes in occupational composition over the 40 years in these industries, rather than merely an earnings-rate change appropriate for use in extrapolating servants' earnings.

[5] Gainful worker figures by occupation and state appear in 1900 Census, *Occupations,* table 33.

[6] U.S. Commissioner of Labor, Seventh Special Report, *The Slums of Baltimore, Chicago, New York and Philadelphia* (1894). Averages were computed from the distributions in table XVII.

[7] The ratios in both Baltimore and New York were 33 percent, reaching to 37 percent in Philadelphia and 55 percent in Chicago. Since most domestic servants were employed in the South, an average of 35 percent was used. A United States laborers' average of $1.53 for 1900 is derived elsewhere in the study.

cent in 1939—years when we have reasonably complete data.[8] By assuming 40 percent in 1899 and using earnings of janitors reported in the 1901 Cost of Living Survey, we arrive at an average of $3.04 for a 50-week year.[9]

Given figures of $3.16 and $3.12 by two reasonably reliable procedures, and $3.04 and $3.21 by check procedures, we can be somewhat more confident of making a benchmark 1900 estimate than first appears when the problem is considered. We take an average of (*a*) the Industrial Commission figure (which is based on direct reports, but on reports that may have a distinct bias) and (*b*) the derived occupational average (which broadly reflects the actual labor market but is indirect) and, with a 50-week year, estimate a full-time earnings rate of $157.

The cash wage total for 1900 was increased 52 percent to allow for the value of board paid in kind, on the basis of data from a survey of employers in Massachusetts in 1906.[10] This percentage is almost identical with the ratio of 49 percent developed for the 1930s by the National Income Division.[11] It is also similar to the 68 percent figure for a closely related measure as of 1897, namely, the ratio of wage rates inclusive of board to those exclusive of board.[12]

Estimates for 1909, 1914, 1919, 1925, and 1927 were made by using census data on earnings in laundries to interpolate between 1900 and 1929.[13] Laundry earnings ran to 121 percent of domestic service earnings

[8] For janitors: 1940 *Census of Population,* part III, vol. 1, table 73, using data for 12-month employees, and Miller, *op. cit.,* table C-2. For the domestic service industry: 1940 Census, *Wage and Salary Income in 1939,* table 9a. Medians were computed from these sources and the ratios based on the medians.

[9] 1901 *Annual Report* of the Commissioner of Labor, p. 283. These data relate to male heads of families, hence tend to overstate the occupational income. On the other hand, they include all employees, rather than merely full-time employees.

[10] "Trained and Supplemental Workers in Domestic Service," a reprint from *Second Annual Report,* Massachusetts Bureau of Labor (1906), p. 23.

[11] Unpublished data kindly provided by the Division indicate the value of full board for those receiving full board as against cash wages paid in 1935, the valuation of board being based on the consumer expenditure data of the National Resources Committee.

[12] Lucy M. Salmon, *Domestic Service* (1897), p. 96. Salmon reports data provided by a sample of women's club and university graduate association members, giving an average wage of $2.94 for general servants per week and a day rate for laundresses of $0.82. The weekly equivalent for the latter group, on a 6-day basis, is 167.5 percent of the former.

[13] Census reports on earnings of wage earners in power laundries appear in the 1929 *Census of Manufactures,* vol. II, p. 1393. For 1900, no such estimate is available. It was assumed that since laundry earnings were 70 percent of dry cleaning earnings in 1919 and 1925, the same ratio could be applied to reported census data on earnings in dry cleaning in 1899. The resultant estimate of $298 for laundry earnings was 118 percent of domestic service earnings in that year—the percentage assumed to apply equally in 1900.

in 1900 and 135 percent in 1929. The ratio interpolated for 1909 leads to a figure of $331. This result may be compared with an estimate of $360 for earnings of waitresses in selected cities surveyed by the Department of Labor about 1910.[14] Ratios for other years in which laundry earnings were reported in the census were similarly interpolated. (The resultant estimate for 1915 is within 10 percent of a figure to be derived from an extremely crude study for that year.)[15]

For intercensal interpolation, we rely on the earnings trend for sectors including large numbers of nonwhite women who would normally be in the same competitive labor market as domestic servants. Thus to interpolate between the 1899, 1909, 1914, and 1919 estimates, we use the trend in earnings of employees in tobacco manufacturing; while for interpolation between the 1919, 1925, and 1929 figures, we use the trend for employees in confectionery manufacturing.[16] (Since the 1899 level for confectionery workers is virtually identical with that for both domestics and laundry workers, the trend in earnings for this group would have been a preferred guide for the early period as well. Unfortunately, the sample of state earnings prior to 1909, as from 1914 to 1919, is exiguous and leads to silly results.[17] We therefore use the more broadly based series for tobacco earnings, having as it does a great similarity of movement to that for domestics.)[18]

Comparison with prior estimates is an easy matter because there are no explicit estimates for the years prior to 1919, and only Kuznets has made estimates for later years.[19] We show in the table below the trend implicitly given in King's 1909 to 1927 estimates for "unclassified" and Kuznets's estimates for 1919 to 1929 estimates for domestics. King reports a higher initial level and a greater gain than do the present estimates. Since the

[14] *Report on Condition of Woman and Child Wage Earners in the United States,* vol. V, p. 192. Data for women receiving three meals a day indicate an average of $7.19 a week including the value of meals.

[15] *Final Report of the Commission of Household Employment,* to the Fifth National Conference of the YMCA (May 5–11, 1914), p. 15. This figure relates merely to a survey of 137 women workers, whose estimated average weekly earnings in domestic service were $4.52 per week, equivalent to $225 annually.

[16] Tobacco and confectionery earnings data are from Douglas, *op. cit.,* pp. 252, 303.

[17] The New Jersey reports, used by Douglas for 1900 to 1909, show a 58 percent gain in earnings from 1908 to 1909, but a three-state series for tobacco shows a mere 1 percent rise.

[18] The apparent possibility of using the trend of earnings in trade was rejected since that series derives most of its intercensal movement from domestic service per se.

[19] King, *The National Income and Its Purchasing Power,* tables IV, XXII, XXVI. King estimates wage earners in "unclassified" industries, a group whose size in his 1919 estimate—2.9 million—suggests that it is primarily composed of domestics and those in personal service. Kuznets's data appear in his *National Income and Its Composition,* vol. II, pp. 762, 764. Douglas does not make estimates for this group.

"unclassified" group was necessarily an amorphous residual and no description of his procedures is given, we have no basis for understanding the differences. Kuznets reports considerably higher earnings than do the present estimates, benchmarked as they are for 1929 to the NID figures.[20]

| Date | King unclassified | Present estimates | | Kuznets domestic |
		Personal	Domestic	
1909	$ 586	$ 420	$331	
1919	. . . . .	. . . . .	538	$680
1927	1,202	1,306	756	
1929	. . . . .	. . . . .	731	931
Percent rise				
1909–1927	105	147	129	
1919–1929	. . . .	. . . .	36	37

His percentage gain over the period is much the same but intraperiod movements differ sharply. For example, he shows a marked rise in earnings from 1919 and 1920 to 1921, relying on earnings trends in appropriate occupations as reported in "various state and city reports." The present estimates report a fall in the 1921 recession, deriving this movement from the underlying trend of earnings by employees in tobacco manufacturing.

[20] Since Kuznets utilized the NID 1929ff. data, he presumably worked with earlier versions of the NID estimates.

APPENDIX

MANPOWER TABLES

WAGE AND PRICE TABLES

NOTE ON USE OF MANPOWER TABLES

A wide variety of series are currently provided for the analysis of changes in employment, labor force, and unemployment. Since these series differ from one another for both definitional and procedural reasons, it is not possible to provide a single set of consistent historical series. The tables below seek to provide one set of data comparable with the labor force materials issued by the Current Population Survey of the Census Bureau, and the others with the establishment data of the Bureau of Labor Statistics. As a rough guide to the user we note the following.

Current Population Survey (Monthly Report on the Labor Force). For maximum comparability with the monthly and annual CPS series on labor force, employment, and unemployment, use Tables A-3, A-4, A-6, A-7, A-9, A-10, and A-15.

Bureau of Labor Statistics (Employees in Nonagricultural Establishments). For maximum comparability with the total series and its components, use Tables A-5 and A-8.

Decennial Census Data. These provide useful geographic, occupational, and related details available from no other source. Although differing from the more accurate control totals from the Current Population Survey, they may be used to provide further breakdowns of the data in Table A-1.

Department of Agriculture: Agricultural Employment. These data differ conceptually from the CPS figures. They provide area detail and, for 1925 to 1939, monthly detail not available in other sources; as such they may be used to elaborate the measures in Tables A-1, A-3, and A-6.

National Income Division, Office of Business Economics. The NID estimates (annual) of full-time and part-time employment are generally consistent with the data in Table A-5 but will differ somewhat because of differences from the BLS procedure of adjusting to benchmarks. The NID estimates for "persons engaged in production" will differ significantly from data in our Tables A-1 and A-4 primarily for two other reasons, however. (1) NID estimates of self-employed and own-account workers are not consistent with the CPS total for this group 1940ff., nor with our estimates for 1930 to 1939. (2) NID significantly reduces the number of employees in agriculture, trade, service, and government to arrive at a "full-time equivalent" basis.

Employment Service, Department of Labor. Measures of the insured employed are not consistent with the total unemployment series issued by the Department of Labor as part of CPS results. However the geographic detail provided may, as the decennial census results, be used to elaborate the unemployment measures in Table A-3.

It will be obvious to the reader who works through the preceding pages on methodology that the estimates for different categories and periods are of differing quality. In general, the figures prior to 1900 were computed in greater detail but rounded on the tables shown here. Those since 1900 are generally not rounded because they report official data published to the detail shown, or because otherwise the series shown would not sum to a control estimate available in such detail.

Table A-1. The Labor Force, 1800–1960*
(In thousands)

Year	Labor force (10 & older) Total	Free	Slave	Agriculture (10 & older)	Fishing	Mining	Construction	Manufacturing Total persons engaged	Cotton textile wage earners	Primary iron & steel wage earners	Trade	Ocean vessels	Railway	Teachers	Domestics
1800	1,900	1,370	530	1,400	5	10			1	1		40		5	40
1810	2,330	1,590	740	1,950	6	11		75	10	5		60		12	70
1820	3,135	2,185	950	2,470	14	13			12	5		50		20	110
1830	4,200	3,020	1,180	2,965	15	22			55	20		70		30	160
1840	5,660	4,180	1,480	3,570	24	32	290	500	72	24	350	95	7	45	240
1850	8,250	6,280	1,970	4,520	30	102	410	1,200	92	35	530	135	20	80	350
1860	11,110	8,770	2,340	5,880	31	176	520	1,530	122	43	890	145	80	115	600
1870	12,930			6,790	28	180	780	2,470	135	78	1,310	135	160	170	1,000
1880	17,390			8,920	41	280	900	3,290	175	130	1,930	125	416	230	1,130
1890	23,320			9,960	60	440	1,510	4,390	222	149	2,960	120	750	350	1,580
1900	29,070			11,680	69	637	1,665	5,895	303	222	3,970	105	1,040	436	1,800
1910	37,480			11,770	68	1,068	1,949	8,332	370	306	5,320	150	1,855	595	2,090
1920	41,610			10,790	53	1,180	1,233	11,190	450	460	5,845	205	2,236	752	1,660
1930	48,830			10,560	73	1,009	1,988	9,884	372	375	8,122	160	1,659	1,044	2,270
1940	56,290			9,575	60	925	1,876	11,309	400	485	9,328	150	1,160	1,086	2,300
1950	65,470			7,870	77	901	3,029	15,648	(350)	(550)	12,152	130	1,373	1,270	1,995
1960	74,060			5,970	45	709	3,640	17,145	(300)	(530)	14,051	135	883	1,850	2,489

* Persons engaged (employees, self-employed, and unpaid family workers), except as specified. Age 10 and over.

510

Table A-2. The Farm Labor Force, 1800–1960*
(In thousands)

Year	Total (age 10 & over)	Farmers				Laborers*				Percent of free to total in agriculture
		Total	Owners	Tenants	Percent owners	Total	Free	Slave	Percent slave	
1800	1,400	600				800	310	490	61	65
1810	1,950	830				1,120	415	705	63	74
1820	2,470	1,040				1,430	515	915	64	63
1830	2,965	1,235				1,730	610	1,120	65	62
1840	3,570	1,440				2,130	720	1,410	66	60
1850	4,520	1,800				2,720	850	1,870	69	59
1860	5,880	2,540				3,340	1,120	2,220	66	62
1870	6,790	3,130				3,660				
1880	8,920	4,300	2,980	1,320	69	4,620				
1890	9,960	4,890	3,290	1,600	67	5,070				
1900	11,680	5,830	3,710	2,120	64	5,850				
1910	11,770	6,230	3,870	2,360	63	5,540				
1920	10,790	6,560	4,000	2,560	62	4,230				
1930	10,560	6,150	3,490	2,660	57	4,410				
1940	9,575	5,480	3,330	2,150	61	4,095				
1950	7,870	4,346	3,160	1,186	73	3,521				
1960	5,970	2,802	2,210	592	79	3,171				

* Age 10 and over.

Table A-3. The Labor Force and Its Components, 1900–1960*
(In thousands)

Year	Total labor force* Number	Total labor force* Percent of noninstitutional population	Armed forces	Civilian labor force	Employment Total	Employment Farm	Employment Nonfarm	Unemployment Total	Unemployment Percent of Civilian labor force	Unemployment Percent of Nonfarm employees
1900	28,500	55.5	124	28,376	26,956	11,050	15,906	1,420	5.0	12.6
1901	29,268	55.8	115	29,153	27,948	10,916	17,032	1,205	4.0	10.1
1902	30,012	56.0	108	29,904	28,807	10,753	18,054	1,097	3.7	8.6
1903	30,804	56.2	106	30,698	29,494	10,869	18,625	1,204	3.9	9.0
1904	31,548	56.3	107	31,441	29,750	11,076	18,674	1,691	5.4	12.0
1905	32,408	56.5	109	32,299	30,918	11,187	19,731	1,381	4.3	9.5
1906	33,321	56.8	109	33,212	32,638	11,479	21,159	574	1.7	3.9
1907	34,295	57.2	112	34,183	33,238	11,493	21,745	945	2.8	6.0
1908	35,039	57.2	123	34,916	32,136	11,238	20,898	2,780	8.0	16.4
1909	35,855	57.2	134	35,721	33,897	11,163	22,734	1,824	5.1	10.3
1910	36,850	57.4	141	36,709	34,559	11,260	23,299	2,150	5.9	11.6
1911	37,623	57.6	145	37,478	34,960	11,107	23,853	2,518	6.7	13.0
1912	38,081	57.4	149	37,932	36,173	11,136	25,037	1,759	4.6	9.0
1913	38,832	57.3	157	38,675	37,004	10,974	26,030	1,671	4.3	8.2
1914	39,564	57.3	163	39,401	36,281	10,945	25,336	3,120	7.9	14.7
1915	39,774	56.8	174	39,600	36,223	10,953	25,270	3,377	8.5	15.6
1916	40,238	56.6	181	40,057	38,014	10,802	27,212	2,043	5.1	9.1
1917	40,742	56.6	719	40,023	38,175	10,788	27,387	1,848	4.6	8.2
1918	41,980	57.7	2,904	39,076	38,540	10,674	27,866	536	1.4	2.4
1919	41,239	56.4	1,543	39,696	39,150	10,498	28,652	546	1.4	2.4
1920	41,720	55.6	380	41,340	39,208	10,440	28,768	2,132	5.2	8.6
1921	42,341	55.9	362	41,979	37,061	10,443	26,618	4,918	11.7	19.5
1922	42,772	55.7	276	42,496	39,637	10,561	29,076	2,859	6.7	11.4
1923	43,699	55.8	255	43,444	42,395	10,621	31,774	1,049	2.4	4.1
1924	44,502	55.5	267	44,235	42,045	10,599	31,446	2,190	5.0	8.3
1925	45,196	55.4	262	45,169	43,716	10,662	33,054	1,453	3.2	5.4
1926	45,885	55.3	256	45,629	44,828	10,690	34,138	801	1.8	2.9
1927	46,634	55.2	259	46,375	44,856	10,529	34,327	1,519	3.3	5.4
1928	47,367	55.2	262	47,105	45,123	10,497	34,626	1,982	4.2	6.9
1929	48,017	55.1	260	47,757	46,207	10,541	35,666	1,550	3.2	5.3
1930	48,783	55.0	260	48,523	44,183	10,340	33,843	4,340	8.9	14.2
1931	49,585	55.2	260	49,325	41,305	10,240	31,065	8,020	16.3	25.2
1932	50,348	55.4	250	50,098	38,038	10,120	27,918	12,060	24.1	36.3
1933	51,132	55.6	250	50,882	38,052	10,090	27,962	12,830	25.2	37.6
1934	51,910	55.7	260	51,650	40,310	9,990	30,320	11,340	22.0	32.6
1935	52,553	55.6	270	52,283	41,673	10,110	31,563	10,610	20.3	30.2
1936	53,319	55.7	300	53,019	43,989	10,090	33,899	9,030	17.0	25.4
1937	54,088	55.9	320	53,768	46,068	10,000	36,068	7,700	14.3	21.3
1938	54,872	56.0	340	54,532	44,142	9,840	34,302	10,390	19.1	27.9
1939	55,588	56.0	370	55,218	45,738	9,710	36,028	9,480	17.2	25.2
1940	56,180	56.0	540	55,640	47,520	9,540	37,980	8,120	14.6	21.3
1941	57,530	56.7	1,620	55,910	50,350	9,100	41,250	5,560	9.9	14.4
1942	60,380	58.8	3,970	56,410	53,750	9,250	44,500	2,660	4.7	6.8
1943	64,560	62.3	9,020	55,540	54,470	9,080	45,390	1,070	1.9	2.7
1944	66,040	63.1	11,410	54,630	53,960	8,950	45,010	670	1.2	1.7
1945	65,290	61.9	11,430	53,860	52,820	8,580	44,240	1,040	1.9	2.7
1946	60,970	57.2	3,450	57,520	55,250	8,320	46,930	2,270	3.9	5.5
1947	61,758	57.4	1,590	60,168	57,812	8,256	49,557	2,356	3.9	5.4
1948	62,898	57.9	1,456	61,442	59,117	7,960	51,156	2,325	3.8	5.1
1949	63,721	58.0	1,616	62,105	58,423	8,017	50,406	3,682	5.9	8.0
1950	64,749	58.4	1,650	63,099	59,748	7,497	52,251	3,351	5.3	7.1
1951	65,983	58.9	3,097	62,884	60,784	7,048	53,736	2,099	3.3	4.4
1952	66,560	58.8	3,594	62,966	61,035	6,792	54,243	1,932	3.1	4.0
1953	67,362	58.5	3,547	63,815	61,945	6,555	55,390	1,870	2.9	3.8
1954	67,818	58.4	3,350	64,468	60,890	6,495	54,395	3,578	5.6	7.1
1955	68,896	58.7	3,048	65,848	62,944	6,718	56,225	2,904	4.4	5.7
1956	70,387	59.3	2,857	67,530	64,708	6,572	58,135	2,822	4.2	5.4
1957	70,744	58.7	2,797	67,946	65,011	6,222	58,789	2,936	4.3	5.6
1958	71,284	58.5	2,637	68,647	63,966	5,844	58,122	4,681	6.8	8.7
1959	71,946	58.3	2,552	69,394	65,581	5,836	59,745	3,813	5.5	7.0
1960	73,126	58.3	2,514	70,612	66,681	5,723	60,958	3,931	5.6	7.1

* Age 14 and over.

Table A-4. Farm and Nonfarm Employment, by Class of Worker, 1900–1960*
(In thousands)

Year	Employees			Self-employed			Unpaid family workers			Domestic service employees
	Total	Nonfarm enterprise	Farm	Total	Nonfarm	Farm	Total	Nonfarm	Farm*	
1900	12,466	10,086	2,380	9,679	3,849	5,830	3,011	171	2,840	1,800
1901	13,182	10,956	2,226	9,969	4,063	5,906	2,968	184	2,784	1,829
1902	13,917	11,834	2,083	10,119	4,177	5,942	2,913	185	2,728	1,858
1903	14,538	12,319	2,219	10,206	4,228	5,978	2,864	192	2,672	1,886
1904	14,779	12,333	2,446	10,251	4,237	6,014	2,805	189	2,616	1,915
1905	15,847	13,270	2,577	10,371	4,321	6,050	2,756	196	2,560	1,944
1906	17,315	14,426	2,889	10,636	4,550	6,086	2,714	210	2,504	1,973
1907	17,858	14,935	2,923	10,722	4,600	6,122	2,656	208	2,448	2,002
1908	16,893	14,205	2,688	10,628	4,470	6,158	2,585	193	2,392	2,030
1909	18,458	15,825	2,633	10,836	4,642	6,194	2,544	208	2,336	2,059
1910	19,141	16,391	2,750	10,845	4,615	6,230	2,483	203	2,280	2,090
1911	19,489	16,854	2,635	10,959	4,693	6,266	2,422	216	2,206	2,090
1912	20,551	17,859	2,692	11,161	4,859	6,302	2,371	229	2,142	2,090
1913	21,299	18,735	2,564	11,307	4,969	6,338	2,308	236	2,072	2,090
1914	20,716	18,149	2,567	11,242	4,868	6,374	2,233	229	2,004	2,090
1915	20,881	18,275	2,606	11,198	4,788	6,410	2,162	225	1,937	1,982
1916	22,805	20,316	2,489	11,223	4,777	6,446	2,111	244	1,867	1,875
1917	23,212	20,689	2,523	11,171	4,696	6,475	2,024	234	1,790	1,768
1918	23,857	21,377	2,480	11,112	4,608	6,504	1,911	221	1,690	1,660
1919	24,618	22,235	2,383	11,065	4,532	6,533	1,807	225	1,582	1,660
1920	24,866	22,536	2,330	10,919	4,359	6,560	1,763	213	1,550	1,660
1921	22,715	20,331	2,384	10,854	4,345	6,509	1,756	206	1,550	1,736
1922	24,820	22,261	2,559	11,217	4,762	6,455	1,787	240	1,547	1,813
1923	27,309	24,636	2,673	11,392	4,989	6,403	1,805	260	1,545	1,889
1924	26,963	24,254	2,709	11,307	4,959	6,348	1,810	268	1,542	1,965
1925	28,330	25,509	2,821	11,525	5,229	6,296	1,819	274	1,545	2,042
1926	29,377	26,446	2,931	11,542	5,298	6,244	1,791	276	1,515	2,118
1927	29,418	26,561	2,857	11,495	5,298	6,197	1,749	274	1,475	2,194
1928	29,638	26,791	2,847	11,457	5,292	6,165	1,758	273	1,485	2,270
1929	30,676	27,785	2,891	11,350	5,188	6,162	1,758	270	1,488	2,423
1930	28,905	26,195	2,710	11,258	5,108	6,150	1,750	270	1,480	2,270
1931	26,355	23,795	2,560	11,119	4,959	6,160	1,788	268	1,520	2,043
1932	23,538	21,158	2,380	10,909	4,729	6,180	1,829	269	1,560	1,762
1933	23,657	21,327	2,330	10,864	4,684	6,180	1,854	274	1,580	1,677
1934	25,707	23,457	2,250	10,858	4,698	6,160	1,848	268	1,580	1,897
1935	26,880	24,550	2,330	10,894	4,754	6,140	1,910	270	1,640	1,989
1936	28,954	26,494	2,460	11,014	4,994	6,020	1,889	279	1,610	2,132
1937	30,899	28,369	2,530	11,021	5,141	5,880	1,886	296	1,590	2,262
1938	29,309	26,789	2,520	10,861	5,131	5,730	1,879	289	1,590	2,093
1939	30,703	28,203	2,500	10,913	5,303	5,610	1,895	295	1,600	2,227
1940	32,470	29,990	2,480	10,870	5,390	5,480	1,880	300	1,580	2,300
1941	35,480	33,150	2,230	10,820	5,660	5,160	2,050	340	1,710	2,100
1942	39,280	36,690	2,590	9,870	5,290	4,580	2,450	370	2,080	2,150
1943	40,670	38,420	2,250	9,280	4,750	4,530	2,700	400	2,300	1,820
1944	40,120	38,160	2,000	9,460	4,720	4,740	2,610	400	2,210	1,730
1945	38,970	37,210	1,760	9,530	4,850	4,680	2,540	400	2,140	1,680
1946	41,005	39,335	1,670	10,430	5,620	4,810	2,240	400	1,840	1,575
1947	43,253	41,576	1,677	11,018	6,045	4,973	2,043	427	1,616	1,714
1948	44,881	43,135	1,746	10,810	6,139	4,671	1,957	401	1,556	1,731
1949	44,154	42,309	1,845	10,826	6,208	4,618	1,959	396	1,563	1,772
1950	45,715	43,982	1,733	10,415	6,069	4,346	1,831	404	1,427	1,995
1951	47,274	45,627	1,647	9,891	5,869	4,022	1,786	400	1,386	2,055
1952	47,990	46,464	1,526	9,606	5,670	3,936	1,773	431	1,342	1,922
1953	48,981	47,514	1,467	9,615	5,794	3,821	1,696	423	1,273	1,920
1954	47,942	46,490	1,452	9,701	5,880	3,821	1,675	445	1,230	1,919
1955	49,537	47,837	1,700	9,617	5,886	3,731	1,823	524	1,299	2,216
1956	51,210	49,518	1,692	9,506	5,936	3,570	1,904	581	1,323	2,359
1957	51,431	49,744	1,687	9,393	6,089	3,304	1,857	626	1,231	2,328
1958	50,546	48,875	1,671	9,272	6,185	3,087	1,691	605	1,086	2,456
1959	52,019	50,330	1,689	9,325	6,298	3,027	1,718	597	1,121	2,520
1960	53,353	51,487	1,866	9,169	6,367	2,802	1,669	615	1,054	2,489

* Age 14 and over.

Table A-5. Employees in Nonfarm Establishments, by Industry, 1900–1960 (In thousands)

Year	Total	Mining	Contract construction	Manufacturing	Transport and utilities	Trade	Finance	Service	Civilian government
1900	15,178	637	1,147	5,468	2,282	2,502	308	1,740	1,094
1901	16,294	703	1,274	5,817	2,404	2,765	322	1,880	1,129
1902	17,395	685	1,393	6,305	2,754	2,827	337	1,903	1,191
1903	17,858	834	1,290	6,527	2,666	2,979	351	1,982	1,229
1904	17,640	801	1,257	6,199	2,743	2,992	369	2,002	1,277
1905	18,707	889	1,208	6,739	2,905	3,170	385	2,076	1,335
1906	20,069	894	1,391	7,226	3,110	3,442	405	2,215	1,386
1907	20,523	1,051	1,436	7,322	3,114	3,486	423	2,243	1,448
1908	19,259	900	1,308	6,570	3,069	3,299	442	2,164	1,507
1909	21,203	998	1,376	7,661	3,229	3,585	464	2,326	1,564
1910	21,697	1,068	1,342	7,828	3,366	3,570	483	2,410	1,630
1911	22,093	1,052	1,249	7,870	3,426	3,813	520	2,491	1,672
1912	23,191	1,083	1,337	8,322	3,552	4,073	568	2,539	1,717
1913	24,143	1,182	1,412	8,751	3,570	4,232	613	2,626	1,757
1914	23,190	1,027	1,267	8,210	3,445	4,128	657	2,647	1,809
1915	23,149	1,022	1,195	8,210	3,439	4,091	694	2,637	1,861
1916	25,510	1,168	1,208	9,629	3,579	4,476	738	2,796	1,916
1917	25,802	1,267	1,027	9,872	3,722	4,320	771	2,783	2,000
1918	26,432	1,311	928	10,167	3,877	4,110	809	2,769	2,461
1919	27,270	1,067	1,011	10,702	4,055	4,213	868	2,905	2,449
1920	27,434	1,180	850	10,702	4,317	4,012	902	3,100	2,371
1921	24,542	906	1,035	8,262	3,929	3,960	968	3,085	2,397
1922	26,616	880	1,315	9,129	3,897	4,708	1,081	3,151	2,455
1923	29,231	1,181	1,408	10,317	4,185	5,194	1,175	3,247	2,524
1924	28,577	1,091	1,556	9,675	4,063	5,047	1,211	3,298	2,636
1925	29,751	1,065	1,680	9,942	4,018	5,717	1,264	3,300	2,765
1926	30,599	1,168	1,756	10,156	4,077	5,864	1,328	3,397	2,853
1927	30,481	1,100	1,761	9,996	3,997	5,942	1,380	3,360	2,945
1928	30,539	1,038	1,704	9,942	3,886	6,047	1,484	3,399	3,093
1929	31,339	1,087	1,497	10,702	3,916	6,123	1,509	3,440	3,065
1930	29,424	1,009	1,372	9,562	3,685	5,797	1,475	3,376	3,148
1931	26,649	873	1,214	8,170	3,254	5,284	1,407	3,183	3,264
1932	23,628	731	970	6,931	2,816	4,683	1,341	2,931	3,225
1933	23,711	744	809	7,397	2,672	4,755	1,295	2,873	3,166
1934	25,953	883	862	8,501	2,750	5,281	1,319	3,058	3,299
1935	27,053	897	912	9,069	2,786	5,431	1,335	3,142	3,481
1936	29,082	946	1,145	9,827	2,973	5,809	1,388	3,326	3,668
1937	31,026	1,015	1,112	10,794	3,134	6,265	1,432	3,518	3,756
1938	29,209	891	1,055	9,440	2,863	6,179	1,425	3,473	3,883
1939	30,618	854	1,150	10,278	2,936	6,426	1,462	3,517	3,995
1940	32,376	925	1,294	10,985	3,038	6,750	1,502	3,681	4,202
1941	36,554	957	1,790	13,192	3,274	7,210	1,549	3,921	4,660
1942	40,125	992	2,170	15,280	3,460	7,118	1,538	4,084	5,483
1943	42,452	925	1,567	17,602	3,647	6,982	1,502	4,148	6,080
1944	41,883	892	1,094	17,328	3,829	7,058	1,476	4,163	6,043
1945	40,394	836	1,132	15,524	3,906	7,314	1,497	4,241	5,944
1946	41,674	862	1,661	14,703	4,061	8,376	1,697	4,719	5,595
1947	43,881	955	1,982	15,545	4,166	8,955	1,754	5,050	5,474
1948	44,891	994	2,169	15,582	4,189	9,272	1,829	5,206	5,650
1949	43,778	930	2,165	14,441	4,001	9,264	1,857	5,264	5,856
1950	45,222	901	2,333	15,241	4,034	9,386	1,919	5,382	6,026
1951	47,849	929	2,603	16,393	4,226	9,742	1,991	5,576	6,389
1952	48,825	898	2,634	16,632	4,248	10,004	2,069	5,730	6,609
1953	50,232	866	2,623	17,549	4,290	10,247	2,146	5,867	6,645
1954	49,022	791	2,612	16,314	4,084	10,235	2,234	6,002	6,751
1955	50,675	792	2,802	16,882	4,141	10,535	2,335	6,274	6,914
1956	52,408	822	2,999	17,243	4,244	10,858	2,429	6,536	7,277
1957	52,904	828	2,923	17,174	4,241	10,886	2,477	6,749	7,626
1958	51,423	751	2,778	15,945	3,976	10,750	2,519	6,811	7,893
1959	53,380	731	2,955	16,667	4,010	11,125	2,597	7,105	8,190
1960	54,347	709	2,882	16,762	4,017	11,412	2,684	7,361	8,520

Table A-6. Farm Employment, by Class of Worker,* 1900–1960 (In thousands)

Year	Total (age 14 & over)	Family	Self-employed	Unpaid family workers	Wage or salary workers
1900	11,050	8,670	5,830	2,840	2,380
1901	10,916	8,690	5,906	2,784	2,226
1902	10,753	8,670	5,942	2,728	2,083
1903	10,869	8,650	5,978	2,672	2,219
1904	11,076	8,630	6,014	2,616	2,446
1905	11,187	8,610	6,050	2,560	2,577
1906	11,479	8,590	6,086	2,504	2,889
1907	11,493	8,570	6,122	2,448	2,923
1908	11,238	8,550	6,158	2,392	2,688
1909	11,163	8,530	6,194	2,336	2,633
1910	11,260	8,510	6,230	2,280	2,750
1911	11,107	8,472	6,266	2,206	2,635
1912	11,136	8,444	6,302	2,142	2,692
1913	10,974	8,410	6,338	2,072	2,564
1914	10,945	8,378	6,374	2,004	2,567
1915	10,953	8,347	6,410	1,937	2,606
1916	10,802	8,313	6,446	1,867	2,489
1917	10,788	8,265	6,475	1,790	2,523
1918	10,674	8,194	6,504	1,690	2,480
1919	10,498	8,115	6,533	1,582	2,383
1920	10,440	8,110	6,560	1,550	2,330
1921	10,443	8,059	6,509	1,550	2,384
1922	10,561	8,002	6,455	1,547	2,559
1923	10,621	7,948	6,403	1,545	2,673
1924	10,599	7,890	6,348	1,542	2,709
1925	10,662	7,841	6,296	1,545	2,821
1926	10,690	7,759	6,244	1,515	2,931
1927	10,529	7,672	6,197	1,475	2,857
1928	10,497	7,650	6,165	1,485	2,847
1929	10,541	7,650	6,162	1,488	2,891
1930	10,340	7,630	6,150	1,480	2,710
1931	10,240	7,680	6,160	1,520	2,560
1932	10,120	7,740	6,180	1,560	2,380
1933	10,090	7,760	6,180	1,580	2,330
1934	9,990	7,740	6,160	1,580	2,250
1935	10,110	7,780	6,140	1,640	2,330
1936	10,090	7,630	6,020	1,610	2,460
1937	10,000	7,470	5,880	1,590	2,530
1938	9,840	7,320	5,730	1,590	2,520
1939	9,710	7,210	5,610	1,600	2,500
1940	9,540	7,060	5,480	1,580	2,480
1941	9,100	6,870	5,160	1,710	2,230
1942	9,250	6,660	4,580	2,080	2,590
1943	9,080	6,830	4,530	2,300	2,250
1944	8,950	6,950	4,740	2,210	2,000
1945	8,580	6,820	4,680	2,140	1,760
1946	8,320	6,650	4,810	1,840	1,670
1947	8,266	6,589	4,973	1,616	1,677
1948	7,973	6,227	4,671	1,556	1,746
1949	8,026	6,181	4,618	1,563	1,845
1950	7,507	5,773	4,346	1,427	1,733
1951	7,054	5,408	4,022	1,386	1,647
1952	6,805	5,278	3,936	1,342	1,526
1953	6,562	5,094	3,821	1,273	1,467
1954	6,504	5,051	3,821	1,230	1,452
1955	6,730	5,030	3,731	1,299	1,700
1956	6,585	4,893	3,570	1,323	1,692
1957	6,222	4,535	3,304	1,231	1,687
1958	5,844	4,173	3,087	1,086	1,671
1959	5,836	4,148	3,027	1,121	1,689
1960	5,723	3,856	2,802	1,054	1,866

* Age 14 and over.

Table A-7. Nonfarm Self-employed, by Industry, 1900–1960
(In thousands)

Year	Total	Construction	Manufactures	Trade	Service	Other
1900	3,849	518	427	1,337	1,132	435
1901	4,063	576	437	1,442	1,170	438
1902	4,177	631	447	1,449	1,208	442
1903	4,228	584	456	1,500	1,243	444
1904	4,237	569	466	1,481	1,277	447
1905	4,321	546	476	1,540	1,311	448
1906	4,550	630	485	1,642	1,341	452
1907	4,600	649	495	1,632	1,371	455
1908	4,470	592	504	1,516	1,398	460
1909	4,642	622	504	1,630	1,425	461
1910	4,615	607	504	1,591	1,450	464
1911	4,693	564	504	1,689	1,472	464
1912	4,859	605	505	1,794	1,486	469
1913	4,969	639	505	1,848	1,510	468
1914	4,868	573	505	1,792	1,530	469
1915	4,788	540	504	1,760	1,512	472
1916	4,777	548	498	1,760	1,493	478
1917	4,696	506	494	1,760	1,471	465
1918	4,608	465	489	1,760	1,447	447
1919	4,532	424	488	1,759	1,431	430
1920	4,359	383	488	1,666	1,407	413
1921	4,345	469	429	1,614	1,420	414
1922	4,762	596	406	1,883	1,420	458
1923	4,989	637	383	2,038	1,436	497
1924	4,959	703	361	1,942	1,456	497
1925	5,229	760	338	2,149	1,475	507
1926	5,298	794	338	2,159	1,498	510
1927	5,298	797	339	2,143	1,506	515
1928	5,292	771	339	2,136	1,519	527
1929	5,188	677	341	2,115	1,541	513
1930	5,108	616	322	2,114	1,534	522
1931	4,959	531	286	2,073	1,556	513
1932	4,729	395	235	1,942	1,671	487
1933	4,684	303	224	2,036	1,654	467
1934	4,698	349	237	2,067	1,544	501
1935	4,754	377	246	2,081	1,539	512
1936	4,994	489	265	2,160	1,552	528
1937	5,141	479	296	2,239	1,585	542
1938	5,131	467	287	2,270	1,574	533
1939	5,303	548	316	2,328	1,590	521
1940	5,390	582	324	2,344	1,589	551
1941	5,660	526	339	2,333	1,566	536
1942	5,290	485	346	2,224	1,560	495
1943	4,750	416	353	1,966	1,440	507
1944	4,720	392	360	1,935	1,440	531
1945	4,850	439	372	2,049	1,570	559
1946	5,620	583	415	2,266	1,750	569
1947	6,044	695	447	2,377	1,960	565
1948	6,139	695	466	2,490	1,921	567
1949	6,208	687	425	2,657	1,908	531
1950	6,069	696	407	2,562	1,883	521
1951	5,868	691	417	2,445	1,765	550
1952	5,670	687	390	2,359	1,759	475
1953	5,747	655	385	2,409	1,761	537
1954	5,880	699	424	2,481	1,745	531
1955	5,886	727	423	2,378	1,784	574
1956	5,936	708	435	2,403	1,806	584
1957	6,090	736	430	2,465	1,875	584
1958	6,185	745	408	2,449	1,984	599
1959	6,298	769	393	2,431	2,083	622
1960	6,367	758	383	2,443	2,175	608

Table A-8. Civilian Government Employment: Federal, State, and Local, 1900–1960
(In thousands)

Year	Total	Federal civilian*	Public education	Nonschool State	Nonschool Local
1900	1,094	239	487	95	273
1901	1,129	239	499	101	290
1902	1,191	264	512	107	308
1903	1,229	270	521	114	324
1904	1,277	287	529	120	341
1905	1,335	312	538	126	359
1906	1,386	328	546	132	380
1907	1,448	344	566	138	400
1908	1,507	357	584	145	421
1909	1,564	372	600	151	441
1910	1,630	389	622	157	462
1911	1,672	396	635	162	479
1912	1,717	400	654	167	496
1913	1,757	396	677	172	512
1914	1,809	402	696	177	534
1915	1,861	395	727	182	557
1916	1,916	399	751	186	580
1917	2,000	438	769	191	602
1918	2,461	854	787	196	624
1919	2,449	794	807	201	647
1920	2,371	655	835	211	670
1921	2,397	561	879	215	742
1922	2,455	544	917	236	758
1923	2,524	537	941	239	807
1924	2,636	543	971	244	878
1925	2,765	553	1,010	263	939
1926	2,853	549	1,047	270	987
1927	2,945	547	1,070	292	1,036
1928	3,039	561	1,099	299	1,080
1929	3,065	533	1,143	1,389	
1930	3,148	536	1,173	1,449	
1931	3,264	560	1,184	1,520	
1932	3,225	559	1,171	1,495	
1933	3,166	565	1,144	1,457	
1934	3,299	652	1,145	1,502	
1935	3,481	753	1,174	1,554	
1936	3,668	826	1,198	1,644	
1937	3,756	833	1,231	1,692	
1938	3,883	829	1,265	1,789	
1939	3,995	905	1,293	1,797	
1940	4,202	996	1,327	1,879	
1941	4,660	1,340	1,392	1,928	
1942	5,483	2,213	1,411	1,859	
1943	6,080	2,905	1,388	1,786	
1944	6,043	2,928	1,378	1,738	
1945	5,944	2,808	1,380	1,757	
1946	5,595	2,254	1,415	1,926	
1947	5,474	1,892	1,499	2,083	
1948	5,650	1,863	1,550	2,237	
1949	5,856	1,908	1,620	2,328	
1950	6,026	1,928	1,680	2,418	
1951	6,389	2,302	1,712	2,375	
1952	6,609	2,420	1,787	2,402	
1953	6,645	2,305	1,893	2,447	
1954	6,751	2,188	2,005	2,558	
1955	6,914	2,187	2,100	2,626	
1956	7,277	2,209	2,262	2,806	
1957	7,626	2,217	2,446	2,963	
1958	7,893	2,191	2,608	3,094	
1959	8,190	2,233	2,777	3,181	
1960	8,520	2,270	2,983	3,266	

* Prior to 1929 includes Philippine scouts.

Table A-9. Nonfarm Self-employment, by Detailed Industry, 1929–1940*

Year	Nonagricultural self-employed domestics and unpaid family workers	Forestry	Fishery	Mining					Construction	Manufacturing	Taxicabs
				Bituminous	Anthracite	Metal	Nonmetallic	Oil and gas			
1929	7,004,480	889	36,411	4,513	1,604	4,331	3,149	11,051	559,305	281,800	32,115
1930	6,780,926	914	35,439	4,559	1,635	5,066	2,960	10,035	508,766	265,810	31,379
1931	6,425,589	939	35,691	4,445	1,667	5,350	2,665	7,874	439,454	236,350	30,642
1932	5,987,853	990	33,602	4,031	1,699	8,824	2,178	7,312	325,860	194,180	29,906
1933	5,839,609	1,066	34,610	4,471	1,731	9,933	2,237	7,949	249,810	185,236	25,817
1934	6,057,775	1,142	36,123	5,501	1,762	17,812	2,725	10,345	287,835	196,286	21,729
1935	6,200,230	1,231	36,915	6,060	1,794	17,852	2,756	10,334	310,939	203,021	21,355
1936	6,551,170	1,333	36,879	6,700	1,826	13,055	3,445	10,506	403,836	218,929	20,981
1937	6,820,800	1,447	37,203	7,389	1,858	13,069	3,992	11,784	395,653	244,031	20,608
1938	6,635,382	1,574	37,636	7,047	1,889	11,887	3,676	10,730	386,027	236,546	20,234
1939	6,939,612	1,726	37,780	7,022	1,921	12,759	4,313	9,977	453,413	261,423	19,860
1940	7,134,412	1,917	36,015	8,715	1,953	13,099	4,911	9,964	481,330	267,560	19,487

Year	Trucking	Other transportation and utilities	Wholesale trade	Retail trade (including automotive)	Banking and other finance	Insurance and real estate	Services			Domestic	Unpaid family workers
							Business repair except automotive, personal, and amusement	Medical and other health	Legal, engineering, educational, and other professional		
1929	157,844	15,630	173,289	1,571,000	34,108	131,035	757,820	301,154	214,043	2,423,000	251,782
1930	159,609	15,804	166,641	1,580,000	32,005	132,721	733,007	294,643	219,735	2,273,000	249,823
1931	158,903	15,734	150,734	1,564,000	29,173	131,378	774,862	283,430	226,241	2,043,000	247,641
1932	144,178	14,276	136,392	1,504,000	26,687	128,930	884,870	268,339	227,256	1,762,000	249,340
1933	140,295	13,892	136,047	1,546,000	25,412	125,705	872,907	263,150	230,374	1,677,000	253,781
1934	146,094	14,466	145,832	1,561,000	25,079	130,748	778,028	265,997	231,037	1,897,000	247,845
1935	149,523	14,806	145,315	1,574,000	24,319	136,090	770,682	265,830	234,505	1,989,000	249,729
1936	158,550	15,699	153,882	1,630,000	25,288	141,534	777,257	268,480	236,215	2,132,000	258,667
1937	161,324	15,974	169,442	1,680,000	25,724	147,464	802,934	267,251	238,962	2,263,000	274,097
1938	154,364	15,285	170,488	1,705,000	24,038	152,108	794,828	263,174	241,714	2,093,000	267,565
1939	155,676	15,415	174,863	1,748,000	23,537	160,087	807,528	261,255	244,460	2,227,000	273,348
1940	154,314	15,280	182,059	1,754,000	23,885	165,538	804,050	260,864	247,204	2,365,000	277,994

* All series are at April 1 Census of Population levels.

Table A-10. Families and Servants, 1790–1960

(In thousands)

Year	Number of white families	Number of Domestic service employees*
1790	558	
1800	755	40
1810	1,025	70
1820	1,380	110
1830	1,870	160
1840	2,520	240
1850	3,540	350
1860	5,100	600
1870	6,650	1,000
1880	8,680	1,130
1890	11,255	1,580
1900	14,064	1,800
1910	18,002	2,090
1920	21,826	1,660
1930	26,983	2,270
1940	31,680	2,300
1950	38,429	1,995
1960	47,766	2,489

* Free servants only.

Table A-11. Female Worker Rates, by Marital Status, Color, and Age, 1830–1960

Year	All ages						Age 35–44			
	White			Nonwhite			Native white		Nonwhite	
	Total	Single	Married	Total	Single	Married	Single	Married	Single	Married
1830	(7)	....	....	(90)	(90)	(90)	....	....	(95)	(95)
1890	12.1	35.2	2.5	39.5	56.4	22.5	39.3	2.3	81.0	22.0
1940*	26.9	47.9	14.6	43.2	45.1	33.5	(73.6)	17.9	(71.1)	34.9
1951*	31.5	50.5	24.3	41.1	41.3	36.0	(76.5)	29.4	(65.8)	43.1
1960*	34.1	45.5	29.6	41.2	33.6	40.8				

* March.

Table A-12. Employment of Women, by Industry-Occupation, 1832–1960 (In thousands)

Year	Manufacturing						Domestic Service	Teachers
	Total	Cotton	Wool	Hats	Shoes	Clothing		
1832	80	39	3	3	5	25	150	20
1850	210	59	19	8	33	62	330	55
1870	324	70	39	6	19	69	880	85
1890	804	107	65	6	40	102	1,330	245
1900	1,030	127	52	12	50	156	1,500	325
1910	1,517	147	70	15	66	230	1,720	477
1920	2,229	190	74	13	80	207	1,480	635
1940	2,644	174	68	4	109	648	2,140	860
1960	4,345	197*		4	150	960	2,201	1,235

* Includes (standard industrial classification) groups 221, 223, 224, 226, 228.

Table A-13. Female Labor Force and Fertility Trends, by Nativity, Color, and Age, 1890–1940

Nativity	Age	Change in children ever born per 1,000 women	Change in worker rates		
			Single	Married	Excess of married over single rates
Native white.......	25–34	− 707	+34.9	+15.5	−19.4
	35–44	−1,195	+35.7	+12.2	−23.5
	45–54	−1,477	+30.6	+ 9.0	−21.6
	55–64	−1,584	+22.0	+ 5.9	−16.1
	65+	−1,319	+ 3.4	+ 2.2	− 1.2
Foreign white.......	25–34	− 966	+ 8.5	+15.6	+ 7.1
	35–44	−1,831	+24.9	+14.8	−10.1
	45–54	−1,851	+32.1	+ 8.9	−23.2
	55–64	−1,966	+13.1	+ 3.7	− 9.4
	65+	−1,818	− 1.0	− 0.3	+ 0.7
Nonwhite..........	25–34	− 968	+ 0.1	+14.2	+14.3
	35–44	−2,036	− 3.8	+14.5	+18.3
	45–54	−2,843	−12.7	+ 9.2	+21.9
	55–64	−2,912	−25.2	+ 0.5	+25.7
	65+	−2,322	−22.9	− 3.7	+19.2

Table A-14. Male Worker Rates, by State, 1850, 1880, and 1890*

	1850	1880	1890
United States................	90.2	90.62	88.65
North Atlantic................	....	90.41	90.15
Maine.....................	88.4	88.63	87.86
New Hampshire..............	90.6	90.40	90.62
Vermont...................	89.7	89.29	88.76
Massachusetts..............	89.5	91.25	90.26
Rhode Island...............	90.8	93.26	91.70
Connecticut................	88.0	90.31	90.96
New York..................	88.7	90.13	90.20
New Jersey.................	86.4	90.11	91.01
Pennsylvania...............	98.4	90.69	89.95
South Atlantic................	....	92.96	89.16
Delaware..................	85.0	95.12	90.84
Maryland..................	84.2	91.30	90.09
District of Columbia..........	81.7	87.71	87.95
Virginia...................	84.0	92.61	87.82
West Virginia..............	....	90.70	85.63
North Carolina.............	88.3	92.28	88.22
South Carolina.............	86.6	95.17	91.23
Georgia...................	87.1	95.60	91.13
Florida....................	88.7	90.48	88.41
North Central................	....	89.34	87.10
Ohio......................	91.2	85.69	86.91
Indiana...................	89.8	90.52	86.60
Illinois....................	86.0	88.83	87.44
Michigan..................	88.6	90.84	88.99
Wisconsin.................	79.0	87.50	87.11
Minnesota.................	90.6	88.08	88.42
Iowa......................	90.6	91.82	85.00
Missouri..................	80.8	90.85	86.79
North Dakota..............	....	94.74	91.29
South Dakota..............	....	....	88.49
Nebraska..................	....	91.48	87.99
Kansas....................	....	91.65	85.01
South Central................	....	91.74	88.09
Kentucky..................	86.8	92.43	86.68
Tennessee.................	82.2	84.64	87.48
Alabama..................	84.3	94.22	89.68
Mississippi................	89.1	93.42	88.44
Louisiana.................	80.8	94.75	91.82
Texas.....................	88.0	93.09	87.77
Oklahoma.................	....	....	88.50
Arkansas..................	90.2	91.31	86.14
Western.....................	....	91.36	91.09
Montana...................	....	93.37	94.52
Wyoming..................	....	74.61	94.35
Colorado..................	....	92.73	92.49
New Mexico................	....	91.68	91.06
Arizona...................	90.9	96.10	92.36
Utah......................	88.3	87.34	87.96
Nevada....................	....	90.53	92.40
Idaho.....................	....	93.34	91.86
Washington................	....	91.36	92.65
Oregon....................	71.2	91.24	88.77
California.................	95.2	91.49	90.26

* Percent gainfully occupied of white males aged 15 and over in 1850, and of all males aged 15 and over in 1880 and 1890.

Table A-15. Unemployment, Labor Force, and Related Series, 1890–1900*

Year	Present Estimates				Percent of labor force unemployed	Percentage of unemployment (Douglas)	Union construction workers: Percent unemployed		Relief recipients in Mass. (000)	Manufacturing production (Frickey)	BLS employment index
	Labor force		Employment (000)	Unemployment (000)			Jan.	Dec.			
	Total (000)	Civilian (000)									
1890	22,811	22,772	21,868	904	4.0	5.1	12.5	37.1	43.4	71	82
1891	23,380	23,342	22,077	1,265	5.4	5.6	24.8	37.2	45.2	73	84
1892	23,949	23,910	23,182	728	3.0	3.7	18.7	37.6	44.1	79	86
1893	24,518	24,479	21,619	2,860	11.7	9.6	22.2	67.7	67.8	70	86
1894	25,087	25,045	20,433	4,612	18.4	16.7	49.6	54.6	70.2	68	81
1895	25,656	25,614	22,104	3,510	13.7	11.9	28.1	43.2	60.7	81	83
1896	26,224	26,182	22,400	3,782	14.4	15.3	33.3	55.9	66.9	74	85
1897	26,793	26,749	22,859	3,890	14.5	14.5	41.4	51.7	73.1	80	87
1898	27,362	27,126	23,775	3,351	12.4	13.9	38.8	47.6	76.3	91	92
1899	27,931	27,831	26,012	1,819	6.5	7.7	18.2	31.2	64.0	100	97
1900	28,500	28,376	26,956	1,420	5.0	6.3	29.8	34.7	63.7	100	100

* More speculative estimates, for 1800ff., appear in Tables 4-2 and 4-3.

Table A-16. All Employees,* Annual Earnings, 1900–1960

Year	Money earnings		Income loss from unemployment	Consumer price index (1914 = 100)	Real earnings (1914 dollars)	
	After deduction for unemployment	When employed			After deduction for unemployment	When employed
1900	$ 375	$ 418	$ 43	84.3	$ 445	$ 496
1901	401	438	37	85.4	470	513
1902	437	472	35	86.3	506	547
1903	441	477	36	88.0	501	542
1904	432	482	50	88.8	486	541
1905	451	490	39	88.5	510	554
1906	488	504	16	90.2	541	559
1907	502	529	27	93.8	535	564
1908	446	519	73	91.5	487	567
1909	496	545	49	91.3	543	597
1910	517	575	58	94.7	546	607
1911	520	587	67	95.2	546	616
1912	554	601	47	97.2	570	618
1913	587	633	46	98.9	594	640
1914	555	639	84	100.0	555	639
1915	547	635	88	101.1	541	628
1916	647	705	58	108.7	595	648
1917	748	807	59	127.7	586	632
1918	972	994	22	150.0	648	663
1919	1,117	1,142	25	172.5	648	662
1920	1,236	1,342	106	199.7	619	672
1921	1,009	1,227	218	178.1	566	689
1922	1,067	1,190	123	166.9	639	718
1923	1,231	1,278	47	169.7	725	753
1924	1,196	1,293	97	170.3	702	759
1925	1,253	1,317	64	174.8	717	753
1926	1,310	1,346	36	176.2	743	764
1927	1,312	1,380	68	172.8	759	799
1928	1,297	1,384	87	170.9	759	810
1929	1,356	1,425	69	170.9	793	834
1930	1,207	1,388	181	166.4	725	834
1931	995	1,298	303	151.5	657	857
1932	754	1,141	387	136.1	554	838
1933	678	1,045	367	128.8	526	811
1934	758	1,066	308	133.3	569	800
1935	799	1,115	316	136.7	584	816
1936	874	1,146	272	138.1	633	830
1937	1,008	1,259	251	143.1	704	880
1938	901	1,221	320	140.6	641	868
1939	967	1,266	299	138.4	699	915
1940	1,052	1,315	263	139.5	754	943
1941	1,261	1,492	231	146.5	861	1,018
1942	1,665	1,778	113	162.5	1,025	1,094
1943	2,053	2,107	54	172.5	1,190	1,221
1944	2,260	2,292	32	175.3	1,289	1,307
1945	2,303	2,364	61	179.3	1,284	1,318
1946	2,343	2,473	130	194.4	1,205	1,272
1947	2,468	2,602	134	222.7	1,108	1,168
1948	2,788	2,933	145	239.5	1,164	1,225
1949	2,769	3,000	231	237.2	1,167	1,265
1950	2,963	3,180	217	239.5	1,237	1,328
1951	3,305	3,452	147	258.5	1,279	1,335
1952	3,518	3,660	142	264.4	1,331	1,384
1953	3,710	3,852	142	266.7	1,391	1,444
1954	3,679	3,953	274	267.5	1,375	1,478
1955	3,899	4,128	229	266.9	1,461	1,547
1956	4,115	4,342	227	270.9	1,519	1,603
1957	4,301	4,546	245	280.3	1,534	1,622
1958	4,308	4,707	399	287.9	1,550	1,635
1959	4,626	4,965	339	290.5	1,592	1,709
1960	4,780	5,130	350	294.9	1,620	1,750

* Excludes armed forces.

Table A-17. Nonfarm Employees,* Annual Earnings, 1900–1960

Year	Money earnings		Income loss from unemployment	Consumer price index (1914 = 100)	Real earnings (1914 dollars)	
	After deduction for unemployment	When employed			After deduction for unemployment	When employed
1900	$ 441	$ 483	$ 42	84.3	$ 523	$ 573
1901	466	497	31	85.4	546	582
1902	503	528	25	86.3	583	612
1903	506	534	28	88.0	575	607
1904	493	538	45	88.8	555	606
1905	515	550	35	88.5	582	621
1906	557	566	12	90.2	618	627
1907	575	592	23	93.8	613	631
1908	499	577	75	91.5	545	631
1909	551	600	38	91.3	604	657
1910	576	634	58	94.7	608	669
1911	583	644	67	95.2	612	676
1912	602	657	47	97.2	619	676
1913	642	687	45	98.9	649	695
1914	613	696	65	100.0	613	696
1915	597	692	93	101.1	591	684
1916	706	760	59	108.7	649	699
1917	805	866	76	127.7	631	678
1918	1,041	1,063	25	150.0	694	709
1919	1,174	1,215	26	172.5	681	704
1920	1,343	1,426	104	199.7	672	714
1921	1,105	1,330	230	178.1	620	747
1922	1,148	1,289	129	166.9	688	772
1923	1,313	1,376	44	169.7	774	811
1924	1,284	1,396	98	170.3	754	820
1925	1,336	1,420	61	174.8	764	812
1926	1,411	1,452	33	176.2	801	824
1927	1,399	1,487	64	172.8	810	861
1928	1,394	1,490	80	170.9	816	872
1929	1,462	1,534	74	170.9	855	898
1930	1,294	1,494	194	166.4	778	898
1931	1,068	1,406	328	151.5	705	928
1932	807	1,244	423	136.1	593	914
1933	722	1,136	401	128.8	561	882
1934	789	1,146	351	133.3	592	860
1935	851	1,195	339	136.7	623	874
1936	932	1,226	293	138.1	675	888
1937	1,072	1,341	268	143.1	749	937
1938	956	1,303	357	140.6	680	927
1939	1,029	1,346	320	138.4	743	973
1940	1,113	1,392	280	139.5	798	998
1941	1,332	1,561	212	146.5	909	1,066
1942	1,740	1,858	119	162.5	1,071	1,143
1943	2,125	2,181	57	172.5	1,232	1,264
1944	2,323	2,360	38	175.3	1,325	1,346
1945	2,364	2,424	61	179.3	1,318	1,352
1946	2,394	2,529	134	194.4	1,231	1,301
1947	2,532	2,657	125	222.7	1,137	1,193
1948	2,867	2,999	132	239.5	1,197	1,252
1949	2,855	3,075	214	237.2	1,204	1,296
1950	3,047	3,255	208	239.5	1,272	1,359
1951	3,392	3,526	134	258.5	1,312	1,364
1952	3,607	3,732	123	264.4	1,364	1,411
1953	3,804	3,927	122	266.7	1,426	1,472
1954	3,781	4,033	250	267.5	1,413	1,508
1955	4,106	4,224	211	266.9	1,538	1,583
1956	4,236	4,445	209	270.9	1,564	1,641
1957	4,410	4,657	247	280.3	1,574	1,663
1958	4,413	4,818	405	287.9	1,533	1,673
1959	4,728	5,069	341	290.5	1,626	1,748
1960	4,908	5,260	352	294.9	1,665	1,785

* Excludes armed forces.

Table A-18. Annual Earnings, 1900–1960:
Full-time Employees, by Industry

Year	Agri-culture	Manu-facturing	Mining			Con-struction	Transportation			
			Total	Coal	Metal		Total	Railroad	Water	Local
1900	$ 178	$ 487	$ 479	$ 459		$ 593	$ 505	$ 536	$ 390	$ 510
1901	182	511	531	509		590	505	537	393	508
1902	191	537	532	494	$ 794	611	472	550	400	487
1903	191	548	619	595		637	528	580	403	492
1904	221	538	599	575		644	540	587	407	516
1905	199	561	610	586		659	543	576	410	546
1906	219	577	636	611		693	560	594	417	559
1907	220	598	697	670		714	592	646	427	556
1908	220	548	590	568		721	591	652	427	549
1909	221	599	625	602	865	731	583	630	423	567
1910	223	651	668	644		804	607	662	420	575
1911	225	632	671	647		779	624	690	417	579
1912	232	651	723	697		791	634	705	437	570
1913	236	689	749	722		827	667	743	467	595
1914	234	696	666	638	923	838	695	778	484	623
1915	236	661	716	688	976	827	711	797	531	632
1916	259	751	889	845	1,152	882	768	848	669	674
1917	327	883	1,138	1,123	1,352	1,001	885	968	851	737
1918	401	1,107	1,399	1,426	1,499	1,191	1,265	1,393	1,086	938
1919	463	1,293	1,370	1,329	1,611	1,387	1,352	1,477	1,305	1,172
1920	528	1,532	1,684	1,668	1,639	1,710	1,645	1,807	1,499	1,435
1921	344	1,346	1,757	1,827	1,482	1,380	1,533	1,664	1,339	1,470
1922	331	1,283	1,300	1,261	1,345	1,297	1,461	1,630	1,088	1,394
1923	372	1,403	1,822	1,891	1,497	1,614	1,484	1,631	1,132	1,413
1924	375	1,427	1,703	1,747	1,378	1,620	1,509	1,627	1,219	1,472
1925	382	1,450	1,580	1,555	1,455	1,655	1,539	1,655	1,227	1,502
1926	386	1,476	1,597	1,587	1,463	1,664	1,562	1,671	1,238	1,530
1927	387	1,502	1,590	1,546	1,485	1,708	1,579	1,687	1,220	1,549
1928	385	1,534	1,478	1,464	1,516	1,719	1,607	1,720	1,255	1,553
1929	378	1,543	1,526	1,398	1,613	1,674	1,643	1,749	1,275	1,598
1930	369	1,488	1,424	1,272	1,551	1,526	1,610	1,717	1,214	1,587
1931	291	1,369	1,221	1,071	1,291	1,233	1,549	1,661	1,153	1,500
1932	228	1,150	1,016	887	1,060	907	1,373	1,461	1,038	1,328
1933	213	1,086	990	884	1,040	869	1,334	1,439	1,059	1,219
1934	235	1,153	1,108	1,019	1,133	942	1,393	1,505	1,055	1,310
1935	268	1,216	1,154	1,041	1,239	1,027	1,492	1,645	1,088	1,361
1936	290	1,287	1,263	982	1,380	1,178	1,582	1,724	1,373	1,433
1937	338	1,376	1,366	1,208	1,630	1,278	1,644	1,774	1,536	1,505
1938	348	1,296	1,282	1,097	1,453	1,193	1,676	1,849	1,299	1,529
1939	362	1,363	1,367	1,194	1,515	1,268	1,723	1,877	1,557	1,569
1940	385	1,432	1,388	1,245	1,610	1,330	1,756	1,906	1,648	1,559
1941	473	1,653	1,579	1,494	1,771	1,635	1,885	2,030	1,854	1,664
1942	643	2,023	1,796	1,721	2,045	2,191	2,183	2,303	2,729	1,990
1943	837	2,349	2,162	2,115	2,333	2,503	2,493	2,585	3,388	2,280
1944	992	2,517	2,499	2,533	2,458	2,602	2,679	2,714	3,624	2,458
1945	1,089	2,517	2,621	2,637	2,551	2,600	2,734	2,711	3,583	2,596
1946	1,166	2,517	2,719	2,752	2,636	2,537	2,948	3,055	3,415	2,689
1947	1,243	2,793	3,113	3,198	3,000	2,829	3,145	3,216	3,748	2,833
1948	1,298	3,040	3,387	3,388	3,327	3,126	3,456	3,611	4,006	2,935
1949	1,272	3,092	3,207	2,924	3,400	3,211	3,556	3,706	4,129	2,987
1950	1,281	3,300	3,448	3,242	3,567	3,339	3,696	3,782	4,413	3,096
1951	1,403	3,606	3,879	3,760	4,098	3,711	3,994	4,164	4,678	3,255
1952	1,453	3,828	4,057	3,718	4,544	3,991	4,205	4,338	5,076	3,387
1953	1,437	4,049	4,353	4,067	4,888	4,225	4,398	4,418	5,898	3,515
1954	1,398	4,116	4,377	3,970	4,614	4,324	4,503	4,545	5,768	3,591
1955	1,428	4,351	4,701	4,466	4,962	4,414	4,697	4,701	5,869	3,727
1956	1,407	4,584	5,015	4,855	5,315	4,674	4,972	5,084	6,083	3,824
1957	1,451	4,781	5,218	5,069	5,459	4,923	5,243	5,421	6,443	3,927
1958	1,460	4,939	5,220	4,770	5,418	5,060	5,490	5,816	6,463	4,053
1959	1,515	5,215	5,540	5,227	5,841	5,254	5,765	6,058	6,589	4,175
1960	1,555	5,342	5,685	5,306	6,108	5,488	5,928	6,228	6,832	4,223

Table A-18. Annual Earnings, 1900–1960:
Full-time Employees, by Industry (Continued)

Year	Communication and Utilities			Trade	Service				Government			
	Total	Gas and electric	Telephone and telegraph		Total	Personal	Professional	Domestic	Total	State and local—general	Public education	Federal civilian
1900	$ 470	$ 506	$ 433	$ 508	$ 340	$ 330	$ 543	$ 240	$ 584	$ 590	$ 345	$ 940
1901	496	506	433	510	344	332	540	243	572	605	354	974
1902	473	518	444	521	361	344	542	264	584	612	364	967
1903	483	544	443	537	370	354	548	270	602	621	377	1,009
1904	487	550	448	551	379	364	551	277	614	640	397	971
1905	477	538	450	561	385	376	553	278	628	646	412	976
1906	497	575	460	569	393	381	556	286	651	664	430	999
1907	521	617	471	580	420	394	581	316	675	694	453	1,014
1908	516	589	482	593	429	403	580	328	683	695	479	1,001
1909	531	612	488	609	439	420	579	331	710	696	501	1,071
1910	516	616	461	630	447	435	567	337	725	699	518	1,096
1911	658	641	488	666	462	453	587	343	739	712	535	1,113
1912	527	635	467	666	469	453	597	350	757	724	556	1,140
1913	560	654	515	685	479	459	605	357	788	779	575	1,169
1914	579	644	557	706	487	471	620	355	798	788	593	1,197
1915	607	637	614	720	493	490	638	342	753	804	608	1,224
1916	640	672	647	760	523	524	656	357	844	826	636	1,273
1917	727	844	675	828	571	580	692	389	880	832	682	1,318
1918	866	1,081	753	941	646	669	757	432	1,023	902	725	1,415
1919	1,035	1,278	906	1,070	757	780	830	538	1,156	1,022	852	1,609
1920	1,238	1,489	1,115	1,270	912	940	979	665	1,245	1,164	970	1,707
1921	1,276	1,497	1,161	1,260	905	932	1,198	649	1,317	1,296	1,109	1,683
1922	1,265	1,423	1,176	1,261	908	933	1,174	649	1,358	1,316	1,206	1,694
1923	1,292	1,429	1,199	1,272	942	941	1,137	711	1,378	1,336	1,239	1,704
1924	1,371	1,544	1,250	1,314	965	972	1,154	732	1,400	1,346	1,269	1,747
1925	1,378	1,552	1,257	1,359	984	1,006	1,234	741	1,425	1,377	1,299	1,762
1926	1,427	1,571	1,317	1,416	1,005	1,048	1,213	748	1,482	1,422	1,342	1,888
1927	1,440	1,558	1,343	1,480	1,046	1,095	1,291	756	1,531	1,488	1,393	1,907
1928	1,474	1,591	1,378	1,573	1,065	1,164	1,314	725	1,550	1,500	1,433	1,916
1929	1,474	1,589	1,386	1,594	1,079	1,177	1,332	731	1,551	1,549	1,445	1,916
1930	1,497	1,603	1,410	1,569	1,066	1,165	1,330	676	1,553	1,576	1,455	1,836
1931	1,514	1,600	1,436	1,495	1,008	1,103	1,300	584	1,547	1,541	1,463	1,904
1932	1,438	1,542	1,335	1,315	918	971	1,227	497	1,477	1,479	1,399	1,807
1933	1,351	1,453	1,245	1,183	854	870	1,113	460	1,328	1,413	1,300	1,625
1934	1,426	1,510	1,338	1,228	857	896	1,136	473	1,284	1,391	1,265	1,677
1935	1,486	1,589	1,378	1,279	873	907	1,138	485	1,292	1,425	1,293	1,768
1936	1,522	1,615	1,420	1,295	898	938	1,163	506	1,279	1,457	1,329	1,885
1937	1,601	1,705	1,481	1,352	938	897	1,192	558	1,355	1,493	1,367	1,818
1938	1,674	1,749	1,580	1,352	942	1,013	1,215	527	1,336	1,517	1,406	1,823
1939	1,692	1,766	1,600	1,360	952	1,041	1,225	544	1,337	1,530	1,403	1,873
1940	1,718	1,795	1,610	1,382	953	1,062	1,207	554	1,344	1,552	1,435	1,866
1941	1,766	1,870	1,633	1,478	1,020	1,095	1,239	601	1,388	1,574	1,462	1,910
1942	1,883	2,040	1,715	1,608	1,132	1,199	1,354	706	1,623	1,628	1,512	2,097
1943	2,075	2,284	1,878	1,781	1,347	1,386	1,476	919	1,777	1,756	1,608	2,459
1944	2,248	2,467	2,035	1,946	1,538	1,575	1,603	1,140	1,924	1,855	1,730	2,628
1945	2,425	2,596	2,246	2,114	1,688	1,725	1,725	1,312	2,052	1,986	1,822	2,607
1946	2,567	2,697	2,413	2,378	1,872	1,881	1,907	1,411	2,341	2,144	2,025	2,716
1947	2,792	2,994	2,583	2,632	2,005	2,011	2,112|	1,463	2,574	2,327	2,261	3,021
1948	3,002	3,223	2,776	2,832	2,114	2,120	2,256	1,500	2,758	2,528	2,538	3,149
1949	3,153	3,383	2,907	2,899	2,172	2,189	2,355	1,498	2,863	2,665	2,671	3,340
1950	3,318	3,571	3,033	3,034	2,220	2,254	2,452	1,502	3,015	2,725	2,794	3,506
1951	3,547	3,851	3,214	3,171	2,367	2,355	2,619	1,588	3,114	2,906	2,998-	3,781
1952	3,799	4,125	3,437	3,284	2,545	2,462	2,806	1,707	3,282	3,112	3,169	4,050
1953	4,039	4,404	3,651	3,446	2,677	2,573	2,937	1,805	3,388	3,249	3,314	4,225
1954	4,229	4,579	3,824	3,558	2,786	2,682	3,026	1,832	3,501	3,390	3,510	4,306
1955	4,426	4,757	4,043	3,702	2,867	2,766	3,134	1,874	3,710	3,523	3,608	4,581
1956	4,612	5,000	4,177	3,860	3,004	2,872	3,375	1,962	3,894	3,676	3,827	4,775
1957	4,813	5,247	4,348	4,014	3,146	2,999	3,408	2,050	4,048	3,847	4,085	4,918
1958	5,063	5,543	4,528	4,135	3,262	3,140	3,540	2,131	4,330	3,985	4,343	5,427
1959	5,385	5,815	4,883	4,301	3,420	3,248	3,670	2,190	4,500	4,149	4,522	5,570
1960	5,642	6,116	5,113	4,445	3,587	3,390	3,700	2,336	4,683	4,330	4,752	5,836

Table A-18. Annual Earnings, 1900–1960: Full-time Employees, by Industry (*Continued*)

Year	Finance, insurance, and real estate	Mining Anthra-cite	Bitumi-nous	Copper	Iron	Oil	Service Medical	Non-profit	Educa-tional services
1900	$1,040	$ 340	$ 516	$ 842			$ 256	$ 652	$ 469
1901	1,037	420	548				258	651	483
1902	1,051	289	577	842	$ 512	$ 772	267	657	489
1903	1,078	544	615		512		275	679	532
1904	1,099	638	554		512		283	677	509
1905	1,115	579	589				292	677	511
1906	1,146	550	633				296	689	528
1907	1,180	633	683				306	741	544
1908	1,218	553	574				313	743	545
1909	1,263	556	617	989	599	801	326	741	546
1910	1,301	604	657		628		338	715	549
1911	1,355	633	652		662		352	763	560
1912	1,338	616	723		692		352	784	568
1913	1,349	659	743	1,111	725		357	802	603
1914	1,368	636	640	1,051	701	1,056	366	837	610
1915	1,399	671	694	1,129	729		381	876	623
1916	1,406	711	884	1,344	874		407	907	631
1917	1,439	1,019	1,150	1,541	1,091		451	953	679
1918	1,438	1,426	1,427	1,629	1,429		520	1,058	721
1919	1,589	1,508	1,276	1,587	1,696	1,515	606	1,104	784
1920	1,758	1,777	1,633	1,580	1,780	2,121	752	1,286	894
1921	1,860	1,868	1,808	1,428	1,764	1,698	983	1,392	1,022
1922	1,932	1,814	1,165	1,445	1,334	1,658	912	1,446	1,109
1923	1,896	2,014	1,848	1,605	1,486	1,848	845	1,454	1,130
1924	1,944	2,117	1,621	1,417	1,497	1,877	845	1,507	1,148
1925	1,997	2,129	1,427	1,537	1,485	1,874	916	1,578	1,173
1926	2,008	2,124	1,434	1,534	1,519	1,840	857	1,607	1,214
1927	2,019	1,851	1,446	1,564	1,527	1,902	931	1,647	1,252
1928	2,043	1,825	1,342	1,616	1,503	1,978	930	1,675	1,284
1929	2,062	1,728	1,293	1,743	1,526	2,019	925	1,712	1,312
1930	1,973	1,750	1,119			1,980	933	1,698	1,329
1931	1,858	1,602	909			1,890	919	1,653	1,323
1932	1,652	1,452	723			1,600	865	1,545	1,279
1933	1,555	1,435	748			1,427	810	1,442	1,189
1934	1,601	1,500	900			1,472	801	1,440	1,175
1935	1,632	1,414	957			1,558	829	1,435	1,162
1936	1,713	1,408	1,103			1,594	851	1,465	1,180
1937	1,788	1,388	1,170			1,734	876	1,497	1,211
1938	1,731	1,315	1,050			1,734	899	1,529	1,228
1939	1,729	1,409	1,197			1,684	908	1,546	1,234
1940	1,725	1,297	1,235			1,714	927	1,408	1,240
1941	1,777	1,467	1,500			1,779	955	1,379	1,264
1942	1,885	1,753	1,715			1,940	1,036	1,482	1,344
1943	2,041	2,119	2,115			2,299	1,127	1,679	1,469
1944	2,191	2,525	2,535			2,601	1,262	1,795	1,562
1945	2,347	2,685	2,629			2,762	1,401	1,876	1,641
1946	2,570	2,890	2,724			2,819	1,605	2,070	1,802
1947	2,740	3,125	3,212			3,157	1,821	2,172	2,113
1948	2,954	3,420	3,383			3,584	1,918	2,334	2,261
1949	3,034	2,896	2,930			3,746	1,995	2,465	2,364
1950	3,217	3,107	3,268			3,861	2,067	2,578	2,473
1951	3,356	3,386	3,831			4,109	2,143	2,720	2,642
1952	3,503	3,500	3,760			4,432	2,262	2,898	2,808
1953	3,663	3,389	4,194			4,615	2,365	3,041	2,924
1954	3,828	3,550	4,044			4,749	2,417	3,179	3,005
1955	3,968	3,871	4,550			4,933	2,488	3,291	3,094
1956	4,145	4,167	4,944			5,193	2,532	3,395	3,174
1957	4,306	4,345	5,162			5,425	2,612	3,533	3,327
1958	4,495	4,261	4,831			5,599	2,751	3,672	3,454
1959	4,714	4,368	5,322			5,802	2,881	3,815	3,688
1960	4,840	4,533	5,376			5,924	3,045	3,918	3,886

Table A-19. Earnings of Nonfarm Employees, 1860–1900

Year	Daily	Annual earnings Money (when employed)	Annual earnings Real (1914 dollars)	Consumer price index (1914 = 100)
1860	$1.09	$363	$457	79.5
1861	1.11	370	439	84.3
1862	1.15	383	398	96.2
1863	1.38	459	382	120.1
1864	1.52	506	421	150.3
1865	1.54	512	328	155.9
1866	1.47	489	322	151.9
1867	1.44	479	338	141.6
1868	1.50	499	367	136.0
1869	1.49	496	380	130.4
1870	1.47	489	375	124.9
1871	1.45	482	386	116.9
1872	1.46	486	416	116.9
1873	1.40	466	407	114.5
1874	1.32	439	403	109.0
1875	1.27	423	403	105.0
1876	1.21	403	393	102.6
1877	1.17	389	388	100.2
1878	1.14	379	397	95.4
1879	1.12	373	391	95.4
1880	1.16	386	395	97.8
1881	....	409	415	98.6
1882	....	428	431	99.4
1883	....	438	459	95.4
1884	....	441	478	92.3
1885	....	446	492	90.7
1886	....	453	499	90.7
1887	....	462	509	90.7
1888	....	466	505	92.3
1889	....	471	510	92.3
1890	....	475	519	91.5
1891	....	480	525	91.5
1892	....	482	527	91.5
1893	....	458	505	90.7
1894	....	420	484	86.7
1895	....	438	520	84.3
1896	....	439	521	84.3
1897	....	442	529	83.5
1898	....	440	527	83.5
1899	....	470	563	83.5
1900	....	483	573	84.3

Table A-20. Mining Wages, 1811–1902*

	Coal		Iron		Lead		Copper	
Year	Penn-sylvania	United States	United States		Missouri	United States	Michigan	United States
	Daily	Annual	Daily	Annual	Daily	Annual	Monthly	Annual
1811					$ 1.60			
1816–1817	$1.20				15‡			
1826					1.60			
1832	1.00							
1840	1.00			$200				
1850	1.20	$269		224			$32	$375
1860	1.15	264		284			33	352
1870	1.91	469		450	1.50	$351	46	501
1880	1.91	326	$1.90	314	1.10	360	49	532
1889	2.15	361	1.91	368	1.25	†	49	678
1902	2.22	†	2.00	554	1.30	550	62	813

* Annual: all employees. Daily, monthly: miners.

† Data not available.

‡ Monthly.

Table A-21. Able-bodied Seamen, Monthly Wages, 1800–1875

Year	Coasting trade and Europe	To China and Pacific ports	U.S. Navy	Year	Coasting trade and Europe	To China and Pacific ports	U.S. Navy	From San Francisco
1800	$20	$19		1840	$14		$12	
1801	17	17		1841	14			
1802	15	14	$12	1842	13			
1803	18	17	10	1843	13			
1804	20	17	12	1844	14			
1805	20			1845	14			
1807	20			1846	14			
				1847	15			
1810	19			1848	15			
1811	20			1849		$12		
1812			12					
1813				1850	15		12	
1814				1851	15	12		
1815			16	1852	15	12		
1816	13			1853	15	12		
1817	11	12		1854	15	15		$30
1818	12	12		1855	15	15		
1819	12			1856				
				1857	15	15		15
1820	10			1858				
1821	11			1859				
1822	12							
1823	12			1860		12	15	20
1824	12			1861		12		20
1825	13	11		1862		14		
1826	14			1863		15		20
1827	14			1864				20
1828				1865		50		20
1829				1866		25		30
				1867				
1830	13		12	1868				
1831	14			1869	18	20		25
1832	14							
1833	13	12		1870		25		
1834	13			1871				
1835		12		1872				32
1836	15	12		1873		25		
1837	14			1874		25		25
1838	14	12		1875				25
1839	14	12						

Table A-22A. Wages of Seamen, by Occupation and Voyage, 1795–1875

Date	Wages							Destination (and duration)	Ship
	Able Seaman	Captain or master	Mate	Second mate	Cook	Ordinary seaman	Boy or green hand		
1795	$20	$40	$23					Charleston	*Sch. Industry*
1798, Oct.	20	28				$11		Martinico	*Brig Hitty*
1799, Jan.	20	15	25		$ 7	8	$ 8	Demerara, West Indies	*Brig Hitty*
1799	17					12		Europe	*Essex*
1800, Jan.	20	17	30	$17	8		4	Europe	*Wonolancet*
1801, Jan.	18, 15½	17	17					Calcutta, 8 mo.	*Wonolancet*
1801, May	14½, 15½				12				*Wonolancet*
1801, Dec.	15	20	18				9	Cadiz	*Sch. Betsey*
1804, July	15, 30						8	from Guadaloupe	*Sch. Silvius*
1810, Feb.	19	25	25				12	Europe	*Brig Jason*
1810, Oct.	19							Europe	*Brig Jason*
1811*	20	25	25	25		16			*Ship Horace*
1811	21	25	25	23	21	16	11		*Brig Rover*
1812	14							Coastal fishing	*Boat Jefferson*
1815, Apr.	17, 18		28		10	12		West Indies, 3 mo.	*Brig Henry*
1815	13	12	14					Charleston	*Sch. Favourite*
1816, Oct.	12							Edgartown, 5 mo.	*Brig Nancy*
1816, Dec.	11½		23		8	9			*Brig Lucy*
1817, July	10		20				5	Eastward, 3 mo.	*Martha and Jane*
Sept.	10		15					Eastward, 3 mo.	*Martha and Jane*
Oct.	10	30	15			5		West Indies, 3 mo.	*Sch. McDonough*
Dec.	11		20			8		4 mo.	*Martha and Jane*
1818, Apr.	11	30	22				6	Portugal, 4 mo.	*Sch. McDonough*
Aug.	11	25	22		5	8			*Martha and Jane*
Nov.	14	25	23			8		Philadelphia, etc., 8 mo.	*Martha and Jane*
1819, Jan.	12		25						*Ship Marmion*
June	14							Pernambuco, 5 mo.	*Ship McDonough*
Oct.	11	20	20						*Martha and Jane*
Dec.	12½		25		12	11		Cuba, 9 mo.	*Brig Lucy*
1820, Apr.	12		20		10			West Indies	*Martha and Jane*
Oct.	10		20		10	8		Cuba, 9 mo.	*Brig Lucy*
Dec.	10		18					West Indies	*Martha and Jane*
Dec.	10							from Norfolk	*Hodgson, Letters*
Dec.	11	30	16						*Sch. Olive Branch*
1821, Nov.	11	20	20		11	9½		Europe, 12 mo.	*Martha and Jane*
1822, Jan.	12		24		12	10	5	Cuba, 9 mo.	*Brig Lucy*
Nov.	12	20	21		11	10		New Orleans	*Martha and Jane*
*	12						6	St. Petersburg, 6 mo.	*Alling, Sea*
1823, Apr.	12				13			Europe	*Martha and Jane*
Dec.	12	20	20		11			West Indies or Europe	*Martha and Jane*
Dec.	12		22		13	9		West Indies	*Brig Lucy*
*	12					8		Europe, 9 mo.	*Brig Brutus*
1824, June	11		22			8		West Indies	*Brig Lucy*
Dec.	12	12	23			11		West Indies	*Brig Lucy*

* No month specified.

Table A-22A. Wages of Seamen, by Occupation and Voyage, 1795–1875 (Continued)

Date	Wages							Destination (and duration)	Ship
	Able Seaman	Captain or master	Mate	Second mate	Cook	Ordinary seaman	Boy or green hand		
1825, May	$13, 14		$23		$14	$11, 12		Campeche & Europe	*Brig Lucy*
Oct.	13		23		15	8, 11		Brazil, etc., 12 mo.	*Brig Lucy*
Dec.	13	$10	20		12			West Indies, 4 mo.	*Martha and Jane*
1826, May	14	10	20		9			West Indies, 6 mo.	*Martha and Jane*
1827, Jan.	14		25		15	12, 11		Havana	*Brig Lucy*
July	12, 14	10	20		14			West Indies	*Martha and Jane*
Oct.	13, 16							Fishing, 4 mo.	*Sch. Hope*
1830, July	13		25	$20	13		$8	New Orleans to Marseilles	*Meteor*
1831, June	14		28		10		4½	Liverpool	*Yeaton*
1832, Apr.	15, 18	28	17		15	8, 9	5	West Indies, Europe	*Yeaton*
1832, Sept.	16	30	18		13			(one month)	*Sch. Hiram*
Oct.	10, 14	30				10			*Sch. Adeline*
*	14	35	23		9	10, 13		West Indies, 1½ mo.	*Brig Lavinia*
*	10	25	20			5			*Sch. Enterprise*
Dec.	14	35	18		14			1 mo.	*Sch. Hiram*
1833, Jan.	15	27	18			5, 7		West Indies, 2 mo.	*Yeaton*
Jan.	14	35	18		12	12		3 mo.	*Sch. Hiram*
May	12, 13	28	18			5, 7, 9		5 mo.	*Yeaton*
May	10, 14, 15, 16	35	16		8	8		3 mo.	*Sch. Adeline*
June	12, 13	25			12	10			*Brig Lavinia*
July	14	35	16		8			1 mo.	*Sch. Adeline*
July	14								Serial Set 373
July	12	45	22					Lubec	*Brig Atlantic*
Aug.	12	35	22		14				*Brig Lavinia*
Sept.	12	35	16		10			1 mo.	*Sch. Adeline*
Oct.	12	50	30	20	13	6		China, 36 mo.	*Ship California*
Oct.	10, 16, 17	30						2 mo.	*Ship Hiram*
Dec.	14, 14, 16	35	18		14			1 mo.	*Ship Hiram*
1834, Jan.	16	20	23		15	15			*Brig Lavinia*
	8, 13				13				*Sch. Paramount*
1835, Aug.	12	60	30	20	13	5, 7, 10, 10	6	China	*Ship California*
1836, Feb.	17				20			Cuba and Europe, 10 mo.	*Ship Timoleon*
Sept.	12, 10							Helsingfors	*Ship Archimedes*
Nov.	15	26	25		7				*Sch. Edward*
1837, Nov.	14	27	25		9½				*Sch. Edward*
1838, Mar.	13		20		10½				*Sch. Amelia*
Oct.	14		30						*Sch. Red Robin*
1839, Jan.	7	15	20		7			1 mo.	*Sch. Red Robin*
*	7	35	22		8			1 mo.	*Sch. Amelia*
Nov.	7	10	9					Norfolk, 3 mo.	*Sch. Equator*
1840, *	14	30	20		7				*Sch. Frances*
Oct.	14				12				*Sch. Equator*
1841, Jan.	14	30	22		9				*Sch. Frances*
Feb.	15, 16	30	22		10				*Sch. Equator*
Mar.	13	30	22		10				*Sch. Amelia*
May	14	30	22		10				*Sch. Miriam*
June	14	30	20						*Sch. Frances*
Sept.					10			Fishing	*Sch. Armida*
Nov.	14		20						*Sch. Armida*

* No month specified.

Table A-22A. Wages of Seamen, by Occupation and Voyage, 1795–1875 (Continued)

Date	Wages							Destination (and duration)	Ship
	Able Seaman	Captain or master	Mate	Second mate	Cook	Ordinary seaman	Boy or green hand		
1842, Jan.	$14, 15	$30	$22		$10				*Sch. Equator*
Sept.	2-0-0			$4			$0-14-0	Liverpool to U.S.	*Ship Medford*
Oct.	12	30	20		10				*Ship Equator*
1843, Jan.	14	30	20		8				*Ship Amelia*
Feb.	13	30	20		7				*Sch. Equator*
Sept.	12, 14								Philadelphia Shipping List
Nov.	12	30	16		10				*Sch. Equator*
1844, Jan.	12	30	16		8				*Sch. Governor*
Sept.	13	20			8				*Sch. Amelia*
Oct.	13, 14		20		8				*Sch. Amelia*
Oct.	13, 14		20		8				*Sch. Amelia*
Nov.	14	30	16		9				*Sch. Governor*
Nov.	14		20		9				*Sch. Frances*
Dec.	14	30	20		9				*Sch. Equator*
1845, Jan.	14	30	17		12				*Sch. Equator*
Jan.	15	20			8			Newcastle	*Sch. Albion*
Jan.	14	30	20		12				*Sch. Governor*
May	16								*Sch. Albion*
Oct.	11, 15	20			10				*Sch. Amelia*
Nov.	10, 14	30	20		14				*Sch. Albion*
Nov.	14	30	20		11				*Sch. Governor*
1846, Jan.	14, 15	30	20		10				*Sch. Amelia*
Mar.	14, 12		20						*Sch. Kanawha*
Mar.	14	30	20		12				*Sch. Governor*
Mar.	14		20		11				*Sch. Equator*
May	13, 15	30	20		11				*Sch. Amelia*
Sept.	15		15		13½				*Sch. Equator*
Dec.	15	30	18		11				*Sch. Equator*
Dec.	15	20	20	18			50¢	West Indies, 3 mo.	*Sch. Sarah*
1847, June	16, 15	25						8 mo.	*Sch. Sarah*
1848, Jan.	16	30	18		10				*Sch. Governor*
Feb.	16		22		12				*Sch. Governor*
Oct.	14	30	20		8				*Sch. Governor*
Dec.	15		20		8				*Sch. Governor*
1849, May	12		30		15			San Francisco, 36 mo.	*Ship Jacob Perkins*
1850, Jan.	15	24	15					Charleston	*Brig Albert Perkins*
Mar.	15	25			16			Norfolk	*Brig Albert Perkins*
Dec.	16	33	20		10			Chesapeake, 6 mo.,	*Sch. General Warren*
1851, Jan.	15		20		16			Virginia, 3 mo.	*Sch. General Warren*
May	15		30		20			New Orleans, 3 mo.	*Ship Medford*
July	15, 13							from New Orleans	*Ship Medford*
Sept.	12		30, 60	20	14	$10	8	Calcutta, 11 mo.	*Ship Medford*
Dec.	15		20		16				*Sch. General Warren*
1852, Apr.	15			20	20			New Orleans	*Ship Timoleon*
May	15		32	20	20			Boston	*Ship Timoleon*
Sept.	12		30	20	14	10	7, 9	China, 15 mo.	*Ship Medford*
Nov.	16		22		15			2 mo.	*Sch. General Warren*
1853, Feb.	16	35	22		14			Virginia, 1 mo.	*Sch. Oliver*
May	15							from New Orleans	Ashbridge

Table A-22A. Wages of Seamen, by Occupation and Voyage, 1795–1875 (Continued)

Date	Wages							Destination (and duration)	Ship
	Able Seaman	Captain or master	Mate	Second mate	Cook	Ordinary seaman	Boy or green hand		
1853, Oct.	$20	$35	$25		$16			Philadelphia, 1 mo.	Sch. General Warren
Oct.	15, 12		30	$20		$10	$7, 9	from Calcutta	Ship Medford
1854, Jan.	18	35	25		18			Virginia, 3 mo.	Sch. Oliver
Jan.	15		50	35	25	13, 14	10	South Pacific, 24 mo.	Ship Herald of Morning
Nov.	15		50	25	25	12, 14		San Francisco, 20 mo.	Ship Medford
1855, June	15			35				to New York	Ship Herald of Morning
Dec.	15			40	26	12		San Francisco	Ship Electric Spark
1856, Nov.	20							Callao to Chincha	Ship Herald of Morning
Nov.	20								New York Post
1857, July	15		50	35	25			from New York	Ship Herald of Morning
Dec.	15							from San Francisco	Ship Herald of Morning
1860, *	12			28	22		9	to San Francisco	Ship Herald of Morning
June	20							San Francisco to New York	Ship Herald of Morning
1861, *	18, 14, 15		50	25	25			Havre	Ship Electric Spark
May	15							from Havre, 1½ mo.	Ship Electric Spark
1862, Mar.	£2/10/0		£6		£4	£2		Callao–London, 10 mo.	Ship Herald of Morning
1863, Feb.	£2/10/0							from London	Ship Herald of Morning
Nov.	15		45	30	25	15, 16		to San Francisco	Ship Swallow
1864, Apr.	20		45	30	20 (Chinese)			San Francisco to Europe, 18 mo.	Ship Swallow
1865, Mar.	20							San Francisco to Europe	Ship Herald of Morning
Nov.	12							Hamburg to U.S.	Ship Herald of Morning
Dec.	£3/10/0							Newcastle to U.S.	Ship Herald of Morning
1866, June	25		55	40	30			to San Francisco, 5 mo.	Ship Herald of Morning
Nov.	30			35	30			San Francisco to Europe	Ship Herald of Morning
1867, June	30		55	40	30	8		Liverpool to New York	Ship Herald of Morning
1869, Apr.	20			40	30	10		to San Francisco	Ship Herald of Morning
Sept.	25				35			San Francisco to Europe	Ship Herald of Morning
1870, Apr.		200							
June	25		55	40		18		to San Francisco, 4 mo.	Ship Herald of Morning
1871, Apr.	20							to Europe, 5 mo.	Ship Herald of Morning
1872, Apr.	15		65	35	30			Marseilles to San Francisco	Ship Herald of Morning
Sept.	30, 35				35	15, 20		San Francisco to Europe	Ship Swallow

* No month specified.

Table A-22A. Wages of Seamen, by Occupation and Voyage, 1795–1875 (Continued)

Date	Wages							Destination (and duration)	Ship
	Able Seaman	Captain or master	Mate	Second mate	Cook	Ordinary seaman	Boy or green hand		
1873, May	$25		$60	$40	$35	$20, 15		New York to San Francisco, 5 mo.	*Ship Herald of Morning*
1874, June	25		60	40	35			New York to San Francisco, 5 mo.	*Ship Herald of Morning*
1875, Jan.	25		60	40	35	20		San Francisco to Tahiti, 7 mo.	*Ship Herald of Morning*

Table A-22B. Wages of Seamen, by Occupation and Voyage, 1788–1869

Date	Able seaman	Captain or master	Mate	Second mate	Cook	Ordinary seaman	Boy or green hand	Steward	Carpenter	Destination (and duration)*	Ship
1788	$38	$60	$54	$22	$14					Hamburg	Peggy
1795	20	12	25		10					Cape	Rose
1796	20+	20+	25+								Katy
1797 Sept.	18	23	22								Katy
1798 Apr.	16	16	20							Surinam, 3 m 16	Katy
Dec.	18 + 6 cwt	20 + 5%	25 + 2½ t††	20 + 20 cwt	20 + 6 cwt	$10	12 + 5 cwt			East Indies	Hannah William
1799 Nov.	19	12	25	22	18	12	10	$17	$22	Madeira &	John
1800 Mar.	20 + 8 cwt	12 + 5%	25 + 2 t	22 + 1½ t	18 + 8 cwt	13 + 6 cwt	10 + 5 cwt	12 + 6 cwt	20	Indies	Henry
1801 Mar.	17	12	25	22 + 1½ t	18	12, 8		12	16		John
July	20	12	25		16	15, 10					Henry
June	20	30	30				4		20	Europe & West Indies	Mary
Sept.	12	25 + 5%	25 + 2 t	23	15			10		12 m	Three Friends
1802 Apr.	13 + 6 cwt	12 + 12 t	21 + 2½ t	18 + 1½ t	8					Calcutta	Martha
July	15	10	20							West Indies, etc., 4 m 27	Mary
July	14	40	20		10					Europe	Three Friends
Aug.	15	12	20 + 2 t	18 + 1½ t		9 + 5 cwt		8 + 6 cwt	17	Amsterdam	Henry
Nov.	14	12	20	17	11	10				Sumatra	John
Dec.	14	30	25			10, 11				South & East	Mary
1803 July	17	30	24	21	17		9		19	West Indies & Europe, 20 m	Susannah
July	17	12	23		20			17 + 6 cwt	22 + 12 cwt	(Indies)	Henry
Oct.	18	50 + 4 t	25 + 1½ t		20						Derby
Dec.	20	25 + 3 t	24 + 2 t	22 + 1½ t	12		10 + 5 cwt			Naples, 5 m 16	John
1804 May	20	10	30	24			8			South & Europe	Reward
Nov.	20	50 + 4 t	30		19	13				South, Europe, etc., 7-8 m	Susannah
Nov.	17	30	23		20	14, 18				Europe, India	Derby
1805 May	20		33		15	10		18 + 6 cwt	24 + 12 cwt	South & Europe, 24 m	Reward
Aug.	24	30	30							Savannah, 4 m 13	Susannah
1806 Jan.	27	35	35		17					Jamaica, 4 m	Susannah

536

Date										Destination	Ship
1807 Jan.	20	12	30	25	12					Jamaica, 3 m 15	*Susannah*
June	19	35	30							Lisbon, 3 m 27	*Reward*
May	23	30	30						20	Alexandria	*Susannah*
1816 Apr.	14	14	25 + 1½ t	15	13	9	5	12		East of Cape, 14 m 20	*Trader*
1817 July	12	20	23 + 2 t	20 + 1¼ t		10, 11	8	9		"Globe"	*Coromandel*
Sept.	12	12	25 + 2 t	20	12	10, 11			20 + 10 cwt	East of Cape	*Trader*
1818 Oct.	13	14	23 + 2 t	20 + 1¼ t	14	4, 6	4		11 + 5 cwt	East of Cape	*Coromandel*
1825 Nov.	11	12	23 + 2 t	20 + 1 t	11					(East Indies), 14 m 24	*Tezel*
1836 Nov.	12	60	22	19						Cayenne, 5 m 3	*Borneo*
1837 Dec.	11		25	18	12					South America, 5 m	*Pactolus*
1838 May	15		28	20	15	11	5	8		East Indies, 14 m 15	*Shawmut*
July	13		25	20	13					Cayenne	*William & Henry*
Sept.	14		28	20	16					East Indies, 8 m 20	*Hope*
Nov.	12		30	20	14		4		14	East of Cape	*Eliza*
Dec.	12		28	19	15		6			West Indies, 3 m 20	*Rolla*
1839 Mar.	17	45	26	20						Cayenne, 2 m 26	*Hope*
Apr.	17	40	28	20	19	6, 12		4		9 m 25	*Pactolus*
Sept.	14		28	19	15	5, 10				East of Cape, 11 m	*Pactolus*
Oct.	12		30	20	14					West Indies & Cayenne	*Eliza*
Dec.	12		25 + 2 t	20	20					Cayenne, 3 m	*William & Henry*
1840 Feb.	15		28	19						Cayenne, 5 m	*Pactolus*
June	15		28	20	16						*Pactolus*
Sept.	14		28	19							*Pactolus*
1841 Dec.	14									from Gibraltar, 10 m	*Eliza Ann*
1846 Dec.	17		30	20	18	8, 12		17		Africa	*Northumberland*
1847 Apr.	19		32	22	20					Africa	*Northumberland*
Apr.	12										*Sappho*
Nov.	16		30	20	20	8, 12		10		Africa	*Northumberland*
1848 Nov.	15		30	20	15						
1853 Oct.	12									San Francisco, 14 m	*Syren*

Table A-22B. Wages of Seamen, by Occupation and Voyage, 1788–1869 (Continued)

Date	Able seaman	Captain or master	Mate	Second mate	Cook	Ordinary seaman	Boy or green hand	Steward	Carpenter	Destination (and duration)*	Ship
1854 Jan.	$30		$60	$40	$40		$12	$40	$30	from San Francisco, 3 m	Augustine Heard
1861 Apr.	12					$18	6				Syren
May	12		45	27	22			25	20	to San Francisco, 5 m	
1862 Aug.	12				28			30	30	6 m	Sooloo
Dec.	20			30							Derby
1862 Sept.	25	$100	50	30	22	12, 13	10, 12	26	25	from San Francisco, 7 m	Sooloo
Nov.	15		55	30	23	12	1, 7	27	30	from Calcutta, 13 m	Indian
Nov.	14									San Francisco, 11 m	Sooloo
1863 Dec.	20		55	30	30	15	2	30	32	from San Francisco	Derby
1864 July	20		50	30	25‡	15	10	25‡	30	San Francisco to Hong Kong, 9 m	Derby
1865 Feb.	50		75	60	50	20, 40	12	55	55	San Francisco, 7 m	Derby
Sept.	20		75	35	30	12, 15	12	35	30	San Francisco to Hong Kong, New York, 8 m	Mindoro
1866 Mar.	25	150		33	28	20		35	30	Batavia, 9 m 17	Mindoro / Ocean Rover
1869 Mar.	18					16				9 m	Ocean Rover

* Months and days.
† Ton.
‡ Chinese.

TABLE A-23. Farm Laborers, Average Monthly Earnings with Board, 1818–1899

Region	1818	1826	1830	1850	1860	1870	1880	1890	1899
United States	$ 9.45	$ 8.83	$ 8.85	$10.85	$13.66	$16.57	$11.70	$13.93	$14.56
New England	11.90	11.65	11.60	12.98	14.73	19.84	13.94	17.78	18.20
Maine	12.43	12.43	12.43	13.12	14.34	19.65	12.80	17.50	18.00
New Hampshire	10.16	10.16	11.66	12.12	14.34	16.87	13.00	17.60	18.48
Vermont	10.00	10.00	10.00	13.00	14.14	20.98	14.33	17.35	18.74
Massachusetts	13.50	13.50	12.00	13.55	15.34	22.24	15.44	18.50	18.32
Rhode Island	11.93	11.93	11.93	13.52	16.04	17.98	14.00	18.00	18.35
Connecticut	13.11	11.61	11.61	12.72	15.11	17.70	13.00	17.33	17.52
Middle Atlantic	9.82	8.38	8.52	11.17	12.75	17.89	13.71	15.76	15.98
New York	10.00	8.00	8.00	11.50	13.19	18.39	13.81	16.65	17.52
New Jersey	8.50	8.50	8.50	10.18	11.91	17.14	12.80	16.00	15.19
Pennsylvania	11.00	9.00	9.50	10.82	12.24	17.30	13.80	14.60	14.32
East North Central	8.86	8.73	8.73	11.44	13.79	16.94	15.48	15.92	16.90
Ohio	9.00	9.00	9.00	11.10	13.11	15.88	14.66	15.10	15.27
Indiana	9.00	9.00	9.00	10.50	13.71	17.31	14.52	14.78	15.45
Illinois	12.00	10.00	10.00	12.55	13.72	17.67	16.25	16.35	17.76
Michigan	—	—	—	12.00	15.27	16.91	16.58	16.75	16.95
Wisconsin	—	—	—	12.69	13.96	16.02	15.87	16.75	19.20
West North Central	10.15	10.15	10.15	12.00	13.76	17.10	14.88	15.84	18.04
Minnesota	—	—	—	17.00	14.10	18.98	16.44	16.60	19.98
Iowa	—	—	—	11.80	13.18	17.23	16.38	17.00	19.32
Missouri	10.15	10.15	10.15	11.81	13.63	16.13	13.34	14.00	14.57
North Dakota	—	—	—	—	—	—	19.55	17.10	21.82
South Dakota	—	—	—	—	—	—	—	—	20.41
Nebraska	—	—	—	—	17.45	18.81	14.53	16.60	18.87
Kansas	—	—	—	—	16.12	18.04	14.06	15.05	17.46
South Atlantic	8.10	7.18	7.16	8.20	11.08	9.95	8.81	9.46	9.32
Delaware	6.00	6.00	6.00	8.79	10.66	12.99	—	11.15	11.98
Maryland	12.00	10.00	10.00	7.88	9.71	10.87	10.10	11.25	11.53
Virginia	6.00	6.00	6.00	8.43	11.43	9.32	8.43	9.47	10.43
West Virginia	—	—	—	—	—	15.14	11.71	12.95	13.55
North Carolina	6.00	6.00	6.00	7.21	10.37	8.39	8.78	8.80	8.56
South Carolina	10.00	8.00	7.00	7.72	11.37	10.33	7.95	8.62	7.34
Georgia	11.44	9.44	9.44	9.03	11.95	10.83	8.47	8.37	8.05
Florida	—	—	—	10.00	14.29	9.99	9.26	12.59	11.32
East South Central	10.36	9.39	9.37	9.60	14.06	12.78	10.16	10.58	10.72
Kentucky	11.00	10.00	10.00	10.00	13.57	14.37	11.19	11.70	12.24
Tennessee	8.50	8.50	8.50	8.67	11.94	12.86	9.58	10.12	10.33
Alabama	11.00	9.00	9.00	9.62	12.41	10.82	9.38	9.85	8.63
Mississippi	15.00	10.00	10.00	11.00	16.66	13.38	10.24	10.50	9.27
West South Central	—	—	—	11.28	15.53	14.05	12.90	12.84	11.86
Arkansas	—	—	—	10.63	14.25	13.52	13.03	12.55	10.54
Louisiana	—	—	—	12.80	17.00	14.34	12.26	11.79	10.30
Texas	—	—	—	12.00	16.02	14.05	13.31	13.30	12.94
Mountain	—	—	—	—	—	—	24.74	21.67	26.33
New Mexico	—	—	—	6.00	14.54	—	21.00	17.83	18.45
Utah	—	—	—	22.00	23.33	—	25.00	21.00	25.72
Nevada	—	—	—	—	—	—	35.00	23.00	31.76
Pacific	—	—	—	68.00	34.16	29.19	24.77	22.64	25.10
Washington	—	—	—	—	43.00	—	24.17	24.40	25.06
Oregon	—	—	—	75.00	—	—	21.60	22.00	22.89
California	—	—	—	60.00	33.28	29.19	25.67	22.40	25.64

Table A-24. Farm Laborers, Average Monthly Earnings with Board, 1899–1948, and Composite Hourly Wage Rate, 1950 and 1954

Region	Average monthly earnings (with board)						Composite hourly wage rate	
	1899	1909	1919	1929	1940	1948	1950	1954
United States.............	$14.56	$21.30	$41.52	$40.40	$28.05	$ 91.00	$0.52	$0.73
New England.............	18.20	25.82	46.16	50.93	33.54	104.00	0.65	0.93
Maine..................	18.00	26.71	49.40	45.56	31.50	94.00	0.67	0.93
New Hampshire.........	18.48	25.18	44.90	48.88	31.50	100.00	0.64	0.86
Vermont...............	18.74	25.93	45.00	48.81	31.50	105.00	0.47	0.75
Massachusetts..........	18.32	26.52	45.00	50.94	34.00	109.00	0.66	0.99
Rhode Island...........	18.35	24.62	48.00	53.50	37.00	106.00	0.68	0.97
Connecticut............	17.52	24.61	45.00	54.19	36.00	109.00	0.73	0.97
Middle Atlantic..........	15.98	22.21	41.17	45.72	30.00	99.00	0.56	0.84
New York..............	17.52	24.78	43.30	48.69	31.50	104.00	0.55	0.87
New Jersey.............	15.19	20.50	44.00	49.69	34.00	107.00	0.67	0.86
Pennsylvania...........	14.32	19.69	37.80	39.19	27.50	90.00	0.52	0.79
East North Central........	16.90	23.59	42.21	41.73	29.40	101.00	0.51	0.82
Ohio..................	15.27	21.35	39.40	38.06	26.50	98.00	0.55	0.86
Indiana................	15.45	21.40	38.20	36.81	28.00	89.00	0.53	0.81
Illinois................	17.76	24.52	43.50	42.56	32.50	106.00	0.53	0.82
Michigan..............	16.95	24.36	42.00	42.44	29.00	99.00	0.57	0.86
Wisconsin.............	19.20	27.52	48.70	46.94	29.50	109.00	0.41	0.73
West North Central.......	18.04	26.47	50.81	42.10	28.12	107.00	0.52	0.82
Minnesota.............	19.98	28.30	53.70	42.94	30.50	109.00	0.49	0.83
Iowa..................	19.32	28.14	55.00	47.69	33.00	118.00	0.53	0.82
Missouri...............	14.57	20.56	37.00	33.75	23.50	81.00	0.46	0.73
North Dakota..........	21.82	32.33	56.00	42.38	28.50	125.00	0.56	0.87
South Dakota..........	20.41	30.38	65.00	44.38	28.00	115.00	0.54	0.79
Nebraska..............	18.87	27.50	56.80	43.50	26.50	111.00	0.56	0.86
Kansas................	17.46	25.21	49.50	38.13	25.50	105.00	0.62	0.91
South Atlantic..........	9.32	14.64	30.23	25.23	17.46	57.00	0.42	0.57
Delaware..............	11.98	17.12	34.00	35.69	27.00	80.00	0.59	0.84
Maryland..............	11.53	15.96	32.00	35.25	27.50	82.00	0.49	0.73
Virginia...............	10.43	15.00	31.00	30.25	22.00	72.00	0.43	0.59
West Virginia..........	13.55	20.33	40.00	32.19	22.00	59.00	0.45	0.63
North Carolina.........	8.56	14.05	32.40	27.19	17.50	60.00	0.40	0.56
South Carolina.........	7.34	11.96	27.00	19.19	13.00	41.00	0.30	0.43
Georgia...............	8.05	13.21	26.70	19.00	13.00	45.00	0.32	0.48
Florida................	11.32	17.86	28.00	23.31	16.00	59.00	0.57	0.74
East South Central........	10.72	15.05	29.09	23.28	16.34	49.00	0.35	0.53
Kentucky..............	12.24	17.13	33.00	26.62	19.50	60.00	0.39	0.62
Tennessee.............	10.33	14.98	29.00	23.88	17.50	51.00	0.33	0.52
Alabama...............	8.63	13.19	25.50	21.50	14.00	44.00	0.32	0.48
Mississippi............	9.27	14.21	26.50	22.38	14.50	43.50	0.34	0.52
West South Central........	11.86	17.33	36.19	27.67	19.61	73.00	0.43	0.61
Arkansas..............	10.54	16.31	31.70	25.00	16.50	55.00	0.38	0.55
Louisiana..............	10.30	13.94	30.20	25.00	15.50	46.50	0.38	0.55
Oklahoma.............	14.52	20.87	40.50	26.38	21.00	82.00	0.55	0.78
Texas.................	12.94	18.47	38.80	29.00	21.50	84.00	0.44	0.62
Mountain...............	26.33	34.34	59.20	49.96	36.11	129.00	0.64	0.83
Montana..............	32.12	38.05	62.20	53.88	39.50	137.00	0.60	0.84
Idaho.................	28.13	39.38	69.00	55.06	40.00	151.00	0.73	1.02
Wyoming..............	29.64	34.53	60.50	50.94	37.00	124.00	0.60	0.79
Colorado..............	23.23	31.53	55.50	42.31	31.00	118.00	0.64	0.87
New Mexico...........	18.45	25.62	40.50	35.50	28.50	104.00	0.52	0.67
Arizona...............	28.23	35.28	60.00	51.50	37.00	135.00	0.68	0.79
Utah..................	25.72	40.77	70.00	59.24	45.00	144.00	0.76	0.93
Nevada...............	31.76	40.30	68.00	61.56	43.00	133.00	0.63	0.86
Pacific.................	25.10	34.28	65.30	59.90	42.84	158.00	0.85	1.04
Washington............	25.06	35.43	66.30	50.81	38.00	149.00	0.83	1.17
Oregon................	22.89	33.11	64.00	50.06	36.50	147.00	0.79	1.05
California.............	25.64	34.17	65.30	62.50	46.50	161.00	0.86	1.02

Table A-25. Common Laborers, Average Daily Earnings, 1832–1940*

Region	1832 (With board)	1850 (With board)	1850	1860	1869	1880	1890	1919 (Hourly)	1929 (Hourly)	1940 (Hourly)
United States	$0.62	$0.61	$0.87	$1.06	$1.55	$1.23	$1.46	$0.41	$0.44	$0.51
New England	0.68	0.77	1.01	1.03	1.56	1.28	1.49	0.38	0.48	0.51
Maine	0.74	0.76	1.00	1.05	1.54	1.25	1.33	0.35	—	0.47
New Hampshire	0.60	0.63	0.89	0.94	1.30	1.20	1.42	—	—	0.50
Vermont	0.60	0.72	0.97	1.02	1.44	1.17	1.24	—	—	0.44
Massachusetts	0.74	0.84	1.09	1.02	1.60	1.28	1.52	0.39	—	0.53
Rhode Island	0.65	0.72	0.95	1.05	1.50	1.17	1.45	0.36	—	0.53
Connecticut	0.67	0.76	0.98	1.05	1.62	1.42	1.53	0.39	—	0.54
Middle Atlantic	0.71	0.60	0.90	1.06	1.58	1.27	1.45	0.45	0.46	0.55
New York	—	0.67	0.90	1.02	1.50	1.29	1.46	0.41	—	0.53
New Jersey	—	0.65	0.88	1.07	1.64	1.32	1.44	0.44	—	0.55
Pennsylvania	—	0.51	0.80	1.11	1.65	1.25	1.45	0.49	—	0.56
East North Central	0.48	0.58	0.87	1.01	1.58	1.30	1.51	0.42	0.48	0.57
Ohio	0.50	0.56	0.78	0.98	1.60	1.29	1.48	0.43	—	0.58
Indiana	0.46	0.55	0.78	0.98	1.56	1.24	1.38	0.39	—	0.57
Illinois	—	0.62	0.85	1.05	1.60	1.40	1.62	0.46	—	0.58
Michigan	—	0.66	0.88	1.04	1.57	1.36	1.37	0.39	—	0.57
Wisconsin	—	0.71	1.00	1.05	1.54	1.21	1.37	0.40	—	0.54
West North Central	0.52	0.56	0.77	0.98	1.55	1.43	1.48	0.41	0.42	0.53
Minnesota	—	0.86	1.37	1.20	1.75	1.50	1.57	0.37	—	0.56
Iowa	—	0.61	0.83	0.99	1.69	—	1.33	0.42	—	0.54
Missouri	0.52	0.55	0.75	0.98	1.48	1.44	1.50	0.43	—	0.55
Nebraska	—	—	—	1.37	2.13	1.50	1.62	—	—	0.50
Kansas	—	—	—	1.22	1.87	1.25	1.47	0.43	—	0.47
South Atlantic	0.45	0.48	0.68	0.84	1.06	0.96	1.19	0.36	0.30	0.39
Delaware	—	0.51	0.78	0.87	1.56	1.17	1.31	0.50	—	0.48
Maryland	—	0.49	0.69	0.84	1.54	1.08	1.23	0.45	—	0.49
District of Columbia	—	0.63	0.98	1.00	—	—	1.17	—	—	—
Virginia	—	0.47	0.65	0.81	1.01	1.00	1.13	0.36	—	0.36
West Virginia	—	—	—	—	1.27	1.33	1.47	0.47	—	0.55
North Carolina	—	0.42	0.54	0.77	0.82	0.51	0.94	0.34	—	0.31
South Carolina	—	0.49	0.66	0.82	1.01	—	1.00	0.30	—	0.32
Georgia	0.54	0.50	0.72	0.89	1.09	0.89	1.05	0.29	—	0.32
Florida	—	0.68	1.03	1.16	1.20	—	1.00	0.26	—	0.32
East South Central	0.49	0.49	0.68	0.92	1.28	1.10	1.32	0.31	0.27	0.37
Kentucky	—	0.50	0.69	0.97	1.39	1.25	1.35	0.43	—	0.44
Tennessee	—	0.43	0.58	0.84	1.15	0.95	1.22	0.30	—	0.34
Alabama	—	0.49	0.70	0.96	1.21	1.06	1.37	0.29	—	0.39
Mississippi	—	0.69	0.95	1.26	1.45	—	0.89	0.30	—	0.36
West South Central	—	0.70	0.95	1.27	1.61	—	1.44	0.33	0.36	0.36
Arkansas	—	0.54	0.75	1.04	1.39	—	1.06	0.27	—	0.32
Louisiana	—	0.73	1.04	1.39	1.70	—	1.26	0.31	—	0.36
Texas	—	0.75	1.00	1.25	1.27	1.00	1.68	0.36	—	0.39
Mountain	—	—	—	2.00	2.71	—	—	0.42	0.45	0.47
Montana	—	—	—	—	6.00	—	—	—	—	—
Idaho	—	—	—	—	3.50	—	—	—	—	—
Wyoming	—	—	—	—	—	2.00	—	—	—	—
Colorado	—	—	—	2.00	2.50	(1.75)	—	—	—	—
New Mexico	—	0.33	0.53	1.02	1.50	—	—	—	—	0.36
Arizona	—	—	—	—	3.25	—	—	—	—	—
Utah	—	1.32	2.00	1.94	—	—	—	0.59	—	0.49
Nevada	—	—	—	—	3.00	—	—	—	—	0.60
Pacific	—	4.00	5.00	2.65	2.30	—	1.96	0.49	0.48	0.60
Washington	—	—	—	2.92	2.50	—	—	0.52	—	0.63
Oregon	—	4.00	5.00	—	2.12	(1.50)	—	0.53	—	0.60
California	—	4.00	5.00	2.62	2.31	(1.75)	1.96	0.44	—	0.59

* For annual estimates, 1860 to 1880, see Table 6-2.

Table A-26. Domestics, Average Weekly Wage, 1850–1900

Region	1850	1860	1870	1900
United States	$1.08	$1.34	$2.00	$3.14
New England	1.35	1.50	2.45	3.48
Maine	1.09	1.32	2.53	3.24
New Hampshire	1.27	1.63	2.58	(3.58)
Vermont	1.19	1.31	2.44	(3.00)
Massachusetts	1.48	1.58	2.37	3.61
Rhode Island	1.42	1.50	2.78	(3.75)
Connecticut	1.36	1.50	2.44	3.16
Middle Atlantic	.96	1.24	2.08	3.14
New York	1.05	1.25	2.22	3.09
New Jersey	.97	1.23	2.05	3.55
Pennsylvania	.80	1.22	1.83	3.09
East North Central	1.06	1.33	2.14	3.06
Ohio	.96	1.22	1.98	2.93
Indiana	.90	1.28	2.11	(2.95)
Illinois	1.14	1.46	2.19	3.55
Michigan	1.10	1.40	2.30	2.89
Wisconsin	1.27	1.30	2.05	2.50
West North Central	1.28	1.44	1.95	3.00
Minnesota	2.25	1.58	2.08	2.94
Iowa	1.07	1.27	2.16	2.82
Missouri	1.17	1.47	1.75	3.24
Nebraska	—	1.72	3.36	3.19
Kansas	—	1.82	2.20	(2.62)
South Atlantic	.99	1.20	1.50	1.86
Delaware	.84	.92	1.86	(2.25)
Maryland	.89	1.17	1.82	(2.22)
Virginia	.96	1.14	1.27	(2.00)
West Virginia	—	—	1.48	3.00
North Carolina	.87	1.08	1.16	(1.66)
South Carolina	1.42	1.82	1.72	1.83
Georgia	1.52	1.67	1.61	1.10
Florida	1.83	2.32	1.62	(2.00)
East South Central	1.18	1.63	1.88	2.78
Kentucky	1.09	1.47	1.87	2.97
Tennessee	1.00	1.28	1.54	(2.33)
Alabama	1.41	2.08	1.93	—
Mississippi	1.52	2.25	2.42	—
West South Central	2.30	2.95	2.22	2.60
Arkansas	1.67	1.91	2.29	(2.00)
Louisiana	2.57	3.36	2.33	(1.77)
Texas	2.00	2.50	1.97	(3.67)
Pacific	—	—	—	—
California	13.00	7.45	6.47	4.80
Oregon	10.00	5.40	—	—

Table A-27. Cotton Manufacturing, Average Annual Earnings, Full-time Equivalent, 1832–1899

Region	1832	1849	1859	1869	1879	1889	1899
United States............	$163	$176	$201	$298	$244	$302	$286
New England............	166	194	206	303	255	325	341
Maine................	178	188	202	272	250	303	316
New Hampshire........	172	198	227	318	262	322	330
Vermont..............	159	165	207	277	225	283	256
Massachusetts.........	169	199	203	312	258	332	351
Rhode Island..........	156	186	202	312	247	318	334
Connecticut...........	166	180	194	269	251	321	333
Middle Atlantic..........	172	161	184	281	243	331	339
New York.............	153	159	183	287	216	294	298
New Jersey............	188	151	185	287	277	352	342
Pennsylvania..........	175	163	185	275	254	346	360
East North Central.......	—	136	196	238	225	262	229
Ohio.................	—	141	180	246	218	292	263
Indiana..............	—	111	231	225	230	237	228
West North Central......	—	—	—	—	—	—	—
Missouri..............	—	125	180	333	193	—	—
South Atlantic...........	—	119	168	200	177	202	181
Delaware.............	—	161	198	262	243	317	373
Maryland.............	—	136	217	235	190	248	251
Virginia..............	—	100	181	132	157	188	228
North Carolina........	—	92	109	126	136	173	169
South Carolina........	—	126	138	229	189	187	168
Georgia..............	—	122	148	215	183	210	195
East South Central.......	—	112	156	210	171	207	187
Kentucky.............	—	143	168	215	184	209	208
Tennessee............	—	96	154	200	159	210	201
Alabama.............	—	117	152	210	166	193	178
Mississippi...........	—	124	169	233	191	229	203

Table A-28. Woolen Manufacturing, Average Annual Earnings, Full-time Equivalent, 1832–1899

Region	1832	1849	1859	1869	1879	1889	1899
United States............	$183	$214	$232	$335	$306	$372	$361
New England............	199	224	233	360	317	380	385
Maine.................	—	205	256	344	336	378	379
New Hampshire........	211	217	275	361	304	378	389
Vermont..............	—	216	199	345	261	394	389
Massachusetts.........	192	229	234	355	318	382	385
Rhode Island..........	205	219	253	350	305	369	407
Connecticut...........	208	226	252	392	339	390	377
Middle Atlantic.........	159	197	234	333	309	376	362
New York.............	137	204	235	322	316	373	347
New Jersey............	—	195	243	306	283	347	344
Pennsylvania..........	240	189	232	343	308	381	371
East North Central......	—	218	261	286	246	311	303
Ohio..................	—	214	246	249	196	314	317
Indiana...............	—	231	282	294	266	284	293
Illinois...............	—	229	272	308	285	343	303
Michigan.............	—	211	243	304	219	314	321
Wisconsin............	—	—	257	296	254	332	301
West North Central......	—	233	228	236	195	306	276
Minnesota............	—	—	—	312	201	355	302
Iowa.................	—	—	197	248	236	352	252
Missouri..............	—	261	282	191	160	239	267
Kansas...............	—	—	—	337	210	—	—
South Atlantic..........	—	199	207	220	201	263	234
Delaware.............	—	223	242	289	418	347	—
Maryland.............	—	201	226	251	178	324	252
Virginia..............	—	189	216	211	197	263	287
West Virginia.........	—	—	—	189	125	216	258
North Carolina........	—	150	237	157	124	201	200
South Carolina........	—	—	124	72	133	—	—
Georgia..............	—	251	165	217	176	179	173
East South Central......	—	184	185	202	198	309	252
Kentucky.............	—	173	236	233	202	298	234
Tennessee............	—	195	247	147	167	240	180
Alabama.............	—	—	172	119	169	178	139
Mississippi...........	—	—	96	248	243	283	183
West South Central......	—	—	—	—	—	—	—
Texas................	—	240	179	203	172	387	304

Table A-29. Iron and Steel Manufacturing, Average Annual Earnings, Full-time Equivalent, 1832–1899

Region	1832	1849	1859	1869	1879	1889	1899
	Full time		Full-time equivalent				
United States............	$313	$292	$346	$524	$394	$522	$543
New England............	311	349	368	594	404	483	549
Maine................	311	329	414	483	—	—	—
New Hampshire........	286	392	364	564	—	—	—
Vermont.............	289	309	389	452	—	—	—
Massachusetts.........	311	365	380	634	396	474	557
Rhode Island..........	311	356	422	552	—	—	—
Connecticut...........	311	324	310	587	483	558	525
Middle Atlantic.........	314	296	344	529	418	530	553
New York............	—	327	385	578	358	482	565
New Jersey...........	311	274	373	585	377	495	470
Pennsylvania..........	314	283	311	486	433	536	558
East North Central.......	—	315	348	506	416	560	579
Ohio.................	—	312	344	506	412	563	586
Indiana..............	—	310	320	554	422	435	560
Illinois..............	—	318	411	556	478	601	579
Michigan.............	—	349	360	500	299	530	477
Wisconsin............	—	329	351	378	467	519	633
West North Central......	—	268	438	720	234	516	539
Minnesota............	—	—	481	508	—	—	—
Iowa.................	—	388	373	506	—	—	—
Missouri.............	—	265	443	742	234	516	539
Nebraska.............	—	—	—	106	—	—	—
Kansas...............	—	—	—	629	—	—	—
South Atlantic..........	—	233	300	366	315	408	444
Delaware.............	—	280	372	484	397	467	473
Maryland.............	—	273	304	304	328	298	482
District of Columbia....	—	325	360	552	—	—	—
Virginia..............	—	189	271	298	264	371	317
West Virginia.........	—	—	—	577	374	462	513
North Carolina........	—	156	237	312	—	—	—
South Carolina........	—	163	200	437	—	—	—
Georgia..............	—	236	340	404	142	263	249
Florida..............	—	—	463	—	—	—	—
East South Central.......	—	238	303	398	293	411	356
Kentucky.............	—	283	380	407	328	467	477
Tennessee............	—	162	226	380	214	446	273
Alabama.............	—	337	319	444	352	388	339
Mississippi...........	—	455	535	269	—	—	—
West South Central......	—	438	453	639	198	—	172
Arkansas.............	—	—	171	389	—	—	—
Louisiana............	—	427	467	650	—	—	—
Texas................	—	521	—	578	198	—	172
Pacific................	—	—	—	—	—	—	—
California............	—	280	106	598	557	622	590

Table A-30. Average Price of Labor, by Occupation, 1832

Average price of labor, including board	Con-necticut	Maine	New Hamp-shire	Rhode Island	Ohio	Indi-ana	Mis-souri	Geor-gia
Per month throughout the year....	$11.61	$12.43	$11.66	$11.93		$9.02	$10.15	$9.44
Per day........................	0.67	0.74	0.60	(0.65)*	$0.50	0.46	0.52	0.54
Per day in harvest time..........	1.00	0.91	0.88	0.91		0.72	0.73	0.80
Value per day for construction and repair of roads and bridges......	0.84	1.08	0.78	0.81	0.75	0.50	0.55	

* Revised from original source. See text, p. 269.

Table A-31. Occupational Earnings, Daily Rates, 1832

	United States	New England	Middle Atlantic	Connecticut	Maine	Massachusetts	New Hampshire	Rhode Island	Vermont	New Jersey	New York	Pennsylvania
Male												
Blacksmiths	$1.09*	$1.00	$1.00	$0.95	$0.89	$1.20	$0.90	$(0.95)	$(0.90)	—	—	—
Ship bldg	(1.20)	1.25	—	—	—	1.26	1.25	—	—	—	—	—
Coach bldg	—	1.10	—	—	—	1.14	0.98	—	—	—	—	—
Iron mfg	0.86†	1.01	0.81†	1.00	1.00	1.11	0.92	(1.00)	0.93	1.00	$0.81†	$0.81†
Cotton mfg	1.01	1.02	1.01	1.00	1.20	1.03	1.13	0.87	0.95	1.00	1.00	1.00
Wool mfg	0.90	0.95	0.82	1.00	0.98	0.93	0.82	—	1.00	—	—	(0.70)
Shoe mfg	—	0.81	—	0.89	1.00	0.80	0.76	—	0.84	—	—	—
Paper mfg	—	0.92	—	0.90	—	0.95	0.79	—	—	—	—	(0.48)
Tanning mfg	—	—	—	—	—	0.75	0.78	—	—	—	—	0.47
Common labor	0.62	0.68	0.71	0.67	0.74	0.74	0.60	0.65	0.60	—	—	—
Female												
Cotton mfg	0.37	0.41	0.33	0.35	0.36	0.44	0.45	0.37	0.33	0.33	0.33	0.34
Wool mfg	0.35	0.34	0.36	0.35	(0.48)	0.45	0.34	—	0.36	(0.42)	0.41	(0.31)
Shoe mfg	—	0.32	—	0.42	(0.49)	0.28	(0.35)	—	0.50	—	—	—
Paper mfg	—	0.33	—	0.33	0.38	0.33	0.34	—	—	—	—	(0.21)
Hats	—	0.34	—	(0.37)	—	0.32	0.33	—	—	—	—	—
Domestics	0.32‡	0.32‡	—	—	—	—	—	—	—	—	—	—
Industry averages												
Iron	0.86†	1.01	0.81†	1.00	1.00	1.11	0.92	1.00	0.93	1.00	0.81	0.81
Wool	0.55	0.62	0.43	0.67	0.72	0.63	0.52	0.66	0.50	0.57	0.44	0.39
Cotton	0.52	0.53	0.55	0.53	0.57	0.54	0.55	0.50	0.51	0.60	0.49	0.56
Shoes	(0.76)	0.70	—	0.79	0.75	0.61	0.75	—	—	—	—	0.80
Paper	—	0.64	—	0.49	0.62	0.74	0.56	—	—	—	—	—
All manufacturing	0.79§											

* Above averages for New England and Middle Atlantic, reflecting high Midwestern rates.
† Average allowing for monthly rates. Daily rates, $1.00.
‡ $1 a week and board, valued at $1.25.
§ Allowing for monthly rates in iron. At $1 daily rates, United States manufacturing is 82 cents.

Table A-32. Retail Price Trends: 1800–1860
(1830 = 100)

Item	1800	1810	1819	1830	1840	1850	1860
Five items (weighted).....	168	197	156	100	91	73	78
Textiles...............	172	214	158	100	94	70	74
Shoes.................	108	95	107	100	73	73	78
Rum, whisky..........	206	224	166	100	98	95	99
Coffee...............	211	199	239	100	92	89	119
Tea..................	134	109	119	100	68	56	47
Board.................	163	163	131	100	—	114	148
Textiles:							
Massachusetts.........	246	230	160	100	99	64	70
Vermont.............	—	217	169	100	96	55	55
Philadelphia, wholesale .	169	210	160	100	90	83	90
New York, wholesale...	—	198	144	100	89	78	81
Shoes:							
Massachusetts.........	120	93	106	100	98	73	81
Massachusetts, boots...	—	89	—	100	67	56	40
Massachusetts, leather..	88	100	76	100	—	—	—
Vermont.............	108	108	120	100	73	73	75
Philadelphia, leather....	79	94	117	100	94	83	123
Coffee:							
Massachusetts.........	207	185	252	100	104	101	148
Vermont.............	200	228	239	100	89	78	100
Philadelphia, wholesale .	216	172	216	100	86	86	109
Tea:							
Massachusetts.........	111	107	129	100	43	74	47
Vermont.............	143	112	104	100	94	66	72
Philadelphia, wholesale .	143	108	120	100	64	70	57
New York, wholesale...	147	111	123	100	77	57	
Rum:							
Massachusetts.........	200	215	160	100	—	—	—
Vermont.............	—	226	213	100	—	—	—
Philadelphia, wholesale .	222	221	173	100	97	88	109
Rye whisky:							
Philadelphia, wholesale .	225	246	135	100	100	102	89

Table A-33. Consumer Prices: 1860–1880
(1860 = 100)

Year	All items	Food	Clothing	Rent	Fuel and lighting	Other
1860	100	100	100	100	100	100
1861	106	106	110	101	107	102
1862	121	119	143	104	119	105
1863	151	143	197	125	143	115
1864	189	177	261	153	166	141
1865	196	194	238	166	173	147
1866	191	199	194	177	173	146
1867	178	191	166	162	159	144
1868	171	187	148	158	153	144
1869	164	176	148	155	155	145
1870	157	168	141	147	150	143
1871	147	154	128	148	148	142
1872	147	154	126	154	145	141
1873	144	150	122	153	145	142
1874	137	145	115	137	140	141
1875	132	141	105	136	135	140
1876	129	140	104	125	131	138
1877	126	140	99	120	118	138
1878	120	132	95	116	112	135
1879	120	129	94	125	113	134
1880	123	132	94	130	116	133

INDEX OF TEXT TABLES*

* See also list of Appendix tables, pages 507, 508

SUBJECT INDEX

Individual citations of United States government publications have not been given, since references to them are too numerous to be usefully indexed. This includes, in particular, works published by the Congress, the Bureau of the Census, the Bureau of Labor and Statistics, and the Office of Business Economics.